# Mountain Fires

♦   ♦   ♦

A

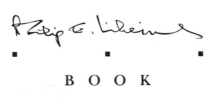

B O O K

The Philip E. Lilienthal imprint
honors special books in commemoration of a man whose work at the
University of California Press from
1954 to 1979 was marked by dedi-
cation to young authors and to high
standards in the field of Asian Studies. Friends, family, authors, and
foundations have together endowed
the Lilienthal Fund, which enables
the Press to publish under this imprint selected books in a way that
reflects the taste and judgment of a
great and beloved editor.

# Mountain Fires

## The Red Army's Three-Year War
## in South China, 1934-1938

• • •

## Gregor Benton

**UNIVERSITY OF CALIFORNIA PRESS**
Berkeley   Los Angeles   Oxford

The University of California Press gratefully acknowledges support from the
China Publication Subventions program.

University of California Press
Berkeley and Los Angeles, California

University of California Press, Ltd.
Oxford, England

**Library of Congress Cataloging-in-Publication Data**

Benton, Gregor.
  Mountain fires: the Red Army's Three-Year War in south China,
1934–1938 / Gregor Benton.
    p.   cm.
  Includes bibliographical references (p.   ) and index.
  ISBN 0-520-04158-5 (cloth : alk. paper)
  1. Communism—China—History.   2. China—Politics and
government—1928–1937.   I. Title.
  HX418.B46   1992
  951.04'2—dc20                                                    91-26012
                                                                        CIP

Printed in the United States of America
1 2 3 4 5 6 7 8 9

*For Zheng Chaolin and Wang Fanxi,
Chinese revolutionaries, in celebration
of their seventy-year war (still going)
against injustice and oppression.*

# CONTENTS

# MAPS

# FOREWORD

This remarkable book tells stories better read about than lived through. It evokes pity, admiration, horror, and other strong reactions to the terrible dramas it recounts without diminishing them into propaganda or trivializing them for the sake of scoring academic points. Although words on the page can never recreate the extremes of human experience, Gregor Benton comes close to letting us imagine what it must have been like to be one of the survivors of the rural revolutionary state in south China who were left behind amid the ashes of defeat.

The stories end with a triumph as most of the survivors of three years of attempted extermination march down from the hills to form the New Fourth Army in 1937. They begin with a great disaster, the catastrophe from which the badly beaten main forces of the Red Army marched away when they retreated from the rapidly shrinking heartlands of the Chinese Soviet Republic in October 1934. They left the territories and people of the soviet state virtually unprotected from the counterrevolution being imposed by the victorious government forces. Communist rule had been bloody enough; the slaughter with which it was ended was probably even greater.

The officials and soldiers left behind to carry on the struggle when nearly all the regular forces slipped out of the soviet areas were for the most part only the wounded and others who were dispensable. In the secrecy with which the evacuation had been organized little or no warning was given to those who were suddenly expected to cope with the consequences of a defeat so massive and total. The men and women left to pay for their party's mistakes must have felt abandoned if not betrayed, though to complain in their comrades' hearing would have been to risk summary execution.

For many it was all too much. Some gave up a hopeless struggle and drifted away from the Revolution. A few succumbed to the sort of pressures the Gestapo later applied in occupied Europe and helped their former enemies to destroy their former comrades, with the result that the guerrilla bands were haunted by mutual suspicion and a fear of betrayal so intense that they often became lethal.

Conditions were grim. Yesterday's officials and activists were today's quarry to be hunted down and killed, unless they fled far from towns and villages to live for years on mountaintops, in forests, in caves, or anywhere else that might shelter them from the elements while leaving no signs behind to guide their pursuers. As Red power collapsed there was no longer an accessible rural population that could be urged or forced to provide recruits, food, and other forms of support. The excesses of Communist rule, especially in its dying months, followed by harsh and effective repression by the Guomindang, meant that few peasants were both willing and able to help the remnants of the former revolutionary regime. The guerrillas were on their own, having to feed themselves as best they could by hunting and gathering or else by kidnapping hostages for ransom just as any other bandits might do. The sick and wounded had to recover without medicines or die. Few guerrilla bands were in touch with national Party organizations or even with one another, such was the fear of betrayal and the effectiveness of the blockades. Newspapers were rarely seen.

These were circumstances that brought out the best and the worst in human nature. The widely scattered handfuls of survivors had to find their own ways to keep themselves and their cause alive in the absence of instructions from higher Party authority. Living like old-fashioned outlaws under the greenwood tree, guerrilla bands often behaved like bandits, with their chiefs as autocratic "kings of the mountains." Continuing to do things the way they had been done under soviet power was suicidal in the absence of the regular army. Making deals with people who would previously have been regarded as targets for execution risked harsh punishments from Party comrades when contact with the organization was restored. But when forced to depend on their own resources, local leaders had to learn flexibility and compromise, finding friends and allies where they could even while preserving as best they could the integrity of their organizations. Thus we find one group organizing an old-fashioned Daoist sword-wielding militia of its own as the most effective way of coping with local armed millenarians.

By taking us through the story of each guerrilla region in turn instead of lumping them all together, Benton brings out the great variety in local conditions, in the tactics and strategies adopted by the different Communist leaders, and in their varying degrees of success in coping with crisis. He shows that we cannot easily speak in generalities about what was happening even in a province when, for example, circumstances, policies, and outcomes in the several guerrilla zones of Fujian differed as widely as they did. This is an invaluable corrective to the tendency to overgeneralize about the history of the Communist Revolution in China, or to take what was happening in one particular area, such as the Shaanganning region around Yan'an, as representative of what the Communists were doing everywhere.

This book is also an essential contribution to breaking down the Mao-centered unilinear historical mythology of the Chinese Revolution. In the tunnel-vision view of history, central and southern China drop out of sight once the main Red Army forces set out on what (though none of them knew it at the time) was to become the Long March, to be noticed again briefly only when three years later Mao's wise leadership in the north makes it possible for the survivors of those left behind to come down from the hills to become the New Fourth Army in the war against Japan. Even then they are often treated in orthodox Chinese historiography and Western writing derived from it as if they were somehow less authentic than Mao's Eighth Route Army in the north. This book—like Benton's sequel on the early years of the New Fourth Army that will, I hope, follow before long—should help to replace mythology with a more trustworthy history. But for the stubborn survivors in the south and the military units they contributed to the Communist side during and after the Japanese war, it is arguable that the Guomindang might never have been driven from the mainland.

How the groups of survivors in their different mountain retreats or strongholds flourished or were destroyed from 1934 is a story that Gregor Benton has been patiently piecing together for about twenty years. The immense quantity of information he has gathered is deployed with masterly selectivity and judgment. His sense of the local and particular makes him acutely aware of factors such as linguistic and ethnic divisions among Han Chinese that are often played down. Benton offers here a model of how to use the evidence of memoirs, articles, and monographs on revolutionary history officially published in China to recover something of what actually happened and what it meant at the time. He handles a complicated and many-stranded narrative with a skill that is rare in writing on Chinese history. The characters of some of the more remarkable figures emerge with striking, and at times appalling, clarity: the dour, self-important Xiang Ying, the pathologically but understandably suspicious Gao Jingting, and the debonair gangster-poet Chen Yi. The legendary and near-fatal encounter between the latter two in 1937, when Gao came close to killing Chen as a renegade for trying to persuade him that the war with the Guomindang was for the time being over, is one of the best of many stories in the book that bring out the nature of the struggle in the south and what it did to those who waged it.

Whatever one may now think of the cause for which the Communist rearguard killed and died, there can be no doubting the heroism of those who carried on a hopeless struggle in impossible circumstances. Their experience is as much worth studying as that of those who made the Long March, especially when their story is reconstructed with the skill and empathy that Benton shows in these pages. If only books of this quality on Chinese history were not so rare.

W. J. F. Jenner
Australian National University

# PREFACE

That there ever was a Three-Year War in the dark backward and abysm of the Chinese Revolution will come as news to many China scholars and historians of Communism.[1] "We should write the history of the three-year guerrilla war in the south to educate later generations," said one veteran of it in 1985.[2] Nearly forty years earlier, Guo Moruo, welcoming a small memoir on one region of the southern struggle, had said: "We all know about the Long March, but no one knows much at all about the three-year guerrilla war."[3] Even so, until the 1980s in China, the Three-Year War was but a short footnote to the main story of the revolution, itself preposterously rewritten as a life of Mao; and even now to my knowledge no comprehensive study on it has been published.

Why the Three-Year War was screened from sight is explained in detail in the last chapter of this book, but I will briefly rehearse the reasons here. One is that Mao played no part in it, having left southern China to go on the Long March, so it could have no function in the Mao cult. Another is that it happened in places where grave strategic errors had been committed, before the start of the Long March, on which no main leader of the Party could afford to dwell. So it was associated with past failures; but also, as ties to the Long Marchers broke, with new unorthodoxy, indiscipline, and insubordination. Later, important leaders of it came to stand at various times under ideological clouds, especially after the Wannan Incident of January 1941 in which part of the New Fourth Army (born in 1938 of the Three-Year War) was destroyed by the Guomindang after failing to heed Mao's warnings.[4] So the Three-Year War became associated with dissidence and was often treated with disapproval. This disapproval reached its zenith in the Cultural Revolution, when its anarchic ethos jarred with the totalitarian strivings of Lin Biao and the "Gang of Four." The Three-Year War vanished from history books; "radical" politicians vilified its leaders.

In the early 1970s, when I first began my study on the New Fourth Army, my search for the key to issues in its early history took me in two directions. One was to Moscow, where Wang Ming had begun in 1935 to formulate for the Party back in China a "right-opportunist" policy that strongly influenced the early New Fourth Army and led to friction between it and Mao. The other was to the old Soviet bases in southern and central China and the rearguards left behind there by the Long March in October 1934, for remnants of these rearguards had formed the nucleus of the New Fourth Army at the end of the Three-Year War.

## THE SOURCES

My research on the "Second Wang Ming Line" was soon completed, for many of the relevant documents were available in editions of the works of Mao Zedong and Wang Ming.[5] The history of the southern rearguard proved far more elusive. I found no systematic studies, general analyses, or collections of materials on it, and only very few on its regional components (of which there were around fourteen). This lack was not just the result of official disapproval. Though the Three-Year War has never been commemorated in the same way as the Long March, there was a period in the 1950s and the early 1960s when historians put some effort into an honest accounting of it, mainly by collecting oral and written testimony from veterans. But most historians were more easily drawn to the well-documented, prestigious affairs of the Party's central leaders. The Three-Year War had been fought by small groups acting in isolation along the borders of eight provinces. Consequently, research on it had to be coordinated across two, three, and even four provinces at a time. Such coordination did happen, but it was not easy, and the border gangs eluded the historians of the 1950s just as they had eluded the Nationalist "pacifiers" of the 1930s, who had also found it hard to act in concert across provinces. Military records published in the 1930s by the Guomindang were even more devoid of information than later Communist publications. They dealt almost exclusively with the successful mop-up of Communist remnants in Gannan in the first six months after the start of the Long March and had little or nothing to say about later Communist activities in the old soviets.[6] This silence reflected Nationalist claims that Communism had been snuffed out in southern China after the soviets' collapse.

For contemporary materials, I had to make do with a bare handful of press reports and of interviews with rearguard leaders taken by Western journalists in the late 1930s, at the end of the Three-Year War and the start of the new war against Japan. My main sources of information were a few dozen short memoirs published before the Cultural Revolution. I had little chance to check them against other, less fallible, evidence.

Even on the basis of these limited materials, I suspected that without a grounded understanding of the Three-Year War, many gaps in our grasp of Chinese Communism and the Chinese Revolution would remain. They needed to be filled—and not just to write the prehistory of the New Fourth Army or to complete the biographies of some main leaders of the Chinese Communist Party. Writings on the Chinese Revolution tend to be preoccupied with visible success: but defeat is the nursery of change, and Communism in defeat in central and southern China after 1934 holds many clues to the nature of the Party and the secret of its endurance. The Three-Year War was waged in a decentralized way, without the resources of a vast military machine, by small groups largely native to the hills they used as bases. The problems they met were special but not unique in the story of the Chinese Revolution: the methods they evolved to meet them were the stock-in-trade of the Party in the villages, or became so after 1937. The Three-Year War was not directed in all its regions by men of "light and leading." Only a minority of its leaders went on to make careers on the national stage. This phenomenon, too, makes the war worthwhile to research. If you are a Chinese, you are more likely to have had dealings with the Tan Yubaos and Gao Jingtings of the revolution than with the Mao Zedongs and Zhu Des. The story of the Three-Year War is in many ways more typical of Chinese Communism, and more revealing of its causes, its strengths, and its weaknesses, than a library of Politburo minutes. It is also an epic of human perseverance with few parallels in the history of the Chinese Revolution.

My discovery of the truth about the Three-Year War came slowly. I started my Ph.D. dissertation with a chapter on what had happened in it; I was far from satisfied with the evidence that this chapter was based on, but, like many other historians researching the Chinese Revolution, I thought it better to compromise than to abstain.[7] In 1980 I went to Taiwan to consult archives on the New Fourth Army held by the Guomindang's Bureau of Intelligence in Taibei. It had not crossed my mind that I might find original materials on the Three-Year War there. I had read in memoirs about political statements on national and international questions that were issued from mountain caves and about conferences held among the trees between 1934 and 1938, but I had thought them exaggerated, and I had never dreamed that material evidence of them might exist. Yet there they were in the Taibei archive: crumbling leaflets, tattered pamphlets, and even a run of *Hongqi* put out by stay-behinders in Minxi'nan. Not all bases of the Three-Year War were represented;

and a good 90 percent of the documents were from Minxi'nan. But their contents closely bore out some of the claims in memoirs, which I now viewed with a new respect. This discovery of correspondences between memoirs and contemporary documents did not, of course, mean that all memoirs were credible, or that I could write my history out of memoirs without individually scrutinizing them. But it dispelled my automatic skepticism about their claims, which now seemed to conform to Paley's dictum that human testimony is mostly "substantial truth under circumstantial variety."

In 1978, the Third Plenum of the Party's Central Committee in Beijing decided to set up a special body to call conferences on Party history, publish articles, collect materials, and encourage veterans to record their experiences in the revolution. At more or less the same time as I was uncovering new materials in Taibei, the trickle of information generated by the Beijing decision grew to a flood. It included memoirs (both new and old, among them some previously held back from publication or suppressed), studies, documents (many of them collected before the Cultural Revolution), maps, and photos. Originally I had intended to confine my discussion of the Three-Year War to an introductory chapter of a larger study on the New Fourth Army, but when the full extent of the material became clear to me, I decided to devote a separate volume to it. On trips to China, I fleshed out the published record with visits to sites of the Three-Year War, interviews with veterans of the revolution, and visits to museums (which in China display documents, maps, and written analyses as well as material remains). Inevitably, geographical biases in the materials available in Taibei and in the direction of my fieldwork influenced the shape of this book, and they help explain why some chapters (for example, that on Minxi'nan) are longer, and based on better evidence, than others. In some places (for example, Mindong), regional leaders energetically promoted research on the Three-Year War; in others (for example, Minyue), research started relatively late. These variations, too, are reflected in the book's shape.[8]

The Three-Year War figured conspicuously in new Party history publishing after 1978, the more so as the 1980s progressed and the fiftieth anniversaries of events in the war came and went. There are other explanations, too, for the war's new visibility. In the past, scholars both in China and abroad had written about the revolution as if it were more or less synonymous with Mao, but in the revisionist climate of the 1980s, Mao's role has been scaled down, and other neglected leaders, like those who fought the Three-Year War, have received long-overdue recognition. The rehabilitation of the Three-Year War returned a missing file to the public record and righted a grave political wrong, for over the years many local veterans of the Three-Year War had been stigmatized and discriminated against. Another possible explanation for the new interest in the Three-Year War is that it seemed to some people to embody virtues of renewed relevance to China after Mao, in particular the virtue of pragmatic adaptation to circumstance.

After 1978, much political and economic power in China was decentralized and returned to the provinces and the regions. This change, too, had its impact on the historiography of the Chinese Revolution. The Three-Year War was an affair of the regions, fought and led by people in their native places. Veterans of the Long March stood a greater chance of rising to national power after 1949 than did those of the Three-Year War, who were more likely to take power in the provinces and the localities. Elderly men and women thrust back into government in the provinces after the Cultural Revolution began to look to their places in the history books and to speak to posterity through memoirs and commissioned studies. Earlier, historical materials on the revolution were usually published centrally. The authorities apparently suppressed unorthodox recollections or brought them into conformity with the prescribed view. In the 1980s, provincial and local presses became more active in memoir publishing. History, which had once served only the state, began to serve the interests of smaller, regional groupings too. Party leaders in the provinces and the counties encouraged their history committees to publish bulletins and books containing articles, documents, chronologies, and memoirs. In the past, publishing of this sort, even where it happened, rarely reached foreign scholars, but in the new, more casual climate of the 1980s it often did, through formal and informal contacts with Chinese colleagues. Local historians became avid accomplices in the campaign to promote their local Party's contribution to the revolution, not just to "seek truth from the facts," but also to please their patrons, to gratify local pride, and not least to raise their own profile in Party history circles by discovering a regional tradition. (History boards no less than trade boards need a marketable local product.)

The new history valued special circumstance and originality: a competition arose to be best, and different. Regionalism, "being a jealous mistress, demands . . . a particularistic history, a private affair, as it were," between the local Party and the people.[9] The Three-Year War had been a period of local experimentation in the south. Southern historians out to promote their region's past probably turned with a sense of relief from the difficulties of negotiating the early 1930s, when even peripheral bases were under the sway of a "leftism" out of sympathy with China's current politics, to the Three-Year War, which marked the start in the south of an era more in tune with the new orthodoxy.

## MEMOIRS AND HOW TO USE THEM

For the Three-Year War, memoirs are by far the most common source of information; analytical studies (insofar as they exist) are written largely from these memoirs rather than from contemporary documentation, which is in scant supply. Memoirs written in China since 1949 share many of the weaknesses of the genre as we know it in the West. Most Western historians follow the rule that memoirs (like letters) should be used to complement evidence gained from other sources, not to form its frame. Memory "is not a storehouse, it is a selecting machine."[10] It is incomplete and unreliable. When the events it sifts concern revolution and class struggle, self-exculpation and political animosity inevitably distort the record. Political memoirs "labor under a complex personal equation": they have an axe to grind.[11]

Chinese memoirs since 1949 have all these drawbacks and several more. They are winners' history written in a society where "the loser is a thief," the losers in this case being not only the defeated Nationalists but also the losers in the Party's endless internal conflicts. On broader questions, these memoirs cleave closely to the dominant political line. They are designed not to stand alone as records of integral, independent lives but to furnish "concrete" illustrations of the general truths of Party history that dictate their framework and their setting. (Thus for many years the only veterans of the Chinese Revolution who could write full-length autobiographies were its dissidents, like Wang Fanxi and Zheng Chaolin, and its renegades, like Zhang Guotao and Gong Chu.) Party memoirs are often edited or ghostwritten on the basis of oral testimony collected on tape recorders or by stenographers. The typical memoir is short, confined to one or two incidents or issues, and often grossly stereotyped. To quarry the few apparently hard facts from it, you must first hack through a dense layer of political shibboleths, editorial embellishment, and edifying anecdotes; even then, what remains is not necessarily the unvarnished truth.

Does this mean that memoirs must be ruled out as sources? No, for that would be to close a main—in some cases the only—door to the past. The question is not whether but how to use them: by what techniques to appraise their evidential value.

Some of these techniques are identical to those applied by Western historians to autobiographical evidence about their own societies. What are the author's antecedents, character, and environment? It he efficient in transmission, knowledgeable, truthful, accurate, alert, and painstaking? What did he know? How did he know it? And what "remained quite unknown to him"? If other data are to hand, how do the author's recollections square with them? Is the text internally consistent, or is it rent by contradictions? Is it intact, or has it been in some way changed? Precise and stringent controls of text and context are the main ways of verifying evidence, supplemented, of course, by feel, faith, doubt, common sense, and educated guesswork.[12]

But in important ways, autobiographical writing in the People's Republic of China is not like autobiographical writing in the West, and different techniques of scrutiny and appraisal must be applied to it. A political historian in the West will set great score by evidence independently attested by several witnesses, on the grounds that the greater the number of testimonies, the more likely the evidence is to be true. But in China, even people remembering independently of one another many sometimes commit identical untruths because they are subject to the same internal constraints. In China the group—based on blood, faith, age, name, school, place, tongue, or some other bond of sentiment and experience—is valued infinitely more than the individual. Personal modesty and self-deprecation are features of both Communism and of China: small wonder that whereas in the West, writers of memoirs strive to advance themselves, in China under the Communists they strive to glorify the group. This distinction also explains other differences between memoirs of the two traditions. Political memoirs everywhere are compost for the lie, but lies take many forms. One relevant distinction (drawn from theology) is that between the formal and the material lie. In a society where the lie is material and officially prescribed, cover-ups are more easily recognizable than in one where the lie is formal and individually improvised. The predictability and transparency of the Chinese lie help the historian, who can more easily do justice to the residual truth; but because they cannot be separated from the Chinese habit of writing to partisan stereotypes, Chinese memoirs, page for page, yield less satisfying evidence than Western ones. In the West, memoirs are largely an individual enterprise and in the personal domain. They are of uneven competence: some are painstakingly researched from diaries, papers, and consultations, some are not. In China, where the Communist Party takes its collective history seriously, resources are made available to elicit and edit the testimony of veterans.[13] The quality of editing and research is not always high, and the fact of editing gives scope to censorship: but it is sometimes an aid to truth, and it results in the collection and verification of materials (including the testimony of illiterates) that would otherwise be lost. Sometimes Chinese memoirs are edited from group discussions. In theory, these collective memoirs—a form virtually unknown in the West—correct personal bias and pool complementary information, but they are even more likely than individual testimony to conform to received opinion.

Taken singly, most Chinese memoirs since 1949 are of limited value and dubious reliability. Veterans of the Three-Year War formed close-knit

groups that over the years have evolved a common stock of loyalties, legends, and tall stories. Yet because their recollections are a unique source
on otherwise largely unrecorded business, we must pay them serious attention, though with greater than usual vigilance and discrimination.

What special techniques must be applied to coax their secrets from
them? To adepts, it is a question of feel and intuition, or automatic and
unconscious habits of scrutiny. Intuition will cause you to linger over
passages containing numbers, statistics, names, dates, and similar apparently hard facts. It will arrest you at quotations from historical documents directly related to the content of the memoir, for experience suggests that such quotations are not invented (though they are sometimes
anachronistically embellished with references to Chairman Mao; and
even when genuine and credible, they are rarely textually intact). And it
will hurry you past pages of stereotyped dialogue, edifying comment,
anonymous incidents, exaggerated accounts of virtue, quotations from
Mao and the Marxist classics, episodes transparently designed to illustrate Party dogma, and "explanations" that resort to general axioms
rather than to specific facts.

Truth in these memoirs is like a faint flickering signal in a sea of
words, whose bearings can only be plotted from two or more places simultaneously. Today, fortunately, memoirists and their editors are less
likely to elide or embellish the truth. Though it is hard to corroborate
testimony in these memoirs by historical documents, there are other
ways of obtaining reasonably reliable running fixes on the truth. These
memoirs are partly (sometimes largely) a construct of current politics;
they rarely strive for independence and objectivity. Officially approved
truth in China changes over time, as do the limits within which it may be
exercised, and the historian's recognition of these shifts allows a reconstruction of one reasonably dependable truth from many partial truths
established by as stringent a control of the evidence as conditions allow.
Voltaire's injunction that "extreme skepticism" is just as objectionable as
"ridiculous credulity" is one useful maxim in this work; another is that
the fuller and more particular the detail, the greater the presumption of
its accuracy.[14] Some detail in Chinese memoirs is indisputably invented,
but invented according to literary and political conventions that are for
the most part recognizable to the practiced eye.

Detail not prescribed by literary or political convention and specifying incidents involving named people is a different matter. Experience
in checking and cross-checking scores of memoirs against other forms of
evidence and against each other has convinced me that in China under
the Communists, memoirists and historians alike are far more likely to
distort the record by not saying what they know to be true than by say-

ing what they know to be untrue. In short, they sin by omission, not commission. This tendency need surprise no one. Witnesses in any society who testify in public are often kept by fear of contradiction from wandering too far from the truth: the more they make up, the more easily they can be found out and discredited. In China, the risk of exposure is rarely worth running; the penalties and sanctions are too great. As regimes change, today's indiscretions can become tomorrow's capital offenses.

What of studies on the revolution by Chinese historians? Broadly speaking, historians are reluctant to base original work on the work of others, for they are secondary authorities, "which is to say, no authorities at all."[15] But this excellent advice cannot apply to historians of the more obscure episodes of the Chinese Revolution, who often have no primary sources and are sometimes as dependent on secondary accounts as are historians of antiquity on Thucydides and Caesar.

Chinese historians of the Party and the revolution work under constraints rarely encountered in the West, for, like Lenin's "cogs and wheels in the Party machine," they are expected to be committed and partisan rather than neutral and objective. In the decade of the Cultural Revolution, history in China degenerated into what Vladimir Dedijer terms "atheistic theology."[16] During those ten years, the few studies that did appear conformed more or less to the canons of what Thomas J. Heffernan (writing about Europe's Middle Ages) has called sacred biography: they were designed to "synthesize complex ideologies in narrative"; to teach "the truth of the faith through the principle of individual example"; and to "excite the minds of listeners to emulate [the life of saints]."[17] During this period more than any other, historians invented, exaggerated, and suppressed important details to raise up Mao and cast down his rivals. Today facts are in theory inviolable, cult biography is no longer universal, and writers quote Mao Zedong less frequently.[18] In practice, however, Chinese historians are still rarely free to say exactly what they think; they mostly follow the orthodox, monolithic view (though this is now broad enough to accommodate disputes and differences of opinion). Today, historians have greater access than in the past to Party archives and informants, and, like their counterparts in Taiwan, devote meticulous attention to preserving documents and compiling records.[19] (In Taiwan, as on the mainland, the grand tradition of Chinese historiography, with its twin stresses on didacticism and the amassing of vast numbers of documents, is entirely compatible with the modern-day strong state.) But the histories they write are still bound by politics, and the documents they publish are selected and not necessarily intact. However well a study is researched, it is still rare to find in it the range of references expected as a matter of course in a Western study. Relying on it is still a matter of trust, based either on intuition or on personal acquaintance with the historian's methods, contacts, resources, and scruples. But the close correspondence between history writing and the official point of view is not an unrelieved inhibition on the truth, for it makes uniform and predictable the intentions that inspire authors and the conventions that bind them.

Scholars in practically no other field of modern history would be satisfied with evidence of the sort on which this book largely rests. But after starving in the 1970s, I was grateful for whatever crumbs of information fell my way in the 1980s, and I was prepared to treat them with techniques that better-off colleagues might dismiss as alien to the spirit of critical scholarship. The relationship between historians in general and historians working on the revolution in the Chinese countryside is analogous to that between earth scientists and lunar geographers or even (during the Cultural Revolution) stellar spectroscopists.

The project of which this study is an unexpectedly heavy spin-off began in the barren early 1970s and has lived through several changes in official views on the Three-Year War. It has drawn on successive waves—and trickles—of reminiscences and scholarship, as well as on original materials from the 1930s. It has grown over the years like a coral thicket, through the constant accretion of fresh buds. The coral analogy captures the limits of the project, too, for the fringing reefs that grow in surface waters are shaped not only by the base on which they fasten but also by the direction and force of the currents that bring their food. Just as the framework of a coral reef is formed by the skeleton secreted by dead generations, so too in this book I have tended to let old references stand and simply joined the new ones to them. The study was built up by running corrections made as I went along, by the slow increment of detail and certitude. Critics might wish that I had pruned my references more systematically instead of duplicating them. But many of the sources I consulted (especially archives in Taiwan and restricted publications on the mainland) are no longer available to me save through my notes, so in working up my data I could not compare earlier and later materials to see how far they overlap. Often old, less dependable data in sources published before 1966 subtly complement and extend stronger data published in the 1980s (though to explain how in each separate reference would be pedantic).

The late Jack Belden predicted in an article in the *Shanghai Evening Post and Mercury* in 1939 that "the full tale of the Red Armies left behind [in southern China by the Long March] will probably never be written."[20] He was almost right. The Three-Year War was thrust into oblivion for nearly half a century; even today, no integral and comprehensive study of it has appeared in China (let alone anywhere else, in any language, before this book).[21] There are reasons besides politics for the slighting of the Three-Year War. It was waged in fourteen different places by scores of different groups. They included no Mao or Stalin with teams of journalists and stenographers hanging on his every word. They lived in caves and forests—and even if there was a fugitive stenographer among the troglodytes, there was not necessarily any ink or paper, or a chance to use it, or a place to keep it. (The exception to this statement is Minxi'nan, where Communists kept up a steady stream of documents and publications.) Most veterans of the Three-Year War are dead; most of them probably died without adding their memories to the pool. In 1978, according to one expert, there were just 4,600 Red Army veterans still alive; probably about a quarter of them were veterans of the Three-Year War. In 1986, fewer than twenty veterans of the Three-Year War in Xianggan were still alive. The generation that fought the Three-Year War will not be with us much longer.[22]

My main aim in writing this book was to recover lost events (and prove Jack Belden wrong) by telling the story of the Three-Year War "as it actually was." Though I make no effort to hide my theoretical preconceptions about the Chinese Revolution, this study is as much a narrative and an ethnography (defined as the "thick" description of the customs, habits, and differences of groups of people) as a history in the analytical, interpretative sense. It is so partly because I believe (with Elton) that "history is a story and its proper method is narrative."[23] But it is also because my task was to reconstruct the facts of the Three-Year War rather than to reflect on an existing body of knowledge.[24]

The structure of this book is quite rudimentary. It is a journey in time, from 1934 to 1938, and in space, through the fourteen or so regions in which the Three-Year War was fought (see Map 1). From an analytical point of view, the direction of the journey is arbitrary. It starts in Gannan, the powerhouse of Chinese Communism between 1930 and 1934; it follows the route in 1934 of the Seventh Red Army Corps' Anti-Japanese Expedition through Fujian into Anhui; it crosses the Chang Jiang northward into Eyuwan; and it returns south through Xiang'egan into Xianggan and Xiangnan, ending up quite close to its original starting point. In each place, it follows the same basic form: a short history of the base (insofar as it is relevant to events after 1934) and a look at the Three-Year War there. Since the different chapters are not different stages in a single argument but could equally well stand alone, it is better that they are named rather than numbered.

# ACKNOWLEDGMENTS

Bill Jenner, a polymath and model of good writing and scholarly scruple, guided me by precept and example through the thesis whose first chapter grew into this book (on which, however, he had little direct influence); for twenty years he has been a true friend.

Wang Fanxi, 86, a veteran revolutionary and an implacable opponent of all established authority, would in another age have excelled as a scholar or a writer. He left Macau in 1975 and came to live with me, Dora, and Katie in Leeds. Though he too had little direct influence on the way this book was written, through his nurturant presence he has taught me more about China and the world than any other person.

I did most of the thinking and writing for this study during my ten years at the University of Amsterdam's Anthropological-Sociological Centre. Researching it was at first a lonely odyssey in a university where I was the sole sinologist, but later I found that my isolation from the world of Chinese studies had freed me into a bigger one. China specialists are notoriously parochial and monomaniac, a result of the stupefactive drudgery of memorizing thousands of characters at an age when others are experimenting with ideas and of the huge effort needed to keep even minimally abreast of the great flow of books from and on China, which leaves small time for other reading. My colleagues at Amsterdam took pity on my disability and tried hard to cure it by teaching me things of wider use.

The person who helped me most, with gentle but disturbing questions, was Rod Aya, the epitome of intellectual stringency, an outstanding editor, and a gifted theorist and generalist, who lightened my days in Holland with his optimism, good company, and feudal sense of loyalty.

Others, too, in Amsterdam played the game of dialectic with me and helped speed the completion of this book. My colleagues in the Department of South and Southeast Asian Studies under Otto van den Muijzenberg introduced me to new methods and intellectual traditions and released me more than was my strict due from teaching for research. Laszlo Sluimers, with his usual generosity and zeal, translated a long pamphlet for me from Japanese into Dutch. Frans Huesken and Hans Vermeulen did their best to make an anthropologist of me and taught me concepts that lit up new areas of the Chinese Revolution.

Over the years several men and women whose opinion I value have helped persuade me that it was worth keeping at this book, though few of them probably know quite how much their support meant to me. They are Lucien Bianco, Chen Yung-fa, John Gittings, Kathleen Hartford, Chalmers Johnson, Don Rimmington, John S. Service, Margaret Sleeboom, Lyman P. Van Slyke, and Wei Hongyun. Margaret Sleeboom also read and commented on the concluding chapter.

This research has been supported at various times by the Department of Chinese (now East Asian) Studies and the Publications Committee at the University of Leeds; the Anthropological-Sociological Centre and the Foreign Affairs Bureau at the University of Amsterdam; and the Dutch Organization for Scientific Research. In 1985–86 I exchanged the stress and bustle of Amsterdam for the tranquillity of Wassenaar, where as a Fellow of the Netherlands Institute for Advanced Study in the Humanities and Social Sciences I drafted some chapters of this work.

The libraries where I did most of my reading are at Leeds University, where David Arrandale has assembled a distinguished collection of books on Chinese Communist history; London's School of Oriental and African Studies; John Dolfin's University Services Centre in Hongkong; Taibei's Bureau of Intelligence (actually an archive); Leiden's Sinological Institute; and Xiamen University. The History Department at Xiamen organized field trips for me to Longyan, Changting, Ruijin, and other sites of the Three-Year War, where local Party historians put me up, showed me around, and took to me meet informants.

John Dixon (who died tragically young, in December 1991) and Tim Hadwin drew the maps. Peter Nix, Anne Simpson, Ada Tieman, and Maartje Uneputty helped technically to produce various drafts of the book.

James H. Cole, who directs China Publication Subventions in New York, gave the book his annual award, an unexpected honor.

Sheila Levine, Amy Klatzkin, and Erika Büky at the University of California Press assisted with unflagging patience, care, courtesy, and editorial exactitude in the birth of this volume.

To all these people and organizations, I return my warmest thanks. Writing this book took me away more often than I should have allowed from my daughter Katja and my son Daniel. Dora, their mother, shared my life for most of the years it took to complete this study. She must have wondered at her own patience as she encouraged and endured my work. To the three of them, my apologies and special thanks.

# A NOTE ON TERMS

## NAMES OF PLACES

Chinese provinces each have a full name, generally consisting of two characters (or syllables), and an abbreviated name, derived from some geographical feature (for example, a river or a mountain) or an ancient name associated with the province, consisting of one character. In Chinese, the abbreviated form is generally used when the province is named in conjunction with one or more other provinces (including in lists); in other special combinations; or when part of the province is specified using the suffix *zhong* (central) or a point on the compass. Thus the abbreviated name for Fujian is Min and for Jiangxi, Gan; and the region along the border between these two provinces is called Min'gan, while northern Fujian is called Minbei, that is, Fujian-north. This book follows Chinese usage in most respects, and for two main reasons: first, because combining abbreviated names (as in Min'gan) creates a distinct identity for border regions that juxtaposing the full forms (Fujian-Jiangxi) does not, and second, because is produces forms that are shorter and more memorable. For example, Eyuwan (a combination of three abbreviated forms) is easier to recognize than "the Hubei-Henan-Anhui border region," which for Western readers has the added disadvantage that Hubei and Henan are easily confused with Hebei and Hunan (also provinces). Conformity to Chinese usage, brevity, and ease of identification—these, then, are the reasons why I have, where applicable, opted for the abbreviated names of Chinese provinces. The following list explains the abbreviations used in this book.

| | |
|---|---|
| Anhui | Wan |
| Fujian | Min |
| Guangdong | Yue |

| Henan | Yu |
|-------|-----|
| Hubei | E |
| Hunan | Xiang |
| Jiangxi | Gan |
| Shaanxi | Shaan |
| Zhejiang | Zhe |

The cardinal points are attached to these forms, singly or in combinations, as suffixes. They are as follows in Chinese.

| dong | east |
|------|------|
| xi | west |
| nan | south |
| bei | north |

Using these two lists, the place-names used in this book can be converted where necessary into full forms. But most readers will not need to do so. Specialists will recognize the combinations anyway; nonspecialists can analyze them if they wish or accept them as place-names in their own right.

## THE WAR AND THE BASES

The "Three-Year War" is my own coinage, used to render the Chinese term *nanfang basheng sannian youjizhanzheng* (three-year guerrilla war in eight southern provinces). Both terms are inexact. Even if we take south to mean the entire region south of the Chang Jiang, the Three-Year War was fought not only in southern China but also in Eyuwan, which is north of the Chang Jiang and southerly only in relation to Yan'an, which became the Party's capital in 1936. The term "guerrilla" applied to units in the Three-Year War has also been disputed in some contexts, though less convincingly. Some people have objected that the troops left behind in Eyuwan were not guerrillas but members of a main-force unit and that they kept their regular designation throughout the Three-Year War.[1] But whatever their background, they fought almost exclusively on irregular lines after 1934. Three years is also inexact, for the guerrilla struggle started at different times in different places. In Eyuwan, it was a five-year war; elsewhere, it fell several months short of three years.

Another problem concerns the number of regions in which the Three-Year War was fought. Conventional accounts list fourteen. For example, one standard account lists the Changting-Ruijin border area, Yuegan, Xiangnan, Xianggan, Xiang'egan, the Tongbai Mountains, Eyuwan, Gandongbei, Zhe'nan, Minbei, Mindong, Minnan, Minzhong, and Qiongya;[2] other studies use different names for some of these places, but other than that they are the same. Earlier accounts, however, do not list Qiongya (Hainan Island) as a region of the Three-Year War,

and some omit Minnan too. The omission of Qiongya is easily explained
if the Three-Year War is defined as a stage in the evolution of the New
Fourth Army, for Qiongya is the only region on the conventional list
that did not contribute a body of troops to the New Fourth Army nucleus. Minnan illustrates a different problem: how to delimit regions in
a war with no fixed fronts. The same is true of Eyu, which sometimes
comes under Eyuwan; of Minzhong, which usually disappears into Mindong; and of Xiangnan, which is sometimes included under Ganyue,
sometimes under Xianggan. There is no orderly solution to this problem, for the division between one region and the next is not always clear,
and sometimes different groups within one region are counted separately. The historian Yan Jingtang (1986) has tried to resolve the problem by classifying regions on the basis of a combination of the name of
the local Communist and guerrilla organization and its geographical location. This approach does not cancel all the anomalies, but it provides
a unitary framework within which they can be clarified.

In disagreements on the number of regions of the Three-Year War,
even the conventional figure of fourteen is reached in different ways by
different studies. My own classification, explained below, accepts the
conventional estimate of fourteen regions but substitutes Minzhong
(usually omitted from Chinese lists) for Qiongya (nowadays often included in them). I have already explained why Qiongya should not be
listed as a region of the Three-Year War.[3] Below I justify the rest of my
list and offer solutions to various problems of terminology.[4]

Studies of the Three-Year War conventionally divide the old Central
Soviet area into Min'gan, meaning the area around Ruijin and on the
border between Ruijin and Changting; and Minxi or Minxi'nan, meaning the area to the west and south of Changting. Min and Gan are the
abbreviated names of the provinces of Fujian and Jiangxi, to which
Changting and Ruijin belong. After 1934, guerrillas slipped to and fro
across the border between Changting (Tingzhou) and Ruijin and at one
point called themselves the Tingrui Guerrillas. Their base is therefore
often called Min'gan. This name has the advantage of suggesting historical continuity with the Central Soviet, which also spanned the border.
But though guerrillas were active in Changting after 1934, they operated mainly on the Gannan (southern Jiangxi) side of the border, from
bases around Ruijin. Other Communist remnants were active further to
the west, in and around Ganxian and other counties of central Gannan,
one hundred miles from Changting. The term Min'gan ignores these
groups and directs attention exclusively to the border area between the
provinces. Moreover, Communists in two other places north of Ruijin
used the name Min'gan to describe their committees after 1934. To
avoid confusion, I refer to the old Central Soviet area (excluding the

part east of Changting) as Gannan, which is the abbreviated name for southern Jiangxi commonly used in Chinese studies to describe the region around Ruijin. Strictly speaking, it does not include that part of the Tingrui base around Changting, but otherwise it meets most of our requirements.

Ganyue (the Jiangxi-Guangdong border region) is sometimes called Yuegan in contemporary reports, but most sources call it Ganyue. This name is preferable because the larger part of the base was in Jiangxi and because it came under the leadership of the Gannan Provincial Committee and Military Region.

Minyue (the Fujian-Guangdong border region) is sometimes called Minnan (southern Fujian), but it was known at the time of the Three-Year War as Minyue. Though it was mainly on the Fujian side of the border, it was garrisoned by guerrillas from both Fujian and Guangdong, and it stretched into a small part of Guangdong. It is treated here in the chapter on Minxi'nan.

Minxi'nan (southwestern Fujian) is sometimes called Minxi (western Fujian) in sources. Minxi is the old, pre-1935 name of the base, which even after 1934 did not extend into Minnan (southern Fujian). But the Party authorities in Minxi called themselves the Minxi'nan Committee after 1934; this committee existed until October 1937, when it was replaced by a new body called the Minyuegan Committee. Where I am talking about the committee, I say Minxi'nan; where I mean the region, I use Minxi.

Minzhong (central Fujian) is usually subsumed under Mindong, but it had its own independent Party organization and guerrilla army with bases in a strategic part of Fujian not far from Fuzhou, the provincial capital. This Minzhong base should not be confused with the Minzhong outpost set up further inland by Minbei guerrillas after 1934. Minzhong is treated here in the chapter on Mindong.

Mindong (eastern Fujian) is sometimes called Mindongbei. Like Zhe'nan, it is also sometimes called Minzhe or Zhemin (the Fujian-Zhejiang border region) because of its proximity to the border and because at one point Mindong guerrillas were active in part of Zhejiang and tried to merge with guerrillas there.

Minbei (northern Fujian) originally came under the Gandongbei Provincial Committee, later renamed first Minzhegan and then Min'gan. In May 1935, after the collapse of the Min'gan Committee, the Minbei Subcommittee carried on independently. In April 1936, the Minbei and Mindong Communists decided to merge in a restored Min'gan Committee, but the merger failed in practice and the new body represented only Minbei. So Minbei is sometimes known as Min'gan in Party sources, though I reserve this term for the committee that was active further south along the same provincial border.

Wanzhegan (the Anhui-Zhejiang-Jiangxi border region) is sometimes called Gandongbei (northeastern Jiangxi) or Minzhegan (the
Fujian-Zhejiang-Jiangxi border region) by historians, but the first title
was superseded in 1932 and the second in April 1936, when the committee adopted the name Wanzhegan. Wanzhegan is geographically more
accurate, for by 1935 forces under this committee were no longer active
in Fujian (Min) and had expanded into Anhui (Wan).

Zhe'nan (southern Zhejiang) is sometimes known as Zhemin or Minzhe (see Mindong, above), but its center was in Zhejiang and the attempt
to set up a Minzhe Committee with the Communists in Mindong failed.
The Red Army units that ended up in Zhe'nan spent much of 1935 trying to set up a base in Zhexi'nan (southwestern Zhejiang); later they established a presence in Zhedong (eastern Zhejiang).

Eyuwan (the Hubei-Henan-Anhui border region) is sometimes called
the Dabie Mountains region. Eyu (the Hubei-Henan border region) is
sometimes called the Yu'nan (southern Henan) or Tongbai Mountains
region, where the guerrillas lived and fought after 1934. But they
came under the leadership of the Eyu Provincial Committee and called
themselves the Eyu Guerrillas. They are treated here in the chapter
on Eyuwan.

Xiang'egan is the Hunan-Hubei-Jiangxi border region.

Xianggan is the Hunan-Jiangxi border region.

Xiangnan (southern Hunan) is sometimes called Xiangyuegan (the
Hunan-Guangdong-Jiangxi border region) or Xiangyue. Four main
guerrilla bands were active here after 1934: one was in Xiangyuegan,
the rest were mainly in Xiangnan. In January 1936, the Xiangnan and
Xiangyuegan Committees merged in a new Xiangnan Committee, so the
region is best called Xiangnan. Originally, the leaders of the Xiangyuegan Committee were part of the Ganyue base, so their base in Xiangyuegan is sometimes classified under Ganyue.

## POLITICAL TERMS

The Guomindang is the Nationalist Party of Chiang Kai-shek, considered by Chinese Marxists to represent the political interests of the bourgeoisie, the landlords, and the big bureaucrats. It is spelled Kuomintang
in older Western studies and is often abbreviated to KMT. The Chinese
Communists twice formed a united front with the Guomindang, once
between 1924 and 1927 and again after 1936. Between 1927 and 1936,
and again between 1946 and 1949, the two parties fought each other in
civil wars.

The Chinese Communist Party, like the Russian one, had its soviets
(transliterated as *suweiai*) and its Red Army. Chinese Communists saw
themselves as part of a world revolution directed by one center (the

Comintern, or Communist International, also called the Third International, with its headquarters in Moscow) under one flag (the Red Flag, with the hammer-and-sickle emblem). Soviet government, unlike other forms of government, was based on mass participation by the workers, peasants, and soldiers in a vast pyramid of soviets (meaning councils in Russian) from the village to the national level. The goal of the soviet was to establish a dictatorship of the toiling classes over the bourgeois and "feudal" classes. The Chinese Communists stopped using the names "soviet" and "Red Army" in 1936, when they temporarily reunited with the Guomindang.

"Leftism" is a term that appears frequently in this book. In China, it is short for " 'leftist' opportunism" and is usually placed in quotation marks to distinguish it from orthodox leftism. I have followed this usage and kept the punctuation to indicate Chinese "leftism" in the 1930s as opposed to leftism more generally. Communist historians distinguish three "leftist" lines between November 1927 and January 1935, under Qu Qiubai, Li Lisan, and Wang Ming. "Leftist" leaders promoted policies that were ideologically rigid and politically sectarian. They exaggerated the significance of the economic struggle against capitalists and rich peasants and of political struggle against "enemies of the revolution" inside and outside the Party. Because they denied or neglected the existence of intermediate classes, their policies alienated potential allies of the Party in the villages and polarized society in places where "leftists" wielded power. They underestimated the strength of the Guomindang and refused to recognize that their social and political base had been temporarily exhausted by their defeat at the hands of the Guomindang in 1927. On the contrary, they believed that the Guomindang was deep in crisis and that new revolutionary forces were growing up that would help propel the Communists into power.

Denying that the revolution was at a "low ebb" and arguing that it was on a "continuous upsurge" toward a "new high tide," they opposed any suggestion of an "orderly retreat," either political or military, and they planned to seize cities in a "decisive fight" against the Guomindang. They believed that the time was ripe after 1927 for a "national offensive" across the whole of China, and they refused to recognize that the revolutionary forces were not everywhere equally strong. They slighted Mao's guerrilla tactics and favored a more centralized and regular form of warfare. They are associated with excessive use of terror, exhortation, and "commandist" (i.e., arbitrary) methods. They imported Stalinist-style purges and show trials to the parts of the Chinese countryside that they controlled and used them against both "class enemies" and "political enemies," including oppositionist and dissident factions in the Party. They frequently accused their political enemies of being Trotskyists or members of the Social Democratic Party, the Anti-Bolshevik League, or some other "counterrevolutionary" organization; but the charges were almost always groundless. In the Three-Year War, *sufan* (the purging of counterrevolutionaries) was mainly directed against real or supposed dissidents in the Party and the Red Army.

According to Party historians, Mao Zedong resisted the three "leftist" lines, promoted more realistic policies, opposed excessive "struggle" both in society and in the Party, recognized the "uneven" nature of the revolution, favored adapting policies to specific circumstance, preferred persuasion to coercion, and tried to create broader, more inclusive alliances. Actually, Mao and his supporters used the term "leftist" to discredit their rivals in the Party. The line between them and the "leftists" was never as sharp as they made out. Mao and his followers shared responsibility for many "leftist" excesses and atrocities, and they held many "leftist" views and attitudes themselves.

Some of the actions criticized as "leftist" were spontaneous outbreaks of indiscipline by rank-and-file activists going too far. But inasmuch as "leftism" represented a political program and an intellectual outlook, it was an import from the Soviet Union, though Chinese historians rarely admit as much. Mao at this stage had never been to Moscow; he had earned his reputation as a revolutionary leader exclusively in China. He was naturally prejudiced against the "foreign dogmas" upon which his rivals tried to build their careers, and he was more sensitive than they to moods and issues in the villages. To that extent, a distinction between Mao and the "leftists" is admissible.

"Mountaintoppist" is Chinese Communist jargon used to describe someone who suffers from "mountain-stronghold mentality, a type of sectarianism," that is, a tendency on the part of individuals or groups to stress their own importance and identity and to act independently of central Party authority. By no means is everyone in this book a mountaintoppist, but the Three-Year War probably had more than its share; for though they are not necessarily people who live (like the heroes of the Three-Year War) on mountaintops, away from Party discipline and control, they are quite likely to be. Mountaintoppists are often accused in Party literature of wanting to set up "independent kingdoms."

In the 1930s, "democratic personages" were those people (especially well-known scholars) who sympathized with the Communist Party and the Soviet Union; they were also known as "friends of the Soviet Union." After mid 1935, particularly after the outbreak of war with Japan, democratic (or patriotic) personages usually opposed the Chiang Kai-shek regime and always opposed the Japanese invasion. Democratic personages included not only ex-Communists, liberal scholars, and business leaders but also Guomindang leaders and military figures (like Feng

Yuxiang) who had been defeated by Chiang in internal struggles. After 1949 these people became ornaments on the Mao regime.

In Chinese Communist class analysis, hired hands (or agricultural laborers) derived more than half their income from farm labor. Poor peasants (who together with hired hands made up roughly 60 percent of rural families) rented or owned land but produced too little to subsist on. Middle peasants (roughly 30 percent) were able to subsist from the land they owned or rented, though some also worked for others. Rich peasants (roughly 8 percent) derived more than half their income from hired labor but were often themselves tenants; they produced more than enough to subsist on. Landlords (roughly 3 percent) derived their main income from rent. Between them, landlords and rich peasants owned roughly half the land in China as a whole, and more than half in the south. According to Party theory, poor peasants and hired hands were "brave fighters" for the revolution, middle peasants generally welcomed and joined the revolution, rich peasants vacillated between left and right, and landlords were feudal and counterrevolutionary. The "enlightened gentry" (also called the "patriotic gentry") were landlords and rich peasants "of a democratic hue" who opposed Chiang Kai-shek and imperialism and supported land revolution and Communist power.

China's twenty million bandits (*tufei*), or "men of the greenwood," were by origin predators, but many enjoyed popular prestige and were viewed more as Robin Hoods than as common criminals. Religious sects (*huimen*) like the Red Spears and the Great Knives, led for the most part by local notables, evolved as an extralegal form of defense against bandit predators in the absence of effective government control over the villages, but sects also resisted tax-gatherers and press-gangs. In time, the distinction between predation and protection became blurred as sects turned to banditry, bandits adopted names, rituals, and other paraphernalia of the sects, and both sects and bandits rebelled against the increasing encroachments on local society by warlords and the state. Perry (1980:21) calls this coalescence the "predatory-protective synthesis." Neither Communists nor Nationalists always distinguished between sects and bandits in their descriptions of rural society.

## OTHER TERMS

A *tuhao* is a local strongman, often comparatively rich and literate, who "bullie[s] others as if the law were nonexistent."[5]

The *baojia* system is "a centuries-old bureaucratically organized police system built on the principle of mutual guarantee and collective responsibility, as a comprehensive method for buttressing existing security

forces and extending governmental authority into the countryside."[6]
Each *jia* consists of ten households, each *bao* of ten *jia*.

The *mintuan* is the rural militia.

I have translated the Chinese word *xian* as county; others translate it
as district or simply transcribe the Chinese word either as *xian* or (if using the old transcription) as *hsien*.

A *qu* is a subdistrict below county level.

A *xiang* is a rural township or administrative village.

A *li* is one-third of an English mile.

A *mu* is one-sixth of an English acre.

A catty (*jin*) is half a kilogram. A picul (*dan*) is fifty kilograms.

*Jiang* and *He* in proper names mean river. The Chang Jiang is the
Long River, known in the West as the Yangtze.

Under the Nationalists, Beijing (Peking) was known as Beiping (Pei-
ping), but for the sake of simplicity and consistency, I have called it Beijing throughout this study.

I use the *Hanyu pinyin* spelling for all Chinese names save Chiang Kai-
shek and Ch'en I, the governor of Fujian Province in the 1930s, whose
name I spell in the old form to distinguish it from that of Chen Yi the
Communist.

# CHRONOLOGY

| | |
|---|---|
| July 23–31, 1921 | The Chinese Communists hold their First Congress. |
| 1924 | The Guomindang and the Chinese Communist Party form the first united front. |
| July 1, 1926 | Chiang Kai-shek orders the start of the Northern Expedition to overthrow the warlords and reunify China. |
| April 12, 1927 | Chiang Kai-shek eliminates the Communists in Shanghai after the city falls to him. |
| April 27, 1927 | The Communists decide to maintain the united front, this time with the Guomindang's left wing, in Wuhan. |
| July 25, 1927 | The Wuhan Guomindang turns against the Communists and the first united front comes to an end. |
| August–September 1927 | Communist-led insurrections fail. |
| October 1927 | Mao Zedong retreats to the Jinggang Mountains, where he sets up China's first Red state. |
| February 1929 | After fleeing to the Jinggang Mountains, Mao and Zhu De found a new base at Ruijin in Gannan, which later becomes the Central Soviet. |

| | |
|---|---|
| October 11, 1932 | Zhang Guotao withdraws his forces from Eyuwan and moves to Sichuan. |
| January 1933 | The Central Committee of the Chinese Communist Party moves from Shanghai, where it had gone underground, to Ruijin. |
| October 6, 1933 | Chiang Kai-shek begins his Fifth Encirclement campaign against the Communists. |
| November 20, 1933 | Dissident politicians and leaders of the Nationalists' Nineteenth Route Army proclaim a revolutionary government in Fujian. |
| January 21, 1934 | The revolutionary government in Fujian is brought to an end. |
| February 19, 1934 | Chiang Kai-shek launches the New Life Movement. |
| July 7, 1934 | The Red Seventh Army Corps leaves Gannan on its Anti-Japanese (or Northern) Expedition. |
| July 23, 1934 | The Red Sixth Army Corps leaves Xianggan on its Western Expedition. |
| September 12, 1934 | The Twenty-fifth Red Army leaves Eyuwan on its Long March. |
| October 16, 1934 | Around this time, the main Long March starts from Ruijin. |
| November 4, 1934 | Fang Zhimin takes command of the Anti-Japanese Expedition after it reaches Gandongbei, and is routed a week later. |
| January 15–18, 1935 | The Zunyi Conference, convened during the Long March, criticizes previous military policy and elevates Mao into the top leadership. |
| May 1935 | The Long Marchers cross the Jinsha River into Sichuan. |
| June 10, 1935 | Chinese troops and officials withdraw from Hebei under the He-Umezi agreement with Japan. |
| June 13, 1935 | The Red First and Fourth front armies, under Mao and Zhang Guotao respectively, unite in Sichuan. |

| June 18, 1935 | Qu Qiubai is executed in Changting. |
| August 1, 1935 | The Chinese delegation to the Comintern, led by Wang Ming, calls for a national united front against Japan. |
| August 20, 1935 | The Maoergai Conference, convened during the Long March, confirms Mao's strategy and resolves to establish a new base between Shaanxi and Gansu. |
| October 19, 1935 | The Central Red Army reaches the Shaanganning base, ending the Long March. |
| November 5, 1935 | Beijing students protest government persecution. |
| December 9, 1935 | Beijing students trigger nationwide agitation against Japanese imperialism. |
| December 1935 | The Party leaders in China, at the Wayaobao Conference, adopt the call for a national united front and begin to moderate their land policy. |
| February 17, 1936 | The Central Red Army announces its Eastern Expedition into Nationalist territory. |
| May–July 1936 | The warlords of Guangdong and Guangxi revolt against Chiang Kai-shek in the Liang Guang Incident but are eventually defeated. The Communist leaders in Shaanbei initially support the revolt. |
| October 22, 1936 | Armies under Zhang Guotao and He Long join Mao in Gansu. |
| December 1936 | The Chinese Communists in Shaanxi move their capital to Yan'an. |
| December 12, 1936 | Chiang Kai-shek is arrested in the Xi'an Incident, staged by the dissident Nationalist general Zhang Xueliang. Chiang is subsequently forced to agree to an alliance with the Chinese Communist Party. |
| February 10, 1937 | The Chinese Communists formally call on the Guomindang to enter into a second united front with them and in return offer to stop trying to overthrow the |

|  | government, to drop the names "soviet" and "Red Army," to bring in democracy in the regions they control, and to stop the land revolution. |
|---|---|
| June 1937 | Chiang Kai-shek and Zhou Enlai reach broad agreement on all major issues in their talks at Lushan. |
| July 7, 1937 | The Lugouqiao (or Marco Polo Bridge) Incident marks the start of all-out war between China and Japan. |
| August 13, 1937 | The Japanese attack Shanghai. |
| August 22–25, 1937 | At the Luochuan Conference, the Chinese Communist leaders decide on their strategy in the war. |
| August 25, 1937 | The Eighth Route Army is established from former Red Army forces in the north. |
| September 25, 1937 | Lin Biao defeats Japanese forces at Pingxingguan in Shanxi. |
| October 2, 1937 | The New Fourth Army is established from Communist guerrillas in south and central China. |
| November 9, 1937 | The Nationalists evacuate Shanghai. |
| November 27, 1937 | Wang Ming flies back to China and proposes a less radical version of the united front than Mao's. |
| December 13, 1937 | The Japanese occupy Nanjing and massacre up to two hundred thousand of its inhabitants. |
| May 12, 1938 | The New Fourth Army fights its first battle north of the Chang Jiang. On the same day, Xiamen falls to the Japanese. |
| June 17, 1938 | The New Fourth Army fights its first battle south of the Chang Jiang. |
| May 1939 | The New Fourth Army sets up a base on the southern bank of the Chang Jiang. |
| January 1941 | The New Fourth Army headquarters in Wannan are destroyed; two months later |

|                    | Xiang Ying, in hiding, is killed by a Communist defector. |
|--------------------|-----------------------------------------------------------|
| August 14, 1945    | Japan surrenders.                                         |
| July 12, 1946      | The civil war resumes.                                    |
| October 1, 1949    | Mao proclaims the People's Republic of China after winning the civil war. |

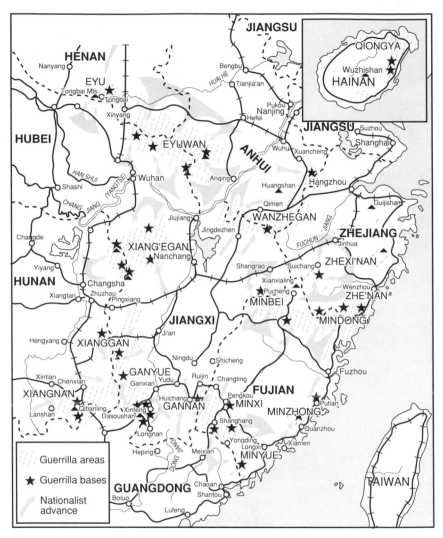

Map 1. The Three-Year War in southern China, 1934–37. *Based on a map in Wu Zaowen, ed., 1987.*

# The Soviet Falls,
# the Three-Year War Begins

❖ ❖ ❖

When the main body of the Chinese Red Army set out on the Long March from Gannan (southern Jiangxi) in October 1934, it left behind a smaller army to harass and tie down the enemy, coordinate with the field armies on their march west, defend the soviet, and restore the soviet if it fell. Similar tiny armies were left scattered here and there throughout southern and central China (map 1) as the majority marched first west and then north. Three years later, after the start of the war against Japan, survivors of these death legions climbed down the mountains to a heroes' welcome from Party leaders who had long given them up for dead.[1] These remnants regrouped as the New Fourth Army, which expanded prodigiously after 1937; by 1945 it had three hundred thousand people under arms and controlled much of central China.[2] Their Three-Year War after 1934 has been left deep in shadow by the legendary Long March. This book aims to rescue them from oblivion by examining their experience in the dark years between their apparent self-immolation in late 1934 and their miraculous resurrection in late 1937.

The events described in this study have no distinct beginning. Periods are a historian's convenience, "useful of course, and legitimate as devices, but still quite unreal."[3] The Three-Year War is a label that attaches to campaigns in more than a dozen places connected by little other than shared beliefs and a shared plight. The subject of this book is the Three-Year War in all its regions, but it starts in Gannan, for Gannan has a special place in the war. Home of the Central Soviet, it was Communism's nerve center in China until October 1934.

The Long March from Gannan was not an isolated event. It was supported by evacuations of other bases where rearguards were left, and it

*1*

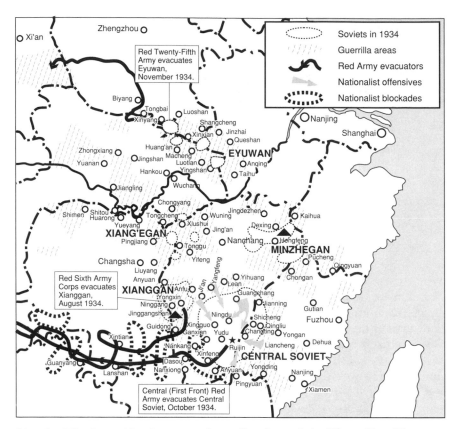

Map 2. The Long March: evacuations of regions of the Three-Year War, August–November 1934. *Based on a map in Junshi kexueyuan 1987, vol. 1.*

was preceded by an expedition into eastern China that brought turmoil (and reinforcements) to the soviets of Minzhewan'gan, a main site of the Three-Year War (map 2). Xiang Ying, leader of the rearguard in Gannan, was nominally commander of rearguards throughout southern China. Though he had no direct line to remnants elsewhere after 1934, he did manage to send batches of leaders to bases in Fujian and Hunan before he was eventually cut off from the outside world altogether in early 1935. In late 1937, he negotiated terms on behalf of stay-behinders everywhere and called them down from the mountains. Even though Gannan was in no real sense a general headquarters of the Three-Year War, it remained a symbol of Communism even after 1934 and continued for a while to be the source of small impulses and initiatives. So for want of a better place, this story begins in Gannan, atop a small hill west of Ruijin, capital of the Central Soviet, on October 16, 1934.

On this hill stood Xiang Ying, reviewing the marching columns of the Western Expedition, whose departure was later taken to mark the start of the Long March and, for those who stayed behind, of the Three-Year War. Leaders of the expedition, including Mao Zedong, climbed the hill to take their leave of Xiang. They would not see him for the next thousand days. The parting struck some marchers as sad and even tragic. Those in the know (a tiny minority) thought Xiang's chances of survival thin.[4] Xiang himself looked firmly on the bright side. He saw the marchers off as heroes; the marchers saluted him and the stay-behinders as heroes, too.

Shortly before his public leave-taking from Xiang Ying, Mao had taken private and sadder leave from Chen Yi, his old comrade-in-arms and now Xiang's second-in-command. Chen Yi was in hospital recovering from battle wounds. Mao handed him two boxes. One held silver for financing the struggle; the other, some of Mao's manuscripts.[5]

In the week before the evacuation, Red Army units poured into the central staging area from all directions and collected along both banks of the Yudu River. As new troops wheeled onto the meadows, others marched off to clear the way. The troops, who mainly came in only after dark, could hear the hubbub and see the gleam of torches and lanterns from miles away. They were puzzled why such a mighty force had been assembled. Women threaded their way through the crowds of soldiers, handing out straw sandals, conical sun-rain hats, oil-paper umbrellas, food, tea, peppers, dried vegetables, and cloth shoes with rope soles tipped and heeled with metal and twice as thick as usual (few knew why). By the river, another group of women sang songs praising the Red Army. The troops, too, sang and chanted as they thronged the river banks and milled around the assembly points. Each night for several nights, a steady stream of advance units crossed the river by pontoon; a stream of stretcher-bearers carrying wounded from the nearby front and porters carrying sacks of salt seized in raids on Nationalist territory crossed back the other way. Each dawn, troops dismantled these floating bridges and hid the boats and cylinders along the river banks, out of sight of enemy planes. Those departing passed quietly through the villages at dead of night. They left strips of paper on the ground, the walls, and the trees saying "Chang Jiang" and "Yellow River" to spur on later units by signaling that great victories lay ahead. Each morning, more and more of these paper signposts littered the way as the hour of the main evacuation neared.[6]

There has been much competition to invent a simile for the Long March. Some plunder the past for inspiration: the hegira, the anabasis, the exodus, the flight of the Torgut, Napoleon's retreat from Moscow, the campaigns of Huang Chao, Li Zicheng, and Zhang Xianzhong. "Hannibal's march across the Alps looked like a holiday excursion beside it," said Edgar Snow.[7] The Chinese Communists, criticizing the evacuation of Gannan during their stopover at Zunyi in January 1935, called it a "panicky flight" and likened it to a house removal.[8] But later Mao said that the Long March was "the first of its kind in the annals of history"; it was "a manifesto, a propaganda force, a seeding machine."[9] The German Otto Braun, Moscow's man in China in the 1930s, preferred a matter-of-fact description: the Long March was "a carefully planned operation that in the further course of its development took on the character of a retreat."[10]

At the other extreme, an angry Chen Yi, speaking for the people left behind, compared the departure to a house burning: "They were like Xiao En in *The Fisherman Kills the Tyrant*. They burned the house down without regard for anyone or anything."[11] In the West, for decades the most influential view of the Long March was that of Snow, who described it in *Red Star over China* as the migration of a nation.

According to the most reliable estimate, eighty-six thousand people set out on the first stage of the Long March (though this figure was commonly rounded up to a hundred thousand in Party propaganda).[12] The sections of the central column of marchers bore names that together formed a roll call of the Soviet Republic: Ruijin, Tingzhou, Huichang, Xingguo, Shicheng, and so on. There were between twenty and thirty thousand noncombatants on the march. These included teachers, printers, minters, doctors, nurses, and tailors. There was a convalescent company of frail old Party leaders and people newly out of hospital. Some rode horses, and others were carried on stretchers, of which there were 120, each attended by four carriers. Fifty to sixty thousand of the marchers were fighting men; the overwhelming majority of noncombatants were Party officials and Red Army porters.[13]

## HOW AND WHY THE SOVIET WAS ABANDONED

War has a rhythm and logic of its own, incompatible with social movements. Marxists quote Clausewitz saying that "war is just a continuation of politics by other means" to show that militarizing the revolution need not change its social and political nature. But Leon Trotsky, founder and leader of the world's first Red Army in 1918, insisted on the independent character of war. "War continues politics," he wrote in 1924, "but with special means and methods."[14] Trotsky organized his Red Army similarly to other armies. He was concerned with the problems created for the Red Army by Russia's technical and cultural backwardness as much as with the crisis created in Russian society by all-out promotion of war. But if war continues politics, politics can also continue war once the war ethos gains a universal hold. It was Trotsky who, casting about for a radical solution to Russia's economic crisis, called in 1920 for the complete militarization of Soviet labor, if necessary by extreme compulsion.[15]

In China, too, after the Communists founded their Red Army in 1927, a strong tension grew up between the army's needs and the Party's obligations to China's "soviet nation" in the villages. Many describe the intimate connection between war and revolution in China in terms of Mao's gentle image of the peasants as water, the army as a fish. But military imperatives were often at odds with the needs of social revolution and nearly always overrode them. This subordination of social revolution to war was a predictable outcome of Mao's idea that "political power grows from the barrel of a gun." If the army is to be the brutal midwife of the old society pregnant with the new, then its forces must be expediently and economically distributed to overwhelm the enemy at the right moment by concentrated blows. "The army is by its very nature an all-state enterprise," Trotsky reminded his commanders.[16] China's Red Army leaders marshaled their divisions nationally, as if on a single battlefield, regularly transferring soldiers and cadres from one place to support a concentrated effort elsewhere, with scant regard to the consequences for their social base. The Long March was an extreme case of this stripping of the revolution to its military core. The Party tore Gannan's young men from the villages and removed them—in many cases forever—to distant battlefields.

To liken the marchers to a "migrating nation" obscures this truth about the Long March and minimizes its tragedy. All but a handful of those who left were able-bodied men. Those who stayed were women, children, invalids, and old men. There were almost no women among the eighty-six thousand marchers: about thirty-five women went with the First Front Army, together with some female nurses. Most of the women nurses at Jiangxi's Red Star Hospital were replaced by men in preparation for the expedition.[17] All but one hundred arsenal workers and all but fourteen officials of the Soviet State Bank were left behind.[18] Party leaders put their children in the care of peasant families before leaving.[19] Many thousands—perhaps tens of thousands—of the sick, the wounded, the crippled, and the dying were abandoned. The house was not removed, it was deserted—but not (as we shall see) before it had been stripped of a large part of its food, furniture, and fittings.

Chen Yi criticized the Long March as an act of wanton destruction against the soviet. Otto Braun's description of it as a military operation that went wrong is not irreconcilable with this view. Braun refuses to give the Long March a romantic meaning of the sort that propagandists lent it after the event; he focuses instead on its narrow military goals. At the start of the expedition, Braun and others expected to found a new soviet within easy reach of the old one, using resources borrowed from it. The project was never likely to succeed, as Chen Yi realized at the time; neither the resources nor the Red Army were ever seen again in Gannan.

On October 21, just five days after the central columns of the First Front Army had crossed the Yudu, advance units pierced the first line of the Nationalist blockade in Xinfeng, and the main phase of the Long March started.[20] Here the Long Marchers march forever from this book, except where they are relevant to my wholly different focus, the rearguards they left behind. Unlike the marchers, the rearguards consisted mainly of natives; many, if not most, of their supporters were women; their natural fighting style was irregular; and they were weighed down by invalids and dependents.

## THE SIZE AND COMPOSITION OF THE REARGUARD

Few documents have survived from the first four or five months of the rearguard action in Gannan. Accounts conflict about such basic questions as how many troops stayed to defend the Central Soviet. A comparison of sources suggests that the rearguard in Gannan was made up of between thirteen and eighteen regiments, including three belonging to the main force's Twenty-fourth Division, and a number of independent battalions at the county level.[21] Both Nationalist and Communist sources conventionally put the overall size of the rearguard at around thirty-seven thousand, but different sources compute this figure in different ways. The Communist renegade Gong Chu and others exclude local forces and include 3,300 troops in Minxi under Wan Yongcheng.[22] But according to recent Communist estimates, the figure of thirty to forty thousand includes both regular and local forces.[23]

Earlier estimates by both parties were far lower. Zhu De, speaking around 1937, mentioned units totaling 13,400 men in the vicinity of the Central Soviet, together with twenty thousand wounded. Early estimates by Chen Yi are compatible with Zhu's. In 1940, Chen Yi said that besides the Twenty-fourth Division, there were guerrillas with three thousand rifles. In 1952, he said that more than thirty thousand troops were left behind, but this figure included Red Army invalids (of whom there were between ten and thirty thousand) and local Party officials. Later he said that the rearguard consisted of ten thousand troops backed by two to three hundred guerrillas in each soviet county, implying a total of between two and three thousand irregulars.[24] This estimate is only partly compatible with Otto Braun's report of ten to twelve thousand fighters in "independent units" plus a "much bigger" number of peasant self-defense forces.[25] Early Nationalist sources say that between thirteen and twenty-seven thousand "bandit remnants" were left behind in the Central Soviet.[26]

What are we to make of this jumble of numbers? The oft-repeated figure of thirty-seven thousand probably comes from the memoir by Gong Chu, published in Hongkong in 1954. This memoir, which gives an early and detailed view of events in Gannan after the start of the Long March, was published without the constraints that inhibit memoir writers in the People's Republic. But it must be read with caution.[27] After his surrender to the Nationalists in 1935, Gong Chu, a military leader of the rearguard, inflated his previous role in the Communist movement. He may have thought that it was in his interest to present himself as a leader of important forces.

Communist sources that put the strength of the rearguard at between thirty and forty thousand are suspect for another reason. They almost certainly include a huge number—probably a majority—of Red Army invalids. Red Army leaders prided themselves on their treatment of wounded soldiers. Communist studies of the rearguard must find it hard to reconcile this pride with the deliberate discarding of a huge army of cripples in Gannan, defended by a tiny army of the fit. The higher Communist estimate of the rearguard's size is a conflation of figures for wounded and able-bodied. Chen Yi was a realist as well as a witness and largely truthful chronicler of the Three-Year War. His estimate, which comes out at between ten and fifteen thousand men, is compatible with Zhu De's and also with a recent definitive history that says that sixteen thousand regular and local troops were left behind, together with more than thirty thousand wounded.[28] Chen Yi's figure can be squared with Nationalist statistics from 1935. The Nationalists claimed to have

TABLE I    Rearguard Forces, Late 1934 and Early 1935

| | |
|---|---|
| Central Soviet (Gannan) | 15,000 |
| Ganyue | 500 |
| Min'gan | 1,000 |
| Minxi | 10,000 |
| Minyue | 1,000 |
| Zhe'nan | 700 |
| Minbei | 3,000 |
| Mindong | 2,000 |
| Minzhewan'gan | 2,500 |
| Eyuwan | 1,200 |
| Xiang'egan | 2,000 |
| Xianggan | 5,000 |
| Xiangnan | 1,000 |
| Total | 44,900 |

NOTE:  These estimates are approximate. For sources, see the relevant chapters of this book.

captured 16,684 Communists in Gannan up to April. A large number were sick or wounded;[29] thousands more were soviet officials and pro-Communist civilians. If we assume that several thousand Communists melted back into civilian life or became guerrillas after 1934, on the basis of these Nationalist statistics we can accept Chen Yi's estimate of around ten thousand armed regulars backed up by a smaller number of irregulars.

If we take the rearguard in its broadest sense, as the aggregate of all guerrilla forces in southern and central China, its initial size was of course much bigger. Its size can only be computed roughly, since estimates for the different bases are often unreliable. The Three-Year War started at different times in different places, so the aggregate is in any case only notional. It is also largely academic, since these different forces were for the most part out of touch with one another and cannot be reckoned even loosely as one army (though they became one in 1937). Even so, it is useful to add them up in order to plot the overall distribution of Communist forces at the start of the Long March and their changing proportions over the years. If we add together starting numbers, excluding wounded, in the fourteen main guerrilla bases, we reach a total of around forty-five thousand (table 1).[30]

Another troublesome issue is the structure, composition, and competencies of the rearguard leadership. On the eve of the Long March, a sub-bureau of the Central Committee was set up under Xiang Ying to lead the Party in Jiangxi, together with a Central Government Office under Chen Yi, and to administer the soviet and a new Central Military

District. Some say that Xiang was both commander and political commissar of this military district, others that Chen Yi was the rearguard's supreme military commander.[31] Whatever the case, with Chen Yi in hospital for the first few weeks of the rearguard action, Xiang Ying, the Party's plenipotentiary in Gannan, had the final say. Neither the size nor the composition of the sub-bureau is known for certain. In December 1943, Zhou Enlai said that its members were Xiang Ying, Qu Qiubai, Chen Yi, Chen Tanqiu, and He Chang.[32] Sources imply that it was later enlarged by coopting Deng Zihui, Zhang Dingcheng, Tan Zhenlin, Liang Botai, Mao Zetan, Wang Jinxiang, and Li Cailian. Recent research discounts as unrealistic suggestions that the bureau was charged with leading all guerrilla areas in the south. Even so, the Party's Military Affairs Council directed the new Central Military District to "take command of the Military Districts of Jiangxi, Fujian, Min'gan, Gannan, and Minzhegan (including Minbei)."[33] In the long run, even this limited commission proved impossible, but in early 1935 it was acquitted in part when news of the Long Marchers' important Zunyi Conference was transmitted to Minxi and Ganyue.

## THE CRISIS IN THE CENTRAL SOVIET

Despite the hardship and human cost, the Long March was a spiritual break with failure and a physical break with a society in terminal decline. Some started out on it in fear, but their spirits lifted as they put past troubles behind them and looked toward the future. Those who remained did not enjoy this luxury; instead they had to stay with the dying soviet, bear it to the grave, and cope with the consequences of its demise. Their Three-Year War began not as a new strategic venture but as the last chapter of an old one. To understand the setting of this war and the constraints within which it was fought, we must first look at events in Gannan in the period before October 1934 and at the multiple crisis—of economy, morale, unity, security, and confidence—that occasioned the Long March and that, for those who stayed behind, was greatly worsened by it.

The two main interacting causes of the crisis were the Guomindang blockade, which wasted the soviet economy and caused an epidemic of illness and disease, and the soviet leaders' drive to raise ever more massive levies of people and goods in a territory that was shrinking daily because of the encirclement.[34] During the blockade, fewer goods and less capital flowed into the soviet than left it. The trade deficit with Nationalist areas grew, soviet cash holdings drained away, and the market, already reportedly undermined by the passive resistance of the rich, collapsed still further. The price of grain in the soviet was low, and after land reform the grain trade dwindled.[35] An economy that before 1929 had been largely self-sufficient found it increasingly difficult to support the soviet's swollen administration and the huge Red Army, which grew from forty thousand to more than one hundred thousand after September 1933.[36] In 1933 and 1934, officials of the Soviet Food Board and the Soviet State Bank could barely maintain the food supply. By January 1934, granaries were less than half full despite the issuance of bonds and certificates payable in grain, and less than 10 percent of the grain tax had been gathered. Grain rations for troops, officials, and citizens were cut, and, in a desperate attempt to enliven the economy, eight million soviet dollars were pumped into circulation in the period up to October 1934, driving up inflation.[37] In the summer and early autumn of 1934, the soviet government campaigned to "borrow" 840,000 piculs of grain and to bring the Red Army stockpile up to one million piculs by purchases and by the immediate levy (announced on July 26) of the entire grain tax for 1934. By then, the soviet territory had shrunk to under nineteen thousand square miles, with a population of between two and three million, some 80 percent of them dependents of Red Army soldiers.[38]

The first campaign was not completely successful. Only 42 percent of the 240,000 piculs targeted for June and July had been collected by July 14. The second campaign collected all but 3 percent of its target in less than one month.[39] The crash grain campaigns of 1934 raised a total of 1,800,000 piculs, more than enough to feed an army of a hundred thousand men for three years. Compare this figure with the total levy of 1933, when only 200,000 piculs were levied from the soviet base. Around 90 percent of the grain raised in 1934 was in the form of "loans"; only 10 percent was tax grain. In the past, the Red Army had fed itself partly by raiding *tuhao* in the White villages. By September 1934, such raids were no longer possible, so the entire burden fell on the backs of the peasants of Gannan and Minxi.[40]

By October, the Soviet Republic spanned less than thirty miles from east to west. "You could almost cast a spear across it," said Chen Yi. Not only was it drained of provisions, but its hard-pressed citizens were also required to manufacture a record quantity of shoes, clothes, and equipment for the campaigns ahead.[41] The pragmatic majority of civilians were by now less moved by the Party's calls for hard work and frugal living. People who had once been prepared to give the Communists the benefit of the doubt no longer cooperated with them freely. As the crisis deepened, even the Party's close supporters became frightened and disheartened. But the immediate problem for those who stayed behind to defend the soviet was less the lack of goodwill than the shortage of resources.

Even before the Long March, Xiang admitted privately that the soviet economy was in grave straits. The rearguard had been left with just $100,000 in Nationalist banknotes (but with mountains of soviet currency). According to Gong Chu, the economy was in ruins. The peddlers and the food store owners had packed up and gone, the shops and markets had closed down. Reports spoke of poverty and destitution throughout the soviet.[42]

Gannan had been stripped of a large part of its population. The repeated conscription of new generations of peasant boys after 1929 was a main cause of the failure to fill the granaries in 1934. The Red Army recruited more than 120,000 men between August 1933 and July 1934, more and more frequently by force. According to its critics, it neglected to develop local forces and excessively enlarged central forces. This strategy eroded its support, discipline, and morale. On May 12, 1934, Red Army leaders launched a new campaign to recruit 50,000 troops in just three months. In the event, 63,000 enlisted. A further campaign begun on September 4 was less successful, yielding only 18,204 of the planned 30,000 new recruits. A recent Communist study concludes from failures of this sort that by late 1934 the soviet had been exhausted by repeated exactions. By late October, it was difficult to find a single able-bodied male between the ages of ten and fifty in the Central Soviet. Some peasants took to the mountains to escape the draft; others killed or maimed themselves. By 1935, the population in counties previously under soviet control had reportedly declined by 16.3 percent over 1931 and in Communist-influenced counties by 24.7 percent.[43]

Propaganda accounts of the departure from the Central Soviet tend not to dwell on the misery of 1934 and instead skip cheerfully from the early prosperity and reform to the Red Army's "victory march" to the northwest. Chinese Communists have always found it hard to provide a satisfactory account of the crisis in the soviet. For the first ten years after the start of the Long March, their public stance was that the soviet had collapsed because of bad generalship, not bad politics. The criticism of the "military mistakes" said to have caused the collapse began in January 1935 at Zunyi. Few people at the time can have taken seriously the distinction, made for tactical reasons, between the "military line" and the "political line" pursued in the Central Soviet under the old Bo Gu leadership. Chen Yi's reaction was probably typical. "That's a compromise," he told Xiang Ying when the news from Zunyi reached Gannan. "How can there be military mistakes divorced from political mistakes? The military mistakes happened under the influence of political mistakes."[44] Even after Mao extended the public criticism in 1945 to the "political line," which he said was "leftist," there was no systematic repudiation of the merciless squeeze on the soviet in 1933 and 1934. On the contrary, the grain levies and the conscription are still a matter of pride. However, accumulated evidence in memoirs and in studies detracts from the official view of the soviet in 1934 as a "free, peaceful, and happy paradise."[45]

Less tangible than these facts and figures, but equally crucial, is the question of Red Army morale, for (to paraphrase Zhang Yu) "it is heart by which the general masters."[46] Sunzi, whose *Art of War* profoundly influenced Mao Zedong and other Red Army leaders, saw moral strength as the first and most decisive of the five fundamental factors of warfare; it is expressed in union of purpose between the ranks, and it is the product of the general's wisdom, sincerity, humanity, courage, and discipline, of the effectiveness and trustworthiness of his orders. Sunzi's comments are a useful framework for discussing the morale of the Red Army in late 1934. Red generals shared the belief that morale, produced by Communist moral influence, is decisive in war. They saw education, ideological indoctrination, "military democracy," and the kind, fair treatment of recruits as essential to strong morale. They valued operational secrecy no less than White generals, but their troops were better informed about plans and goals than those in conventional armies and showed greater initiative in battle. The Red commanders encouraged "military democracy" in groups and committees that met before, during, and after battles to discuss tactics and assign tasks.[47] The ideal Red Army soldier was enlightened, loyal, collectivist, and confident of the invincibility of his cause. However, the morale of the Red Army in October 1934 was not equally strong at all levels and was not the same among the rearguard as among the Long Marchers.

If clarity, effectiveness, and trustworthiness of orders are necessary for good morale, then decisions made in panic, without due preparation and reflection, will harm it. For decades, Chinese Communists have criticized the first stages of the Long March, before Mao took over, as a sudden disordered flight. Chen Yi rehearsed these criticisms in talks in the late 1950s. His thesis was that the "leftists," namely Bo Gu and other supporters of Wang Ming who controlled the Party before Mao, abandoned the soviet because they believed that the situation was beyond hope.

> They fled helter-skelter to the west, where the gaps were widest and there was much water. At first sight this was a clever tactic, but actually it was stupid. . . . We simply ran ourselves to death, starved to death. What's more, we could not hit the enemy where it hurt. . . . The worst thing was that people were acting in panic. They made no preparations. Having lost the soviet, we simply took to our heels. There were no preparations at either the general or the particular level. Next, let us look at material preparations. The troops were about to transfer to White areas and fight outside the base. What about food and clothing? What routes should they take through mountains and across rivers? What bridges? This way? That way? Everything needed preparing, but it was rushed through at the last

minute. What about ideological preparation? There were none of the usual conferences, there was no political mobilization, soliciting of opinions, or discussions with experienced people. They did not even ask a brilliant leader like Mao Zedong for his views. No one with any sense would have chosen the direction that they chose. Anyone else would have got things properly prepared. They would not have let the Long March take place in panic, and Jiangxi would not have suffered such a tragedy. That is not to say that you can be sure you will never lose a battle. But if a defeat is to be glorious, it needs much organization, rhythm, and composure. . . . There is no point in endless weeping and wailing, fleeing the battle in defeat, scattering like birds and beasts. That is not just wrong, it is criminal. . . . Military affairs were also badly prepared. It was like a house removal. They took everything. . . . They also took too many porters: fifty to sixty thousand troops and ten to twenty thousand porters. The march was like a dragon. When the head pierced White lines, the tail was still here. From head to tail was three days' march. . . . With so many people, you were bound to fail. Light packs would have been better, and fewer people. Speed was of the essence. . . . What about personnel? There was no proper discussion or study of who should go and who should stay.[48]

Finally, there was the question of what to do in Gannan after the start of the Long March. "There had been even fewer preparations for carrying on the struggle in the soviet area."[49]

## CHEN YI'S CRITICISMS OF THE LONG MARCH

Chen's criticisms express with characteristic clarity and vigor what for decades was received but muted opinion about the Long March in China. I shall restate the criticisms as six questions, which I shall then try to answer. When was the idea of an evacuation of the Central Soviet first mooted? Was the route well chosen and well planned? Was the expedition properly supplied? Was public opinion prepared for the evacuation? Who went, who stayed, and why? How well was the rearguard operation in Gannan prepared? Some of these questions are about the marchers, but they are all relevant in one way or another, directly or indirectly, to the morale of Xiang Ying's rearguard.

### The Planning of the Evacuation

When was the idea of an evacuation mooted? According to Chen Yi, there were no preparations even "at a general level": the decision was taken in haste and without forethought. But we know that the Party's inner core, consisting of Bo Gu, Zhou Enlai, and Otto Braun, first "fomented" the idea of a strategic transfer in the spring of 1934, possibly in response to a Comintern proposal. (Certainly the Comintern, on June 25, 1934, agreed with the plan to quit Gannan.)[50] Preparations at the strategic (but not yet at the tactical) level began in May 1934. By then, Zhang Wentian, Xiang Ying, Zhu De, and Wang Jiaxiang had probably been drawn into the discussions;[51] by August, so had Mao Zedong, Li Weihan, and one or two others.[52] So the decision to leave Gannan was not taken at the eleventh hour: it was the outcome of discussions that went on for more than half a year.

Was the route of the evacuation well chosen and well planned? Here we must distinguish between strategy and tactics. The strategic aspect concerns the general direction of the evacuation. According to Mao, Chen Yi, and others, the Red Army should have thrust north toward Nanjing and Shanghai in late 1933 to take advantage of the turmoil created by the Fujian Incident and to threaten the Nationalists in their heartland. According to another of Mao's criticisms, they should have thrust into central Hunan in mid-1934. Instead, says Chen, they headed west in October 1934 and got bogged down in regions of marginal importance. There is no point in discussing Mao's retrospective second thoughts about strategy in this period, since they would have depended for success on a host of imponderables, though it is worth remembering that expeditions in both the directions that Mao suggests were defeated in late 1934.

We do not know when the soviet leaders took the decision to head west, but clearly the march west from Xianggan by the Sixth Red Army Corps in August 1934 was a preparatory step for the Long March proper that started two months later.[53] The evacuation of the central armies from Gannan was not a single event but part of a pattern of linked and coordinated movements, not only from the Central Soviet and its vicinity but also from outer soviets like Eyuwan. It was part of a national marshaling and upgrading of forces during which peasants became guerrillas, guerrillas were grouped into independent battalions, battalions were grouped into regiments, regiments were grouped into armies, and armies went on expeditions. So the Long March was not planned overnight, nor was its direction chosen overnight, although it may have seemed so to people like Chen Yi who were not in on its planning. There are signs that the tactical aspect—the actual line of march—was also carefully prepared. According to Otto Braun, the route and the positions of the Guangdong Army along it were closely reconnoitered. The breakthrough was staged at a weak point in enemy lines between Ganzhou and Huichang; it was a success, and losses were minimal. The marchers then headed toward Niedu in southwestern Jiangxi, near the border with Guangdong and Hunan. Niedu had been a guerrilla base ever since 1927; its terrain suited the Red Army.[54] So both the general direction and the specific route were planned in advance, and Chen's criticism falls.

Was the expedition properly supplied? Under this heading fall two related criticisms on Chen's list. One is the question of day-to-day supplies, which Chen suggests fell short of needs; the other is capital equipment, of which he says too much was taken. Chen's first point is easy to refute. Measures to supply the troops with food, new clothes, and ammunition were probably planned as early as May 1934. Throughout 1934, the Soviet Food Board campaigned frenetically to fill the granaries. Each soldier going on the Long March was issued with two pouches, each holding five catties of provisions. The Long March probably carried off one-tenth of the entire year's grain target and even more of the stockpile (for grain targets had not been met). Just before the start of the expedition, the Soviet Women's Department was told to mobilize women to make two hundred thousand pairs of grass sandals and several tens of thousands of rice bags. The departing troops were issued with new clothing from head to foot, one or two spare pairs of strong shoes, a blanket or a quilt, and a quilted winter uniform. "Each man had a drinking cup," recalled one Long Marcher,

> a pair of chopsticks thrust into his puttees, and a needle and thread caught on the underside of the peak of his cap. All men wore big sun-rain hats of two thin layers of bamboo with oiled paper between, and many had paper umbrellas stuck in their packs. Each man carried a rifle. Everyone going on the Long March was dressed and equipped the same. Everyone was armed.[55]

Though it is not true that the marchers all had rifles,[56] they were far better armed than Xiang Ying's rearguard and were loaded down with as much ammunition as they could carry, including strings of hand grenades.[57]

Chen's second criticism, about capital equipment, is better founded. The marchers carried off printing presses, banknote machines, arsenal equipment, heavy artillery, sewing machines, the hospital's X-ray equipment, and huge piles of printed material, documents, currency, and bullion strapped to the backs of an army of coolies and a cavalcade of donkeys, mules, and horses. As a result they were forced to mobilize thousands of porters, and their pace was slowed. Parts of the column covered less than ten miles a day on the small mountain tracks along the provincial borders during the first stages of the march.[58] Even so, Chen's criticism is probably wisdom in hindsight; no one seems to have raised it at the time. As things looked then, it made sense to carry off precious equipment, for leaders believed that a new soviet could be planted on the Hunan-Guangxi border, less than two hundred miles to the west; probably none guessed that they were about to walk the length of China.[59] Chen Yi's criticism is also questionable from another point of view. It undermines his earlier charge that "material preparations" for the march were rushed through at the last minute.

*The Preparation of Public Opinion*

Was public opinion prepared for the evacuation? According to Chen Yi, there was too little "ideological preparation," discussion of issues, and political mobilization. Here we must distinguish between different levels of command and between expeditionaries and stay-behinders. As we have seen, discussions at the very top began quite early but were held in secret. In early September 1934, the leaders of some army groups were called to Ruijin and told of the plans for an evacuation. But leaders below this level responsible for specific tasks connected with the preparations were kept in the dark at least until the end of the month. For example, Mao Zemin was detailed to deliver soviet funds, including gold, valuables, and Nationalist banknotes, into the safekeeping of the different army groups, but without being told why.[60]

The first heavily veiled public hint at an imminent withdrawal came on September 29 in an article by Zhang Wentian in *Hongse Zhonghua* (Red China). Zhang said that offensives alone would not bring victory, that retreats were sometimes also necessary, that final victory might still be years away, and that it was "opportunistic" to call for the defense of every inch of soviet territory. On October 3, *Hongse Zhonghua* published a second article calling on soviet citizens to launch all-out guerrilla war in defense of "freedom, land, and soviet" at a moment described as critical and urgent.[61] These articles fall short of an open admission that the soviet was about to be evacuated, though some people have interpreted them as such.[62] The October 3 article still spoke of a "decisive battle" to smash the encirclement and called for the soviet's defense. Even then— and for weeks to come—the overwhelming majority thought that these were the Party's two main aims.[63] "The enemy is located in more and more hostile circumstances," the article went on. "Pillboxes in the enemy rear are thinly guarded and their soldiers are wavering. That is obvious to anybody."[64] Three weeks after the appearance of Zhang's article, Xiang Ying, writing in *Hongse Zhonghua* on October 20, still kept quiet about the evacuation, even though it had already happened.[65] The Red Army leaders did everything in their power to maintain stealth; to let slip that a withdrawal was under way would have been high treason. We can conclude that the Long March was not announced beforehand.

Even so, by early October, experienced Party officials guessed that something big and dramatic was afoot. They could not miss the massing of forces and supplies and the reorganization of troop positions to fit in with the plans for a main-force breakout. The security blackout was not entirely effective, and they noticed many unusual and inexplicable events. For old hands who knew the code, the editorials in *Hongse Zhonghua* were the final clue. "They did not inform us," said Chen Yi, "but we knew that they were about to go." The knowledge created a subterranean shock, though none dared to talk about it.[66]

Most rearguard leaders, with the exception of Xiang Ying, probably first got wind of the evacuation by piecing together these random clues. Chen Yi, still in hospital with wounds that he had suffered at Xingguo in late August, was the highest-ranking Red Army invalid and destined to be Xiang's second-in-command. He was commander of a military region and of a local army group, and he regularly attended meetings of the Central Committee. Even so, he was not officially told of the evacuation until the day before it started, though he had several visits from Party leaders. "Some high-ranking cadres did come to see us," Chen Yi recalled, "but they did not like to talk, nor I to ask. It would just have put them in an awkward position. If they talked about it, they would be letting out military secrets, which in those days could cost you your head. All the same, I knew."[67]

Ordinary soldiers, without Chen Yi's experience, acumen, and contacts, were less likely to guess the truth. Naturally, they were not blind to what was happening around them, and they too were puzzled by the build-up of forces, the unusual bustle in the Red Army hospitals, the discharging of large numbers of walking wounded, the shifting of valuables and stockpiles, the return of Red Army dependents to the villages, the destruction (in late September) of some heavy arsenal machinery and guns, the dispersal of the rest of the arsenal across the central armies and parts of Jiangxi and Fujian, and other strange goings-on. Troops destined to leave Gannan were puzzled—and delighted—by the sudden abundance of new equipment in the second week of October. Before, they had been lucky to get even summer clothes; many had dressed in rags. Now they were issued with brand-new cotton-padded winter clothes whose appearance was doubly puzzling, since autumn days in Gannan are generally mild, and unlined uniforms would have sufficed. Salt and oil were also suddenly available for the first time in months. As the troops tried on their new uniforms at the end of the day in the flickering half-light of tea-oil lamps, swapping and swapping until they found clothes and shoes that fitted, their spirits rose, and a wave of excitement rippled through the Red Army camps along the river. There was no longer any question that a major campaign lay ahead; rumors abounded that the Red Army was "about to leave." Who was going and who was staying became a main talking point. Privately, people began to weigh the comparative advantages. But it did not occur even to veterans that they were about to leave Gannan forever.

The march began around October 16, but it was still some time before the marchers learned its purpose. In part they were misled, albeit unintentionally, by Party propaganda, which ever since July (when the Anti-Japanese Expedition had marched north toward Anhui) had been delicately preparing public opinion for the possibility of a strategic turn by playing up the need for resistance to Japan in the north. Many people expected a follow-up to the July expedition and were therefore confused by the direction of the march, to the southwest; this strengthened the belief that the campaign was no more than a short-term sally. Not until after crossing into Nationalist territory did rank-and-file marchers finally learn that they could not expect to return to the Central Soviet in the foreseeable future, that they were embarked on a strategic transfer.[68]

For those left behind, the deception was crueller and longer-lasting. The evacuation was carried out at night, some say for fear of enemy attacks and reconnaissance from the air, others say to accustom the troops to night marching before breaching Nationalist lines. The night march and the gentle night winds braced the marchers, but the secrecy deepened the disquiet of the stay-behinders, who had literally been left in the dark.[69] They were also denied the chance to say good-bye to their departing brothers, husbands, fathers, and sons, who learned of the departure too late to tell their relatives. This sudden departure had a bad effect on morale both in Gannan and among the marchers, who were upset about leaving their families behind with little protection. Optimists in Gannan continued to believe that the expedition was part of a plan to sally into White areas, break the blockade, seize grain and property, and return to the soviet. Some even gave the marchers money to buy salt, tobacco, and other goods in short supply at home and told them to "go quickly, come back quickly."[70] From past experience, they expected the Red Army columns to return after a month or two with prisoners and supplies.[71] They were to be bitterly disappointed. Others, less optimistic, stood by the roadside or in the doorways of their houses searching the marchers' faces for clues about what was happening. "Some seemed to want to ask us something," recalled one marcher, "but for reasons of military secrecy, we could not respond. We could only gaze back in silence."[72]

### The Reasons for the Secrecy

So though the Long March was preceded by several months' discussion, this discussion was confined to a tiny circle of the Party's most powerful leaders. There was no broad canvasing of opinions and no effort to enlighten the rank and file, who were left to puzzle out for themselves what was going on. Later, Mao and others criticized this secrecy as "mechanical" thinking.[73] Party leaders believed with Confucius that "to lead an uninstructed people to war is to throw them away." Why, then, did they fail to prepare their troops and supporters for this momentous change?

One reason was their drive between June and October 1934 to "borrow" huge amounts of grain in Gannan; any hint that they were about to leave would have jeopardized their chances of success. More important, Red Army leaders believed that only speed, surprise, and deception could enable a small, weak army like their own to gain the advantage over a large, strong army, especially one like Chiang Kai-shek's, which stuck to a strategy of tortoise-like advance and predictable campaigns.[74] By moving swiftly, the Red Army could take the Nationalists off guard; by creating false appearances, it could win time and heighten the surprise. Speed and deception are complementary. As an ancient Chinese folk manual on warfare explains, "Deception is when something is dressed up as nothing; if it lasts too long, it will easily be spotted."[75] According to Griffith's exposition of Sunzi's thought,

> A skilled general must be master of the complementary arts of simulation and dissimulation; while creating shapes to confuse and delude the enemy he conceals his true dispositions and ultimate intent. When capable he feigns incapacity; when near he makes it appear that he is far away; when far away, that he is near. Moving intangibly as a ghost in the starlight, he is obscure, inaudible. His primary target is the mind of the opposing commander; the victorious situation, a product of his creative imagination.[76]

The Chinese Red Army survived because it took Sunzi's precepts to heart while its opponents in Chiang Kai-shek's military academies ignored them.

The Red Army's strategy in October 1934 was a modern enactment of the cicada trick described thus by Wu Gu:

> The form is kept, the power is gone. Friends doubt nothing, the enemy does not move. "The golden cicada sheds its skin" . . . refers to the art of dividing your body. The greater part of my body leaves, but my flags, banners, gongs, and drums announce that I am holding to the original line. So my first enemy dares not move. . . . Only when I return from destroying my second enemy does he learn of it, if even then.[77]

But if the way back is barred (it was) and the distant army is not defeated (it was not), then those holding the drums, gongs, banners, and flags will be sacrificed, for "when loss is bound to be, let it be in the parts, so that the whole prospers."[78] The agents of this planned deception were the stay-behinders; its target Chiang Kai-shek. The secrecy was meant to stop news of the deception leaking out to Chiang. Speed being a main condition of deception, there was no time between muster and departure to rest and reorganize, mobilize the troops behind new goals, or train them in new tasks and tactics.[79]

The stay-behinders, military and civilian, were not only agents of deception but were themselves objects of deception by the Party leaders. Xiang Ying knew that the goal of the evacuation was to transfer the bulk of the Red Army to a new base outside Jiangxi, but it was weeks before he publicly admitted the fact. Instead, he tried to stabilize his military and civilian support by deceiving the deceivers in order to stiffen their morale and let them act their part with confidence.[80] This deception within deception violated the maxim that deception should harbor truth, so that at a critical moment "something is born from nothing . . . and the enemy is defeated."[81] Both deceptions were quickly penetrated, as we shall see. But as a result of the mental inflexibility of the Nationalist generals, who continued at least for a short while to inch forward into territory that they could have taken at high speed, the deception lasted for long enough to fulfill its purpose, which was to let the main force get away.

### The Selection of the Rearguard

Who went on the Long March, who stayed in the soviet, and why? The way people were sorted into goers and stayers in October 1934 has been the subject of bitter comment in China and of tendentious speculation elsewhere. Much of the comment and the speculation share a common assumption: the decision on who should be left behind was motivated by factional vindictiveness. According to this view, the rearguard was chosen from a blacklist of dissidents and undesirables. In China, critics say that Mao's opponents used the evacuation to rid themselves of his supporters in order to erode his power base. "They wanted to discard me," said Chen Yi, a Mao supporter.[82] The children of He Shuheng, one of the Party's "five old men" in 1934, say that their father and Qu Qiubai were abandoned in Jiangxi because they were out of favor with Party leaders, even though Mao thought that they should join the march. The same authors imply that Deng Zihui, Zhang Dingcheng, and Zeng Shan were left behind because of their Maoist sympathies.[83] A recent Chinese study concludes that "leftist" likes and dislikes determined many assignments: the rearguard was used to "dump burdens and to discriminate against those who held different views."[84] Non-Communist writers, happy to borrow the Manichean idea of "two-line struggle" to back their factional analysis of Chinese Communism, have generally used a similar drama and a similar cast.[85] Only the villain sometimes changes. According to the renegade Communist Li Ang, it was not the "leftists" but Mao who abandoned Qu Qiubai, because Mao was "deeply jealous" of Qu. Li Ang and others explain Xiang Ying's appointment to the rearguard in a similar way.[86]

There is a grain of truth in this discrimination thesis, but it is buried in a heap of nonsense. "A connection with Mao," writes Harrison Salisbury, summarizing the view of Chinese historians, "was a ticket for staying in the soviet area at a time when the chances of survival there were . . . about one in ten."[87] This sentence begs several questions. It assumes that factional lines were clearly drawn in 1934, but they were not. True, Mao opposed the Central Committee under Bo Gu on several issues, but even though the differences were real, they were probably not as great as they were later claimed to be. Between 1932 and 1934, these differences sharpened, and finally a distinctly Maoist opposition began to take shape in the Party leadership. Even so, Mao's position remained strong; his loss of power is often exaggerated. The Comintern continued to regard him highly. Most Chinese Communist leaders had a practical view of policy and were prepared to weigh the objective strengths of competing viewpoints. Only a minority of dogmatists and factionalists were blind to pragmatic considerations. How else could Mao have captured enough support within three months of the start of the Long March to emerge from a leadership struggle as first among equals?

The change in the balance of power that ended in Mao's victory was not sudden. The crisis of 1934 had led to the return to office of people previously in the wilderness. The leadership majority had itself begun to split: in the summer of 1934, Zhang Wentian and Wang Jiaxiang, members of the Moscow-inspired "Russian Returned Students" group, formed a "Group of Three" with Mao.[88] Salisbury's informants imply, again wrongly, that Mao's friends and relatives were automatically discarded in October 1934. Mao's youngest brother Zetan stayed behind (and died), but his younger brother Zemin marched and even directed the transportation of "revolutionary assets" (that is, the soviet hoard). Chen Yi stayed, but Chen Yi's political commissar Nie Rongzhen helped lead the Long March, even though he was sick with malaria.[89] Many influential Communists conventionally called Maoists were left behind, but others were not. The most striking example of one who was not is Luo Ming, a target of "pitiless struggle" in 1933 and 1934 and seen by many as a stand-in target for Mao. If the Long March was used to ditch dissidents, why was Luo Ming allowed to leave? Clearly, the criteria for selection were more complex than factional affiliation. And why was a large contingent of orthodox Party leaders, starting at the top with Xiang Ying, left behind? Again the demonological view collapses.

Where a theory fails to fit the facts, it is best to change it. But people are more often wedded to theories than to facts, so they change the facts instead. For example, because He Chang was left behind (and martyred), he has been posthumously converted to the Maoist faith.[90] In fact, He Chang, far from being a Maoist, was dropped from the Central Committee as a supporter of Li Lisan in January 1931 and restored to it in January 1934 when Mao was dropped. He joined the witchhunt against Luo Ming, spoke of a "decisive final battle," and called for a study of defense through blockhouses—policies that Mao allegedly criticized as "leftist." After the start of the Long March, however, this "leftist" joined

the Maoist Chen Yi in calling for a switch to guerrilla warfare, showing once again that the idea of a Party rigidly divided into factions is
quite wrong.[91]

If a link to Mao was a ticket for staying, then the "Maoist" credentials
of those who left (but presumably not of Mao himself) are by implication
open to question. Here, the theory is rescued by an extra twist. "Maoists"
like Deng Xiaoping who theoretically should have stayed but who went
are said to have been discriminated against by being made to march as
common soldiers or even to join the porters. (But Mao himself began the
march on a litter.)[92]

The second part of the discrimination thesis implies that it was better
to go than to stay and that people knew this at the time. I show in the
chapter on the war in historical perspective that in late 1937, both
marchers and stay-behinders commanded forces one-quarter the size of
those they started out with in 1934. A similar picture obtains if we define
the rearguard more narrowly, as the ten to twenty thousand troops under Xiang Ying in Gannan, and restrict our comparison to the twelve
months that it took the marchers to get from Gannan to Shaanbei. According to Salisbury's informants, eighty-six thousand troops started out
on the Long March, but only four thousand (i.e., fewer than one in
twenty) finished it.[93] A similar proportion of the Gannan rearguard
(and a far bigger proportion of the rearguard as a whole) survived until
October 1935. However, the rearguard probably lost a larger proportion
of its leaders, through deaths and desertions, than the marchers did.
Among those who died were Qu Qiubai, He Shuheng, He Chang, Ruan
Xiaoxian, Liu Bojian, and Li Tianzhu.[94]

How people saw their chances in October 1934 is another matter.
Writers imply that Red Army leaders had little hope that the rearguard would pull through. Red Army leaders, said Edgar Snow in
1941, "did not wish to sacrifice in the rearguard any more first-line
troops than the minimum necessary. Already surrounded on all sides,
those who stayed faced total extermination."[95] But there is no evidence
of this foreknowledge. To many, the fate of stayers and goers looked
equally bleak—or equally bright, depending on your frame of mind.
"It was dangerous to go, and it was dangerous to stay," recalled Chen
Yi. "As long as I kept my wits about me, I could stay out of enemy
hands."[96] For Xiang Ying, who struck observers as "thoroughly optimistic" in October 1934, "the political and military situation was not
unfavorable."[97] Few could say for sure at the time where greater safety
lay, though the question was on everyone's lips. In any case, it made no
difference what people thought, since the decision was not up to them.[98]
Most took a fatalistic view.

To return to our initial questions, was too little thought given to the
composition of the rearguard, and on what grounds were people as-

signed to it? No single reason explains why some were left behind and others taken along. The stayers fall into several categories, and the assignments were rarely punitive (though one cannot rule out some settling of scores).

Xiang Ying, the rearguard's supreme commander, was chosen for his administrative experience, his great energy, his sangfroid, and above all his unswerving loyalty to the Party center. Loyalty was probably decisive in many appointments: most rearguard units persevered for a while in "leftism" before switching to policies and tactics of the sort that Chen Yi favored. Chen Yi disapproved of Xiang's appointment, believing that Xiang "understood nothing of military affairs, vacillated politically, and within the Party was always making mistakes."[99] Chen's criticism is understandable: the two disagreed on many questions. But Chen would have been the first to complain if Party leaders had left the Central Soviet in the hands of a lesser person than a vice chairman of the soviet government.

Liang Botai and others not known as core supporters of the Party's ruling group were assigned to the rearguard for their administrative talents. Xiang chose Liang after the Central Committee decided in early October that someone with authority should stay behind to "take specific responsibility for government work," though Liang had originally been assigned to the evacuation. Liang Botai was not a Mao supporter, but he was on good terms with most people, including Mao and Zhang Wentian.[100]

Chen Yi, a "guerrillaist"[101] and a Mao supporter, was not discarded, as he claimed in his 1957 talk, but left behind for other reasons, as he admitted later in the same talk. Leaders visited him and said, "You are a high-ranking cadre. We should actually take you with us. But you have been in Jiangxi more than ten [*sic*] years, so you have influence and a reputation. You understand warfare. If we do not leave you behind when the Central Committee goes, how can we justify ourselves before the masses?" Chen, laid up with battle wounds in October, was the highest-ranking officer among the bedridden. Later, he played the main role in rallying patients after the collapse of the soviet. Had he been removed from hospital and taken on the march, the rest would even more surely have lost heart. Shortly after the start of the Long March, Xiang Ying asked Chen if he wanted to slip through White lines to the safety of the cities. Chen refused to answer either yes or no. Chen is the most frequently cited example of discrimination; but the facts do not bear it out.[102]

Qu Qiubai, He Shuheng, and others were left behind because they were too ill to march. Qu was dying of tuberculosis; He Shuheng was nearly sixty and walked with a stick.[103] They are often cited as victims of heartless discrimination, but the evidence shows otherwise. Qu Qiubai himself said after his capture by the Nationalists and a fortnight before his execution on June 18, 1935, that though the decision to leave him behind was taken without his knowledge, he had agreed to it because he feared that his "sick body could not stand the hardships of a long, long journey."[104] In any case, the aim was not to keep Qu and He in Gannan come what may, but to smuggle them if necessary to Shanghai to do secret work for the Party, together with a group of women leaders and "important personages" too frail to fight.[105]

Women of all ranks were a fifth and major category of stayers. The wives of Xiang Ying and Liang Botai were among the group that left with Qu Qiubai.[106] Nurses, actresses, teachers, Party officials, soviet employees, and dependents of Red Army men (who accounted for four out of five people in the soviet heartland[107]) made up the ranks of the soviet women's home guard in October 1934. Many were raped by members of the occupying army and the returning legions and sold to the brothels of Guangdong and the Nanyang or to Guomindang officers and soldiers.[108] Others, cowed by the army or won over by the teams of educated young women sent to the villages to indoctrinate them, turned their backs on Communism and called home their sons and brothers.[109] But some stayed loyal to the Party and became the mainstay of guerrilla communications and supply after 1934.

The biggest group of male stay-behinders (apart from Red Army invalids, whom I discuss later) were Communists and Red Army men native to the soviet areas.[110] Almost all local Party and government officials were left behind; most of the troops left behind were local peasants organized in self-defense armies. The rearguard leaders, especially outside Gannan, were also mainly local people. These appointments made sense. Local leaders could survive more easily if the soviet collapsed. They were generally more committed to and better at guerrilla warfare than officers of the central Red Army. For the same reason, most of them were Mao supporters.[111] Mao saw the value of leaving people like this behind. "You should go back to Minxi," he told Zhang Dingcheng on the eve of the Long March. "You know the region well. You can hold out there and develop it."[112] So the preponderance of Mao supporters among leaders of the rearguard, especially in Minxi, can be explained better by coincidence than by discrimination. It was perhaps to balance their influence that overall direction of the rearguard was vested in the orthodox Xiang Ying. Local troops at first fought poorly during the period of regular warfare in late 1934, and many deserted to their homes. They lacked experience of this style of fighting, and their discipline was poor. Later, however, stay-behinders drew strength from their local ties and knowledge.

A final group left behind in the Central Soviet were purge victims being held in a dozen or so concentration camps around Ruijin. The purge, begun during the build-up to the Long March, aimed to strengthen discipline and stop desertions by marchers and defections by stay-behinders. Several thousand people, including large numbers of Communist intellectuals, were removed from office and investigated. Executions of purged officials continued a month after the Long Marchers had left. Xiang Ying, Chen Yi, and Tan Zhenlin all helped in the purge, which extended to people sent back from the Long March after getting injured.[113] It was both a product of extreme tensions in the Central Soviet and a further blow to the morale of the rearguard and to people's confidence in the Party.

### The Preparation of the Rearguard

Chen Yi's final criticism concerns preparations for the rearguard action in Gannan, which he says were rushed through even more quickly than preparations for the evacuation. Detailed arrangements probably started in early September 1934, when Xiang Ying learned that he was to lead the rearguard.[114] Chen Yi and the rest were not informed until a month or so later. For them, the change came suddenly. Only Xiang Ying had time to prepare mentally for the upheaval. Simplified structures, including a sub-bureau of the Central Committee, were set up to run the soviet, and these structures were to be simplified even further by unifying Party, government, and army in a new Military and Political Committee if worst came to worst.[115] In fact, several regions eventually set up committees of this sort. But the people who were to run these bodies were not informed until the last minute. The preparations paid more attention to forms of organization than to their staffing.

### MORALE

What does Chen Yi's criticism reveal about the state of soviet morale after the start of the Long March? It shows that decision making about the evacuation was confined to a tiny group, that the vast majority of both marchers and stay-behinders were unaware that the soviet was to be abandoned, and that Party leaders did nothing to relieve supporters of their various misconceptions about the expedition. The preparations that did take place were almost exclusively logistical and bureaucratic; their purpose was kept secret. Inevitably, rumors abounded, whipping up an undercurrent of fear in the villages and in the army.

For the marchers, there were compensations. In the weeks before the evacuation the mood was grim, mainly because of a series of defeats that had swamped the hospitals with wounded soldiers.[116] The mood in the field armies reflected and influenced the mood in the villages and among the stay-behinders. But after October 1934, the morale of marchers and stay-behinders traced opposite courses, one lifting like a rocket into a clear sky, the other plunging to earth in a ball of flames like the rocket's exhausted first stage. The marchers were freed from constraints of space and, as a result, from the social consequences of their war. Inconsolable "grumblers" peeled off and were swallowed up in the vastness of China. "Grumblers" under Xiang had nowhere to go but the villages of the soviet, where they stoked the discontent and made life impossible for Xiang.

For the marchers, the revival began during mobilization week in October, as the congregating troops were borne down to the river by a throng of shouting, singing, chanting people. The sudden availability of supplies after months of shortages gave them hope that the period of setbacks was nearly over. The anxiety changed to excitement as the idea slowly dawned that they were on the threshold of a great undertaking. For the stay-behinders, there was no revival. Those who cherished illusions—probably a minority—soon saw them shattered. They had the worst of both worlds. Deprived, like the marchers, of information, they were also deprived of equipment and provisions, and there was little hope of replenishment. The marchers' good fortune was deliberately planned at the stayers' cost. The evacuation was not a stampede, as Chen Yi implies, but the preparations, far from making things easier for those who stayed behind, made things much worse. The eighty-six thousand marchers carried ten catties of grain each; once outside the soviet, they could live off purchases and plunder. The thirty thousand or so stay-behinders, including the wounded, had three hundred thousand catties for themselves and their civilian dependents and no prospect of getting more.

The marchers had three or four rifles for every five soldiers.[117] The stayers were far worse equipped: most estimates suggest that only a third were armed. After the soviet's final collapse, Nationalist troops dug up eight thousand rifle barrels, two hundred light machine guns, ten pieces of artillery, seven hundred bayonets, thirty trench mortars, and two hundred piculs of ammunition near the site of the old soviet arsenal.[118] Either the rearguard was deliberately denied these arms, which is unlikely, or too little attention was paid to preparations, so that there was no time to hand out the stocks left by the marchers.

The fighting quality of the rearguard was also comparatively poor. Agnes Smedley was exaggerating when she said that 80 percent of the marchers were "seasoned, disciplined veterans"; at least half of them had been recruited within the previous ten months.[119] But back in the soviet, far more than half the troops were either unfit or untrained. According to Edgar Snow, several thousand were "mere children, Young Vanguards from eleven to fifteen . . . ; many actually participated in the bayonet charges."[120] Otto Braun thought that far too few men were left to defend the soviet, which was "largely stripped of serviceable troops." He proposed a smaller evacuation but only succeeded in reducing it by 10 to 20 percent.[121]

After October, the marchers came to form a compact community of interests, feelings, ideals, and action. Their shared experience of danger and delivery from danger strengthened their camaraderie and solidarity. The defeatist strain receded, together with the battlegrounds on which the defeats had happened; the initial deception was forgotten as new goals formed. The marchers became lighter (by shedding unnecessary burdens), more mobile, and—with a reunited leadership—less troubled by a sense of aimless wandering. For those left behind in Chen Yi's burning house, with an empty armory, dwindling grain supplies, and no manpower to replace losses in battle, nothing remained to offset the disillusion. The farther the marchers got from Gannan, the closer they were drawn together. But the rearguard was splintered into tinier and tinier fragments both spiritually, by the loss of morale, and physically, by tactics of the Nationalist encirclers. They were a "blind army," cut off from the world outside.

The collapse started almost immediately after the main force left. Stay-behinders lost heart, became terrified of the enemy, and disintegrated; whole regiments threw down their guns and took to their heels. "The combat effectiveness and will of the soviet area troops was no longer what it had been," said Chen Yi. "A battalion of Guangdong warlord troops occupied a pass in southern Yudu. We wanted to win it back. We sent in eight regiments or about ten thousand troops against them, but failed to take it even after four days and nights of fighting." Eventually the Communist regiments fled. Chen's response was, "Let them run," for their morale was broken.[122]

## CHIANG'S ARMIES OCCUPY THE SOVIET

In early October 1934, Nationalist political and military leaders of Jiangxi and four other provinces troubled by insurgents met at Lushan to discuss plans—drawn up several months earlier, reportedly with German advice—for the final drive on the Central Soviet. The campaign was to be known as "encircling and destroying in a metal bucket." The plan, laid with great precision, envisaged a "sudden encirclement" of the soviet by one and a half million troops, with Ruijin at the center. The rate of advance was set at just over half a mile a day. Troops were to lay a thick barbed-wire entanglement every five hundred yards, with minefields in between, and to build a complete line of forts (with civilian help) every three miles. Had the plan been followed, Ruijin would have fallen within six months, enclosed by three hundred lines of entanglement and thirty lines of forts.

The sudden emptying of the bucket in mid-October, when the Red Army marched away, and the fall of Changting on November 1 and of Ruijin on November 9, five months ahead of schedule, led to a general acceleration of timetables and the lapsing of previous battle orders, though the idea of "pacification" was kept much the same. On November 24, new plans were announced to purge Jiangxi and Fujian. The soviet was cut up into twelve pacification zones. Troops sealed these zones to prevent trapped Communists from sneaking off and crisscrossed the region with lines of stone and concrete blockhouses, telephone lines, and roads. Once strong units had secured key points, smaller units fanned out across the mesh of small squares formed by the lines, catching or killing the people in them; snipers harassed the Communists to exhaust, demoralize, and weaken them. Once an area had been declared clean of Communists, "their chiefs caught and their ranks reduced," the majority of troops moved forward to quarantine and purge an adjacent area. It was not enough, wrote an official historian of the campaign, simply to rout and scatter the Communists.

> The bandits' independent regiments, battalions, and guerrilla units were made up of local elements well acquainted with local topography. They could disperse as civilians and congregate as bandits. True, they had little power to resist, but they were more mobile than the main force. In wiping them out, the emphasis had to be on destroying their real forces and capturing their chiefs.[123]

Blockhouses and roads played a key role in subjugating the Central Soviet. Some thirty thousand blockhouses were built around it in 1933 and 1934, averaging three per square mile. In November 1934, 729 blockhouses were built in Jiangxi alone, and a further 2,454 were built between December 1934 and March 1935. On the army's heels came officials of the Highway Bureau to build new roads. More than five thousand miles of modern highway and an equal length of long-distance telephone line were laid in Jiangxi in 1933 and 1934; 180 miles of highway were completed in the first five months of 1935. The telephone lines connected the villages to central military intelligence. The blockhouses were situated along roads and projected roads and at strategic places within easy reach of roads, so that they could be easily relieved if brought under siege. Blockhouses varied in strength and size. Some could house a battalion, others a platoon or less.[124]

By the end of January 1935, the area west of Ruijin and Shicheng had been declared free of Communists. By late March, the areas north of Xingguo and Gulonggang, southwest of Yudu and Huichang, and between Ruijin and Huichang had also been purged. By April, "the task of extirpating Communists in the twelve zones had been accomplished," and by May, Gannan as a whole had been "completely cleared of ban-dits." Nearly seventeen thousand prisoners had been taken, together with nearly twelve thousand rifles (eight thousand of them retrieved from secret caches).[125]

The failure of earlier encirclements had convinced Chiang Kai-shek to change the emphasis of his strategy and to "use a method of '30 per-cent military, 70 percent political,' while combining government, party and military resources in a new style of total war."[126] The watchword was reunification by reconstruction, rather than reconstruction by force. Po-litical reforms would consolidate military gains; rural Jiangxi would be-come the crucible for a new China. Past encirclements were said to have failed because they had relied on military means to crush the Commu-nists. Under the new approach, military encirclement would be just one aspect of a blockade. The mobilization of the villages to support the war against the Communists would become the basis for their reconstruction after peace.

## THE NEW SYSTEM OF VILLAGE SECURITY

*Sanbao* (the three *bao*s) was the cornerstone of this new approach. The term refers to the *baojia* system of village security, which bound villag-ers together as mutual guarantors; the *baoweituan*, or defense militias, which rural power holders set up to oppose the Communists; and the *baolei*, or blockhouses (also translated as forts or pillboxes), through which the blockade was physically enforced. Besides these measures, there were the *baoxue*, or community schools, designed to "right the wrong thoughts of the masses, to lead them in self-defense," and to teach skills that would help rehabilitate war-torn regions.[127] The *baojia* heads, trained and supervised by army officers, were charged with look-ing out for subversive activities, registering households, policing peo-ple's movements, organizing defense militias, and recruiting unpaid la-bor for public works and security tasks. The *baojia* hierarchy was based on a module of ten. Ten households made a *jia*, ten *jia* a *bao*. The func-tions of the defense militia paralleled those of the *baojia*. Militias were responsible for defending fortified village settlements. They were cheap (because not professional) and at least for a while they were efficient, for they were fighting on their home ground.[128]

Most officers of the *baojia*, commanders of the defense militia, and teachers in the community schools belonged to the rural elite.[129] During the late Qing dynasty the countryside had been largely run by local gen-try who derived their status from degrees gained in the imperial exam-inations. By the early years of the twentieth century, this "upright gen-try" had begun to disintegrate. In its place emerged a class of rich and literate *tuhao,* variously translated as village strongmen or local bullies, who plundered the villages with the help of hired thugs and monopolized the *mintuan,* or defense militias. Nationalist leaders had an uneasy relationship with this "new gentry" or "evil gentry," which many blamed for the success of the Communist insurgency. After 1927, the new government in Nanjing at first tried to limit the power of the *tuhao* by introducing modern policing into the villages, but its new security forces were incompetent, corrupt, inadequately funded, and largely ineffective. The government eventually abandoned its efforts to undermine the *tuhao* and instead awarded them and their militia a star role in "pacifying" the villages. "The underlying assumption," wrote G. E. Taylor in 1935,

> appears to be that the way to defeat Communism is to strengthen, both politically and economically, those classes of the population that have most to fear from Communism. It is difficult to see at what point the programme gives real hope to the poor and landless. . . . Strategically considered, . . . the Government policy is directly opposite to that of the Communists, who sought to strengthen the poor against the rich.[130]

But though *sanbao* crushed the Communists in early 1935, it was unable to prevent the revival of guerrilla pockets throughout southern and central China between late 1935 and 1937, partly because the government failed to address root causes of peasant distress after 1934. Many Nationalists recognized that land hunger was among Jiangxi's biggest social ills. Chiang Kai-shek promised during his final campaign against the Central Soviet to "solve the land problem."[131] But after the Communists had retreated from Gannan, landlords returned to the villages to reclaim their land, and the government supported them.[132] For the first six months after the start of the Long March, most landlords kept clear of old soviet areas, and the Nationalists tried to buy stability by what Communists called "cheating propaganda." Only after June did landlords start returning in large numbers. Many had collected no rent or interest for several years; they now demanded large back payments. In lieu of debts, peasant women were sold, and debtors were forced to build houses for these landlords. Chiang Kai-shek did not disapprove of this agrarian Thermidor. "If we are going to take the land away from the landlords," he is reported to have said, "why are we driving out the Communists?" Foreign critics observed that he had done nothing to remove the causes of Communism. "The Long March removed the most pressing argument for land reform," concluded one historian.[133]

To unite all classes of society behind new patriotic goals, Chiang Kai-shek launched his fascist-inspired New Life Movement in 1934. This movement stressed "national" culture and "traditional" moral virtues, which Chiang thought would speak more directly to the peasants than class struggle and Communist internationalism.[134] It was a reactionary irrelevance to the problems of poverty, violence, and deeply entrenched corruption. Despite its rhetoric about removing dirt, beggary, robbery, and graft, it brought about only superficial change. In the words of one study, it aimed to build "a mass campaign for national regeneration . . . on the toothbrush, the mouse trap and the fly swatter."[135]

Far from relieving the peasants of excessive burdens, *sanbao* imposed new hardships on them. Militarizing the villages laid claim to resources that otherwise might have been used locally to rehabilitate the economy. "Most provincial resources were mobilized to fuel the military machine," said Hung-mao Tien.[136] The *baojia* were meant to form the basis for the economic reconstruction of the villages as well as for rural policing, but they lacked the capital to finance big projects. Thousands of people lost their lives building roads for the government; tens of thousands lost land and resources to the roads. "Many miles of roads and dykes have been built . . . by forced and unpaid labor," wrote Taylor, "and nearly two hundred playgrounds and parks have been constructed by the same means. Most of these parks stand out in the countryside, . . . untrodden by the unforced foot of man, mocking the hills and rivers with their desolate and unhappy civil pride."[137]

*Sanbao*'s second weakness was the nature of the coalition upon which it rested. *Sanbao* was officially aimed at extending government power into the villages, for example by making local procedures uniform, increasing coordination between the provinces and the counties, and centralizing local administration in the hands of county magistrates.[138] But the government's agents in the "evil gentry" resisted such measures, which they saw as a threat to their local rule.

Here then were two conflicts on which the Communists could play after 1934: between the villagers and the petty tyrants who oppressed them, and between these petty tyrants and the Nationalist authorities. Before 1935, class conflict between rich and poor had been the Party's main political focus in the villages. After the start of the Long March, conflicts of interest between local powerholders and higher authorities became a second focus for stay-behinders in the south. Through a combination of tact and terror, the Communists managed, after a short period of strategic rethinking, to undermine all four *bao*s: by inveigling officials of the *baojia*, officers of the militia, and teachers in the community schools to "turn round" at least halfway; by infiltrating their own supporters into *bao* organizations; and by destroying the blockhouses— undermining them (literally, with tunnels), burning them, tearing them down, and blowing them up where they did not "fall" by peaceful means. However, other openings that the Communists had exploited in the past had closed. Several years of war had concentrated military power in government hands in Jiangxi. The Nationalists were no longer troubled by deep divisions in their army and could devote their undivided attention to pacifying Communists.

Even though acorns of discord were wedged in the new political stonework, the peasants were at first in no frame of mind to listen to the Communists, and they were too weak and demoralized to resist revenge by the *tuhao*. The rural economy was exhausted, tens of thousands of households had been scattered or destroyed by war, and one-third of the arable land in the old Central Soviet lay idle.[139] The economic blockade had created terrible shortages. Nationalist troops rushed grain, salt, food, medicine, vaccines, and tools into recovered areas, in line with the plans agreed on at Lushan in October. The villagers welcomed government rehabilitation measures in the weeks and months after the fall of the soviet. Government health bureaus provided "perhaps the easiest entrance into the confidence of the farmers."[140] Rearguard leaders realized that the Nationalists would at first tread lightly in the villages. "The enemy knew that those who wore the red hats had long since gone," said Chen Yi, "so they thought that they could start by buying people over. The repression could be left till later."[141] Reports—not wholly naive—spoke of a new mood of idealism and commitment to change in Jiangxi and of an improvement in military discipline as a result of stricter training and better officers. "Hosts of refugees were provided for and all official and military exactions ceased," reported the *Times* in an article which, though bordering on the gullible, gives some flavor of the spirit of the period.

> Soldiers were ordered to be polite and considerate, and to help farmers in harvesting their crops, and a number of young officials were stationed throughout [Jiangxi] for the express purpose of giving a new impression of officialdom by fair and helpful administration. The services of foreign missionaries were engaged to advise upon and to supervise the good work.[142]

This attempt to gain the people's trust is only one side of the picture. The occupation of the soviets was often cruel and violent, especially outside Gannan, which Chiang Kai-shek used for a while as a showpiece to impress foreigners. Even in Gannan, Communists and their sympathizers were treated harshly unless they recanted and actively collaborated with the occupiers. According to Chen Yi, they were killed unless they supplied the names of three fellow Party members.[143] But nationalist officials did succeed for a few months in winning the confidence of some war-weary peasants and thus made the Party's task there doubly difficult. It was some time before the Communists could latch onto reemerging social tensions. Meanwhile, they faced a host of awesome new obstacles and dangers.

## XIANG YING AND CHEN YI:
## TWO PATHS TO REVOLUTION

The two main protagonists in the Communist movement in Gannan after October 1934, and later in Ganyue, were Xiang Ying and Chen Yi. Before we look at the history of the rearguard in Gannan between October 1934 and April 1935, we must first consider the lives of these two men and their contrasting characters and views. For the six and a half years between the start of the Long March and Xiang Ying's murder by a traitor in early 1941,[144] Xiang's fate and Chen's were intimately entwined, both in the Three-Year War and in the first three years of the New Fourth Army, formed from southern guerrilla remnants in late 1937. History books in China are dictated by winners on the principle that "the victor is king, the loser is a rebel." As a loser—and a dead loser, who died in disgrace after opposing Mao—Xiang Ying has been the subject of much false witness and unfair comment in China; whereas Chen Yi, a Mao supporter who rose to become mayor of Shanghai (a city he captured from the Nationalists in 1949), one of China's ten marshals, a doyen of education and science, and foreign minister of the People's Republic, became a popular romantic hero and a favorite of many Chinese historians. Needless to say, the conventional view that Chen Yi matched each of Xiang Ying's vices with a virtue, and was always right where Xiang was always wrong, is a caricature. "On many questions I differed from Comrade Xiang Ying in my views and actions," said Chen Yi, probably in 1941, "but I would not venture to say that in my heart I had a line that was clear, complete, and encompassing both general and specific issues."[145]

Chen's personal relationship to Xiang was also far more complex than caricatures allow. Their natures were in almost every way opposed, as we shall see. But though they quarreled constantly during the Three-Year War and afterwards, whenever possible they slept in the same room, ate at the same table, and apparently took pleasure in their endless wrangling (though apparently Xiang sometimes bore grudges).[146]

For years, it would have been impossible in China to publish Chen Yi's confession of fallibility, except perhaps during his temporary disgrace in the Cultural Revolution. Since the death of Mao, however, more and more historians in China have begun to look first at the facts and only then at their political implications. In the process, their view of Xiang has slowly changed. His reputation can be gauged at a glance from the way people name him. Early texts called him comrade and put his name before Chen Yi's, who was after all his second-in-command. Later this order was inverted, though Xiang remained a comrade. Then the word "comrade" was dropped, and in the Cultural Revolution Red Guards talked of "traitor Xiang." In 1977, when tens of thousands of Xiang

Yings, dead or alive, were in limbo awaiting rehabilitation, his name vanished altogether from the handful of publications that appeared on the Three-Year War. Historians attributed its leadership solely to Chen Yi as they waited to see which way the political wind would blow.[147] Since then, Xiang has climbed back up the nomenclature ladder. By the mid-1980s, his titular comeback was complete, and he was Comrade Xiang again.

The contrast between Xiang and Chen begins with their physical appearance. Xiang was "short, shorn of head, and a bundle of closely knit sinew," said Evans Fordyce Carlson, who met him in Hankou in 1938.[148] Edgar Snow gained a similar impression: for him, Xiang was

> a Treaty-Port foreigner's idea of a "typical coolie." His lips and nose are broad and thick; his teeth, some of which are missing, jut out irregularly and unsightly; his hands are stubby and calloused; his big broad feet are most comfortable in peasant straw sandals. Everything about this wiry and muscular figure suggests primitive strength and a life of toil and sweat.[149]

Xiang would have been happy with this unflattering view of him: it tallied with his self-projection as a son of toil. Xiang was one of only two workers in China's Communist elite (the other being Chen Yun). His proletarian credentials won him attention and support in a Party nominally of the working class but in reality embarrassingly short of workers, especially at the top.

Chen Yi presented the very different appearance of a man of learning, though observers differ on the moral impression that his looks conveyed. For Colonel David Barrett, Chen had a "cruel hard face; the face of a killer." For Xu Xingzhi, he had a noble look: sparkling strong eyes that radiated warmth; a high-bridged nose; a firm resolute mouth; a fine voice; a shaved chin, "as in France."[150] Photos of the period admit both descriptions. Barrett, an army man, is struck by the ferocity and ruthlessness of Chen the soldier. Xu, a writer, notices the sensitivity of Chen the poet.

Xiang Ying's background is not as unambiguously proletarian as it is sometimes painted. His father was an impoverished scholar who had slid into shop work (according to one source) or office work (according to another). Xiang Ying, originally called Xiang Delong, was born in Wuchang in 1898. His father died when he was ten, but his mother managed to buy him four years' education by spinning and embroidering. Xiang's father's family was not without wealth and influence. His uncle was director of the Wuchang Charity Association, but Xiang had no dealings with him and cursed him as a "people-eating hoodlum." Xiang can better be described as part of the ousted lowest level of a class in swift decline than as a proletarian pure and simple. His severance from the world of formal learning was completed by his fifteenth birthday, when he started a three-year apprenticeship in the Wuchang Model Factory. Disappointment and personal resentment were probably the fuses that lit his strong class hatred. After finishing his apprenticeship, he became a textile worker and a revolutionary.[151]

As a child and a young man, Chen Yi, too, was part of a family in decline, but its slide was gentler and started from further up the social slope. Family feuding—between his rich maternal relatives and his poor father's family—helped form his rebel nature as it had helped form Xiang's. "In my childhood I personally experienced this class struggle within the landlord class," recalled the older Chen.[152]

Chen Yi was born near Chengdu, the Sichuan capital, in 1901, a ninth-generation descendent of an immigrant from Hunan. His father was a scholar and small landlord who went bankrupt. When Chen was five, he attended a small private school. He read the Four Books[153] and could soon recite them by heart, thanks to his photographic memory. When he was seven, he and his father went to Hubei, where his maternal grandfather, Huang, had bought a minor position in the government bureaucracy. Grandfather Huang, disappointed in his own son and having no grandson by him, sought substitutes in his daughter's menfolk. Chen senior started to work in Huang's yamen. At first he was enthusiastic. "We are going to be officials," he told his son. "We will ride everywhere in sedan chairs." But he and Huang soon fell out, so he sold up and went back to Chengdu.

Chen Yi stayed for more than two years with his grandfather before rejoining his father. As an even younger child, he had heard stories about his great-great-grandfather on his father's side, a wealthy *xiucai*,[154] who lent money at usurious rates and forced repayment by holding a knife to his own throat and threatening to kill himself. Chen Yi's paternal grandfather was a kindhearted man who fed people he caught pilfering from his stores or tied them up loosely so that they could slip free. Later, Chen Yi the Marxist branded this as "false humanity" designed to "buy hearts," but the story moved him as a small boy and taught him compassion. In the yamen, he witnessed ferocious beatings that planted in his mind "the first seed of hatred for the old society." During these beatings, he was sometimes instructed to plead for mercy on a prisoner's behalf; at other times, pity drove him to plead for it of his own accord, but he was then ignored.

After his father left, Chen's position in the yamen changed; his grandfather's kindness turned to coldness. Chen went barefoot and ragged and was scolded as a parasite. Chen's compassion, his revulsion at the beatings, Huang's disparagement of Chen's father, and Chen's feeling of rejection combined to produce in him a strong sense of justice

and of his own personal identity. He developed not only a poetic sensitivity but also an iron will and an indomitable self-confidence. The final
break with his grandfather came when he was nine. Caught embezzling
public grain, the grandfather invited local bigwigs to a banquet in the
hope that they would intercede for him. Little Chen Yi, who had been
hidden from sight, used the occasion to take his revenge. He put on his
worst rags and stood in the doorway to shame his grandfather in front of
his important guests. That night, he was beaten. Shortly afterwards, he
returned to Sichuan.

After the revolution of 1911, Huang, too, went back to Sichuan, but
he kept up his business contacts in Hubei and bought Sichuan slave girls
to sell there. Chen Yi agreed with those who cursed Huang as a trader
in human flesh. In Hubei, Chen had learned to sympathize with the oppressed and to rebel against injustice, but he had also learned other
skills that he put to use in later life. For example, he had learned to
make appeals and entreaties and to manipulate petty tyrants. He also became versed in the "etiquette of official circles," which he used as a boy
to charm local dignitaries. These skills served him well in the Three-
Year War and the founding years of the New Fourth Army.

In Chengdu, Chen Yi returned to school, where he became an avid
reader of classical verse. His family encouraged him to "stand out head
and shoulders above the rest," to become a big official, and above all to
outshine the Huangs. For a while, he became arrogant and competitive.
Soon, new crises and conflicts rent his family. For years, his father and
uncles were in litigation with their landlord over rent; by the end, the
family was on the edge of bankruptcy. At school, children of "warlords
and bureaucrats" mocked him as a "country bumpkin," a "poor boy,"
and the son of a "bankrupt landlord."[155]

The revolution of 1911 and the events leading up to the May Fourth
Movement of 1919 struck a chord in Chen, though he was too young and
too ignorant of politics to grasp their full meaning. In 1915, he went to
study at an industrial college and emerged as a leader of the poorer students, representing them in disputes. In 1918, family funds dried up.
Chen Yi wanted to become a soldier; his family refused to let him. Instead, he joined a school that prepared students for training in France
under the Part Work and Part Study Program. His ambition was "to
make China strong by learning science."[156]

In 1919, he and his brother won scholarships to go to Paris. En route,
Chen passed through Shanghai, Singapore, Ceylon, and the Suez Canal,
extending his mental horizons and freeing himself of some national
prejudices. In Paris, he learned about socialism and French literature.
He earned his keep by loading barges, washing dishes, and working in a
factory, where he took part in a strike. Earlier he had seen going abroad

as a chance to escape bankruptcy and the hard life of the factory. "Getting the chance . . . was a big liberation," he recalled. "But actually it was nothing more than going abroad for work. Facts show that unless you take part in the revolution, there is no way out." In Paris, he had expected a paradise of social order, clean streets, and civilized behavior. The realities of inequality, anti-Chinese racism, and the harsh factory regime offended him. Earlier, he had "looked down a little on the toilers"; experience on the shop floor changed his mind. He began to sympathize and identify with the workers, especially the rebels. Even then, a wage raise and promotion to technician briefly revived his hopes of an "individual way out," and for a while he turned his back on the revolutionaries. But in late 1921, he and 103 other students were deported back to China under armed escort after protesting against plans for a new Chinese school in France that bypassed students like them already in the country. Chen soon gave up his dreams of personally saving China, and himself, through literature and science.[157]

Xiang Ying's path to revolution was in most respects unlike Chen Yi's. Xiang never went abroad before 1928 (when he went to Moscow), and his further political education was confined to the Workers' Night School in Wuhan run by Dong Biwu and Chen Tanqiu, which he began attending in 1919. In 1920, he led his first small strike, of Wuhan mill women, with the help of a revolutionary cell in Hubei that he immediately joined. The strike—the first ever in Wuhan's textile industry—was a brilliant success. Xiang soon became a professional agitator. In the summer of 1921, he sought out Bao Huiseng, the Communist Party's labor organizer in Wuhan, and applied to join the Chang Jiang branch of the Party's labor movement. In early 1922, Bao recruited him to the Party.[158] Xiang committed himself at once and forever to Communism.

Chen Yi moved more slowly toward the Party. He had a wider experience of political organizations, he had not yet entirely put the search for a "personal solution" behind him, he was by nature more skeptical and individualistic than Xiang Ying, and, despite his disillusion with French capitalism, he had developed a soft spot in Paris for "bourgeois freedom, equality, and universal fraternity." In Shanghai and in France, he had met anarchists, reformists, and bourgeois democrats as well as Marxists. He had sipped from every flower. "At that time, our thinking literally changed daily," he later said. When Cai Hesen, already a Communist, suggested in late 1921 that Chen go to Russia, he refused and instead returned to his native Sichuan, where he started work in early 1922 as editor on a Chongqing newspaper. Not only did he refuse to go to Russia; he was also of two minds about the Communist Party, though he promised Cai Hesen to distribute its literature. He was wary of being used, and he knew the dangers of a revolutionary career. He had not yet conquered his arrogance, and he planned to join the Party only as a leader, if at all; certainly he would not first join its youth wing. So he vacillated, despite attempts to recruit him. Back in Chongqing, he discovered that his spell abroad, far from advancing him, was a cause for discrimination. Seeing no future for himself, he became disheartened. In the winter of 1923, after losing his editor's job for criticizing the Sichuan warlords, Chen went to Beijing, where he studied at the Franco-Chinese University. Only then, in November, did he finally allow himself to be pressured into joining the Party. It was not until 1925, the year he graduated, that he became a professional revolutionary in Beijing and gradually set aside his literary career.[159]

Unlike Chen Yi, who was a freethinker and individualist, Xiang Ying had no difficulty in complying with the Party's centralist regime. The qualities that he brought to it were orthodoxy, "class purity," and a phenomenal gift for organizing. His first job in Bao Huiseng's labor movement, in December 1921, was to build a workers' club for railwaymen on the Beijing-Hankou line. Nominally, he was the club secretary, but he turned his hand to all sorts of jobs and became its main pillar and driving force. He rose rapidly in the national trade-union movement and the Communist Party and led many of the big strikes of the 1920s in Shanghai and Wuhan. "To tens of thousands of workers [he] soon became a symbol of hope," wrote Edgar Snow.[160] In 1928, he attended the Sixth Party Congress and the Sixth Congress of the Comintern in Moscow. He was elected to the Party's Standing Committee and to the Supervisory Committee of the Comintern. He returned to China in 1929 and took overall charge of the Party's trade-union work. By then, he was a bête noire of the Guomindang. "He has a natural talent for stirring up trouble," said one writer. "He can dive into society's bottom depths and cause waves where there is no wind. In the Communist Party, he is considered to have a formidable capacity for work. . . . He is a Party hatchet man."[161]

In 1930, Xiang was transferred from Wuhan to Gannan, where he stood in as secretary of the Central Committee's Southern Bureau until the arrival of Zhou Enlai. Over the next four years, he put his organizational talents to work building the soviet, for whose daily operations he was largely responsible. He was minister of several departments, including labor, land, finance, and investigation; from the very start, the existence of the soviet owed a great deal to his work. Though he was never known as an important theoretician, he has been described (with Zhou Enlai) as one of the chief "indigenous" collaborators of the "Twenty-eight Bolsheviks," Chinese who had studied in the Soviet Union and took their cue from Moscow. The Twenty-eight preached an orthodox "proletarian" Marxism that appealed to Xiang's self-image.

Xiang, too, derived authority from his Comintern link. Many of the students who returned from Moscow were former members of his workers' picket in Shanghai and Wuhan. He is said to have distributed these people around the soviet as his "mass base." He opposed the liquidation of Mao's opponents in the 1930 Futian Incident and argued that the so-called AB's (anti-Bolsheviks) should have been dealt with not as counter-revolutionaries but as a "contradiction within the people," a view now widely supported in China. But Xiang approved and helped carry out later purges. Together with Chen Tanqiu, he was responsible for crash-collecting one-quarter of a million piculs of grain in 1934.[162]

Xiang Ying was a cautious man who by training and inclination believed in orderly structures and fixed routines. He was a town Communist who had spent the hard years in Shanghai and Wuhan. He only arrived in Gannan when the revolution there had been under way for more than a year, and he had no direct experience of guerrilla warfare. Here, too, Chen Yi was his opposite. Chen was a fighting man, a poet who composed verses in the heat of battle, a man of stubborn temper, impetuous and easily swayed by feeling. In 1926, Chen went to Guangzhou and joined Zhou Enlai in the Political Department of the Whampoa Military Academy. When he first told the Party's Beijing Branch of his wish to go to Guangzhou, he was criticized as a "petty bourgeois . . . and a military opportunist" and sent to work in a blanket factory instead, to "steel himself" politically. He was sacked when it was discovered that he had had an education.[163] In Guangzhou, he began the military career that he had dreamed of in his teens. He took part in the Northern Expedition, the Nanchang Uprising, and the retreat to Shantou, probably in a political rather than a directly military role. He then fled with Zhu De and Lin Biao to the Jinggang Mountains, where he helped Mao set up the Fourth Red Army.

"Preparations were made for me to go to the Soviet Union," he later recalled,

> but I did not want to go. I could have gone to Beijing or Shanghai to do underground work, but I knew too many people there. I could have gone to France, but that would have meant leaving the Party, and anyway I had no money. There was nothing for it but to make the switch to guerrilla war. So I stripped off my long gown, burned myself black under the sun, learned the speech of the common people, took up the hoe, and helped till the people's fields, spread nightsoil, and sow seeds. I asked my way through the mountains. I learned to fire a gun, to track, to scout. And so I made the turn. . . . But Xiang Ying had not had that experience.[164]

As a result, concluded Chen, Xiang was not equipped to make the necessary adjustments after 1934; instead, Xiang clung to the structures and routines of the soviet he had done so much to build.

Two sayings spring to mind in connection with Xiang's place in the Chinese Revolution after 1934. One is the maxim that present wars are fought with the tactics of past wars. The other is the quip about the restored Bourbons: they had learned nothing and forgotten nothing. Xiang Ying was a Chinese Bourbon. Even after the collapse of the soviet and the removal of the Central Committee from Gannan, he clung to outworn forms and procedures. His military strategy was a replica in miniature of the fighting style of Bo Gu and Otto Braun before they were put to flight. Not until several months after the start of the Long March did Xiang finally yield to those who wanted change. At the end of the Three-Year War, he again found it difficult to switch to new policies and tactics, and as a result, he lost his life. "There was no problem about Xiang's staunchness," said Chen Yi. "It was his policies that were wrong, his rigidity and his inability to change line."[165] Others, too, saw Xiang as a man of little flexibility or imagination. He was an "austere, unyielding personality," said Agnes Smedley. Lacking originality and breadth of vision, he became a master of intrigue and cunning "who would adopt any method to reach his goal."[166] His obsession with hierarchies and routines made it difficult for him to take decisions independently after his comrades had marched away. He became more and more irresolute as the gap grew between reality and the simulated motions of the soviet government.[167]

Chen Yi's approach to most issues was generally the opposite. Chen was a man of numerous accomplishments: a horseman, a marksman, a chess player, a poet (classical and modern), and a translator of poems from the French.[168] He was a rebel long before he was a Communist; during the Cultural Revolution, he told his Red Guard inquisitors that he would stay a rebel all his life, "even after death."[169] He was never rigidly attached to ideas or bureaucratic forms. In his youth, he had become acquainted with a large number of radical and libertarian philosophers whose writings lent range and pliancy to his thinking. Xiang Ying also valued flexibility, but he thought that Chen Yi sometimes took it too far and ended up on the wrong line. Whereas Xiang Ying behaved like "a factionalist and a patriarch" and was considered aloof, Chen Yi had a winning nature and a tolerant style.[170] He won praise for his ability to delegate authority. Communists with creative talents and the courage to take on responsibility felt that under Chen Yi, they could prosper, even if they labored under "political problems" (like the remnants of Xiang's defeated command who escaped north to join Chen Yi in 1941).[171] "Chen Yi was amiable and easy to approach," enthused one survivor of the 1941 rout.

> He was a frank and open man; bighearted, bold, grand of vision; wise and farsighted, with an eye to the whole; resolute and resourceful; well versed in both the polite letters and the martial arts; . . . warm and loving toward

us; . . . skillful and patient; factual and rational; not given to slapping on labels and waving big sticks; good at uniting with other comrades. . . . So we who had worked for years under Xiang Ying could quickly see Xiang's faults.[172]

Xiang became increasingly irresolute as the soviet collapsed around him; Chen kept calm and spoke of the need—a favorite theme of his—to "be heroes in defeat."[173] Xiang was good at marshaling resources and regimenting people; Chen was good at holding people together of their own free will. Chen's childhood experience in his grandfather's yamen was useful to him after 1934, when it became necessary to compromise and even ally with the rich and powerful in the countryside.

It is not enough to explain the differences and conflicts between Xiang and Chen by their previous factional affiliations. True, Xiang had been a supporter of the Moscow-inspired majority, and Chen had "suffered ostracism and attack" for advocating "guerrillaism." Chen's faith in Mao and Xiang's opposition to Mao played a role in their confrontations. But in their case, labels like "leftism" and "Maoism" are only useful as shorthand for a range of attitudes that preceded and transcended politics.[174]

## THE DIFFICULT TRANSITION TO GUERRILLA WAR IN THE SOVIET AREA

The switch to guerrilla warfare in the Central Soviet did not take place everywhere simultaneously; it was a protracted process. Regular units continued to fight large-scale battles until several months after the start of the Long March. Some units left behind in the soviet had never fought anything but guerrilla war and continued to do so during the soviet's last months. Others were upgraded and used to replenish regular units. New guerrilla units were set up under officials released from bodies disbanded during and after the evacuation. These units were established later in some places than in others because of poor communications, slow decisions, and general chaos.

Luo Mengwen, Party secretary in the strategic Yanggan base, the northwestern doorway to the Central Soviet, was only told of his new military duties a month after the start of the Long March; others heard much sooner. Zeng Shan, rearguard leader of the Jiangxi Provincial Soviet, was directed in mid-October to wage guerrilla war in the region between Ningdu and Yongfeng. At a hurried meeting of the Gannan Provincial Committee on October 15 at Yudu, Mao told more than two hundred officials that they should "unite with the people, quickly organize guerrilla forces, expand guerrilla forces, develop guerrilla war, and mobilize the masses to strengthen the defenses and hide everything beyond the enemy's reach"; go underground if necessary and work secretly for the Party; and stay optimistic, for "the Red Army will definitely return." After this meeting, officials began sabotaging enemy communications, blowing up bridges, hiding grain, millstones, and pestles, and generally mobilizing for war. Other local Party workers from peripheral parts of the soviet had been attending training classes in Ruijin run by the Department for Work in White Areas in the summer of 1934. One such group graduated in October and returned to the villages after setting up a revolutionary committee and a guerrilla army. But they were probably unique; there is no evidence of any special effort to train large numbers of people for the new conditions. Some Party committees, like that at Ruixi, were not instructed until December 1934 to change to guerrilla tactics; others were left completely without instructions.[175]

The key to understanding the debates that accompanied the transition to guerrilla warfare in Gannan is the concept of "revolutionary optimism," in which Xiang Ying was a great believer. Optimism has been called the prerogative of a revolutionary, but optimism, as the Party promoted it in the 1930s, was not of the *dum spiro, spero* sort and even less the "optimism of the will, pessimism of the intellect" that critical Marxists like Gramsci recommended. Instead, it was "scientifically founded" optimism of the sort that "approves of everything, submits to everything, and believes everything."[176] Optimism of this sort was no longer a prerogative but an article of faith. Pessimism, in contrast, was a badge of opportunism and rightist deviation; in extreme cases it could be a capital offense. Stalin said that under wise leaders revolution was inevitable; to cast doubt on the revolution's prospects was to cast doubt on the leadership. So Xiang Ying was on firm ground when he made optimism the issue in his arguments with Chen Yi about strategy and tactics, and he used pessimism and "shaky morale" as a stick with which to beat Chen. Optimism oozed from Xiang's statement of October 18, 1934, in which he told skeptical citizens that Chiang Kai-shek would soon run out of troops to man his forts and that Chiang's army would "collapse completely" if every man, woman, and child acted against it.[177]

Xiang's optimism stemmed from his general assessment of the war. He did not believe that the soviet had been abandoned. The Long Marchers had not, as some studies imply, deliberately deceived him; they could not have known in advance that they would be unable to settle in Hunan. "The Red Army main force will win a string of victories in Hunan," Xiang told Chen Yi. "It will set up new soviets and draw most of the enemy away. Once it turns around, we can smash the enemy's offensive and restore soviet territory already lost." Chen Yi disagreed and thought that Xiang was wrong to "pin all his hopes on the field armies."[178] Three years later, in a report on the Three-Year War to the Party center in Yan'an in December 1937, Xiang admitted that he had been wrong to count on help from outside Gannan. To his credit, he took the blame himself and uttered no word of reproach against the Long Marchers who had abandoned him.[179]

Xiang's unrealistic optimism had important practical implications for the rearguard. During the first few weeks after the evacuation, with giant armies bearing down on him from all directions, he behaved with an exaggerated nonchalance. He spent much of his time chatting with the soviet librarian, the hospital director, and the leader of the cultural troupe. He carried on as if nothing much was happening and tried to reassure people, telling them not to be pessimistic. Far from streamlining the leadership in preparation for coming storms, he enlarged it with new members.[180] He even planned to set up a military academy. Under his direction, He Chang and Liu Bojian continued to publish *Hongse Zhonghua* until February 1935 (though Chen Yi thought that the time for newspapers was over).[181] Xiang's failure to show a sense of urgency, drop unjustifiable pretensions, and scrap unwieldy structures increased the support for Chen Yi among the other leaders.

Since Xiang believed that victory over Chiang Kai-shek was around the corner, he naturally opposed breaking up the Twenty-fourth Division. He even called for "new divisions and new armies" to be formed by reorganizing local troops into independent regiments, and he reckoned that his forces were strong enough to destroy an enemy division. He massed his troops in so-called passive defense in the area between Ruijin, Huichang, Yudu, and Ningdu. On more than one occasion, he massed them offensively, though they were by then disheartened and outgunned. On November 21, 1934, more than five thousand troops of the Twenty-fourth Division and the Ruijin and Huichang Independent Battalions joined to attack the Third Division of the Guomindang's East Route Army at Wantan'gang in order to "rouse the masses and boost their self-confidence." The attack was costly: it destroyed half an enemy brigade but led directly to the deployment of four enemy divisions against the Red Twenty-fourth, which lost its last positions.[182] In Yan'an in 1937, Xiang criticized this and similar battles as "very unwise" and "a serious mistake."[183]

Chen Yi started from the opposite premise. He believed that the soviet was doomed, that Xiang was daydreaming to think that the rearguard could coordinate a counteroffensive with the field armies. Chen pointed out that if the main Red Army had been unable to stem Chiang Kai-shek's advance, then it was unrealistic to expect Xiang's much smaller force to do so—unless of course the Nationalists withdrew in large numbers from Gannan, which was improbable. Unlike Xiang, Chen could afford to take a realistic view of the crisis. As an old "guerrillaist," he had no reason to defend the policies of the leadership in which Xiang had served. He could take grim satisfaction from confronting Xiang with the consequences of its misgovernment. Chen agreed that the problems of the Central Soviet could be solved within two to three months if the field armies got a foothold in Hunan, but he did not believe that they would do so, and he thought that it was enough to hope that they would escape destruction. So he opposed any strategy that depended for success on outside intervention; the stay-behinders should look only to themselves.[184]

Chen resisted the charge of pessimism, but his hopes were for the future rather than the present. His model was the course pursued after the Nanchang Uprising of August 1927, when an army a dozen times smaller than Xiang's had survived and later multiplied. "There will be a great storm over Jiangxi," he told Xiang in October 1934, "but in the end victory will be ours. We must work out ways of saving as many as possible from the storm."[185] After the storm would come a new high tide of revolution. What would bring it? Not the field armies, as Xiang thought. Conditions had changed since the early 1930s; the next high tide would look very different from the last. Its main cause would be the spread of Japanese aggression across China. Meanwhile, Xiang should not squander his resources on futile adventures; he should husband them for the battles ahead.

Chen urged Xiang to begin by changing his methods and his style of work. Xiang was a main architect of the Jiangxi Soviet bureaucracy and a student and admirer of its Russian model. He was used to large-scale administration, shock campaigns, an endless flow of documents and publications, conferences that went on for a week or a fortnight (with teams of stenographers working in shifts to record them), and speeches that lasted for hours or even days. He found it hard to tear himself away from all the accessories and trappings of high office; he clung to forms of statehood now emptied of content and imperturbably acted out his role in them. He was for all the world like Henry Pu Yi after 1911, presiding over a shrunken court within the four walls of the Imperial Palace as if the dynasty were still intact. The difference was that Xiang's ministers would not humor him, and the Nationalists, far from subsidizing him, were preparing to batter down his gates.

Chen Yi himself, after his discharge from hospital, was installed in a house lined high with books. As a veteran guerrilla, he viewed Xiang's conduct as an extravagant fantasy that would require endless transfusions of blood to sustain. Now as in 1927, he told Xiang, only a timely switch to guerrilla war could stop the destruction of the soviet's "living forces." The troops should throw off their insignia and regroup in units of a dozen. Party secretaries should put down their pens, take up guns, burrow deep into the towns and villages, set up yet more guerrilla bands, and give the occupiers no rest. The Nationalists would then be faced with hundreds of small targets rather than one large target. "We will fight the war of the sparrow," said Chen, "in dozens and tens of dozens of small flocks. They might net one, but they cannot net them all." "The enemy was about to enter the soviet," he said later.

> The revolution was once more on the ebb. The soviet was bound to fall. A defeat is a defeat and should be recognized as such. If you recognize it, you may avert it, or reduce its size. To recognize defeat is not pessimism or disillusion but a sign of political resoluteness. You must coldly face up to reality, conscientiously organize the retreat, swiftly and resolutely adapt to the situation, abandon the old set-up, make a thorough turn. Politically, you must prepare to confront severe storms and to carry out a hard, long-term struggle behind enemy lines; militarily, you must decisively disperse and develop extensive mass-style guerrilla warfare; organizationally, you must change methods of leadership and work. From regular war to guerrilla war, from concentrated to dispersed, from ruling to being ruled, from open activity to secret and hidden activity. Make these changes, retreat, preserve forces, hold out in the long term, influence the situation in small ways, and prepare to meet the revolution's next high tide.[186]

Xiang Ying was not in principle opposed to guerrilla strategy. In the first two weeks of October, he evacuated some civilian personnel from endangered points on the plains to fight as partisans in the mountains and was planning to decentralize some military operations even further once the main force had left. For a long time, he was of two minds about overall military strategy. If the Nationalists continued to attack in large numbers, he would withdraw to the Wuyi Mountains and wage guerrilla war. If they lessened their offensive, he would mass his forces and fight to preserve the soviet's territorial integrity.[187] But his heart was not in withdrawal; it was two to three months before he finally came down in favor of it. In the meantime, he kept the machinery of government intact and pursued two different military strategies at once. Regular troops continued to fight in big formations and by regular means.[188] But "the masses" were urged to defend their lives and property by guerrilla warfare; to arm themselves "with spears, hunting guns, native cannon, revolvers, and old and new weapons of all sorts in defense of our government, our lives, our land, our grain, our cattle, our chickens, and our ducks, and to resist slaughter, destruction, looting, and rape."[189]

So the difference between Xiang and Chen was about not the principle but rather the extent and tempo of the switch to guerrilla warfare. Chen Yi wanted to switch right away and to disperse all of the rearguard, including the three regiments of the Twenty-fourth Division. Xiang Ying had a more elastic view. Perhaps he seriously believed that he could stave off collapse in the war of attrition against the Nationalists until relief arrived. According to intelligence reports passed on to Ruijin by a mole in Chiang's general command, the Nationalist generals were not planning to reach Ruijin until the end of March.[190] But this timetable was drastically curtailed as soon as news of the evacuation reached Nationalist headquarters, and Ruijin was taken in weeks rather than months. Even so, Xiang refused to speed up his plans. It was several weeks before he began to listen seriously to contrary opinions and several months before he finally gave up his losing battle altogether. At first he told his critics that he was only prepared to consider further decentralization in November or December, by which time the intentions of the field armies would be clearer.[191] But in December, he was still loath to disperse his best regiments; on the contrary, he tried to strengthen them.

## XIANG YING'S DILEMMA

Xiang Ying was not a madman, though he sometimes seemed like one. His job was to hold on to the soviet for at least as long as it took to cover up the dangerous first stages of the Long March. He had to trick the Nationalist generals into thinking that Red Army strength in Gannan remained more or less unchanged. To do so, he rotated his small and shrinking army in a mad dash around positions and along lines abandoned by the main force. The better he acquitted himself, the smaller were his chances of survival. For several weeks, he tried to hold on to old positions, at tremendous cost. The weaker his forces grew, the harder they had to fight; the harder they fought, the harder they were pressed; the longer they survived, the closer the field armies came to the safety of the west.

Did Xiang's juggling trick take in the Nationalists? Pro-Communist sources claim that Chiang Kai-shek suffered an intelligence fiasco in Jiangxi and that it was not until late November that his generals finally rumbled what had happened.[192] Nationalists say that Chen Cheng, commander of the Reserve Army in Jiangxi,[193] already knew on October 24 that the Red Army was heading west.[194] Recently published military archives show that the Nationalists knew about the evacuation in October, not long after it had started, and that they also knew the precise disposition of forces in the Central Soviet. "It has already been verified," said one report in late October, "that the bandit army is sneaking west. Will it return? That is not yet clear. But in and around Changting today only the Communists' Twenty-fourth Division and various guerrilla forces are putting up a desperate resistance." The report went on to say that it was unclear whether these stay-behind units "want to protect the main force as it sneaks west" or intend to "form the basis for a future comeback." Chiang Kai-shek knew, then, that an evacuation was under way. But he did not yet know how many people it involved. Some said fifty thousand, others a hundred thousand.[195]

How could the government have known about the evacuation just a week or two after it happened? At the beginning of October, leaders of the Party's Shanghai Bureau had defected to the Nationalists after being arrested; these people probably told their captors about the general intention to evacuate Jiangxi, although not about the specific details (which they did not know). Other political and military developments in August and September 1934 show that even before October, Chiang Kai-shek had more than a glimmering of the Red Army's plans.[196] After the start of the Long March, the bulk of Chiang's army hurried west in pursuit, leaving a smaller force of around two hundred thousand behind in Gannan.[197] This force reorganized and resumed the offensive a month later, at the end of November.[198]

Even so, in one sense the deception worked. Though the evacuation had not escaped the attention of Chiang's generals, at first they had no clear idea of how many Communists were left behind. According to Chen Yi, there was not even a consensus in Chiang's headquarters about whether more had gone than stayed (though Chen's surmise is unconvincing).[199] There were rumors in the Nationalist press that Mao Zedong had remained in Gannan.[200] The Nationalists had fought their way into trouble often enough in past encirclement campaigns to be wary of tricks and ruses. Instead of rushing Xiang, they crept gingerly forward from one position to the next, sensing traps everywhere and shrinking back into their shells at every unexpected contact.[201] So their probes lacked penetration, and it was some time before they had convinced themselves that it was safe to chase Xiang. Even when Xiang's nakedness had been fully exposed, they continued to mass huge forces against him. They knew from experience that even a small nucleus of Communists could grow quickly if left unchecked. "They were a motley crew, incapable of attacking," said an official history. "But our armies could not afford to let up for one moment in the campaign to exterminate and pacify the bandits, for a single spark can start a prairie fire." Chen Yi agreed: "The Guomindang knew that even though only a few guerrillas were left behind in the soviet, the fire would eventually sweep the entire prairie unless put out."[202]

## NEW METHODS AND NEW TACTICS

By late November 1934, Xiang Ying was under pressure to give up postures that were increasingly at odds with the facts. Deceptions cannot last for long without relief; Xiang had little left to conjure with. The Nationalists had overrun most of the soviet and were compressing Xiang's forces into an ever smaller space, which the Nationalists had sealed and were preparing to invade.[203] On December 4, Chen Cheng received reports that the Communists' main force in Gannan was by then less than six thousand strong, with just three thousand rifles.[204] He prepared to act more boldly. By this time, Chen Yi was out of hospital. At meetings, he argued openly (from a stretcher) for all-out guerrilla warfare.[205] Defeat is a school in which the truth grows strong. The bloody battle at Wantan'gang on November 21 convinced a majority of rearguard leaders that Chen Yi was right and that the time had come for a change. Xiang Ying reluctantly agreed. "At present, the Party's only central task is to lead guerrilla war," he told his people on December 29, 1934.[206] Decisions were taken to scatter units and leaders rather than monopolize them for a concentrated effort.[207] However, these decisions were not fully carried out and still did not affect the core Twenty-fourth Division. On January 12, 1935, four thousand men of this division, plus guerrillas, attacked a regiment of the Guomindang's Twenty-seventh Division but were driven off after two hours' fighting. The attack led to a further strengthening of Nationalist forces in the region. The last big assault on Nationalist positions was during the Spring Festival in late January, when, according to a Nationalist officer, "Red troops streamed in continuously, . . . swarming forward over the hills and dales" in an attempt to seize Niuling. The battle raged throughout the night. The Communists had superior forces but were thrown back with unusually heavy losses.[208]

In late November, probably, Xiang commissioned Chen to write a directive on new tasks and measures. The directive had a military and a political part. The former advocated dispersal in small units and a turn toward mass-based guerrilla warfare waged from the mountains in order to "ride out the storm and preserve forces." The latter addressed an issue that urgently concerned Communist supporters in villages overrun or soon to be overrun by the Nationalists, namely how to make the switch from "ruling to being ruled" without betraying the revolution. This question was paramount for Communists everywhere during the Three-Year War. Chen Yi was probably the first to try to answer it. His message, which he and others later elaborated into a comprehensive set of tactics, was that compromise with the occupiers was justified. For many, this concession was a repeal from certain death. It was one thing to be "a hero in defeat" high in the mountains, quite another to be one in the villages. But to surrender to the Nationalists without permission was risky, too: traitors could expect short shrift from Communist assassins.

Chen offered a way out of this dilemma. He said that Communists should try to "seize hegemony over the Guomindang's Voluntary Surrender Brigades in order to protect the masses and avoid senseless losses." These brigades were an essential part of the "pacification" of the soviet. They followed the army into the villages and issued "Fresh Start Certificates" to those who voluntarily surrendered to them and cooperated by supplying information. Such people were called Fresh Start Elements. They were not investigated by the brigades and were eligible for government relief aid. Chen thought that if Communists could infiltrate these brigades before they got their bearings in the villages, "the masses would then 'surrender' to us, so we can preserve our forces." (Party members, however, were forbidden to surrender.)

Chen also suggested other ways, including bribery, by which Communists could come to terms with the loss of power. Where landlords could not be kept from the villages altogether, they should be given back some land and allowed to live in peace. It should be made clear, however, that they would be killed if they caused trouble.[209]

Xiang had agreed to Chen's proposal under pressure; his conversion was incomplete. He still had not entirely given up hope of saving the soviet, and he wanted to delay a final decision until he received instructions from the Party center. At first, he strongly disagreed with parts of Chen's draft directive on guerrilla warfare and voluntary surrender. He held up its publication for several days; it was only with "the greatest reluctance" that he agreed to distribute it, and it was probably not until the end of the year that it was finally sent out. His reluctance is not hard to fathom. Chen's directive was a death certificate for Xiang's soviet. If Xiang released it without authorization from the Party center, purists might later use it against him as evidence of "rightism" or "capitulationism." When the directive finally went out, it was too late for many Party outposts, which by then had collapsed or lost contact with Xiang's command. Only the Party's Ruijin, Huichang, and Yudu committees received the directive and could act on it.[210]

Officials of the Central Soviet were accustomed to centralized command and the close coordination of military front and civilian rear. Ideally, the dismantling of the machinery of state and the switch from complex structures to simple structures, or even no structures, would have been preceded by a long period of political and material preparation, but there was no transition period in Gannan. In other regions with flimsier soviets and stronger guerrilla traditions, there was no abrupt transition or radical break. Regions that had already abandoned or had never had strong soviets took advantage of periods of quiet during which the Nationalists ignored them, particularly in the dangerous months immediately after the start of the Long March. The Central

Soviet, however, as the hub of Communist revolution and the main target of the Nationalist encirclers, was crushed.

Under these circumstances, Xiang's prolonged indecision and procrastination were particularly damaging. Thinking back in 1940 on Xiang's secretiveness, Chen Yi said that one of the most important things in making a strategic turn is to ensure that lower officials understand what it is about. Because Xiang informed these officials either too late or not at all, there were no channels to the millions of ordinary peasants mobilized in Gannan after 1929, who were left confused and disoriented.[211]

### "CLASS TERROR"

So the soviet was plunged into chaos and anarchic terror. Party leaders proclaimed that soviet laws, currency, names, and symbols were still valid, but most of the Party workers responsible for upholding them had fled to the mountains or to White areas. Gong Chu reported after his inspection tour of the dying soviet that "gangsters and hoodlums" were taking advantage of the collapse of order to rape and rob Red Army dependents, extract grain "contributions" at gunpoint, and make off with Party funds.[212]

Chen Yi and Liang Botai, the two leaders of the Central Government Office in Gannan, tried to hold the line and win back confidence by issuing proclamations that threatened drastic penalties against traitors. On December 1, 1934, they warned that "wicked merchants and rich peasants who refuse soviet bank notes, raise prices, and devalue the currency" would be arrested and severely punished as counterrevolutionaries, adding that soviet notes and coins were "valid world currency." "If workers and peasants are deceived into refusing this currency," they went on, "the government at various levels should persuade them on the one hand and punish counterrevolutionary elements on the other."[213] On December 20, Chen and Liang issued another "urgent instruction" about "a minority of revolutionaries who are turning traitor" and announced measures to crush them. The instruction warned that officials who betrayed the Party and soviet citizens who went over to the enemy would be killed and their property and that of their dependents would be seized; the same fate awaited people who knew about such betrayals but failed to report them. Others, the instruction continued, "have the right to kill them on the spot and then report it to the soviet, which will reward them. Their dependents will get the title of Model Soviet Citizen" as well as the property of the people they killed.[214]

In those few places where the Party still wielded power, these were more than empty threats. In December 1934 in Longquan, by then the seat of Xiang Ying's bureau, a new purge was launched to maintain vigilance and enforce soviet discipline on "wavering elements." As one participant recalls, "We took energetic measures to attack the sabotaging activities of elements who had defected to the enemy. We especially assigned people to exercise strict supervision over landlord and rich peasant elements. We plugged the leaks."[215] Outside Longquan, if the proclamations had any effect, it was probably other than that intended. By December, all towns and most big villages had fallen to the Nationalists. However, in some areas that were in transition between soviet and Nationalist rule, ruffians and people out to settle old scores could use the right to "kill first and report afterwards" as an excuse for murder, robbery, and terror.

## DRAMA WITHIN A DRAMA

For millions of Chinese, the fall of the soviet under Xiang Ying was a personal and political tragedy, but for Chen Yi, the tragedy was lightened by moments of high farce.[216] For much of the time, Xiang Ying was not so much exercising power as conjuring its illusion by ridiculous, inflated gestures. It is an ironic comment on Xiang's regime that actors played a prominent part in trying to uphold it. Many actors performed heroically during the terminal chaos in February 1935, rising to the occasion while soldiers and officials were taking to their heels. Chinese Communists are well aware of the mobilizing power of the stage. Their speech and writing is rich in theater imagery. They see themselves as acting epic roles on a world stage in a drama scripted by history and directed by philosophers. During the evacuation in October, a greater proportion of actors than of soldiers stayed in the soviet. Large numbers of actors were not needed on the march, which was already overburdened with noncombatants. Other leaders must have realized that Xiang would need all the propagandists he could muster to make up for his lack of guns. After the start of the Long March, members of the Gorki Drama School and the Central Drama Corps regrouped into three separate Workers' and Peasants' Drama Troupes that dispersed to different parts of the Central Soviet to "console the troops." In the first two months, these troupes spent much of their time rehearsing victory songs and sketches to welcome the Red Army "after its return," which they thought would come before the end of 1934. In the evenings, they staged shows to stiffen morale. In just a few months, they performed more than twenty new plays and dance dramas and several hundred new "folk songs"; Qu Qiubai edited and published many of them in *Hongse Zhonghua*. The actors, like the band on the Titanic, kept playing until the end. At the Lantern Festival on the fifteenth night of the first lunar

month of 1935, the three troupes met up at Xiang Ying's headquarters
in Yudu to give a marathon joint performance of their new numbers.
The stage, which consisted of planks laid across tree trunks and table
tops, was rigged up in the open air and was dimly lit on either side by
hurricane lamps borrowed from Xiang's office. The scene was swept by
a biting wind and steady rain that turned into a torrent as the evening
wore on. Actors and audience, sheltering under umbrellas, bamboo
hats, straw capes, and waterproofs to keep out the worst of the rain, sang
to one another in what was actually a festival of farewell, though few
knew it. Shortly after the performance, these actors played a main role
in evacuating Red Army invalids from the hospitals. Some took up
spears and tried to restore order among the hordes of refugees rushing
this way and that to escape the final battles. A great number of actors
died in the mountains around Yudu. Others started a new life as guerrillas or escaped to Shanghai.[217]

### THE RED ARMY WOUNDED

After the collapse of the soviet, able-bodied stay-behinders had the
choice of taking to the mountains as guerrillas, fleeing to other places,
or returning to the villages and passing as refugees. Invalids had none of
these options. Their wounds immobilized and incriminated them. When
Xiang Ying finally conceded that defeat was certain, his greatest practical problem was what to do with the Red Army wounded.

The number of invalids left behind in the Central Soviet is variously
put at between ten and thirty thousand.[218] The Red Army was able to
muster a total of between sixty and eighty thousand able-bodied troops
(including both marchers and stay-behinders) in October 1934. Probably
as many as twenty thousand of them were new men recruited in the
campaign that began on September 4. Assuming that for every three
men wounded at least one was killed, we can infer that the Red Army's
casualty rate in the months before the start of the Long March must
have been extraordinarily high, perhaps as high as one in two.[219] This
figure shows the enormous depth of the military crisis facing Red Army
leaders on the eve of the Long March and helps explain the broken morale of Xiang's rearguard.

The Red Army command had no choice but to leave behind this
army of invalids, with instructions to report for duty on recovery.[220]
Even ten thousand wounded would have needed forty thousand
stretcher bearers to transport them, for each stretcher was attended by
four men working in two shifts. It cannot have been an easy parting.
Later, Red Army generals and Communist historians pretended that
elaborate arrangements had been made to care for people left behind in

the hospitals. They tried to play down the tragedy by underestimating the number of wounded and overestimating the number of able-bodied troops left to defend them. Zhu De told Agnes Smedley in Yan'an: "We also left behind 20,000 of our wounded, scattered in mountain hospitals. After recovering, these men left the hospital and reported for duty. Maimed men were given money, sent to their homes, and allotted a pension of $50 a year. These pensions were paid out so long as our comrades in Kiangsi [Jiangxi] had money."[221] Informants told Harrison Salisbury a similarly reassuring story, based on memoirs of Chen Pixian: "Within half a day, every wounded man had been placed with a peasant family, dispersed invisibly in the countryside, each equipped with several silver dollars, medicine for treating their wounds and five jin of salt."[222]

Stories such as these are part of a general mesh of half-truths used to cover up the tragedy of the fall of the soviet. The reality was different. Minimal resources were allocated for wounded stay-behinders, who outnumbered their able-bodied defenders. According to Gong Chu, the rearguard had only $100,000 to cover its expenses.[223] If he is right, it is hard to see how several thousand sick and wounded can have been paid a pension. Doctors in the Jiangxi Provincial Hospital, who according to Chen Yi were slapdash and incompetent even at the best of times, were desperately short of equipment on the eve of the Long March. The soviet's battery chargers were monopolized by the Red Army radio teams, who were busy sending and receiving messages night and day in the weeks before the evacuation, so that hospital staff were unable to take X rays and doctors were often unable to operate. Even Chen Yi was refused an operation on his shattered leg until Zhou Enlai intervened to see that a charger was made available for his old comrade. After Chen had had his operation, the doctors packed their instruments and left to join the Long March.[224] Others without Chen's pull could not hope for such privileges. After the start of the Long March, specialist care became a thing of the past even for Chen Yi.

A directive from the Party's Military Council on October 22 charged Xiang Ying with helping the wounded in Gannan, but there is no sign that they had much claim on his attention. He left the evacuation of the hospitals until the end; reports suggest that he made no effort to take the wounded into his confidence. Even invalided Party officials were kept "in a drum" for several months. Some hospital workers did not hear about the start of the Long March until the spring of 1935, two or three months after it had happened. They were not told what was going on in the world outside, and they found it hard to counteract a wave of unease and incipient panic in the hospitals. It was not until mid-February that steps were finally taken to deal with their plight. By then, it was too late.[225]

Accounts imply that there were still more than ten thousand sick and wounded soldiers in hospital in February 1935, that between seven and eight thousand soldiers who had lighter wounds or were on their way to recovery left hospital to "follow the troops," and that between two and three thousand heavily wounded were dispersed to the villages. One actor who helped organize the evacuation says that seven thousand sick and wounded were dispersed. Because Chen Yi and He Chang were themselves wounded and walked on sticks, Xiang Ying detailed them to visit the hospitals and make rousing speeches. "I was a high-ranking commander," said Chen. "Because I had wounds too, it was all right for me to talk. There was nothing the wounded soldiers could say."[226]

Chen Yi spoke bluntly:

> The Central Soviet has been defeated, but the revolution will not be defeated. The spark of revolution is unquenchable. The revolutionary tide will rise again. Now is a dangerous time. The situation in the Central Soviet may improve, but it may also worsen. We cannot take you with us. We can only make arrangements for you among the masses. Go home, or go to the homes of the common people. It is unimportant whether you till the land or fight guerrilla war. When things improve, we will come back for you. You are precious beyond words. Look after yourselves. Be heroes in defeat. Should you come across the enemy, sacrifice only yourself: do not implicate others. As long as there are comrades living, they will avenge us.[227]

Chen Yi also made speeches to groups of people appointed to take care of the evacuees: "Carry these comrades to your homes. Keep them as your sons or sons-in-law. After their wounds have healed, you will have one more unit of labor power, one more person to avenge you."[228]

Party officials issued minutely detailed instructions on how billeting families should treat their charges. Every invalid should be given a portable bamboo brazier and a quilt, preferably padded. His clothes should be washed once every five days; if he had nothing to wear in the meantime, he should be lent clothes. He should be bathed at least once every three days, and once or even twice a day if his wounds wept. He should receive hot tea and hot food. The masses should be mobilized to console him at New Year; women and children should visit him once every ten days to show sympathy and solicitude. He should be inspected every ten days. Every recuperating person should have a stretcher and four bearers.[229]

Chen Yi's speeches were brave, dignified, and moving, and they were said to have rallied his audiences. "The masses were courageous," he recalled, "and after a long while we resolved the problem."[230] But Nationalist accounts say that 3,300 "assorted bandits" (with only three hundred rifles) were captured under the Communists' hospital director. This claim suggests that the evacuation was far from complete.[231] Of those

dispersed across the villages, a handful recovered and joined the guerrillas; others returned to their native villages and either gave up politics
or took part in underground activity; large numbers were caught or
butchered.[232] The wonderfully elaborate directive on how to treat recuperating soldiers looked fine on paper, but it is improbable that it was
carried out. The more intricate the instructions, the less likely they were
followed. Had the evacuation started earlier, losses would have been far
fewer. As it was, the hospitals were emptied in great haste while the soviet was surrounded. The evacuation was necessarily restricted to a
small and besieged territory. The evacuees, far from being "dispersed
invisibly in the countryside," were easy prey for the enemy and a source
of great danger for the people tending them.

### CHEN YI AND THE SWITCH TO GUERRILLA WAR

Communist historians dissociate Chen Yi from the rout of the soviet and
credit him with alternative proposals that would have cut the losses.
Chen Yi himself says that if the rearguard had dispersed earlier rather
than as a last resort, the soviet would have preserved far more "living
forces." To prove his point, Chen cites the case of Zhong Desheng,
leader of the Ruijin guerrillas, who survived the Three-Year War with
more than one hundred followers. According to Chen Yi, Zhong succeeded because he—and he alone—received the December directive on
guerrilla warfare and spent a whole day and night discussing it with
Chen. Chen concludes that if the directive had reached the twenty or
thirty counties in Jiangxi where the Party had support, they could each
have kept two to three hundred people under arms, and ten or even
twenty thousand Communist guerrillas would have remained in Jiangxi
in late 1937. Could such a dispersal have been accomplished in the four
to five months between the start of the Long March and the soviet's last
stand? Yes, says Chen. Xiang had more than enough time because of
Chiang's policy of "go slow" and "serene advance." But Xiang threw the
chance away, and the rearguard was destroyed.[233]

   Chen's proposal—to scatter units, end fanatical class struggle, and allow some measure of coexistence with landlords and occupiers—antici-
pated the policies that stay-behinders everywhere adopted after 1934.
But Chen would not necessarily have succeeded where Xiang failed between October 1934 and March 1935. Two things limited Xiang's freedom of action. Because his main concern for several weeks was to cover
up the evacuation, he massed his forces to create a false appearance of
strength. After that, the huge size of the invasion wrenched the initiative
from his hands. Xiang was gambling that Chiang Kai-shek would eventually relax his siege and transfer forces to pursuing the Long March.
"He thought that after the Red Army had left, the Nationalist Army

would follow it," said Zeng Shan.[234] Xiang's gamble failed: the Nationalists kept a powerful army in Gannan until they knew for certain that the rearguard had been annihilated. Xiang's army had lost the will to fight. Could he be sure that if it scattered, it would ever return to his command? In October and November, Xiang massed his forces to conceal his weakness, both from the enemy and from the soviet citizens whose spirits he hoped to lift. After November, when the encirclers had smashed great holes in his defenses, he massed his forces on several new occasions.[235] His aim was no longer to create illusions of strength but to break through the elaborate gridiron of forts and entanglements.

Had Chen Yi commanded the rearguard, he would still have had to "hold up the banners and strike the gongs and drums" while the main force got away. The problems of war-weariness, sinking spirits, poor resources, and a huge, rich, triumphal Nationalist army would have plagued him no less than they plagued Xiang. It is not only bad generalship that creates defeats; even brilliant strategies fail when the odds against them are too long. According to Chen Yi, only Zhong Desheng switched to guerrilla warfare in Gannan and survived with "living forces." But in fact several units adopted guerrilla tactics even earlier than Zhong. The two hundred cadres of the Gannan Provincial Committee rallied by Mao in October 1934 to organize partisans achieved little or nothing. The same is true of the three hundred guerrillas and four hundred guerrilla-minded officials who set out for Xunwu in October 1934 after two months' training in the Central Soviet.

Even more instructive, since we know more about it, is the case of Zeng Shan, a local man (born in Ji'an in 1899) who was chairman of the Jiangxi Provincial Soviet in 1934.[236] Zeng was left behind in October 1934 to lead the Jiangxi Provincial Committee and wage guerrilla war between Ningdu and Yongfeng. After the fall of Ningdu on October 26, he headed west toward Donggu (Gonglüe) to open a new guerrilla base behind enemy lines but failed to break through. His guerrilla band continued to slip this way and that, but by early 1935 he had been routed, and by May 1935 his Jiangxi Provincial Committee was no more. He divided his remaining troops into forty teams of "traveling traders" to do secret work in the Shangyou-Chongyi area of Gannan. By late 1937, there was little trace of them left. Zeng himself turned up in Moscow late in 1935.[237]

Chen Yi could not have switched to guerrilla warfare before late November or early December 1934 without letting down the field armies; even then, he could not have wished away Chiang's lines and forts. So it is unlikely that he could have salvaged ten to twenty thousand guerrillas from the holocaust. Size is not everything, however. Chen thought that it was futile to maintain the pretense of military might by chaining soldiers to the parapets: far better to preserve a core of volunteers in a secret scattered army, however tiny. An army fighting from choice and conviction is less likely to crumble under pressure than an army of faint-hearts, skeptics, and malcontents. Had Chen been able to put his proposal into practice in December, fewer people would have died, and the Party would probably have preserved more support and at least a few more guerrillas in Gannan.

### XIANG FINALLY AGREES TO TRY TO
### BREAK THE ENCIRCLEMENT

As we have seen, Xiang Ying had agreed to Chen Yi's proposal in December, but he was still reluctant to disperse his main force without first reporting to Party leaders on the Long March. He also wanted time to reorganize his troops. So instead of scattering at once, he took what remained of his army to the Renfeng Mountains in Yudu, where he spent much of his time requesting instructions by radio. At first, all he got in reply was a demand for a report on conditions in the Central Soviet. The tone of his messages became shriller, and he began to send them in his own name, rather than the bureau's. "I am a member of the Politburo," he protested. "You cannot treat me like this." In late January and early February, he radioed a series of increasingly desperate pleas for a directive on what strategy to follow.

To Chen, Xiang's preoccupation with reports and instructions was irrational. The two men continued to quarrel frequently. Chen Yi doubted whether it was worth waiting for a new directive; he wanted to act independently. "[The Long Marchers] are in a very difficult position," he told Xiang.

> What with marching and eating, how can they find time to answer your messages? You should stop bothering them. Even if they rest for two or three days, they will need to hold a meeting before they can reply, and there will be no time for that. If things went wrong, they would get the blame. Any ideas they come up with, we too can think of. If we cannot think of anything ourselves, how can we expect them to think of something? They have enough problems of their own, how can you expect them to concern themselves with yours?[238]

It was not until February 1935 that Xiang finally made specific plans to break through the encirclement and set up new guerrilla bases outside the soviet. Three things decided him: Chen Yi's unremitting criticism and persuasion; the desperate military situation; and a series of directives from the Central Committee.[239] Different sources give different dates for the arrival of these directives, of which there were at least three and perhaps six or more. They were written in the spirit of decisions taken at a leaders' meeting at Zunyi in Guizhou in mid-January 1935. This meeting, which launched Mao on his rise to power, criticized the military strategy followed by Bo Gu and Otto Braun in the campaign against the Fifth Encirclement and during the first stages of the Long March. The main message of the February directives was that the rearguard should scatter as guerrillas.

The first, which arrived on February 5, instructed Xiang to set up and lead a branch of the Revolutionary Military Council in Gannan. This body would take all important military decisions, though Xiang's sub-bureau would continue to decide overall strategy. The Party leaders had apparently found fault with Xiang's earlier report, which they had discussed before sending the directive, for they were implicitly critical of Xiang: "You should immediately change your methods of organization and struggle to make them consonant with guerrilla struggle. At present there are too many bloated rear organs and organizations and very many inappropriate old methods of struggle."[240] On February 13, a new directive called for the setting up of one hundred guerrilla companies that should mass only when conditions allowed and operate independently under the Party's "best cadres" in and around the soviet.[241] Big organizations should be slimmed down or wound up. Large numbers of revolutionaries should be sent to the coastal cities to set up secret liaison points. "Generally speaking," it said, "you should change from soviet-area methods to guerrilla-area methods." According to Chen Yi, this directive criticized Xiang's earlier messages on the grounds that "their morale is poor, they are too passive."[242]

On February 17, Xiang discussed the directive of February 13 with Chen Yi and Chen Tanqiu, who later told Zhang Dingcheng in Minxi about it.[243] Xiang and Chen Yi quarreled bitterly over the meaning of the directive, which had explained the criticism at Zunyi of the "purely defensist" military errors of the old Bo Gu leadership. According to Xiang, the way in which the criticism was expressed meant that the mistakes had not been political. Chen Yi said that Xiang's distinction between the military and the political was imaginary and that he now looked forward to Mao Zedong's taking over the leadership. Even so, Xiang and Chen put aside their differences and Xiang criticized himself in the light of the directives. Xiang then started organizing the details of the breakout, the evacuation of the sick and wounded, and the burial of books, machines, medicine, and the soviet's hoard of tungsten ore.[244] On February 21, he radioed Zhu De and Zhang Wentian about his preparations and about the deteriorating conditions in the soviet. Earlier, on October 22, 1934, the Party's Central Military Council had instructed Xiang to take overall charge of rearguards everywhere south of the

Chang Jiang. On a fresh note of realism, Xiang radioed back that under the circumstances it would be better if the Central Committee took direct responsibility for the guerrillas in Minzhegan (although in fact it was in no better a position than Xiang to do so).[245]

By now, the rearguard in Gannan had been driven from big villages everywhere except in parts of Xunwu, several hours' march to the south of the Renfeng Mountains. February is part of the rainy season in this region. Xiang's remnants were penned in on all sides by hostile forces and swollen streams and rivers.[246] At first, they intended to escape the ring in a compact group, but later they decided to burst out simultaneously in several different directions. According to Gong Chu, the original plan was to break out to the west, follow the Long March, and try to join up with it, but the plan was scrapped when Red Army leaders radioed back advising against it;[247] according to Chen Yi, the plan was to go north to Xingguo "and suddenly pop up behind the enemy's buttocks," but it was betrayed by a Communist leader captured by the Nationalists.[248]

## THE PLAN EXPLAINED

The new plan, reconstructed here from several sources, was to march columns to Minxi, Xiangnan, the Dong Jiang region, Xianggan, Gandong, Min'gan, southern Xunwu, and southern Yudu; and to keep two main columns in or around the heartland of the old Central Soviet.[249] How big the various columns were is unclear. By then, the designations of the units assigned to them were nominal, for their ranks had been thinned by losses and desertions. According to Chen Yi, five main columns, each about one thousand strong, were sent to Minxi, Xiangnan, Dong Jiang, Xianggan, and Gandong. Exactly when the columns left Renfeng is also unclear. "Some expeditions have already set out," Xiang told the Central Committee on February 21; "others are preparing to do so."[250]

The Minxi column, comprising four companies of the Twenty-fourth Division, was led by Chen Tanqiu and Tan Zhenlin. After arriving in Minxi, Chen Tanqiu was to continue to the cities to work underground for the Party and attend the Comintern's Seventh Congress in Moscow. The Communist movement in Minxi was by now at least as strong as in Gannan, and its base was close to Zhangzhou and other ports through which contact could be made to other Party branches. But to reach Minxi, the escapers would have to cross high mountains and difficult terrain.

The Xiangnan column under Gong Chu (who defected to the Nationalists in May 1935) was probably the biggest of the ten. It was 1,200 strong and comprised nine companies of the Twenty-fourth Division, plus radio personnel. Xiangnan was ten days' march from Gannan. The route to Xiangnan crossed the Gan Jiang, which the Nationalists patrolled closely.

The Dong Jiang column, comprising four companies of the Twenty-fourth Division, was led by Li Tianzhu and Sun Fali; it would first pass through former Communist strongholds in Xunwu. The Dong Jiang region was only two days' march from Gannan. It was not an ideal guerrilla region, for it was covered by an extensive network of communications, including roads, rivers, and telephone lines. Its indigenous guerrillas had been practically wiped out (as was Li and Sun's column).

The Xianggan column, led by Xu Ming, consisted of the Red Third Regiment. Xianggan was an ideal hideout with a long and continuing guerrilla tradition, but it was hard to reach, for, like Xiangnan, it lay beyond the Gan Jiang. A minority of escapers reached it.

The Gandong column headed north toward Jiangxi's Nanchang, Fuzhou, and Guangchang. The Min'gan column under Li Cailian, made up of the Red Seventh Regiment, headed for northern Ningdu. Smaller groups headed for southern Yudu and the Xingguo-Longgantou region of Jiangxi. The Sixth Regiment, under Cai Huiwen, Ruan Xiaoxian, and Liu Bojian, was to stay behind to fight guerrilla war in Gannan. The Seventieth Regiment of the Twenty-fourth Division was to stay in the old Central Soviet area under Xiang Ying, Chen Yi, and He Chang. On February 21, Xiang Ying told the Central Committee that He Chang would go to Zheyuegan [*sic*] and that Xiang and Chen would go to Wufu in southwestern Jiangxi, not far from the border with Hunan.[251]

## NERVING THE TROOPS

Once the decision had been taken to try to crack the ring at several points, the next step was to nerve the troops. This task was far from easy. The proposed action was fraught with risk. Most troops had no experience of acting independently in small teams behind enemy lines.[252] For them, it was a leap in the dark. No one had told them explicitly until the last moment that a change was in the offing. People who had asked awkward questions—for example about the size of the encirclement—that implied a lack of confidence in the future were browbeaten and threatened with investigation. No end of words must have been eaten in the days that followed. Even Chen Pixian, a top leader of the Communist Youth League in the Central Soviet, was taken by surprise when Liu Bojian suddenly announced that there was about to be a "big turn." Shortly beforehand, Chen had heard a propaganda official telling a skeptical audience of Red Army men that the "final and decisive battle" for China was being fought right now, that the counteroffensive in Gannan would start as soon as news came of victories by the main Red Army, and that the Communists would take Nanjing.[253]

Inevitably, it was difficult to march these troops toward the front. "The change in the situation was a severe test of all comrades," recalled Chen Yi in 1952.

> It is easy to be a hero when you are winning; when you are defeated and on the run, then you really need to be a hero. The road ahead is full of pitfalls. The revolutionary masses have been butchered in their thousands and tens of thousands. The troops' morale is shaky. Many are vacillating. They have lost their revolutionary confidence. . . . Those scattering and breaking out suffer anguish. Some fail and return. You rally them. They try again. Some burst through only to find that the enemy is everywhere, that it is impossible to get food or sleep. They are like helpless children. They return midway. We leaders severely criticized this sort of thinking that clings to old forms and cannot adapt to new conditions. We pointed out that even if only one person is left, that person is a living force of the Party, that to stay within the blockade was a dead end. Then the troops, after a filling bowl of rice and a good night's sleep, would break through to the outer line. For a whole week people left and returned, until finally no one returned.[254]

The poor morale and the splitting into columns lessened the momentum and impact of the rush. Few got through; most were killed or captured. Nationalist sources say that of the seven thousand Communists who tried to escape, three thousand were taken prisoner; an unspecified number died.[255] According to Chen Yi, of one column, only two or three survived; of another, only a few dozen.[256]

## THE FINAL BREAKOUT

Finally, only two thousand or so troops of the Sixth Regiment (under Cai, Ruan, and Liu) and the Seventieth Regiment (under Xiang, Chen, and He) were left at Renfeng.[257] These remaining columns decided to abandon Gannan and to strike out instead toward Youshan on the Ganyue border to the southwest, where Li Letian had a guerrilla base.[258] It was probably not altruism that kept Xiang and Chen from leaving sooner. They were, after all, the brains of the rearguard, responsible to history for the fate of Communism in southern China. They may have calculated that if they waited, the blockade would be thrown into confusion by the fighting and they could slip to safety. In fact, the delay worked against them. The encirclers, emboldened by their easy victory over the early columns, came pouring from their blockhouses and started closing in for the kill. Xiang had to move fast. But first, he insisted on radioing news to the Long Marchers of his decision to leave Gannan. He had already urgently requested a directive on February 21, for he was not planning to take his radio with him, and he would have no means of communicating with the Party center for the foreseeable future.[259] He was still waiting nearly a fortnight later. While Xiang stayed glued to his receiver, 1,800 troops under Cai Huiwen, Chen Pixian, Ruan Xiaoxian, and Liu Bojian tried to break out on March 3 or 4. The column was smashed at Maling by troops outnumbering it five to one. After a week of bloody battles, 1,400 officers and men had been taken prisoner, and all but eighty of the rest had been killed or scattered.[260] Ruan died on the battlefield; Liu was caught and killed. A month later the eighty survivors, plus stragglers they collected on the way south, turned up on Mount Youshan.

Now only Xiang, Chen, and He remained in the Renfeng base, together with a few hundred troops belonging to three depleted battalions of the Seventieth Regiment. As Xiang tried again and again to raise the Long Marchers on his radio, his troops kicked their heels on a nearby road. He Chang was a man of action, fearless and headstrong, who thought that Xiang was being overcautious and should address himself instead to getting as many troops as possible through the circle. Finally, Chen Yi told He Chang to go on ahead with two of the three battalions to the Huichang River and wait there to give Xiang and Chen cover when they arrived.[261]

At last, probably on March 6 at around four o'clock in the afternoon, Xiang Ying got through to the Long Marchers and told them of his plans. An hour later, his receiver crackled to life with a reply. Xiang's long wait had been in vain. This message, the last he was to receive from the Party center for nearly three years, was transmitted in a code for which he had no key. He destroyed the radio, buried it, and led what remained of the last battalion into battle.[262]

By the time Xiang and Chen set out, night had fallen, and it was raining heavily. In two hours, they covered less than two miles. Chen Yi hobbled on his injured leg, slipping often in the mud. The column came under fire. A large part of it scattered. Xiang and Chen lost contact in the dark. It turned out that some of the shooting came from Red Guards, who fired random shots in all directions and then fled. For fear of hitting his own people in the melee, Chen Yi ordered his men to hold their fire.

The chaos was compounded by crowds of panic-stricken civilians blocking the mountain paths. Earlier, refugees had fled from the towns to the villages to escape the fighting. Now they were fleeing from the villages to the forests. Old people, women, children, Red Army stragglers, wounded soldiers, oxen, horses, mules, and dogs stampeded along the muddy paths and across the fields, jostling and crashing into one another in the dark. People too tired or too scared to move huddled together by the wayside and in the valleys and the gullies. Chen Yi came across a lost group of actors vainly trying to keep order. "As soon as they opened their mouths they were swept along by the tide of humans and animals," and their shouts were lost on the wind, said Chen. "It was the tragedy of a state in ruins, of the collapse of a nation."[263]

A group of escapers under Chen Yi gathered higher up the mountain to eat and rest. Many others deserted along the way. Hearing sounds of battle not far ahead, Chen feared for He Chang, who would by then have reached the river, seven miles further south. The sky lightened. Xiang Ying turned up, agitated. After midday, some of He Chang's men found their way back to Xiang and Chen. It was as Chen Yi had thought: He Chang had crossed the river and been overwhelmed on the further bank. Wounded, he killed himself rather than fall prisoner. His forces had been largely wiped out.[264]

### XIANG AND CHEN SLIP SOUTH

Xiang and Chen continued their march south. At one point, they neared a village. A light flashed, a shot rang out, and the column scattered. Xiang and Chen rounded up as many armed men as they could and sent them into the settlement. It turned out to be full of refugees and "local riffraff" who had hoisted a white flag thinking that Xiang and Chen were the Guomindang. When they realized their mistake, they said, "Comrades, we had no choice. Now you are here, we welcome you equally." With the Nationalists' northern and southern drives meeting at the middle, villages throughout the former soviet were burying red flags and hoisting white ones.

Xiang and Chen decided that it was too dangerous to continue their journey in a large group. They chose a bodyguard of five men, disguised themselves as refugees, and went off on their own after arranging to meet up again in Ganyue with the rest. "This was to reduce the burden on our troops," said Chen Yi.[265] A cynic might say that Xiang and Chen were shedding a burden as much as relieving others of one, that they were motivated not by gallantry but by a wish to save their own skins and continue the revolution. This is the construction that Communist writers put on similar behavior by Xiang Ying during the Wannan Incident of January 1941, when Xiang slipped off with a handful of fellow leaders under the slogan (so it is said), "Take the officers, leave the men, scatter for guerrilla war."[266]

Neither Xiang nor Chen knew the region they were crossing, and they quickly lost their way. Suddenly, a man with long matted hair and loose yellow skin hobbled up to Chen Yi shouting "Senior cadre, senior cadre!" The man was thin as a rake and in rags. Like Chen, he walked on a stick. On his head he wore a chipped Guomindang steel helmet discolored by smoke and ash. (Later they learned that he also used the helmet for cooking. The inside was encrusted with burnt rice.) Three others joined him. They too wore smoke-stained helmets and carried clubs.

This ghost was Zeng Jicai, who had been Party secretary of Niujing in Ganyue when Chen Yi organized the Twenty-second Red Army there in the early 1930s. Later, Zeng had transferred to Daiying, where Xiang and Chen now met him. Chen recognized him. He remembered him as an intellectual, "frank in manner and straightforward in opinion." Zeng was a godsend: as a local Party organizer, he knew every house and mountain for miles around. Chen asked him, "What are you doing here?" Zeng needed food and water before he could reply. Then he told his story.

"When I was Party secretary in Daiying, some people came to inspect me and said I was an opportunist. They organized a long struggle against me. They said that I had done this wrong, that wrong. I was removed from office and given two years' reform through labor. I was sent to bear stretchers for the Red Army. I did that for two or three months. They said I was working well and made me captain of a stretcher team. These men here are my bearers. When the Red Army left, they told me to escort a batch of local tyrants and evil gentry to a certain place. On the way a plane bombed us and my prisoners escaped. That was my undoing. It proved beyond doubt that I was an opportunist. They no longer wanted me in Daiying. No one was prepared to accept me with a letter of introduction saying that I was an incorrigible opportunist. Everyone agreed that I should be kicked from the ranks of the revolution. When the soviet fell, the Reform through Labor Brigade fell too. There was no one left to do any more reforming. It was everyone for himself. I had no idea where the Party was or what its policies were."

"Why did you not go home?"

"My family had been wiped out by the reactionaries. My home had been burned down. The local tyrants and evil gentry where I come from hate me. I would not stand a chance against them. My wife used to be with the Red Army. When it left, she was sacrificed. I would like to rejoin an armed unit, but I am afraid that they will think I am an opportunist and not want me, that they will take me out at night and kill me."

"They would never kill you. It was wrong to struggle against you as an opportunist. Now you are no longer one. Now that the soviet has fallen, your case can be reopened and there can be a new verdict. We are all in the same boat now. The best thing is to renew the guerrilla struggle."[267]

These fragments of dialogue are reconstructed from passages recalled by Chen Yi thirty or so years after the event; they cannot be taken as an accurate record. Still, they are worth quoting, for Zeng's story dramatizes aspects of the soviet tragedy that conventional accounts ignore.

After the fall of the soviet and the collapse of old constraints, swarms of people like Zeng crushed by the revolution roamed the Jiangxi countryside, some seeking revenge, others fleeing it. Communists in trouble with the Party could expect attacks from more than one direction: disgrace in the soviet was no guarantee that old enemies would drop their grudges. But Zeng was different from most casualties of the purges. He stayed true to the cause and nursed no bitterness. "There are bound to be mistakes in a revolution," he told Xiang and Chen. "You cannot expect local committees to be right all the time. . . . This is not the time to reckon up old scores. We must make the best of the defeat, and hope that in future the Central Committee will reconsider its verdict."[268]

With Zeng Jicai to guide them, Xiang and Chen resumed their journey south. They skirted roads and followed obscure tracks through the forests, out of sight of the searching troops whose shouts drifted up from the valleys and the lower slopes. The searchers set fire to trees and bushes to burn the Communists from their hideouts. Mountainsides went up in smoke and flames, darkening the sky by day, lighting it by night. Only when it rained did the fires stop, the quiet return. Normally Chen hated rain. Now he prayed for it.

As the fugitives hurried on toward Ganyue, they met with suspicion and little help. People in old soviet areas were mistrustful of them, though they did not directly harm them. The controls at river crossings were perfunctory; the escapers passed them without challenge. By the time they left what had been soviet territory, two desertions had cut their number to five. People watched them with frightened eyes, guessing that they were on the run. Along the way, they visited the house of Zeng's wife's family. Zeng's mother-in-law confirmed that guerrillas were still active on Mount Youshan and that they sometimes ventured down onto the roads to attack *tuhao* or ambush soldiers. She revealed that thirty miles away, there lived a bamboo carpenter who had been arrested as a Communist suspect and then freed. The escapers went to find him. The carpenter said that an old crop-watcher who guarded bamboo groves on a mountain another thirty miles away might be able to lead them to the guerrillas. "After you have reached the liaison station, you can walk about even in broad daylight," he told them. Sure enough, the crop-watcher was in contact with guerrillas under Li Letian, who sent a small party to fetch Xiang and Chen. After threading their way through many twists and turns from one liaison station to the next, the two finally reached Li's headquarters sometime in April. "The old life has ended," said Chen Yi in the forests on the way south. "The new life has begun."

After reaching Mount Youshan, Zeng was sent back to lead a county committee and organize guerrillas. He was caught and tortured by the Nationalists. He stood firm and was shot on February 21, 1936.[269]

## PERSPECTIVES ON THE COLLAPSE
## OF THE CENTRAL SOVIET

The transition to guerrilla warfare was nowhere so abrupt and bloody as in the Central Soviet, which was the nearest the Communists had to a sovereign state. Of the ten to twenty thousand troops assigned to Xiang in October 1934, just a few hundred turned up on Mount Youshan in the spring of 1935; a tiny number remained at large in Gannan, mainly individuals and small groups wandering aimlessly through the mountains trying to renew links to the Party. Xiang's rearguard, though small, was far bigger than the Zhu-Mao army that had laid the foundations for the Central Soviet in 1929. Xiang initially had the support of tens of thousands of officials and supporters organized in local networks and the counsel of a distinguished team of leaders. But conditions had changed radically in six years. Even an army twenty times the size of Zhu and Mao's could not now have achieved the same success. The Nationalists had learned from their earlier mistakes. They took the Communists in deadly earnest and applied a new strategy combining economic quarantine with military strangulation. The Communists, too, had changed, becoming more bureaucratic and dogmatic. A gap had opened between the interests of the Party and of the villages. The stronger the Communists became, the more ruthlessly they preyed on Gannan's resources, draining the region of men and goods. This despoilment, together with the Nationalist blockade, destroyed morale and undermined support for the Party among villagers, who switched sides by the tens of thousands in late 1934.

Isolation and the prospect of defeat shattered the confidence of the Communists. Crises were upon them as soon as the Long March left. They had no time to reflect or reorganize. Where they should have moved quickly and decisively, they moved slowly, talked too much, and quarreled too often. They missed their chances and invited disaster. Between October 1934 and March 1935, their victories were few and costly; crushing defeats were the rule. It took them just short of six months to enact the thirty-sixth and final trick in China's classic book of tricks, which says that when all else fails, "it is best to leave."[270]

The Long March swept across the whole of China and ended up in a place where the revolution was still vigorous. The stay-behinders, trapped in the ruins of the soviet, rushed about in ever-smaller circles in a futile attempt to escape the many-fronted Nationalist advance. The Long March shook off alien, discredited ideas and became a symbol for the birth of a new, Chinese style of Communism. For a long time the Three-Year War was ignored in Chinese history books and even scorned as "useless roaming." Lin Biao and the "Gang of Four" were said to have vilified the southern guerrillas as "local bandit troops."[271] In the Cultural Revolution, zealots cast a slur on the probity of many of those who had fought in the Three-Year War. It was not hard to criticize, for these people had often survived by innovating in unauthorized ways and sealing unorthodox alliances. Not surprisingly, they were embittered by the stigma and by having missed out on the Long March. They projected their feelings back onto the events of October 1934, planting the idea that discredited "leftist" leaders had used the rearguard and the Central Soviet as a penal colony for truehearted Maoists.

Books that take the Long March as their focus have helped promote a myth about the Chinese Communist Party in the 1930s as an infinitely resourceful and irrepressible Monkey King that could survive fire and sword, surmount all dangers, work miracles, frustrate mighty armies, leap great distances, be everywhere at once, strike terror into demons, and make the enemies of good submit. Popular movements thrive on such legends; but the stuff from which the legends are constructed often looks less extraordinary under closer scrutiny. The Long March cannot be understood apart from the crisis that engendered it and the people that it left behind. At least as many ordinary officials of the Party stayed in Gannan as went away. Together with the secret Party in the cities, they formed a majority of the Communists. The wrecking of the soviet and the Party's loss of power were crucial events in the Communist experience in the 1930s. They should not be consigned to obscurity.

The rearguard crisis soldered Xiang and Chen into a quarrelsome intimacy that lasted for six years. Their qualities were in many ways complementary. Xiang was staunch and obstinate; Chen was adaptive, flexible, and imaginative. Chen's shrewd evaluation of the odds and his early anticipation of the Zunyi directives won Xiang's grudging respect. Xiang was mentally less agile: he was used to regular procedures, not to improvisation. Chen's motto from the old days in Ganyue was that "As long as the mountains are still green, there will be firewood enough."[272] He had no doubt that the next step should be guerrilla war. By early 1935, Xiang was willing to concede that the time had come for a fundamental change. But his disastrous last stand in the Renfeng Mountains and his experience fleeing south through hostile villages sapped his confidence; for a while, as we shall see, he wanted to suspend armed struggle altogether. By then, however, the balance of power, and of the argument, had swung Chen's way. Chen was increasingly in his element the closer he came to Ganyue. Resistance to him fizzled out as more and more Red Army professionals either came around to his point of view or turned their backs on the revolution.

In April 1935, the Nationalists announced that they had finished "extirpating Communists in the twelve pacification zones." Likely sanctuaries were systematically destroyed. "There is not a dwelling that has not been burned," said a government report, "there is not a tree that has not been felled, there is not a fowl or dog that has not been killed, there is not an able-bodied man remaining, no smoke rises from the kitchen chimneys in the alleys and the lanes, the only noise in the fields is the wailing of ghosts."[273] So the main phase of the Three-Year War began. According to one Nationalist historian, it amounted to "nothing more than the desperate flight of a handful of defeated Communist remnants" in the rugged mountains.[274] But though Communist activities in the Central Soviet itself died down to a flicker after 1934, numerous small bands slipped through Nationalist lines all over the south.[275] These survivors managed, more or less successfully, to develop new strategies appropriate to the new conditions. They held out in small parts of old soviet and guerrilla areas and even built new bases. The rest of this book tells their story.

# Gannan:
# Seeds of Fire

◆ ◆ ◆

During the Three-Year War in the old Central Soviet area, guerrillas were active in Ruijin, Changting, Wuping, Shicheng, Yudu, Shengli, Dengxian, Ruixi, Xingguo, Changsheng, Huicheng, Ganxian, Yanggan, and Ningdu.[1] At its peak in the early 1930s, the Central Soviet extended to eleven counties in Gannan (or southern Jiangxi) and to ten in Minxi (or western Fujian). Its capital was Ruijin in eastern Gannan, the soviet's political and economic hub (map 3). Authors refer to Changting in Minxi as Ruijin's twin capital, but Minxi was less securely controlled by the Red Army than the area around Ruijin and was reckoned as part of the soviet periphery.

The Communist movement in Gannan began along lines similar to those in many other parts of rural China but developed differently. It was founded by Communist refugees fleeing the cities after the Party's defeat by the Nationalists in 1927. These people were mainly educated offspring of local gentry families. After the failure of an uprising at Wan'an, south of Ji'an, large numbers of intellectuals belonging to the hill country elite fled west to the Jinggang Mountains, where they joined Zhu De and Mao Zedong, or east to Donggu in Gannan. The Communists at Donggu, led by Lai Jinbang, a former official of the Ji'an Education Bureau, began a struggle for power after winning the support of a gang of bandits armed with fifteen rifles. Alliances of this sort between radical schoolteachers and outlaws sprang up throughout China in this period. In Yanfu, near Ji'an, most Communists came from richer families with large landholdings and bought their guns directly.[2] The power base of these Gannan revolutionaries was personal and parochial. Their constituencies were in schools, lineages, sworn brotherhoods, bandit gangs, and the peasant associations that they themselves called into being.

Map 3.  Gannan (southern Jiangxi).

In January 1929, Mao and Zhu's Fourth Red Army marched into Gannan and set up a base that became the revolution's main home until October 1934. In 1929, Red Army leaders started land revolution in Gannan. Indigenous leaders had up to then followed mildly reformist land policies—for example, rent and interest cuts—so as to avoid antagonizing their powerful relatives, friends, and allies. Many Gannan Communists did not welcome the Red Army's radical intrusion. Red Army leaders criticized them as localist and conservative; tensions between the two groups ran high. The differences were about power as well as policy. After Zhu and Mao had settled down in Gannan, they began to consolidate their control over the region and to gather more and more power at the center. Local leaders saw this move as a threat to their own position. In December 1930, the tensions culminated in a bloody purge of thousands of Communists around Donggu and Futian. The victims included large numbers of local leaders who had joined the Party in the mid-1920s and helped found soviet bases in Gannan. This purge, known as the Futian Incident, ushered in a new radical centralist phase of the revolution in Gannan.[3]

Elsewhere, too, local Communists founded bases that rested at first on personal followings and unorthodox alliances. We will see later that the class profile of Communist movements all over rural China was strikingly similar to that of the movement around Gannan's Donggu. However, some important differences are clearly brought out by a comparison of Gannan with neighboring Minxi. Minxi was nominally joined to Gannan in the Central Soviet, but soviet power was never so firmly established in Minxi as in Gannan, which was the site of the central government of the Chinese Soviet Republic, often called the Jiangxi Soviet. The confrontation between central and local leaders was never so extreme in Minxi as in Gannan during and after the Futian Incident. Purges in Minxi and elsewhere at around the time of that incident were smaller in scope and different in character. They resulted from power struggles among local Communists as well as between local Communists and outsiders, and they were directly linked to the purge of Li Lisan's supporters. Local Communists in Minxi were more radical than their Gannan cousins and more inclined to support an intensification of the revolution after the arrival of the Zhu-Mao army in 1929, so that it was neither physically possible nor politically necessary for radical centralizers to confront and transform the Minxi movement as they confronted and transformed the movement in Gannan. Partly for that reason, a local leadership and ethos survived relatively intact in Minxi.

In those parts of Gannan around Ruijin where the Party headquarters was based after 1929, the Communist movement started later than in the region around Donggu; it coincided with the arrival of the Fourth

Red Army.[4] When Zhu and Mao arrived in Minxi in early 1929, they were able to link up with an existing Communist network, but when they appeared in Ruijin at around the same time, people fled to the mountains, "cheated by the enemy's propaganda."[5] Ruijin before 1929 was a "stronghold of the landlords"; their ancestral temples crammed the county capital.[6] In Ruijin, said a Fourth Red Army report on March 20, 1929, "there is as yet no [Communist] organization; in Changting it is just beginning to develop. The best place, Yongding [in Minxi], is still three hundred *li* away." The report added that in Changting "the masses are very good: after we distributed the grain and property of *tuhao* and reactionaries and spread propaganda, workers and peasants near the town rose in large numbers."[7]

In 1941, the Communist leader Zheng Weisan, talking about the Three-Year War, made an interesting comment on the implications of this difference between Ruijin and Minxi. "The past soviet movement," he said, "shows that soviet areas created by local peasants fighting as guerrillas did not collapse during the three-year guerrilla war, whereas soviet areas created by the Red Army 'conquering the world' collapsed easily. For example, the Minxi Soviet area was created by local guerrillas led by Director Deng [Zihui] and Comrade Zhang Dingcheng, so it could hold out during the one-year [*sic*] guerrilla war. But Ruijin in the Central Soviet was conquered by the Red Army and collapsed easily."[8] Ye Fei said the same thing about Gannan to underline the merits of his own indigenous movement in Mindong.[9]

Communism came to Ruijin by the gun. Red Army leaders—and the Party leaders who arrived in their wake in 1931—could impose their vision of the revolution on Gannan free of the constraints that held them back in other parts of southern China. They built a powerful military machine and a strong administration that efficiently taxed Gannan's resources. Gannan, as the seat of central power, lost its local character and therefore its ability to withstand meddling intruders. Because of its protected position at the center of a cluster of soviets, it was for several years an impregnable fortress of the revolution. Paradoxically, the more vulnerable regions to the east in Minxi proved in the long run to be more durable, and preserved a strong local movement under local leaders after 1934.

## GANNAN: THE REARGUARD OF THE REARGUARD

The Communist remnants left behind in the Central Soviet by the main Red Army's Long March north and then by Xiang and Chen's short march south were the rearguard of the rearguard. Stay-behinders in Minxi outside the immediate vicinity of Changting were well schooled in guerrilla tactics; important units in Minxi were waging guerrilla war even before the autumn of 1934. These Minxi guerrillas were led by outstanding Party veterans, natives of Minxi, specially primed for the tasks that awaited them. They knew of the Zunyi directives, which gave them a free hand to pursue policies suited to their temperament and experience; and they had personally witnessed the failure of "leftist" tactics in Gannan. The stay-behinders twice over in Gannan enjoyed none of these advantages save the last, which was a disadvantage insofar as they also had to endure the outcome of the disaster.

Communists in Gannan between 1935 and 1937 fall into several categories. Thousands of individuals who had lost contact with the Party roamed the countryside seeking a way back to the ranks. Some found one; others settled down under assumed identities and marked time for three years. Large numbers forced to give up the armed struggle sat out the storm in groups, sheltering from the authorities under collective disguises and preparing for the next "high tide." A profusion of armed bands fought guerrilla war around Ruijin and along the border with Fujian. They were served by teams of agents and suppliers who worked under cover in the villages or in mountain industries. Some bands at first numbered in the hundreds. A few faded away; the rest were whittled down to just a handful in 1935, after which the survivors briefly linked up, scattered again, lost touch, and finally regrouped for good in 1937.

Many of the Communist stragglers playing hide-and-seek among the refugees in early 1935 were women. These were no ordinary women, but women "who had received a revolutionary education."[10] Some had been left behind "in the care of the masses" because they were pregnant at the time of the evacuation of the Central Soviet, but they soon absconded to rejoin the struggle. Tiny groups of women on either side of childbirth toiled through the mountains trying to find the Party or the Red Army. One group of four women, an infant, and a horse, moving only at night, headed for Changting after learning that the guerrillas had retreated to the Wuyi Mountains, but they returned to Ruijin after losing the horse and hearing that hordes of Daoist Great Knives were rampaging through Changting, killing indiscriminately. Eventually, they found the Party's Ruijin Committee and its guerrillas in the mountains at Baizhuzhai. They stayed there for several weeks "grazing" on the mountains and moving off like nomads to find fresh pasture once the crop of plants had been exhausted. These women at Baizhuzhai held out better than the men, some of whom went down the mountains and surrendered. The women gave birth in the wild rather than join the exodus to the plains and give up the struggle.[11]

In Gannan, as in other regions of the Three-Year War, women played a special role in "burrowing deep among the masses" to obtain supplies for the guerrillas, target people for them to kill, and inform them about enemy movements. The Tingrui Guerrilla Detachment, set up in late 1936 or early 1937, had a special seven-woman squad that took care of logistics, cooking, washing, sewing, making grass sandals, gathering plants, and fetching food. The guerrillas in the mountains kept up regular contact with women agents in the villages, mainly through women guerrillas, who could move around less conspicuously than men. Agents smuggled supplies to the guerrillas during expeditions into the forests to gather firewood. The authorities were suspicious of these expeditions and sent escorts to watch over them. The classic way to spirit rice, batteries, and other supplies into the mountains undetected was to hide them in the hollows of bamboo carrying-poles and leave the filled poles behind after cutting new ones. To get intelligence to the guerrillas, women spies wrote notes on scraps of paper and left them under the seat of Buddha in the local temple, hidden among the religious messages.[12]

## THE SEDENTARY COMMUNISTS

Not all stayed under the gun after 1934 or worked directly for the guerrillas from bases in the villages. In various parts of Gannan, isolated groups of Communists set up small communities and lived like dharma families under father-masters who preserved and transmitted Party doctrines. The main purpose of these communities was to enable the revolutionaries to survive among kindred souls rather than return to everyday life and give up their politics. Like monks, community members sometimes went out into the wider world to lecture to the devout, proselytize, or earn money as wage laborers and entrepreneurs to help meet communal living expenses, pay for travel, bribe officials, and rehabilitate victims of government campaigns. Gannan was probably the only region where this sort of revolutionary hermitage survived. Groups in most regions of the Three-Year War pondered the idea of giving up the gun and switching to other forms of struggle, but most who went down the mountains either lost touch with the Party or were caught and turned by the authorities. Those who stayed together in an organized way were less likely to abandon the revolution. Even less likely to do so were those who stayed under arms: they were harder to track, beyond the pale, and under group control.

The main congregation of sedentary civilian Communists in Gannan was that under Luo Mengwen in Yanggan. Soviet leaders had set up the Yanggan Special Region under Luo during the campaign against the Fifth Encirclement. Yanggan, an area of more or less continuous mountain peaks, comprised parts of Ganxian, Wan'an, Taihe, and Xingguo. It had originally served as the Central Soviet's northwestern gateway. In October 1934, seven hundred armed men of the Red Thirteenth Independent Regiment and various local forces stayed behind under Luo to defend Yanggan. Support for the Party was said to be strong among the region's two hundred thousand inhabitants. In January 1935, four or five Nationalist divisions purged the base, and in March Luo led his men to Gongwanxing, where they met up with forces under Zeng Shan. Some time after March, Luo and his men broke back through Nationalist lines to Yanggan in the hope of joining up with Li Letian in Ganyue. They held out for three months in Yanggan with little or no ammunition, defending themselves as best they could by throwing stones. They hid in head-high grass, scything swathes in it to break the fires lit by their pursuers. By then, they were outnumbered by several hundred to one. Finally they crumbled, and the last flicker of armed resistance in Yanggan died.[13]

In 1936, Luo went to a place in Taihe where he met fugitives from the Yanggan Soviet. This group included some who had become woodcutters high up in the mountains, where they lived relatively unmolested by the authorities. From these people, Luo came up with the idea of organizing a secret Communist camp of woodcutters. He sent agents to negotiate with a local capitalist and settled a contract to run four huts in the mountains, each with between a dozen and several dozen workers. Luo wanted not just to provide an income and a sanctuary for his people but also to strengthen their Communist identity by meetings, joint living, and mutual aid. This second aim was not easy to achieve. The huts were scattered as much as a day's journey apart, and lumbering was so unprofitable that Luo's men had to work long hours simply to secure a living. They solved the problem by switching to the more profitable trade of charcoal burning, which also enabled the Communists to move their huts closer together. They set up a Party cell in each hut and ran classes in revolutionary theory and other subjects. To provide a cover and spread the word, they set up a Gannan Fellow Provincials' Association. (They were all Gannan men.) At its first general meeting, Luo's hut stood the treat with a banquet of fish from a nearby stream and a choir to sing to delegates from other huts. News of the "men in the mountains" reached the ears of the local *baojia* chief, who began to make enquiries but was silenced by veiled threats. In January 1937, Luo made contact with other Jiangxi Communist leaders and reestablished a provisional committee that set about restoring Party organization in the province. Back in the mountains, Luo sent his woodcutters and charcoal burners out into the villages to work as casual laborers, carpenters, and the like, and to recruit people for the movement. Luo's Gannan Association became active in the towns and won support by taking up popular issues. In the summer of 1937, Luo went to Ganyue and renewed his ties to rearguard leaders there.[14]

Tinier embers of revolution smoldered on here and there in the towns and villages. In Shangyou and Chongyi, in the southwestern tip of Jiangxi, guerrillas under Zeng Shan abandoned the armed struggle and regrouped in forty teams of peddlers who traveled about the region for the Party. Guerrillas in the Jiu Mountains on the Xingguo border were largely smashed in early 1935. A couple of dozen gunmen held out, but the main Communist center was a tobacco shop in Xingguo. Other Communists, scattered across the region from Taihe in the north to Anyuan in the South, earned their living as blacksmiths, tinkers, and quiltmakers while working secretly for the Party.[15]

## THE ARMED STRUGGLE IN GANNAN

Most memoirs and studies of Gannan in the Three-Year War are about the groups that persevered in armed struggle. At least a dozen different groups were active between Ruijin, Huichang, and Changting.[16] It is hard to trace their ancestry and connections through the sources, which are fragmentary and frequently contradict one another. Zhong Desheng, a Communist youth leader left behind in the Central Soviet because his arm was crippled, set up the Ruijin Guerrillas (also called the Red Capital Guerrillas) on the direct instructions of Chen Yi.[17] Zhong started out with one thousand guerrillas. By May 1935, they had been cut by losses to a motley collection of thirty people: Red Army men, Party cadres, militiamen, and a handful of women. At first Zhong's group was isolated from all bases of support and had to storm the villages for supplies. In the early summer of 1935, the group broke through to Dabaidi in northern Ruijin and hid in the mountains. Liu Guoxing, also a local man who joined the Party in 1929, led a group of guerrillas in southern Ruijin on the border with Huichang.[18] Peng Shengbiao, Party secretary of the Gucheng-Taoyang district on the border between Ruijin and Changting, started out with a group of more than one hundred guerrillas in the mountains around Gucheng.[19] Sometime in 1935, Hu Rongjia from Ruijin and Zhang Kaijing from Fujian fused with Peng and set up the Tingrui Guerrilla Command. Zhang was a graduate of the Whampoa Military Academy.[20] Another group, under Deng Haishan and Zhong Min, fought from a small base somewhere in northern Ruijin. Lacking experience in guerrilla fighting, they initially massed their forces in one village, where all but twelve of them were wiped out by an anti-Communist militia.[21] By the late summer of 1935, none of these groups numbered more than a few dozen people.

The guerrilla remnants around Ruijin were at first divided into two commands, one east of the Mian Shui (at Baizhuzhai) and one west of it (in the Tongbo Mountains). In March 1935, the guerrillas west of the Mian Shui fled east to escape a mop-up and became active around Simaoping. In May, those units in direct contact with one another at Simaoping broke up into nine different teams, each with twenty or so members, and dispersed along the Min'gan border and both banks of the Mian Shui. In June and July, they suffered heavy losses and re-grouped in three brigades.

In late 1936 or in 1937, three separate groups came together under Zhong Desheng, Zhang Kaijing, and Peng Shengbiao and called them-selves the Tingrui Guerrilla Command.[22] Most sources identify these three groups with the three brigades set up in 1935, but to do so gives a false impression of continuity, coordination, and communication. The three groups had been constantly on the move and out of touch with one another for more than a year. They split and regrouped sev-eral times between 1935 and 1937, swapping one set of supporters for another and teaming up with armed groups from other areas like that under Liu Guoxing from southern Ruijin. Even after their fusion in 1937 under Zhong, Zhang, and Peng, they split up once again into three companies.[23]

The main political strategies pursued by Communists in most regions of the Three-Year War were localization and the creation of a secret class of collaborators or double-dealers among local power-holders. Lo-calization meant adapting to local conditions, learning local languages and customs, and generally adjusting to the loss of power; it was easier for some than for others. Double-dealers were turned around by vari-ous means: terror, infiltrating agents, mobilizing social pressure, aban-doning extreme forms of class struggle, and adopting new and more conciliatory policies. In other regions, people who doubted the need for these new approaches clashed heatedly with the pragmatists who fa-vored them. In Gannan, however, localization and class collaboration never became issues of obvious dispute. The overwhelming majority of guerrillas and their leaders were born and bred in Gannan.[24] No explicit decision seems to have been made in Gannan to practice class collabo-ration and adopt more moderate policies, though there were pragmatic adjustments.

The collapse of the rearguard and the occupation of the soviet by government troops left many small groups of Communists cut off in the mountains under inexperienced leaders. Some gave up politics alto-gether, robbing *tuhao* and spending the takings on food and drink.[25] Others acted with blind disregard for the enemy and suffered heavy losses.[26] Many groups were burdened at first by huge numbers of civilian refugees. According to Liu Huishan, an old Tingrui veteran, as many as fifty thousand people climbed the mountains with the guerrillas in the early days of the Three-Year War. But the overwhelming majority soon trickled back to the villages and towns because of hunger or fear for the safety of relatives they had left behind, or lest their children's cries gave the guerrillas away.[27]

Losses and defections eventually brought the handful of surviving guerrillas to their senses. Then began a series of flights through the mountains that lasted in some cases right through to the winter of 1935. In 1936, after a brief rest, the guerrillas again headed off into the forest when Zhang Shiheng, vice-chairman of the Fujian Provincial Soviet, defected. Conditions in the mountains were harsh. The fugitives' health and morale deteriorated. They were completely cut off from inhabited settlements by the Nationalist blockade. The villages they passed through had been robbed clean and depopulated, though slogans on the remaining walls predicted that "the Red Army will certainly return!" They guessed the months by the budding, blooming, and fruiting of plants. "Our cheeks hollowed out, our hair grew two feet long, our faces lost their youthful shine, our beards thickened, our lips became two dry strips of skin through malnutrition," recalled Peng Shengbiao. Usually, the guerrillas ate wild plants. If they were lucky, they found edible roots left unharvested in the fields or grains of rice in abandoned hullers. By late 1935, many of the tiny bands roaming the borders of Ruijin were generals' armies, made up almost exclusively of senior cadres. They saw their role less as resisting actively than as preserving "revolutionary embers" for the Party. The members of one group symbolized this mission in their last remaining matchstick, which they wrapped like a precious jewel in oiled paper. They kept this icon in a bamboo container and reserved the driest spot for it whenever they pitched camp in the rainswept mountains.[28]

After months of aimless flight, the runaways began to question the point of running. A plenary meeting of guerrillas under four of the main Gannan leaders resolved to stop rushing round in circles, to split into several columns, and to set up huts in the mountains. By now, the Nationalists, believing that the guerrillas had been destroyed, withdrew from around Ruijin. Communists organized schools, training courses, and sports events and revived the old soviet tradition of entertainment evenings. But they were still cut off from the outside world. Their biggest problem was getting food. In one area they set up a paper factory in the mountains. The factory provided an excuse to bring supplies of food through the blockade and generated revenue. The food was smuggled past the checkpoints in factory ash and dumped at prearranged spots. The guerrillas mounted new attacks on the villages, kidnapping hostages for ransom and extorting money from landlords. They began by seizing an "enlightened" *baojia* chief who had once been chairman of a village soviet. They freed him on condition that he would give them information at all times, report their presence in his area only after they had left, refrain from oppressive acts, guarantee the safety of Red Army dependents, and provide supplies for the guerrillas. To press their message home, they assassinated several other *baojia* chiefs and gave away the victims' property.

The guerrillas traded with peddlers on the highway between Changting and Ruijin and bought food and supplies from them at market prices. Most small shopkeepers were said to have done business with the guerrillas. The period between early 1936 and late 1937 was one of "victorious development," claimed Peng Shengbiao, during which the guerrillas "punished" some *baojia* officials, subverted others, and set up "double-dealing governments." By late 1936, more than thirty Party branches had been restored in the Ruijin area with six hundred members. "We had freedom within a circumference of thirty miles," said Peng. An exaggerated report of the guerrillas in the Gucheng Mountains even reached Xiang Ying's headquarters in Ganyue. "People were saying there are several hundred in all," a messenger reported. But no reports of guerrillas in other regions reached Gannan.[29]

Unlike other stay-behinders, the Communists in Gannan were known less for moderating their policies, manipulating "contradictions among the enemy," infiltrating local government, and subverting the local elite than for their unreconstructed attachment to class violence. Where other guerrillas adapted creatively to the new conditions after 1934, the guerrillas in Gannan lived like hermits and outlaws in the forests and compromised only as a matter of need, hanging fire until the time came to restore the soviet. Instead of alliances, they practiced terror. They caused a wave of panic among local security officials, who fled from the smaller villages to the larger ones and raised defense walls around their houses.[30] The Gucheng Guerrillas under Peng Shengbiao assassinated a number of *baojia* officials in retaliation for the overturn of land revolution. Peng himself personally axed one to death.[31] Guerrillas in other regions also behaved ruthlessly at times, but their violence was generally more selective.

## THE UNITED FRONT

In most places, news of the united front against Japan between the Communist Party and the Guomindang led to far-reaching changes in guerrilla policy, but the Communists in Gannan responded less flexibly when they read about it in a newspaper in July or August 1937. Instead of launching a political offensive, they decided to step up their military attacks until they had received precise instructions from the Party center. In Gannan, it was the Nationalists rather than the Communists who, in

October 1937, proposed talks on ending the civil war. The guerrillas reluctantly agreed, but only because they hoped that talks would help them get back in touch with the Party center. Hu Rongjia and Peng Shengbiao took a tough position in the negotiations, claiming the entire stretch between Ruijin and Changting as their garrison and demanding the right to enter the capital of Ruijin. In the meantime, they continued their attacks and widened their territory. Around this time, when agreement between the two parties had already been reached in other places, the Tingrui Guerrillas killed a dozen or so militiamen and the wife of the Nationalist commissioner of Changting in a holdup on the highway between Changting and Ruijin.[32] The Nationalists published articles angrily attacking the guerrillas for "wrecking the united front" and protested furiously to Xiang Ying and Chen Yi, with whom they were negotiating a cease-fire to cover guerrillas everywhere in the south. In late November, Xiang and Chen sent a team headed by Chen Pixian to talk with Hu and Peng, overcome their hostility to the united front, and mobilize them for war against Japan. This was the guerrillas' first direct contact with the Party in nearly three years. Chen Pixian, himself a Changting man, renewed many old friendships during his visit to the border. Nationalist officials also protested about the Tingrui Guerrillas to Zhang Dingcheng during talks in Minxi, so that Minxi envoys, too, soon arrived at the guerrilla camp. Between them, Chen Pixian and the Minxi people convinced the guerrillas that the united front was not a trap and that they should negotiate seriously with the authorities. The guerrillas' tactic had paid off. By contacting the Nationalists and continuing their attacks, they had found a way back to the Party.[33]

Shortly after Chen Pixian's arrival in Tingrui, a delegation under Hu Rongjia and Peng Shengbiao went to Ruijin for new talks. Hu and Peng dropped their more extreme demands and reached an agreement to set up an office in Ruijin and assemble their troops at Lantian, a village they already controlled. Despite the agreement, the atmosphere remained tense and angry. The Nationalists accused the Communists of making "Red propaganda" and tried to force them to remove their posters from Ruijin. They also accused them of illicitly enlarging their forces.[34]

The Tingrui Guerrillas had expanded quickly in 1937, from perhaps as few as eighty in January to more than seven hundred in July. They grew partly through establishing contact with previously lost groups and partly through recruitment. The negotiators had agreed at Ruijin that the Nationalists would send observers to count the guerrillas and assess their needs. The Communists mobilized three hundred teenage boys to go to Lantian just for the count, bringing the size of the muster to more than one thousand. At the same time, forty guerrilla leaders attended a meeting called by Tan Zhenlin at their new office in Ruijin. The decision to call the meeting was unwise; Tan was severely criticized for it during the Cultural Revolution. It gave the Nationalists the opportunity for revenge. They surrounded and attacked the meeting, arrested those present, and seized their radio and supplies. The next day, they surrounded the guerrillas at Lantian and reduced them by nine-tenths, to just one hundred. The Communists avoided an even worse outcome only by mobilizing political pressure in Ruijin and getting the Party's Minxi'nan Committee to intervene.[35]

In February 1938, the survivors, along with some supporters who had found their way back to the ranks, arrived in Minxi, where they merged with the Minxi'nan guerrillas to form the Second Detachment of the New Fourth Army. By then, they numbered three to four hundred, armed with 150 rifles. Not all the guerrillas and Communist agents in Gannan left for the front; some, including twenty-five women, stayed behind to work for the Party under Liu Guoxing. Liu himself was killed in action in 1942. The Tingrui Committee set up in the region after 1937 was destroyed in 1946.[36]

## PERSPECTIVES ON THE THREE-YEAR WAR IN GANNAN

The Three-Year War in Gannan was strikingly unsuccessful in terms of the goals set by the departing soviet leaders and by comparison with other regions. Gannan had been China's reddest place in the early 1930s; the Gannan rearguard was initially the biggest of all the soviet rearguards. But Gannan preserved fewer "living forces" for the New Fourth Army than any other main region of the Three-Year War, and the guerrillas' political impact there was negligible. They failed partly because they were exceptionally isolated and fragmented after 1934, with a dozen tiny units fighting independently and largely out of touch with one another. They did not manage to coordinate their activities until 1937, and not until November 1937 did they restore ties to the outside world. One reason that they could not break from their isolation was that they looked mainly to the past and had few new ideas of the sort that helped restore Communist fortunes elsewhere. That is why memoirs and articles about the Three-Year War in Gannan are few; those that exist harp on a limited number of standard themes and lack the rich detail and strong flavor of experimentation and nonconformity of similar writings from elsewhere. It is also why this is the shortest of the main chapters of this study.

By March 1935, the Communist movement in Gannan was practically spent. Its social base in the villages was exhausted by war and counterrevolution; it had earned the reputation of an agent of catastrophe. Its isolation was increased by the Nationalist blockade, which was tighter in Gannan than in other regions. Guerrillas in what had once been China's main hotbed of Communism lived like hermits after 1934, "going for three years without a haircut, mosquitoes above, ants below, snakes in bed."[37] They fought under the severest conditions and were led by minor Party officials without experience in acting independently or the confidence to develop new initiatives. They clung rigidly to old ideas rather than run the risk of making mistakes by unauthorized innovation. The old Central Soviet had been the main home of doctrinaire "leftism" and extreme uniformity. Other approaches and traditions had been crushed; no alternative repertoire could be called into play when old ways failed.

Important new ventures in any sphere are often sanctioned by a mythical charter; it is a telling comment on the political sterility of Red Gannan that it is one of the few regions of the Three-Year War with no legend of a "founding conference" at which strategy was rethought and the basis laid for a resurgence. The tight military controls that shut the guerrillas off from the villages made it hard to experiment and blacked out news of crises in the outside world (such as the Liang Guang Incident of 1936 and the growing confrontation with Japan) that might have caused guerrilla leaders to reexamine tactics. No one in Gannan was capable of injecting new life into the Communist movement through the power of his personality or ideas. Gannan in the Three-Year War was short of Communists of authority. After 1937, none of its leaders assumed positions at the regimental level or above in the early New Fourth Army. Under different circumstances, a collective leadership might have remedied the problem, but the Communists on their different mountains around Ruijin came together only briefly after 1934, once near the beginning and again at the end of the war. There was little opportunity for the exchange of ideas, and currents of creative thought ceased to flow.

The Gannan Communists lacked the brawn to engage the Nationalists on the battlefield or the brains to engage them in the teahouses and the temples by secretly contacting their malcontents. Lacking politics, they resorted instinctively to terror. Violence was their method; revenge their motive. Because they could inspire fear and fury, but not confidence, they were unable to subvert their enemies with alliances of the sort that undermined them elsewhere. Their violence was a mirror image of the violence done to their relatives and supporters by the government. Tens of thousands of people were killed in and around the old Central Soviet during the Three-Year War, eighteen thousand of them in Ruijin. The kinfolk of guerrillas suffered worst. The families of Zhong Desheng and other guerrilla leaders were massacred, and their property was seized.[38]

# Ganyue:
# Heroes in Defeat

◆ ◆ ◆

Ganyue is the name of the rocky uplands between Jiangxi (Gan) and Guangdong (Yue) that form part of southern China's massive Nanling range (map 4). After 1934, guerrillas were active here in Nanxiong, Dayu, Xinfeng, Nankang, Anyuan, Quannan, Longnan, and Dingnan.[1] Ganyue's mountains, lower than surrounding chains, are forested with pine, bamboo, and camellia and crossed by deep passes, through one of which China's main north-south route has run since ancient times. To the east, they join the huge Wuyi fold and to the west, the Luoxiao range, in whose Jinggang Mountains Mao and Zhu De set up China's first Red base in 1927; to the south, they abut the Dong Jiang region, where a soviet government, together with the Eleventh Red Army, was founded in April 1930. After 1930, the revolution ebbed in the south but stayed alive in these mountains to the north.[2]

The main site of Communist activity in Ganyue after the start of the Long March was Youshan in the Meiling Ridge, where revolutionaries first appeared in 1925. The slopes of Youshan, whose main peak rises to around six thousand feet, house numerous small villages.[3] Youshan's main crops include turpentine, bamboo, timber, native paper, mushrooms, and tea oil, whence the name Youshan (Oil Mountain). In ancient times this region was known as Tree Ocean.[4] Song Shengfa, Chen Yi's bodyguard after 1934, described it in a memoir:

> Youshan is a big mountain area sitting astride Ganyue and stretching for one hundred *li*. It bristles with trees reaching to the sky, bamboo as wide as the mouth of a rice bowl, wild grass as tall as a person; big snakes, mountain oxen, and leopards move about it at night in search of food. . . . Youshan changes its attire each season: in summer, it is green like a jade ocean; in autumn, the grass and leaves turn yellow like a field of ripe

Map 4. The Three-Year War in Ganyue, 1934–37. *Based on a map in Yang Shangkui 1978b.*

wheat and the wind sings through the bamboo and the trees, setting the leaves a-dance; by October, harsh winter has covered the rocks and plants with a thick quilt of snow and foot-long icicles hang from the mountain trees, tapping against one another and creaking in the chill wind; by February, in the foothills the wind is softer, the sun is warm, and spring has come, but the mountain tops are still deep in winter and the peaks and slopes are under ice and snow; by April, the ice has melted, the snow has thawed, the bushes and trees are budding, and Youshan puts its green dress back on.[5]

Xiang Ying and Chen Yi had several reasons to choose the Ganyue highlands as their new base in 1935. Ganyue was strategically placed between the Central Soviet and the bases of Minxi'nan, Yuedong (eastern Guangdong), and Xianggan.[6] Chen Yi had first visited this region in September 1927 after the failure of the Nanchang Uprising, and he stayed for several months. He had spent three years as a guerrilla in Ganyue after 1928 and had lived in many of its villages. Most borderers knew his name; many knew him in person.[7] To the northwest of Ganyue, in Jiangxi's Niedu, Communists had led peasant uprisings in 1927 and founded secret trade unions and peasant associations.[8] Further to the south, around Haifeng, the Communist Peng Pai had begun organizing peasants as early as 1922, when he founded the regional movement of which Ganyue was the northern edge.[9] In Ganyue itself, Chen Yi had set up the guerrilla band that later swelled into the Red Twenty-second Army. When that army was transferred to the Central Soviet, some guerrillas stayed behind to fight under Li Letian.[10]

Before October 1934, the Ganyue Communists kept close ties to the Central Soviet in Gannan and regularly sent local men and women to Ruijin to attend conferences and make reports. Li Letian, who had ambitions for the Ganyue base, several times asked the Central Committee to send a division to stiffen his local forces so that he could expand, and Ruijin finally agreed to his request; but in the end, all he got was a battered remnant of the Gannan rearguard.[11] At the start of the Three-Year War—actually a two-year, eight-month war here—Ganyue was relatively empty of government troops.[12] It lay between territories controlled by rival armies of Chiang Kai-shek and the Cantonese militarist Chen Jitang. Administratively, Youshan belonged to Jiangxi, but politically and economically, it belonged to Guangdong; Chen Jitang took its taxes.[13] The Communists hoped to exploit the rivalries between these two systems. Should they become hard pressed on both sides of the border, they could try to reach the Jinggang Mountains a few days' march to the north.[14]

The events of the winter of 1934–35 in Gannan had little direct impact on Li Letian's guerrillas in Ganyue, save that the last Ganyue delegation to visit Ruijin before the soviet's collapse failed to return home. Li Letian, who had worked in the Ganyue mountains ever since 1926, was a veteran of the region's 1928 Nanxiong Uprising.[15] In November or December 1934, he became chief of the newly formed Ganyue Committee, with Xiang Xianglin as his chief of staff. His main force was quite weak. Ganyue, like other bases on the Central Soviet's periphery, was used by central Red Armies as a military reservoir; when Red units crossed Li's territory during shunting movements in the autumn of 1934, they tapped it yet again. In return, they left Li a few dozen of their wounded. Later, some Long March stragglers turned up at Li's camp, and other sick and wounded soldiers paid off by the Red Army in early October made their way to Youshan. They hobbled through the mountains, taking turns at carrying those too ill to walk and wading or swimming rivers from which Guangdong Army patrols had removed the boats. In late 1934, Li Letian led a battalion of six hundred troops and a team of cadres from Yudu to Youshan with instructions to expand the base, make contact with guerrillas along connected provincial borders in places like Xianggan, Xiang'egan, and Minxi'nan, and strive to restore the Central Soviet. This new force joined up with a smaller group of guerrillas under Zeng Biao and Liu Fujie already on Youshan.

In February 1935, the Red Army's Seventy-first Regiment, under Gong Chu (soon to defect), passed through Ganyue on its way to Hunan.[16] In April, Xiang Ying and Chen Yi turned up with a small armed escort. They were joined over the next few days by Cai Huiwen and the Jiangxi Young Communist leader Chen Pixian. Cai and Chen had set out from the Renfeng Mountains in Gannan on March 4 at the head of 1,800 troops, but their number had been reduced to eighty after a week of bloody battles. (Survivors joked that their divisional commander had been demoted to company captain.) A month later, they reached Youshan, having meanwhile picked up three to four hundred lost troops. With stragglers trickling in from all sides, the number of guerrillas in Ganyue eventually approached a thousand;[17] together with local Red forces, there were two to three thousand. During the first few months after the fall of the Central Soviet, Chen Jitang's generals were wary about committing their forces to battle against these Ganyue Communists. They had no clear idea of the enemy's strength, and they were worried that Guomindang generals north of the mountains might try to profit from any clashes.[18]

## REGULAR OR GUERRILLA WAR?

Before Xiang and Chen arrived in April 1935, two courses of action were being debated in the Communist camp in Ganyue. The local leader, Li Letian, wanted to split his forces into smaller units and wage guerrilla war around Youshan, as he had done for the previous several years. Xiang Xianglin, chief of staff of the Ganyue military subarea, who had gone to Youshan with other officers in late 1934, opposed guerrilla warfare as "passive hiding": for him, strength lay in numbers. Views like Xiang Xianglin's are now explained as emanations of the Wang Ming "left" line, but at the time they must have seemed quite sensible to many Communists in Ganyue, and for a while, most supported them. Many outsiders who arrived in Ganyue from Gannan were used to field campaigns and thought that decentralization would leave them dangerously exposed. They were not prepared to abandon heavy equipment, and they had even brought a printing press with them.[19] Most came from Xingguo, Ruijin, or Fujian and were strangers to Youshan; they did not even know its language. Few realized that the retreat from the Central Soviet was in reality a defeat. Many thought that the Red Army would soon return; at the time, none even dreamed of a Long March to the northwest.

The remnants of the troops in Youshan followed a routine not unlike that in the Central Soviet before its collapse. Each morning, after reveille and a parade, their commanders met to plan the day's activities, which were orderly and measured, marked by bugle calls and three regular meals. Because the enemy was as yet largely inactive, this routine continued unchecked for some time. On the rare occasions when enemy soldiers did appear, the Communists shouldered their backpacks and marched off into the mountains, never once stepping outside an area just a few miles across.

This aimless marching weakened their morale. For two months, they had not found a single *tuhao* to expropriate. Funds that the Central Soviet fugitives had brought with them were running out, and the Communists had to rely more and more on resources accumulated locally by Li Letian. Even small towns were by now in enemy hands; it was hard to see how these resources could be replenished.

At first, the dissatisfaction expressed itself mainly in private grumbling; Xiang Xianglin's "cruel warlord style" is said to have prevented an open discussion of problems. Soon troops began deserting. Most deserted to their homes, but some left in protest at the Party's lack of direction in Ganyue and went to Gannan to seek more active units. When news of the collapse of the Central Soviet reached Ganyue, some concluded that without a change of policy the Youshan base too would soon collapse, more under its own deadweight than from external pressure.[20]

Urgent decisions therefore awaited Xiang and Chen when they arrived on Youshan in April 1935. Food was giving out, while the number of mouths to feed had more than doubled. By then, it was clear that the

Red Army would not soon return to Jiangxi. Enemy troops—Cantonese regulars, several regiments of the Jiangxi Peace Preservation Corps, and various local landlord forces—were beginning to act more boldly against the Communists. How should the Party act? Local leaders looked to the men from Gannan for an answer.[21]

## THE CHANGLING CONFERENCE

Shortly after Xiang Ying and Chen Yi reached Youshan, they and the local leaders held a meeting on Changling in the nearby Beishan range. The Changling meeting is described as "key and decisive" in later studies and depicted as a Ganyue version of the Zunyi Conference, about which Xiang Ying had learned shortly before fleeing south. No documents of this conference appear to have survived. The version of the event that Chinese sources now promote is the one consistent with today's orthodoxy. The losers in the debate did not necessarily hold the views now attributed to them. This point should be borne in mind when reading my reconstruction of the discussion.

The majority at the meeting believed that there was no immediate hope of restoring Party fortunes against such great odds; it would be victory enough to stay alive and at large. The political line they adopted was essentially that defended by Chen Yi against Xiang Ying in the last days of the soviet, which was at first branded as pessimistic. It began from the premise that the revolution was at its lowest ebb. The Party in Ganyue should scatter and retreat to preserve its forces and its main cadre but should fight guerrilla war whenever it was confident of winning.

Some of those present, including Xiang Xianglin, rejected this proposal as "shameful skulking." Xiang thought that the Communists should continue to concentrate their forces, arguing that "the revolution is not at present at a low ebb and the Red Army could fight its way back at any time."[22] They believed that the Party should show some daring, even if doing so meant taking losses. They could not convince the rest, probably because of the disastrous failure of Xiang Ying's similar strategy in Gannan.

Even so, Xiang Xianglin refused to follow the tactic of dispersal. Shortly after the Changling meeting, he led three hundred troops into battle near Nanxiong; within a few months all but a handful of them were lost, and Xiang Xianglin himself defected after being wounded and taken captive. Most at Changling, however, agreed with Chen Yi that "a soldier preserved today can become a platoon commander tomorrow, a county secretary can lead a province, a handful can become a crowd."

A few opposed Chen's strategy for reasons opposite to Xiang Xianglin's. They proposed a policy of inaction on the grounds that the soviet was defeated and the enemy was temporarily invincible. They argued that the Communists should lie low in the mountains until conditions improved, for if they exposed themselves as targets now, they risked obliteration. Xiang Ying is said to have shared this view, though he finally agreed to Chen's proposals. At first, Xiang's opinion carried weight, for he represented the Central Committee; but his proposals were eventually rejected as too passive. Most agreed with Chen that a policy of preserving existing forces should not rule out winning new ones and that guerrillas should respond flexibly to new openings, tie down and wear down enemy units wherever possible, influence the situation in small ways, and prepare to handle big incidents and crises in coming months and years; that they should plant the Red Flag on the mountain, uphold the stoic traditions of the Red Army, and prepare for the next high tide. This tide would rise, said Chen, when the Japanese invaded northern China. If the guerrillas held out until then, a few would become a few hundred, a few hundred would become a few thousand, and in the end the Guomindang would be forced to send a military band to play them down the mountains. Chen explained that three factors would sustain the Party: the continuing existence of imperialism, the people's continuing wish for change, and the guerrillas' bravery.[23]

The conference resolved to "disperse guerrilla forces, undertake mass work, and build and consolidate bases." New methods were needed to "maintain the struggle without being defeated or dispersed, to preserve the Party's forces in a period of difficulties for the revolution," and to tie down enemy forces and so lessen pressure on the main Red Army. Special efforts should be made, said Chen Yi, to "localize cadres" and to explain the new situation both to the troops and to the Party's local supporters (who had been kept in ignorance of its plans since the fall of the soviet).[24]

Chen Yi was not himself a "local" Communist. He had made his career on the Party's national stage. Though he had links to Ganyue, he had no special loyalty to it. His concern, like Mao's, was to keep the Red Army going, as the necessary vehicle of revolution. Like Mao, too, he was flexible and pragmatic and prepared to compromise to a far greater extent than Xiang Ying, who was a centralist of the purer sort.

The Nationalists were aware of potential conflicts between "local" and "outsider" Communists and tried hard to exacerbate and exploit them. "You only came here because you had no choice," they told outsiders in their propaganda leaflets. "You are the ones Mao Zedong did not want." To "insiders" they said, "The people from east of the [Tao] river [i.e., Central Soviet refugees] have come to make their homes west of the river. We should beware that we do not fall into traps set by others."

Chen Yi took great pains to meld the two groups and stressed their reciprocity and interdependence. Indigenous guerrillas, he said, had flesh-and-blood ties to local people, knew the area intimately, and had many years' experience of guerrilla warfare; members of the Red Army from the Central Soviet knew little of guerrilla tactics or of local people, language, conditions, or geography. But, he added, local guerrillas had studied little and tended to put their immediate interests first, while Red Army troops and cadres had experience of large-scale political movements and "a high political level." He concluded that each group should learn from the other's strengths and weaknesses. Even so, "special emphasis should be put on outside cadres learning from local cadres, outside troops learning from local guerrillas." He admonished his people "quickly to become Youshan experts." As a result of the Changling decisions, the Ganyue Communists split their forces into teams of between ten and twenty guerrillas. But despite this strategy, the transition to guerrilla warfare was not easy.[25]

## THE GUERRILLAS DISPERSE

Even while this conference was going on, enemy troops were starting to bear down on Ganyue. To escape this pressure and carry out the Changling decisions, Ganyue was divided into five main regions. A Red unit was assigned to each of them and instructed to act independently. Cadres from the Ganyue Special Committee and the Central Committee's sub-bureau were distributed over the five regions to lead them politically. The Youshan and Beishan mountains became the twin centers of the Ganyue system.

Beishan, to the north of Nanxiong, was covered by a blanket of forest so dense that it was said that "you could walk through it for days without ever glimpsing the sky." This natural fortress was an ideal headquarters for top guerrilla leaders like Xiang Ying, Chen Yi, Li Letian, and Chen Pixian, who lived sometimes together, sometimes on separate peaks, depending on the level of alert. From Beishan to Youshan was two days' march across the Nanxiong plain. A line of liaison stations was formed to connect these two bases; if one base was attacked, its guerrillas could flee along this line to the other. Lesser lines were strung out to link these central bases to the three outer ones. The Nationalists aimed to isolate the various bases and pick them off one by one; this intricate liaison network was designed to forestall such attacks. Each base in turn had its own separate system of communications.[26]

One outer base lay between Chongyi and Shangyou in Jiangxi near the Hunan border. Its leader, Cai Huiwen, was directed to contact guerrillas further north along this same border, in Xianggan. Guerrillas throughout the southern provinces strove to break from their isolation during the Three-Year War and planned their activities with an eye to larger national and regional frameworks. Cai's army of three hundred quickly grew by incorporating local guerrillas in Guidong across the border in Hunan. Cai set up a Xiangyuegan Committee and a Xiangyuegan army that by 1936 had more than one thousand guerrillas. In the autumn of 1935, he sent a contingent of guerrillas back to Ganyue to help relieve the pressure on Xiang and Chen and another, smaller unit north to Xianggan. But in the long run, his mission failed. He did not make lasting contact with Xianggan, and eventually he lost touch with Ganyue. In the spring of 1936, he was captured and killed after the Nationalists hunted him down with three main-force divisions.[27]

A mission from Ganyue to the old Central Soviet in Gannan was more successful. A Communist agent disguised as a peddler reported that several hundred guerrillas were still active around Ruijin. This agent then went to Xingguo and helped set up Communist cells in several places.[28] These moves were directed toward resurrecting collapsed networks in the old soviet areas in preparation for the eventual restoration of the soviet, which was the long-term task of all rearguard units.

## THE SANNAN GUERRILLAS

One group under Huang Chengze and Zhang Riqing (aged eighteen) was sent to open up a new guerrilla base in the Sannan area (that is, Longnan, Quannan, and Dingnan) of Gannan, to relieve pressure on the Youshan base. This group was small but well armed; one in three of its members was in the Party or its Youth League. Sannan was an area of high peaks and forests well suited to guerrilla war. In 1925, the Party had set up a branch in nearby Nanxiong. In late 1930, the Thirty-fifth Red Army passed through the region and stimulated a peasant and guerrilla movement. In 1931, the guerrillas were crushed, but in July 1932 the Red Army seized Longnan and in October, a new guerrilla army under Li Letian started operating there.[29] However, few Communists had worked in the rest of Sannan, which was a main garrison of Chen Jitang and Yu Hanmou's Guangdong Army. Ferociously anti-Communist militias ruled the area and had defeated an attempt to set up a guerrilla unit in late 1934. The Sannan mountains were infested by outlaws and opium barons who preyed on the many small towns and villages supported by the harvests of this "treasure house throughout the four seasons." Even the tiniest settlements were fortified with earthworks and ruled by "mountain hegemons." Most mountain people had primitive guns to hunt wild pigs and defend themselves and their hegemons against the bandits.

Thirty-eight guerrillas marched into these mountains in early May 1935, without so much as a map of the area but with thirty dollars between them and Chen Yi's advice to become "local experts" ringing in their ears. They were not only to fend for themselves by attacking *tuhao* but also to hand a hundred dollars a month to "higher levels." It is unlikely that they did so regularly, for they were isolated for months on end from the Youshan center, despite plans to maintain two separate lines of liaison stations. However, they did their best to secure a steady income by "fining" owners of the ubiquitous opium dens and marching great distances to rob rich landlords or hold their wives and children to ransom.

Their first requirement was a network of local contacts. They tried to set one up by sending people down to the villages, but inhabitants simply shot at them from guntowers and embrasures, taking them for bandits; other villages round about were instantly roused to join the fighting. The guerrillas were forced to adopt other measures to make themselves heard. They surrounded a papermakers' cabin in the mountains, sealed off the approaches to it, held up the papermakers at gunpoint, and lectured them on Communism and class struggle.

Sannan was close enough to soviet areas for these papermakers to have heard of the Red Army; they warmed to the guerrillas and gave them grain and information. The guerrillas then began a campaign of armed propaganda attacks on *tuhao*, distributing clothes and grain to the poor. To spread their message, they wrote leaflets and composed ballads about class oppression and won enough support to help them survive an extermination drive in the spring of 1936. In the darkest days of that year, their leaders organized an education campaign to stiffen morale and convince the ranks that better days lay ahead. Guerrillas were called in from all over Sannan, and comrades who had left the mountains were recalled for a plenary assembly among the trees at which local leaders rallied spirits and stressed discipline. Of the original core of thirty-eight guerrillas who had set out for Sannan in May 1935, not one had deserted.[30]

## COUNTERREVOLUTION AND THE RESISTANCE

By the spring of 1935, Chiang Kai-shek's armies had finished mopping up the Central Soviet in Gannan. Nationalist generals and politicians escorted groups of Chinese and foreign journalists round the "former bandit areas" to show them that the government had regained control; the journalists informed the world that "China's Red kingdom has perished." But Nationalist troops continued to hunt down Communist remnants holding out along nearby provincial borders. In April 1935, three divisions of Yu Hanmou's First Army arrived in Ganyue. Together with local forces, they numbered between thirty and forty thousand men. In the winter, according to Communist accounts, they increased their garrison to one hundred thousand.[31]

The Nationalists patrolled the river crossings and the highways. They emptied mountain villages that might otherwise have supplied the guerrillas, and they herded villagers into shanty settlements on the plains. They calculated that by stopping the flow of intelligence and supplies into the mountains, they could destroy the guerrillas within a year. They strictly rationed the sale of essential goods along the border and gave the landlord-controlled *mintuan* a free hand in the villages. These *mintuan* were in some ways more effective than regular army units, for they were themselves local people; they could distinguish accents and knew the region well. Troops and *mintuan* made spot checks at dawn and dusk and regularly stopped and searched travelers on the roads. Sometimes troops pretended to be guerrillas and killed or arrested people who revealed themselves as Communist sympathizers. Soon few dared open their door to the guerrillas, though some Communist supporters are said to have turned the tables on troops masquerading as guerrillas by killing them when they asked for "shelter" and then claiming a reward from the authorities.[32]

The Nationalists also used political propaganda and persuasion to root out Communist influence. Applied intelligently, this approach was deadlier than military sanctions and the blockade. Officials distributed leaflets telling the peasants that the soviet had fallen, the main Red Army had fled, and there was no longer any hope for Communists in southern China. They spread the idea that Zhu and Mao were the only true Red Army, that the Ganyue guerrillas were not wanted by Zhu and Mao, and that if Zhu and Mao returned, they would hunt down Xiang and Chen. Officials handed out money, medicine, and small gifts to guerrillas' relatives and supporters to shake their resolve and, through them, that of the guerrillas.[33]

After consolidating the blockade, the Guangdong troops turned their attention to the inner mountains. They chopped down the trees or sprinkled petrol about and set fire to the forests. River deer, muntjacs, and wild pigs stampeded through the trees, and huge snakes slithered about to escape the flames. Trackers brought up hunting dogs to scent out the guerrillas and tear them apart. At night, they illuminated the mountain slopes with powerful searchlights. "They treated us like wild pigs," said Chen Yi. "Their soldiers said that they were going into the mountains to fight wild men, that the Communists had long hair and went naked."

In the valleys, Nationalist searchers disguised themselves as guerrillas to test local people; on the mountains, they disguised themselves as woodcutters, boar hunters, mushroom gatherers, bamboo farmers, or charcoal burners to draw out the Communists. Sometimes they sent Communist renegades into the mountains to call down the guerrillas or forced guerrillas' wives to call their husbands down.

Few places in the mountains were now safe for the guerrillas. Yu Hanmou's troops built forts or posted lookouts on the peaks to watch for smoke by day and flames by night. They hid in the woods and bushes to listen for sounds of movement. They watched the earth, the grass, and the stones. Whenever they found signs of human presence, they intensified the search. They left rice or meat on the mountains as bait. If the guerrillas found it, they left it well alone. If they were unlucky, a tiger or a wild pig took it and triggered the hunt.[34]

Chen Yi said of this period,

> When two armies engage in conflict, that is known as war. But the three-year guerrilla struggle in Ganyue was not like a war, viewed in the military sense. The discrepancy between our strength and the enemy's was too great. Sometimes the enemy massed thirty to forty regiments, whereas the guerrillas had only three to four hundred people under arms. That is why the guerrillas had to adopt a policy of "long-term lying low," of preserving their forces and awaiting opportunities.[35]

What few weapons the guerrillas had were antiquated and badly maintained; they had no arsenal to repair them.[36] They were desperately short of ammunition. Sometimes they seized guns and ammunition from the Whites, but not often enough to equip more than a few guerrillas. Each guerrilla had only a handful of bullets, mostly recycled from spent shells and sometimes primed with scraped-off match heads. After they had fired a few of these, their rifle barrels became so hot that the bullets—said Chen Yi, who liked to enliven a story with hyperbole—dropped to the ground straight from the muzzle, or flopped harmlessly short of target. Often, the hand grenades failed to ignite (throwing them was like throwing stones, said Chen Yi), or they went off too soon, removing the thrower's fingers.[37]

Speed, quick wits, flexibility, stratagems, and evasion were the essence of Communist strategy in the Three-Year War in Ganyue. The guerrillas fought neither often nor long. They rarely fought save for political impact or to get supplies, and they avoided battles in which they might expect losses. If they came across the enemy by accident, they scattered and hid. Their main tactics were the ambush, the surprise attack, and the night or dawn raid, undertaken by units of between three and a dozen. They planned their attacks meticulously on the basis of reconnaissance reports or intelligence reports by underground helpers. They fought on split-second decisions, rarely for more than a few minutes.

After fighting, they headed back into the forest, sometimes marching for days on end to throw off their pursuers. Often they marched through the night to launch dawn raids on small enemy positions, to smash up district offices, or to grab *tuhao* for ransom. When they attacked, they scattered propaganda leaflets or painted slogans along the road.[38]

## A WAR OF TRICKS AND RUSES

The Three-Year War in Ganyue was largely a war of tricks and ruses. Government troops tried to trick the guerrillas into showing themselves; the guerrillas tried to confuse their pursuers about their movements. The Whites disguised themselves as guerrillas or as local people when they climbed the mountains; the guerrillas disguised themselves as Whites or as log traders, chicken gelders, pot menders, or peddlers when they descended to the plains. Each side fought more with silence than with guns. "We could never raise our voices," said Chen Yi. "We spoke together in whispers, like lovers."[39] Guerrillas squatted motionless in the bushes or in dense reed clumps from first light to nightfall while enemy troops combed the mountains in search of them. If a guerrilla spoke, the game was up; because most had bad chests from sleeping in the wet mountains, some gave themselves away by coughing. But if they kept still, they were generally safe. Even if the searchers had seen them vanish into the bushes, few had much stomach for going in after them, and they often only pretended to search unless officers were standing directly over them. Sometimes, when hunts failed to flush the guerrillas out, White officers blew whistles, shouted orders, and made a noisy show of retiring, but secretly left some men behind. If the guerrillas then broke cover, they were caught or shot. But most saw through this trick and had more patience than their pursuers, who eventually started firing wildly into the undergrowth or challenged them to come out and fight. At dusk, the enemy left in earnest. Then the guerrillas regrouped, gathered up their wounded, and marched off quickly through the night.[40]

At first they bivouacked in the gullies, near water, but as the searches intensified they moved further up the slopes and finally onto the peaks, where they could see in all directions. The searchers sent listeners, smoke watchers, and scout teams to live in the mountains and track them down. To throw them off the scent, the guerrillas sent a decoy to an opposite mountain to light a cigarette, start a small fire, scatter tin bowls, or loose off a shot.[41]

The guerrillas followed eight rules to avoid detection while on the march: (1) Choose your time with care. (2) Go where there are no paths. (3) Skirt level ground. (4) Always look out for signs of the enemy. (5) At night keep together by marching slowly; never use a flashlight. (6) March closely together; but stay at least ten paces ahead when first in line, in case the enemy is about. (7) Keep silent. (8) Sleep fully dressed and make sure your belongings are bundled so that you can leave at once in an emergency.[42]

Xiang Ying coupled these eight rules with six principles of warfare that renounced previous military practices: (1) If you can make a profit, do so; but do not take a loss. (2) If you are in control, fight; if not, slip away. (3) If you cannot escape victorious, then hide; we did not understand this in the past. (4) Mass and fight when the advantage is with you; otherwise, disperse. (5) Attack the enemy's gaps and weak spots. (6) Do not go where there are roads; go only where there are no roads.[43] Finally, there were the five considerations for choosing a site to bivouac: (1) Was it secluded? (2) Were there retreat routes? (3) Were there numerous paths into the mountains along which the enemy might approach? (4) Were there settlements nearby on which the guerrillas could depend? (5) Had the enemy already searched the place? (If so, he was unlikely to return.)[44]

After silence, fleetness was the guerrillas' main defense and their main means of attack. "We were like wild men," said Xiang Ying, "living and fighting by instinct. . . . We knew every corner of the mountains. We . . . became strong and agile as savages. . . . Our young men could go up and down mountains at incredible speed."[45] When the Nationalists entered one base, the guerrillas fled to another. If the enemy operated in all four bases at once in such force that it was impossible to hide in any of them, the guerrillas fled to the outer line and lay low close to the enemy's lair, where he would least expect to find them, or attacked redoubts and sabotaged electricity cables in places where the enemy was weak.[46]

During the whole Three-Year War, Chen Yi only twice stepped inside a house and only four times set eyes on anyone other than a guerrilla.[47] For three years, the mountains were his "house." "It was like living in eight rooms," Chen recalled. "One for sleeping in, one for retreating to, one for eating in, and so on. Our dogs [the sentries] were well trained. They barked as soon as the enemy appeared." Xiang Ying's mountain was rather more hospitable than Chen's. Some two thousand people lived round its slopes. Even so, Xiang also lived in well-aired rooms.[48] "For two years I never undressed at night," he said. "We . . . made our beds in the forests of the mountains. . . . We were constantly moving and were unable to build a base anywhere."[49]

Xiang Ying and Chen Yi were not typical of the guerrillas. They were marked men and needed to be especially vigilant. But there is little sign that any of the Red units in Ganyue could ever have called on widespread support between 1935 and 1937. During the first twenty months, their ties to the outside world were frayed or broken. The rhetorical insistence in memoirs of this period that the guerrillas relied on "the masses" refers mainly to their secret, tiny network of Party workers.

## GUERRILLA LINKS TO SOCIETY

However, the guerrillas could not have survived without any links to society, and as the political climate in Ganyue gradually brightened, so they remade small ties. The authorities knew that Communism in southern China had been dealt a severe blow by the events of late 1934 and the mop-ups of 1935, and in due course they relaxed some of their controls. Gradually, families began to return to the valleys from the plains to which they had been forcibly exiled, and their return gave the Communists the chance to revive some of their old support.[50] They devised unconventional methods to spread their political message. In one place, they carved slogans on sharpened bamboo slips that they planted near the villages at night, or on fir planks that they coated with tung oil and pushed into the river, in the hope that boatmen downstream would fish them out.[51] In other places, guerrillas slipped down into the valleys, where they organized secret peasant associations and collected lost comrades.

In early 1936, Chen Pixian and others left Youshan to work in Pengkeng. Even though Pengkeng had never been a soviet and enemy troops were stationed near it, Chen and his comrades eventually won some support there and laid the basis to expand in mid-1936. But the Communists realized that more generally, "the masses had temporarily lost direction" because of Nationalist propaganda and that the authorities would crack down on them again if they became openly active, so they channeled their contacts with the plains largely through underground intermediaries.[52]

Still, from the Pure Brightness festival in early April until the autumn harvest, there was always someone in the forests, even at the height of the blockade. Ganyue's Hakka peasants had lived off the mountains for centuries; they could never be wholly excluded from them. In the spring, the papermakers came; in the autumn, the charcoal burners. They stayed in cabins scattered throughout the forests. Most worked for employers and had special permits to enter the mountains; their provisions were officially rationed, but if the guerrillas befriended them, they shared their food. Ganyue is famous for its *beigu* mushrooms, marketed throughout Guangdong. When these mushrooms were in season, local folk, with or without permission, climbed the hills to pick them. Sometimes the military authorities let peasants into the forest to gather firewood under military guard. In the spring of 1936, the authorities first turned down a request by peasants to be allowed back into the mountains to plough their fields, but underground Communists mobilized a protest movement, and permission was eventually granted. The tiny handful of Communist agents in Ganyue took advantage of the constant human trickle into the hills to smuggle rice, salt, newspapers, and intelligence reports to the guerrillas. At first people going into the mountains "lost" these things among the trees; when the guards grew wise to this ploy, they hid the goods in the stopped hollows of bamboo carrying-poles, cut new poles on the mountains, and left the old ones behind. But in winter most of this mountainbound traffic stopped, and guerrillas either risked fetching their own rice from the valleys or starved.[53]

Sometimes troops brought crowds of peasants into the mountains to search the forests or to chop down the trees and burn the vegetation that hid the guerrillas. After the spring ploughing of 1936, eight columns, each two to three hundred strong, filed into the mountains between Dayu and Xinfeng on such a mission, watched over by a company of troops. The guerrillas adopted two main defenses against these searches. They fled into Nationalist areas to lie low or create diversions; or their underground supporters secretly organized the peasants to search slowly and noisily so that the guerrillas were forewarned. Communist supporters did their best to sabotage the tree-chopping and brush-burning by persuading peasants to arrive late or leave early; to chop slowly; to use only the backs of their blades; and to blunt their axes, so that, though the sound of chopping rang out everywhere, few trees fell; and to wet their matches so that they failed to light. When the troops checked, everyone was chopping; when the troops' backs were turned, so were the ax blades. But there is much ideological embellishment to these stories. Reality was harsher. In early 1936 two of Ganyue's main Red leaders, Li Letian and Zeng Jicai, died as a result of one such search.[54]

Sometimes the guerrillas sent people down into the villages to contact supporters or to pass on instructions to the liaison stations. If the authorities suspected that a village maintained secret links to the guerrillas, they put it under hidden watch and waited to make arrests. The Party's supporters in the village then left covert signs on the treetops, on the walls, and on the doors, a whip stuck in a pile of hay, a straw hat hung on a bamboo pole, an ox tied to a nut tree, or paper flowers stuck to a window—and the guerrillas slipped silently away.[55]

Women and children—relatives of the guerrillas, dependents of the Long Marchers, and widows and orphans of the Red Army—were a mainstay of the liaison stations strung out across the nearby plains. A typical contact point included a liaison official, a mimeograph operator, and a cook, grouped together in a "revolutionary family." Women took food up into the mountains, gathered intelligence, spread leaflets, wrote up slogans, and maintained communications between the four guerrilla bases. If local activists, plainclothes guerrillas, or liaison workers were seized, this entire network sprang into action. Communist supporters organized campaigns—where possible fronted by local bigwigs susceptible to Communist pressure—to request the release of those arrested. They started lawsuits; persuaded Daoist priests, Buddhist monks, and old women to wail in front of the local magistrate's office; or bribed local officials to drop the charges.[56]

The guerrillas had plenty of cash; at one point Chen Yi carried more than thirty thousand dollars in bullion, gold coins, and paper money strapped to his waist. When Communists or their sympathizers were arrested, the guerrillas provided money for bail or to help their families. When the houses of Communist supporters were burned down by troops, the guerrillas paid for the materials to rebuild them. Robbing *tuhao* was the main source of such funds. In some parts of Ganyue, small cells of mountain youths were set up to help the guerrillas wage this economic war. The Youshan and Beishan bases included more than fifty such cells. The youngsters who joined them worked in the fields by day and joined the guerrillas at night to rob *tuhao*, chop down telegraph poles, and let off firecrackers in oil drums to announce their presence.[57]

## GUERRILLA MORALE

By any reckoning, the fall of the soviet hit the standing and morale of Communism in Ganyue far harder than the 1927 defeat. In 1927, Communism was all but stamped out in the great cities, but in places like Ganyue it was only just beginning to flourish. After 1934, "a small state had gone under . . . and there was no news of where the Red Army was," said Chen Yi. "During the 1927 defeat, tens of thousands were butchered; now, hundreds of thousands were butchered. . . . Even though we leaders mobilized every day, the air of pessimism and demoralization was still hard to dispel."[58] From the plains came reports of the arrest of one leader after another and of the destruction of liaison stations and whole networks of Party agents.[59]

Most of the Red troops who arrived at the border in early 1935 had been borne into the Red Army on the crest of the great soviet wave, when the Communists were growing stronger and smashing Chiang Kai-shek's campaigns against them. They had rarely known defeat and were not equipped to cope with it. It is not surprising, noted Chen Yi, that when the soviet tide ebbed, their confidence ebbed with it. They could see only the dwindling numbers, the unrelenting hardship, the raining blows, and the isolation.[60] They feared for their homes and relatives in Gannan, which they had left defenseless against reprisals. Hunger made some surrender or desert. During the first few months of the rearguard action, many of their leaders had been unwilling to concede defeat or to scale down their plans to match their shrinking means. Some troops knew that their leaders were deeply divided on basic policy. Xiang Ying and Chen Yi had supported different lines in the past; the rivalry between them resurfaced again and again after 1934. Although they tried to hold their quarrels in private, they could not hide their differences from their followers.[61]

Pessimism and self-doubt, expressed in grumbling, vacillation, cynicism, and, at worst, desertion and betrayal, were rife in the guerrilla camps at certain times.[62] Pessimism was more destructive than the mopup; in severe cases, excising it was the best remedy, but where it was not yet malignant, persuasion and education proved more effective than "class dictatorship." "At that time," wrote Chen Yi in 1959,

> two methods were proposed for consolidating the ranks. One was force: if someone showed bad qualities or grumbled, we held a struggle meeting; we suppressed vacillators and deserters by extreme methods. When posting sentries, we increased the watch to two or three people if we suspected that one person was not reliable. Clearly, this was wrong. It created terror and suspicion in the ranks and destroyed unity. Some areas collapsed entirely because of such methods. Of course, it is necessary to repress resolutely renegades who endanger the revolution. But within the ranks, the important thing is to stress democracy, voluntariness, and persuasion. The revolution is voluntary, people cannot be made to take part in it. Persuasion should be used on people whose thought is vacillating . . . ; if they can persevere, fine—through testing and steeling they can become the mainstay of the future revolutionary struggle. But if they still want to go, then let them go—help them to go, even. Give them the money for the journey, help them to change into civilian clothes, find them a good route, let them return safely to their homes, if they are arrested by reactionaries on the way, organize people in the yellow villages[63] to vouch for them. . . . This method is best. After you have publicized it, people who at first vacillated a lot say openly that they no longer want to leave, and those who do leave cannot bring themselves to betray their friends and endanger the revolution. Even more important, this method raises the troops' political awareness and strengthens their unity.[64]

Not everyone could be persuaded to go quietly with the Party's knowledge and assent. Large numbers, including senior Red Army officers like Xiang Xianglin, went over to the Guomindang. The authorities encouraged such desertions by offering generous fixed prices for every rifle, bullet, and hand grenade turned in, and by offering deserters jobs in specially formed squads. Renegades wreaked enormous damage on the

Ganyue guerrillas. In October 1935, the renegade Gong Chu told the Nationalists that Xiang Ying and Chen Yi were hiding in Ganyue.[65] Xiang Xianglin stood at the city gates of Nanxiong pointing out guerrillas and their supporters to his captors. He and others led searches of the mountains and drove the guerrilla leaders deeper and deeper into the forests, where they were increasingly cut off by their own intricate system of security.[66] Though the Ganyue bases were connected after 1934 by lines of liaison points, the various Party organs were not directly linked, so that if one collapsed the rest would not necessarily collapse with it.

The Ganyue network was unlike that in neighboring Minxi and Minyue. It linked bases not to cities but merely to other bases on nearby mountains: it was insulated and for the most part self-contained. Sentries were everywhere, in the trees and on the roads. "Some of our lookouts practically lived in trees," said Xiang Ying.[67] These measures achieved their immediate aim, but they isolated the guerrilla bands even further from one another and from the towns and villages. At times, the guerrillas were forced to concentrate so single-mindedly on survival that they neglected their political goals. In that sense, the Guomindang achieved its aim.

## GUERRILLA LIFE

One resource of which the guerrillas had more than enough was time. Revolutionaries traditionally turn their prison cells into studies; Communists in Ganyue turned the mountain slopes into universities. Their first aim was to stanch the desertions by showing that the revolution had a future. They could only hope to succeed if they dropped their wilder claims. The Changling meeting of April 1935 proposed a more sober timetable than that implied in the final declarations of the soviet. Their second aim was to use the enforced idleness of the guerrillas to train them in basic skills and indoctrinate them politically, so that by the time they left the forests they would be transformed from a beaten remnant into a nucleus of future Red Army officers and political leaders.

Whenever conditions allowed, school started up among the trees. The curriculum included military affairs, the history of the Chinese Soviet, Chinese language and culture, mathematics, guerrilla tactics, and Marxism-Leninism.[68] The guerrillas had only two books—Lenin's *Two Tactics*[69] and another by Stalin (not named in the source)—a handful of pamphlets, and some tattered copies of the old soviet newspaper *Hongse Zhonghua,* which they studied and restudied. On rare occasions, they got hold of up-to-date newspapers through the liaison stations. Those who were literate taught the others to read and write, and Chen Yi edited a

*Soldier's Reader* to help this effort. Both he and Xiang Ying wrote textbooks on general knowledge and political theory that were mimeographed on local paper by a tiny guerrilla print shop on Mount Shangleshan in Xinfeng, using ink and wax stencils provided by friendly schoolteachers and *baojia* chiefs.[70]

In these textbooks, guerrillas read about the need to work among the peasants, attack *tuhao*, divide the land, destroy counterrevolutionary armies, set up soviets, and create Red Armies (the "Five Great Tasks"); to obey orders, respect the interests of the people, "cleave to the class line" when attacking *tuhao*, love one's weapon as oneself, and not beat or curse people (the "Five Great Disciplines"); to have one's weapon always by one's side, speak carefully, stick together while marching, stay with the ranks except in special circumstances, hand over "common property" after attacking *tuhao*, speak courteously, buy and sell fairly, return borrowed things, recompense damage, respect prisoners' personal belongings, and love one's comrades (the "Ten Points for Attention"). A typical handbook also explained the different responsibilities of officers and ranks and the structure of the rank-and-file soldiers' committee; and it gave tips on marksmanship and bayoneting.[71]

In the last months of the Three-Year War, when war with Japan was approaching swiftly, the guerrillas leveled out a parade ground in the mountains and drilled in sections and platoons.[72] They learned, through practice, basic principles of economic management and public accounting. Accounts were kept centrally and published at regular intervals. They showed income ("fines and contributions") and expenditure on supplies, political campaigns, and liaison work.

The guerrillas amassed money and gold by the bagful through their marauding. They operated in such tiny units that no waste or embezzlement could go unnoticed. Their budgets were generally democratic and egalitarian, and this equitable sharing enhanced their sense of solidarity. In principle, each guerrilla received $12 a month regardless of rank, less $6 for food and $3 to $4 for tobacco. Normally, they had few chances to spend this money, but they carried small amounts around with them at all times in case—as often happened—they got lost or left behind. Cash was distributed among the most reliable guerrillas for safekeeping. The only exception to the general principle of equality was Xiang Ying, who as a heavy smoker was allowed more tobacco than the norm; but even Xiang sometimes had to smoke wild leaves.[73]

When the remnants of the Jiangxi rearguard first went up Youshan, they hid in empty houses. When these were burned down or demolished, the guerrillas moved to papermakers' cabins higher up the slopes. When these too were destroyed, they put up bamboo, fir-bark, or reed huts. Even these huts eventually proved too conspicuous, and instead the guerrillas strung up canopies of cloth covered with one or more layers of oiled paper between the trees, cutting channels across the upper ground to drain away rainwater; or they slept back-to-back under giant paper umbrellas treated with persimmon gum and wood oil. Bamboo sun-rain hats and palm-fiber capes were their normal attire in the rainy season. "A pistol at his waist, a cloth bundle on his back, an umbrella at his side—that was your guerrilla," one recalled. Summer was the best season in the mountains; the air was pleasantly cool, and there were no mosquitoes. On cloudless nights, the guerrillas sometimes stretched out on flattened tombstones, "watching the stars and the moon, at one with heaven and earth."[74]

Sleeping deep in the forest was less tranquil. The forest night was alive with the howls, the humming, and the clatter of wild animals and insects. The canopy of trees cut out the night light, and in the inky blackness it was easy to confuse the tread of large animals with that of searching men. Sometimes guerrillas were jolted awake by the terrified clamor of mountain goats or other animals being attacked by tigers or leopards. As they stole through the mountains, they sometimes came across these predators sitting on rocks. The forests teemed with snakes great and small. Often a guerrilla found on waking that one had coiled up on his stomach for warmth.[75] Fires in the mountains were easily spotted by enemy lookouts, so it was dangerous to light them. During the worst of the winter, the guerrillas huddled together in the snow to hide from searchers, knocking and prizing their frozen food from its containers.[76]

At first, when communications between the highlands and the lowlands were still open, the guerrillas sent people down to the villages to buy rice, salt, pepper, and meat, or to obtain supplies by armed foraging. In those days, each guerrilla carried a week's rations, burying any surplus. Being mostly on the move, they often had no cooking pots, so they boiled their rice in bamboo segments over campfires. Later, when the blockade tightened and civilian sources of provisions dried up, they harvested wild vegetables, fruit, and nuts, shot or trapped wild animals, and scratched around for grubs. The pupae of hornets, which abound in the Ganyue forests, became a staple. To gather them, a guerrilla squeezed his head into a bamboo-strip basket, smoked out the adult hornets with a brushwood torch, and smashed open the nest. The grubs were fried, roasted, or boiled into a soup. On summer nights, the guerrillas shone flashlights into the grass to draw fat bullfrogs toward the beam and fished in the mountain streams. When government troops were not around they shot muntjac, hare, and wild boar and trapped snakes. Once they had learned to harvest the mountain, they generally had enough to eat. The best thing, said Chen Yi, was the water: pure, clean, fresh, and constantly available.[77]

In healing and curing, nature was less provident. Many Gannan veterans were sick or lame when the Long March began. They had no doctors and few medical workers. Some, like Chen Yi, had had cursory operations before the Red Army surgeons finally packed their bags, but the
haste of the evacuation meant that most guerrillas had had no treatment, and others were crippled by bad surgery. Many limped about the
mountains on sticks, afflicted by bone splinters or badly set bones that
stuck out at unlikely angles. Scabies, ulcers, malaria, and pulmonary tuberculosis were occupational diseases of the guerrilla. For hunger there
was always a remedy, but the mountains could provide no relief for illness or deformity. Sometimes guerrillas seized medicines and ointments
from *tuhao,* but normally they had only all-purpose balms like *wanjinyou*
to treat their wounds; when all else failed, they washed them in herbal
juices, chili water, and brine, sucking out the pus to stop maggots breed-
ing in it.[78]

## THE LIANG GUANG INCIDENT AND ITS AFTERMATH

In June 1936, a grave political crisis in southern China gave the guerrillas their first chance to expand. In the winter of 1935, they had gone
into virtual hibernation, taking shelter wherever they could from the elements and the enemy's attacks and slowing down their vital processes to
the minimum necessary for survival. By early 1936, only two to three
hundred remained. For Communists in many places, the June crisis was
the first stirring of a political spring; in Ganyue, too, it led to a quick-
ening of the Party's pulse.

Ever since the start of the Three-Year War, Communist leaders in
Ganyue had confidently predicted that "contradictions" among the
enemy—among the imperialists, between imperialists and the Chinese
ruling classes, and among the Chinese ruling classes—would recur and
that the Party's fortunes would then improve. The contradiction that
emerged in June 1936 was of the third sort. The Cantonese warlord
Chen Jitang attacked Chiang Kai-shek in what became known as the
Liang Guang Incident and called for an active resistance to Japan. The
Communists in Ganyue debated how to respond. Some thought that
Chen Jitang's opposition to Chiang Kai-shek should be supported even
though he was an anti-Communist. The Ganyue Committee held that
Chen Jitang's call for resistance to Japan was purely demagogic and that
the war was a reactionary diversion from the fight for a united
resistance.[79]

The withdrawal of a dozen regiments of Yu Hanmou's First Army
from Ganyue to join in the attack on Chiang, and the ensuing flight of

local reactionaries to the cities, nonetheless provided an opening for the Communists. Views on how to use it differed. Some hotheads thought that the time had come to restore the soviet, but the committee opposed this idea at a meeting of guerrilla chiefs and liaison officials from a dozen or so counties. Xiang Ying argued that the incident was a "contradiction among the enemy" and that, despite their differences, Chiang Kai-shek and Chen Jitang would unite to crush any challenge from the left. Instead of restoring the soviet, the Communists should continue to fight guerrilla war and raise the slogan "Turn the warlord war into a revolutionary war against Japan." A recent Chinese assessment of Xiang Ying's career concluded that "this decision played a very important role in preserving the revolution's forces."[80]

Some guerrillas opposed even this proposal for a political campaign on the grounds that it would draw attention to the Communists' continuing presence in Ganyue and invite retaliation. But on this issue, Xiang Ying and Chen Yi agreed, and the campaign went ahead. Chen Yi wrote an "Open Letter to the Masses" explaining the Special Committee's view of the incident. This letter was copied a dozen or so times and sent down the mountains to the Party's liaison workers, who made further copies and stuck them up on walls and bridges and at crossroads. During this campaign, some new Party branches sprang up.[81]

Xiang Ying and Chen Yi were united against proposals to restore the soviet, but on other issues, they still differed. Chen Yi wanted the Communists to mass their forces against local landlord militia while Chen Jitang's armies were busy elsewhere; Xiang favored lying low, save for a small political offensive, and he is even said to have opposed making contact with the Party center on the grounds that conditions were too dangerous. Chen Yi's view reportedly prevailed, and the decision to mass forces scored some notable victories. The Ganyue guerrillas doubled and trebled in strength to more than six hundred in less than a month. They widened their area of operations, spilling over onto the plains and into the towns, and at one point, they were fighting in units of two hundred, backed by hundreds of civilian supporters. They destroyed large numbers of enemy redoubts with homemade bombs.[82] Some "reactionary villages" and landlord militia sent representatives to negotiate with them. At the Chongyang Festival, shortly after the Liang Guang Incident, the Communists held a parade and a big meeting at Dayangkeng in Pengkeng. The Party grew rapidly: Communists set up a district committee in Meishan and more than twenty branches in Sannan.

The longer-term benefits of the incident were minimal, however. Within a few weeks, Chen Jitang's rebellion had collapsed after his air force and Yu Hanmou's First Army deserted him for Chiang Kai-shek. In September, the Central Army's Forty-sixth Division arrived in Ganyue to resume the blockade and "root out bandits." The guerrillas were driven back into the mountains, where they were chased from peak to peak, and over the next few weeks they lost what strength they had gained.[83]

## THE GUERRILLAS CHANGE THEIR METHODS

The defeats of the autumn of 1936 led to a profound change in Communist strategy and tactics. Practices that they had previously followed incidentally and pragmatically now became general policy. This strategic turn tided them through the even worse storms that followed, when hunger, isolation, night marches, bivouacking on the mountains, and constant pursuit again became the rule.[84] During the incident, the guerrillas had reminded the government that they could still make trouble given the chance; afterwards, the government showed the guerrillas that its capacity for quelling troublemakers was far from spent. The newly arrived Forty-sixth Division pursued the guerrillas more systematically than the Cantonese, who by now had been transferred elsewhere. But because they were strangers to Ganyue and in some respects less resolute than the Cantonese, they were easier to outwit and ultimately less effective. The guerrillas' morale rose when news came of the main Red Army's arrival in Shaanxi. Some proposed "meeting White terror with Red," but Xiang and Chen opted for a strategy that would take political advantage of the Forty-sixth Division's lack of local ties and knowledge.[85]

The policies adopted by the Communists during their sudden expansion in mid-1936 had led to a polarization of Ganyue society into Red villages and White: those that the Communists influenced and those controlled by the government or the landlords. "The guerrillas turned into an agent of catastrophe," said Chen Yi. "They were fire-gods—wherever they appeared, the enemy burned houses and killed people." The Communists had to find a way to widen their support without exposing their supporters to unnecessary danger.

Their solution was the "gray" or "yellow" village tactic. They encouraged their contacts in the villages to set up "gray, two-faced governments" (as opposed to red) and even to pretend to oppose the Party. In the past, they had planted the flag too widely and killed or threatened too many people. Now they switched to a less drastic policy. They "visited" *baojia* heads on dark or rainy nights, befriended officials prepared to compromise with them, and instructed their secret members and supporters to obtain appointments to *baojia* posts. Now they killed only a few diehards, "as a warning to the rest." Soon "double-dealing" became widespread in the mountains, and under the shield of "double agents of an intermediate color," the Communists began to organize political campaigns of a legal and semilegal sort.

This set of tactics was not new in Ganyue; the Party had begun its political retreat as early as 1935. But after 1936, restraint played a far more central role in its strategy. In Chijiang, Communists even engineered the appointment of one of their wealthy contacts as district chief. Through him, they got intelligence, newspapers, and, during the harsh winter of 1936, padded clothes, blankets, footwear, and medicine. One advantage of double-dealing was that when conditions within the blockade worsened, guerrillas could slip down into the villages to lie low for a while. Another was that they could more easily learn of enemy plans. The change in tactics came later in Ganyue than in other regions. If "class struggle" had been mitigated earlier, Xiang and Chen might have broken from their isolation and played a more active political role.[86]

Throughout the Three-Year War, the guerrillas funded their activities mainly by "fining" *tuhao*. "Attacking *tuhao* had two meanings," said Chen Yi. "Politically, it dampened their arrogance and made them afraid to harm the people. Economically, it was a way of collecting donations of grain and provisions." But catching *tuhao* was far from easy. The richer ones had armed bodyguards, walled forts, and crowds of followers of the same lineage, and others had either been robbed clean or had moved beyond the guerrillas' reach. Under the yellow-village policy, the Communists began to differentiate more finely among different sorts of *tuhao* and government official. They calculated "fines" and "contributions to the anti-Japanese resistance" on the basis of estimates of their victims' wealth and property, and they tried to avoid asking for too much. By then, the anti-Japanese theme had become a main plank in their political platform. Where possible in the villages, they sealed anti-Japanese "alliances" with "progressive landlords, enlightened gentry, and intellectuals." By giving their stickups a new and respectable political coloring, they hoped to shed their bandit image. But from the point of view of "anti-Japanese" *tuhao*, the line between a stickup and a whip-round was probably quite thin. Communists in neighboring Minxi'nan, who had direct ties to Party bureaus, dropped the last vestiges of "leftism" as early as January 1937, when they stopped kidnapping and robbing *tuhao* and asked them instead for "contributions." At the same time, they formally adopted the policy of confiscating only "traitors' " land (though in reality they had already stopped confiscating land of any kind). In Ganyue, similar policies were formally adopted only after July.[87]

## DEFENDING THE GAINS OF LAND REFORM

As part of their policy to "rehabilitate" old soviet areas, the Nationalists had published special land regulations stipulating that land divided after 1929 should be returned to its original owners. Some landlords even tried to claim five years' back rent for the period up to 1935. During the Three-Year War in Ganyue, Communist leaders fought hard to resist the canceling of land reform. Campaigns to resist paying rent and taxes, providing grain, repaying debts, and conscription (the "Five Resists") became the main content of their work in the villages whenever they could get into them.

In the mountains and the old soviets, agrarian counterrevolution was easier to proclaim than to implement. In many villages, land nominally restored to its previous owners continued in practice to be farmed by arrangements reached under the soviet; landlords' forests continued to be communally exploited, and the Party continued to assign de facto rights over the fields. Apart from "tearful pleading," landlords had two ways of asserting their rights to land: they either sent rent collectors into the villages under Nationalist armed guard, or they waylaid peasants leaving the mountains to attend market. The Communists responded by threatening to kill the rent collectors. If landlords or their agents did manage to collect rent or grain, the guerrillas tried to ambush them on roads from the villages and to return the takings to the peasants. Where outright resistance failed, they adopted other tactics. During the spring famine of 1936 (caused by a poor harvest in 1935 and the predations of the landlords' "restitution league"), the Communists asked landlords to return grain they had already collected or to make interest-free loans to tenants. If they refused, the guerrillas tried to organize tenants to break open the storehouses and help themselves. At first, no steps were taken to disguise the identity of the grain raiders, who were traced and punished. Later, landlords' families were locked in their houses during raids. Even so, land reform was effectively overturned in Ganyue.[88]

The Communists' new strategy of ducking confrontations and subverting the local administration from within widened their civilian network. Relations between villages in Red and White areas were often strained and hostile. Many on the plains believed the propaganda of the Guomindang and had been alienated by Communist "left excesses." Because of the blockade, it was difficult for mountain people to leave the mountains and for plains people to enter them. Two worlds had grown up in the early 1930s, and the antagonism between them remained. Still, as the tension eased, more and more people returned from the plains to the valleys, swelling the poor peasant associations whose instigators hovered in the surrounding mountains; some joined the Communist Party and its Youth League.

## REACHING DOWN ONTO THE PLAINS

It was important for the Communists to extend their influence beyond the mountains, which were too thinly populated to sustain them. The Ganyue uplands were traditionally linked by business and family ties to the surrounding plains. The economic blockade of guerrilla areas was only partly effective, and yellow villages were not greatly affected by it. Many people, especially hawkers, traders, and artisans, circulated round the marketing communities of Ganyue, forming grids that the Communists used to spread their political message and organization to the lowlands. For example, they recruited two itinerant barbers to work for the Party in a ring of markets around Youshan. They also infiltrated their people into the towns and villages to spread Party influence. Many cadres learned a trade, such as tailoring or carpentry. Others did casual work or went down the mines. In cities like Dayu, Nanxiong, Dasou, and Xincheng, the Communists set up shops as fronts for their liaison stations and made friends among workers and soldiers. "In the mines, our ears and eyes were everywhere," said Chen Pixian. They also spread northward into Jiangxi, opening a button factory in Ganzhou and a tailor's shop in Yudu in the hope of contacting remnants of the Central Soviet. At one point, they were even preparing to open secret offices in Hongkong and Shanghai.[89]

From other directions, too, Communist feelers reached into the Guangdong cities. In the autumn of 1935, the Party's Shanghai bureau sent people to Guangzhou to form a branch of the Chinese Youth League as a first step toward rebuilding the Party there; later, agents of the Northern Bureau formed another front organization. Through these bodies, the Communists mobilized students at Zhongshan University and elsewhere to stage patriotic protests in late 1935 and early 1936. They also secretly infiltrated and controlled various official organizations. But it was only after changes at the national level that the movement down from the hills converged with the movement inland from Hongkong and Shanghai to rebuild the Party's city structure, in ruins since the defeat of 1927. It was not until January 1938, several months after Zhang Yunyi and others had arrived in Guangdong, that a provincial committee was reestablished.[90] In the three years after the winter of 1934, small groups of lost Communists roamed Guangdong under assumed identities seeking the Party in areas where Communist guerrillas had been reported. The Party's Southern Bureau sent people to look for these lost groups, but they were too well hidden to be found. It was not until late 1937 and early 1938 that they were finally gathered back into the Party fold.[91]

Some Communists who had had enough of eating wind and drinking dew saw the yellow-village campaign as a chance to quit the hard and dangerous life of the mountain guerrilla and switch instead to underground town and village work. But the Special Committee argued strongly that the underground political struggle depended for success on the guerrilla and the gun, without which it would lack credibility, and it opposed phasing out armed activity.[92]

## AFTER THE XI'AN INCIDENT

In early 1937, Ganyue guerrillas learned from a Hongkong newspaper about the Xi'an Incident. They rejoiced that Chiang was "going to get his head chopped off" and were furious when they learned of his release, though Xiang Ying had not ruled out a peaceful resolution of the crisis (and was consequently branded behind his back as a "rightist"). Only after they heard of Mao's Wayaobao report, made more than a year earlier, did they begin to see the need for a new political direction and a thorough reschooling of troops and cadres. A special Youshan conference announced that "national contradictions have transcended class ones" and decided to mobilize in the towns and villages around a unity manifesto calling on the Guomindang to "let the guerrillas go to the resistance front." They continued to stress the need for vigilance. Their unity declaration had no immediate effect except to prompt local newspapers to announce that the "Youshan Communist bandits have surrendered." As part of their campaign for a united front, the Ganyue Communists infiltrated Guangdong Army units and Chiang Kai-shek's Forty-fifth Division. But their cells were betrayed, and their man in the Forty-fifth, Chen Hai, was arrested and became a double agent for the government.[93]

After a brief lull following the truce between Communists and Nationalists in northern China, the Nanjing government renewed its campaign against Communist pockets in old soviet areas, including Ganyue. Having patched up relations with Yan'an, Chiang wanted to destroy the guerrillas in the south before going to war against Japan. Chen Yi described how the Guomindang might justify this policy: "Zhu and Mao are the true Communist Party, among their troops are many with lofty ideals. But those in the mountains are not true Communists. The true Communists cast them off. They are bandits. Not one of them has lofty ideals. And bandits must be stamped out."[94]

Chiang was worried that the southern guerrillas might create a second Communist focus in the south after restoring ties to the Red Army in the north.[95] The guerrillas were few, but they were hard and able; given the chance, they might revive their bases and sow trouble behind Guomindang lines in the coming war. The Communists in Ganyue were as keen to restore contact with their Central Committee as Nanjing was to prevent it. Their radio links had been cut throughout most of the Three-Year War. They had tried to contact the Long Marchers by sending letters through the writers Lu Xun and Mao Dun in Shanghai, but the letters were lost or intercepted. The authorities took advantage of Xiang and Chen's eagerness to find the Party by setting a trap for them, baited with the renegade Chen Hai, who pretended that he had news of the Central Committee. Chen Yi almost fell into it but escaped by a whisker.[96]

The Forty-sixth Division's post-Xi'an campaign in Ganyue lasted from February 7, 1937, until the outbreak of war with Japan in July. It came in two main drives. January 1937 was quiet, the lull before the storm. Once the campaign started, it moved immediately into top gear and barely slackened until May. For the Communists, the intervening months were the worst of the whole Three-Year War. There was hardly a day or night that they were not under attack or on the run; forest after forest went up in flames. The government troops used their old tactics but with new energy and resolve.[97]

## MOVES TOWARD A UNITED FRONT

Though the Communists had had no direct news or instructions from the Party, Xiang Ying read of the peaceful settlement of the Xi'an Incident while on a secret visit to Nanxiong and called on the Nationalists for a cease-fire. His call was ignored; the drive continued. It was not until late July 1937 that Xiang and Chen received detailed information about the united front. They called a conference of Party leaders in Ganyue to tell them about the new policy of allying with Chiang Kaishek and sent out word of the change to guerrilla units in other places. On August 8, they issued a statement calling for a joint resistance. Even then, the authorities at first treated their statement with contempt and declared that the guerrillas should either submit to reeducation and reorganization or go home to become farmers.[98]

In July, government troops began withdrawing from Ganyue. After Japan's sudden attack on Shanghai in August, the guerrillas' troubles quickly lightened. Xiong Shihui, Governor of Jiangxi, set up an "amnesty committee" in Nanchang and similar offices in Ganzhou and Ningdu. The local authorities told the guerrillas that the Communists in the northwest were already cooperating with Nanjing and urged them to come down the mountains to negotiate a truce. On Governor Xiong's instructions, some county magistrates sent representatives to contact the guerrillas. According to Chen Yi, some praised the guerrillas as patriots and denounced the campaign against them; others said that the Communists would be treated leniently only if they recanted. The guerrillas, unhappy about negotiating without higher instructions, ignored the first two communications from the Nationalists, but they feared that if they delayed too long in leaving the mountains, they might miss the chance to link up with other guerrillas in southern China. After a third letter, Chen agreed to meet a representative of the Dayu magistrate in a lonely temple.

At first, other leaders stayed in the mountains recruiting troops and sent people down into the valleys only as spies. After much discussion, they adopted the slogan, "Extend our influence, recruit troops, and seize the chance to unite the southern guerrillas and become a real force, so that north and south can act in concert." Even then, they insisted that negotiations should stick to the issue of a cease-fire. They demanded facilities to enable them to make contact with guerrillas in inaccessible places. They also declared that future political arrangements and decisions on military reorganization should be dealt with by the Party's national leaders.

Talks soon followed in the nearby city of Dayu (where the Communists were greeted, as Chen Yi had foretold three years earlier, by a military band) and later in Ganzhou and Nanchang, where Chen reestablished contact with the Party's Central Committee and agreed to cooperate with the Guomindang.[99]

## THE GUERRILLAS REORGANIZE

In late September, Xiang Ying held talks in Nanchang at which it was informally agreed that the guerrillas would be reorganized as the Anti-Japanese Volunteer force, that old and new debts in the guerrilla areas would be canceled, and that the Jiangxi authorities would pay the costs of reorganization.[100]

Chen Yi and four other Ganyue leaders spent some weeks in hospital in Dayu, recovering from scabies and other illnesses. Chen worked hard to win the support of "enlightened personages," including the headmistress of Dayu Girls' School. In Ganzhou, the first thing he did was to make a tour of the bookshops; for three years he had read nothing save newspapers and the same old set of pamphlets. After that, the Ganyue leaders, who still formally commanded Communist units throughout the old soviet areas, spent much of their time calling in guerrillas all over southern China.[101]

In northwestern China (and even in some other regions of southern China, such as Mindong), the switch from civil war to a united front was preceded by a long period of discussion, maneuvering, and political readjustment. In Ganyue, it was sudden and abrupt, and it resulted from decisions taken elsewhere. Perhaps the signals coming from Yan'an were partly contradicted by others from Party bureaus in the coastal cities, which may have taken a different line under the influence of Wang Ming in Moscow. Not surprisingly, the Ganyue Special Committee floundered politically in the first days after the cease-fire. Chen Pixian remembers that Xiang Ying began to call for "cooperation to the end," while Chen Yi—having reportedly learned the need for "proletarian independence" from his tattered volume of Lenin's *Two Tactics*—called only for "long-term cooperation" and warned that unless the Communists kept up their guard, *hezuo* (cooperation) could become *huozhuo* (catching alive).[102] On August 25, 1937, the Ganyue Committee issued a "Letter to the Masses about the Resistance War" that lacked the fiery ring of leaflets put out by other southern guerrillas.[103] It asked people to give money to the government for the resistance and told "all able-bodied men to enthusiastically await the government's conscription." It was not an attempt to shape events but rather a passive commentary on them. However, the Ganyue Communists had fewer troops and a narrower political base than their more assertive, vociferous comrades across the border in Minxi'nan, where Japanese pressures helped create tensions useful to the Party.

Chen Pixian wrote in a memoir that Xiang Ying was more rightist than Chen Yi in the period immediately after the cease-fire in Ganyue, but elsewhere he summarizes an article published in Xiang's name in 1937 (but drafted jointly with Chen Yi and others) that was far from rightist. This article, called "The New Stage of the Chinese Revolution and the Party Line," said that cooperation with the Guomindang presupposed that the Party would keep its "special areas," its Red Army, its independence, and its right to criticize the Guomindang, and that it would strive for hegemony in the resistance.[104] Even so, after the Wannan Incident of January 1941, Xiang was accused by the Party center of making speeches in September 1937 that diverged from the Yan'an position.[105] After the He Ming Incident, when Communists in Minnan were disarmed and disbanded by the Nationalists, the Central Committee resolved that "Xiang Ying apparently does not yet understand the principle of maintaining independence within the united front and understands even less the principle that we should not unconditionally concentrate our forces and should preserve strategic support points in the south."[106]

After the negotiations, between three hundred and six hundred guerrillas from all over Ganyue gathered, in early 1938, at three separate points around Chijiang (each five *li* apart in case of attack) and were incorporated into the New Fourth Army's Second Regiment.[107] Some were new recruits; their numbers were artificially swelled in a battle of wits with the authorities. According to Yang Shangkui,

The Kuomintang asked us how many men we actually had, and we gave the figure of more than a thousand because the troop was still being enlarged. They were sly enough to ask us for the roster, giving the reason that pay was allotted accordingly, but actually they just wanted to find out our real strength. After some expansion, we had over six hundred men, who had been re-organised and were beginning gradually to spread out toward the plain.

This number was brought up to one thousand, explained Yang, with the help of sympathetic peasants who came "just to answer the roll-call."[108] (Actually, some Nationalist officials sympathized with the Communists and were prepared to accept their blatantly false claims).[109] Among the last to arrive at Chijiang were one hundred troops from Sannan, including the thirty-eight veterans who had set out for Sannan with Zhang Riqing in early 1935. These diehards had not seen a newspaper, heard of the Long March, or slept in a bed for three years, and they had been hunted longer than any other unit in Ganyue. According to one, "we had been cut off from the outside world for so long that when Nationalist cargo planes flew over the mountains, we thought it was the Red Army coming back."[110]

The Ganyue leaders expected problems in persuading the guerrillas to leave their home villages. "We therefore organised a series of get-togethers and send-offs before they left," said Yang Shangkui. "At these the scene which took place several years earlier of young wives bidding farewell to their husbands who were joining the Red Army was re-enacted."[111] On their march to Wannan, they avoided towns and moved mainly at night. Cadres stood watch over the troops "to avoid cheating propaganda and attacks by the Nationalists." Camp was always pitched within easy reach of the mountains. The guerrillas did not try to win new recruits on their way north (though Chen Yi boasted that they could "easily have recruited a hundred thousand" if they had been allowed to do so).[112] Some two hundred Communists stayed behind when the guerrillas left for the front; they were joined by others sent down from Yan'an. They set up underground Party cells in Ganzhou, Ruijin, and other towns of the old Central Soviet.[113]

## PERSPECTIVES ON THE THREE-YEAR WAR
## IN GANYUE

In other areas of the Three-Year War, including Eyuwan and parts of Fujian, the Communists maintained their organization and influence until 1949. Their success was partly due to the impact of the Japanese invasion on these areas; it was also a consequence of the greater strength of the Communist tradition there. The Three-Year War left few traces in

Ganyue after 1937. One proof is the experience of the 1,300 Communist troops under Wang Zuoyao sent to set up a "strategic base" around Youshan in the summer of 1945, just eight years after Xiang and Chen had left. Local Hakka peasants, far from welcoming Wang's troops as long-lost comrades, were in a "state of anxiety" and stood silently at their doors as the Communists marched by. Later they broke their silence to ask, "How long will you stay?" They wanted to know whether the Communists were planning to remain permanently or whether they would soon march off again, leaving the field clear for yet another change of regime. They wanted reassurance on this point before they were prepared to drop their guard.

The Communists' answer was unequivocal: "We will not be leaving. Now we have won the war, this country is ours. Why should we go? Should we leave for abroad?" The peasants' response is not recorded. In any case, the promise was broken, for within a year, Wang and his soldiers had left for Shandong aboard United States landing ships under the terms of the Party's postwar agreement with the Nationalists. Wang left just two hundred people underground in Ganyue. Only in 1949 did Wang's men return south to take part in the liberation of Guangdong and—for the third time—Ganyue. (By then, the two hundred had grown to one thousand.)[114]

In 1977, on the fiftieth anniversary of the founding of the Chinese Red Army, Chen Yi's comrades in the Three-Year War from across the border in Minxi offered a generous assessment of his achievements between 1934 and 1937. (Xiang Ying's name was omitted from the encomium, though a later assessment said "his achievements [in the Three-Year War] outweighed his errors.")[115] "The struggle waged by the guerrilla units on the Kiangsi-Kwangtung [Ganyue] border under the leadership of Chen Yi and other comrades," wrote the Minxi veterans, "kept alive the embers of the revolution, sapped the arrogance of the Kuomintang reactionaries, pinned down and depleted the enemy's effectives, complemented the struggle going on in the other guerrilla base areas and supported the Red Army in its Northward march to resist Japanese aggression."[116]

In reality, however, the stay-behinders in Ganyue were among the least successful of the pockets of resistance in and around old soviet areas after 1934. Ganyue was never a consolidated soviet before 1935 but rather a gateway to the soviet. Ganyue peasants who rallied to the guerrillas in the early days were systematically drawn off to replenish and expand the main Red Army; requests by local leaders for an upgrading of their region were ignored.

Being close to the Central Soviet, Ganyue could hardly avoid the effects of its collapse. After 1934, it became the site of the headquarters of

the two main leaders of the southern rearguard. Xiang Ying and Chen
Yi managed to keep Party organization intact in their guerrilla army
and also at the county and district levels. They kept in touch and reacted
to China's major political crises between 1934 and 1938. They were particularly successful at uniting different sorts of guerrillas, despite efforts
by the Guomindang to sow dissension between "insiders" and "newcomers." As a result, most guerrillas stayed loyal.[117]

The three years after 1934 were not, however, a time of unremitting
and indiscriminate terror for the Communists in Ganyue. There were
four main periods of tension: between April and September 1935; in the
spring of 1936, when mountain searches resumed; after July 1936, when
the Nationalist rebel Yu Hanmou defected to Chiang Kai-shek; and between February and July 1937.[118] During these times, the guerrillas
were chased relentlessly, and their social ties were methodically cut. In
between, when pressure slackened, the movement immediately started
to revive and new recruits took the places of those who had fled or
fallen. Even so, Xiang and Chen were special targets for the Nationalists
after 1934, and with a big price on their heads they could do little more
than hide in the forests even when the heat was off them. In Ganyue—in
contrast to other regions—periods of tension outlasted slack periods,
and Xiang and Chen were unable to build on the gains they made, for
example in the summer of 1936. Until late 1936, they were unimagina-
tive in their choice of policies. Only in the autumn of 1936 did they begin to switch systematically to a policy of flexible alliances.

This conservatism was a main cause of their political isolation and
their inability to expand their forces. It can partly be explained by the
fact that neither Xiang nor Chen was a local man, and the main local
leader in Ganyue, Li Letian, died early in the Three-Year War. The
Ganyue leaders, especially Xiang Ying, lacked the necessary feel for local
conditions and the political, social, and kinship networks that sustained
stay-behinders in other regions. Xiang and Chen's main achievement
was to stay alive and keep intact a small core of veterans; throughout the
Three-Year War, their emphasis was on survival, and they were seldom
able to launch initiatives of the sort that reinvigorated rearguards elsewhere. They were isolated for more than two years from the Party's national leaders. "At times we believed our western armies had perished,"
said Xiang Ying.[119] It was only after the Liang Guang crisis that they
learned clearly about the united front,[120] and even later that they
learned the precise details of the new policy toward the Guomindang.

## APPENDIX: CHEN YI, POEMS, 1935–40

In a book that strives for objectivity and dispassion, this appendix is exceptional, for in it Chen Yi, nerve of the soviet nation, speaks from the

heart about how it felt to fight the Three-Year War. It is no clinical photograph, but a portrait of the adventures of Chen's impassioned soul, a yin aspcct in a yang book.

Chen Yi wrote these poems in bivouacs or in the heat of battle and stored them in notebooks or in his head. The poems treat the span of events covered in this book: the collapse of the soviet, living and fighting in the wild, coming down from the mountains, entering the plains, and meeting up again with old comrades after many years of separation, when, in the autumn of 1940, the Eighth Route Army and the New Fourth Army finally joined forces in northern Jiangsu. Chen's poems are the secret history of the Three-Year War, its lunar echo, its human counterpoint.

Chen Yi was not a great poet, but in China his poems are widely considered to be the best of the genre jokingly referred to as "generals' poetry." Many high officials of the Chinese Communist Party, emulating Mao, dabbled in traditional verse, but few mastered its techniques. Chen's poems are not the "cogs and wheels" of revolution that Stalin ordained as the role of literature. Rather, they are a private record of despair, hope and defiance. Chen's poems are less natural and flowing than Mao's, and their imagery is more contrived, but in them Chen lives up to his reputation as the Chinese Communist leader with the biggest heart.[21]

### In Mourning for Comrades Ruan Xiaoxian and He Chang

Among our comrades
Ruan and He may be called virtuous and able.
Ruan was well known in southern China,
He's name was famous in the north.
In planning and checking they were diligent and tireless,
in administering they had authority and influence.
I am grieved that when we tried to crack the ring
they fell, and only I survived.

April 1935

### Climbing Dayu Mountain

[Written in the autumn of 1935, when Chen Yi got news of the Tanggu Agreement.]

The sky lowers on Dayu Mountain,
storms over Europe and Asia cloud my eyes.
Traitors have sold the last handful of our soil.
The sky fills with red banners raised among war's
    beacons.

### Bivouacking

Storm-lashed and homeless
we sleep in the wild and every day change base,

with nothing but cold food to still our hunger.
Quietly we catch lice among the mountain flowers.
Pebbles can fill the sea of blood,
we rejoice that our distant army crossed the Jinsha.
As we peer out into the long lampless nights,
our hair grays with the anguish of our love for China.

Spring 1936

### Guerrilla Fighting

First light nears, our troops wake early.
Dew soaks our shirts and quilts:
it is summer, but still cold.
In the trees, cicadas sing.
Blades of grass cling to our clothes.

The sun is near its noontime peak. Our bellies
beat like drums. For three months
the blockade has stopped supplies.
Counting the grains of rice,
we boil wild vegetables.

The sun is setting in the west. We sit
and talk of war. We have no news
of our liaison man. He left at dawn.
He should be back by now. We strike camp.

Night marching is a test of fortitude. For two weeks now
it has rained relentlessly. Tentless, we camp
beneath a spreading tree.
Sleep does not come easily.

The weather clears. We bivouac
under the beaming moon. Breezes speed our sleep.
Ten thousand pines shield us from the sky, like clouds.
We dream of the enemy.

Speak in whispers, do not laugh or joke.
Beyond the woods lurk spies.
Before, coughing betrayed our whereabouts.
By sincerely recognizing our mistakes, we can improve.

We sigh for lack of grain. For months on end
we've fed on nature's store.
In summer months we eat wild strawberries,
in winter months bamboo.
We chase wild boar across the mountains
and snare huge snakes.

Be tactical, angle with confidence.
Fight when the enemy won't,
don't when he will;
then we're his master.

The mountain is surrounded and besieged.
Trees go up in flames. The enemy
slaughters us in our thousands; we resist.
We shall fight and fight.

Do not complain; march steadily on.
The Japanese have overrun our country from the north,
but our men have crossed the Jinsha River.
The Resistance will win.

Depend on the people, never forget their support.
They are our parents, we their good sons
in the fight.
The revolution will advance from strength to strength.

Study hard, and pity those who lag behind.
Let us refine our skills,
so that another year
we can march victoriously forward.

Summer 1936

### On My Thirty-fifth Birthday

In 1936 I was leading the guerrilla struggle in the Wuling Mountains in
Gannan and went through hard times. In August I became thirty-five
and wrote this poem to express my feelings. [Chen Yi's note]

Our main army has marched splendidly west,
while for us in the south war breaks out again.
Half the fatherland is drowned in blood,
many of my good friends lie in their graves.
Enemies track and attack us night and day.
By luck I am still alive;
ten thousand died as heroes.
When carried to extremity, everything must change;
the earth will turn and redden.

### Three Stanzas Written at Meiling

In the winter of 1936, we were besieged at Meiling, and I lay wounded
in the bushes for more than twenty days. Not expecting to escape, I
wrote these three stanzas and kept them in my pocket. But the siege was
lifted. [Chen Yi's note]

What if my head falls now?
Revolution is hard; it takes a hundred battles.
I shall rally my old comrades in the nether regions,
a mighty host to kill the King of Hell.

Beacons have blazed in the south ten long years;
this head of mine may dangle from the city gate,
but you who live on must make redoubled efforts:
news of your victories will be our paper coins.

This revolution has been my home;
though heaven rains blood, slaughter must sometime end.
Today the just cause claims our lives,
sowing flowers of freedom over all the earth.

### To Friends

In the spring of 1937, the Japanese were daily stepping up their plans
to invade China. At the same time, the Guomindang reactionaries carried out an even more frenzied "campaign of annihilation" against us. I
was leading the guerrilla struggle in the Wuling Mountains. The Red
Army main force had marched west to Shaanxi and Gansu; news was
hard to get. Comrades Ruan Xiaoxian, He Chang, and Liu Bojian had
been sacrificed one after the other. Nightly they came into my dreams.
In death as in life, our comradeship has never changed. My guerrilla
comrades were scattered here and there in small groups, so I wrote this
poem to let them know my feelings. [Chen Yi's note]

Wind and rain soak our clothes.
We hide by day and march by night,
scarcely ever meeting others.
Whom can we ask for news of Shaanxi and Gansu?
Ghosts of dead comrades reach me in my dreams.
Even innocent relatives and friends are tyrannized,
the common people drown
in a sea of troubles.
Brother fights brother, while the invader grows fat.
Renegades and traitors should be put to death.
On the southern front the nation's fate is in our hands.

### Lines Improvised While Coming Down from the Mountains on the Occasion of the Second United Front between the Guomindang and the Communists
[To the tune of *Shengchazi*]

After ten years' war
Nationalist and Communist collaborate again.
As I recall past fallen comrades
tears stain my sleeve.

Our main task is to resist Japan,
but our salvation hinges on democracy.
We should insure ourselves by swearing that
we won't behave like Chen Duxiu.

                                                    August 1937

### Arriving at Gaochun for the First Time during the Eastern Expedition

Ripples reflect the sun's rays.
Countless creeks and rivers break the land.
A small boat floats slowly by,
the people as if painted on it.
In the midst of war, peace.

Willows bending on the river pattern the shafts of light.
Peasants take supper, talking of mulberry and jute.
When our soldiers' boat arrives
people suspect that we are Japanese.
When they learn that we are their compatriots
they talk and laugh with us.

This is my first time in Jiangnan.
For twenty years I've dreamed of Suzhou.
Today I sit beneath the sail and gaze
at hills and water everywhere.

I pass freely through the reeds and rushes,
fires of fishermen reflected in the waves.
Lookouts give the signal, men awake
happy to find themselves in Gaochun at midnight.

                                              June 1938

### Ten Years

[This is Chen Yi's draft of the New Fourth Army song. It is followed by
the collectively rewritten official version.]

In the glorious ranks of the Northern Expedition
people remembered our respected name.
Inheriting the revolutionary's martyr spirit
our isolated troops were tempered
and steeled in the Luoxiao Mountains of the south.
The voice of revolution, loud and clear,
was heard abroad and in the villages.
We saw the vanguard march ten thousand miles to fight Japan
and stayed behind to keep the struggle going
so that we could eventually reunify our nation.
Like cocks at dawn we issued the great call
to fight Japan.

We started amid the wind and snow and pitched our tent
in the deserted mountains, hardship tempered us;
for three years we were cut off from the world,
but this increased our courage and our will
to carry on alone.
In long years of ambushes and maneuvering
we linked guerrilla war with secret work.
Our only reliance is on the people,
we are the son, they the mother;
they are the furnace of our iron discipline.
Today we leave to fight Japan:
the bandit enemy is truly scared.

We flit to the north and the south of the Chang Jiang
and penetrate enemy lines.
Our resistance banner flutters outside Nanjing's walls.

We are politically united, living and dying for each
    other.
It is this that inspires the people under enemy rule
to confidence in final victory.
We thread the Japanese blockade
and engage the enemy in his city forts.
We fight at night
hand-to-hand with bayonets,
torching the enemy lair.
Small wins accumulate and become great victories.
First stalemate, then on to the counteroffensive.
Strike with lightning speed, wipe out the Japanese!
March on, march on! We are the New Fourth Army Ironsides!
Lift high the flag of the new China, and march on!

March 30, 1939

### The New Fourth Army Song

During the glorious Northern Expedition
our names were written in blood
outside the city walls of Nanchang.
We fought alone in the Luoxiao Mountains,
upholding the achievements of our martyrs.
We fought a hundred thousand battles
in the wind and snow, hungry and cold.
We marched a hundred thousand marches
through the bare mountains, camping in the wilderness.
We acquired a rich experience of war
and tempered our spirit of sacrifice.
For the welfare of society and the survival of our nation
we have persisted in the fight.
We rallied from eight provinces to form an iron current.
March east! March east!
We are the New Fourth Army Ironsides!

We march freely to and fro
on both banks of the Chang Jiang and the Huai;
piercing deep behind enemy lines,
we have won a hundred fights.
Everywhere our battle cry is heard.
We should attack bravely
to destroy the enemy;
we should raise our voices high
to rouse the people.
Develop the excellent traditions of our revolution
and create a modern revolutionary new army
for the welfare of society and the survival of our
    nation.

We must consolidate our unity and persist in struggle!

Resist the invaders and reconstruct the country,
hold high the banner of independence and freedom!
March on! March on!
We are the New Fourth Army Ironsides!

                                                        1939

*Reunion with Comrades of the Eighth Route Army Sent South,*
    *Some of Whom I Have Not Seen for More Than Ten Years*

Few survived the ten years' war
but now I am reunited with some comrades;
we ride back side by side to camp.
Who controls the Chang, Huai, Han, and Yellow Rivers now?
Red flags flutter throughout the October sky.

                                              November 1940

# Minxi'nan:
# Mountain Marxists

• ◆ •

Fujian (Min) is a maritime province locked off from China's interior by an almost unbroken chain of mountains (the Wuyi) whose passes are few, high, and difficult. In the old days, these formidable barriers shielded Fujian from the mainstream of Chinese politics and culture. Not only were the threads slight that bound it to the rest of China; so too were the links between its parts. Of its many rivers, only one, the Min Jiang, was navigable deep into the rocky hinterland. Of Fujian's people, all but 1 percent are Han Chinese, yet a great profusion of cultures and mutually unintelligible tongues flourishes in its separate valleys. All but 5 percent of its surface is mountainous: per person, less of Fujian is cultivable than of any other Chinese province. Because of its resulting poverty, its people for centuries have looked to the sea and beyond for a living as pirates, pilots, smugglers, and traders: a living in which, says Meskill, "unorthodoxy and illegality co-mingled."[1] But Fujian's cellularity has generally prevented the emergence of strong regionalist movements.

In the south of Fujian in the 1930s, ancient pines, larches, and firs coated the hills and mountains, which abounded in endemic species and even families of vegetation. Jungles of bamboo, tree fern, sword grass, and brambles choked the ravines to a height of ten feet and gave cover to the muntjac or barking deer and to a great variety of cats, civets, and other viverrids. Tigers stalked through twisting tunnels pressed into the tangle of grass and thorns; traders who climbed the higher slopes in search of porcupine quills and the bony scales of the pangolin shouted as they went to scare off these and other dangerous predators. The summer can be swelteringly hot and humid, as moisture is borne in by the sea winds; but the mountain winter can be raw and damp. In the first

half of the century—but probably less so today, after decades of deforestation—the forests were alive at night with the scurry of feet, the bark
of the muntjac, the yelp of the fox, and the roar of the tiger and the
leopard. Each mountain dawn was greeted by a great shriek of birdsong
and by the wails and squeals of monkey packs swinging through the trees
or up sheer rock walls.

It was in such forests that the Communists of Minxi'nan, or southwestern Fujian, spent much of their time in the three years after 1934.
Whenever possible, they moved down into the valleys and onto the small
coastal plains, but the granite and clay hills around Xiamen are generally bare of vegetation and offered little cover from pursuers.[2] The counties in which guerrillas were most active were Shanghang, Yongan,
Longyan, Liancheng, Yongding, Pinghe, Raoping (across the border, in
Guangdong), Yunxiao, Zhangpu, Nanjing, and Zhangping (map 5).[3]

## THE BACKGROUND TO THE THREE-YEAR WAR

Before 1949, Fujian was a province of dissidents and rebels; the Fujianese were a "bold and lawless race," according to the botanist Robert
Fortune.[4] In late 1933, powerholders in the province declared the Fujian People's Revolutionary Government in opposition to Chiang Kai-
shek; even after the defeat of this government in January 1934, support
for its ideas lingered in corners of Fujianese society. At the time of the
revolt, Communist leaders in Jiangxi failed to back the rebels, and local
Communists had few direct links to them after January 1934. But after
its collapse, there were instances of dissident Nationalists providing
Communists in Fujian with arms and men. Leaders of the defeated
revolutionary government organized a "Party of Production and the
People" that was friendly to the Communists and criticized Chiang's
campaign against the Soviets.[5]

Communist accounts of the Fujian Incident portray it as a military
action without strong local roots. They criticize its leaders for "not daring to mobilize the masses" and describe the dissident party as a ragbag
of bourgeois cliques. But at the height of the rebellion, tens of thousands
of soldiers, local officials, and members of local organizations massed in
its support in Fuzhou, Longyan, Xiamen, and other cities. The rebellion
gave urban Communists the chance to become openly active and lessened the pressure on Red troops in rural areas. Party morale strengthened during the rebellion, even in places where Communists were
unaware that it had happened. In southern Fujian, Communist guerrillas took advantage of the crisis to give land to ten thousand people. According to a recent study, the revolutionary government created a "democratic climate" in Fujian that aided the Communists' struggle after

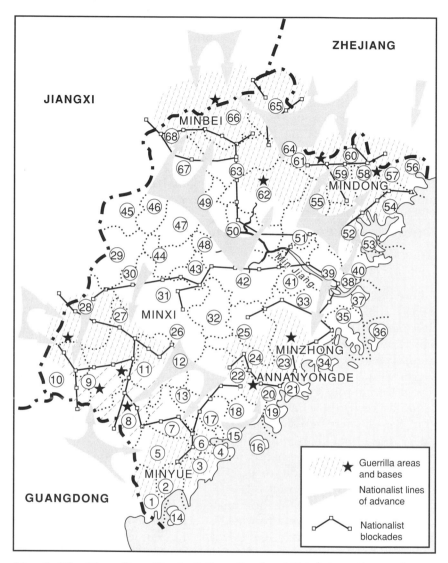

Map 5. The Three-Year War in Fujian, October 1934–July 1937. *Based on a map in Liao Kaizhu, ed., 1986.*

1934. Its impact explains in part why guerrillas in Minxi'nan campaigned with some success in 1937 among Fujianese businesspeople and intellectuals on their political demands.[6]

This dissidence at the top had its match in Fujian's folk tradition. Outlaws and rebel sects were active everywhere in Fujian. Many religious sectarians opposed the Communists; some—especially those whose teachings and leaders had come from Taiwan[7]—supported the Japanese, but others came to form one of the Communists' main bases in the Three-Year War.

Though Fujian's political history under the Guomindang was in many ways peculiar to the province, one of its most pressing problems in the 1930s would become the burning issue of China's national politics in 1937: Japanese aggression. South of the Great Wall, for some years this issue truly burned only in Fujian. In most of China beyond the northeast, the Japanese invaders were perceived before 1937 only as a distant threat; not until the mobilizations of late 1935 did Japanese imperialism become an issue to be disputed on the streets, and not until 1937 did it engage more than a tiny radical minority. In Fujian, however, which had a long history of anti-imperialist movements, the Japanese exerted direct and constant pressure. After seizing Shenyang in 1931 as a step toward

*Key*

| | | |
|---|---|---|
| 1. Zhao'an | 23. Xianyou | 46. Taining |
| 2. Yunxiao | 24. Yongchun | 47. Jiangle |
| 3. Zhangpu | 25. Dehua | 48. Shaxian |
| 4. Haicheng | 26. Shuangyang | 49. Shunchang |
| 5. Pinghe | 27. Liancheng | 50. Nanping |
| 6. Longxi | 28. Changting | 51. Gutian |
| 7. Nanjing | 29. Ninghua | 52. Ningde |
| 8. Yongding | 30. Qingliu | 53. Luoyuan |
| 9. Shanghang | 31. Yongan | 54. Xiapu |
| 10. Wuping | 32. Datian | 55. Pingnan |
| 11. Longyan | 33. Yongtai | 56. Fuding |
| 12. Zhangping | 34. Putian | 57. Zherong |
| 13. Hua'an | 35. Fuqing | 58. Fuan |
| 14. Dongshan | 36. Pingtan | 59. Zhouning |
| 15. Xiamen | 37. Changle | 60. Shouning |
| 16. Jinmen | 38. Fuzhou | 61. Zhenghe |
| 17. Changtai | 39. Minhou | 62. Jian'ou |
| 18. Tongan | 40. Lianjiang | 63. Jianyang |
| 19. Jinjiang | 41. Minqing | 64. Songxi |
| 20. Nan'an | 42. Youxi | 65. Pucheng |
| 21. Huian | 43. Sanyuan | 66. Chongan |
| 22. Anxi | 44. Mingxi | 67. Shaowu |
| | 45. Jianning | 68. Guangze |

occupying the whole of northeastern China, they became increasingly active around Xiamen. A lively anti-Japanese political movement sprang up in Fuzhou, Xiamen, and Zhangzhou in the early and mid-1930s.[8]

Xiamen was a main base from which Taiwan was settled, and it kept its links to the island even after the Japanese took over Taiwan in 1895. From Taiwan, the Japanese strove to set up a Hua'nanguo, or south China state, just as they had set up a puppet Manzhouguo in China's northeast. Local criminals and Taiwanese gangsters with Japanese citizenship were enlisted to promote an "autonomy" campaign by organizing associations and armies in Minnan (southern Fujian). Collaborationist organizations went virtually unchecked; by the time the Japanese renewed their pressure on Xiamen in 1936, their supporters had become an effective fifth column in the region.[9]

Apart from this political and military pressure, the Japanese occupation of Taiwan harmed the Fujianese economy, which could not compete with Japanese or Taiwanese imports. The market for Fujian's traditional products—tea, timber, mushrooms, bamboo shoots, sugar, and especially native paper and tobacco—shrank dramatically after 1895, putting large numbers of people out of work. By 1936, Fujian's imports exceeded its exports by 38 percent; in Minxi (western Fujian), even daily needs like cloth, oil, salt, and medicine were imported. Powerful firms in Xiamen came increasingly under the control of Japanese, who also ran newspapers, schools, and hospitals. Japanese political delegations, tour groups, and representatives of mining and quarrying companies constantly visited Fujian, which, according to Communist propaganda of the 1930s, was "in Japan's pocket."[10]

Ch'en I, sent to Fujian by Chiang Kai-shek in early 1934 to quell the Nationalist rebels, stayed on as governor of the province until 1942. Far from resisting the Japanese, Ch'en fronted clandestine trade with them. "In the period of Chen Yi's [Ch'en I's] governorship," wrote George H. Kerr, "the Province of Fukien [Fujian] was systematically looted. Hotheaded students demonstrated, rioting broke out again and again, and Chen Yi reacted without mercy. The brutality with which students were tortured and killed in Fukien set something of a record even for China."[11] The Communists' call for resistance to Japan won wide support. After 1935, their Xiamen Association had members in many schools and colleges and could stage large demonstrations in the city. Communists in Xiamen set up a whole series of anti-Japanese committees, including a League for the Liberation of Taiwan.[12] By the time Japanese aggression had become the central focus of Chinese politics, the Communists of Minxi'nan were well equipped—with arguments, tactics, and networks—to organize against it.

Minnan lies at a main junction of the great sea lanes of east and southeast Asia and has strong ties to the cosmopolitan Chinese societies of the Nanyang and to Hongkong and Taiwan.[13] In the early part of the century, new and radical ideas flowed into the region to give modern form to its rebel temperament and unorthodox tradition. The Communist movement began in Fujian in the early summer of 1925, four years after the Party's founding; it soon flourished. Communist pioneers started their agitation in the treaty ports of Fuzhou and Xiamen, but in early 1926, Party workers spread to Minxi, where the movement sank its deepest roots. Because Minxi and Minnan border on Guangdong, the hotbed of Nationalist revolution in the early 1920s, politics here were more turbulent during the Great Revolution than in other parts of Fujian. In 1919, young patriots in Longyan, the birthplace of many important Communist leaders, and in other towns of Minxi read Beijing journals of the May Fourth Movement and set up their own journals and study groups. In October 1921, a progressive organization was founded in the region. By 1926, large numbers of local youth had been convinced by the Communists' explanation of the region's social and economic decline. When, in October 1926, the eastern route of the Northern Expedition crossed from Guangdong into Minxi, it was preceded by political workers who rallied local militias against the Fujian warlords. The expedition passed through several areas that later spawned strong Communist movements, including Longyan, Yongding, and Changting.

The sudden collapse of the warlord regime in Fujian removed constraints on Communist organization in the province. In October 1926, a Special Committee of the Party was set up in Minnan under Luo Ming. This body was temporarily knocked out during the counterrevolution of April 1927, when many Communists were killed in Minxi'nan, but within months it was restored. In July 1927, Zhang Dingcheng, a student of Chinese medicine, went home to Yongding after taking part in Guangdong's Dabu rising and set up a Party branch and a peasant movement while teaching at a local school; a year later, he led thousands of peasants in an Iron-and-Blood League to storm Yongding jail. In August 1927, insurrectionaries fleeing south after the failure of the Nanchang Uprising rebuilt the Communist network in parts of Minxi and left behind fifty rifles. Within months, the number of Party members in Longyan alone had grown from twenty-five to 150. In December, the Special Committees of Minnan and Minbei (northern Fujian) merged to form a Provisional Committee for the province as a whole; after unsuccessful local risings and agitation on land rent, loans, and taxes, Minxi acquired its own Special Committee (in July 1928) and its own army, the Nineteenth Division of the Seventh Red Army.[14]

## A PARTY OF LOCAL PRAGMATISTS

Though soldiers played an important role in founding the Communists' early base in Minxi, this base was not imposed by outside armies but grew up mainly through the efforts of homegrown Communists like Zhang Dingcheng, Deng Zihui, Luo Ming, and others who led political movements and guerrilla units in the region in the early 1930s and during the Three-Year War. When the Zhu-Mao army fought its way east into Minxi in March 1929, bringing soviet power to Changting and other towns, it built on foundations laid by local leaders. Even before the arrival of Mao and Zhu, the Communist Party had 755 members in six counties of Minxi; by July 1929, it had three thousand.[15] In the first three to four months of 1929, Minxi Communists opened up new areas of work in Yongding, Longyan, Shanghang, Changting, and Pinghe and connected their five main bases. This arrangement created excellent conditions for growth after the arrival of Mao and Zhu. From this base in Minxi, the Communist main force secured the adjoining area of Gannan, where it eventually set up its capital (at Ruijin).

In Minxi, especially in Yongding, the Party's social base was stronger than in neighboring Gannan. In Gannan, political power was seized principally by armed outsiders. When the Zhu-Mao army first entered Gannan in early 1929, it even had problems in finding guides. "At that time, the masses generally did not understand the Red Army," wrote a historian of the Central Soviet. "They were not keen to guide it."[16] In Minxi, in contrast, the Party had six county committees by late 1926. The path to political power was paved by a series of uprisings organized by local Party leaders. Six such uprisings took place between March and June 1928, and by August 1928, soviets had been set up in a dozen or so villages. Local Communists set up guerrilla units on the basis of these revolts. That is why Mao and Zhu crossed quickly into Minxi after entering Gannan, and why they returned to Minxi after their second sortie into Gannan. So although Minxi eventually became the southern sector of the eastern flank of Gannan's Central Soviet, its soviets preceded Gannan's, as did its Special Committee (set up in December 1926, ten months before Gannan's). Its Communist movement probably started out with more local cadres than Gannan, and it began land revolution sooner.[17]

Land revolution started in Minxi even before the Party center or the Provincial Committee in Fujian issued specific directives. Deng Zihui, Zhang Dingcheng, and other Minxi leaders decided on policies and methods of reform at a roundtable discussion with a wide spectrum of villagers, ranging from rich peasants to hired hands. The method they chose was *chouduobushao* (take what is in excess and supplement deficits), which they first tried in one small area and then extended to nearly twenty thousand people in Xi'nan. They adapted it to local conditions and avoided extreme measures: characteristic procedures, as we shall see, of the Minxi Communist tradition, especially after 1934, when "native Communism" again came to the fore in the region.

The main land revolution in Minxi was launched after the First Congress of the Minxi Committee in July 1929, a key event in the early history of the Minxi base. It was attended by Mao and other Fourth Red Army leaders, back in Minxi after their brief excursion into Gannan. After the Congress, eight hundred thousand peasants acquired land in just a few months. The membership of the Communist Party trebled to ten thousand people organized in five hundred branches, seven county committees, and fifty-three district committees. By June 1930, soviet governments had been proclaimed in six counties, sixty districts, and 557 villages, with a reported population of 850,000. The base was by now strong enough to withstand the combined attacks of Cantonese and Fujianese forces starting in January 1930.

In March, Minxi formed its own main-force Red Army, the Ninth (reorganized in May as the Twelfth), with six regiments and more than three thousand troops under Deng Yigang and Deng Zihui. In June, after the Fourth Red Army had again returned to Changting, Mao, Deng Zihui, and Zhang Dingcheng called a joint conference of the Fourth Red Army and the Minxi Committee. This conference passed various resolutions drafted by Deng on the basis of the Party's experience in Minxi and revised by Mao.[18]

Mao valued his links to the Changting and Minxi borderers and sent Deng Zihui to address the Fourth Red Army on Party achievements in the region. The Minxi leaders can best be described as local pragmatists, which does not mean that they considered the interests of the national and local movement to be counterposed. Mao, on the other hand, represented the Party center, but he was a pragmatic centralizer who believed that the future of the revolution lay with the Red Army, to protect which he was prepared to compromise with local leaders. He and the Minxi Communists shared a common mistrust for purists who tried to make the revolution conform to abstract dogmas worked out in Moscow. Mao was not above ditching local allies when the interests of his army so dictated, but for a while, his links to Minxi became close, and Minxi leaders were one of his main bases of support in the Party. While Ruijin was known as Little Moscow, Minxi's Changting was known as Little Shanghai.[19] The names are apt: they symbolize the gap between China's two revolutions, one guided by imported dogma, the other by Chinese concerns. In the early 1930s, many of Fujian's local leaders were temporarily ousted or demoted by the ruling faction in Ruijin, but most reappeared in leading roles after 1934.

Like Mao, leaders of the Minxi Soviet were skeptical about the chances of Li Lisan's insurrectionary line in mid-1930. In July, they opposed the official strategy of marching west toward the Dong Jiang and argued that the newly established Twenty-first Army (formed from units left behind after the incorporation of the original Twelfth Army into the First Red Army Group in June) should first consolidate its position in Minxi and only then spread east toward the coastal cities. For this stand, they were accused of "new rightism," and their views were suppressed. The Twenty-first Red Army marched east, where it was badly mauled; on returning to Minxi in October 1930, it merged with other forces into a New Twelfth Red Army. In Minxi, the local branch of Li Lisan's Operations Committee carried out a "leftist" version of land reform and organized young people to attack temples and smash religious symbols. By the time the Li Lisan line was finally wound up later in the year, military defeats and "leftist" excesses had led to big losses in Minxi, including the fall of Longyan.[20]

In December 1930, the Minyuegan (Fujian-Guangdong-Jiangxi) Committee, incorporating the Minxi Committee, held its First Congress in Yongding, shortly after the closing down of Li Lisan's Operations Committee in Minxi. In Gannan, Mao Zedong is said to have been a prime mover in the bloody campaign to liquidate Li Lisan supporters under the pretext that they belonged to a "counterrevolutionary anti-Bolshevik conspiracy." But in Minxi, Zhang Dingcheng opposed the purging of "Social Democrats" and was accused of "vacillating." Zhang is said to have reported his misgivings about the purge to Mao, who "quickly ordered the freeing of arrested comrades." Mao was apparently acting to defend his friends in Minxi against attack by "leftists" in the newly formed Minyuegan Committee. This halt to the purge stopped the bloodshed, which had led to a flight of population, a loss of territory, and the deaths of several thousand Party members. At the same time, the arch-purger Deng Fa was removed as leader of the Minyuegan Soviet. In 1986, the purges of 1931 and 1932 in Minxi were criticized as "completely wrong," and it was announced that more than 6,300 purge victims had been rehabilitated and their families compensated.[21]

In 1932 Luo Ming, a native of Dabu in Guangdong, just across the border from Fujian, was appointed (perhaps with Mao's help) as secretary of the Minyuegan Committee.[22] The following spring, Party leaders in Ruijin ordered an "offensive" line in Fujian. Luo Ming wrote back asking to be allowed to follow policies appropriate to the special conditions in Minxi. He pointed out that border areas like Shanghang, Longyan, and Yongding were different from areas where the soviet was strong. He said that excessive recruiting had damaged morale both inside and outside the Party in Minxi; he accepted that the Minxi Red Army should expand but opposed transferring it to Jiangxi. It was wrong, he added, to ascribe Minxi's problems to insufficient mobilization, purges, or class struggle; even Stalin and Lenin would be unable to overcome the mood of pessimism in Yongding. Nor would a policy of unyielding resistance restore confidence; on the contrary, battles against the Guomindang's main forces should be avoided. The number of mass organizations in peripheral areas should be cut. Fewer of Minxi's taxes should be "centralized"; more should be left to meet the expenses of the local movement.[23]

Luo Ming was criticized as a petty bourgeois vacillator, a pessimist, a liquidationist, and a flightist. A struggle began in Minxi against the "Luo Ming line." However, he had strong support in the Fujian Party. At a meeting of the Provincial Committee that he attended in March 1933, most said that they did not understand the campaign against him, but a minority opposed to Luo overruled the majority by saying that the meeting was bound by a higher directive. After this meeting, large numbers of officials at the provincial and the county level were purged. Zhang Dingcheng was stripped of his posts, including his chairmanship of the Fujian Soviet, and transferred to Ruijin. Others in Minxi replaced by supporters of the "offensive line" included Deng Zihui, Tan Zhenlin, Chen Tanqiu, and Fang Fang, all of them prominent in the Three-Year War. The purge spread to the Jiangxi Party and the Red Army, where Deng Xiaoping and Mao's youngest brother, Mao Zetan, were among its casualties. In Minxi, a "great majority" of cadres are said to have been attacked as "opportunists." The attacks continued from February 1933 until the end of 1934. They did not entirely stop even after the Long March began.[24]

Today, the campaign against Luo Ming is seen as an attack by Party leaders on Mao's influence in the soviets.[25] They were not yet ready to attack Mao frontally, so they attacked him through Luo Ming. The identity between Mao and Luo is often exaggerated (the attacks on Luo barely affected Mao's position), but on some issues, the criticisms against the two were similar.[26] Between June 1930 and November 1933, Mao visited Shanghang three times and had several opportunities to influence Luo and others in Minxi. After being criticized at the Ningdu Conference in August 1932, Mao spent several months in hospital at Changting recuperating from an illness. During his convalescence, he advised Luo on how to fight the Fourth Encirclement. Luo and others in Minxi, including Fang Fang, stuck closely to Mao's political formulas and fighting style, and Luo passed Mao's views on to local cadres.[27]

The 1931 campaign to root out "counterrevolutionaries" did great damage to the Fujian Party. The "pitiless attacks" on Luo Ming and his supporters heightened the terror. The new "offensive line" drained the soviet of grain and men: in one township in Shanghang, only seven able-bodied men were left in a population of two thousand. Much of the support gained by earlier reforms evaporated as the Party's squeeze on local resources tightened. But though the Party and the soviet in Minxi were ravaged and demoralized on the eve of the Long March, they had started out with a strong local identity that the purges, imposed by metropolitan officials who believed that "there is no Marxism in the mountain valleys," may even have strengthened.

Compared with the region around Ruijin, seat of the Communists' main government, the bases in Minxi and Minnan were less directly steered by the Party center and less uniformly committed to its policies. When some Shanghai leaders passed through Minxi during their retreat to Ruijin in early 1933, they reproached Luo Ming for behaving more like a guerrilla chief than a provincial leader and criticized other local cadres too.[28] Yet though they could remove Luo Ming, and soon did, they could not remove the tradition that he stood for. This tradition, which was revived shortly after the fall of the Central Soviet, was better suited to conditions in the Three-Year War than was Ruijin's centralism. "['Leftist'] areas were quickly recovered by counterrevolutionary forces [after 1934]," concluded Wen Yangchun, noting that in such areas the masses had become indifferent to the revolution. "But in the Longyan-Yongding-Shanghang region [of Minxi] and in other old soviet bases where the 'leftist' line did not rule for long and where its influence was shallow, the masses' consciousness was high; they had a rich experience of struggle and understood how to apply different methods of struggle against the enemy."[29]

In late 1934, Xiang Ying sent exiled Minxi leaders home to keep losses in the base there to a minimum. Very soon, the original core of the Minxi Communist movement was largely reconstituted, and old policies were restored. Most Minxi Communists were local people, said Zhang Dingcheng, and even those who were not, like the Hunanese Tan Zhenlin, were "localized" after the Long March.[30] This continuity in group identity, together with a sounder grasp of guerrilla principles, a more immediate political focus (Japanese aggression), and stronger links to the cities, helps explain why Minxi resisted Chiang Kai-shek's mop-up in 1935 more successfully than other rearguard areas. Another reason is that though Fujian was brought firmly into the Nationalist camp after the collapse of the 1933 rebellion, Nanjing placed less strategic or symbolic value on "rehabilitating" it than on neighboring Jiangxi and devoted correspondingly fewer resources to pacifying Fujian. Finally, the Communist movement in Minxi was not borne in by the Red Army, as in Ruijin, but was "created by local guerrillas."[31] Because of its sturdier, deeper roots, it could hold out longer under pressure than Gannan, which the Red Army controlled better and milked more efficiently until the start of the Long March.

## THE COLLAPSE OF THE SOVIET

The momentous events of October 1934 around Ruijin, when twenty thousand sons and a handful of daughters of Minxi set out with sixty thousand others on the Long March,[32] had less immediate impact on Minxi'nan than on the Central Soviet. At first, Nationalist military pressure on Minxi'nan was weaker than on Gannan. In Minxi, the switch to guerrilla war had started as early as April 1934, when the Red Independent Eighth and Ninth Regiments, as well as other smaller units, were sent to Yongan, Liancheng, Zhangping, and Longyan. Their task was to slip behind enemy lines, even into areas where the soviet movement had not yet reached, and to tie down troops there as part of the complicated series of military movements started during preparations for the Fang Zhimin expedition. Because of the earlier start to guerrilla war and the later start to "bandit extermination," Minxi did not experience the same abrupt transition as Gannan between soviet government and chaos.[33]

In December 1934, Xiang Ying sent Zhang Dingcheng back from the Central Soviet to work for the Provincial Committee in Minxi. Mao, too, wanted Zhang sent back. He told him on the eve of the Long March, "You should return to Minxi, you know the region well. You can hold out there and develop it." Once in Changting, Zhang and three others were sent on by the Provincial Committee to the Longyan-Yongding area to fight guerrilla war and coordinate with "the defense of the soviet." But though Zhang got the commission, he was given no troops to help him put it into practice. Instead, he rallied a handful of Yongding refugees then in Changting and marched off west with eight rusty rifles and a string of hand grenades. Because all towns and most big villages along the way were by then under the Nationalists, Zhang and his team went by mountain paths. Occasionally they came across starving, half-naked Red Army stragglers. Some they sent into the hills as partisans; others they took in tow. By the time they reached Yongding, their number had grown to one hundred.[34]

The roads around Longyan and Yongding were clogged with refugees and their families who had earlier fled to Changting after the collapse of the soviet to the east. Now that Changting, too, had fallen, they were flooding back again. They brought with them chilling tales of White terror in Changting and Ruijin. "Some spread defeatist thinking," recalled the Communist veteran Wu Hongxiang. "This provoked pessimism and disillusion among the masses."[35]

In and around Yongding were the four-hundred-strong Red Eighth Regiment and two hundred Longyan guerrillas. The commander of the Eighth, Qiu Jinsheng, was a native of Longyan, where he had started his political life in a peasant association. Qiu's Eighth was in every sense a local unit: most of its leaders were from Minxi, in particular from

Longyan and Yongding. Qiu had taken charge of the Eighth after studying at Ruijin's Red Army University while recovering from battle wounds. His mission was to break the blockade of the Central Soviet. To help him do so, batches of cadres were detached to his regiment from the Party school, the Red Army University, and other organizations.

Qiu's troops' morale was poor. In the past, they had fought on the periphery of the soviet, where they could dive back to safety whenever necessary. Now they were deep behind White lines, fighting along the highway between Zhangzhou and Longyan. They were troubled by a host of questions. When would they return to the soviet? How would they get supplies? What would happen if they were wounded? Now that they were back near their homes, could they visit their families? Qiu answered these questions and doubts as best he could. He explained that though the area his troops were fighting in was now under Nationalist control, it had once been a soviet; the Party was still strong there and would provide guides and spies.[36]

Zhang Dingcheng's arrival in Yongding stabilized and strengthened the leadership of Qiu's regiment, which spearheaded the Three-Year War in Minxi. Zhang had prestige and authority in the region. He sent searchers to call in Red soldiers hiding out in the mountains. He spoke out against "passive skulking" and persuaded troops to operate in smaller, lighter, more mobile units. By late 1934, the Independent Eighth was more than six hundred strong and had reestablished a base northeast of Yongding; these successes largely dispelled the initial doubts and fears. For the time being, Gannan remained the Nationalists' main target; at the year's end, only one Nationalist division was in action against Qiu, and only two were active between Longyan and Changting. In February 1935, after news arrived of the fall of Ruijin, the Independent Eighth merged with the Longyan Guerrillas and resolved to fight on independently. The Eighth had moved behind Nationalist lines and started fighting guerrilla war several months before the soviet's collapse. The presence in Minxi of this war-hardened local regiment eased the transition to guerrilla warfare.[37]

Around Changting, the Communists adopted an opposite strategy. Changting was the capital of the old Minxi base and, with Ruijin, formed the soviet's twin center. Before October 1934, Changting was the seat of the Fujian Provincial Committee under the "leftist" Wan Yongcheng. In October, Wan fought to defend Changting under the slogan "Not a cabbage, not a piece of meat, not a grain of rice, not a drop of water for the enemy" and ordered the destruction or removal of the town's provisions. After Changting fell, Wan retreated to Sidu in the mountains between Ruijin and Changting. Directly under him were two main-force regiments (the Nineteenth and Twentieth) and various local units, numbering four to five thousand soldiers. In November, after the fall of the Communists' last county seat in Gannan, several White divisions equipped with planes, artillery, and plenty of grain began pressing down on Wan. By December, the Minxi Soviet was just a name; its officials and their dependents had taken to the mountains.

During this period, Zhang Dingcheng passed through Sidu but was immediately sent on to Yongding. He was then criticized by letter for encouraging isolated groups along the route to "leave their posts" and become guerrillas. Wan's treatment of Zhang and other founders of the Minxi base is today described as "sectarian."

Among those who stayed in Sidu was Mao Zedong's brother Zetan, who proposed that Wan's two regiments abandon Sidu and flee south in small detachments to the border between Fujian, Guangdong, and Jiangxi. Wan disagreed and stuck to his line of "pinning down the Guomindang main force" from fixed positions. In the ensuing battles, more than half of Wan's men were wiped out; in April, the survivors were surrounded in Huichang to the east and routed.[38]

The other main Red force in Minxi in late 1934 was the Independent Ninth Regiment, active between Yongan, Liancheng, and Zhangping, to the north of the Eighth Regiment. The Independent Ninth, like Qiu's Eighth, was composed mainly of local people from Longyan, Yongding, and Shanghang. One of its main early leaders was the Cantonese Fang Fang, who took charge in April 1934. Fang's tasks were to ensure that Yongan's steel, cloth, and salt got through enemy lines to the Central Soviet, to harass government road-builders in Yongan, and to build guerrilla bases. Fang was told to set up a military and administrative committee in the Ninth and to operate autonomously. He soon commanded a base along the northern border of Longyan with a population of forty thousand, and he divided land and raised morale with a string of victories. By October 1934, the Red Ninth had 1,500 men.

Other leaders in the Ninth opposed what they saw as Fang's "going independent" and replaced him with Zhu Sen, soon to defect. Zhu, a middle-ranking Nationalist officer who had gone over to the Red Army after being captured, had no experience of guerrilla fighting and opposed Fang's advocacy of it. He also criticized Fang's prediction that Ruijin and Changting would soon fall and sent a hostile report on him to Ruijin. Fang was called to Ruijin for investigation, but he could not get through the blockade and was instead demoted.[39]

So the party in Minxi was still deeply split on the eve of the Three-Year War, though it had important advantages over stay-behinders elsewhere. Apart from the four thousand troops under Wan near Changting, there were up to four thousand guerrillas scattered across the region in small groups. Counting local forces, there were more than ten thousand Red guerrillas in Minxi in late 1934. According to Zhang Dingcheng, more than thirty thousand Communists were left behind in Minxi after the evacuation of the Central Soviet. By April 1935, Wan's troops were reduced to fewer than two hundred, but most guerrillas survived, and their leaders came together briefly to decide new policies and directions just before the start of the Nationalists' first main drive against them.[40]

In mid-February 1935, Xiang Ying had decided that troops and cadres hemmed in around the Renfeng Mountains in Gannan should break out in five directions, including toward Minxi. The Minxi column was made up of former Central Soviet leaders like He Shuheng, Deng Zihui, and Qu Qiubai and a reinforced battalion of the Red Twenty-fourth Division, led by Chen Tanqiu and Tan Zhenlin. The column was attacked even before crossing the border into Fujian. During the fighting, He, Deng, and Qu lost contact with their escort but managed to find their own way to Sidu. There Wan Yongcheng gave them a new escort for the journey to Yongding, where they should either join the guerrillas or go on to Shanghai. Again, their column was attacked and their escort practically wiped out. He Shuheng died; he is said by one source to have jumped from a high cliff, though according to other reports, he was killed.[41] Qu Qiubai was caught, identified by defectors, and eventually shot. "In life there are short rests and long rests," he wrote in jail: "my rest will be long." Deng Zihui, who knew Changting better than He and Qu, managed to escape back to Sidu. There he was reunited with Chen Tanqiu and Tan Zhenlin, who had meanwhile turned up with what remained of their unit. Together they pressed on to Yongding, where, after a fortnight's march and further heavy losses, they finally met up with Zhang Dingcheng sometime in late March.[42]

At around the same time, the Red Independent Ninth Regiment moved south toward Yongding to escape a large Nationalist force that appeared north of Longyan. The proposal to go south was Fang Fang's. Though he had been demoted, losses caused by his critics' tactics had left the regiment on the brink of destruction, and new splits appeared in its command. When Fang proposed to leaders of the regiment that they should go to Yongding and ask Zhang Dingcheng to resolve the issues at dispute, they agreed.[43]

### THE TURN TO GUERRILLA WAR

By April 1935, a small Communist army had gathered in or near Yongding. Besides the Ninth, Qiu's Eighth, and the remnants of Chen Tanqiu's battalion of the Red Twenty-fourth Division, they included several hundred local guerrillas active along the border between Yongding and Shanghang. Further to the south in Minnan and out of contact with these forces was the Red Third Regiment, which between 1934 and 1937 remained in the richer southern tip of Fujian, between the mountains and the sea, south of Xiamen. This Minnan base had been founded by the ten-thousand-strong Red Eastern Route Army that captured Zhangzhou across the Jiulong River from Xiamen in April 1932 and held it till late May; in the wake of the battle for Zhangzhou, one thousand local guerrillas were reorganized into the Third Regiment.[44]

During the Fujian Rebellion, leaders of the Red Third took advantage of the vacuum in Minnan to extend their influence; in January 1934, Huang Huicong formed a Special Committee for the region. This committee was called the Minyue Committee, for though it was mainly active in Fujian (Min), it also extended into neighboring Guangdong (Yue). In late 1934 and early 1935, small units of this regiment were active southeast of Zhangzhou, with orders to link up Minnan and Party bases in eastern Guangdong. After a debilitating purge in March 1935, this Minyue (Fujian-Guangdong) base began to grow and within a year claimed a population of twenty thousand.[45]

Two conferences were held in Minxi in the spring of 1935 to discuss unresolved issues and reorganize forces. A small meeting under Zhang Dingcheng in March unified and simplified Party leadership by setting up a Minxi Military and Administrative Committee, but the meeting failed to settle various policy differences. Leaders of the Ninth Regiment were still under attack for excessively concentrating their forces, fighting pitched battles, neglecting to build bases or mobilize local people, and lacking political flexibility. The meeting postponed decisions on these matters and agreed meanwhile to close ranks against the enemy. It chose Zhang Dingcheng as its chairman and Fang Fang as its political director. Not until the arrival in Yongding in late March of remnants of the Central Soviet escapers did the Communists complete the switch to new tactics.

The key person among the escapers was Chen Tanqiu, who was carried on a stretcher for the last stages of the journey. "Marx's spirit in heaven helped you reach Minxi," Zhang Dingcheng told Chen and Tan Zhenlin. Chen had been secretary of the Fujian Provincial Committee in 1933, possibly as successor to Luo Ming, but he too was apparently infected by Fujian's "wavering opportunism" and lost the job; after the start of the Long March, he is said to have helped Chen Yi overcome Xiang Ying's "leftism." Chen Tanqiu had kept his place on the Central Committee and was named to the important post of people's commissar for food. In early 1935, he was the senior Communist in Fujian; he held cabinet rank in the soviet and had strong local ties. He played an important role in the second meeting of Minxi leaders held in April 1935.[46]

This meeting was announced as the First Congress of the Minxi Party, Government, and Army; Minyue Communists were not represented.

The Minxi and Minyue (Minnan) bases were separated by nearly two hundred miles of Nationalist territory. Normally, Minyue came under the Party's Shanghai Bureau, but now its link to Shanghai was broken.[47] Chen Tanqiu proposed that the Military and Administrative Committee set up by the Minxi Congress should strive to link Minxi and Minyue (Minnan) and should therefore call itself the Minxi'nan Committee, a name that it kept until 1937. By this time, the Long Marchers were already in Sichuan. The Central Soviet had collapsed, and the Minxi Communists had been expelled from their strongholds. The old slogan of pinning down the enemy to protect the main Red Army rang extremely hollow; "there was little we could do by way of direct coordination," Fang Fang later wrote. The new line was defined as "developing widespread, victorious, mass-style guerrilla war . . . in order to await the chance to restore the Soviet area," preserving essential forces, protecting the gains of land revolution, and strengthening ties to local people.[48] The meeting adopted a "double-edged" policy for dealing with government officials in the villages. It mapped out four independent battle zones and set up various independent county committees to spread the new policies to the villages and avoid losses caused by over-centralization.

Units of the Red Ninth, in the second battle zone, were sent south to liaise directly with the isolated Third Regiment, in an effort to give some substance to the idea of a single movement for the whole of Minxi'nan. Previously, communication between Minxi and Minyue had been poor. Few Minxi people ever went to Minyue; the committee lacked even a map of the region. The expedition had to fight its way through practically every village on its journey south and found few people who had even heard of the Red Army. As a result, it suffered losses.[49]

After the Minxi'nan Congress, the leaders of the new committees dispersed, but they set up a communications system based on the old soviet liaison network so that they could continue to coordinate their plans.[50] At the Congress, Zhang Dingcheng was confirmed as chair of the committee by Chen Tanqiu. Tan Zhenlin and Deng Zihui were appointed as Zhang's deputies, and Fang Fang became political director.[51] These appointments resulted in the rebirth of a pragmatic "Maoist" leadership of the sort knocked out in Minxi by the purges.

The First Congress of the Minxi'nan Committee has been the subject of controversy in China. The issue is whether Chen Tanqiu transmitted to it the "spirit of Zunyi." For veterans of the Three-Year War, this question was—and is—of great consequence. A recent study of the Zunyi Conference, held in January 1935 on the Long March, sums up the "two merits" ascribed to it by the Party: "it changed the leadership of the Chinese Communist Party, making Mao the leader of the whole Party, and it changed the Party's political and military line, establishing the correct line to replace the former 'left' or 'right' wrong lines."[52] If true, this assertion would mean that the Minxi'nan Committee departed—as we shall see—often and grossly from the line decided on at Zunyi. During the Cultural Revolution, the difference between the line followed in Minxi and the supposed merits of Zunyi was used by radicals to attack Zhang Dingcheng, Deng Zihui, Tan Zhenlin, and others for opposing Mao after 1934. To be in the wrong on such an issue could cost you—and your colleagues, friends, and kin—the comforts associated with the honorable status of "old comrade." Defenders of Zhang, Deng, and Tan have tried to rebut this accusation by arguing that Chen Tanqiu did not transmit "Zunyi's spirit" to Minxi and that the so-called First Congress was a hurried meeting held, as it were, among falling shells and flying bullets.[53]

The charge that the Minxi leaders disobeyed Mao rests on false assumptions about what happened at Zunyi. Documents show that the conference there criticized only the Party's military line and not its "general political line," which it called correct. The idea that Zunyi marked a clear break with the "leftism" of the Jiangxi period is a myth; the criticisms formulated at Zunyi were quite limited in scope. The spirit of the real Zunyi, with its incomplete attack on Party "leftists," was not incompatible with the patchwork of old and new ideas put together in Minxi after 1934. The defense formulated by friends of the accused leaders is unnecessary. The First Congress can be reinstated as an important meeting of the Party in Minxi'nan.

As we saw earlier, Xiang Ying in Gannan received directives from the Central Party leaders with precise instructions on what to do in old soviet areas. On February 13, 1935, he was told to set up several hundred company-sized guerrilla bands in and around the Central Soviet and to "switch from soviet-area methods to guerrilla-area methods." Xiang discussed this directive with Chen Yi and Chen Tanqiu before Chen Tanqiu left for Minxi. So Chen Tanqiu was able to transmit the "spirit" of the directive to Minxi, where it fell "like timely rain." The meeting at which he did so lasted two and a half days and was attended by some fifteen "major leaders." Chen Tanqiu talked about the "rising contradiction" between China and Japan and outlined appropriate new policies.[54]

Despite Chen Tanqiu's credentials and his knowledge of the Zunyi decisions, not everyone at the meeting agreed with him. Heated discussions erupted about whether the campaign against the Fifth Encirclement had failed and whether it was wise or necessary to change strategy. Some argued that the Nationalist occupation of the soviet was "superficial" and that "armed defense of the soviet" was still an appropriate slogan. This debate echoed others held elsewhere in southern China after the start of the Long March. Red Army officers in several places quixotically proposed "pinning down the enemy inside the Soviet." Having once received the instruction to do this, said Wen Yangchun, "they dared not cancel it." This rigidity was a product of the old regime of "leftist" intimidation. Even the Minxi'nan Congress could not escape this tradition of unthinking deference: its turn away from "leftism" was far from uniform or complete. Still, from the ample clues encoded in the message Chen Tanqiu took to him, Zhang Dingcheng was able to piece together fragments of a new, more flexible and realistic plan.

Later studies and reminiscences have summed up the Three-Year War in Minxi as "the restoration of Mao Zedong's line for the Party," but at the time, Zhang's switch was very much a gamble. He and other southern leaders approached Yan'an in trepidation at the end of the Three-Year War in 1937. When they found that the Party approved of their innovations, it was as if "a cloud had been dispelled."[55]

On his flight through the mountains to Fujian, Chen Tanqiu was wounded. In May 1935, he went to Shantou to convalesce, and from there to Hongkong and Shanghai. His eventual goal was Moscow, where he was to represent the Chinese Communists at the Seventh Congress of the Comintern; but he and Chen Yun did not arrive in Moscow until late August, by which time the Congress was over.[56]

The liaison network set up by the First Congress had its roots in the old Minxi Workers' and Peasants' Correspondents' Societies, which passed on secret messages, escorted cadres, helped obtain military supplies and vital goods, and cooperated with other liaison stations in Shantou and Hongkong. This Fujian-Hongkong nexus became the Central Soviet's main link to the outside world after the line through Xiang'egan was broken by the Fourth Encirclement in 1933. After October 1934, the Minxi line was also broken for several months when defecting liaison officials gave away stations, "base villages," and "contact households," and five Communist shopkeepers in Yongding were killed. The old Minxi Correspondents' Societies were resurrected as Minxi'nan Armed Communications Stations. These stations were directly controlled by the Minxi'nan Committee and staffed by Red Army and guerrilla cadres. They were linked at the center to a general station. Intermediate stations were set up in each of Minxi'nan's four battle zones, served by strings of lesser ones. In addition, each county and district committee had its own station. To avoid unnecessary risks, links between stations were single lines, without intersections. In a year, several hundred people might pass through an intermediate station.[57]

## COUNTERREVOLUTION AND THE RESISTANCE

The decisions and measures of the April Congress were well timed. Even before the Congress, in February and March, Communist units in

Minxi'nan had begun a series of forced marches similar to those made by rearguard units evacuating the Central Soviet—though with less catastrophic results, for they were better prepared for the new conditions. No sooner was the Congress over than one hundred thousand Nationalist troops, organized in eight or nine divisions, having finished off the Central Soviet, started an "extermination drive" in Minxi aimed at wiping out the Communists within three months. These divisions rallied a further hundred thousand local landlord forces and Daoist Great Knives. According to one study, at least forty thousand households were wiped out in Minxi during this campaign. According to another, at least fifteen thousand Communists and their supporters were killed, more than five hundred villages were forcibly evacuated, more than eight thousand houses were burned down, and more than ten thousand farm cattle were taken.[58]

Revanchists set out to undo land revolution in the villages. Village restoration committees were formed in every county, district, market town, and village, in a great pyramid of counterrevolution. Their aim was to restore land to its previous owners in accordance with the Guomindang's Special Land Regulations and to enforce rent collection and the settlement of old debts, including some that went back to the start of land revolution in 1929. The committees began by ordering peasants to put up notices in their fields showing the names of the original owner and tenant so that the land could be registered and a rent set. The restoration committees harassed the families of Red Army soldiers and soviet officials.

Altogether, 563,000 people in 267 villages returned land to its previous owners after 1934. But the Communists put up a dogged and effective resistance to this campaign, in some villages right up until 1949. They trained peasants to answer vaguely or inconsistently if they were asked to name the original owner of their fields, to say that the fields had become too jumbled for clear boundaries to be marked out, or to pretend that the land had always been theirs. At night, the Communists spread leaflets threatening with death any landlords who pressed their demands, and they assassinated prominent members of the restoration committees.

In principle, they chose their victims carefully, putting each landlord into one of three categories: officials, or diehards who would pursue their claims to the end; those with "lingering fears"; and those—a majority—who would take rent if others did, but only if there was no chance of trouble. Ideally, those in the first category were killed; those in the second group were in principle left alone, and members of the third were befriended. Landlords who made no attempt to take back land were visited, praised, helped financially, and encouraged to "transform themselves into members of the toiling masses." If landlord agents turned up in the villages to collect rent or debts, peasants were told to drag their feet or say that the Red Army had forbidden them to pay. If the agents seized tools, household goods, or animals in lieu of payment, drums and gongs would call back peasants from the fields to attack them in areas where the Party was strong. Tens of thousands of peasants are said to have been mobilized in actions of this sort, with strings of villages linked in mutual-defense pacts. When rent or goods were taken anyway, guerrillas attacked the collectors on roads from the villages. Through such measures, many restoration committees were intimidated or out-witted and their aims thwarted.[59]

Even in some places where land was restored, the effects of counter-revolution were mitigated by campaigns to restrict rent and taxes. Land-lords in some villages were persuaded to sell part of their land cheap to the *gongtang,* or village councils. Amazingly, the number of middle peas-ants grew in some parts of Minxi after 1934 as a result of rent and tax resistance.[60]

Communists agitated on other economic issues, too. They organized landless paupers or hired laborers into grain squads or fraternities to plunder local *tuhao.* "In White areas and towns," said one directive, "mo-bilize the masses after dusk to take cloth bags and knives to seize grain, but be sure to set armed watches. After seizing the grain, distribute it. Those who do not take part get nothing." Most peasants were afraid of retaliation if they joined in these raids, so guerrillas distributed grain di-rectly to peasants' houses and warned *tuhao* that they would be punished if they intervened. Party members were expected to be at the fore dur-ing expropriation and to the rear during division of the spoils. When one or two of the poorest villagers had divided *tuhao* property, others could be spurred on to do the same. Ideally, the struggle was to con-tinue—in the words of one declaration of the period—until the land, the forests, and the houses had all been taken over. The Party inter-vened in the smallest disputes to spread its influence: a herdsboy de-manding a New Year bonus, or a hired hand demanding better pay. Communists produced special posters to spread their message to the vil-lages, where their agents displayed them last thing at night and demon-stratively ripped them down first thing in the morning to prove their loyalty to the authorities.[61]

During the drive against the Communists in Minxi, the Nationalists built forts and blockhouses throughout the mountains. It was important for the guerrillas to defeat this Nationalist campaign to immobilize them. At first, they tried to stop the forts being built by firing into the air whenever building parties climbed the slopes or by ensuring that only old people, small children, pregnant women, and women with bound feet reported for building duty, and that their tools were broken and their building baskets leaked. This tactic could not work forever: the forts were built in the end. The guerrillas then tore them down at night, set fire to them, or tunneled under them. This tactic, too, was soon abandoned; it simply increased the burden on people to whom the Communists looked for support. Eventually, the guerrillas settled on "replacing the beams with rotten timbers," or allowing their supporters to garrison the forts.

This tactic had a number of advantages. Guards were supposed to beat gongs whenever they caught sight of guerrillas. To confuse the Nationalist regulars and deprive them of sleep, Communist infiltrators beat gongs in several places at once, at all times of the day or night. The guerrillas themselves could move freely and sleep soundly. They even used the forts as safe houses for their wounded and as bases from which to launch attacks on blockhouses that they had not yet managed to control.[62]

Through this combination of military dispersal and defensive political struggle, the Minxi Communists survived the first extermination drive even though their social base was largely demolished. Only the Red Ninth faltered; in 1934, it had scored some victories under Fang Fang, but in 1935, even after the First Congress, it operated in too centralized a fashion and suffered heavy losses. The second extermination drive, launched in September 1935, all but brought the Communist movement in Minxi to its knees.[63] Before the year was up, the Party was convulsed by betrayals, weakened by demoralization, and reeling from well-aimed blows.

The Nationalist garrisons redoubled their efforts to isolate the guerrillas by besieging the mountains. They rounded up local people in strategic hamlets or in timber and bamboo stockades in the market towns and larger villages. Watchtowers overlooked these camps, and their single exits were well guarded. People leaving and entering had to report to military gatekeepers. The old Communist stronghold at Baitu was sealed by seventy-three blockhouses. Its ten thousand inhabitants were mobilized to deforest the nearby hills. A timber stockade several layers deep was erected at the foot of these hills and hung with thousands of tiny bells. Outside the camps and stockades, farming stopped over large areas in which land had previously been divided. Wild pigs and tigers were said to roam the deserted fields.[64]

During this period, the Nationalists persuaded large numbers of Communist leaders to defect. The most significant defector was Zhu Sen, leader of the Red Ninth Regiment. Zhu had been in on all the Minxi'nan Committee's plans and knew the location of its units. A war of leaflets started between Zhu's agents and the guerrillas. Zhu told the guerrillas that they "had no secrets" and would be hunted down; the guerrillas replied that they would survive and that Zhu's days were numbered. Zhu recruited whole teams of Communist renegades and sent them to live rough in the mountains, where they grew long hair and beards like the guerrillas. Communist assassins were sent to gun Zhu down, but without success. Zhu wrought enormous destruction on Party organization and morale as he rode from village to village in a sedan chair at the head of a regiment of troops.[65]

Most guerrillas scattered to new positions after Zhu's defection. Within days, Chen Xincai, chair of the Longyan revolutionary committee, had defected to Xiamen with two other leading Communists. Local Party networks throughout the region were destroyed. "In the crisis, very many turned traitor," recalled one Minxi veteran. "Traitors and militiamen were even harder to deal with than the Nationalist army. They were crueler and more savage, and they knew our situation and our regulations. They often ambushed us. They killed our supporters, our liaison officers, and the popular masses who supplied us with intelligence, food, and medicine. This led to many serious defeats."

During this repression, one link after another in the liaison chain was smashed. The severed heads of station workers and of members of contact households were displayed in the villages. Those station workers who managed to escape moved from mountain to mountain, banding together in huts or in tiny mountain villages. In some areas, Communists deserted the villages altogether, demoralized by the ceaseless arrests and the return of landlords and *tuhao*. This flight from the villages became so general that the Minxi'nan Committee launched a campaign of expulsions to root out the "pessimism," "panic," "vacillation," "passivity," and "work-slacking" that had supposedly caused it. This witch-hunt, carried out by Communist leaders who themselves had been persecuted as "right opportunists" in the early 1930s, did not resolve the crisis and in fact probably deepened it.[66]

## ON THE RUN

Like guerrillas throughout the south, the Minxi'nan guerrillas chose a course of "sheltering under the big trees until the sky brightens." Many died from lack of salt and medicine. For remedies, they improvised. When their feet were sore from constant marching, they massaged them with bamboo powder gnawed out by moth grubs. In the mountains, even tobacco was often a luxury. Sometimes a whole company of guerrillas shared just one cigarette; often they smoked wild leaves. Finding vegetables to eat was no great problem, for every season is like spring in the Minxi mountains. Mainly they ate their food raw, but sometimes they cooked beside tumbling streams so that the smoke mixed with the spray and was dispersed. They ate from bowls that quickly lost their enamel and turned into blackened iron crocks; for chopsticks, they used twigs.[67]

Fire was for a time the main enemy of these "fire-seeds" of the revolution. During fires started by their pursuers to burn them from the mountains, they hid among the bare rocks, away from the trees. They shielded with mats the fires that they lit to keep warm on winter nights, lest the smoke or glare alert the teams of searchers who entered the mountains disguised as peasants or woodcutters.[68] As they fled through the forests, they systematically removed all traces of their passage, brushing the ground behind them with reed bundles and trying not to disturb the dew or spider's webs or to trample the grass. They buried their excrement and urine and avoided eating pungent roots. Infants born on the mountains could give the guerrillas away by crying. One was hidden deep in the forest; another was suffocated by its mother to still its noise.[69]

For months on end, the fugitives slept among the trees, where they were in danger from wild animals.[70] During the endless mists and plum rains of the early summer, they slept under umbrellas or lengths of cloth tied between branches. Only later, when conditions improved, could they safely build bamboo huts in the mountains. Because they could not afford to sleep too soundly, they stuck smoldering joss sticks between their toes to wake them like alarm-clocks. Sometimes they moved several times a night.

After traitors, snakes, which abound in Minxi, were their worst enemy. They had no antidotes for snake bites. As they moved among the mountains, their trailblazers beat the grass each side of the track to scare snakes away. Survivors claim that tigers, too, were a frequent danger. If the guerrillas used guns against them, they risked detection, so they had no choice—or has memory improved the tale?—but to try to face them down by puffing out their chests and brandishing their fists.[71]

Women played a special role in infiltrating the blockade. They could slip more easily than men into the villages, where they bought flashlights, umbrellas, medicine, clothes, and food. Along the roads, Nationalist troops or local security forces checked peasants returning from the fairs and markets and arrested as suspected Communist sympathizers people who bought excessive quantities. To defeat these checks, buyers organized village men to go barefoot or bare-chested to the market and return wearing new shoes or shirts. For cash, the guerrillas kidnapped *tuhao* and held them to ransom in "*tuhao* huts" dotted around the forests. Women ran a secret factory in the mountains that turned out hundreds of pieces of padded clothing as well as cloth shoes and woven bamboo hats, and they cared for wounded guerrillas in secret sanctuaries.[72]

Women were by then in the great majority in many parts of Minxi, for huge numbers of men had been either killed or conscripted by Reds or Whites. Minxi women had lived for several years under the soviet which—on and off—had propagated free choice in marriage and other feminist ideals. Many women in old soviet areas had attended literacy classes and night schools. During the counterrevolution, these women suffered special humiliations. Many were raped or forced back into "feudal" marriages from which the soviet had delivered them. Female dependents of Red Army men were special targets of the restorationists, who killed or sold large numbers of them. Some escaped to the hills to live with the guerrillas; others who stayed behind in the villages could often be persuaded to work secretly for the Party.

In the old soviet heartland, where "feudal thinking was less," the guerrillas did not think separate women's organizations necessary, but in other places special associations were set up with names like "the Society of Sisters" or "the Goddess of Mercy Sect." The Communists encouraged women to participate in the Party's general campaigns, for example by wailing in front of government offices to protest against land recovery, excessive taxation, road-building, and the stockading of villages. Party members also campaigned on issues of special concern to women. For example, they protested against the compulsory annulment of divorces obtained under the soviet and helped women kill rapists.

Women influenced by the Communists encouraged their menfolk in the militia to connive at the guerrillas' presence in the mountains. The Nationalists knew that the guerrillas needed above all to keep up their morale, so they tried hard to put pressure on Communists through their families. Here, too, the Party's women supporters in the villages were of use. They raised Red Army children and shielded Red Army wives and mothers so that they were less tempted to "call their husbands and sons home to certain death." By protecting Red Army dependents from abuse, these solidarity networks helped to allay the anxiety of the men in the mountains.[73]

The First Minxi'nan Congress had adopted a policy of subversion, not confrontation, in dealings with enemy classes and officials, but some Communists reverted to the old "leftist" ways as the repression increased. The Shanghang leader Liao Haitao killed numerous village, *baojia*, and *mintuan* officials after his house was burned, his property was seized, and a dozen members of his family were murdered in an attempt to force him down the mountains. The killings by the authorities had already alienated local villagers from the Communists, who were seen as indirect agents of the calamity. Liao's revenge killings drove villagers further into the arms of the diehards. On Zhang Dingcheng's orders, Liao stopped indiscriminately slaughtering his opponents and switched to a policy of political persuasion.[74]

Whatever measures the Communists adopted, for the time being they could do little to stop the erosion of their support. To some extent, they were themselves to blame. "Leftist" policies in 1934 had won them many enemies in the old soviet heartland, and Wan Yongcheng's last stand around Changting had inflicted further suffering on the region. After the fall of Changting, the Communists retreated to guerrilla regions further east. Even there, the mood had hardened against them by the summer of 1935. The guerrillas, constantly on the move, had few opportunities to speak to their supporters, and in any case, they were still in the dark about the Party center's further plans. In the event, people pieced together their own conclusions from the reports of refugees ("The Red Army has gone, the soviet has fallen") and from the victory claims of Nationalist generals. Few people any longer believed in the Party. Many threw in their lot with the victors; others collaborated with the government for fear of punishment. A spiral of discord tightened as some guerrillas recklessly shot down villagers who led search parties through the mountains. Later, Communist agents taught sympathetic villagers how to search without finding and to shoot without killing; in the meantime, Deng Zihui tried to repair the damage by compensating the families of the dead.[75]

Fang Fang and his guerrillas lost touch completely with the Minxi'-nan Committee after the defection of Zhu Sen in the autumn of 1935, and they did not restore contact until the following summer. Shortly after Zhu's defection, Fang sent out search parties to collect the sick and wounded of the Ninghua military district's Seventeenth and Eighteenth Regiments, which had been defeated while trying to break through toward the Fujian coast, and recovered forty of these "precious assets." In the summer of 1935, Fang had already lost two-thirds of his main force in battle; by winter, his troops were without food or padded clothes, and their morale was low. By December, he had fewer than two hundred men, whom he divided into four small columns and dispersed. He adopted a policy of extreme decentralization: his guerrillas were equipped to hold out in tiny groups, with individual supplies of rice and salt and two cooking pots per squad. The guerrillas attacked the enemy only outside their strongholds, to prevent reprisals against Communist supporters. They befriended local religious sect or bandit leaders, concluding mutual nonaggression pacts with them on condition that they did not collaborate with the Nationalists, demand protection money from Communist supporters, or rape women.

During and immediately after the collapse of the soviet, sects were extremely active against the Communists in parts of Minxi and Minbei, attacking in mass formation after drinking alcohol and performing religious rites. Among the rearguard's original tasks was to destroy the troublesome Great Knives sect.[76] But in areas like Minxi, hard times led to big changes in Communist policy toward sects and bandits. Fang Fang's chief of staff, Huang Zhiping, a native of the area in which Fang's troops were active, became a blood brother of one "man of the greenwood" who fought alongside the Communists against the Guomindang and let them use two small villages as sanctuaries for their wounded. If the Nationalists entered a guerrilla area in force, the Communists fled to a bandit stronghold for protection. Since many bandits and sect members had ties to local officials at the county level "and were hence an indestructible force," sipping blood with them had great advantages. The Communists set clear limits to these pacts and alliances and maintained distinctions between themselves and the outlaws. They explained their land policy to their allies, told them to stop plundering and robbing local people, and sent propaganda teams into their villages. In one place, the Communist Eighth Regiment won sympathy for destroying bandits who, despite warnings, continued to rob peasants. Communist leaders warned their followers to be vigilant in dealing with bandits, "especially those of a political coloring." Such warnings were not always heeded; excessive fraternization eventually led to the betrayal of Huang Zhiping to the Nationalists by his bandit "ally."[77]

Fang Fang's bandit policy was later singled out as a model for the rest of Minxi. Fang's guerrillas established support points and even a health center and a "general rear" in dozens of small villages. "Once the enemy withdrew," said Fang, "the entire 'world' was still ours." Alongside Red areas, they maintained "gray areas" in which they kept their activities completely secret. In these gray areas, they collected intelligence, sheltered their sick and wounded, and bought provisions. When Guomindang forces occupied the Red "inner line" in August 1935, the Communists slipped safely into the gray-specked outer line, "leaving them to patrol a few mountaintops."[78]

Even so, in the autumn and winter of 1935, the main picture throughout the old and new Red bases of Minxi was one of contraction and retreat. Nationalists controlled the bigger villages, the roads between them, and the main strategic points. The initiative belonged for the time being to the Guomindang, and the Communists were reduced to a strategy of passive defense waged from the mountains or the smaller settlements (of which there were still several hundred) not permanently under government control.[79] The armed actions they initiated were mainly propaganda efforts. When the chief Guomindang "exterminator" had the town of Longyan decked out with lanterns and colored streamers in December 1935 and invited leaders of the village restoration committees to a "victory" parade, guerrillas spoiled his celebrations by a spectacular raid on Longyan military hospital, where they seized arms and medical supplies.[80]

## NEW OPENINGS, NEW POLICIES

The Party's prospects in Minxi brightened a little in early 1936. The second extermination drive had run its course by the end of 1935. Four Nationalist divisions had been moved from Minxi to counter Red Army and Japanese pressure in the north. Because the forces brought in to replace them were far weaker, the local militia units became less cocksure and aggressive.[81] The Communists further improved their chances of survival by switching to policies and tactics appropriate to local conditions and to their own shrunken resources.

Some of these new policies and tactics originated outside Fujian. In late 1935, a messenger of the Minxi'nan Committee brought back documents from Shanghai outlining the new united-front policy started in Moscow by the Comintern; at around the same time, the committee learned of the Red Army's arrival in Shaanbei and of the anti-Japanese student demonstrations in Beijing and other cities.[82] On December 25, the day that the Party's Politburo in Shaanbei approved the call for a united front against Japan and Chiang Kai-shek, Communists in Minxi finished drafting a statement on similar lines. They criticized the Minxi'nan Committee's old approach for making unity conditional on support for the soviet and for treating the anti-Japanese movement in Fujian as if it were a second Communist Party, rather than an autonomous political movement. They urged Party members to break from sectarian isolation and to spread the Party's new message to the factories, the villages, the schools, the White armies, associations led by Guomindang officials, and yellow unions.[83]

In early January 1936, the Second Congress of the Minxi'nan Committee met on a mountain in Shanghang to fix a new course and set new tasks. It criticized the lack of freedom and heavy taxes under the Nationalists. It made much of the Japanese threat to China and especially to Fujian, where the pro-Japanese Autonomy Movement was then spreading, and the complicity in it of "the traitor Chiang Kai-shek." Previously, it had called for the destruction of the *baojia* system, the *mintuan*, and the armies of the Guomindang. Now it decided to work to "transform the enemy's *baojia* into a Red Defense Federation" and to "transform White blockhouses into secret Red ones."

The Communists exploited old personal and political ties to achieve these aims. Many people driven from the movement by the purges of the early 1930s had since begun working for the provincial government, some at high levels. Such people had at first been denounced out of hand; now they became the main targets of this subversion.[84] In some villages, Communist sympathizers and Red Army dependents were forced by the authorities to act as officials of the *baojia*. Earlier, the Communists would have punished them as traitors; now they encouraged Party supporters to rotate such posts among themselves and use them as a cover for Party work. The alliances even extended to Fu Bocui, former commander of the Fourth Column of the Fourth Red Army, who had gone home and organized an armed force now collaborating with the Nationalists. Living in the space between the Communists and the Guomindang, Fu had no interest in seeing the guerrillas destroyed. The Communists sealed a nonaggression pact with him even though he was a renegade, and guerrillas hid in his territory when their own bases were under fire.[85]

Instead of calling for the "dissolution" of White armies, the Party now called for cease-fire agreements and spoke of winning Whites to the resistance. "Go of your own accord to Zhangzhou and Xiamen," it told Nationalist soldiers. "Defend this important gateway into southern China. Fight in alliance with the Red Army. Jointly resist the Japanese dwarf bandits." It addressed classes other than the workers and peasants in its search for allies: the urban petty bourgeoisie, students, merchants, intellectuals, "all parties," even landlords, rich peasants, and "part of the bourgeoisie." "Among the brothers of the greenwood there are no few patriots," it added. As a token of sincerity, the committee grandly renamed its armed forces "Resistance Detachments of the Chinese Workers' and Peasants' Red Army's Minxi'nan Anti-Japanese, Anti-Chiang Army" and told them to "restore the Soviet areas and . . . advance south to strengthen the defenses of Zhangzhou and Xiamen."[86]

Minxi'nan Communists saw no contradiction between campaigning for alliances and agitating on class issues. Wage raises should still be fought for; gains of the land revolution should be defended; land should, where possible, still be divided. Communist statements of the period insisted on the need for alertness in dealing with enemy armies and classes. The struggle against renegades was to be intensified; so, too, was the drive to eliminate counterrevolutionaries.[87]

The Congress, and the military respite, created the conditions for a slight revival of Party fortunes in Minxi in early 1936. The new Resistance Army unified its command, reversing the earlier trend toward extreme decentralization. Fang Fang, after reading in a newspaper about the Long March and the united front, went to Longyan and Yongding to look for the Minxi'nan Committee. By the time he had tracked it down in June, units in all areas were growing again after their earlier losses; the Eighth Regiment controlled parts of an important highway and had restored old bases and developed new ones.[88] To celebrate the respite, Deng Zihui remarried. He had divorced his first wife, who had three children, to protect her against Nationalist reprisals. His new wife, Chen Lan, had joined the guerrillas—as mimeographer, intelligence agent, sentry, needlewoman, and cook—after the Nationalists wiped out her family in late 1934.[89]

To signal its revival, the Minxi'nan Committee reorganized its forces into four detachments; together with various county guerrillas (renamed Anti-Japanese Volunteers), they numbered more than two thousand, according to a Communist source, though a government intelligence report put their number at less than six hundred. The committee restored Party organization in the region, setting up committees at the county and district level; by now, even many villages had secret Party branches.[90] This revival was reflected in the quality of the Party press. Copies of Minxi'nan Communist publications from this period held in the Intelligence Bureau archives in Taiwan are well mimeographed and produced; their covers are well designed; and they appeared far more regularly than Communist publications elsewhere in the south.

The new turn was not immediately accepted by all the Communists. To convince doubters, the Committee organized study sessions in Party branches and slogan-shouting in the villages. To get the message to an even wider public, Red Army officers disguised as merchants or peddlers slipped into the river ports and sea ports of Minxi'nan to scatter leaflets or visit "targets," and they mailed leaflets and personal letters to targets in towns too dangerous to enter. Earlier, they had tried to kill anti-Communist *baojia* officials; now they wrote them warning letters. Earlier, guerrillas had robbed the rich; now they asked for "contributions." If an urban merchant traded across territory they controlled, they "protected" him. Thus they slowly widened their influence and even won the support of some "patriotic personages."[91]

By early 1936, most *baojia* officials in Minxi were double-dealers, and some were revolutionaries; only a small minority were "bad." Guerrillas paraded openly in many mountain areas, and "plainclothes" Communists were active in most big villages, some permanently. The Party took the opportunity to rectify its "backward branches." Some branches, said Zhang Dingcheng, had met the tests of 1935 less resolutely than others. "Hard strugglers and the poor" were propelled into the leadership of inactive branches previously dominated by "middle peasants who dragged their feet and were depressed and cowed."[92]

To carry the message to White troops, the Communists switched from shooting to shouting at them. The shouting was carefully planned. Guerrillas were taught appropriate slogans, clear articulation, and the art of quick retort, as well as a range of retorts for all foreseeable needs.

Some shouted the slogans; others pretended to be Whites and shouted back complicated replies. The guerrillas were trained to project their voices crisply, vigorously, and at the right speed; to use plain words in short sentences; and not to swear back when sworn at. The slogans concerned the need to resist Japan or other issues of importance to Nationalist troops. Party journals published transcripts of such "conversations" between shouters and respondents for readers to study and learn. Men with loud voices were trained to shout in chorus so that they could be heard above gunfire during battles. Before shouting at a blockhouse, guerrillas secretly observed its exits. To wake or alert the soldiers in it, they yelled or fired into the air. If a "fascist officer" tried to shout back counterpropaganda, they urged his soldiers to oppose him. Later, they met to evaluate their shouting.[93]

The Communists also reached Nationalist troops through leaflets. They developed various tricks for getting these into the troops' hands. Guerrillas or local Party members pasted them on electricity poles along roads leading to blockhouses; wrapped them around food or cigarettes and left them near enemy posts; scattered them on the ground around enemy positions and lured soldiers out by firing into the air; slipped them into the pockets of soldiers' laundry hanging up to dry; smuggled them into the towns in bags with false bottoms; put them up in toilets or scattered them at plays and operas; and persuaded friendly *baojia* officials to take them directly to the blockhouses and say, "Look, the Communists have been spreading leaflets again."[94]

The most effective propaganda was the sort that touched on the troops' specific grievances and concerns. This type required inside knowledge. The Party had to know a unit's history, its factional affiliations, the political parties it represented, the places from which it recruited, its pay and conditions, its view of the Japanese and Chiang Kai-shek, its view of the Communists, and the relations between its officers and ranks. Some of this information appeared in books and newspapers, but most could be learned only by direct contact. Catching and interrogating Nationalist troops was one approach, but violence was both risky and, given the Party's new strategy, self-defeating. Instead, the Communists began "mobilizing the masses" to talk with soldiers or eavesdrop on them. This approach, too, was risky. Those recruited to do it were taught to move in on their quarry slowly and in stages and to leave clear lines of retreat. "Do not start talking straight away about the revolution and the Red Army. First, talk to a soldier about his family or his daily life. After several conversations, he should have revealed his attitude to politics. Only then talk to him about the revolution. Having chosen someone as a target and found him safe, cultivate a relationship with him. Swear brotherhood with him. Introduce him to a football club or a mah-jongg group." Party publications carried much advice of this sort, together with fictitious transcripts of conversations in which undercover agitators coaxed White soldiers into revealing their views and grievances while keeping their own beliefs well hidden.[95] The aim (to paraphrase Samuel Griffith) was to place the soldier on a lighted stage, closely observed by unseen eyes in the surrounding darkness. "When he strikes out, he hits the air; his antagonists are insubstantial, as intangible as fleeting shadows in the moonlight."[96]

This investment in techniques of enticement did not pay off as well in Minxi as in northern China, where large numbers of Zhang Xueliang's Manchurians were won over by Communist propaganda. Japanese pressure on Minnan was mounting. Intimidating visits to Xiamen by the Japanese fleet began in February 1935; in August 1936, dozens of Japanese warships sailed there with twenty-eight thousand men aboard.[97] The troops pitted against the Communists were local Fujianese who might have been expected to respond sympathetically to a campaign against Japan. Many had acquired land under the Communists or served in the Red Army; others had fought as anti-Japanese volunteers in the 1932 Battle of Shanghai.[98] But the Communists in Minxi'nan were weaker than in the north, and so they had less attractive power and less chance of capturing Nationalists and "educating" them. Moreover, they had no Zhang Xueliang or Yang Hucheng with whom to ally.

## THE LIANG GUANG INCIDENT AND THE REVERSION TO "LEFTIST" POLICIES

In the summer of 1936, the Minxi'nan Committee plunged into a crisis partly of its own making, from which it emerged shrunken and discredited. This crisis was connected with the Liang Guang Incident of June 1936, when long-simmering rivalries between Chiang Kai-shek and leaders of Guangdong and Guangxi came to the boil. After defeating this challenge, Chiang removed Fujianese divisions from Minxi'nan and replaced them with thirty thousand Cantonese belonging to Yu Hanmou's 157th and 158th Divisions, to cut their ties to Guangdong.[99] This move broke any links between the Communists and the Fujianese, and it removed from Minxi'nan divisions that were native to the province and more susceptible to calls for its defense against Japan. The Liang Guang crisis also caused the Minxi'nan Committee to lurch to the left, a shift that undid most of the gains from the spell of realism and moderation.

Few Communists resisted the leftward turn in the summer and autumn of 1936. Even Deng Zihui, who had earlier spoken out against "narrow sectarianism,"[100] could not stand up against it; on the contrary, he formulated its theses. In the early days of the southern generals' rebellion, Minxi Communists believed that the mobilization of troops in Guangdong and Guangxi on ostensibly patriotic grounds would stoke the anti-Japanese movement throughout China, that large parts of the rebel forces were likely to join the Red Army, and that the war would be long and might even spill over into open war against Japan (though Deng conceded that the rebel leaders were holding back from such a course). Deng concluded that the Communists should try to help the Liang Guang rebels by staging political demonstrations and harassing Chiang's armies. At the same time, they should try to expand toward the south, for only a strong Red Army would hold the generals on course against Chiang.[101]

Policies and tactics should also change during this new period of "counteroffensive": from resisting rent and tax and dividing grain to "the whole program of land revolution"; from legal and peaceful methods of struggle to armed ones; from "turning" blockhouses to "dissolving and destroying" them; from winning over *baojia* to smashing them. In short, said Deng, "Minxi'nan has reentered the period of land revolution," and Minxi'nan Communists must "decisively attack and destroy all those who are enemies of land revolution, even those in allied armies."[102]

Zhang Dingcheng also believed that the victory of the revolution was now around the corner, and he implied that the peasants would start it with or without the Party. In 1935, he wrote, the Communists in Minxi'nan had used "relatively peaceful means of struggle," but now they were using "methods of intense armed struggle." He claimed that the masses in many areas no longer waited for the Red Army to help them out but actively demanded guns from it.[103] Communists who resisted Deng and Zhang's new line were punished. When Qiu Jinsheng, Commander of the Red Eighth, refused an order to concentrate his forces and intercept Nationalist divisions marching west into Guangdong, he was sacked—a decision criticized today.[104]

During this "leftist" interlude, Minxi'nan Communists "restored and expanded" the territory under their control, set up soviets in many villages, and organized fifty guerrilla cells with a membership of several thousand. Between July and August, their Anti-Japanese Volunteer Army topped three thousand. They also restored Party organization, which had been largely destroyed during the second "extermination drive" of 1935. At one point, no Party branch had been left in the whole of Yongding, and only a dozen or so survived in Longyan and Shanghang. By late 1936, the Party had more than three thousand members in Minxi, organized in four hundred branches.[105]

Land revolution was again carried out in many villages, often in its most extreme form of "no land for landlords, bad land for rich peasants." Land already divided was further "readjusted"; some landlords, gentry, double-dealers, and *baojia* officials were killed; and *mintuan* units already secretly under Communist control were ordered to stage insurrections, destroy their pillboxes, and join the Reds. This policy violated earlier pledges and left Party supporters exposed after the swift resolution of the crisis. Communist morale collapsed in some areas, and the number of people "recanting and turning traitor" rose.[106]

In October, units of three divisions of the defeated Guangdong Army arrived in Minnan to replace Central Army units there. Shortly before, guerrilla leaders had decided to concentrate their forces in two columns, each consisting of three detachments, and to become active politically in big towns like Zhangzhou and Xiamen in preparation for all-out war with Japan. These political preparations were later approved, but as the military odds against the guerrillas lengthened, the decision to mass in central columns was rescinded. The guerrillas found the newly arrived Cantonese divisions harder to deal with than the previous Nationalist garrison. The Cantonese were better equipped than the Central Army they replaced; they fought bravely and flexibly in small units and excelled at ambushing; they were good at climbing mountains and at night fighting; and they were prepared to fight to the death, apparently because of "past mistakes in prisoner policy" by guerrillas in Guangdong. They were politically more astute than other armies and made better use of defectors. Their arrival emboldened local reactionaries to attack the Communists, who by late 1936 had lost many of their leaders and were once again deep in crisis.[107]

The Cantonese were particularly good at tracking. They watched for smoke by day, fire by night, the debris of guerrilla bivouacs (such as discarded vegetable leaves in streams or flattened grass), and natural signs of disturbance, like a flock of birds taking suddenly to the air. The guerrillas developed the usual set of countertactics: they wore their sandals back to front on the march, brushed away their footprints, burned only dry wood to reduce the smoke, and tied themselves together with lengths of rope when marching after dark so that they could dispense with flashlights. They, too, observed the movements of birds and animals to avoid surprise attacks.[108]

Though the Party and its detachments had grown between July and September, they had mainly kept to the smaller villages and were later criticized for their "conservative" reluctance to enter larger villages or towns. They were also criticized for letting the united front "stagnate." These omissions were, of course, related. The Communists did not expand quickly into the vacuum left by the departing Fujian divisions during Chiang's mobilization against the rebel generals because they thought the crisis would last longer. It is hardly surprising that cadres told to resume land revolution kept to the villages and neglected the anti-Japanese movement among the educated urban elite. In some areas, they even dragged their feet on land war for fear of provoking new burning and killing in the villages. Party leaders called this restraint "right opportunism" and "tailing after the masses," but it is easy to see why it arose.[109] For several months, the Party in Minxi'nan had steered clear of confrontation and made new friends; now friends made in the spring suddenly became enemies, and reconciliation again yielded to class struggle.

During the left turn, some Communists lost all hope of a quick growth of the movement. One "opportunist" wrote that "the masses have defected and turned tail, they take to the hills whenever they see the Red Army, there's no way of getting food, . . . there's no hope. . . . As soon as the masses see us, they flee in panic." Local leaders launched ferocious attacks on "flightists" and "boundless pessimists" of this sort. "We can categorically assert," wrote one,

> that after the Guangdong Army comes to Minxi'nan . . . there will be no way of preventing the advance and development of our partial counteroffensive and even progress toward a situation of general counteroffensive. The viewpoint of all those opportunists who do not realize their own strength, who do not see the whole situation, and who exaggerate the strength of the enemy must be subjected to an assault of Bolshevik firepower.[110]

At first, the guerrillas cherished illusions in the politics of the Guangdong Army. According to Deng Zihui's biographer, they "continued to overestimate its anti-Japanese, anti–Chiang Kai-shek morale and to underestimate its anti-Communism; so they decided on a policy of first attacking and then winning over, and concentrated three detachments to fight the Guangdong Army at Yongding."[111] But it soon became clear that the Cantonese posed a grave threat to Communist positions in Minxi'nan. Shortly after their arrival, they scattered an entire Communist detachment (the Third).[112] Within weeks, the Minxi'nan Committee had abandoned its extreme positions and reverted to policies similar to those worked out in January 1936. Once again, it recognized that politics, not bullets, was the best way of dealing with the enemy.

This change did not produce the desired effect. Some Cantonese took the Communists' unilateral cease-fire as a sign of weakness and redoubled the attack.[113] In the three months after November 1936, Communists in Minxi fought more than forty battles with the Nationalists, who launched a nonstop offensive to defeat the Red Army in its strongholds. But because the Nationalists were no more capable of seizing the mountains than the Reds were of driving them back onto the plains, a stalemate ensued.[114]

## MINYUE

While the Communists in Minxi were endangering their survival by polarizing the villages and tilting at the Cantonese, in Minyue the Party held to a steadier course and preserved its gains. The Minyue Communists were active after 1934 in Chao'an, Zhangpu, Nanjing, Pinghe, Raoping, Zhao'an, and Yunxiao.[115] To understand their position, we must look briefly at the history of the Communist movement in Minyue. Until the 1980s, far less was published about the Communist movement in Minyue than about its sister movements in other parts of China. This neglect was probably due to the He Ming Incident of July 1937, discussed below, which tarnished the Minyue Party's reputation and led to an information blackout. Recently, however, local historians and Party veterans have begun to publish writings about Minyue between 1932 and 1938. A conference in October 1985 was specifically devoted to Minyue's Three-Year War.[116] The resulting studies and memoirs reveal telling differences between Minyue and Minxi and show that until 1937, the Minyue guerrillas were among the most successful of the Party's southern forces.

The Party in Minyue, like its Minxi neighbor, was staffed at most levels by local people (though Huang Huicong and He Ming, its two main leaders, were outsiders from Hainan). The Minyue Party retained its local character despite attempts by Ruijin to change it. Minyue's Red Third Regiment, founded in 1932 after the retreat from Zhangzhou, had at first been led exclusively by outsiders, with local Communists confined to the Party's lower rungs. In the summer of 1933, a well-known local leader "of bandit origin" committed suicide after his arrest by purist high-ups, and some local guerrillas were killed. These deaths provoked a wave of resentment against outsiders. Many were hacked down; others fled to the cities.

Conflicts of this sort between local Communists and outsiders were common in the early stages of the Three-Year War. They were generally resolved in favor of the locals, who after 1934 held the trump cards. In Minyue, this ethnic conflict got out of hand. It became a main issue in purges in 1935, when many Cantonese outsiders were killed in a purge of "Social Democrats," and in 1936, when more than one hundred Red Army officers and ninety district-level officials were liquidated. After the bloodletting, which devastated the guerrillas at their time of greatest need, "careful attention was paid to uniting outsider and insider cadres," and further clashes were avoided.[117]

The purges were not entirely harmful. The outsiders eliminated by the feuding were natural carriers of the "Bolshevism" that caused such havoc in the Party in southern China. Local revolutionaries had little knowledge of or interest in this style of Marxism. It is no accident that of the various southern bases, it was the archetypically local bases of Minyue and Mindong that were least encumbered by Party dogmas after the start of the Long March. In its "external work," Minyue was virtually free of "leftism" after 1934. Minyue had never been much more than an outer gate on the Central Soviet's southern flank; the combination of guerrilla fighting and pragmatic politics that was the hallmark of Communism in the Three-Year War was second nature to the Communists of Minyue, who did not need to rethink policies after the fall of Ruijin. Even before they realized the extent of the defeat, they were using tactics that only later became widespread in other areas. They had no objection to "collective recantations" where there was no realistic alternative. Instead of shooting at former Red Guards forced to man the watchtowers, or harassing their families, they secretly won them back to the revolution by manipulating lineage or social ties: in Wunan, sixteen of twenty-two blockhouses were "turned around" in this way.[118] Policies of this sort were implemented sooner and more consistently in Minyue than in other guerrilla areas after 1934.

Veterans of Minyue's Three-Year War pride themselves on their mastery of the united-front tactic and their exemplary grasp of the anti-Japanese issue. The 1985 Minyue conference concluded that Minyue Communists achieved "Three Firsts" after 1934: they were the first to do united-front work, the first to set up an Anti-Japanese Volunteer Army, and the first to start talks with the Guomindang.[119] They decided as early as September 1935 that their main project should be to build a strong "anti-Chiang, anti-Japanese" armed force; before long, they had set up Anti-Japanese Volunteer units throughout the region. On December 25, 1935, the day that Mao's famous resolution was passed at Wayaobao, Huang Huicong called for a broad-based anti-Japanese movement in Fujian that would admit "all layers, . . . including those with status." A few weeks later, he spoke to supporters about Japanese pressure on Fujian and said that they should try to win the Guangdong Army to the resistance rather than to dissolve it.

Huang made his case "against closed-doorism" before he had even heard of the Party's August First (1935) Manifesto. His committee criticized those in the Party "who neglect setting up united fronts and who think that in the villages the peasants have no need for anti-Japanese policies." It also criticized "dogmatists" who want to set up soviets and divide the land "even in villages of just fifty or sixty households."[120]

The Minyue Party's local character and its strong focus on Japan's threat to China pose no contradiction. In Fujian, Japanese aggression was not a distant menace or a political abstraction. The role of Huang Huicong was of course central in setting political priorities, for Huang was a leader with courage, clear vision, and creative energy. He promptly postponed agrarian revolution after 1934 and devoted himself to educating his supporters. His committee brought out five regular and numerous occasional publications. He started up his anti-Japanese campaign despite being completely out of touch with the Party center. He was, above all, a pragmatist. He believed, for example, that in promoting cadres "class background is important, but not in itself sufficient."[121]

His early advocacy of the united front reflects his sensitivity to issues vibrant in Minyue. This region, which lies between Xiamen, Zhangzhou, Shantou, and Chaozhou, was an important center of Nationalist rule in southeastern China. During the Great Revolution of 1925 to 1927, Communist influence spread to Minyue from neighboring Guangdong, particularly through Shantou, where Peng Pai became active in the spring of 1925.[122] After 1934, the Minyue Communists were largely cut off from the Party elsewhere. The Ninth Regiment set up a liaison line between Minyue and Minxi after its expedition south in the summer of 1935, but the line was rarely open, and it was more useful to the Communists in Minxi (who received Central Committee documents through it in late 1936) than to those in Minyue.

Minyue Communists, on the other hand, had better links to coastal cities, and through them to Hongkong and Shanghai, than other stay-behinders. Minyue is one of China's main points of overseas migration. Chinese from southeast Asia, Hongkong, and Taiwan played an important role in the early years of its Communist movement.[123] In 1935, Minyue guerrillas set up an extensive network of "economic committees" and "consumer cooperatives" using pooled funds and under the protection of Overseas Chinese and other groups. This network linked the Minyue Party to liaison stations in Zhangzhou and Xiamen. Another important link to these cities was formed by "outsider" Communists who had fled the villages in 1933 to escape the purges.

The strength of this Minyue network, unmatched anywhere in regions of the Three-Year War, can be measured by the flow of helpers that it channeled to the villages: more than three hundred people arrived from overseas to work in the Minyue base between 1934 and 1938, including two hundred from Malaya and Singapore; others—students, workers, and medics—came from Xiamen and Zhangzhou. Though Huang Huicong had independently realized the need for an anti-Japanese united front, news and documents of the united front that reached him along these routes confirmed his view.[124]

By 1936, the Minyue Communists had organized a great army of peasants under the flag of resistance to Japan and could campaign openly in the villages. It is unlikely that anti-imperialism appealed directly and urgently to ordinary peasants, but it certainly appealed to the patriotic offspring of local gentry and to other key sections of the

Minyue elite, who in this most open part of southeastern China had frequently spearheaded the struggle against foreigners. Though Minyue was an economic and political center, its Nationalist garrison was relatively small, with between seven and ten thousand troops. At their peak, the Communist-controlled national salvation associations and peasant associations in Minyue during the Three-Year War had more than thirty thousand members; in addition, seven thousand peasants joined the Anti-Japanese Self-Defense Army and more than one thousand became Red Army guerrillas.[125]

The Party, too, prospered in Minyue in 1936. It had 1,400 members in more than three hundred branches—fewer members by half than in neighboring Minxi, but there the Party had started from a far stronger base in 1934. One-third of all guerrillas were members of either the Communist Party or the Communist Youth League. By 1936, the Communist Party had been wiped out in most White areas; by May 1937, it had only fifty thousand members in all of China, including in the Red Army. By that measure, the Communist Party in Minyue scored rather well after 1934. Elsewhere, Party organization was in ruins; in Minyue, it was largely intact, right down to the district and branch levels.

The Minyue Communists were in direct contact with their Zhangzhou Committee. In January 1936, they were able to organize demonstrations in Zhangzhou in support of the earlier demonstrations against Japan in Beijing in December 1935. They masterminded the infiltration of a drama group that subsequently toured Xiamen, Zhangzhou, and other cities staging performances that propagated the Party line on the need to resist Japan. They even won a response from Chinese overseas. Their strong urban connection after 1934 distinguished them from other stay-behinders. By the summer of 1936, they were one of the Party's most successful branches, with extensive support in the villages, a two-tier peasant army, a flourishing and well-organized Party, and a record of political moderation and consistency.[126]

The eruption of the Liang Guang Incident did not throw Communists in Minyue off balance and destroy their gains as it had done in Minxi. The committee's first reaction to the crisis was to reorganize its forces along more regular lines and fight an ill-advised encounter that cost it sixty-four lives.[127] But it continued to focus on resistance to Japan, especially after it received a copy of the August First (1935) Manifesto at the height of the incident. While the Minxi'nan Committee was calling for a return to land war, the Communists in Minyue were restating their more moderate position. In late 1936, they received news through their coastal stations of the new policy of "uniting with Chiang Kai-shek" and put out a call for the armed defense of Fujian. In the aftermath of Liang Guang, they started to seek direct ties to the Party center. In Pinghe, the

Party-influenced National Salvation Movement, which was strong in 1936, forged links to the National Salvation Movement in Shanghai.[128]

In October 1936, Huang Huicong left Minyue for Shanghai and Beijing, for health reasons and to report to higher Party bodies; he died of illness a few months later, either in Hongkong or in Shanghai. Huang left behind a movement seemingly poised on the brink of even greater victories, but in fact destined for a great defeat. Huang's personal role in directing the movement in Minyue was crucial to its success. Some historians believe that if he had not died, the 1937 incident might have been avoided.[129]

### THE UNITY OFFENSIVE

The arrival of the Guangdong Army in Minxi forced the Minxi'nan Committee to bow to military reality and give up its dream of a "general counteroffensive." This new approach was doubly realistic, for the Cantonese, though good at fighting, were vulnerable to political attack. They could not speak local dialects, they lacked local ties, and they roused local fury by burning down bamboo groves and pine forests in their hunt for the guerrillas, jeopardizing the livelihoods of several hundred thousand papermakers and scores of merchants.[130] The Cantonese had been exposed to anti-Japanese propaganda in the Liang Guang Incident. Many of their officers resented Chiang Kai-shek's efforts to impose his views and system on them and his seizing control, after the incident, of the Guangdong treasury. So the Communists believed that some Cantonese junior officers and men might respond favorably to their propaganda. In its statements, the Party called for unity against Japan; it denounced Chiang's milking of funds earmarked for the Guangdong Army and his imposition of a regime of "fascism" on it. Party leaders hoped that the impact of this propaganda would be reinforced by Red Army advances in the northwest and by the National Salvation Movement in the cities.[131]

A host of Communist letter-writers wrote to officers of the Guangdong Army reminding them of their "glorious" role in the Liang Guang revolt and the treachery of its two main leaders, Chen Jitang and Li Zongren. The Minxi'nan Committee ordered its guerrillas to retreat before Cantonese advances but to send out sniper teams against units that penetrated too far into guerrilla areas. It reverted to a policy of an alliance of all classes and strata, including some landlords (especially small ones). It called a halt to "the struggle to destroy feudalism," to land revolution, and to attacks on *tuhao*, switching once again to "requests for contributions." It freed kidnapped landlords and rich peasants and proposed measures to restore prosperity to the villages, including an end to mountain searches, forced evacuations, and speculation in rice prices. It fired a barrage of letters at the towns and cities stressing the economic harm caused by the Guangdong Army's war against the Communists, the fraudulence of its leaders' anti-Japanese rhetoric, and the patriotism of its officers and men.[132]

Under the new conditions, winning women to the revolution became especially important. Women were already a mainstay of guerrilla liaison, supplying daily needs and caring for the sick and wounded.[133] Now that the Party once again intended to use open, legal channels of political activity, it needed women—and children—in even larger numbers to smuggle leaflets into the towns and to post propaganda letters. The "opportunist" failure to recruit and train women in the past had, said one directive, "enormously lessened the Party's ability to win the masses, and was a main reason for our inability to complete Red Army expansion and stem desertions."[134]

Even the campaign to "eliminate counterrevolutionaries" was suspended and replaced by a campaign to "eliminate [pro-Japanese] traitors." But within the Party, those who espoused "opportunist" viewpoints continued to serve as scapegoats. The main focus of this campaign was the "rightist" Li Hua, but the charges brought against Li were so varied and contradictory that he was probably elevated to a more general symbol for "deviants" of many sorts.

The area to which the committee had assigned Li Hua was northwest of Zhangzhou, on the eastern flank of the old Minxi system of bases, nearest to the coastal cities and to Minnan. Li had the formidable task of bridging the Communist movements in Minxi and Minyue, which, despite the existence of a Minxi'nan Committee to cover both, had never been more than fleetingly linked.[135]

In its campaign against Li Hua, the committee claimed that his detachment had been cut (mainly through desertions) by two-thirds since the arrival of the Cantonese, that local guerrilla cells in his area had disintegrated, that the "overwhelming majority of the masses" had registered with the authorities and set up baojia, that in some areas district committees had collapsed as a result of wholesale defections, and that in several counties political activity had virtually ceased. The committee claimed that these crises had come about not because the Cantonese "used especially harsh methods of repression and were especially competent," but rather because of "internal panic and vacillation," "flightism," and "right opportunism." Li Hua had overestimated the strength of the enemy and underestimated his own, so his cadres had taken to their heels, and the masses had gone with them. He had made matters worse by not "decisively adopting methods of Red terror to suppress those who had already deserted." Instead he excused them, saying that "they are all newcomers to the revolution, if you seize and kill them, politically it will have a bad effect; the best thing is to let them go." (In Ganyue, Chen Yi's approach was the same as Li's.) Curiously, Li was also accused of opposing the kidnapping of *tuhao*, a tactic that the committee had already dropped.

Quite apart from these "rightist" errors, Li Hua's guerrillas were censured for stealing and destroying property, being unruly and ill-disciplined, and engaging in waste, corruption, "departmentalism," egalitarianism, petit bourgeois heroism, and "roaming without attacking." All this, said the committee, was "ceaselessly happening."[136]

What can we make of this jumble of accusations? The obscure campaign against Li Hua had some features in common with other classic campaigns in the history of Chinese Communism. Though its immediate occasion was a real difference of opinion, it was quickly inflated into an instrument for dealing with all kinds of problems and "deviations." Thus Li Hua was criticized not only for "rightist" errors but also for "leftist" offenses like egalitarianism and individual heroism, an amalgam readily permitted under the "dialectical" law of the "interpenetration of opposites." Other charges had to do with Li Hua's alleged disrespect for higher authority, his lack of discipline, and his "small-group" mentality. In principle, the committee encouraged detachments to fight independently, according to local conditions. But flexibility and dispersal carried with them the constant risk of "deviation."

The committee used its campaign against Li Hua to tighten its grip on the guerrillas. It started a campaign of education to "consolidate the Party and oppose new vacillation." It stepped up the "anti-defector struggle"; defectors were to be seized and killed. It intensified military resistance, tax resistance, and the struggle for free grain: these were "leftist" themes that provided a necessary corrective to Li Hua's "rightism."[137] It called for the searching out of "flightists" and "individual heroes" through individual introspection and the minute collective examination of cadres' conduct. The political awareness and military skills of the troops were to be raised by daily study and training. Waste and inefficiency were to stop; hygiene was to be improved; the wounded were to be duly cherished, both on and off the battlefield; the masses were to be better shielded against enemy reprisals; leadership was to be unified; reporting was to be made systematic; and scouting and vigilante work were to be strengthened. Working-class revolutionaries known for their combativeness, bravery, political steadfastness, flexibility, and responsibility were to be groomed for promotion.[138]

From the persecution of Li Hua, then, plans emerged for a comprehensive reform to restore unity to the movement. This unity was achieved partly through terror, by eliminating defectors and crushing deviants.

Party historians associate the terror of the 1930s with Wang Ming "leftists," but in Minxi'nan after 1934, terror was more than once used by would-be Maoists against their critics.

So much for the Party's official campaign against Li Hua. The real causes of the differences between him and the committee remain obscure. The Communists of Minyue were consistently less radical in the Three-Year War than those in Minxi; their leader, He Ming, is still described as "rightist." Some Communists apparently construed the quarrel with Li Hua as a product of the factional rivalry between Mao and Wang Ming. On December 15, 1936, the Minxi'nan Committee "completely accepted" Wang Ming's views on the united front,[139] but twice it accused Li Hua of "wanting only to talk about Comrade Wang Ming's report" and of omitting to mention opportunism and failing to take steps to strengthen the Red Army. This criticism recalls Mao's later campaign to correct Wang Ming's one-sided emphasis on unity with the Nationalists by stressing the simultaneous need to fight them.

The real explanation of the differences between Li and the committee is probably simple. Not only were the Minxi and Minyue Communists cut off from one another, but the conditions in which each group operated were quite different. The Minyue movement was younger, having been set up in 1932, and its bases were closer to the cities, the coast, and garrisons of the Nationalists. Though Li Hua belonged to Minxi, he too was more directly exposed to the Nationalists than the rest of the committee was; he was therefore cautious and pragmatic, like the Communists in Minyue. After the Xi'an Incident, the Nationalists hit hard at Communist bases throughout southern China; in Minxi'nan, Li Hua's vulnerably placed detachment was apparently hardest hit. Li asked the committee for permission to move further inland and further north to open up a new base between Yongan and Shaxian, where he hoped to ally with twenty thousand Great Knives. He was unconvinced by the committee's new "leftist" policies and its plans to build a Red Army of ten thousand in Minxi'nan. He had seen the consequences of the "leftist" turn of mid-1936, and he knew that by late 1936 the national Party was sounding a milder note. But the Minxi'nan Committee was intolerant of difference, suspicious of Communists operating semi-independently far outside the guerrilla heartland, and prepared to pay whatever cost in lives was necessary to carry out what it saw as Party policy.[140]

The central issue in the Li Hua affair foreshadowed the national Party's debate on how to reconcile national unity with class struggle. The affair suggests that the balance varied from place to place and from time to time and could not be decided conclusively. That is not to say that the dispute between Mao and Wang Ming was without substance; they were debating the general form of national policy, not its local content. But it does show the need for caution in assigning factional labels to Communists who worked in widely differing conditions.

The measures decided on in late 1936 restored the Communist movement in Minxi to health. Further south, the Minyue Committee's new stress on "economic work, mass work, . . . and fighting the 'political war' " also consolidated the Party. It resulted in closer ties between Party branches; in the restoration of ties to former Red Guard units in the villages, most of which had become watch teams for the Guomindang during the repression; and in a growth of Communist influence among the *baojia*.[141] In December, Minxi'nan leaders learned from a Hongkong newspaper of Chiang Kai-shek's arrest at Xi'an. Fang Fang shaved his beard in celebration; the secretary of the Yonghebu Committee pledged to fast for three days in thanksgiving; others got drunk. Most "could not believe their ears" when they heard of Chiang's safe return to Nanjing. For a while, their morale sank. The Yonghebu secretary resumed his fast, this time in protest.[142] The Xi'an Incident temporarily pitched the Communists back onto a "leftist" course. Despite their earlier resolution to stop attacking the Cantonese, they decided after Xi'an that the time was again ripe for a "partial counteroffensive" and "village insurrections." In some places, they reverted to a policy of expropriating rich peasants, landlords, and merchants, and they abandoned political overtures to the Guangdong Army. Several weeks after the Xi'an Incident, with the help of the National Salvation Society, they restored links for the first time in more than a year to the Party office in Shanghai, which sent them documents setting out the latest line. Meanwhile, they had learned from newspapers that the Party slogan had changed from "Oppose Chiang" to "Unite with Chiang against Japan." An emergency meeting of the Minxi'nan Committee supported the Shanghai documents, and shortly thereafter—probably in February—the committee sent Fang Fang to Yan'an to report and seek instructions. New, moderate policies were adopted in January and February 1937, when the committee resolved to protect the interests of classes they had only recently decided to attack. They freed rich peasants they had just arrested and promised to allow landlords—but not pro-Japanese traitors—a "reasonable life" and to give preferential treatment to rich peasants who actively opposed Japan. But it was not until May 1937, when new documents came their way, that they finally cast off the last vestiges of "leftism."[143]

## LINKS ARE RESTORED TO THE PARTY CENTER

Fang Fang took a roundabout route to Yan'an via Shantou, Hongkong, and Shanghai. En route, he braved various perils, military and moral. In

Shanghai, he was pestered by prostitutes, but he resisted them. "Obviously I had always thought about women during those three years," he later wrote. "But I feared first that I would harm the cause of the Party, second that I would sully my good name, and third that I would get VD."

Fang arrived in Yan'an in June 1937, "as happy as a child returning to its mother's arms."[144] There he met Mao, Zhu De, Zhang Wentian, and others and reported to the Party School and the Anti-Japanese University on the Three-Year War in Minxi-nan. Mao said to him, "It is a great victory that you held out in the three-year guerrilla war, kept so many cadres, kept and developed so many troops, kept two hundred thousand *mu* of land, and defended the interests of the broad masses of the soviet area." Mao also urged vigilance: "Quietly immerse yourselves in hard work, conceal yourselves long-term, accumulate forces, await opportunities." With this and other messages and advice, Fang Fang left for the south on August 2 and arrived back in Minxi in September.[145]

Also in early 1937, the Central Committee set up a Southern Working Committee in Hongkong. On the advice of this committee, the Minyue Communists formed a Special Committee. They proposed an alliance with the Guangdong Army to defend Minnan and dropped their call for the downfall of Chiang Kai-shek. This Minyue Committee was separate from the old Minxi'nan Committee and remained so until the latter's abolition in October 1937.[146]

This coexistence of two committees shows that Communists in Minxi and Minyue were still out of touch with one another, though each committee was separately restoring contact to the Party center. Both committees were swiftly reinstated into regional and national Party networks in early 1937. This re-reticulation began simultaneously at the middle and the edge. The threads that reeled out in both directions thickened, proliferated, and crossed, weaving eventually into a tissue through which advice, information, instructions, material, and people flowed.

Even before Fang Fang's arrival in Yan'an, his passage to the coast reactivated a link to Communist leaders in the south. In mid-April, an anonymous "urgent communication," perhaps sent by the Southern Committee, was addressed to Zhang Dingcheng, Deng Zihui, and Tan Zhenlin. It began, "Our years of struggle after parting in Jiangxi will soon number three. Even though we have been working in different places, our tasks and activities have been completely unified. . . . The news of your situation in Fujian made me boundlessly happy." The letter went on to explain the Party's tasks in the new phase and illustrated the problems and possibilities by pointing to experiences in Minnan. It said that the Minyue Communists had already started peace negotiations with the Guangdong Army and urged the Minxi'nan Committee to "absorb their experiences and lessons and to use them as a mirror in future dealings with the opposite side." But it counseled against uncritically copying the tactics of the Minnan guerrillas, who had wrongly failed to make "reform of the people's livelihood and aid to famine victims" an issue in the negotiations. "There must be a close link," it said, "between peaceful resolution work on the one hand and mass work and work directed toward the opposing army on the other. Only if the masses (including the soldiers of the opposing army) understand and urgently demand peace can there be peace, only then will peace be guaranteed. . . . There must be absolutely no wavering from our fundamental position just because of some small hardship or trifling setback."[147] But this cautioning was largely superfluous, for there was no sign that the Minxi'nan committee was about to abandon class struggle in its quest for peace.

Encouraged by this directive, the Minxi Communists returned to the course upon which they had set out before December 1936. In May 1937, they received Central Committee documents via Minyue; in June, they sent out a new round of open letters and draft programs. Their proposals were inventively centered on local issues and realities, unlike the sloganeering and generalities of other southern remnants. Before receiving the new directives, the Minxi'nan leaders had no clear idea about the Party center's negotiations with Nanjing or what their own role should be. The urgent communication and the Central Committee documents enlightened them. "We have already reported on southern China to the Central Committee," explained the communication, "and we have asked the Central Committee to negotiate with Nanjing to resolve the problems of our southern forces. But it will require action from many angles before it can become effective, so on no account adopt a 'waiting' attitude."[148]

The Minxi'nan Committee acted on this instruction. "In the past," it told its troops, "we were not active enough toward the Guangdong Army. We committed the error of waitism, that is, we waited for Nanjing and the central Red Army to unite. We did not understand that the united front can only be founded on the basis of many small unities."[149]

"Many small unities," to be achieved by "small talks within big talks," puts in a nutshell the strategy of the Communists in Minxi in the two months before negotiations started.[150] Within Minxi, they sought small unities as a precondition for a regional version of the national united front; within the broader national context, they saw their struggle in Minxi'nan as one stone in a mosaic of small unities upon which the balance of forces in China as a whole might someday depend. During their second letter-blitz in the summer of 1937, they wrote to every county, township, and *baojia* official, every school, gentry leader, merchant, newspaper, and army officer in the region. Gao Jingting, leader of the

Three-Year War in Eyuwan, tossed his insolently written letter to Wei Lihuang in a mat awning. The Minxi leaders approached their targets with refinement and restraint, politely requesting views and comments. They took care to seal and address the letters properly. Where possible, they delivered them by hand. Partly as a result of their punctiliousness, they received many positive replies. They also started a new campaign of shouting at forts and blockhouses.[151]

To win the Guangdong Army, they stressed the central Red Army's alliance in the north and played on Guangdong Army chauvinism. They argued that the Cantonese could only "revive last year's call to save the nation and avoid cuts in your own forces" if they stopped their drive against the guerrillas and began resisting the Japanese. "Your army is the biggest military bloc in southern China," they continued. "As soon as you unite with us, . . . we can organize a southern China allied anti-Japanese army." They unilaterally stopped all action against the Guangdong Army during this propaganda campaign.[152]

To win local patriots, they stressed that Fujian was in the front line of the struggle for southeastern China and that the Japanese wanted it declared a special zone from which political parties would be excluded. Here, too, they tried to use the Party's national successes as a bandwagon. They pointed out that the negotiations in Nanjing had brought the Communists and the Guomindang closer and had isolated pro-Japanese politicians. They proposed a "Fujian People's Government of National Salvation" formed by representatives of all parties, all armies, and "all walks of life" that would eventually merge with the provincial government, and they called for civil liberties and the arming of the people.

To win the business class, they pointed to the great material loss and destruction caused by years of "bandit extermination" and the consequent weakening of Minxi'nan society and the sapping of its will to resist, adding that as long as civil war continued, the losses could not be made good. They called for the removal of all taxes on trade and industry, especially paper, timber, tobacco, and tea; for an increase in import duty; and for lower shop rents.

To win the Overseas Chinese—a key community in the region that was becoming increasingly hostile to Ch'en I's corrupt provincial government—they demanded measures to encourage overseas investment in the province and guarantees of its security. In the first few years of the Resistance War, Overseas Chinese raised valuable levies of educated recruits for the New Fourth Army.

To win women, especially educated women, the Communists called for sexual equality before the law and in politics, schools, the economy, and the professions, and for free choice in marriage and an end to the system of child brides.

In the countryside, too, they tried to rally support among classes other than the rural poor, but here their switch to "democratic" policies consisted of more style than substance. In the cities, they could freely champion the interests of classes oppressed by bad government; in the villages, their hands were tied by financial considerations, for the villages were the main source of their income. They could not afford to stop squeezing the rural rich. Here, only their terminology changed. Instead of "attacking *tuhao*," they now "earnestly requested funds." They renamed their guardhouses reception centers and their jailers "reception officials"; they freed, at reduced ransoms, *tuhao* captured before the change of line. "Treat rich peasants who come to discuss contributions as you would a member of your family," said one directive. "Treat them as you would a Red soldier. Be especially kind to weak, sick, old people, pregnant women, and scholars who are not used to manual labor." In villages where they were strong, they set aggregate contributions and let richer householders discuss among themselves how best to raise them.[153]

Through these proposals, they began to make political headway in Minxi. Between May and September, they held peace talks with every military and administrative unit in the region down to the village level. They stuck to small issues more likely to produce agreement: that each side stop kidnapping, that mountain people deported to the plains be allowed to return home, and so on.[154] Their impact on the Guangdong Army was limited, though some troops were said to have searched the mountains in a deliberately offhand way and even to have refused orders to attack guerrillas. During subsequent negotiations, the Communists had sympathizers among lower-ranking Nationalist officers, including one who had given the Minxi Red Army twenty men and rifles after the defeat of the Fujian Rebellion in early 1934.[155]

But the constant barrage of letters and leaflets did not have the same effect as the Party's campaign among Manchurian troops in northern China. One reason was that Yu Hanmou shook up his command before sending it to Minxi and appointed the archreactionary Huang Tao, an old-style military man, as new commander of the 157th Division. Huang had no intention of seeing his army go the way of Zhang Xueliang's Manchurians. He purged it from top to bottom, appointing new officers at the regimental, battalion, and company levels. He personally supervised these new appointees, who vied to win his confidence and justify their promotion.[156]

The Communists' letter-writing campaign to Fellow Townspeople's Associations, local scholars, and well-known local people in Zhangzhou, Xiamen, Shantou, and as far away as Hongkong, Guangzhou, Nanxiong, and Ganzhou was more effective than their efforts to subvert the Guangdong Army.[157] Many Minxi exiles in the coastal cities planned to return to the interior if the Japanese invaded and were therefore keen to reach an agreement with the Communists. Some recipients of Party propaganda wrote to Guangdong Army officers supporting the call for peace talks and collected several thousand dollars for the Minxi'nan Committee. Some tobacco and paper-factory owners, local gentry, and returned Overseas Chinese maintained secret contact with the Communists. Xiamen's *Xingguang Ribao* printed an open letter from them. Even Zheng Bishan, a powerful Longyan gentry leader who in the early 1930s moved to Zhangzhou to escape the revolution, apparently had second thoughts about "bandit extermination." Zheng, a deputy leader of the Fujian legislature, told the Minxi Fellow Countrypeople's Association in Zhangzhou: "If anyone is a determined anti-Communist, it's me. I have opposed the Communists for ten years, but to no avail. Now that they are proposing peaceful cooperation and resistance, we should approve." Numerous other Townspeople's Associations supported the Communists' peace plans.

The Communists' campaign for "partial peaces in preparation for the greater peace" had the greatest success in the villages, where they had strong networks and guns to back up their propaganda. They concluded nonaggression pacts with district and village leaders and set up joint peace bodies with local *baojia* officials, but at the same time they defended the interests of their supporters in the villages. To give local meaning to their national campaign for unity and security, they stamped out bandits around Yonghejing and settled feuds among lineages and villages.[158]

Their directives now put greater stress on the dangers of "leftism" and in particular of inconsistency. Having lurched more than once from left to right and back again, they knew the harm of "uniting with someone today, killing them tomorrow."[159] Still, if the line changed, the regime did not. "Leftist" excesses were not only denounced but also shown to coincide with the thinking of "pro-Japanese traitors." In a movement geared to "pitiless struggle," the instruction to "destroy conspiracies of Han traitors" easily led to fresh purges.

Besides guarding against "leftism," the Minxi'nan Committee tried to steer clear of excessive class amity. "To absorb great masses of peasants into the resistance," it declared, "it is necessary to carry out a policy of land-to-the-tillers and to guarantee that land will not be taken back in areas where it has been divided." The committee told its supporters that conflicts would not lessen as the two parties moved toward cooperation. The period of preparing the united front would not be peaceful and uneventful. The class enemy would still be out to destroy Communist forces, especially military ones; the guerrillas should not relax their guard but should rectify "pacifist" tendencies. The committee made it clear that it would not surrender control over the internal affairs of its armed forces to the Guangdong Army, though it was prepared to put them under overall Cantonese command. The Red Army needed territory capable of supporting it to ensure that it was not "disbanded or absorbed through reorganization." By the early summer of 1937, there were numerous "small Moscows" in the mountains of Minxi'nan where the guerrillas could parade openly, but they needed more. Requests for territory became a standard theme of their public statements.[160]

### DENG ZIHUI NEGOTIATES WITH THE NATIONALISTS

Formal negotiations began on July 10 in Longyan between Deng Zihui and a Nationalist brigade commander after exploratory talks in May between local Communist liaison officials and the Cantonese. Deng demanded an end to the extermination campaign, to the blockade of guerrilla areas, to the deportations, and to the ban on political parties. He called for democratic rights, the freeing of political prisoners, economic help for disaster victims, help for Red Army dependents, rent and interest cuts, an acceptance of past land reforms, and supplies for the guerrillas. These local negotiations were not just a byproduct of the national ones. The Communists in Minxi had become more than a small nuisance and were now a potential threat to the stability of the region. There could be no question of leaving hardened bands of homegrown troublemakers at large in their old haunts; if they could not be wiped out, then they must be talked out. By now there was some support for the Communists in Fujian among middle-ranking opinion leaders. The Cantonese, under orders to go to the front, needed a quick agreement.[161]

The Guangdong Army was at loggerheads with local representatives of the Fujian administration, so in the talks, Deng Zihui could play the two sides against each other. Liang Guobin, director of the Communists' Longyan office, made contact with Party sympathizers in the Nationalist garrison at Longyan,[162] and Wei Jinshui cultivated relations with officers of the 157th Division. The Communists still believed that they had potential support in the Guangdong Army, which had fought in the 1932 Battle of Shanghai and participated in the Fujian people's government of 1933, but they considered the Fujian provincial government reactionary and hostile. Deng eventually held joint talks with Lian Tisheng, who represented the Guangdong Army, and Zhang Cean, prefectural commissioner for Longyan. Both Lian and Zhang were keen to incorporate the guerrillas so that they could claim extra pay and supplies for them. Each opposed the other, so Deng could ward off the more extreme proposals of both: that Zhang Dingcheng became a provincial commissioner, that Deng go abroad, that other guerrilla leaders either quit the area or carry out reclamation work, or that the guerrillas join a reserve or provincial security regiment under Nationalist command. Instead, the Nationalists had to be content with the right to "inspect" the reorganized guerrillas.[163]

Even so, the terms of the peace were a disappointment to the Communists, who had to abandon many of their demands. On the question of the designation and command of their forces, they could claim only that "our concessions have definitely not gone beyond the lowest limit set by the Central Committee." But they had failed to obtain assurances that the land would stay divided; they could promise only that after the guerrillas had gone, "the Party would still be able to devise new ways of leading the masses' struggle and it will not be difficult to crush landlords' plans to collect rent."[164] They explained that internal peace and cooperation "are the only way the Party can win hegemony in the war of resistance."[165] But though their overall record in defending the gains of land revolution after 1937 was good, they were powerless in many areas to stop rent collectors entering villages where people had stopped paying rent in 1930. The rent collectors' first targets were the families of guerrillas who had gone to fight the Japanese; these families were ordered to pay first as examples to the rest. Many were too poor to pay, having already been repeatedly "expropriated" by the vengeful administration.[166]

Guerrillas in Minxi were understandably tense and angry when Guomindang uniforms arrived for them in August 1937. Some deserted rather than put them on; others returned to the hills as guerrillas.[167] "The ordinary people were very dissatisfied," recalled Wei Jinshui. "They would not let us quarter with them. They even wanted to take back the bed planks and rice straw we had borrowed. . . . They were so angry that the troops stripped off their yellow [Nationalist] uniforms and flung them vigorously to the ground."[168]

## THE ZHANGPU INCIDENT

Of the various incidents that disturbed the negotiations in Minxi'nan, by far the most serious was the Zhangpu Incident of July 16, 1937, when troops of the 157th Division disarmed between six hundred and eleven hundred guerrillas—estimates vary—of Minyue's Red Third Regiment at Zhangpu, south of Zhangzhou. This incident hardened attitudes in Minxi'nan, where Communists launched a strident campaign for the return of the men and weapons seized, and in Yan'an, where Mao used it to illustrate the dangers of "excessive accommodation." When Fang Fang returned from Yan'an in September, he made a special point of criticizing the lack of vigilance of "some Party members" and reinforced

Mao's idea of struggle within unity. To avoid a repetition of the incident, Deng Zihui insisted in his negotiations with the Nationalists that the guerrillas should assemble in isolated areas with no roads, a tactic that was perhaps also useful for keeping the guerrillas' real strength secret until they had recruited up to their claimed levels. Even so, guerrillas all over Minxi'nan were ambushed while heading for assembly points and forced to make long detours through the mountains.[169]

Those connected with the Zhangpu Incident were from the very start targets for criticism; in the Cultural Revolution, they became objects of vehement attack. They have done their best to remove the stigma by trying to justify their roles in the incident and have rightly or wrongly tended to heap the blame for it on He Ming and his associate Wu Jin.[170]

Negotiations between the Minyue Committee and the Guangdong Army started several months earlier than in Minxi, and were held up as a mirror to the Minxi'nan Committee by the anonymous author of the urgent communication.[171] Agreement was reached on June 26, 1937, before talks in Minxi'nan had even started. Shortly after the Lugouqiao Incident of July 7, 1937, marking the start of all-out war between Japan and China, the Cantonese told the guerrillas of the Red Third to hurry to Zhangpu on the coast. The guerrillas were billeted in a temple there. Two days later, they assembled on a sports field to drill and collect their pay. They were surrounded, disarmed, and taken prisoner by a battalion of heavily armed Cantonese who rose suddenly from the bushes. Some wanted to fight their way free; He Ming proposed waiting instead for the Party center to mediate. At the same time, twelve members of the Minyue Committee were seized and killed at Zhao'an, in the extreme south of Fujian, and some local Party leaders were arrested. The extermination drive, the deportations, and the blockade resumed. Attacks continued at least until November. In short, "the revolutionary struggle in Minnan had suffered a big defeat."[172]

In early August, the Minxi Communists published a stinging criticism of the Minyue Committee. Relations between the two committees were probably already strained, for theoretically Minyue came under the Minxi'nan Committee, which may have seen the establishment of the Minyue Committee as a challenge to its authority. In 1935, the Minxi'nan Committee had sent emissaries to Minyue to discuss unifying the leadership, but Minyue's Huang Huicong put them off, saying that he could not act until he received directives from a higher body.[173] This stalling undoubtedly annoyed his comrades to the north. In 1937, the Minxi'nan Committee's criticism focused on the "opportunism" of the Minyue Communists: their lack of class vigilance, their naive trust in the Cantonese, their complete lack of "the will to resist or spirit of self-preservation" when surrounded. It added that though He and Wu bore most responsibility for this "shameful incident," the Minyue Committee was not free from blame and should criticize itself.[174]

In September and November, a reformed Minyue Committee delivered the self-criticism demanded of it by both the Minxi'nan Committee and the Southern Committee in Hongkong. It explained that the internal cause of the "tragic defeat" was "rightist liquidationism," manifested in an overoptimistic assessment of the Guangdong Army, a reliance on interviews with journalists rather than on "mass work" and political agitation among Cantonese troops, irresolution in the face of He Ming's suspicious behavior, and a failure to follow the instructions of the Southern Committee. The "bloody lesson" that it drew from the defeat was that in future it would "not waver from the Party's general direction."

The strategy and tactics it now adopted were modeled on those of the Minxi'nan Committee, which in September sent an armed unit under Tan Zhenlin to Minyue to help the Communists there restore their organization. The effect of the incident was to draw the two bodies closer together: in October, they merged in a newly elected Minyue Committee under Zhang Dingcheng. "Peace cannot be turned on like a tap," the reformed Minyue Committee told its followers; it can only be achieved through sweat and toil, through the "menace" of a mass movement, through a blizzard of letters and leaflets, and through a stronger Red Army, for "every new rifle is another step on the road to negotiations." It criticized those in the committee who saw the peace movement and the social movement as counterposed and called instead for a close linking of the two. It also called for the simultaneous use of public and secret, legal and illegal channels.[175]

In the immediate aftermath of the Zhangpu Incident, more than one hundred guerrillas escaped to the mountains. Over the next few weeks, another two to three hundred joined them. In September, an armed unit from Minxi arrived in Minyue to help restore the Red Third, and Tan Zhenlin stayed in Minyue for a month.[176] In late 1937, Zhang Yunyi arrived in Fujian as a representative of the Party center. Shortly before Zhang's arrival, local Communist leaders, still unable to reach new terms with the Nationalists, discussed "reviving the civil war" but were afraid of violating the united front. Zhang's advice was that they should "go up the mountains and fight" if their independence was in the slightest way threatened. Zhang's tough stand secured the release of guerrillas and weapons seized in the Zhangpu Incident and in a separate incident in Minzhong (central Fujian).[177]

As for He Ming, the Nationalists gave him full power over the Red Third (in reality disbanded). Later, they transferred him to the 157th Division's Investigation Department, where he worked for nearly a year.[178] His former comrades, fearful that he might endanger their security, tracked him down despite attempts to keep him incommunicado. They persuaded him that he had a "glorious future" with—and only with—the New Fourth Army. He Ming returned to the Party but was expelled and found guilty by court-martial of "conspiring to . . . destroy the Red Army." He was executed in June 1939 at Yunling, though he denied his guilt and not everyone was convinced by the evidence against him. After 1949, Zhang Dingcheng said that it had been wrong to kill him; Chen Yi implied the same. Today, the Zhangpu Incident is classified as "an error by a comrade within the Party."[179]

Since 1980, various new accounts of the Zhangpu Incident have appeared, including one by Lu Sheng, deputy commander of the Red Third at the time of its disarming and leader of the initial breakout by several dozen captured guerrillas.[180] Some of these articles are aimed at correcting "distortions" made during the Cultural Revolution. This concern to put the record straight is understandable: the whole of the guerrilla period in Minyue became a taboo subject in China after 1949 because of the Zhangpu Incident.[181] Thorny "historical problems" continued to attach to those associated with it well into the 1980s. These problems have created gaps in the history books and given ammunition to factional enemies of the old guard in Minnan, who have been denied the respect and material comforts accorded other old revolutionaries.

Shortly after the incident, the Minyue Committee accused He and Wu of having arranged beforehand to defect to the Guomindang,[182] but Lu Sheng and others do not repeat this charge. Instead, they describe He Ming as a follower of the Wang Ming line who "relaxed his guard" and was taken in by the Guangdong Army's nationalist rhetoric. They reveal that in May 1937, He Ming was captured by the Nationalists and taken off to Zhangzhou, where he negotiated directly with the commander of the 157th Division and signed an agreement. One author reveals that after his arrest, He Ming smuggled a message to the Minyue Committee asking for authority to negotiate, which he was granted.[183] He Ming also agreed, on his own initiative, to accept the designation of Peace Preservation Corps. Accounts describe the agreement He achieved as "basically identical" with the line of the Central Committee in Yan'an.[184] Today, He Ming is criticized not for negotiating the agreement but for proposing to leave the mountains and go to Zhangpu.

After his release by the Nationalists, He Ming was removed as acting secretary of the Minyue Committee but allowed to continue as commander of the Red Third. His proposal to assemble at Zhangpu provoked a heated discussion in the committee. Earlier, Zhang Dingcheng had written to He Ming telling him not to leave his base without instructions from the Party center, and the Southern Committee had warned him against going down onto the plains. A majority in Minyue is said—

often by people with a strong interest in distancing themselves from He's decision—at first to have opposed leaving for Zhangpu.[185] He Ming argued that if the guerrillas stayed in the mountains, they would be unable to influence the towns and would imperil the united front; the newly appointed acting secretary gave in to He's bluster, while the representative of the Southern Committee (who had come up from Hongkong to meet He Ming) changed his position and failed to oppose the proposal.[186] A friendly officer of the 157th Division secretly warned He and Wu that it would be dangerous to leave the mountains. Just before the incident, Communist spies in the division told He that the Cantonese were preparing to disarm him.[187] He kept these reports to himself and failed to act on them. On the contrary, he told the Minyue Committee that the Nationalists had only one battalion of troops within twenty miles of Zhangpu, while the Communists themselves had more than eight hundred men under arms.[188]

Why did He Ming choose to go to Zhangpu? Today all agree that he was a loyal Communist, so we can rule out treachery as a motive. Some explain the incident as a product of youthful hubris (He was twenty-seven at the time). In 1936, He had taken over as commander of the Third after the death of Zhang Changshui; in 1937, he became acting secretary of the Minyue Committee after Huang Huicong left. He had accumulated a monopoly of power, and few in the leadership dared contradict him. For various reasons, he cherished strong illusions about the 157th Division. Indeed, in 1937 and 1938, He Ming was not the only Communist excessively optimistic about the united front.

He had special cause to believe in the Nationalists' good faith. Communists arrested elsewhere in this period were killed or thrown in jail: He Ming was not only freed unharmed but was also convinced by his captors' behavior that they could be won to a Communist conception of the resistance to Japan. Many junior officers and men of the 157th Division were hostile to Chiang Kai-shek; a secret Communist cell worked hard to whip up anti-Japanese sentiment. Huang Tao, commander of the division, was strictly anti-Communist, but he put on a display of anti-Japanese propaganda to deceive He Ming, who was even given the chance to debate issues in the resistance before an audience of officers. Huang Tao's aim was (according to one of his subordinates) "to incorporate the Red Army guerrillas into his own force in order to complete his task of 'exterminating the Communists' "—and, presumably, to increase pay and supplies.

He Ming's vanity blinded him to this deceit. Believing that he had won his freedom by his own persuasive powers, he was deaf to all warnings about Huang's true intentions. In addition, he was young and out of touch with other Party leaders. He had not personally experienced the failure of the first united front, for he had only joined the Party in December 1927, several months after the break between the Communists and Chiang Kai-shek. Consequently, he took his guerrillas to Zhangpu. Once he got there, his illusions were destroyed. Even on the way, his guerrillas were discreetly trailed by Nationalist troops who tore Communist posters from the walls. In Zhangpu, far from "spreading Party influence to the towns," his troops were practically confined to quarters before the incident. Messages are said to have passed from Chiang Kai-shek's headquarters to Yu Hanmou, chief of the Guangdong Army, and to Ch'en I telling them to disarm He Ming's guerrillas.[189]

The Minyue Committee adapted skillfully to the pressures of defeat after 1934 and paraded more than one thousand guerrillas in seven companies and four platoons just a month before the incident.[190] But in a broader view, possible connections become apparent between the committee's early success and eventual failure. The noisy presence of a column of guerrillas in Minyue provoked conservative authorities to take repressive measures. Could Huang Huicong have steered a passage between the twin dangers of "right accommodationism" and "left sectarianism" if he had not left Minyue? Chinese writers today imply that he could. Lu Sheng and others criticize both the Minyue Committee and the Southern Committee for laxness and irresolution rather than complicity in He Ming's actions, and they accuse He Ming of opportunism rather than of treason. But though they lighten the charge, they still narrow the main target to He Ming—an analysis already criticized by the Minxi'nan Committee in 1937.[191]

The wrong decisions may well have been solely He Ming's, and he may have pushed them through against the doubts and opposition of his comrades. But was "rightism" in Minyue exclusively He Ming's failing? It had been detected in the Minyue Committee as early as April 1937; the committee's twelve officials killed at Zhao'an were, like He Ming, accused of a "complete lack of class vigilance."[192] Even the Minxi'nan Communists were not entirely free of "accommodationism." According to their leader Zhang Dingcheng, they should have recruited more vigorously after the negotiations, when Xiamen was in ferment and the Guangdong Army was already withdrawing.[193] Just as the Minxi'nan Communists were not entirely perfect, so He Ming was not an out-and-out "opportunist." "He Ming resisted orders six times, carried on propagating Communism, and carried out Communist political work," said the Nationalist officer who arrested him.[194]

The same factors that allowed the Communist movement in Minyue to flourish before July 1937 also explain its eventual downfall. The strength of the Minyue Communists was that they were "Marxists of the valleys" who lacked dogma. Their inclination was to the right rather than to the left. Their great test came in 1937, when political changes in China made an element of "leftist dogma" indispensable if the Communists were to maintain their identity and even their existence. In 1937, Communists in Minxi were sufficiently immunized with "leftism" to resist the danger of excessive accommodation; those in Minyue were not.

## THE MINXI'NAN VIEW OF THE UNITED FRONT

The Zhangpu Incident was a severe blow, but not severe enough to knock the Minxi'nan Committee off its course. He Ming's Minyue Committee was the first southern guerrilla unit to negotiate with the Nationalists after the call for unity.[195] Its mistakes were a useful lesson for guerrillas elsewhere and for policy-makers in Yan'an. "We must react without anger or hatred," the Minxi'nan Committee told the Minyue regiment. "But we must draw the lessons and step up our guard. . . . Communists in Minyue must neither give up hope nor thirst for revenge.[196]

To be sure, the Minxi'nan Committee was never uniformly orthodox during this difficult period of transition. At the autumn harvest, high-handed junior cadres alienated landlords; others were too quick to label their opponents in the government as traitors; still others tried to set factions in the administration at one another's throats rather than "win merit" by trying to stop conflicts.[197] But these and other "leftist" failings were sternly criticized by Communist leaders.

Why could the Communists in Minxi'nan steer clear of both insular "leftism" and "rightist" appeasement when guerrillas elsewhere failed to do so? One reason is that they were not a lightweight force in regional politics. They were led by a large, experienced team of local leaders and had gone some way toward restoring their political organization. They revived direct links to Party liaison offices in Hongkong and Shanghai sooner than most guerrillas. They changed course earlier and could consult the experience and avoid the mistakes of the Communists in Minyue, who had blazed the trail.

To a certain extent, they were locked on course by circumstance. They were strong enough for some in the government and the Guangdong Army to want to swallow or destroy them; the resulting plots and attacks helped keep them vigilant. But the wish for unity in southern Fujian was exceptionally strong, and the Communists were captivated by it. By countering war with peace after Zhangpu, they won sympathy and support.[198]

Through experience and reflection, the Communists in Minxi'nan arrived at a conception of the united front similar to that defended by Mao against Wang Ming after 1935. "Oppose raising ultraleft slogans that frighten off allies," the reformed Minyue Committee told its cadres, "but

oppose ultrarightist neglect of your own position or the masses' interests, especially the proletariat's. In the movement toward the united
front, class struggle is not halted or weakened. On the contrary, the
united front cannot be achieved without this sort of struggle. Whoever
uses the united front as a pretext for liquidating class struggle is repeating Chen Duxiu's opportunism."[199] Reform without excessive friction,
and well-intentioned criticism: following these two basic policies, the
Minxi'nan Communists steeled their cadre and came to terms with local
officials throughout the region. "Joint programs" proliferated in the villages in the months before the guerrillas finally marched north.

## THE MINXI'NAN GUERRILLAS JOIN THE
## NEW FOURTH ARMY

In September 1937 at Nanchang, Xiang Ying and Xiong Shihui, governor of Jiangxi, representing He Yingqin, started negotiating the southern guerrillas' corporate future. On October 2, they agreed to reorganize the guerrillas into a national army, the New Fourth. But the
Communists in Minxi'nan continued for the time being to call themselves the Anti-Japanese Volunteer Army. It quickly became clear that
they saw their future in Fujian, though they were already part of the
New Fourth.[200] They were an army of Fujianese, led by Fujianese. If
they were to fight Japan, where better to do so than in Fujian, where the
Japanese were opening a front? So their manifestos of the early autumn
of 1937 demanded that the provincial government take urgent steps to
reinvigorate the resistance, promote the National Salvation Movement,
arm the people, clear out pro-Japanese traitors, free political prisoners,
and set up a joint Minxi'nan Command formed by "people of talent
from all parties and factions." They requested a garrison area in which
they could mobilize and recruit and a sector of the front from which
they could cooperate with the Guangdong Army to defend Fujian.[201]

It is unlikely that they independently decided to ask to be allowed to
stay in Fujian, for they made the request shortly after Fang Fang, newly
returned from Yan'an, had conveyed the instructions of the Central
Committee.[202] The Party center was loath to give up its positions in
Minxi'nan. It kept the Fujian option in reserve even after most Minxi'nan guerrillas had marched north and promoted it when the chance
arose. In any case, the request to stay in Fujian was popular with the
guerrillas, many of whom had not seen their families in three years.[203]

At first Ch'en I, the conservative Japanophile governor of Fujian,
seemed to accept the Communists' call for a role in defending Fujian
and offered to send lorries to take them to the front, whether because
he was under pressure from patriotic opinion, because he coveted the

guerrillas for his provincial army, or—as Fang Fang guessed—because he planned to drive them into the sea once they reached the coast. Whatever the case, he soon dropped the idea of keeping them in the province. The Communists, wary of a second Zhangpu, declined his offer of lorries, saying that they would march to the front along routes of their own choosing. They asked for their own defense sector, separate from that of the Cantonese. Clearly, they did not mean to be swallowed. Ch'en I was probably afraid that once they reached the coast, they would link up with Communist remnants there and spread their influence still further. So the arrangement was scrapped; the Communists were told to "await orders" in Longyan and forbidden to act independently.

In November, tension grew when Deng Zihui, again suspecting a trap, resisted an order to send the entire Volunteer Army to Longyan and sent only part of it instead, heavily armed, ready for trouble, and not before the last Nationalist troops had left the town. After the inspection, they returned to their mountain strongholds.

Even before this incident, the provincial authorities had been reluctant to make resources available to the Communists. After it, Ch'en I ordered that supplies and pay should stop. The Communists replied with a "loan extraction movement," "borrowing" money from local merchants and landlords that they promised to pay back as soon as they themselves were paid. They also "borrowed" cloth from local tailors, for it was by now late autumn and they needed uniforms for the winter. They repaid these loans when the authorities restored a flow of cash to them. In their Baitu stronghold in Longyan, they "developed open struggle and various organizations from the former Central Soviet" to which they recruited educated youth from Fujian, Guangdong, and Chinese communities overseas. "This terrified Ch'en I and Zhang Cean," wrote Fang Fang. "They only wished that we would quickly leave."[204]

The Minxi'nan Communists were quite prepared to face up to Ch'en I but were undermined by Xiang Ying, who is said to have played into Ch'en's hands by "naively" agreeing to a time limit for a withdrawal from Fujian. Xiang Ying wanted the Minxi'nan forces for his New Fourth Army; the Minxi'nan leaders hoped to stay in Fujian and build on their existing base. "Xiang apparently does not yet understand . . . that we should preserve strategic support points in the south," said the Central Committee on October 1, 1937.[205] Reluctantly, the Minxi'nan leaders began preparing to withdraw; they found the order unreasonable but felt bound by Party discipline to follow it.[206] So their efforts to repeat the Xi'an alliance in Fujian failed. Most of the Red Army's southern remnants were happy to take the chance to join Xiang Ying in Wannan, for by themselves they were powerless to influence events. In Minxi'nan, however, the pull-out was a reverse, not a victory.

In January 1938, the designation of the Minxi'nan Volunteers as the Second Detachment of the New Fourth Army was confirmed, and in February they and other units marched into Baitu to train and reorganize. From Minzhong came a few hundred guerrillas under Lei Guangxi to form the detachment's special-tasks company. From Ruijin and Changting in the heartland of the old Central Soviet came another hundred, rallied in part by the Long Marcher Deng Zhenxun, newly transferred south by the Party center. From Minyue, in late February, came remnants of the Red Third. Large numbers of Party members arrived in Longyan from the mountain villages of Minxi'nan and from villages across the border in Guangdong and Jiangxi; representatives of anti-Japanese political groups arrived from Hongkong and the big cities of Minnan and Yuedong (eastern Guangdong), together with Overseas Chinese; and cadres came down from Yan'an. In all, several hundred young people turned up at Longyan, including two hundred students. Some left after conveying greetings or receiving instructions and advice; others stayed to train as soldiers or political workers for the New Fourth Army and were sent in batches to the front. This recruiting was done in secret. Special measures were taken to thwart Nationalist spies who infiltrated the new arrivals.[207]

The Communists in Minxi avoided further incidents like the one at Zhangpu. During an inspection by Zhang Cean at Baisha, they marched their troops into the hills and paraded them one company at a time to avoid revealing their true strength and to forestall attacks. They rotated their few good rifles among the companies on show and stuffed their bandoliers with wooden cartridges so that they seemed to bristle with weapons and ammunition.[208]

The final tally of guerrillas from Minxi'nan and adjacent areas incorporated into the New Fourth Army is conventionally put at more than two thousand.[209] However, lower and higher figures are also mentioned. A Guomindang intelligence report said that more than three thousand were reorganized; a study prepared by the New Fourth Army staff office in 1946 says 1,200 were reorganized in Minxi'nan, though it adds that a further three hundred joined from Ruijin; and a recent study says that there were more than five thousand guerrillas in Minxi'nan by the end of the Three-Year War (though many probably never left Fujian).[210] A detailed breakdown of the Red Army in Minxi in early 1937, based on Fang Fang's report to the Central Committee, suggests that there were seven hundred troops in the five detachments backed by 1,500 local forces.[211] These different figures reflect different dates and bases of calculation. Two conclusions can be drawn from their general range. First, this region, along with Eyuwan, was a star performer in the Three-Year War; exceptionally, it felt no need to swell its ranks with the old, the weak, or the very young to impress the Guomindang.[212] Second, and in spite of this strength, it came nowhere near its ambitious goal of recruiting a ten-thousand-strong Red Army; on the contrary, in the first three months of 1938, it recruited only seventy-seven of its target of seven hundred volunteers,[213] partly because of its leaders' excessive political restraint.[214]

The reorganized guerrillas set off from Houtian near Longyan on March 1, 1938, under Zhang Dingcheng, Deng Zihui, and Tan Zhenlin and went north via Changting and Ruijin. By then, Ch'en I was heartily sick of these troublesome Communists and gave them six hundred dollars of "tea money" to speed them on their way. In the Hakka town of Changting, they were greeted with fireworks and confetti by a crowd of several hundred Nationalist officials, merchants, and students. They stayed in Changting for a week and restored Communist organization there.[215] Zhang Dingcheng, himself a Hakka, was recognized everywhere along the route and addressed a rally of two thousand people.

The marchers skirted Ruijin to avoid trouble. The guerrillas had deliberately chosen to march north through the old Central Soviet to demonstrate that the Red Army was not defeated. Overseas Chinese supporters of the Party staged plays and propaganda shows in villages along the route.[216] The Minxi'nan guerrillas were among the last units to arrive at the New Fourth Army's assembly point in Wannan, reaching it on April 18. They were delayed partly because some guerrillas clashed— and were criticized for doing so by the Minyue Committee—with government forces that harassed them along the route.[217] But even under the best of circumstances, traveling the six hundred miles between Longyan and Yansi on foot would take at least a month.[218]

### THE PARTY IN MINYUE AND MINXI'NAN AFTER THE PULLOUT

This Fujianese Long March to the Chang Jiang did not quench the flame of Communism in Minxi'nan any more than the Long March of 1934 had quenched it in southern China as a whole. The Party center often drained resources from Fujian to strengthen its national concentrations but never emptied it completely (though Xiang Ying—allegedly acting for Wang Ming—is frequently accused of wanting to do so in 1938). It is characteristic of the Chinese Revolution that Communist gains were never anywhere wholly relinquished; cells of Communism were left scattered in various states of dormancy all over China to be roused or rallied as conditions required and allowed. Fujian was no exception, and Minxi'nan was kept more wakeful than most southern bases of the Party after 1937. Party leaders appreciated that the movement in

Minxi'nan was deeply rooted and well branched. The special value that they placed on Minxi'nan was a recognition of its strategic position alongside the old Central Soviet, between the great cities of southern and eastern China, and close to the islands of southeast Asia, where the war against Japan would be decided.

While negotiating the withdrawal of the Minxi'nan guerrillas with Ch'en I, the Communists demanded the right to leave behind a rear office and a company of troops to guard Party officials and protect invalid and demobbed soldiers and New Fourth Army dependents. On September 30 and October 1, 1937, Mao instructed guerrilla leaders in old base areas to leave behind two-fifths of their men as "strategic support points" for the future struggle. The Minxi'nan demand for an office and a guard was hardly consistent with these directives. Ch'en I agreed to the request, perhaps only to be rid of the guerrillas. The Communists also left behind an intact Party organization under Fang Fang, then secretary of the region's Minyuegan Committee, in both Minxi and Minyue. Very soon, after continuing friction, the company of guards was ordered by the provincial authorities to leave for Wannan, and the office was first wound down and then closed altogether after accusations that it was plotting a new land revolution and an uprising to seize power. Local conservatives still saw the Red Army in Minxi'nan as a "plague god" (i.e., bringer of misfortune) and wanted to destroy it completely now that its main force had departed.[219]

According to Fang Fang, Ch'en I put pressure on Xiang Ying to have the Communist office and troops removed. In April 1938, Xiang called the guard company to Wannan, rescinding even this minimum compliance with Yan'an's directive. Fujian Communists pointed out that Xiang's directive contradicted Mao's earlier ones, but they eventually complied—their greatest mistake, according to Fang Fang—after rank-pulling by Zhang Wentian. On the way north, in Nanchang, the company's commander called on Zeng Shan, deputy secretary of the Party's Southeastern Bureau, who told him that he personally should return to Minxi, for it was an important base that needed good military leaders. On May 22, the Party secretariat tried again to get Xiang Ying, and Wang Ming in Wuhan, to use the base in Fujian to stiffen the resistance. It told them, "Now that Xiamen is lost and Fuzhou is in danger, the region along the Fujian coast will become a war zone. Please promptly direct the Minyuegan Committee to send capable cadres to lead work in these regions, develop guerrilla war there, organize guerrilla forces, create guerrilla bases." But the directive was not passed on, and the plan came to nothing.[220]

During the earlier campaign for a "joint defense" of Minnan, Minxi'nan Communists had stressed the need to restore and, if possible, widen the movement's social and territorial base, starting with the so-called "three mountains." They wanted to restore contact with people deported to the plains during the civil war and to campaign for their right to return to the mountains. They planned to rehabilitate the mountain economy and use it to support their activities in the region.[221]

The march north, the pull-out of the guard company, assassinations of Communist officials, and the closing down of the New Fourth Army's rear office in Longyan did not mean that these plans were abandoned. The Party center had told Minxi'nan Communists to use the peace to reorganize and expand the Party structure in the region.[222] At first, the idea of repopulating the "three mountains" as a base from which to resist the expected Japanese invasion of Minxi'nan was kept alive, and in April 1938 instructions went out to create a new Communist army to replace the one that had left. During these first few months, the Party ran training courses for young intellectuals from Minnan and Yuedong. Communists set up or participated in lawful political bodies and supported the New Fourth Army by organizing "consoling and contributing" and running charity bazaars. For a while, they changed the name of the Minyue Border Area Special Committee to Zhangzhou Central Committee, symbolizing their coming in from the cold.[223]

During much of 1938, the Communists in Minxi'nan, under the direction of Xiang Ying's Southeastern Bureau, pursued a policy regarded as "rightist" in Yan'an. They put their main emphasis on helping the Nationalists to recruit troops and gather taxes; in their old bases, they came to be regarded as henchmen of the Guomindang and lost much of their support. They even mobilized students sympathetic to the Party to climb the hills and chop firewood for the Nationalists. This collaboration exposed their supporters to the authorities, and many Communists were harassed or arrested in six incidents between March and October 1938.[224]

Fang Fang, a realist, could see that with the guerrillas gone, the Guomindang would gain the upper hand throughout Minxi, even around old Communist strongholds, and that the Party should take precautions. He also recognized, as had Luo Ming five years earlier, that the people of the Minxi'nan "old areas" had suffered greatly over the years and that though "the big villages could shelter us, the masses would face huge difficulties." He decided to lift the pressure on Minxi'nan by switching the focus of the movement to his native Chaomei region in neighboring Guangdong province, "where the seeds of revolution were broadly scattered." He summed up this new policy in the maxim "Consolidate Minxi'nan, energetically develop new areas in Chaomei" and set up two new committees—one for Minxi'nan, the other for Chaomei—to replace the old unified one and embody the new turn.[225]

Recent studies implicitly criticize this retreat. They point out that after the fall of Xiamen, the Nationalists removed their forces from the front, so that whole sections of the Fujian coast fell either to bandits or to the Japanese. They conclude that the Communists could have launched attacks on these territories and infiltrated cadres into them if they had stayed on in Minxi'nan. Yet the Fujian Provincial Committee did little to develop forces along the coast, and it sent no one at all to old bases of the Three-Year War in Mindong and Minzhong. However, it is unfair to blame Fujian Communists for this failure. Even when they tried to set up bases along the coast after the first fall of Fuzhou in April 1941, they did not succeed.[226] They might have done so had more guerrillas been left behind in 1938.

For a while, the bases in Chaomei and Minxi'nan worked in tandem. The Communist organization in Chaomei grew rapidly, and soon both Meixian and Chaoshan had committees of their own. They published local journals and set up the usual range of resistance organizations.[227] Minxi'nan continued to figure in Guomindang intelligence reports as a hive of Communist activity. In March 1939, the New Fourth's Second Detachment was said—groundlessly—to have sent five thousand troops to protect the movement in Minxi'nan and to have transferred all its wounded to Longyan, whence they fanned out across the whole of Minxi'nan. The Minxi'nan Committee was even said at one time to be planning to recruit one hundred thousand members.[228] These reports were ludicrously exaggerated, but they suggest that Guomindang agents took Communist influence in Minxi'nan extremely seriously.

### THE CONTEST FOR THE LAND

A burning issue in old guerrilla areas after 1937 was the two hundred thousand *mu* of land that had been divided under the soviet but not yet restored to its original owners.[229] In some areas, dispossessed landlords set up "proprietors' squads" to collect rent and regain possession. The Communists resisted these groups, often successfully. Tu Jianchen, magistrate of Longyan and an expert on farming, said in his 1944 study on the land problem in Longyan that three-quarters of the land originally expropriated was still in peasant hands.[230] Most of these peasants, unlike those in other parts of the south, kept their land until 1949. The Party "effectively defended" the land of 146,400 beneficiaries of land reform in Longyan, Shanghang, and Yongding.[231]

The local Guomindang administration tried various ways of reclaiming this land. One of the main Communist officials in Longyan was Wei Jinshui (who in 1962 became governor of Fujian). Early on in the united front, representatives of the Longyan magistrate called on Wei to request talks about the land problem. Wei did not respond. His family, which had itself acquired land in the revolution, was then singled out as a target by rent collectors acting for the landlord Du. Wei's father thwarted Du by manipulating local ties; he asked an elder of the Du lineage to agree that there was no proof that Du had ever owned the land in question and to tell him to drop his demand for rent and repossession. This tactic worked, for the elder knew that the lineage as a whole could suffer if it became associated with "evil landlordism."

*Mintuan* leaders tried to intimidate peasants into handing over rent by displaying arms in the villages. The peasants of Longyan were extremely tough and were organized by Communists into secret associations, so that Party supporters could put collective pressure on any peasants who might consider giving in. Minxi Communists had a long experience of dealing with the *mintuan*, which became riddled with their agents. Many *mintuan* members—its backbone, according to Wei Jinshui—were former Communists or Red Army men who had fled the soviet in the early 1930s; many had themselves obtained land in the revolution. In the moderate phases of the Three-Year War, guerrillas had used these links to stem the attacks against their bases. In the war against Japan, they found that they could touch these people even more effectively. They persuaded some to set up secret "sympathizer cells" in the *mintuan*, including one in its general headquarters at Longyan. They also won over large numbers of *baojia* officials by their milder tactics; in some places, they controlled the majority. As a result, they had excellent intelligence and were able to prepare for and react swiftly to hostile moves.

To blunt the landlords' offensive, the Communists tried to isolate the diehards among them. They came to agreements with "patriotic landlords" and gave small plots of land to landlords fleeing inland from the coastal war zone who might otherwise have joined proprietors' squads. They also harassed and intimidated stubborn landlords. At night, crowds of peasants stoned the houses of those who lived in the villages. Some were killed, and their deaths were made to look like suicides. Town-dwelling landlords or their agents were scolded as chicken thieves or cheats and were threatened or beaten if they entered the villages. If all else failed, land recovered by landlords was deprived of water or flooded, or its crops vanished overnight.

Crowds of peasants demonstrated in the towns against the government's role in the land campaign. In December 1939, they stormed the magistrate's office in Longyan. On another occasion, they blockaded the county capital for three days, causing a shortage of food and firewood and a surfeit of nightsoil; for a while the town simultaneously starved, shivered, and stank. In a similar protest in the spring of 1940, more than thirty *baojia* heads from Longyan pleaded with officials on behalf of several thousand protesting peasants.[232]

## THE CONFLICT ESCALATES

After the guerrillas left in 1938 to join the New Fourth Army, clashes in Minxi'nan and other areas of the Three-Year War degraded relations between the Communists and the Nationalists. In November 1939, four months after the Pingjiang Incident, the two committees under Fang Fang decided to "hide, bide their time, and accumulate forces" but not yet to set up an armed force for fear of further harming the united front. They cut ties to Party members "whose consciousness is low" and dispersed their better-known members who were in danger of arrest. Some went to the New Fourth Army; others were switched between Minxi'nan and Chaomei; still others were sent into the mountains to "start production."[233]

In the summer of 1940, the provincial authorities in Fujian sent troops into the mountains on the first stage of a new extermination drive.[234] This move coincided with escalating violence between Communists and Nationalists elsewhere in China. The campaign against the Communists in Fujian was an extension of the undeclared civil war between New Fourth Army and Nationalist units along the Chang Jiang, for the New Fourth still viewed Minxi'nan as one of its rear bases. The killings that resulted were also an expression by local landlords and conservatives of hatred accumulated over a decade of strife in the region and barely suppressed during the first three years of the war against Japan, when the united front still partly held.

The Communists at first adopted a conciliatory tone in their protests against the attacks on "progressive areas." But their message carried a threat as well as a promise. "If your honorable Party can accept our proposals," it told the provincial government on August 12, 1940,

> the nation will be happy and both the people and the local areas will enjoy good fortune. . . . But should you be unable to restrain these national dregs and let them continue to rampage unchecked, there will be turmoil in the local areas, people will suffer hardship, the nation's law and discipline will be destroyed, the rule and prestige of your honorable Party's authorities will disintegrate, and civil war will arise in Minnan. However, the responsibility will be completely that of the anti-Communist elements, not of our own humble Party.[235]

On January 20, 1941, just a week after the destruction of the New Fourth Army headquarters in the Wannan Incident, two thousand troops of the Fujian Peace Preservation Corps and other local forces swept down on the Communist headquarters in Longyan and Yongding and carried out a wave of arrests and killings. This "Minxi Incident" marked the final collapse of peaceful cooperation in Minxi'nan. Places where the Communists had support were again designated "bandit extermination zones." Families of Communists were wiped out. For a while, defections gravely weakened the Party. To save what they could, the Communists dispersed and took cover. For the next two years, Fang Fang, disguised as a merchant, kept up links between the Party's isolated cells and units; at one point, he was kidnapped by bandits and ransomed on the instructions of Zhou Enlai.

Some Communists retreated to the mountains, where they banded together to farm wasteland and put up bamboo huts to house the recruits who came for training. On June 7, 1941, the Central Committee directed Communists in old soviet areas to fight back when attacked, but at first Fang Fang was forbidden to do so by Party authorities in the south, including Zhou Enlai. Later, the Minxi Special Committee resolved to develop "mass-style armed struggle" and set up a guerrilla detachment.[236]

Other Communists took cover in the towns, where the Party went into tortoise posture. It slimmed down its administration, transferred well-known members elsewhere, stopped holding large meetings, set up a system of secret contacts, stopped most recruitment, and instructed its members in the arts of secrecy. Communists working under cover in government jobs or legally recognized associations were told to stay put while their cover held, but their links to the Party's secret sector were suspended or stripped to essentials. Members pushing the Party line as "democrats" or "patriots" at public meetings were taught to plan their interventions to the last detail. Proposers and seconders of motions invented sharp differences on minor issues to disguise their identity of views.

To ensure the security of Party members working underground, links between higher and lower levels were simplified and reduced; horizontal links were cut. Stand-ins were appointed in case local leaders were arrested, and safe houses were kept ready for emergencies. "With your contacts be neither intimate nor aloof," Party members were advised. "Neither ask nor talk about things that you or others do not need to know; keep your membership of the Party secret even from your nearest kin, for they might unintentionally give you away, or their feelings for you might suddenly change."

Meetings were in principle avoided; where they were essential, precautions were advised. The venue—a restaurant, a teahouse, or a club-room—should be unobtrusive but not hard to find. As few people as

possible should attend. The meeting itself should not look like a meeting: some should sit as if chatting, others reading, others playing chess.

> Should an outsider enter, begin at once to talk of other things; under no
> circumstances go silent or appear flustered. Use special codes: call the
> Party a "school" and your comrades "classmates." If the venue is not en-
> tirely safe, avoid glancing about, speak neither too loudly nor too softly,
> spit if you want to ask a question. After the meeting, disperse at intervals,
> by different routes.
>
> Live like the masses. Live according to your professional status. Dress
> normally, wash often, wear your hair short, drop unnecessary habits.
> Avoid walking quickly, even when in danger; do not eat while walking. Live
> away from opium dens, brothels, and other dangerous places. Be sociable
> and neighborly, but never too much so. Avoid a spartan life. Keep a bal-
> anced selection of books.

So in the towns, the Party slipped into a phase of retreat and consolidation to escape arrests and assassinations. By burrowing deep, it survived the repression unleashed in Minxi'nan after the incidents of January 1941, though it could not wholly stop the defections. Its descent
into secrecy was swift and deft; it drew on two decades of practice in
switching gears. "Secrecy is one of our excellent traditions," the Party
told its members. "We know from years of experience how vital it is to
our security. . . . It is as sacred to us as our political line. . . . Wage pitiless struggle against the slapdash individualism of petit-bourgeois
romantics."[237]

In the remaining years of the war, the Party in the towns of Minxi'nan
barely influenced the region's politics. But the urban bases laid in the
1920s and renewed at the start of the war against Japan were secretly
maintained until 1949, when they helped stabilize the transition to a
new regime.

## THE GUERRILLAS REVIVE

By late 1944, the guerrillas in the region had grown to more than eight
hundred and spawned a detachment in Yuedong. The link between the
movement in Fujian (Min) and Guangdong (Yue) was not new; it had
been formalized in the Minyue Committee of 1937 and in other committees before that. Early on in the war, Fang Fang had called for the simultaneous development of the movement in both regions. In the autumn
of 1940, he took charge of a Southern Working Committee responsible
to Zhou Enlai's Southern Bureau and covering Guangdong, Guangxi,
Fujian, Jiangxi, and Hunan. The guerrillas of Minxi were in contact

even then with guerrillas as far west as Guangdong's Dong Jiang. In the winter of 1946, the Party center ordered Communists in Minyue to develop guerrilla war first in Yuedong, then in Minxi'nan, on the grounds that the balance of forces in Yuedong was more favorable.[238]

By 1945, there were more than ten thousand Communist guerrillas along the border between Guangdong and Fujian.[239] In the final stages of the war against Japan, Communist leaders in Yan'an, having consolidated their hold on much of northern and central China, tried to revive strong southern bases, including those in Minxi'nan. A chance to knit Fujian back into the struggle came in August 1944, when Chen Yi (then in Yan'an) proposed some startling new uses for the old Communist bases in southeastern China to John S. Service of the U.S. Dixie Mission.

> If the Japanese close the Canton-Hankow [Guangzhou-Hankou] line, the Kuomintang forces East of the railway will be weakened and cut off from supplies. Since they have proved in North China their inability to live and fight under guerrilla conditions, they may lose most of the territory to the Japanese (if the Japanese want to take it) without much of a fight. This seems all the more likely because of the indications—in the Honan [Henan] and Hunan fighting—that the fighting ability of the Kuomintang forces has sunk to a new low. It will also be likely because the Kuomintang forces will have not the support of the people in these areas, but more likely their active resistance. But this section of Southwest [sic] China may be of great importance to the war against Japan because it must be the site of American landings. If the Kuomintang cannot hold it, the Communists can. They could easily send officers and old cadres into the old bases from their present operating areas in the Yangtze [Chang Jiang] Valley. Organization and training would be incomparably easier than it was in North China. The organizers would be natives of the areas who know it [sic] well from the long years of civil war and subsequent guerrilla fighting. The people would be already indoctrinated and eager to mobilize under a democratic regime. The arms would be plentiful from the Kuomintang forces who have been defeated and scattered all through the area by the Japanese. In six months the Communists could be sure of at least 100,000 well organized and effective guerrilla fighters.
>
> So far the Communists have decided not to do this because they want to avoid more trouble with the Kuomintang, which would consider such expansion an aggressive act by the Communists and resist it violently. The Communists are not afraid of this competition with the Kuomintang, but it would be a stage closer to civil war, and it would interfere with fighting the Japanese.
>
> Now, however, the situation may be changing. The possible near collapse of the Kuomintang in these areas, and the importance of the areas to the United Nations war effort must be considered.[240]

In the event, the prospect of Communist guerrillas greeting American troops on the beaches of Fujian and Guangdong was not realized.

Roosevelt turned down proposals by Service and others for a Yugoslavia-style cooperation with the Chinese Communists and instead gave unilateral support to Chiang Kai-shek.[241] In the civil war, the Communist columns in southeastern China grew vigorously and eventually had more than forty thousand troops. In August 1949, some of these units met up with the Fourth Field Army at Huichang in Jiangxi; in October, while the Fourth Field Army was taking Guangzhou, they independently took Shantou and other cities to the East.[242] This explosive revival of Communism in the southeast suggests that Chen Yi's proposal to Service was not just empty rhetoric.

## THE MINXI'NAN WAY TO REVOLUTION

Many have described the Communism of Yan'an as the essence of the special spirit of the Chinese Revolution; outside China, few have paid much attention to the movement's regional variants. The "Minxi'nan way" after 1934 was quite different in character from its centralized northern counterpart. It eclipsed the Yan'an way as an example of revolutionary loyalty and perseverance: few traveled it in serious expectation of high status and material privilege. Among the guerrillas, duties differed, but lives were on the whole identical. They mostly sewed their own clothes and stitched their own sandals; leaders like Zhang Dingcheng did the communal cooking and washing while the rest fought. "It was a hard life," said Wen Yangchun, "but a happy one."[243] The movement in Yan'an was a movement of government, with a pronounced hierarchy and a sharp division between the leaders and the led; in Minxi'nan after the Long March, as in other regions of the Three-Year War, the movement was internally less differentiated. Its leaders acted more like family heads than Party managers, and its supporters were likelier to take an active part in its affairs. Women provide the best example: in Minxi'nan after 1934, women played a vital role in the resistance.

Without repeated levies of people and things from Minxi'nan and regions like it, the early Red Army and the early New Fourth Army could never have grown as quickly as they did. Minxi'nan was a seed and sapling bed of the revolution and an independent actor in it. In the early days of the soviet, it was a radiant center of land revolution and Communist armed power. After the start of the Long March, soviet power never collapsed as completely in Minxi'nan as it did in Gannan. Its supporters could not withstand the Guomindang's main extermination drives, but they avoided complete destruction and instantly reappeared in the villages once Guomindang divisions were withdrawn.

In most cases, the idea that Communists depended on mass support in the Three-Year War is pious fiction, but Minxi'nan represents something of an exception. Communists there could call on extensive support in the villages whenever the repression lessened. The Communists left behind in Minxi'nan in 1934 emerged from the war stronger than rearguards in other southern provinces and might have emerged stronger still if they had responded more consistently and vigilantly to their chances. They also emerged from the war against Japan stronger than many other Party outposts, even after all but one of their main leaders had gone north as officers of the New Fourth Army.

The best index of Communist strength in Minxi is the government's failure to roll back land revolution there. The emergence of a new guerrilla army in Minyue after 1940, and especially after 1944, gives the lie to the centralist obsession of historians who stress the role of great military machines in chasing out the Nationalists and ignore regional movements like the one in Minxi, where from the start to the finish of the armed struggle "the people of the border area never once put down the gun." Yet the cost in human suffering of these successes was tremendous. In Longyan alone, more than five hundred villages were razed by fire, more than thirty-seven thousand households "became extinct," and more than ninety thousand local people died in the revolution.[244]

One reason why Communists left behind in Minxi'nan after 1934 fared so much better than their comrades along the fringes of nearby Jiangxi is that they stayed closer to the pulse of national politics. Fujian lay outside the Chinese mainstream, but for that very reason Chiang Kai-shek put less effort into suppressing its guerrillas. Fujian's seclusion from the rest of China was offset by its openness to the sea and its proximity to occupied Taiwan. Japanese aggression became an issue in Fujian earlier than elsewhere in the south, and the Communists in Fujian could give local relevance to abstract proclamations against imperialism.

The Minxi'nan Communists also stayed in closer touch with national politics through their better links to the Party center and its bureaus in the cities of eastern and southern China.[245] Unlike guerrillas in other regions, they got word of the "spirit of Zunyi," which legitimized their adoption of new policies in April 1935. These contacts rescued them from dilemmas and false starts and introduced them earlier than other southern remnants to the idea of a second united front.

But Minxi Communists' loyalty to the center diminished their flexibility, their self-reliance, their independence, and their tolerance, and it encouraged a destructive and irresponsible factionalism among them. Their leaders had more than once been objects of "leftist" persecution, but that experience did not apparently teach them the destructiveness of purges. The fight for an identity of aims in the Minxi'nan Committee

sometimes degenerated into a sterile wrangle between "lines" pieced together by a mixture of guesswork and inference from sketchy press reports and sporadic Party directives.

The Minxi'nan Communists were, in a sense, victims of their own success. Communists in some regions of the Three-Year War were so demoralized and weakened that they concentrated all their efforts on sheer
survival and had neither the energy nor the opportunity to attend to national issues. The Communists in Minxi'nan, however, were in a position
to respond to national crises. Twice, after the Liang Guang Incident and
the Xi'an Incident, they reverted compulsively to "leftist" positions.
These lurches from one extreme to the other harmed Party unity and
made democracy impossible.

The Minxi movement after 1934 was on the whole well led by Communists born and bred in the region and loyal to the guerrilla tradition.
The Minxi'nan Committee was easily the strongest leading team in
any base of the Three-Year War. It had the largest number of experienced and capable leaders outside Shaanbei and probably the best collection of Marxist and general literature of any guerrilla base.[246] In the
early 1930s, Minxi'nan was a peripheral soviet. It escaped the worst exactions of soviet commissars and the extremes of demoralization and
alienation that they bred, but the movement was well enough rooted
in the region to rally support after 1934, except during peaks of repression. It had an advantage over bases where Party networks were less
extensive.

The Minyue Communists to the south generally avoided "leftist" excesses after 1934, for they were less schooled in Party dogma and were
attuned to the realities of Minyue politics. They fought more than one
thousand battles, mostly small ones, between 1934 and 1938 (averaging
out at one a day), and they claimed to have destroyed several thousand
enemy troops, to have captured 1,200 guns, and to have burned or torn
down 150 blockhouses.[247] They built a strong Communist Party in
Minyue in the Three-Year War and ran a model campaign against
Japan. But they fell disastrously at the last hurdle, when they were unable to produce the necessary element of political rigidity.

During the Three-Year War in Minxi'nan, the Communists were not
strong enough to take over political arrangements in the villages completely. This set bounds to their intolerance and made them more responsive to local views and needs. For years on end—between 1934
and 1937, and again between 1941 and 1947—they lost direct contact
with the main Party center.[248] Without central support, they were more
prone to compromise, not only with the village poor whose weight in
village councils had been increased by revolution but also with local
"democratic personages" and *baojia* heads. These intact communities

were better able to confront the Party as equals, so Party decisions were more likely to be negotiated, and "leftist" thinking was correspondingly contained.

Despite their strong local ties, the guerrillas promptly marched north when told to do so in early 1938. Though they were a distinct division of the Party with a strong regional tradition and character, they identified unswervingly with the wider movement, especially its Maoist faction, and followed central instructions even when it hurt to do so. Save for their transfer north in 1938, which greatly weakened the Party in Minxi'nan, they might have maintained a robust Fujianese tradition of Communism and with time played a role in the politics of the southeast similar to that played by the main Red Army in the north.

# Minzhewan'gan (I)

◆    ◆    ◆

Minzhewan'gan is a collective name for the border regions between Fujian (Min), Zhejiang (Zhe), Anhui (Wan), and Jiangxi (Gan), where guerrillas were active at one time or another after 1927 in parts of no fewer than fifty-two counties.[1] The bases it encompassed included Wan'gan (Anhui-Jiangxi), Wannan (southern Anhui), Wanzhe (Anhui-Zhejiang), Zhegan (Zhejiang-Jiangxi), Wanzhegan (Anhui-Zhejiang-Jiangxi), Minzhe (Fujian-Zhejiang), Min'gan (Fujian-Jiangxi), Gandongbei (northeastern Jiangxi), Minzhegan (Fujian-Zhejiang-Jiangxi), Zhexi'nan (southwestern Zhejiang), Zhe'nan (southern Zhejiang), Minbei (northern Fujian), Mindong (eastern Fujian), Mindongbei (northwestern Fujian), and Minzhong (central Fujian). These bases, most of which in their prime overlapped with one or more of their neighbors, formed at best no more than a loose cluster; attempts to weld them into a connected system came to nothing. For months and years on end their leaders were out of touch with one another, though some were more isolated than others. However, most were conscious of their common origins and purpose and strove to keep or restore regional ties. The conditions in which each group operated after 1934 were not identical, but as some problems were common to them all and in part peculiar to the region, it makes sense to discuss them in regional perspective before looking at them individually.

The Communist movement in Minzhewan'gan had its origins in the sudden growth of modern education after World War I, when merchants and landowners began sending their sons to study at foreign-style schools in the cities. Among those seeking the new learning were many future Communist leaders of Minzhewan'gan, including its best-known leader, Fang Zhimin.[2] In 1922, Fang went to Shanghai, where he joined the Party. In 1923, he returned to Jiangxi to build the revolutionary movement in his native Yiyang. In the autumn of 1926, many more Communists returned to the countryside when schools closed after Nationalist armies occupied Nanchang and other cities. Some county magistrates who were too closely associated with the Beiyang warlords fled the region; for a time, most reactionary officials kept their heads down.

During this conservative retreat, returned intellectuals worked to organize the peasants. Some set up branches of the Communist Party in the villages of Gandongbei.[3] After the events of April 12, 1927, when Chiang Kai-shek started a bloody coup against the Communists in Shanghai and elsewhere, Fang Zhimin, Shao Shiping, Huang Dao, and others secretly left Nanchang, Ji'an, and Jingdezhen for the countryside around Yiyang and Hengfeng, where they began preparing for land revolution and armed risings. Their activities paved the way for the establishment of the Party's Gandongbei base, whence Communist organizers fanned out across the whole of Minzhewan'gan.

The founding core of the Gandongbei base consisted of parts of Fujian's Chongan, Zhejiang's Kaihua, Anhui's Wuyuan, and Jiangxi's Yiyang and Hengfeng. In November 1927, representatives of five counties set up a joint committee under Fang Zhimin to start an insurrection in the Yiyang-Hengfeng area; it began in January 1928 but was defeated. The Gandongbei Communists then entered a guerrilla phase after setting up a twenty-man "Land Revolution Army." Soviets sprang up throughout 1928 in the villages; in November, the Party's Jiangxi Committee set up a Xin Jiang Special Committee, renamed the Gandongbei Special Committee a year later, to coordinate these village soviets under a Xin Jiang soviet government chaired by Fang Zhimin.[4]

In 1930, the Gandongbei Communists set up their own Red Army, the Tenth, and supported a new base in Minbei under Huang Dao and Huang Ligui. In November 1930, the Gandongbei Special Committee was reorganized as a provincial committee, and in late 1930 and early 1931 this committee used guerrilla tactics to thwart Nanjing's First and Second Encirclements of the base. Later in 1931, the "leftists" Wan Yongcheng and Zeng Hongyi were put in charge of Gandongbei by the new leadership in Ruijin, which criticized the old Gandongbei leaders for "right opportunist flightism," a "feudal local viewpoint," conservatism, and insufficient resolution in carrying out Party policies.

During the "leftist" period in Gandongbei, several thousand people, including many cadres, were killed in purges that ravaged army morale and alienated villagers from the Party, and an extreme form of land revolution was carried out.[5] In July 1931, three hundred thousand government troops attacked the Central Soviet during the Third Encirclement, and twenty thousand more took up positions along the Xin Jiang to prevent Gandongbei's Tenth Red Army from going south to aid Ruijin. During battles near the Xin Jiang in which Gandongbei's new "leftist" leaders fought (wrongly, according to later critics) by conventional methods, the Tenth Red Army and the base shrank, but in November 1932, parts of Fujian and Zhejiang were sovietized by Red Army units that marched north into Gandongbei from the Central Soviet. A month later, the Gandongbei Provincial Committee was formally reorganized as the Minzhegan Provincial Committee in recognition of this change.[6]

In January 1933, Gandongbei's Tenth Red Army received orders to march south to help the Central Soviet break the Fourth Encirclement; after merging with the Third Red Army Corps, it was reorganized as the Eleventh Red Army. Troops and cadres of the border region were unprepared for this transfer; most opposed it. Many of the semiautonomous local guerrillas assembled for the march south had not previously been under the direct control of the Minzhegan command, and they resented this "excessive centralization." "This difference of opinion," wrote Fang Zhichun many years later, "was not unreasonable, and the mood was understandable." His view was apparently shared by Mao. After this reorganization, many officers of the old Tenth were transferred to other units, and some were attacked or purged.[7]

These measures weakened the solidarity of the old Gandongbei forces and stripped the Minzhegan base of defenders. One thousand five hundred Minzhewan'gan guerrillas and Red Guards were hastily reorganized into a New Tenth Red Army under a centrally appointed commander, who persisted with conventional tactics. This army was no match for the Nationalists, and the Minzhegan base was plunged into a crisis from which it never recovered. The crisis was aggravated by a fresh campaign against "right opportunism" modeled on the struggle against the "Luo Ming line" in the Central Soviet. Support for the Party fell away; many of its followers by now believed that "the Party center no longer wants us."[8]

In December 1933, Fang Zhimin was appointed secretary of the Minzhegan Committee. Fang fought more flexibly, abandoning the line of "fixed defense." He stepped back from a "leftist" land policy and slowed down the purges. However, fresh directives from Ruijin led to a new wave of "leftism" in Minzhegan. By early 1934, all but a small part of the base had fallen to the Nationalists, and links between Gandongbei and Minbei were cut. On October 18, 1934, the seat of the Minzhegan Soviet government fell, and by late 1934 Gandongbei was completely in Nationalist hands, save for a few guerrilla enclaves. "We carried out the strategy of the Central Military Affairs Committee too mechanically," concluded Fang.[9] After the defeat, the mood of the Minzhewan'gan Party soured even further. To stop the grumbling and vacillating, local "leftists" killed or arrested still more "counterrevolutionaries"; the purges continued well into 1935.[10]

The Three-Year War in Minzhewan'gan began, then, in a trough of demoralization and defeat. The Ruijin leaders' attack on "Li Lisan vestiges" in the region was actually a way of asserting central control over it; the campaign weakened the Party's regional identity.[11] By late 1934, many people had become hostile to the Communists in old Gandongbei Soviet areas, where the Red Army was all but finished. After 1934, Communist remnants in Minzhewan'gan fled to peripheral soviets like Minbei, where the Communists were still not completely beaten; to places like Zhe'nan, where the Party could build on a tradition established in earlier years but now dormant; or to parts of the region where the Party was known barely or not at all.

This pattern of movement set the scene for the Communist experience in Minzhewan'gan after 1934. In peripheral areas where the Party still had some basic organization and support, it weathered the storm best; in areas where it had little or no previous organization or where its supporters had long been inactive, it flared up strongly, only to fizzle out under the first drenching; and in the old Soviet core areas, it remained more or less extinct.

Communist units that fought the Three-Year War in Minzhewan'gan were of two main sorts. Some were local guerrillas left behind or recruited after the original Tenth Red Army went south in January 1933. Others were remnants of a Northern Expedition (not to be confused with the famous Northern Expedition of 1926–28) carried out by an Anti-Japanese Vanguard, founded by central Red Army units that entered the region in late 1934 and scattered after their subsequent defeat. The diverse origins of the Minzhewan'gan guerrillas after 1934 caused rivalries and tensions that contributed to the "sectarian" reputation of the region's Communists.

## THE NORTHERN EXPEDITION OF 1934

The Northern Expedition into Minzhewan'gan was a curtain-raiser for the Long March, though its leaders did not know it at the time. On July 7, 1934, central military leaders in Ruijin ordered the Seventh Red Army Corps, formed on the basis of the Eleventh Red Army, to march north into Gandongbei, merge into the Anti-Japanese Vanguard with the New Tenth Red Army formed there after January 1933, go to Wannan, and establish bases there. The Eleventh Red Army was historically linked to Gandongbei, for it was the product of an earlier merger between two forces, one of which (the Old Tenth) had marched south from Gandongbei in January 1933. The Old Tenth had been greatly weakened by this merger; many of its officers were criticized or transferred to other units. By July 1934, after suffering heavy losses on the Central Soviet's eastern front, the Seventh Red Army Corps had only four thousand soldiers left; it was restored to strength by the infusion of two thousand local recruits. When it started out from Ruijin in July, it was escorted by the Ninth Red Army Corps, which covered its rear and flanks. The Ninth had never before been outside soviet territory; it was a poor choice to escort an expedition deep behind enemy lines. In the three divisions of the Seventh Red Army Corps, one-third of its six thousand members were noncombatants; less than one-third of its combat troops had guns. So the expedition started off poorly armed and inexperienced.[12]

At the same time, the corps was overburdened with tasks and materials and charged with a mission that it could not hope to fulfill. It was expected to wage guerrilla war deep behind enemy lines, raise a new anti-Japanese army, whip up an anti-Japanese political movement while marching north and after arriving in Minzhewan'gan, and found new soviets just outside Chiang Kai-shek's main political and economic base in the lower Chang Jiang valley (map 6). These political goals explain the large number of noncombatants among the marchers, who carried twenty tons of anti-Japanese propaganda (including 1.6 million leaflets) and twenty-five tons of standard equipment and supplies. The expedition was also expected to reach Anhui within six weeks.[13] What the expeditionaries did not know at the time was that their real purpose was to draw Nationalist troops away from the Central Soviet and thus help the Long Marchers escape west.[14]

On top of being weak and overburdened, the expedition was split into warring factions. Its nominal commander was Xun Huaizhou, who, though still only twenty-two, was a Red Army veteran. But real power belonged to Zeng Hongyi and Yue Shaohua, two "leftists" who had no respect for Xun and often clashed with him. Because of Zeng and Yue's ideological browbeating, leaders of the expedition who favored guerrilla tactics failed to get their way, and the column was drawn into expensive battles on the road north. Disputes among leaders of the expedition went a long way toward wrecking its morale.[15]

Many years later, Su Yu, a leader of the Seventh, summed up his criticisms of the expedition. He concluded that it could reasonably have been expected to act as a lure but not at the same time to found new soviets and launch a vast new political campaign. Such expectations were all the more unrealistic given the direction in which it had set out. If eighty thousand troops had been unable to hold on to Ruijin, how could six thousand hold onto new bases just outside the Guomindang's main political stronghold? According to Su, the original proposal to send a

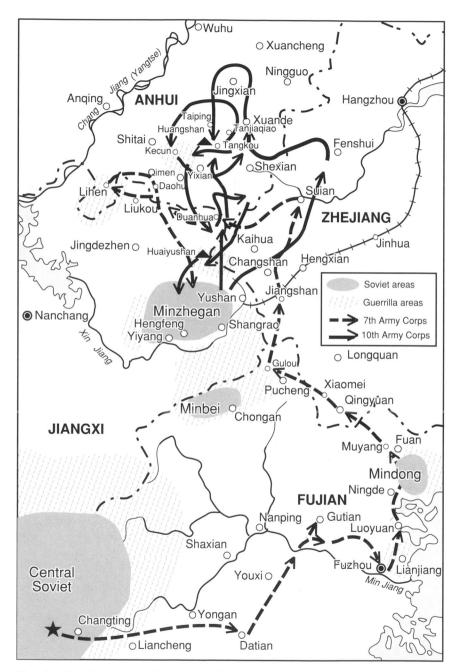

Map 6. The line of march of the Red Army's Anti-Japanese Vanguard (the Northern Expedition), July–December 1934. *Based on a map in Ye Fei 1988.*

Red Army into Zhewan'gan came from Mao at the start of the Nationalists' Fifth Encirclement campaign, but it was not then adopted. Su says that by July 1934, when the expedition was eventually launched, the situation had changed, and Mao's old strategy was no longer appropriate.[16]

The expedition set out from Jianning on July 9, 1934, toward Ninghua. Over the next six months, it covered nearly two thousand miles and fought more than thirty major battles, scaring several big towns and cities along the way. It made contact with Communist guerrillas in Minzhong, Mindong, Minbei, Zhexi, Zhewan, and Wan'gan before reaching Gandongbei in late October. It left behind small groups of wounded in many of these places, seeding the route with more than one thousand troops; its propaganda teams plastered towns and villages with posters calling for resistance to Japan and denouncing the Guomindang dictatorship. Most regular Nationalist forces had by then withdrawn from central Fujian to take part in the campaign against the Central Soviet, but the marchers were harassed and slowed down by local forces. On August 1, 1934, they crossed the Min Jiang and began calling themselves the Anti-Japanese Vanguard. Their escort returned to the Central Soviet with four thousand cases of captured ammunition and great quantities of food and salt. At first, they were poorly armed, with between 1,200 and 1,300 guns. Many had started out with nothing more than a spear. They armed themselves as they marched by overrunning their opponents. On August 7, they rashly attacked the city of Fuzhou on instructions from Ruijin and were beaten off by troops and planes. By mid-August they were carrying nearly eight hundred wounded; and because of their attack on Fuzhou, the Nationalists now knew their exact strength.[17]

When the expedition threatened Fuzhou, Nationalist regulars were transferred south from Mindong to block the Communists, allowing guerrillas in Mindong to expand. It was vital for the marchers to link up with local Communists: they needed help with their wounded and were unable to recruit widely in the areas they crossed. For their part, the guerrillas under Ye Fei in Mindong had never before seen a main-force Red Army unit and were overjoyed when they heard of its approach. The expedition's passage through Mindong was unplanned. Its original route avoided Mindong, but the plan was changed after the unscheduled attack on Fuzhou. Consequently, apart from spreading the Party's general line, the marchers had no particular agenda in Mindong.[18]

Marchers and guerrillas finally met up in a southern outpost of the Mindong base in Luoyuan in August. The vanguard teamed up with local guerrilla chiefs to attack the county capital, where they executed the magistrate and carried off huge quantities of cash and supplies. They left two days later, when French and United States gunboats appeared in Luoyuan Bay, and reached the headquarters of the Mindong Red Army in Ningde on August 19.[19] As the expeditionaries marched into the Ningde base, bronzed by the sun and camouflaged with twigs and leaves, the guerrillas raced down from the hills to stand by the road and cheer them on. Guerrillas shouted greetings to the marchers, and the marchers shouted greetings back, in mutually unintelligible tongues. (This confusion of languages created many problems for the expedition in Fujian: exchanges with local people were carried out mainly by gesture.)[20] The guerrillas were struck by the marchers' technicolor sandals, woven with thread and cloth of many different sorts, and above all by their guns, which the guerrillas were strictly forbidden to touch. On a small mound by the side of the road, members of one of the expedition's propaganda teams beat bamboo clappers and sang to the troops as they swung past. The hundreds of stretcher-bearers in the column sweated freely; so did the porters carrying huge loads of ammunition and propaganda.

After blocking nearby roads with stones and tree-trunks, pulling down telephone wires, and digging simple fortifications, the marchers camped in a village, where they set about painting slogans, sticking up posters, and preparing food. The guerrillas were kept at bay "to avoid confusion and misunderstandings," but the next day they and the marchers joined forces to attack Muyang, a nearby town of some two thousand households. Again, propagandists filled the walls with slogans, while troops removed cases of opium from rich homes; later, the guerrillas returned to collect "contributions" from their owners. A banner slung across a Muyang shop read "Bank of the Chinese Soviet Republic." Here local traders were able to cash in the soviet currency paid them by the marchers.[21]

Government forces were by now hard on the heels of the expeditionaries, who slipped away to the north. They took along a fresh batch of five hundred recruits from Mindong to offset earlier losses, but by the time they reached the perimeter of the guerrilla area, all but three of these recruits had run away. The marchers left behind more than three hundred wounded, who were later to play an important role in the Mindong Independent Division; a like number of rifles and two machine guns (the expedition now bristled with weapons); and word of the slogan "Resist Japan and oppose Chiang," which Ye Fei tried to apply in Mindong.[22] Similar encounters took place throughout Minzhewan'gan. Though the expedition did little to loosen Chiang's grip on the Central Soviet, it electrified local units of the Party and made an indelible impact on the regions it traversed.

In early September, the expedition reached the Minbei soviet area under Huang Dao. Its leaders would have liked to stop to rest and recuperate, but they were told by Ruijin to continue toward Wannan. Many years later, Su Yu said that this decision was wrong; if the aim was to distract attention from the Central Soviet, it was unnecessary to press on into Wannan, especially since the Ruijin leaders (but not the marchers) had known since mid-1934 that earlier risings in Wannan had been defeated. Su concluded that the expedition could have tied down Nationalist divisions far more effectively if it had been allowed to build on the existing Minbei base and to link it to Ye Fei's base in Mindong. It might also have avoided the defeat that awaited it in Wannan.[23] Ye Fei, too, says that it was wrong to go to Wannan and that the expedition should have stayed with him in Mindong: he controlled a large area that was well supplied with grain and salt, was within easy reach of other Minzhewan'gan bases, and could have played an important role in coordinating the Central Soviet's defense.[24] Nevertheless, the expedition marched off to the west.

By this time, the expeditionaries had already missed their deadline for reaching Wannan. Even so, they were burdened with two more tasks: to come to the aid of the Communist New Tenth, under siege in Gandongbei, by attacking enemy communications; and to found new soviets in Minzhegan. At the same time, they were accused of timidity for failing to stay on the offensive. The area along the Zhejiang border that they now entered had no Communist tradition and was controlled by Nationalists. Once again the marchers had to bear their own wounded, for there were no local supporters to carry them to safe places. Because each wounded soldier required two stretcher-bearers and one replacement bearer, carrying them put an enormous strain on the expedition. On September 17, 1934, the marchers were ordered to build a soviet around Quxian and Kaihua, just north of the Zhegan Railway. However, this part of Zhejiang was strategically vulnerable because of the railway and its proximity to Hangzhou. It was, moreover, a stronghold of anti-Communist refugees from Gandongbei. So the leaders of the expedition ignored the directive and pressed on toward Wannan.

In late September, not far from their final destination, they learned of the defeat of the risings in Wannan in mid-1934. But there were still small pockets of Communist resistance in Wannan, which looked more promising as a potential base than Zhejiang's Quxian. The Wan'gan Communists gave the expedition five hundred new recruits to offset its losses in Zhejiang (though they did so reluctantly and on the understanding—quickly overtaken by events—that the marchers would stay close by).

On October 15, the distant steersmen in Ruijin gave a new twist to the expedition's helm that yanked the marchers back south to join forces with Communists in Gandongbei. This constant interference from Ruijin exacerbated tensions in the expedition's leadership, which split three ways among Zeng, Yue, and Xun.[25]

## FANG ZHIMIN AND THE EXPEDITION

By the time the expedition marched into Gandongbei later in October, nearly half of its six thousand troops had fallen by the way. This depleted army was welcomed in Gandongbei by Fang Zhimin as the Old Tenth and was amalgamated with the New Tenth to form the Tenth Red Army Corps. This new joint force is said by one source to have numbered eighteen thousand men and by others (more realistically) between eight and ten thousand.[26] It carried out the final stages of the Northern Expedition of the Anti-Japanese Vanguard. Liu Chouxi, commander of the Minzhegan Military Region, commanded it; Zeng, Yue, and Xun retained important posts. Fang Zhimin, leader of the Minzhegan Soviet, was in effect overall commander of the reorganised vanguard, with Su Yu as his chief of staff.

In November 1934, one of the Tenth Red Army Corps's three divisions, the Nineteenth, marched north under Xun Huaizhou; the other two (the Twentieth and Twenty-first) stayed behind in Gandongbei. Two weeks later, the Twentieth and Twenty-first Divisions followed Xun into Wannan's Huang Mountains after he had won some initial victories and declared the Wanzhegan Soviet on the borders of Anhui, Zhejiang, and Jiangxi. One thousand men were left behind in Minzhegan under Guan Ying and Tang Zaigang. By January 1935, the Minzhegan base had fallen, Tang was dead, and Guan had fled to set up a new base in the Zhanggong Mountains of Wanzhegan.[27]

On December 14, 1934, Xun was killed near Tanjiaqiao. Not long afterward, Yue Shaohua and Liu Ying (a leader of the Three-Year War in Minzhewan'gan) were wounded in further fighting. According to Wang Yaowu, the Nationalist general who defeated the expedition, a total of two hundred thousand men took part in the campaign against Fang's vanguard. By the year's end, Nationalists controlled all the main roads in the region. To preserve his forces, Fang took to the mountains, twisting and turning to throw off his pursuers. His troops were short of ammunition and had scarcely rested since leaving Gandongbei. They were tired, freezing, starving, and largely shoeless; bounty hunters who later dug up Xun's corpse reported that it was small and gaunt, that the bodies of Communist troops who had died of cold or hunger were scattered throughout the mountains, and that "all the captured bandits were thin and emaciated." According to General Yao, their fingers were so cold that they could no longer pull the triggers of their rifles, they were too weak to throw their hand grenades, and thirst had blistered their lips.[28]

Under the circumstances, the expedition would have done better to break into smaller mobile units and disperse, but its leaders were not prepared to take responsibility for such a move, and they decided instead to try to lead the column back into Gandongbei by way of Huawude, a small outer soviet to the north of the main base. Zeng Hongyi proposed abandoning Minzhegan and fleeing to Minbei, but he defected to the government after three days and nights of ideological "struggle" by Su and Liu, who stripped him of his posts and demanded that he confess his errors. On January 12, 1935, units of the expedition arrived on the northeastern border of Huawude, and a few days later its vanguard, under Su Yu, fought its way through into Gandongbei. Fang Zhimin and Liu Chouxi, by now in command of a mere two to three thousand troops, were captured in the Huaiyu Mountains just short of Gandongbei. Altogether 2,700 members of the expedition were captured, and more than one thousand weapons were seized. "Herewith, the Northern Expedition . . . was basically defeated."[29]

This defeat portended the Wannan Incident of 1941, in which New Fourth Army units—including veterans of the Three-Year War in Minzhewan'gan—were also surrounded and destroyed by a huge Nationalist army.[30] The two defeats happened in more or less the same place. The main difference is that by 1941, the Party controlled powerful bases north of the Chang Jiang. In 1935, no strong Communist base was left anywhere, and the main Chinese Red Armies had been put to flight. The effects of the 1935 defeat in the region were far more devastating.[31]

Fang Zhimin was taken in chains to Nanchang, where the Nationalist Gu Zhutong had his headquarters. While Fang was in jail, Chiang Kaishek wrote him a personal letter and Gu, who had studied with Fang, urged him to recant. Fang ignored them. "Fan[g] rejects all proposals," the Nationalist press reported. "He is still incredibly adamant. He will presumably remain so until his death." In early February 1935, the Nationalists organized a "popular rejoicing on the occasion of the seizure alive of Fan" in a Nanchang park. "Not a sound of rejoicing was heard," wrote an American correspondent. "In [the] silence was displayed all the respect and sympathy felt towards the man who stood upon the platform, with head held high and fearless eyes. He was immediately driven away, for the silence of the crowd was too menacing for the authorities. As soon as the armoured car moved away, the crowd began to show signs of agitation. The people were quietened by the machine-guns, which were trained on them."[32]

Fang's role in the Minzhewan'gan Communist movement was not yet over. From jail, he smuggled messages to his fellow prisoners, urging them to stay firm and if necessary to face death with dignity. Prisoners later set up a Communist Party branch in jail that by 1937 had more than thirty members, all of whom joined the New Fourth Army. Fang smuggled letters from his cell before his execution on August 6, 1935. One, addressed to "all comrades" in Gandongbei, Minbei, Wan'gan, Wannan, and Zhexi, said, "I cannot complete my task. I have no choice but to transfer it to your shoulders."[33] More than a year later, in August 1936, this letter reached survivors of Fang's Anti-Japanese Vanguard, who reproduced and distributed it in hundreds of copies.[34]

# Zhe'nan:
# Walking on Two Legs

•  •  •

Among the armed groups onto whose shoulders Fang Zhimin transferred responsibility in 1935, first in line was the unit under Su Yu and
Liu Ying, main commanders of Fang's vanguard and its two highest-
ranking survivors. By the time that Su and Liu broke through in January 1935, Gandongbei was finished as a Communist base.[1] Twice it had
given up its sons to produce a Tenth Red Army; twice they had marched
off to fight largely ineffective battles in other parts of China. The transfer south of the Old Tenth in January 1933 had created unrest and disaffection in the region. The decision by vanguard leaders to swallow up
the New Tenth in October 1934 has also been criticized as a serious mistake and a main cause of the subsequent rout.[2] This double exploitation
of Gandongbei undermined the support that Communists had once enjoyed there. The vanguard was demoralized by its defeat and torn apart
by fierce ideological disputes. The future looked bleak for the battered
remnants of it that wound up in Gandongbei under Su and Liu.

At first they planned to march south into what had formerly been the
Central Soviet, but they changed their plans after receiving a directive
from the Central Committee sub-bureau in Gannan. The directive ordered them to reorganize their remnant forces into an Advance Division
of three detachments and go east into Zhejiang to fight guerrilla war, tie
down Nationalist forces, protect nearby Red bases, create new soviets,
and divide the land (map 7).

Some eight hundred Red Army troops, including a company of infan-
trymen and a company of machine gunners and artillerymen, arrived at
the border of Dexing and Hengfeng under Su and Liu. Many were noncombatants, as were the officials of the routed Minzhegan (Gandongbei)
Soviet who turned up to join them; many, including Su and Liu, had

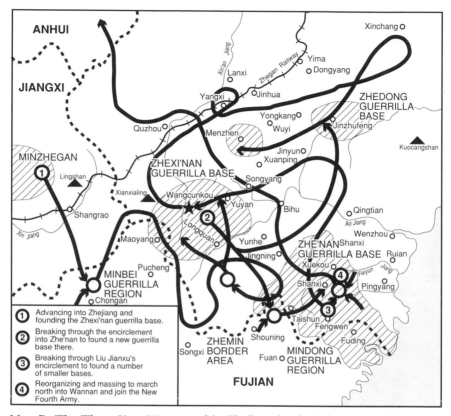

Map 7. The Three-Year War waged in Zhejiang by the Advance Division, 1935–37. *Based on a map in Zhejiang sheng junqu, eds., 1984.*

collected wounds in the January battles. Of those who gathered in Gandongbei, slightly more than half marched east on February 27, 1935.[3]

When the expedition set out, it was 538 strong and well armed (with 445 rifles and twelve machine guns).[4] But it was an army born of defeat, weakened at the very start by a new split. It had been assembled hastily; not all its recruits believed that the move to Zhejiang would succeed, and not enough effort was put into persuading them that it would. Though Zhejiang was in the main orbit of Nationalist power, the march into Zhejiang was preceded by only a fortnight's training.[5] The strongest resistance to the assignment came from Minbei guerrillas previously incorporated into the division. Unlike members of the original expedition, they had homes nearby to which they could return, and they were local people whose loyalties were to Minbei rather than to any grand ideal. As the Su-Liu column marched east through the nights in hostile mountains, some marchers began to waver, and about one hundred Minbei guerrillas deserted.[6] But Su and Liu more than made good this loss when they met up with a further 150 survivors of the Fang Zhimin expedition stranded in Zhexi'nan (southwestern Zhejiang).

The history of the Su-Liu Advance Division falls into four main stages. The first stage runs from early April to mid-September 1935, when the division advanced into Zhexi'nan. Between mid-September 1935 and later May 1936, after the Zhexi'nan venture had collapsed, the bulk of the division marched southeast into Zhe'nan (southern Zhejiang), where it eventually began to pick up strength. Between June and December 1936, the division grew strongly in the wake of the Liang Guang Incident. In 1937, most of this growth was pruned back by a new Nationalist offensive.[7]

## ZHEXI'NAN

Su and Liu spent the summer of 1935 in the area below the Ou Jiang and around the Xianxialing range as far south as Pucheng, just across the border in Fujian. They chose this region for its rugged features and its strategic location close to the border with Fujian and Jiangxi and to the Hangzhou-Jiangshan section of the Zhegan railway, as well as to three main highways and to the Communist bases of Minbei and Mindong. Apart from Pucheng, which the Minbei Communists had held for three days in 1932, this area had never seen a Communist army until the autumn of 1934, when the Seventh Red Army Corps passed by on its way to Wannan and planted a contingent of troops that was later reorganized as the Red Third Regiment.

Zhexi'nan was more or less virgin territory, opened up only after Fang Zhimin's defeat.[8] As such, it had both advantages and disadvantages for

Su and Liu. One advantage was that local people had not been through the same process of disillusion and alienation as those in Gandongbei. Against this benefit, the region was a stronghold of local and national reaction; it was close to the center of Guomindang support and to the birthplaces of Chiang Kai-shek and Chen Cheng; and its economy and communications were better developed than in areas where Communists had previously set up military bases. Apart from having briefly crossed it in 1934, Su and Liu knew nothing about the region, and at first neither they nor their troops (from Hunan, Jiangxi, and Fujian) understood its languages.[9]

Even so, Su and Liu won a string of victories within weeks of arriving in Zhexi'nan. Strengthened by the Red Third Regiment, they set up a Zhexi'nan Special Committee that mobilized peasant support for insurrections in three counties. Zhexi'nan had been hit by drought in 1934 and by floods in the spring of 1935; beggars and refugees swarmed through the region. To win them, the Communists adopted the slogan, "Attack *tuhao,* open granaries to help the people, help the masses to overcome the summer shortage." Guerrillas were soon active in half a dozen counties south of the Zhegan railway, an area at first only lightly garrisoned by the Nationalists. A high official of the provincial Peace Preservation Corps reported in April that Liu Ying had marched into the Jiangshan-Suichang area at the head of more than one thousand armed men; the authorities received similar urgent telegrams from other parts of Zhexi'nan.

Settled peasants were less easily organized than beggars and refugees. At first, they feared the Communists and fled them, leaving them with neither guides nor grain. Su and Liu broke from their isolation by allying with two local leaders of the Green Gang, who opposed the Guomindang and had a reputation for robbing the rich to help the poor. These Green Gang leaders were bandits of a special sort: one had studied in Japan, and both had been exposed to left-wing ideas. Later, some gang members joined the Communist Party, yielding the region's first generation of local cadres.[10]

The Daoist Great Knives, the main sect in Zhexi'nan, were far harder to infiltrate and sway. They had clashed with local Nationalists when forming their lodges in the region and had initially defended the villages against conscriptors and grain collectors. Later their leaders, men "famed for learning and for art," developed ties to the Zhejiang Guomindang: by the time Su and Liu arrived, they were collaborating with the local Peace Preservation Corps. The authorities played on regional xenophobia to isolate the Advance Division, saying that "people from Jiangxi are bandits, they should be seized."[11]

According to the Daoists, Communists were monsters with red hair and red eyes. The Great Knives caused enormous trouble for the Su-Liu column. They controlled many of the villages in Zhexi'nan. Smaller villages were federated into lodges; bigger ones formed lodges of their own. Whenever the Communists approached these villages, their inhabitants took to the mountains. Throughout the night, votaries of the Jade Emperor blew cowhorns on the slopes above the Communist camps; sentries who strayed too far ran the risk of being hacked to death in the dark. Sometimes yellow-turbaned "Magic Soldiers" attacked the Communists in formation, flourishing double-edged swords and red-tasseled spears. Before battle, they swallowed magic pellets concocted from herbs, cinnabar, and the ashes of paper slips on which were written incantations. These pellets were supposed to make the Magic Soldiers invulnerable to bullets ("guns cannot get past knives, fire cannot get near water").

At first, the Communists had no idea how to deal with these attacks. Firing on the Magic Soldiers only further alienated the villagers. During one attack, the guerrillas stood their ground, chanting, "We too are poor," as Daoists came whooping down the hillside. Their words were carried away on the wind as the attackers fell about them. Some Communists were cut down and killed; the rest fled. The Daoists, now convinced that the guerrillas were afraid of them, became bolder still.

Later, the Communists captured a sect member and interrogated him about the sect and its beliefs. They learned about the structure of its lodges, the belief in the inefficacy of bullets, and the sect's fears and taboos. They learned that the Great Knives dreaded bamboo pitchforks, which they believed could vanquish swords, and that they had a taboo against dirty cloth. From then on, the guerrillas were never without a supply of pitchforks decked about with pieces of soiled clothing, which they flaunted at the Knives. Sometimes crowds of Daoists would gather in the valleys and block the Communists' passage. During one such confrontation, a pheasant, disturbed by Daoist cowhorns, whirred up from the bushes and was shot down by a Communist marksman. The marksman turned to the Knives and said, "See that? Don't be cheated." Arguments and slogans were hurled back and forth; the confrontation became more and more heated. Finally, the Communist commander shot dead the sect leader to head off an attack. After this episode, the guerrillas were left in peace, but the villagers continued to shun them. Only a few Daoist lodges were neutralized or won over in Zhexi'nan, unlike those in neighboring Minbei and Mindong. Liu Ying later concluded that the Communists had not sufficiently distinguished between the leaders and the led; because they had been uniformly hostile to the Daoists, their efforts to "dissolve and win them over . . . had little effect."[12]

When the Advance Division first entered Zhexi'nan, it was not a local or guerrilla unit but part of the regular Red Army. Su and Liu were not initially prepared for a switch to irregular tactics, though they soon opted for decentralization. Some founding members of the expedition (especially veterans of the Old Tenth) had once been guerrillas, but they had been reorganized and made regular soldiers after their transfer to the Central Soviet. Those who remained now had to relearn guerrilla tactics, their rationale and their nature. This reeducation was far from easy. At first, small units sent out on their own for a fortnight returned to headquarters in just a day or two without accomplishing their missions. But gradually their confidence grew, and they stayed out on their own for longer and longer periods. After the switch, the guerrillas at first avoided the towns and stuck to the villages, where the Nationalists had scant authority. They also changed their land policy. In June 1935, the secretary of the Zhejiang Provincial Government reported, "[The Communists] have changed their policy toward middle peasants and landlords from one of burning and killing to one of taxing and seducing, and put the emphasis not on capturing the towns but on activity in the countryside; they base their military plans on the principle of avoiding formal clashes with [Nationalist] armed forces. That is why . . . bandits now turn up whenever the army leaves."[13] He Yuelao, a regimental commander in Zhejiang's Peace Preservation Corps, admired the Communists' stamina and courage. "The four to five hundred of you have the mettle to sovietize the whole of Zhejiang," he wrote in a letter to the Advance Division. "This spirit of bold advance is commendable."[14]

By seizing on local grievances and taking advantage of the government's unpreparedness, Su and Liu's army expanded quickly in the summer of 1935. The five hundred troops with which they had started out were joined before long by some 1,500 others, backed by more than one thousand local guerrillas. In the past, wrote a vice commander of the Guomindang's regional military headquarters, "Liu Ying and Su Yu only had several hundred people. Now they have more than three thousand. Investigations show that three-quarters of them are Zhejiang workers and peasants who have been led astray. They have spread to more than twenty counties. They are making more headway even than [the Communists in] Jiangxi." Before long, units of the Advance Division were active in thirty counties and began to establish ties to other guerrilla units along nearby provincial borders. By midyear, they had built a base sixty miles across, thus fulfilling Xiang Ying's directive. "The greater part" of a number of counties has "gone Red," reported Zhejiang's *Dongnan Ribao*.[15] It added that though Zhejiang was normally peaceful, "since Su and Liu slipped in, banditry has spread to the whole province. If the authorities cannot quickly stamp them out, the future is worrying." Huang Shaoxiong, governor of Zhejiang, also took the threat from the guerrillas seriously. In parts of Jinhua, he said, "everyone was in state of utter terror": the rich had fled, the gentry were helpless, local organization had collapsed.[16]

The Advance Division was set up in late January and early February 1935, after the Zunyi Conference. Some Chinese believe that it was formed in line with a directive from Zunyi. But Su and Liu left for Zhexi'nan before the exact contents of the Zunyi decisions were radioed to Gandongbei by leaders of the Central Soviet rearguard; they knew only that they were to switch to guerrilla warfare. Before the week was out, their radio broke down, so it is unlikely that they were acquainted with the more detailed contents of the Zunyi directives. This lack of information may explain why they reverted to soviet-period policies, including land reform and insurrectionary tactics that unnecessarily exposed their forces, whenever they felt strong enough to do so.[17]

In June 1935 the Advance Division killed several dozen members of an inspection force directly under Governor Huang Shaoxiong. It seized towns, killed their administrators, and set up soviets and revolutionary committees. In August, it launched a field inspection campaign to prepare for land revolution.[18]

In the late 1920s, Communists working under Wang Ming in Shanghai had held demonstrations on important anniversaries of the labor movement, a practice derided by Leon Trotsky as "directing the revolution with a revolutionary calendar."[19] In Zhexi'nan, Communist leaders encouraged by the swift growth of their base staged spectacular armed propaganda actions according to this same revolutionary calendar. They commemorated July 1 (the founding of the Party) and August 1 (the founding of the Chinese Red Army) with attacks on nineteen towns, roads, and railways. They also launched a campaign to "build the Red Army" (four hundred youths were recruited) and had fifty thousand leaflets and posters printed. While these demonstrations took place, the alarmed authorities were massing a huge army to crush the Communists.[20]

### THE "PACIFICATION" OF ZHEXI'NAN

To counter the Su-Liu threat, Governor Huang divided Zhejiang into nine "peace preservation subzones" and brought in reinforcements from outside the province. This campaign, waged by eight or nine regiments, petered out in June 1935, but a second and much stronger force bore down on the Communists in late August. This new campaign,

reportedly supervised by Chiang Kai-shek, was directed by a command
drawn from the provinces of Fujian (Min), Jiangxi (Gan), Zhejiang (Zhe),
and Anhui (Wan), known as the Min'ganzhewan Four Provinces General
Bandit Extermination Command.

The command set up headquarters in Pucheng, on the southern edge
of Zhexi'nan. In late August its new leader, the "ever-victorious general"
Wei Lihuang, promised to wipe out Su and Liu before October 15, 1935.
Wei's force, built around crack troops of the Eighteenth Army, was dozens of times bigger than the Advance Division: it commanded more than
seventy thousand regular troops in thirty-two regiments, supported by
forty regiments of landlord troops—an army "of a scope rarely seen in
China's southern guerrilla areas" (for in Zhexi'nan, Chiang Kai-shek was
protecting places dear to him). This army, backed up by warplanes, used
tactics (blockhouses and gradual advance) applied earlier against the
Central Soviet, though the campaign in Zhexi'nan was styled *qingjiao*
(clean up) rather than *weijiao* (encircle and suppress) on the grounds
that the Su-Liu troops were "remnants."[21]

The Party's new support in Zhexi'nan crumbled under this onslaught. At first, Su and Liu continued to expose their division in wasteful battles. It was not until late September (by which time their tiny capital at Wangcunkou had fallen) that they realized the size of the force
ranged against them. They responded by transferring the bulk of their
troops to Zhe'nan, where the second phase of their three-year campaign
began; a few went to Minbei, and up to four hundred local guerrillas
stayed behind in Zhexi'nan: too many, according to Liu Ying, who
thought that fewer than a quarter should have stayed.[22]

The guerrillas left behind in Zhexi'nan suffered heavy losses and were
scattered across the mountains. Su and Liu hoped by marching east to
draw Nationalist troops away from Zhexi'nan and save the base. But the
Nationalists, more interested in cleaning up Zhexi'nan than in chasing
Su and Liu's dwindling army, kept all but five regiments behind. The
purging of Zhexi'nan lasted eight months, until the outbreak of the
Liang Guang Incident in June 1936. Soon after Su and Liu left, the main
Communist leader in Zhexi'nan was killed in action, whereupon many of
his followers lost heart and deserted.[23]

In retrospect, Communist leaders blamed the loss of Zhexi'nan on
misguided policies pursued in the summer of 1935. Within months of
arriving in the region, they had openly set up soviets and Communist
Party branches, begun to divide the land, and indiscriminately attacked
*tuhao* and officials. Despite the switch to guerrilla warfare, they had
squandered their troops in "pitched battles of annihilation" and "pitted
forts against forts." They had built an openly Red base on a tiny island
of territory in the midst of a great White sea, just a few miles from a rail-

way line. If they had kept to more modest policies, they might have succeeded in building a stronger base before the Nationalists started their offensive.[24]

By December 1935, the guerrillas in Zhexi'nan had been whittled down to a few dozen diehards, mostly local people recruited in the summer. Normally this local composition would have been considered an advantage, but in Zhexi'nan, where there was no Communist tradition, the Party's few local converts stood out and were more easily rounded up. So the guerrillas kept well clear of the villages and were cut off for months on end from news and intelligence. At first, they split into teams of a dozen, and later into teams of four or five. When Guomindang troops burned them out of the lower slopes, they fled to the peaks, where sheer cliffs shielded them. The mountains were coated by virgin forests and covered by a three-foot layer of rotting leaves that was extremely difficult to cross: this was the guerrillas' second line of defense. In the forests, they lived on mushrooms, wild plants, monkeys, and wild pigs, which they sometimes roasted in the fires set by their pursuers.[25] Lacking ammunition, they fought mainly with spears. Light, noiseless, and readily available on the nearest tree, spears were ideal in the new conditions. One unit killed more than fifty enemy troops with spears at no cost to itself.[26]

In late 1935, the Zhexi'nan guerrillas read in a captured newspaper that the Advance Division was fighting near Wenzhou. They then fought a battle to make headlines themselves and so send news of their whereabouts to Su and Liu. The trick worked. In February 1936, Su returned to Zhexi'nan to see them.[27] In the summer, he returned again to organize rent and tax resistance. By that time, however, more than two-thirds of the Communists left behind in Zhexi'nan had been wiped out.[28]

Between June 1936, when the Nationalists' Eighteenth Army withdrew from Zhexi'nan to help deal with the Liang Guang Incident, and February or March 1937, Zhexi'nan was largely free of government troops, and the Communists were able to surge up again and rally stragglers.[29] By then, they had learned their lesson. Though they reformed the Zhexi'nan Special Committee and three county committees, they emphasized secrecy and so built a firmer though smaller base.[30] However, between March and October 1937, the Nationalists purged Zhexi'nan as part of a general purge of the Minzhewan'gan border region and wiped out many of these gains.

## ZHE'NAN

On its flight eastward to the coast, the Advance Division was chased by a Nationalist regular contingent that outnumbered it by ten to one. Along the route, landlord and local security forces were on a war footing. The division suffered heavy losses, especially on the small plains that punctuated its line of march.[31] But in the longer term, the transfer to Zhe'nan increased its freedom of movement and its chances of survival, for Zhe'nan had several advantages over Zhexi'nan.

Zhe'nan is the part of Zhejiang north and south of the Ou Jiang, which joins the sea at Wenzhou. Su and Liu were unfamiliar with the region, and there were no soviets or guerrillas to receive them. However, there was a ten-year-old tradition of Communist activity in the countryside around Wenzhou. In the winter of 1924, the Communists had set up an independent division here. In the spring of 1927, tens of thousands of Zhe'nan peasants had joined associations and campaigned for reforms. These organizations had been destroyed by White terror, but in September 1928 two hundred peasants from various parts of Zhe'nan formed a Zhe'nan Red Army that in the spring of 1930 was redesignated as the Red Thirteenth Army.

Commanded by cadres trained in the Soviet Union, the Red Thirteenth had two thousand troops and one thousand assorted weapons. Before long, it had helped establish more than one hundred peasant self-defense teams in a dozen counties around Wenzhou. In late 1930, it was defeated and went underground, but handfuls of Communist agitators continued to visit the villages, and revolutionaries from Mindong were active as far north as Zhe'nan's Pingyang. After the arrival of Su and Liu in late 1935, veterans of the Red Thirteenth again took up the gun, the sword, the spear, the cudgel, and the hammer, and guerrillas reappeared in areas where the Red Thirteenth had once fought.[32]

During the Three-Year War, Communists in Zhe'nan were active in Fuding, Pucheng, Jiangshan, Suichang, Taishun, Pingyang, Ruian, and Wenzhou.[33] Communist historians classify the base after 1934 as one of the Party's youngest and newest, but though there was no unbroken Red Army presence in Zhe'nan before 1935, Su and Liu's task there was to restore Communist organization rather than, as in Zhexi'nan, to create it.[34] Zhe'nan was therefore easier for them to "open up." When the Advance Division had first arrived in Zhexi'nan, local villagers fled in panic; when it appeared along the Ou Jiang in Zhe'nan, peasants gathered round to hear its message and even volunteered help and information. Although there was no Communist organization in most of Zhe'nan, there was some activity around Wenzhou on the coast.[35]

Zhe'nan had two other main advantages for Su and Liu. It was less heavily garrisoned by government troops than other parts of the province (though it too was part of Chiang Kai-shek's backyard and even included Chen Cheng's native village of Gaoshi near Qingtian).[36] And its interior was more mountainous and inaccessible than Zhexi'nan, which was knit together by the Ou Jiang plain and the Zhegan railway.[37]

In the first few months after their flight east in September 1935, Su and Liu spent much of their time organizing search parties to round up guerrillas scattered across Zhexi'nan. They also rallied a group of indigenous guerrillas around Wenzhou. They had soon set up a dozen or so Party branches in Zhe'nan, a number of Red Army liaison stations, and a hospital. By the time the Guomindang's first campaign against them ended in May 1936, they were poised for growth.[38]

The linguistic map (or rather jigsaw) of Zhe'nan is extremely complex. Among languages spoken in the region are Minnanhua and Wenzhouhua. These were at first completely unintelligible to members of the Advance Division, who spoke mainly variants of Jiangxihua. "When the Advance Division first arrived in a place," notes one study, "it was as if they were from a foreign country. . . . Much had to be conveyed by hands and feet." Liu Ying was attended by a team of interpreters until he had mastered enough of the language spoken in his Zhe'nan base to understand and use it; he is also said to have learned a Fujian language.[39]

After establishing an armed presence and a Party network in Zhe'nan, Su and Liu deployed their troops to stretch the small Nationalist garrison to the limit and draw the enemy away from places where they planned to set up their main base. While Liu Ying rallied support in the mountains, Su Yu slipped back and forth across the Fujian border, with government troops in hot but generally futile pursuit.[40] Su and Liu perfected this "walking on two legs" to a high art after 1935. They could rarely coordinate their operations tactically, but even when out of touch, they achieved an extraordinary degree of strategic concert, like dancers on either side of a screen who effortlessly match one another's speed and movement.

The idea of a division of tasks between Liu the base-builder and Su the guerrilla became ingrained in the Advance Division in Zhe'nan. Mountain people marveled at the way the two men seemed to slip in and out of their skins to appear simultaneously in different places and perfectly complemented each other's actions. Villagers got used to interpreting the Party in dualist terms. The idea spread that Liu Ying was not one person but two; the real Liu Ying, according to the story, was a young woman Communist of outstanding beauty and intelligence, accompanied by the young and handsome male Communist Ke Fu (in reality, Liu's alias). When Chiang Kai-shek's soldiers surrounded the mountain on which Liu and Ke lived, the couple stood motionless on the summit to escape detection.[41]

Though it is unlikely that Su and Liu received the details of the decisions of the Zunyi Conference, with their criticisms of military adventurism and their hints of a new political direction, "leftist" policies met resistance in the Advance Division. Su Yu was a veteran of guerrilla warfare under Zhu and Mao in the late 1920s and is thought to have opposed the dogmatists after 1934. He had helped found bases in the Jinggang Mountains, in Fujian, and in Jiangxi, he attended the Gutian Conference, and he was known as an old Mao supporter.[42] By late 1935, Communist leaders in Zhe'nan knew that they could no longer afford pitched battles and radical reform. In Zhexi'nan, they had changed rapidly from old-style "leftism" to a more moderate line and back again, but in Zhe'nan, they seemed at first to have learned from their mistakes and held to a steadier course. Only in the heady days after the Liang Guang Incident did they temporarily revert to their old habits.

In their new base, they abandoned soviets and land revolution and switched to a policy of subverting rather than attacking the *baojia* system; of "requesting contributions" rather than attacking rich households; of resisting rent and debt collection; and of forming secret, rather than open, associations. If a landlord ran away when they approached, they made a rough estimate of his wealth and income and left a note specifying how much grain, clothing, and cash they expected in return for "protecting" him; in principle, they deducted from the specification any food that they had consumed on the spot. They levied "fines" on landlords who refused to cooperate. They also worked hard to stimulate trade in mountain products (clay utensils, timber or bamboo tubs and baskets, haws, nuts, fungi, and the like) by welcoming merchants into their areas.

In some regions of the Three-Year War, Communists were so busy fighting and running that they neglected political work, but in Zhe'nan propaganda teams were often active in the villages. Every literate Communist was expected to paint at least one slogan a day on walls, trees, or bridges and to copy out ten leaflets; illiterates were expected to talk their message across. In Zhexi'nan, the guerrillas had sometimes massed forces against important targets; in Zhe'nan, they at first followed flexible principles "aimed not at destroying the enemy but at wearing him down." In May 1936, the Zhe'nan Communists had enough local support to set up a hospital in seventeen mountain caves, with room for thirty to forty patients.[43]

## THE LIANG GUANG INCIDENT

During the Liang Guang Incident of June 1936, Nationalist troops in Minzhegan marched south toward Guangdong, leaving Zhe'nan practically empty of regular divisions.[44] In many places, local security forces could do little to contain the Communists, who set up Special Committees in Zhe'nan and Zhedong (eastern Zhejiang) and restored the Special Committee in Zhexi'nan. Both Su Yu (in Zhexi'nan) and Liu Ying (in

Zhe'nan) issued statements opposing the "warlord civil war" and calling on Chiang Kai-shek and the southern rebels to resist Japan. June to December 1936 was their second period of rapid growth. The division of labor between Su and Liu continued, now on a tactical as well as a strategic plane. Once again, Su fought on the outer line, while Liu consolidated the Party's base in guerrilla strongholds.[45]

This tactical coordination was carried out by two different sorts of troops, shock units under Liu and diversionary units under Su. Liu's shock brigades seldom took up arms. Their task was chiefly political: to organize local people in associations and to coordinate plainclothes squads. Su's diversionary brigades were the main force of the guerrilla army, responsible for drawing local security troops away from Liu and tying them down elsewhere. Liu garrisoned the central base, which expanded rapidly during the Liang Guang crisis and had soon established pockets of support as far east as the Wenzhou coast, where Liu reestablished contact with a group of local Communists operating independently in Pingyang. Su's forces, operating outside areas of strong Communist influence, constructed a mosaic of "stopover points" and "springboards" in villages with "red-heart, white-skin" governments through which the Communists could safely move and where they could shake off tails—a tactic Su picked up from Ye Fei's guerrillas in Mindong.

Although the Nationalists controlled the heights of local government, they had little inkling of what went on lower down, where the guerrillas held secret sway. By this time, said one veteran, most of the Party's Zhe'nan stronghold was "like an old soviet area."[46] As soon as a dozen or so adjacent villages had reddened, they were linked together in a small guerrilla base; as soon as several bases had been formed in a region, they were amalgamated into one big base where Communist power was either open or an open secret and where Su's guerrillas could rest, reorganize, and plan their next move.

By November 1936, the central base in Zhe'nan was nearly two hundred miles in diameter. The Advance Division had once again more than trebled in size to between 1500 and two thousand troops; a similar number of local guerrillas was said to be active in more than thirty counties. The Party had nearly three thousand Party members in Zhe'nan, and Communist-run mass organizations claimed more than one hundred thousand members led by five hundred local officials.[47]

Su and Liu were able to take advantage of the power vacuum that opened up in Zhe'nan in the summer and autumn of 1936 because they developed new political initiatives mirroring those launched by Communists in nearby cities. Unlike most other southern guerrilla bases, Zhe'nan is linked by an important river, the Ou Jiang, to a nearby city,

Wenzhou, and is within relatively easy reach of Shanghai and Fuzhou. Through various conduits, the Zhe'nan Communists received left-wing publications with articles about the student demonstrations of December 9, 1935, against Japan and the moves toward a restoration of the united front between Communists and Nationalists. The December Ninth Movement had a powerful impact on Wenzhou, where students staged two large demonstrations echoing the demands of the students in Beijing and "actively coordinated" with the Red guerrillas in Zhe'nan. Su and Liu produced a flood of propaganda on the basis of what they read, and they changed their slogans. Where previously they had called on "White Army brothers" to "kill their officers and come over to the Red Army with their guns," now they told the Nationalist troops to "turn their rifles outward and resist Japan." In 1936, they began to infiltrate agents into Wenzhou to "unite with intellectuals" and sent people to Shanghai to make direct contact with the Party. In June, Liu Ying changed his Minzhe Soviet government into a People's Revolutionary Council. By August, he was in touch with Feng Xuefeng, who told him to change his revolutionary committee into a "great anti-imperialist alliance" and to rename his guerrillas anti-Japanese volunteers. He also obtained documents of the Central Committee, the first he had seen since setting out on the Northern Expedition in July 1934.[48]

After hearing of the united front, Liu Ying called a conference at Lijiashan to explain the new policy and to test cadres in it. Those who could read and write were given written tests; the rest were examined orally. Liu gave them marks from one to ten. Some scraped through with a five; a few got eights or nines.[49]

Among the groups Liu and Su contacted in 1936 was an organization of revolutionary youth that had become independently active south of Wenzhou in the winter of 1935, after returning from Shanghai. This group had Party contacts in Shanghai and friends in Nationalist military academies in Nanjing. It is a good example of the special nature of the political scene in Zhejiang, which had both clear benefits and disadvantages for Liu and Su. This Wenzhou group acted as a channel between the Advance Division and Shanghai and developed its own armed column of one hundred rifles; it knocked out a number of blockhouses in early 1937 after recruiting four professional soldiers from a Nanjing army school in 1936.[50]

Central Committee documents of the period up to and around the Liang Guang crisis called for unity against Japan but continued to promote radical class-based policies, including land revolution. This approach may explain Su and Liu's reversion to a policy of dividing the land and attacking *tuhao* in some Zhe'nan villages in the summer of 1936. Emboldened by their forces' sudden growth, they decided around the time they received these documents to continue where possible to "satisfy the masses' demands" until they had secured an end to the civil war.[51] This strategy may have made sense in regions like Shaanbei, which had large Red Armies and were remote from concentrations of Nationalist power, but it made no sense in Zhe'nan. Su and Liu's mindless copying of inappropriate slogans imperiled the movement by provoking a new Nationalist crackdown.

## THE MINZHE COMMITTEE

Chinese Communist historians associate excessive radicalism with frequent and violent Party purges. The connection is logical; unrealistic and unpopular social policies can only be maintained by authoritarian measures, both inside and outside the Party. Party veterans from Minzhewan'gan believe that in Zhe'nan, too, "sectarianism, inability to unite, and even splitting the organization caused great havoc" and give as an example the 1936 split in the Minzhe Provincial Committee. The origins of this committee date from the time of Su and Liu's departure from Zhexi'nan in September 1935. During their flight toward Zhe'nan in early October, Su and Liu briefly passed through Shouning in Mindong. There they met Ye Fei, leader of the Mindong Soviet. The three men agreed to set up a joint Minzhe (Fujian-Zhejiang) Committee, formally proclaimed on November 11, 1935. The Nationalists in Minzhewan'gan had unified their forces in the powerful Four Provinces Command; Liu, Su, and Ye believed that by coordinating their efforts, they could put up a united and more effective defense against them. Ye Fei was at first enthusiastic about linking up with Liu and Su and thus compensating for his lack of ties to the Party center. He "actively sought their leadership" and ceded one of his four bases (the one straddling the Minzhe border between Fuding and Pingyang) to them, together with its guerrillas.[52] He was to regret his generosity.

The three leaders originally planned to extend the alliance by drawing Huang Dao's Minbei into it, but Huang had no intention of taking orders from Liu Ying. He not only refused to join the new committee but also urged Ye Fei to quit it.[53] Far from spreading, the Minzhe initiative stagnated, and the committee was eventually disbanded (though Su and Liu continued to use its name until March 1938). Communist sources attribute this collapse to "departmentalism and mountaintoppism" on both sides.[54] There is evidence of friction between the two forces because of their different origins, of competition for troops and resources, and of political differences (Liu Ying accused Ye Fei of conservatism for not setting up enough soviets; Ye apparently thought Liu an extremist).

Su Yu admits that the Zhe'nan division, as the main force, thought itself a cut above Ye Fei's guerrillas. "The Party repeatedly demanded that we send people to lead Mindong," wrote Liu Ying. He tried to appoint two of his people to lead the Mindong Independent Division, and he and Su Yu took the two top posts in the Minzhe Committee for themselves, fobbing off Ye Fei with two minor posts, including the suitably humble one of leader of the Communist Youth League. This behavior was not out of character: in their own areas, cadres of the Advance Division tended to look down on locally recruited Communists. Later, each party to the committee "wrongly seized or killed the other's people, so that misunderstandings deepened [and] contradictions intensified."[55]

Finally, the venture came to grief amid "unprincipled petit-bourgeois wrangling." Ye Fei disobeyed Liu's order to leave Mindong and build new soviets in Zhexi'nan, and he resisted Liu's "unilateral" decision to remove him from Mindong by "promoting" him to the new committee. In late 1936 or early 1937, Liu instructed Su to arrest Ye after inviting him to a banquet. Fortunately for Ye, an armed clash took place with Nationalist troops, during which he escaped by hurling himself down a mountain. (After this incident, Liu announced Ye's expulsion from the Party.)[56] Even in the face of enemy attacks, the two sides were unable to unite and coordinate their actions; partly as a result, they suffered heavy losses.[57]

The quarrel between Liu and Ye also damaged relations between Liu and Su. Although Su had acted as Liu's hatchet man by seizing Ye and trussing him like a *tuhao* to a pole, he had earlier secretly urged Ye not to leave Mindong and had admitted to him that he and Liu had "suffered greatly" because they had no base. Su's guerrilla background in the Jinggang Mountains was quite different from that of Liu, who identified with the centralist and dogmatic "leftist" school of Communism associated with his native Ruijin (where he first became a revolutionary). Su favored moderate policies and a measure of "class unity": Liu advocated a radical policy of land revolution, class war, an open Communist Party, and an open soviet in the villages of Zhe'nan. Liu accused Su of "small group activity" because of his relations with Ye and put him under official supervision after the banquet incident.[58] Relations between Su and Liu deteriorated to the point where neither was prepared to meet the other without an armed guard in attendance.[59] The conflict was probably more general. Recently Su criticized Liu's 1940 report on the Three-Year War for "important errors" and said that it "represented only [Liu's] own views."[60]

Other factors, too, lay behind the miscarriage of the Minzhe Committee. The leaders of the Advance Division had grown up with purges and believed that it was right to settle disputes by dictatorial means. In the absence of direct links to the Party center, each local chief was free to decide for himself what line to take. Even if contacts between the scattered units had been more systematic, it would have been hard to dissolve the rivalries. As it was, collective discussion was practically out of the question; even within Zhe'nan, Su and Liu went their different ways.[61] Most guerrilla units in the region had a strong local stamp and roots or connections among outlaws, so they had more than their fair share of mavericks and ungovernables.

The Advance Division revived briefly after June 1936 and again began to cause trouble for the authorities. On October 26, the Nationalists reponded by moving the Four Provinces Command deeper into Zhejiang and by replacing Wei Lihuang as commander, first with Zhang Fakui and later, in December, with Liu Jianxu. The deputy commander of the Zhejiang Peace Preservation Corps moved his headquarters to Wenzhou to take personal charge of operations against the guerrillas. In November 1936, eighty thousand regulars massed for a drive against Su and Liu.[62] In other southern provinces, the last main drive against Communist guerrillas did not start until early 1937, after the peaceful resolution of the Xi'an crisis. In Zhe'nan, it started several weeks before the Xi'an Incident, reflecting the greater importance that Nationalist politicians attached to this key region. At around the same time, Huang Shaoxiong was replaced as governor of Zhejiang by the conservative hardliner Zhu Jiahua, a member of the so-called C.C. Clique.[63]

## THE NATIONALISTS RESUME THEIR CAMPAIGN

When the Zhe'nan Communists heard that Chiang Kai-Shek had been seized at Xi'an, they looked forward eagerly to his execution. Nationalists in Zhe'nan held their fire during the crisis; the Communists rushed from their strongholds, knocking out one fort after the other.[64] Successes in the summer and autumn of 1936 had already led them to abandon some of their earlier caution and aim for impact by staging spectacular attacks on symbols of Nationalist power in the region, including the birthplaces of Tang Enbo, Chen Cheng, and Chiang Kaishek. These attacks were a main reason for the early resumption of "bandit extermination" in Zhe'nan.

The Communists saw in the Xi'an crisis a fresh chance to expand and massed one thousand troops in a Nineteenth Division (later scrapped). By late 1936, their numbers had swollen to two thousand, and they took the offensive; at Fengwen, they reportedly wiped out several hundred Nationalist troops. However, they had wrongly evaluated the incident at Xi'an. They expected events to develop in a revolutionary direction and hoped to speed up the crisis by going onto the attack.[65] When the incident was resolved, it did not occur to them that Nanjing would take advantage of peace with Yan'an to launch a new drive against them (though Liu Ying later claimed to have foreseen this outcome). It was some time before they realized that they had exposed themselves by their rash moves.[66]

Liu Jianxu resumed his campaign against the Communists on February 17, 1937. The Advance Division was by then better branched and rooted, so the encirclement tactics used in Zhexi'nan in 1935 were no longer appropriate. Instead, Liu Jianxu organized his forces into two columns that formed simultaneous dragnets in Zhe'nan from north to south and from west to east. He built several thousand small forts along the border between Zhe'nan and Fujian and set up scores of blockades. He had the boats removed at certain times of the day from the southern banks of the Ou Jiang and the Feiyun Jiang to stop the guerrillas slipping north. He reportedly mobilized several hundred thousand local conscripts to stand watch at fifty-yard intervals. By driving the Communists onto this seemingly impenetrable line, he hoped to trap and destroy them. In areas through which his dragnets had been trawled, he applied the usual controls, including *baojia*, strict rationing, and deportations. He emptied the smaller villages and occupied the bigger ones.[67]

At first, Su Yu and Liu Ying underestimated the scale of the offensive. Liu Jianxu continued his campaign for eight months, until the day after the start of full-scale war with Japan. In those eight months, the guerrillas fought harder and more often than at any time since 1934. The worst period was after May, when Liu Jianxu personally directed operations. Then the guerrillas were on the run night and day from pursuers who by now were familiar with their ways. In one twenty-four-hour period, Su Yu marched fifty miles and fought eight times: his guerrillas, desperately short of bullets, waited until the last moment before firing. The area into which they had been driven was served by an extensive network of telephone lines and roads along which the Nationalists could quickly dispatch intelligence and troops. Because the guerrillas had too few explosives to blow up the bridges and block the troops, they concentrated instead on bringing down telephone wires to block intelligence.[68] At first, they sawed the poles off at the base, but the Nationalists simply lifted them into new holes. So the guerrillas set up high benches on either side of each pole and sawed it in half at the middle.[69]

Although there were more Nationalist troops in Zhe'nan in 1937 than in Zhexi'nan in 1935, the guerrillas were better able to defend themselves. They were active across a wider area, they had more local support, and they were served by a patchwork of open and secret bases set up in mid-1936. They had had two years' experience of guerrilla fighting and were by now expert at it. Moreover, in 1937 the political and military situation changed dramatically in their favor. Chiang Kai-shek had to rethink his policy of "peace in the north, suppression in the south" after the outbreak of all-out war with Japan on July 7, and Liu Jianxu relaxed his drive against the Communists. Though the core of the Advance Division in the central bases suffered heavy losses, the peripheral bases suffered less; more cadres were preserved than in 1935.[70]

To escape the columns bearing down on them, Su and Liu marched in opposite directions, Su north and Liu east toward the coast. They split into tiny mobile units—too tiny, according to one observer, who thinks that one or two larger units should have been retained—and fled up the mountains.[71] In any one unit, there might have been a staff officer, a bodyguard, a nurse, a mapmaker, a signalman, a cook, and a barber. In addition to carrying out their normal jobs all would scout, fight, stand sentry, or perform whatever task the circumstances required. In the mountains, these units operated a five-squad system, with one commanding squad at the center and a squad at each cardinal point. From whichever direction the Nationalists approached, one squad could always engage them while the rest escaped. Each morning, squad commanders determined assembly points in case they were scattered. Even so, large numbers of guerrillas were wounded. The government's depopulation measures had robbed them of safe places for their invalids, and caves were regularly searched. Sometimes they removed corpses from coffins on the slopes above the villages, lined the coffins with grass, and concealed their casualties in them—a trick known as "borrowing a house."[72]

For seven months after February 1937, Su and Liu lost all contact with one another (though it is unlikely that they were always very far apart; Su once tried to set up a new guerrilla base on Meishan near Wenzhou Bay, at a time when Liu was probably in Pingyang, just a few miles south). Each moved at a different pace toward negotiations before reuniting in late September. In the spring of 1937, the Zhe'nan Party renewed direct links to the Party in Shanghai after absorbing the well-connected column of revolutionary youth active south of Wenzhou. In March, underground Communists in Zhe'nan received Party documents about the united front. Having failed to track down Liu Ying, they decided to act first and report afterwards and issued a call for peace talks in the name of the Minzhe Committee. Not until September did Su learn of the second united front through rumors that the Party had capitulated.[73]

## THE GUERRILLAS REASSEMBLE

On April 12, 1937, talks began between underground Communists and representatives of the Nationalists. The Communists' "Five Demands and Four Guarantees" were identical with those in the Central Committee's telegram to the Third Plenum of the Guomindang, save for a call

for a Minzhe Special Area.[74] The talks came to nothing. The Nationalists, afraid (according to a Zhe'nan Party report) that Liu Ying would repeat the experience of the Red Army in the north, decided to try once
again to wipe out the guerrillas. In late May, a second stage began in the
military campaign against the Communists. Liu Ying, by then back in
touch with Wenzhou, continued to issue peace proposals, but he had little hope of success. So convinced was he that talks would fail that he "demanded the impossible," offering to "abandon everything" in Zhe'nan in
exchange for funds that would allow him to march north and join the
resistance to Japan. Liu's pistol-squad was then fighting several times a
day, fleeing to the plains when the Nationalists entered the mountains in
force. Some units returned to Zhexi'nan.[75]

Meanwhile, Party leaders in Yan'an tried to bring extra pressure to
bear on Liu Jianxu by instructing He Long, with whom Liu had studied,
to write him a personal letter.[76] In late July, after the Lugouqiao Incident,
Liu Jianxu wrote to Liu Ying and other Communist leaders along the
Fujian border to propose new talks. On September 16, his representatives met Liu Ying in Pingyang and signed a formal agreement with
him.[77] After the decline of his forces in 1937, Liu Ying had abandoned
the earlier call, modeled on Yan'an's, for a special border area in Minzhe,
but he continued to reject a proposal that the Advance Division be incorporated into Liu Jianxu's Tenth Army Corps and posted to the northern
Zhejiang front. Instead, he agreed to rename the Advance Division the
Zhemin Border Area Anti-Japanese Guerrilla Force of the National
Revolutionary Army, which was later split into three detachments.

While Liu Ying was calling on guerrillas to assemble and go to the
front, Su Yu reached Suichang and independently contacted the authorities there. After securing a pledge of supplies and safe passage, he came
down the mountains on September 21 and hurried to Pingyang to meet
up with Liu Ying. Thus ended the Three-Year War in Zhe'nan.[78]

In early 1935, after the collapse of their Northern Expedition, Su and
Liu had struck out into Zhejiang at the head of some five hundred
troops. Now, in Pingyang, a similar number gathered, including two
hundred peasant youth selected from the much greater number who offered themselves as recruits. The composition of the division had
changed greatly. The original expeditionaries had mainly been veterans
of the Seventh and Tenth Red Army Corps; the Zhemin Anti-Japanese
Guerrillas were mostly local people from Zhe'nan and Zhexi'nan, plus a
sprinkling of students from Wenzhou and Shanghai.[79]

While the guerrillas were assembling in Pingyang, Communist representatives sought contact with the Central Committee and took back a
message for Liu Ying from Bo Gu in Nanjing. Bo told Liu not to move
from the mountains until the New Fourth Army had been formally

established, except on personal instructions from Bo. Perhaps as a result, Su and Liu rejected a Guomindang directive to assemble in Wenzhou. After further messages, Liu started up a training course in January 1938 for Party cadres, and Su a school for recruiting students to the Party; both classes were held high in the mountains in the small town of Shanmenjie. Su's school lasted three months and trained two hundred youngsters, many of them members of the "exploiting classes," who had been active on the streets of Wenzhou since August, making anti-Japanese propaganda for the Youth Service Corps.[80]

The Zhe'nan guerrillas left to join the New Fourth Army later than practically all other guerrillas south of the Chang Jiang—later even (by nearly three weeks) than their comrades in Minxi'nan, who left on March 1 (but who had some two hundred miles further to go). Clashes with government troops stopped in 1937, but the two sides remained in a state of armed confrontation well into the spring of 1938, when Huang Shaoxiong (once again governor of Zhejiang) mediated between the guerrillas and Nationalist generals after meeting Zhou Enlai.[81] The guerrillas took their decision to leave Zhe'nan after a visit to Shanmenjie by Zeng Shan of the Party's Southeastern Bureau. After hearing Zeng, Su and Liu decided to leave part of their armed force behind under Liu Ying; Su Yu was to take the rest to the New Fourth Army assembly point in Wannan. By early 1938, more than seven hundred troops and cadres had gathered at Shanmenjie, of whom 409 reached Wannan (it is not clear how many started out); through recruitment, this nucleus quickly grew to five or six hundred, most of whom had guns. This figure suggests that some three hundred guerrillas and their newly recruited supporters stayed behind in Zhe'nan under Liu. Between one and two hundred graduates of Su's school scattered across Zhejiang—some later ended up in Shaanbei and Wannan—to work for the Party.[82]

Communist leaders were keen to maintain a presence in Zhe'nan, and Mao was against even a partial evacuation of guerrillas from what he calculated would become a key region in the war against Japan. Some say that too many guerrillas were evacuated in 1938 because of an overzealous interpretation of the slogan "Everything for the united front" and that the Minzhewan'gan bases were abandoned. The Zhe'nan Communists, who were not prepared to fight for Liu Jianxu in northern Zhejiang, persuaded him to drop his demand that they do so. Even though they failed to live up to Mao's expectations by hanging on to their old base, all of them wanted to keep at least some of their people in Zhe'nan so that if (as expected) the Japanese army came ashore at Wenzhou, they could grow by leading the resistance.

The guerrillas left late to join the New Fourth Army both from Zhe'nan and from Minxi'nan, where the Communists similarly hoped to take advantage of the opportunities that they expected from a Japanese invasion. Collecting forces in the New Fourth Army gave guerrillas in remote inland regions the chance to break from their isolation and join in the struggle against Japan. Elsewhere, however, it helped the Nationalists by uprooting rebel armies, including the large Minxi'nan force and the strategically important Zhe'nan force, from places where they might have prospered. The small number of Communists left behind in Zhe'nan after March 1938 held firm despite Liu Ying's imprisonment and death in Wenzhou in May 1942. They played a useful role on the New Fourth Army's southern flank in the Resistance War and again during the civil war of 1946–49.[83]

On March 18, 1938, relatives and supporters beating gongs and drums and chanting slogans escorted Su Yu and his guerrillas from Shanmenjie. The mood was simultaneously jubilant and sad. Despite their frequent differences, Su and Liu had fought shoulder to shoulder for four years; now they were finally parting (never to meet again). At Dagangtou in Yunhe, Su's marchers, many of them carrying only spears, were greeted by Liu Jianxu and by Governor Huang Shaoxiong, who had travelled from Jinhua to meet them. Huang gave the marchers one thousand uniforms and fifty thousand rounds of ammunition and presented each cadre with an engraved ceremonial sword. Many marchers were at first unwilling to put on the uniforms or to remove their red collar badges and cap stars, which they eventually stored in their backpacks. On April 18, they arrived at Yansi in Wannan, where they became the Third Battalion of the Fourth Regiment of the Second Detachment of the New Fourth Army. Later, Su Yu commanded the New Fourth's first-ever engagement south of the Chang Jiang, at Weigang. Su's battalion survives today as a crack contingent of the People's Liberation Army.[84]

In other regions of the Three-Year War, particularly in Eyuwan and Minxi'nan, the guerrillas became involved in tense confrontations with government forces while they were assembling, but in Zhe'nan reorganization went more smoothly, probably because of He Long's letter to Liu Jianxu and Zhou Enlai's talk with Huang Shaoxiong. In any case, there were fewer guerrillas in Zhe'nan than in Minxi'nan and in Eyuwan, and their top leaders had fewer ties in the region.

PERSPECTIVES ON THE THREE-YEAR WAR IN ZHE'NAN

The Communists had never been strong in Zhe'nan or Zhexi'nan: their attempt to found a soviet there in 1930 had come to nothing. Many villagers had never heard of the Communist Party before the arrival of the Advance Division. Most bases of the Three-Year War were far from modern communications and cities, but Zhe'nan was crossed by highways and close to the heart of Nationalist power. The guerrillas here were doubly unwelcome—it is no accident that the last big drive against them started earlier and ended later than in other areas—and they were dangerously exposed. But they were also less isolated from the Party center (through its Shanghai bureau) than other guerrillas, and they learned sooner of changes in national politics and Party policy.

The Advance Division was staffed at first by Red Army regulars. Most other stay-behinders were guerrillas who knew the local language, customs, and geography and could count on a local Communist tradition. The regular troops who marched north under Liu and Su in July 1934 knew about technical aspects of warfare and were disciplined, politically indoctrinated, and battle-hardened, but they found it harder to adapt to the new conditions than other southern stay-behinders, who had long followed a more flexible and pragmatic approach and often neither knew nor cared about "foreign dogmas." The Zhe'nan Communists acted recklessly in some key phases of the Three-Year War. Liu Ying was later singled out for having continued to fight "foolhardy" battles; but by then he was dead and unable to answer back.[85] "Leftist" interludes coincided with periods of Party growth.

Because Zhe'nan and Zhexi'nan were largely virgin territory for the Communists, the Advance Division was able to grow swiftly once it had overcome local prejudice. Since most villagers had no experience of defeat, they were more likely than the Party's disillusioned supporters in old soviet areas to trust the Communists. Su and Liu at first dropped their more extreme policies, but once they had regained some strength they reverted to class struggle, and the Nationalists cracked down on them. Then the freshness of their roots became a drawback; their support fell away as quickly as it had risen, and they found scant protection against the blows that rained down on them.

This sequence of rapid growth coinciding with a period of enemy inattention, followed by sudden collapse under intense enemy pressure, happened twice after 1934, once in Zhexi'nan and once in Zhe'nan. Each time, the Advance Division grew fourfold to two thousand, only to shrink to its original size within weeks. As a result of Nationalist pressure, the Zhe'nan Communists were often on the run and out of touch with one another for weeks and even months on end; this frequent separation widened the political gap between Liu and Su.

But if the Zhe'nan guerrillas fought more often and lost more heavily than other stay-behinders, they did so less because of "military adventurism" than because of special conditions in the region. Su and Liu, charged with founding a new base in Zhejiang, decided that they could not do so by "hiding the flag, burying their arms, going underground, splitting into tiny units, and abandoning open guerrilla warfare." The

Nationalist crackdown on them was exceptionally severe.[86] Through a combination of intense enemy pressure and their own mistakes, Su and Liu could not fulfill their early promise, and they emerged in 1938 with little to show for three years of hardship.

However, the Advance Division persevered despite its isolation. Of its thirty leaders, only three deserted or defected; of the rest, eighteen were killed.[87] They tied down large numbers of troops for longer than guerrillas in other parts of southern China and fulfilled their task of founding a base in Zhejiang. By doing so, they relieved pressure on Communist bases across the border in Fujian and on the main Red Army in the northwest. "The Long March by the Party center and main force Red Army and the struggle to tie down the enemy main force in the southern guerrilla areas powerfully assisted the struggle in Zhe'nan," concluded a Zhe'nan veteran. "On the other hand, the struggle in Zhe'nan undoubtedly supported . . . the Party center and main force Red Army's strategic operations as well as our brothers' struggle in neighboring guerrilla areas."[88]

Quelling Su and Liu cost the Guomindang dear: in just one short campaign in 1935, the Zhejiang provincial government spent 2.5 million yuan. Because it was fighting in Zhejiang, on Chiang Kai-shek's doorstep, the exploits of the Su-Liu army had exceptional propaganda value and were even reported in Moscow's *Pravda*.[89] By the end of the Three-Year War, the Communist Party had five thousand members, mostly new, in this region. The base that Su and Liu founded became, in the words of the Party's Southeastern Bureau, an "important support of the Resistance War" and a key point in the southward expansion of the New Fourth Army.[90]

# Minbei:
# The Party and the Dao

◆　◆　◆

Communist organization during the Three-Year War in Minzhe-wan'gan is often described as a tripod,[1] but this image wildly exaggerates the degree of unity achieved by Communists in the region, who for much of the time were either out of touch with one another or at each other's throats. Moreover, it wrongly suggests three stable points of support; there were more than three, and none was stable. Still, it accurately conveys the wish of Communist leaders in the region's three main bases after 1934 to coordinate their efforts against the "pacifiers," though in the event the coordination never involved more than two of them at once.

The first Communist organization in Minbei (see map 5) was started at Chongan in 1927 by Chen Geng (not to be confused with the better-known Hunanese Chen Geng, whose name is written with other characters); the first Party branch was also set up at Chongan in 1928. Chen Geng, one of many Minbei youths sent by rich parents for a liberal education on the coast, joined the Communist Party in Fuzhou. Back in Chongan, he was able to build on foundations laid in late 1926, when the Guomindang's Communist-influenced Eleventh Army crossed Minbei on the Northern Expedition. Because the Communists had made little impact on Minbei before 1927, the Nationalists paid scant attention to the region in the 1927 counterrevolution, and the Communists continued their activities practically undisturbed.

In the spring of 1928, news reached Minbei of the campaigns to resist rent and debt in neighboring Gandongbei, where the Communist movement had started a year earlier. Similar campaigns began in Minbei. Although they were soon defeated, they served as a useful dress rehearsal for the "autumn harvest struggle" later in 1928. Elsewhere in China, the Party was losing ground, but in Minbei it gained support. By

April 1929, a Minbei Red Independent Regiment had been formed, with three hundred troops and one hundred rifles; at around the same time, soviets and land revolution were imported from Gandongbei.[2] In 1930, the Communist movement in Minbei spread as a result of better coordination with Fang Zhimin across the border in Gandongbei. It also took advantage of fighting between the Fujian militarists Liu Xingbang and Liu Heding (paralleling the civil war between Chiang Kai-shek and the Yan-Feng group at around the same time).[3]

In July 1930, the Communist Party in Minbei was directed to merge with Gandongbei in a new Minzhegan Provincial Committee. The Minbei Regiment left to join the Gandongbei forces, and Chen Geng was transferred to Shanghai, despite opposition by local Communists to his removal. Huang Dao was sent to strengthen Minbei's depleted leadership. He was a friend of Fang Zhimin and a founder of the Gandongbei base. Though not Fujianese, he was not a complete outsider to Minbei, for he hailed from Hengfeng in Jiangxi, just north of the Fujian border.[4] He was to spend the next—and last—eight years of his life in Minbei.

With the arrival of Huang Dao, Minbei became more closely integrated into the Party's Minzhewan'gan system. Before July 1930, the Communist movement in Minbei had been "riven with localism, petty factionalism, jockeying for position by cadres, and internal confusion." Huang Dao tried hard to end these disputes. According to Ye Fei from nearby Mindong, all local Minbei cadres were "knocked out" by Minzhegan leaders. This outcome is important for understanding some of the problems that Communists encountered in Minbei in the Three-Year War. After July 1930, three different sorts of people led Minbei: central appointees, Gandongbei appointees, and local appointees. Sometimes outsiders and insiders clashed, but on the whole they avoided friction.[5]

Though the Party in Minbei lost much of its autonomy after 1929, it preserved its local character better than in Gandongbei. Being new and weak, it was an uninteresting asset for the centralizers, and it was partly protected by its remoteness. The Minbei Regiment was never as completely uprooted in support of national campaigns as Red forces were in Gandongbei. After September 1930, it was reorganized, replenished, put under the command of Huang Ligui, regularized, and sent back from Gandongbei to Minbei. There it won some victories and widened its territorial base, particularly in 1932. Huang Ligui, who like Huang Dao was a native of Hengfeng in Gandongbei, had joined the Party in 1927; he became Huang Dao's right-hand man.[6]

In April 1933, the Minbei Reds were again reorganized, this time as the Fifty-eighth Regiment of Minzhegan's Seventh Red Army Corps, and sent to the Central Soviet; guerrillas left behind in Minbei were re-

formed as an independent regiment. In early 1934, the Fifty-eighth returned to Minbei and fought alongside this independent regiment.
Consequently Huang Ligui's troops never left Minbei for more than a
few months.[7]

## THE THREE-YEAR WAR BEGINS

In 1934, during Chiang Kai-shek's Fifth Encirclement of the Communists, links between Minbei and the Central Soviet were cut, and even the
link to Gandongbei wore thin. Previously, Minbei had served as a bridge
between Ruijin and Gandongbei. Huang Ligui at first won some victories in Minbei after his return in 1934. He set up the Jiansongzheng Soviet to the northeast of Jian'ou, with a population of ninety thousand
and governments at the county, district, and village levels. Later in 1934,
the situation in Minbei became critical, especially during the evacuation
of the Central Soviet. In October 1934, one hundred thousand Nationalist regular and local troops began advancing on the region. Groups of
retreating Communists converged on Da'an, a big village in the Huanggang Mountains that became the Minbei Soviet's temporary capital.[8] In
Da'an, a fierce dispute flared up of the sort that affected many of the
units left behind in southern China in late 1934.

The Minbei Military Subregion was under the command of Li Desheng, a "leftist" appointed to the post by the Party center in Ruijin
through the Min'gan Military Committee. At Da'an, military officials
led by Li are said to have proposed a dogged defense of soviet territory
"until the main force returns," so for a while the Communists fought
costly pitched battles around the village.[9] Eventually, a majority of
Minbei leaders supported Huang Dao's proposals that Communist
forces in the region disperse in small mobile units and fight guerrilla
war in the mountains; that the Party and its officials go underground or
join the guerrillas; and that Party committees, soviet governments, and
army units merge under new unified guerrilla commands headed by soviet chairmen. The need for such a policy became increasingly obvious
as the winter wore on, as the sides of the soviet triangle around Da'an
shortened, and as losses mounted.[10] It was finally adopted in February
1935. With it started the Three-Year War in Minbei, fought mainly in
Chongan, Shaowu, Jian'ou, Songxi, Zhenghe, Gutian, and Pingnan.[11]
The preparations for it were later described as inadequate. They were
carried out in haste, at a time when Nationalist encirclers were almost
upon the village.[12]

Before evacuating Da'an, one thousand Communists paraded
through the village, joined by groups of local people who locked their

doors and prepared to leave. Piles of books, newspapers, and documents were stacked and burned. All available food was packed for transport; the village was emptied of everything that might serve the enemy; equipment too big to carry was buried in the mountains.

After the main column had marched off, scores of Young Pioneers laid several hundred mines in Da'an: by the side of the road, in houses, toilets, water vessels, rice buckets, bamboo carrying poles, and ovens, and even on walls and in trees. Mine warfare was a speciality of the Minbei guerrillas, and after 1932, mines had become standard Red Army weapons throughout Gandongbei. Fang Zhimin gave a much-praised report to the Second Soviet Congress on their uses. Each soviet in Minbei down to the county level had a department of mine warfare, and each soviet below that ran a mine-warfare team. The Minbei Communists produced their mines in metal, stone, wood, and earthenware. In February 1935, mines of all shapes, sizes, materials, and detonating designs were sown high and low around Da'an.[13]

The retreating Communists, climbing higher and higher above the abandoned village, could hear these booby traps exploding as the Nationalists—five hundred of whom were killed or wounded—advanced along Da'an's empty streets. Among the Communist evacuees were one thousand sick and wounded. To give them and the thousand or so officials accompanying them time to get away, a rearguard stayed behind to engage the enemy. Local youths carrying spears and hunting guns joined the evacuation; large numbers of women and children brought up the rear. Only the old and the immobile stayed behind.[14]

At around this time, Su Yu passed briefly through Minbei. He talked with Huang Dao and incorporated one hundred or so Minbei troops into his Advance Division. But after crossing the border into Zhejiang, these recruits slipped away and went home.[15]

From Da'an, the guerrillas marched east to Kengkou, north of Chong-an. Kengkou had been a soviet since 1929. It was connected to the outside world by a long, narrow, winding defile, a strategic pass since ancient times. Kengkou was by then a village without able-bodied men; every male capable of carrying a spear had long since left for the front. The guerrillas were met at the entrance to the village by teams of women beating gongs and drums. In a ritual gesture of solidarity, the guerrillas dispersed to help the women fetch water, chop firewood, and work the fields. The women in turn brought thread to patch and mend the guerrillas' clothes and bathed the wounded.[16]

In the following months, government troops depopulated the villages in the abandoned soviet and created new settlements sealed off from the mountains by barbed wire. They crisscrossed the region with more than fifty lines of forts; the lines were less than seven miles apart, the forts less than five hundred yards apart. Each morning, teams of searchers left the forts to comb the mountains.[17]

Together with local guerrillas, the Communists at first numbered between two and four thousand. They were relatively well armed, with 1,700 rifles, but they were desperately short of ammunition, having used up most of their explosives at Da'an.[18] To defend themselves, they hid boards studded with spikes dipped in a mixture of chili juice and mud along the approaches to Kengkou.[19] They were no match for their pursuers, who drove them higher and higher into the mountains. There they shared the forest with snakes and monkeys and slept in reed huts, in caves, under trees, or under the stars, "studying astronomy when we could not sleep."

Security became their constant preoccupation. "After waking, we lifted the grass that we had slept on as if to apologize," one veteran recalled. Few guerrillas had padded clothes; some froze to death in the raw Minbei winter. Cut off from normal food supplies, many became emaciated. But in most seasons, edible plants are plentiful in the Fujian mountains. The guerrillas had more than a dozen sorts to choose from, from blueberries to bitter bamboo. Huang Dao called these wild plants "revolutionary vegetables" and joked that after the revolution, they should be exhibited in a memorial hall.[20]

In March 1935, Li Desheng, no doubt a "struggle object" after his defeat in the dispute on strategy at Da'an, defected. Li had been a main leader of the Communists and knew their ways. The search parties he led through the mountains devastated the guerrillas and forced them to move their bases day and night and to shed their heavier equipment. After Li's defection, the Communists combed their ranks for counterrevolutionaries and unnecessarily killed some "waverers."[21]

The Minbei Communist leaders decided to transfer some of their forces, organized in the Minbei Independent Division, to regions free of Nationalist troops. It was pointless to stay holed up in Kengkou, where the guerrillas had so little to do when they were not on the run that they spent most of the time asleep.[22] The guerrilla leaders rejected a proposal to go to Zhexi'nan and join up with Su and Liu on the grounds that to do so would attract enemy attention. Eventually, they decided to send units under Huang Ligui to Mindongbei, which included old soviet areas like Jiansongzheng (where Huang had worked in early 1934), and to new areas west of Gutian. The Independent Regiment had been formally reestablished in February 1935, with up to four thousand troops organized in four regiments each of three battalions. The division, strengthened by an infusion of civilian staff, including officials, nurses, tailors, and arsenal workers, was too large for Kengkou. The Party and the Red Army were in chaos; many were deserting. By sending the bulk of his forces outside the soviet, Huang Dao hoped to regain the military initiative, overcome the general mood of pessimism, and obtain new supplies by attacking *tuhao*.[23]

Huang Dao himself stayed with the Minbei Committee in Chongan.[24] According to Fan Shiren, a leader of the Mindong base, Huang Dao was hobbled by an inflated administration staffed by excessive numbers of women. Huang Ligui's various expeditions were partly designed to distract attention from the Chongan base. According to Ye Fei, it was not only Huang Dao's bloated administration that immobilized him; Huang Dao himself was so fat that he would have needed two men to carry him up the mountains.[25]

## NEW POLICIES

To survive, the Minbei Communists needed both new military tactics and new policies. At first, they suppressed "vacillators and turncoats" in the villages and refused to let their supporters engage in "legal struggle" or feign compliance with the authorities. This rigidity demoralized and disaffected some Communist sympathizers. According to one account, "in some areas the masses did not even dare approach us," and the Party became so isolated that many wounded Red Army men were left to starve to death.[26] Later, the Communists abandoned slogans associated with the period of soviet government; they returned partly to policies of the sort previously developed in peripheral guerrilla areas and designed to lessen opposition.

We are already familiar with these changes from other regions: the switch from land reform to rent cuts, from canceling debts to lowering interest rates, from attacking the *baojia* to subverting it, and from robbing *tuhao* to asking them for contributions. According to veterans, the "red heart, white skin" tactic was particularly useful for keeping up support among people deported from the mountains. In some resettlement camps, "the Communist Party branch secretary, the chairman of the soviet government, and the head of the *baojia* were one and the same person"; at night, he and his supporters lowered bags of rice over the stockade for the guerrillas.[27]

The milder line was accompanied, as in other bases of the Three-Year War, by a campaign to "feminize" the Party. "At that time it was essential for the development of the struggle to pay attention to furthering the participation of women in it," said a Minbei veteran. "Women could move about relatively freely. If men did things badly, the enemy could easily kill them."[28]

It is not clear when this political turn was accomplished. According to Liu Xiao, it was decided on as early as August 1935, but Chen Renhong dates it to mid-1937, after the Nationalists isolated the guerrillas by again mobilizing the villages against them. According to Chen, before this time the guerrillas had continued to expropriate the entire property of landlords, *baojia* officials, and militia members, whereas afterwards they distributed only movable assets such as cash, grain, and timber and spared those local powerholders who were prepared to cooperate with them.[29] One possible explanation of this discrepancy in dates is that the earlier decisions Liu Xiao recalls were implemented unmethodically and unevenly.

Some Minbei Communists developed a milder form of purge after 1934. The practice of purging had been imported to Minbei in 1932 from Gandongbei by the "leftist" Zeng Hongyi. Between 1932 and 1937, Minbei Communists killed more than two thousand "reformists" and "AB's." The purges continued even after the start of the Long March, especially during crises. In February 1935, during the first Nationalist drive against the base, a violent purge was directed against "vacillators, grumblers, people with an insufficient sense of urgency, and people who committed small errors." The purgers killed some veteran commanders in the belief that people who had joined the revolution early were more likely to be "AB's" than those who "passed the gate" during the trials of late 1934 and early 1935.

Leaders of some units eventually recognized the damage that these purges caused and changed tactics. Instead of extorting confessions by violence and indiscriminately slaughtering suspects, they started holding "new-leaf rallies." Rank-and-file suspects who promised at these rallies to make a fresh start were spared even if they confessed to belonging to the "AB's"; only those of group-leader rank and above were executed. But the switch was far from universal. In the summer of 1936, Minbei Communists killed "all but a few" Mindong guerrillas sent by Ye Fei to help Huang Dao. Their crimes were homesickness and "making cynical remarks." According to veterans, leaders like Wang Zhu not only actively implemented purges in Minbei but "did so for longer than anywhere else: it was not until October 1937 . . . that they stopped the killing." In Chongan, the damage done by the purges was not easy to repair. Even in late 1938, lapsed revolutionaries declined to rejoin the Party because of the purges, though they were prepared to cooperate with it.[30]

One main target of the Minbei purges was the Fourth Column, which had its origins in Liu and Su's Advance Division. In Mindong, too, men connected with Liu and Su were systematically purged, suggesting that this conflict was partly between regulars and local guerrillas. But just as important were regional antagonisms; guerrillas in Minbei directed a similar bloody purge against fellow guerrillas from Mindong. The three hundred men of the Fourth Column had arrived in Minbei after the collapse of their base in Zhexi'nan and were kept there because of their "higher material and cultural level and greater battle experience," in the hope that they would impart new skills to the guerrillas. They came mainly from Hunan and Jiangxi and found it hard to adjust to their new units in Minbei, even though they were given leading positions; they hankered after the Advance Division and consequently were branded as "AB's" or "reorganizationists" and subjected to "pitiless struggle." Many were liquidated; others deliberately sacrificed themselves in heroic acts to clear their names. One fled to a mountain temple where he did odd jobs before finally hearing about the New Fourth Army and going off to join it. Even one Minbei leader who had worked with these outsiders came under suspicion and was temporarily removed from office. At the end of the Three-Year War, Huang Dao was persuaded to admit that the purges were "leftist," and he canceled the punishments.[31]

## HUANG LIGUI AND THE DAOISTS

Because lodges of the Daoist Great Knives and Nine Immortals controlled the parts of Mindongbei to which Huang Ligui's Communists had moved, new policy initiatives were especially urgent. Tens of thousands of Magic Soldiers were active in the villages.[32] Their motto was "Rob the rich to help the poor, obey Heaven to gain salvation," but they were often controlled by local powerholders.

The Communists who marched east into Mindongbei in early 1935 were attacked twenty or thirty times along the way by government troops, but when they reached their destination they found only one Nationalist division (under Liu Heding) garrisoning a vast stretch of sparsely populated mountains. They had picked Mindongbei because it was strategically placed between Minbei, Mindong, and Zhe'nan.[33] But wherever Huang's troops went in the area, they were attacked by hordes of armed Daoists, who harassed large groups and surrounded and tried to kill small groups. Mindongbei had no Communist tradition, and the guerrillas could not understand local languages. "As soon as we reached a village," said Rao Shoukun, "everyone would vanish. We could see nothing of the masses' face. We confronted unprecedented difficulties: we were attacked even on the march, and comrades fell. Sometimes crowds of people would pour over the brow of a hill wearing strange Daoist costumes, shouting 'Kill!' and flourishing spears and swords."

The Daoists believed that eating cinnabar made them invulnerable to blades and bullets. The guerrillas found that if they downed the front line of attackers, the rest fled. This "military solution" won battles but not hearts and minds. Local people would not volunteer to guide the guerrillas or take their wounded, of whom there were soon around one hundred. Some Communists lost courage and proposed fighting their way back to Minbei or into Mindong or Zhe'nan. "In several years of revolutionary combat," said Rao Shoukun, "we had never left the masses for one single day. This was our first taste of isolation. It was as if we had been dropped into the thick of a clump of brambles. We were being pricked on all sides and could not sit."[34]

Huang Ligui had had experience fighting Great Knives in the early 1930s and had developed tactics that he now rethought and reapplied. During the purges of 1932, the Communists in Minbei had denounced the Great Knives as counterrevolutionary, but after 1934 they adopted a new and more effective strategy. At dusk, they split into small propaganda teams and combed the hills for an audience. Still the masses stayed elusive, but here and there the search parties came across small groups of older men too frail to flee; to these they preached their message, sometimes into the small hours. Communist leaders appointed people to protect sect altars and taught guerrillas to treat sect members with respect.[35] Eventually, they won converts who told them how the Daoists were organized and who identified local *tuhao* for them. These converts talked about the Communists to their neighbors, who gradually overcame their fear of the guerrillas. Before long, Huang had built secret islands of support in the mountains where his people could buy supplies and get intelligence. To consolidate this support, the guerrillas robbed *tuhao* and distributed the "struggle fruits" among Party sympathizers. But the Daoist threat remained. Though some villagers now responded to a midnight knock, they still feared the authority of the lodges and could not openly befriend the Communists.

The problem of the Daoists required bold measures, but at first Huang Ligui shied away from excessive innovation and tried instead to restore a link to Huang Dao to discuss what steps to take. He failed, and after two months' fighting, he decided to act independently to lessen the confrontation, fearing that otherwise his forces would be eroded by casualties. He adopted a dual strategy analogous to the "united front from above" developed in the cities, that is, uniting with lodge leaders while dissolving their support, and simultaneously preparing for clashes.

The leader of the Daoists in Mindongbei was Lin Ximing, a man in his thirties who was said to have ten thousand disciples and armed forces in several dozen villages. Lin came from a poor peasant family in Zhenghe, on the Zhejiang border. He had fled his village because of debts and joined the Green Gang. Later, he returned home and acquired his own support as a sect leader. To his followers, he was a duke, and his wife was a duchess. He was "of middle stature, not robust," with a short moustache and two rows of gold teeth that flashed when he spoke or smiled. He dressed in imperial robes. His skin was painted with cinnabar and tattooed with coiled dragons. Round his neck, he wore a red cloth bag containing a card bearing the names of bodhisattvas and other saints and supernatural beings; this amulet supposedly obstructed knives and bullets.

According to one account, Lin Ximing was first won to an alliance with the Communists when Huang Ligui rescued him from a Nationalist ambush. Lin's definitive conversion came after a battle in which some Daoists were killed and one hundred fell prisoner. Previously, Huang had freed his prisoners, but now he held them hostage for several days, treated their wounds, and preached politics to them. Among them was an uncle of Lin Ximing. Huang freed this man with a letter for his nephew. The letter requested a cease-fire and friendship, but added that the hostages' lives would not be safe unless Lin "acted righteously."

Lin agreed to a meeting. A company of guerrillas marched into his capital through crowds of turbaned and colorfully garbed Daoists flourishing knives and spears. Lin impressed the Communists, and they him, as frank and honest. Huang's negotiators had primed themselves for the meeting by planning tactics with local supporters. They played up their criticisms of the Guomindang, for they knew from prisoners that the Nationalists had made themselves unpopular in the villages by conscripting only sons. Lin listened in a silence broken only by the gurgle of his hookah. He finally agreed to drink cock's blood with the Communists and unite with them against the Guomindang. He even promised them ministerial posts in the government he was planning to set up after becoming emperor of China.[36]

News of the alliance spread instantly. Villages previously closed to the Communists now opened to them, and safe houses became available for their sick and wounded. Together, guerrillas and Daoists attacked local security forces, with a thousand or so villagers armed with spears and swords luring troops toward the guerrillas' guns. To cement the alliance, the Communists shared the spoils of these attacks—including rifles— with the Daoists. Several hundred peasant youths joined the guerrillas, swelling their number from 1,300 to more than two thousand (though government sources claimed that Huang Ligui's army had been reduced to just five hundred by late 1935).[37]

The Communists set up governments in some villages and campaigned against rent and conscription. Through Lin Ximing, they wrote to Daoist chiefs throughout the region and made links to sects as far away as Zhedong (eastern Zhejiang). Lin remained a loyal ally of the Communists and was made commander of a guerrilla battalion. After the start of the second united front in 1937, the Communists tried to persuade him to leave the mountains and fight the Japanese. He declined and was later killed by the Nationalists.[38]

The Communists in Minbei did not emerge unchanged from their encounter with Lin Ximing. They came to behave in ways that drew frowns from more orthodox leaders. They put their main emphasis on fighting, which they saw as the quickest way of expanding, and they failed to build bases independent of the Daoists in the villages by waging systematic political campaigns. This failure came about partly because of their political contamination by "feudal" allies like Lin Ximing. Later, Huang Dao was criticized for not keeping his distance from Lin, whose "peasant consciousness" he commended. Because of this lack of distance, Communist leaders in Minbei "blurred class lines" and went easy on landlords in Lin's sect. The distinction between them and the Daoists wore dangerously thin. "If the Great Knives want us to swallow magic charms, we'll swallow magic charms," said one leader. Guerrillas elsewhere normally handed out part of their booty to the poor: Communists in Minbei—like their outlaw allies—often kept the "fines" they levied. But they did try to persuade the Daoists to confine their plundering to villages outside their own area on the grounds that "rabbits do not eat the grass around their burrows."[39]

One symptom of the commingling of Communists and Daoists was the filial reverence in which Huang Dao was held. Huang Dao was thirty-four at the start of the Three-Year War; most of the guerrillas were half his age, and none was over twenty-five.[40] When an animal was killed, the heart was first offered to Huang Dao, who, of course, refused it.[41] Such stories, which illustrate the idolization of the leader, also crop up in accounts of leaders in the Three-Year War in other parts of China.

## HUANG DAO, HUANG LIGUI, AND YE FEI

Huang Dao's background was quite different from that of most of his comrades, who were mainly unschooled. Huang had studied at Beijing Normal University to become a teacher. As a guerrilla leader, he kept his passion for education. When he first arrived in Minbei in 1930, he had set up a Lenin Primary School and then a Lenin Training College to provide the teachers for it. Under Huang, each soviet village set up a "literacy station" and a checkpoint at which schoolchildren stopped passers-by and refused to let them go until they had read or learned the chosen character for that day. During the Three-Year War, when the Communist movement in Minbei took on characteristics of an outlaw sect, Huang Dao's concern for education became its anchor of orthodoxy and a key to upholding its goals and morale. During breaks in the fighting, he taught classes in economics, philosophy, mathematics, Chinese history, the Russian Revolution, the life of Fang Zhimin, and the founding of the Gandongbei Soviet. Though he had a few treasured

Marxist classics and Party documents with him in the mountains, he lacked materials to teach basic literacy. He wrote out his own texts for classes to copy, if necessary with twigs in the dust. He also composed stirring ballads about important local incidents such as the defection of Li Desheng, and he ran singing competitions.[42] Huang's teaching skills were crucial for keeping up spirits in the worst days after 1934.

In late 1935, Huang Ligui returned briefly to Chongan in Jianyang to report to Huang Dao on his experiences in Mindongbei. He told Huang Dao that outside Jianyang, vast stretches of territory were empty of enemy troops, and even important towns were garrisoned only by small local security forces.[43] The two men decided that Huang Ligui should lead the bulk of the guerrillas toward Mindong. Some stayed behind in Chongan, others went with Huang Dao to Jinzigui on the border with Jiangxi, and a few went to look for Su and Liu in Zhe'nan. This decision to seek contact with Mindong was consistent with a Central Committee directive of late 1934 or early 1935, probably sent at the same time as the one that led to Su and Liu's abortive alliance with Ye Fei. The two Huangs, like Su and Liu, also had another reason to seek links with Mindong. By 1936, the Nationalist campaign against the Communists in Minzhewan'gan was coordinated across four provincial borders by Liu Jianxu; they hoped to coordinate countermeasures.[44]

But the plan for a joint campaign came to nothing. By 1935, the tiny Minbei army was already thinly spread. The decision of early 1936 to strike out in three new directions while maintaining positions in Jianyang meant that pockets of guerrillas were spread all the way from the Min Jiang in the south to the Xin Jiang in the north, and from Jiangxi in the west to the borders of Mindong in the east.[45] Some initial victories convinced the Huangs that their strategy was working. After five towns in the region were briefly occupied within just one month of Huang Ligui's march east, the Nationalists transferred their units from Jianyang. The rearguard in the old soviet was therefore able to tear down lines of forts.[46]

Later, however, some Communists concluded that they had overreached themselves; they had acted like "adventurists" and had sent too many troops to Mindong. "We had no rear," said one. "We were active everywhere and paid no attention to building a consolidated base, so our troops later suffered losses." This rush from target to target and this drive to found bases everywhere were characteristic of the Three-Year War in Minbei. It stretched the movement to the point of fragmentation. The guerrillas found out about each others' whereabouts mainly by reading reports of battles in the Nationalist press.[47]

In early 1936, guerrillas from Minbei and Mindong met up in the Donggong Mountains. Huang Dao and Ye Fei, the Mindong leader, agreed to restore the Min'gan (Fujian-Jiangxi) Provincial Committee and unite their bases.[48] Ye Fei's earlier merger with Liu Ying's Zhe'nan guerrillas came apart, but this new Min'gan Committee survived intact. Liu Ying outranked Ye and had tried to dominate him; Ye resisted. But the Communists in Minbei and Mindong shared similar backgrounds. Neither region's leaders saw themselves as representatives of the Party center; they commanded no regular forces; and they were joined by regional ties. Though Mindongbei was opened up by the Huangs, it was put under Ye Fei's overall command and led by the Minbei Communist Wang Zhu, who had worked well under Ye before.[49] There is no evidence of friction between Ye and the two Huangs. However, ties between them were never close enough to put their alliance to the test. The Mindong leaders were in no position to participate actively in the Min'gan Committee. In 1937, all contact between the two regions stopped as a result of a renewed Nationalist drive against them.[50]

After the Donggong meeting, the Minbei Communists under Huang Dao grew quickly for a while. They expanded the number of their county committees from eight to more than twenty. Most guerrillas were operating outside the old soviet; the Nationalists, who could no longer blockade them, tried instead to stage converging attacks on them. By now the guerrillas' main problem was not hunger, for food was no longer difficult to find, but fatigue: sometimes they marched thirty miles in a night to shake off enemy tails.[51]

Just four months after the merger with Mindong, in June 1936, large numbers of government troops left Minzhewan'gan for the southwest after the outbreak of the Liang Guang Incident. This mobilization created openings to which the Minbei Communists, as usual, overreacted. In August, Huang Ligui, having marched east earlier, marched west into the Jiangshuntai region near Nanping and crossed the Min Jiang southward into Minzhong (central Fujian). By "manipulating social ties," he spread his influence to new areas. "At that time," recall Minbei veterans, "the Red Army's slogan was: First day grasp the situation, second day make friends, third day set up secret mass associations (called by whatever name best suits local conditions). In this way, the Red Army's ties to the masses took root." Also in August, the Min'gan Committee set up four regional subcommittees nominally covering all Fujian north of the Min Jiang and some parts of the province south of it. By then, the Minbei Communists commanded three thousand troops (including local guerrillas). Again this support lacked depth; most of it collapsed in the trials of 1937.[52]

The frequent upsurges in Minbei between 1935 and 1937 were enough to strike terror into the rich and into White villages near "bandit-infested areas." An article in the *North China Herald* on

May 26, 1937, reported on a three-year epidemic of insurgency in the region, implying that embarrassed officials were covering up the true extent of the insurgency. This is the only contemporary report I have found on guerrillas in Minbei after the Long March. It gives the lie to Nationalist claims to have mopped up Communists in Fujian after 1934.

> In North-west Fukien [Fujian] during the past few years, . . . there has been no improvement of any kind in the bandit situation, and the disorder and confusion of that district is already spilling over into Kiangsi [Jiangxi] and Chekiang [Zhejiang]. Public buses, mail boats, travellers and villagers are being looted by bands of armed men who are agile enough to keep out of the hands of the law. . . . The highways running from the Kiangsi border across into Fukien, down to Shaowu, over to Kienyang [Jianyang], Kien-O [Jian'ou] and Yenping [Yanping, i.e., Nanping], have facilitated communications between these cities, but up to the present they have not succeeded in putting an end to banditry. Within a few miles of these towns, buses are constantly being held up by outlaws. The bus drivers are quite often shot and prosperous passengers taken off into the mountains to be held for ransom. For days on end buses are prevented from making their regular trips, merchants and travellers are being greatly inconvenienced, and important people who have money to spend and constructive projects of reconstruction to carry out are prevented from entering these districts. . . . Just back from the main roads the people of the villages live in a state of uncertainty, not knowing when a band of ruffians will descend from the mountains, loot their homes and carry off their livestock. . . . The young men in the villages who have had some training in the local militia . . . are quite often cruelly beaten and left nailed to the walls of their farmhouses. These so-called Communist bandits seem to have an undying hatred for regulations coming from Nanking [Nanjing], particularly those that are calculated to bring peace and security to the country-side, hence they seek to terrorise all young men lest they throw in their lot too vigorously with the National government. The Central Government troops quartered in North-west Fukien seem quite incapable of dealing with this bandit menace and the people are in consequence once again losing their faith in the ability of the National Army to maintain peace and order in the mountainous region.[53]

This sketch of Minbei guerrillas as ruthless marauders who killed or tortured lesser victims and trafficked in richer ones does not square with the Minbei veterans' own version of their war. Who wrote the article? In the 1930s, most of the *North China Herald*'s reporting from the Chinese interior was by local missionaries, who received small payments if their reports were used. Few of these missionaries were politically knowledgeable, and most got their information from local Chinese contacts—urban people, usually of the merchant or gentry class—in the towns where they were preaching.[54] They would not have had much insight into policy changes in the Communists' mountain strongholds or among their secret circles of supporters, and their reports were probably colored by

Nationalist propaganda. Nevertheless, this passage should caution us against romanticizing the guerrillas.

## MINBEI AFTER THE XI'AN INCIDENT

In Minbei, as elsewhere in southern China, the peaceful resolution of the Xi'an crisis in December 1936 led to a sudden worsening in the position of the guerrillas as government forces massed to crush them before negotiating with the main Communist leaders in Yan'an. Minbei leaders learned of the events at Xi'an soon after they had happened (from a newspaper used by a shopkeeper to wrap a bar of salt), but they did not expect the Nationalists to take advantage of the cease-fire with Yan'an to transfer forces south against them. They were taken unawares by the scale of the offensive. Despite their recent growth, their forces were still quite weak. They were dispersed and out of touch with one another; they could not count on stable bases of support in the villages; and they had not yet set up an effective network of cells and liaison points. At first, believing that the drive against them would be short-lived, they stood their ground. But by February 1937, they had been forced back onto the higher slopes, where they hid in the forests.

The first drive began in Mindongbei in late December 1936, days after Chiang Kai-shek's release at Xi'an and just as guerrilla leaders were preparing to train the new recruits they had won since June. The guerrillas were hit by three divisions. Their base changed color "like a tree at the onset of the frost." Forts rose everywhere around the mountains and "village purgers" again applied the tactics of late 1934 and early 1935.[55]

The days that followed were the hardest of the Three-Year War in Minbei. For two months the guerrillas "ate nature's harvest." "Wild animals became our military targets," said Rao Shoukun; a dead boar or goat was hailed as a "great victory." Their clothes were torn to shreds as they fled through the undergrowth. By the time the worst was over, most were dressed in little more than rags and straw or palm-bark capes; more than one in three went barefoot. "During the winter rain," said Rao, "we burrowed into the dry leaves beneath the trees. When it snowed, we became snowmen." Illness spread quickly, and many guerrillas died or deserted. They suffered their worst losses in these months. A minority of intransigents, stiffened by Huang Ligui's motto "Our eyes must be able to see further ahead," went off in twos and threes and sheltered from the storm in caves.[56]

## THE UNITED FRONT

Specific moves toward a second united front with the Guomindang came later in Minbei than in other parts of Minzhewan'gan, though the Min'gan Provincial Committee issued an anti-Japanese statement on

February 7, 1937, after reading in reports of the December Ninth Movement in Beijing that the political situation in China was in the throes of change.[57] Communists in Zhe'nan and Mindong forged links to Party branches in the cities more easily than Huang Dao, for they were operating closer to the coast. Huang Dao was one of the last Communist leaders to find out about the united front and to issue specific peace proposals, though after March 1937, the Minbei Communists mailed several letters to the authorities in Jiangxi and Fujian calling generally for a cease-fire and a unified resistance.[58] Huang had no link to the Party center for the duration of the Three-Year War, and even his links to Ye Fei were suspended. His units in Mindongbei had read about the united front in captured newspapers even before the Xi'an Incident, but they were unable to get a full picture of what was happening and were afraid to act independently in such an important matter. For more than a year after August 1936, they were even out of touch with Huang Dao.[59]

Huang Dao more than once sent people to the coast to track down the Party and get advice on policy. Sometime in the summer or early autumn of 1936, he sent Wu Huayou to Shanghai to ask the Party to ratify his earlier decision to set up a Min'gan Committee. Wu knew the coastal cities from his days as a seaman. He just missed his Party contact in Shanghai, so he trailed him to Hongkong; once again, he arrived too late. Finally, in February 1937, he received a copy of the August First (1935) Manifesto and other documents from a comrade who had traveled to the United States and obtained them from American Communists. Wu posted them back to Huang Dao—not a moment too soon, for Wu was arrested in Fuzhou in June on his way back to Minbei and held for five months.[60] I do not know when these documents, having traveled twice across the Pacific Ocean, were finally delivered to Huang's cave.

While Wu was away, Huang Dao read press reports about peace moves between the Communist Party and the Guomindang. To find out more, he sent people down to the valleys to buy newspapers and into the cities to make contacts.[61] But he was once again driven deep into the mountains by a Nationalist offensive, so it is unlikely that much news reached him.[62] It was probably not until July or August 1937 that Huang Dao, holed up on the borders of Guangze, Jinxi, and Guixi, received a detailed report about the united front through Zeng Jingbing, whom Ye Fei had briefed.

In September, Huang started negotiations with the deputy commander of Jiangxi's Peace Preservation Corps. By now the Nationalists, too, were keen for an agreement; their two main divisions had already left Minbei for the front. Huang's peace conditions were grossly unrealistic. He demanded that the capitals of Chongan and Shaowu be ceded to his tiny forces and that the authorities recognize a Min'gan Border

Area People's Government. Not surprisingly, the demands came to nothing. Huang got no government, and several months later he lost even the small base that he had painstakingly built up in Minbei over the previous eight years; it was "abandoned" as an area of Communist operations.[63] On pressing problems like what to do when landlords asked for back rent, tried to reverse rent and interest cuts, or demanded their land back, the negotiators were silent. Huang's failure to campaign on issues of this sort, which crucially affected his supporters, says much about the character of his movement, which was better at striking poses than striking roots.

At first, the guerrillas found it hard to understand the new united front. At a meeting called by Huang Dao, "nobody dared propose cooperation between the Guomindang and the Communist Party; all believed that there could be only one cooperation [that of 1924–27], not two." One reason was that fighting continued in Minbei at the time of this meeting (August 1937). By then, Xiang Ying had already finished his Jiangxi talks with the government, but the Communists in Minbei did not even know that the talks had started.

## THE GUERRILLAS MARCH NORTH

Many guerrillas continued to think in old ways. True, they finally marched north, for the careers and loyalties of their leaders were bound up with the national Party. But particular attachments ran deep among the leaders and even deeper among the ranks. National leaders in Yan'an probably approved of their intransigent stand. When the Party center first tried to contact Huang Dao in 1937, it was stopped by the government, which was still bent on destroying Huang. After failing to dislodge the guerrillas, the Guomindang changed its position and asked Yan'an to send people to talk them down from the mountains. Now the Yan'an leaders showed no interest in complying. According to one account, they were happy to see friction in Minbei and told the Communists there to "Act independently and with the initiative in your own hands; pitch your tents in the mountains."[64] The Yan'an leaders were apparently reluctant to give up their base in Minbei.

Why did the Party center in Yan'an want to keep Minbei, and why was it eventually abandoned? The usual explanation for the withdrawal is that Xiang Ying, overall commander of all guerrilla units in the south, interpreted the slogan "Everything for the united front" in a literal sense and forbade the Minbei Communists to leave behind a single combatant or rifle.[65] Many unlikely charges have been leveled against Xiang Ying by the Party, but this one rings true. Xiang Ying wanted to build a strong army under his own leadership. He was more committed to the

united front than other Communists and tried to remove potential obstacles to good relations with the Guomindang. One such obstacle was
the presence in nominally Nationalist areas of fiery pockets of diehard
veterans of the Three-Year War. So Xiang had two reasons to clear the
guerrillas from Minbei (and also from other southern bases): to make
him stronger and to gratify the Guomindang.

As for the Communists in Yan'an, their view of the war against Japan
differed from Xiang's. They planned a more independent role and
wanted to nurture old bases in the south to prepare for the day when
they could expand beyond the limits that Chiang Kai-shek had set. From
this point of view, the base in Minbei, however tiny, was a precious asset.
Like Zhe'nan, it was on the southern doorstep of the Chang Jiang delta,
close to what Party leaders reckoned would become an outer line of
the Japanese occupation. The Communists in Minbei were "natives,"
well suited to the tasks that central Party leaders had in mind for them:
to lie low, accumulate forces, and prepare for the future. The Party center never entirely abandoned hope of a Communist resurgence in Minxi'nan; they believed these Minbei bases might in time serve as springboards to the south.

Huang Dao, too, is said to have opposed Xiang Ying's decision to give
up Minbei. According to one account, he secretly left behind a platoon
of soldiers and twenty or thirty rifles; when Xiang and the Nationalists
protested, he had an equal number of broken rifles dug from a cache
and surrendered them in place of the good ones. But the Communists
maintained no effective presence in Minbei after 1937. The bodyguards
they left behind were new recruits, some barely in their teens. When
they ordered local capitalists to send them contributions, the capitalists
replied, "If you want money, come to town and fetch it." They did
not go.[66]

The Minbei Communists started out in 1935 with one thousand guerrillas and twice as many armed supporters. Despite great losses in 1935,
they had grown again to more than two thousand by the start of 1937.
But in September, only three hundred remained.[67] These losses stemmed
chiefly from casualties and desertions during the pacification drive that
started in March. Many guerrillas born and bred in Minbei probably
melted back to their villages when they learned that they were sched-
uled to march off to the Chang Jiang.

Of the three hundred survivors, some two hundred had been with
Huang Ligui in Mindongbei;[68] just a few dozen remained in Chongan
with Huang Dao. Huang Dao could not impose his views on the Nationalists without strong forces to back him up. It is not surprising that most
of his demands were ignored. However, a policy of holding on in Minbei
after 1937 would not necessarily have failed. After the August 1937 Bat-

tle of Shanghai, the Nationalists cut their garrison in Minbei by a division. Soon all Nationalist regular troops had left the region, and local authorities feared that the Communists would act against them.[69]

By September 1937, the guerrillas in Mindongbei had been out of touch with Huang Dao's Min'gan Committee for more than a year and knew only that Huang was probably holding out around Chongan. They sent missions to look for him, but none returned with news; during one such expedition, in mid-July, Huang Ligui was killed. The Mindongbei guerrillas had no idea whether Huang Dao was alive or dead. After the outbreak of full-scale war with Japan on July 7, 1937, Nationalist troops stepped up their drive against this region. Guerrilla leaders racked their brains for ways to restore contact with the Party in Chongan. Eventually, they pooled the names of all their old civilian contacts in the region and sent searchers to find out whether any of them was still in touch with the committee. This tactic worked. By September, they had received directives from Huang Dao about the united front and the cease-fire and instructions to gather up their scattered units and go to the market town of Shitang, in Jiangxi's Qianshan, to rendezvous with other Communist survivors.[70]

Between three hundred and six hundred Red Army "backbone cadres" assembled at Shitang in December 1937.[71] Each was given a medal. Later accounts say that the Minbei base held up better than that in nearby Zhe'nan because of its wiser policies, but these reports wrongly assume that more than one thousand guerrillas came down the mountains in Minbei in late 1937. In fact, most came later. The Minbei Communists told the Nationalist officer who came to count them that they had between 1,700 and 1,800 men. The inspector "knew that the claim was false, but we had a tacit understanding with him."

In the following days and weeks, the Communists went all out to recruit troops as quickly as possible before their claim could be exposed as false. By late 1937, Huang Dao had recruited several hundred troops in Qianshan, including both former guerrillas or Party members who had lost touch with the movement and raw recruits. This crash recruitment brought the final tally to more than 1,200—nearly two thousand according to some accounts—armed with swords, spears, seven hundred rifles, and a dozen machine guns. Some two to three hundred recruits deserted on the way north, but those who reached Wannan formed the Fifth Regiment of the Third Detachment of the New Fourth Army.[72]

Huang Dao himself stayed behind to become director of the New Fourth Army's Jiangxi office, as well as secretary of the Jiangxi Provincial Committee and a member of the Party's Southeastern Bureau. He was poisoned by Nationalist agents in May 1939, at the age of thirty-nine, while moving his headquarters from Nanchang to Shangrao. He was buried in the Wugong Mountains, where he had lived and fought. The Nationalists destroyed his grave, but local Communists collected his scattered bones and reburied them.[73]

At Shitang, the guerrillas were joined by a group of men and women students from Shanghai. The New Fourth Army recruited large numbers of young students, but to the guerrillas of Minbei these new-comers were a weird, unwelcome intrusion. "Some wore Western suits and leather shoes, others wore cheongsams or long gowns," noted one account.

> They cooed like pigeons, looking everywhere as they wandered along the street, arguing shrilly and roaring with laughter. The worker and peasant comrades could not understand a word they said or bear the sight of them. It was hard to believe that these gigglers had come to resist Japan. Later, when they changed out of their suits and shoes, everything was different. These young people were cultured. They could write and make speeches. They loved to sing. It was a great boost for propaganda and cultural work. They sang constantly wherever we went. They livened things up no end. Comrade Huang Dao criticized some comrades. He pointed out that the young Shanghai comrades had come a long way to serve the revolution, that what they had done was not easy. He told the comrades to learn from their culture.[74]

## PERSPECTIVES ON THE THREE-YEAR WAR IN MINBEI

The Three-Year War in Minbei was in many respects most like that in neighboring regions of Minzhewan'gan. Minbei Communism was young, having emerged only in the late 1920s, under the tutelage of the nearby Gandongbei Soviet; it was almost exclusively local in composition; and, during its early growth, it was equidistant from the Party's two main centers in Shanghai and Ruijin. New, inexperienced, and over-shadowed by Fang Zhimin's stronger base to the west, it had barely be-gun to expand outside its Chongan stronghold before the Nationalists launched a major drive against it in late 1934. Minbei guerrillas owed their loyalty to local Communist patriarchs, though the Party center tried to shake them free of personal and particular ties by imposing on them new leaders from Gandongbei and taking away Chen Geng, their locally born founder.

Unlike Communists in Eyuwan, who were also overwhelmingly local people with local attachments, the Communists in Minbei had not yet built extensive and hardened networks of support before they were swept up into the mountains by the storms of 1935.[75] Unlike Commu-nists in Minxi, they had no large team of experienced leaders, no link to the cities, and no major political focus beyond class struggle. They made matters worse for themselves by striking out in too many directions at once and trying to plant flags everywhere. Communists throughout China were familiar with the tactic of scattering under pressure and creating multiple targets to dissipate enemy offensives and destroy their impact, but the Communists in Minbei dispersed too frequently and roved too widely. They failed to strike a balance between depth and breadth. As a result, they were easily rolled back in 1937, when Nationalist troops once again fixed their attention on them. The dispersal tactic was far more effective in Eyuwan and Minxi'nan, where Communists could rely on a far-flung web of Party workers and a Communist culture nurtured over several years. Only in Chongan did the Minbei Communists maintain a stable presence, and there they committed the opposite mistake of trying to preserve too many offices and bureaus.[76]

Communists in Minbei, like Communists everywhere in southern China, quickly switched to new military tactics after 1934. They simplified their command structure, merged the Party, the army, and the soviets, and abandoned fixed positions. They also abandoned radical policies in the villages. This switch of policies and tactics provoked a switch of leaders. Conflicts flared up in many southern bases after 1934 between regulars and guerrillas, often so bitterly that the losers (mostly regulars) defected with men and guns to the Guomindang. There was an epidemic of such desertions in 1935 in Minbei and elsewhere. The "leftist" Li Desheng, himself a central plant, opposed the switch to guerrilla warfare and fled. His appointment to Minbei had probably wounded the feelings of ambitious local leaders. The qualities that recommended him to Ruijin were the opposite of those needed to lead the Three-Year War: a sensitivity to forms of local power and the people that embody it, pragmatic resourcefulness, and a nose for danger. The trenches that Li Desheng and others dug to defend the soviet "to the last inch" became their own political graves.

The antipathy that men like Li Desheng aroused in "native Communists" in Minbei also fouled relations between Min guerrillas throughout northern Fujian (including Mindong) and the Communist regulars in Zhe'nan, who alienated their Min comrades by trying to lord it over them. But relations between Minbei and Mindong, though tenuous, stayed good.

After Li Desheng's defection, the Party in Minbei was held together less by structure than by the personalities of its leaders. Under their paternalistic rule, functions that had once been defined and differentiated became diffuse, and personal relations became more important than politics. The same was true of relations between the Party and society. Native leaders with a feel for the villages could adapt more easily than outsiders intent on molding the villages to fit abstract models. The survival of the two Huangs depended less on social movements, of which there were precious few in Minbei after 1934, than on a reversion to an older style of politics, one based on personal loyalties and particular solutions rather than on general theories and political machines. Some of the alliances they struck, particularly with Lin Ximing's Daoists, accentuated this pattern. Many of Lin's habits rubbed off on the Minbei Communists, who adapted to local norms almost to the point of assimilating with them completely; "personal" politics easily slipped over into "feudalism."

The rhythm of the Communist movement in Minbei between 1934 and 1938 was similar in all respects but one to that of most other southern guerrilla groups: a crackdown in early 1935; the start of a revival in early 1936, paving the way for a sudden growth in the wake of the Liang Guang crisis; and a major setback after the Xi'an crisis. The two Huangs, like other Communist remnants, began to thrive whenever the pressure on them relaxed, but they succumbed as soon as it revived. The movement in Minbei differed from most of the rest in that its leaders learned comparatively late about the Party's peace proposals because of their remoteness from sources of information, and they apparently held longer to a "leftist" course.

It is hard to say whether things would have turned out differently in Minbei if Huang Dao had called earlier for a united front. Patriotic slogans would probably have made little impression on his allies in Minbei; the Daoist Lin Ximing showed no interest in joining the united front when told of it, staying in the mountains to pursue his millenarian dream. But if Huang Dao had learned sooner of the new developments, he might have broken from his isolation by forging links in the towns and have stemmed the drive against him by appealing to the patriotism of Nationalist officers. He would also have had more time to prepare his guerrillas for cooperation with the Guomindang. Communists in Eyuwan and Xianggan were similarly remote from Party channels, and they, too, learned later than Communists elsewhere of the change in line. But the Eyuwan Committee was deeply enough rooted to withstand the worst of the 1937 offensive, and the guerrillas in Xianggan were so peripheral that little attention was paid to them after Xi'an.

The two Huangs are criticized more frankly and frequently than other, better-known leaders of the Three-Year War, partly because neither of them lived to defend himself. Yet they are also credited with some achievements. At times, they tied down tens of thousands of troops that could have been used against Red Army units elsewhere, and by spreading out in all directions, they took heat off Mindong and Zhe'nan.[77] In the end, Huang Dao loyally rallied the remnants of his army and sent them north, then died for the Party a year later.

# Mindong:
# The Wily Hare

◆    ◆    ◆

The Communist base in Mindong (eastern Fujian) was the youngest of the three main bases along Fujian's northern border (see map 5). It was, says its leader Ye Fei, "China's last soviet."[1] Mindong is a region of "countless mountains skirted by the sea" along one thousand miles of coast; it is ideal for guerrilla warfare, easy to defend, and good for maneuvering.[2] Communists in Mindong after 1934 were active in Fuan, Nanping, Zhenghe, Songxi, Qingyuan, Shouning, Fuding, Xiapu, Ningde, and Pingnan.[3]

Because the smaller Minzhong base to the south was joined to Mindong before the defeats of late 1934, I treat the two together here. The Minzhong base was founded first, and it set up soviets in 1930, three years earlier than Mindong. But its impact after 1934 was smaller, and it is often neglected in Party histories despite its strategic position south of Fuzhou.

A circle of Communists was active in Mindong's Fuan as early as 1927. These people had joined the Party while studying in Beijing or Shanghai. They made scant impression on the region outside the schools, and most soon left for other parts.[4] In 1929, the Fujian Provincial Committee sent Deng Zihui, a native of Longyan in Minxi, to shake up the Party in Minbei and bring Communism to the villages. Fuan, once a minor county capital, had taken to opium farming in a big way in 1922. By 1925, it had become a political, cultural, and economic center of Mindong. The opium boom brought rapid inflation and, for the peasants, indebtedness and swingeing taxes.[5] Deng led campaigns around Fuan against high taxes, rents, and interest. By 1930, the Party had won some support in the Mindong villages; Party branches were also set up in

Lianjiang and Luoyuan to the south, paving the way for a separate Min-zhong organization.

In the winter of 1931, Ye Fei arrived in Fuan from Fuzhou and founded the Party's first army in the region, known as the First Detachment of the Minbei [sic] Guerrillas.[6] In February, two local Communists, Zhan Rubo and Chen Ting, had set up a band of seven guerrillas to support the antitax campaign in Fuan and tried to win "greenwood" gangs by swearing brotherhood with them. The initiative came to nothing, but it was an augury of the Mindong Party's future unorthodox style.[7] Ye Fei, who was to lead the Mindong guerrillas for the next six years, later became an important leader of the New Fourth Army. At around the time that he arrived in Mindong, Minzhong, too, acquired its own armed force, the Ninth Detachment of the Mindong [sic] Red Army Guerrillas, and the Communists set up a second branch of their organization in Shouning in mountains near the Zhejiang border.

In early 1933, the Communists were driven from their Fuan stronghold. Some fugitives fled north to Shouning and others south to Ningde, where the Party had established a base the previous winter. By late 1933, Ye Fei's guerrillas had recovered from their setback in Fuan and posed a greater threat to the authorities. Guerrillas were now organized in two independent regiments in place of the earlier detachments; Communists had set up soviets with a claimed population of two hundred thousand. Between 1932 and August 1934, Communists created seven armed detachments in Mindong composed almost exclusively of local people.[8]

Few Communist units active in Minzhewan'gan in the 1930s have escaped the charge of "sectarianism," understood as a fractious inability to unite internally or—as a result of a myopic and parochial viewpoint—with Party neighbors. This sectarianism at times plagued Mindong with a singular vehemence. Its origins lie partly in the special circumstances under which the Communist movement grew up in Mindong, though over time other factors lent it new form and content. In the late 1920s and the 1930s, much of the region was in the grip of religious sects and bandits. Party veterans explain this situation as a product of military turmoil and of an agricultural crisis brought on by the early impact of imperialism on the regional economy, owing to Mindong's position on the coast between Wenzhou and Fuzhou.

Sects and outlaws put their stamp on Communism in the region. "Non-Party consciousness was reflected in severe form in the Party too," veterans admit, "as were individualism and mutual attacks," including murderous feuds among different factions and committees. In 1931, a feud broke out between the Party's eastern and western branches in Shouning. In 1932, "ruffians, bandits, and other impure elements infiltrated the guerrillas." One group in Fuan went independent, "raping, robbing, and betraying." The Party destroyed these mavericks by armed force.[9] Because it was founded late and its army later still, it had had no experience of the catastrophic effects of "leftist" practices imported into the region from Jiangxi, and it enthusiastically indulged in violent factional struggles and purges when told to by outsiders after 1934 (though it was spared other "leftist" excesses that wreaked havoc in older soviets).

Fujian continued for a while under warlord rule even after the founding of the Nationalist Government in Nanjing in 1927. Mindong was the stamping ground of the militarists Lin Shouguo and Lin Bingzhou. Under the Lins' misrule, more and more impoverished peasants took to the greenwood. In the late 1910s and the mid-1920s, bandits were widespread around Fuan.[10] By 1928, large parts of Mindong had become outlaw territory. Bands up to two thousand, like that of the notorious Zhou Yuguang, roamed across the Zhejiang border and as far south as Gutian. Zhou terrorized Mindong, thrice occupying the town of Shouning, until he was destroyed in 1931. The outlaw bands also had ties to local strongmen and rich landlords. Other landlords set up *mintuan* to oppose them and protected their territories with forts and blockhouses. In villages of Mindong without *mintuan*, a colorful array of religious sects sprang up after 1927. These sects, which went under names like Undivided Heart, Nine Immortals, and White Crane, were divisions of the Great Knives sect, itself an offspring of the Red Spears.[11]

## THE RED BELTS

The Party's military organizers in Mindong were faced from the start with the problem of how to win over peasants steeped in "feudal superstition." It was not only a question of recruiting new members. The Great Knives were a major obstacle to Communist organizers; they preached to the peasants against rent strikes and class struggle.[12] The Communists developed various ruses to discomfit them on the battlefield. Great Knives fought in a state of trance induced by magic potions, charms, and incantations, but their sense of invulnerability wore off if they tripped or entered water. To take the fight out of them, Communists staged their battles on rough terrain or among paddy fields.[13] But in a region like Mindong, where sects were endemic, the idea of a permanent "Red-White confrontation" was unrealistic, and the Communists had to find new ways to deal with the sects.

Eventually, Party activists hit on a novel and ingenious solution. In the autumn of 1931, two young men from Shouning, Ye Xiufan and Fan Jun, returned home from studying in Fuzhou, where they had joined the Communist Party. Ye set up a primary school with himself as principal. In 1931 and 1932, he and Fan founded secret peasant associations in villages around Shouning. In September 1932, a Shouning committee was established. As the peasant movement spread, Ye and Fan set out to provide it with a military arm. Casting around for "an organizational form that would be readily accepted by the masses," they came up with the idea of forming their own sect, which they called Red Belts (or sometimes One Heart).[14] Fan Shiren, who worked closely with the Red Belts for several months, described the sect as a "mass revolutionary armed force set up by the Party in Mindong . . . using a distinctive form that accorded with the concrete circumstances of time and place" and with the "then level of consciousness of the masses."

"We saw that peasants believed in superstitious mass armed organizations like the 'Red Belts'," said another Communist, "so we decided to develop it extensively in order to promote rent resistance."[15] The sect enabled the Communists to recruit secretly and quickly. At its peak, it engulfed whole villages and districts.

Most sects in the Mindong mountains were financed by wealthy patrons, and the Red Belts were no exception. Almost all early leaders of the Mindong Communist movement came from rich local families and gave up wealth and privilege to join the revolution. To finance the Red Belts, Ye took money from his home; Fan stole and sold a family land deed. Other local Communists burned their property deeds and distributed land voluntarily to the peasants farming it. "By their own model behavior," says Chen Ting, "they influenced the masses and convinced them of the morality of Communism."[16] Communists from wealthy families all over China made similar gestures in the land revolution after 1926. In Mindong, however, these gestures were not incidental to the revolution but the occasion for it. More than in most parts of China, the Communist movement in Mindong was formed around personal loyalties.

To the outside world, the Red Belts appeared to be a sect like any other, but their internal structure was different. Ye and Fan adapted a Party tactic used in the trade unions to ensure that the Red Belts stayed under their control. In the cities, Party members formed secret caucuses to steer trade-union branches or other "mass-style" front organizations of the Party. In Shouning, activists of the Red peasant associations did the same in the Red Belts, transmitting Party views to the general membership. In villages where they had support, the Communists selected groups of activists and sent them off to bases in the mountains, where they attended a forty-day training session before returning to the villages to win new members for the sect. Villages organized altars, each with its own name, deity, and incantation, and between twenty and one hundred adepts. Each altar was tended by a master of the fist or foot.

Preferably this was a local person, but if necessary a *wushu* expert was invited in from outside.

The Red Belts suppressed local strongmen in villages that they controlled, and they shared out grain seized from the rich. They helped Communist guerrillas attack "counterrevolutionary" Great Knives and government troops. In a typical action, several hundred or several thousand Red Belts from different altars supported a few dozen guerrillas.[17]

The sect was useful for influencing classes other than the poor. Daoist exorcists (*fashi*) joined peasant associations, and some even joined the Party. By keeping the Red Flag furled, the Party was able to protect its activists and grow quickly. During the Fujian Incident of late 1933 and early 1934, the sect helped win over Nationalist troops, who "everywhere were in great mental confusion." By July 1933, Ye and Fan had won a following of many thousands in more than three hundred villages of Fuan alone, and Party activists began waging land war.[18]

This reliance on traditional forms of organization also had a less fortunate outcome. Villagers outside Red Belt strongholds saw the new sect in traditional terms, as predator and rival, and responded by raising barriers against it. Among the Red Belts' chief local rivals were the Magic Soldiers of another Great Knives Sect. Whenever the sects clashed, boxed adepts spearheaded the Communist attack, and the Red Belts warded off their opponents' knives and swords with poles. In June 1934, when the Red Belts routed a crown of Great Knives in Boyang, Magic Soldiers in villages for hundreds of *li* around laid down their weapons, and a soviet government was formed in Boyang. The Boyang Daoists would not have been so easily absorbed if they had been defeated by Red Army regulars. Their switch of allegiance was based not on a change of heart but on traditional calculations of expediency; it could just as easily be reversed.

Before long, many Red Belts had risen to become Red Guards, and in 1934, large numbers were incorporated directly into a Mindong Red Army regiment. By October 1934, more than one hundred thousand Red Belts had been reorganized into guard companies, independent battalions, and Red Guard units. Soviet governments had been established in regions with a total population of more than three hundred thousand. By the end of 1934, the Red Belts had ceased to exist, "having fulfilled their historical task."[19] By then, the emphasis was on "regularization," and organizations like the Red Belts were viewed as an embarrassing relict. In any case, defeat was looming for the Communists in Mindong, and their quickest gains probably became their quickest losses. But the experience of the Red Belts equipped the Mindong Communists well for the Three-Year War, when they became too weak to act independently.

By the time they were incorporated as guerrillas, many Red Belts had shed some of their feudal thinking under the tutelage of their

Communist teacher-chieftains. At first, Party members had no compunction about using superstition for their revolutionary purposes. A mixture of cinnabar and yellow rice-wine before battle and a mind "deranged" by incantations and kowtows to the altar made peasants "brave and extraordinarily ferocious." "Under the historical conditions of the age," wrote Chen Ting, a Mindong veteran, "this sort of mass armed force played a rather important role in grabbing *tuhao,* attacking *mintuan,* and suppressing Great Knives."[20] But in due course, propaganda, and experience on the battlefield, revealed the inefficacy of charms to Red Belt peasants, and campaigns against landlords instilled "class consciousness" into them. Even so, this class consciousness did not drive out old thoughts entirely. Peasants schooled in Daoist superstition and sectarian organization understood Red Belt campaigns quite differently from their educated patrons. The Communist element was small even in the Red peasant associations that were supposed to act as a leaven of class struggle and Marxist orthodoxy in the sect, and it was all but lost in some sect lodges, especially at times of swift growth.

This laxness may explain why, despite the factional violence of the Mindong Communists, society in areas where sects proliferated was often freer of confrontation between the classes than soviet areas in other places. In this sense, the Red Belts simply reflected tradition, for landlords and peasants in Mindong shared an interest in defending themselves against outlaws, and they expressed it in the sects.[21] Though Mindong Communists carried out land reform in 1934, Yue Shaohua, passing through the region during the Anti-Japanese Vanguard's Northern Expedition in the autumn of 1934, noticed that "the classes in Mindong got on peacefully together, . . . which is not right." Zeng Hongyi, too, criticized the Mindong Communists as "rightist" and said that the "Red-White confrontation" in Mindong was not sharp enough, and "class fronts were not clear enough."[22] The soviet at Boyang was imposed by boxer fists and bamboo staffs on the eve of a great defeat (described below) for the Communists in Mindong. It is hard to believe that the wholesale incorporation of a real Daoist kingdom (of Great Knives) into a fake Daoist kingdom (of Red Belts) led to the automatic rejection of old habits, let alone the assumption of new Marxist ones.

## OTHER SOURCES OF FACTIOUSNESS

The Party in Mindong experimented in the early days with various other ways of building a military shield for their activists. According to Fan Shiren, there were two main ways of acquiring armed forces: by buying guns and by "dissolving" bandit gangs.[23] As a result of the second tactic, the guerrillas were "constantly infiltrated by ruffians" who, though brave, were hard to discipline. These swashbucklers won the admiration and affection of some guerrillas and took over some Party units. According to Ye Fei, "just five or six bandit elements could easily control one hundred guerrillas." So powerful had they become that an attempt to purge them almost led to a split in the Fuan guerrilla army; the target of the purge had to be narrowed.[24] The bandits, then, were another source of the endemic factionalism of the early Communist movement in Mindong.

Two events in the spring and autumn of 1934 are crucial for understanding the Mindong Communist movement in the Three-Year War. One was the passage through Mindong of the anti-Japanese Northern Expedition. The other was the collapse of the Party's Municipal Committee in nearby Fuzhou (capital of Fujian) in March and, probably at the same time, of the Fujian Provincial Committee, which deprived the Communists in Mindong of channels to Shanghai and the Party center.[25]

Shortly before this loss of links, the Mindong Communists had unified their political organization in a Mindong Soviet government and a Mindong Special Committee.[26] The soviet, set up in February 1934 during the revolution's brief golden age in this region, had a population of one million; it was based on eleven county soviets and more than eight hundred village soviets. According to Ye Fei, it was a "concentration of numerous small-scale armed struggles." It gave land to six hundred thousand people. The Party had 570 branches with 2,200 members, 90 percent of them "poor peasants."[27]

In August 1934, the guerrillas fleetingly restored an indirect link to Ruijin when the expedition marched through Mindong. The visitors from the south mightily impressed the guerrillas, who urged them to stay for a while and help build a strong base along the Mindong coast and the Zhejiang border. But the expeditionaries had been commissioned to march north into Wannan; they could not afford to linger.[28] Instead, they asked for recruits to replenish their ranks and directed the Mindong leaders in the name of the Party center to merge their two regiments into a "main-force Red Army" to match their freshly unified political administration.[29] Four thousand peasant youth were mobilized in just one week; 1,500 were selected to join the expedition, and the rest were sent home. But by then the expeditionaries had marched on, and the main batch of recruits were left behind and used to form a new Independent Division in line with the instructions. This muster yielded a force of one to two thousand troops armed with nearly one thousand guns and supported by a roughly equal number of local forces.

These developments did not escape the attention of the government in Nanjing. "The military situation in Mindong is developing apace,"

Chiang Kai-shek warned troops in the region in September 1934. "It is advancing in leaps and bounds. There is no precedent for this."[30] In December the authorities again expressed alarm: "The 'bandit' scourge in Mindong is extremely serious," said *Fujian Ribao* on December 12. "It is no less serious than in Minxi, particularly in Fuan and Lianjiang."

The expedition's failure to make good its losses in Mindong was probably no accident. Its leaders neither understood nor trusted local leaders in Mindong, and after the first flush of enthusiasm, the Mindong guerrillas probably developed similar doubts about their guests from the south, who had more weapons than they could use and threw their weight around. "You have rifles but no people," Ye Fei told them. "With us it is the other way round." Later, relations between the two groups became openly hostile.[31]

Meeting the expedition had several important consequences, both welcome and unwelcome, for Ye Fei and his guerrillas. It strengthened their morale by giving them—and peasants in Mindong—their first glimpse of a main-force Red Army unit; it strengthened their politics by instructing them in the need for a campaign against Japan and by leaving behind Party literature;[32] it strengthened them militarily by teaching them new tactics;[33] it strengthened them organizationally by giving them an address through which to contact Central Committee representatives in Shanghai;[34] it strengthened them financially and logistically by getting them money from the raid on Muyang and leaving guns behind for them; and it strengthened them numerically by leaving behind up to three hundred wounded.[35] These wounded were carried to safety by several hundred peasants and junkmen. At first, they were a burden on the soviet, but many recovered and for a while joined the leadership of the Mindong Division's Thirteenth Regiment.[36] But the arrival of the expedition also brought big trouble for the Mindong guerrillas. When the expedition crossed the Min Jiang in August 1934, the Nationalist garrison in Mindong had hurried off to protect Fuzhou, giving Ye Fei the chance to expand. But after the expedition had passed through Mindong and marched west toward Jiangxi, government troops came on its heels to start a campaign that also marked the start of the Three-Year War in the region. Finally, meeting the expeditionaries helped turn what had originally been an indigenous guerrilla movement into something different. It brought new people and ideas into the Mindong Party, an influx that both braced and alarmed its established leaders.

This last point is important for understanding the difficulties that beset the Communists in Mindong. The history of splits in the Mindong Communist movement goes back almost to its founding; the unification of early 1934 (when the Mindong Special Committee was set up) did nothing to end it. New splits followed almost immediately. The destruction of the Party in Fuzhou led to an exodus of Communists to the rural bases. It is unlikely that these urban newcomers saw eye to eye on issues with their rural cousins, whose pragmatic adjustments to village life were easily interpreted as "tailism." In May 1932, Party leaders in Mindong spirited rejected the Fuzhou Committee's suggestion that previous losses were caused by rightist policies and that they should start up an "intense struggle" against the "rich peasant line." The arrival in Mindong of yet more contenders—this time regular soldiers on an "historic mission" launched by the Party center—for top posts in the movement was a blessing insofar as Ye Fei lacked trained officers and cadres, but one that easily turned into a bane. The Independent Division established in Mindong on the instructions of the expeditionaries incorporated troops from several different regions, including Lianjiang in Minzhong.[37] Add these ingredients to the tradition of banditry and sectarian particularism that Mindong's Communists inherited and you have a recipe for wrangling and dissension.

Of the contending cliques, the biggest threat to the indigenous group in the long run was the wounded expeditionaries left behind in August 1934. This group included at least one regimental commander (who took charge of the Mindong Independent Division), three company commanders, thirty or so platoon leaders, and some squad leaders. It is easy to imagine their impact on the Mindong guerrillas, who had previously been so starved of military know-how that they depended for decisions on a youngster who had once served as a platoon leader in Jiangxi.[38] Under normal circumstances, this infusion of experience and enterprise would have boosted the movement, but in the event, it introduced harmful strains and tensions.

Liu Ying, joint leader of the Zhe'nan Advance Division formed from remnants of the defeated expedition, probably counted on his highly placed plants in Mindong to help him gain control over the movement there. He attached great importance to their health. He gave each twenty silver dollars, clothes, food, and medicine before leaving. During a second visit to Mindong in December 1935, he left behind another hundred dollars to cover the expenses of those who had still not recovered.[39] The role of these wounded in the Three-Year War has become a matter of dispute; Mindong veterans resent the conventional belief that their success depended on these outsiders. In 1959, Fan Shiren said, "I cannot agree that this whole batch of people became the backbone of the Red Army in Mindong. As for our fighting style, even before they came we were neither too weak nor too unyielding."[40] By the end of the Three-Year War, all the expeditionaries left behind in Mindong were dead. Accounts differ about how they died. Ningde historians say that many were buried alive during the White terror of early 1935, but Liu

Ying was convinced that his men were murdered by Mindong guerrillas. According to Ye Fei, speaking in 1982, some who looked unlikely to recover quickly from their wounds were killed (along with invalided guerrillas from Mindong) during the campaign to "suppress counterrevolutionaries," though most died in battle; others recovered and rejoined the struggle. On another occasion, Ye Fei revealed that he killed one expeditionary who, depressed by the capture of Fang Zhimin, was preparing to give up the struggle. Ye believes that many expeditionaries were demoralized by the capture of their old leader. He claims that leaders of the Advance Division approved when he reported this execution to them in early 1936.[41]

## YE FEI

Despite its immaturity and factiousness, the guerrilla movement in Mindong can hardly be counted a failure, The guerrillas feuded their way into intermittent internal crises, yet they avoided destruction and emerged from the mountains in 1937 at more or less the same strength as at their peak in 1934. The main credit for this success belongs to Ye Fei, who grew enormously in stature after "bandit exterminators" had killed several local leaders, including Ma Lifeng, in the spring of 1935.[42]

Ma Lifeng, a Fuan man, was Mindong's Fang Zhimin.[43] His killing by traitors led to a crisis of confidence in which some guerrillas lost heart and quit the movement.[44] But unlike those in Gandongbei, which collapsed after the loss of Fang Zhimin, the Communists in Mindong were instilled with new confidence and roused to resistance by Ye Fei, and the local leadership became relatively strong and united. Before 1935, the factional struggle in Mindong was complex, with insider cliques at one another's throats and at the throats of outsiders who landed in the villages.[45] Thereafter, Ye Fei, in the absence of local contenders, became undisputed leader of the Mindong Communists and more or less put an end to the internal rivalries.

The later purges in Mindong were quite different from the early ones. They were a "foreign import," a last echo of the Stalin-style purges that had decimated the Central Soviet in the early 1930s. The factional rivalries were also of a different order. They were no longer among local people but rather between Mindong Communists and outsiders like Liu Ying in Zhe'nan, together with the wounded soldiers Liu left behind, who came to be viewed in Mindong as Liu's Trojan horse.

There are several explanations for Ye Fei's success in reconciling internal differences after 1934. The Party was under internal pressure from Communist outsiders. This rivalry strengthened the Mindong Communists' local identity and pride, reflected even today in the writings and speeches of Ye Fei. The Communist movement in Mindong was largely the product of rich patrons who won the personal allegiance of their followers by moral acts. Ye Fei was a "moral Communist" of this stamp, a strong leader and a model of self-sacrifice around whom a loyal following could gather. He considered himself a "falling leaf [ye] that settles on its roots": born to a Chinese father in the Philippines in 1914, he "returned" to his ancestral home in Fujian's Nan'an, a county famous for its migrants and a hotbed of revolutionary nationalism in the early twentieth century. Like many other Overseas Chinese, Ye's father had one wife in China and another in his adopted country. Ye's mother, a Filipina, was an independent-minded woman who spoke good English and taught it to her Chinese son. Though Ye Fei was only five when he went to China, his mother kept in touch with him through letters written in English. Later, Ye Fei received a modern education in Xiamen from progressive teachers. So his mental and political horizons were far broader than those of other revolutionaries in Mindong, all of whom (save for the wounded expeditionaries and two more outsiders) were local people.[46]

At first, Ye Fei could not speak the language of Fuan, which was quite different from the Chinese spoken in Nan'an, but he soon spoke it like a native. He served as a focus for local loyalties while at the same time transcending narrow localism and steering the movement by higher lights. His ambiguous status was again of use in 1938, when his monolingual guerrillas clashed with the Mandarin-speakers appointed as their officers. Both groups took their complaints to Ye. "I had to work at both ends," he recalled. "If both sides had not trusted me, things would have been very difficult."[47]

Ye had two other advantages. One had to do with the geography of his base, the other with the peculiar historical origins of the Communist movement in Mindong. In a sense, Mindong's geographical advantages matched the special combination of qualities that Ye Fei brought to the base. Ye was both an insider and an outsider; Mindong was both closed and open to the outside world. In the Mindong mountains, intersected everywhere by a tangle of streams and torrents, the guerrillas were generally safe outside periods of extreme alert after 1934. Because the region was rich in natural resources, the guerrillas did not need to leave it for supplies, and no highways crossed it.[48] Yet the Mindong Communists were still close enough to the coast and to important cities, including Fuzhou, to keep abreast of national politics.

Few other southern remnants shared this advantage; most Red bases after 1927 indeed owed their existence to their isolation from centers of Nationalist power. But the very founding of the Mindong Soviet (in February 1934) was intimately linked to an important crisis in national politics, namely the Fujian Incident, which was the direct occasion for the release from prison of three of its main leaders (including Ma Lifeng).[49]

A striking symbol of the Mindong Communists' openness to the world was their guerrilla navy, which survived well into 1935 and perhaps longer still. Through their urban links, they obtained Party publications and supplies throughout the Three-Year War. Later, when students and patriots along the coast started to organize against Japan, Ye Fei seized the chance to rebuild the Communist movement in the towns.[50]

## THE LOCAL ROOTS OF COMMUNISM IN MINDONG

Some of the special circumstances of the birth of the Communist movement in Mindong harmed its unity. It was homegrown and reflected the character of the society around it, a society that, by Marxist standards, was backward, feudal, factious, and uncultured. But from another point of view, the Mindong Party was well qualified to withstand the trials that awaited it in 1935. Events in Minxi, Minyue, and Eyuwan show that movements with strong local roots fared better in the Three-Year War than regular forces left behind by the main Red Army. Ye Fei's movement was deeply embedded in the Mindong countryside. Unlike the movement in Minxi, it had no important leaders. This apparent drawback could be turned into an advantage. The Mindong Party was like an earthworm, said Ye Fei: it could be cut into parts and each would live. On another occasion Ye compared it to a centipede, "which does not topple over even when dead." Ye wrote:

> Why did some places collapse [after 1934]? The reason Fujian kept and developed more forces [than elsewhere] is that the Fujian movement was locally born and bred. Minxi had its insurrection as a result of the activities of the underground Party, as did Minbei. It was only later that Minxi became the Central Soviet. Mindong was the newest, the reddest, the most local base, it was independent and self-reliant. The eight provinces in the south lost their link to the Central Committee while carrying on the three-year guerrilla struggle. But Mindong lost its link in 1933; its guerrilla struggle lasted four or five years, not three years. It was locally born and bred and extraordinarily close to the masses. It did not come from outside; it came bubbling up from the earth, it grew from the masses. Moreover, it lacked experience, so it had no choice but to seek truth from the facts, to start from reality, to avoid becoming divorced from the masses. Otherwise it would have been finished. The situation forced us to take this path, and the path was correct. It corresponded exactly to the correct thought of Chairman Mao. At the time we understood nothing of Chairman Mao. Even his name was only a vague idea. The reason Mindong history is worth researching is that Mindong is different from bases everywhere else in China.[51]

Similar views were expressed by Communists from Minxi and Eyuwan, quoted elsewhere in this study. In China, discussion of this issue involves more than the respective advantages of centralist and local Communism. Rivalries between "native" and outsider cadres have sometimes been intense since 1949, especially in Fujian; Ye Fei's eulogy to the local movement must be seen in that context. But Ye's analysis of the special character of the Mindong movement is interesting because it goes beyond the usual platitudinous orthodoxies to specify the movement's distinguishing features.

The Mindong guerrillas "understood popular sentiment, spoke the dialect, and had natural flesh-and-blood ties to local people,"[52] but they also had a further advantage: they were able to work out policies for themselves according to local conditions. Even in Shaanbei, in the "backward north," the soviet was established earlier than in Mindong. The Communists in Shaanbei, despite their independent start, were brought firmly under central control at the end of 1935, when Mao's Long Marchers purged indigenous Communists from power.[53] Ye Fei's guerrillas, in contrast, were cut off from the Party center by the wrecking of the Fujian Communist Party in the spring of 1934, and they fought off attempts by Liu Ying to take over in Mindong. In Minbei, local cadres were purged by outsiders from Jiangxi in the early 1930s. But central Party leaders were in no position to do the same in Mindong, of which they learned only after reports in the Nationalist press of the passage through the region of the Party's Northern Expedition in August 1934. (*Hongse Zhonghua* reported the event under the headline "Mindong for one hundred *li* in length and breadth has become Red territory.") Of the handful of outsiders who arrived in Mindong in the early 1930s, none had been sent specifically by Ruijin to impose a line on the region; most arrived accidentally or were sent by underground Communists in Shanghai.[54]

The soviet in Mindong was not suddenly and artificially proclaimed in response to a ukase from the center; it grew and ripened naturally over several years. By the time it was set up, it had extensive local support. It was spared the disaster of wasteful and provocative "regular" warfare. Until the arrival in Mindong of the vanguard, it had only one "military expert," a man called Lai Jinbiao who arrived by accident from Ruijin in 1932 while on his way to Moscow. Lai, though only a platoon commander in the Red Army and a raw youngster, was made commander of the Red Guerrillas in Shouning.[55] For the duration of the civil war, save for one brief campaign in January 1935, the Mindong Communists used exclusively guerrilla tactics; unlike their counterparts in most other regions, they did not switch abruptly from one style of fighting to another after 1934.

In Mindong, as in Eyuwan, the Three-Year War actually lasted five years. As a consequence of its isolation from the Party center, Mindong leaders had no choice but to work out their policies and strategy independently. Their lack of ties often led them into difficulties that Communists elsewhere had already experienced and learned to solve, but on the whole they learned more by reinventing the wheel than they would have done by copying it.[56] So their movement developed a profile strikingly different from that in any other base. Leaders elsewhere often strove, even against their better judgment, to make local reality conform to the latest central directive; Mindong leaders responded inventively and flexibly to opportunities as they arose.

Mindong's revolutionary past was largely hidden from view until the 1980s, when difference again became legitimate and "seeking truth from the facts" was officially promoted. One of the Mindong leaders' "original creations" was the Red Belts. Their early experience in dealing with the Daoists prepared them better for the Three-Year War than rearguards in other parts of China, where Communists had been taught that religion must be crushed. Other examples of Mindong ingenuity are the Seaborne Guerrillas of Ke Chenggui and the close ties that grew up between Ye Fei's Communists and the people of the She minority after 1934.

## MINDONG'S RED NAVY

Ke Chenggui's guerrilla navy was the Red Army's first and last seaborne unit. Xiang'exi also had a guerrilla navy, but it was on a lake. It was not until the early 1940s that Communists again developed navies along the eastern coast, but by then the Red Army had been nominally abolished.[57] Ke's navy was a product of the spread of class struggle from the mountains to the rivers and to the fishing villages of the nearby coast. At first, Communists in Mindong viewed the rivers as barriers to extending and integrating their base. Very soon, they found that under the right conditions revolution could thrive as well on water as on land and that communications by water were quicker and often safer.

The Seaborne Guerrillas had their origins in the founding of a secret liaison station in 1932 on a part of the coast where wooded mountains sloping down to the sea provided cover for people to smuggle supplies into the interior. Many fishermen joined the guerrillas. In 1934, Communist agitators set up trade unions among the junkmen and organized a struggle against "fisher-hegemons" for lower boat rents. The campaign spread quickly. Before long, the Communists claimed the support of most fishers along the Mindong coast for their junkmen's union. They organized the core of their supporters into three guerrilla fleets with shore bases in Fuding, Xiapu, and Lianjiang. One fleet had a secret sea link to Fuzhou and Changle on the Min Jiang estuary, where they could buy medicine, ammunition, weapons, batteries, and cloth.

Traditionally, this part of the Fujian coast was a base for pirates who smuggled opium and preyed on long-distance shipping. The Communists competed with these pirates for control of the coastal villages, the rivers, and the surrounding sea. The first clashes came in March 1934, by which time the three Red fleets had recruited 1,300 fishers armed with seven hundred rifles. The Communists defeated the pirates, and between March and May they extended their control to hundreds of square miles of ocean.

They took over both the tactics and the territory of their competitors. They attacked and hijacked passenger steamers; they intercepted smugglers and took and sold their opium. They intimidated steamer companies into transporting goods for them. On June 1, 1935, the newspaper *Jiangsheng Bao* reported that "from Zhangzhou right up to Mindong, passenger steamers everywhere . . . are shipping guns, ammunition, military uniforms, and other military supplies for the [Communist] bandits."

But the Communists were no mere pirates. Their guerrilla fleets were part of a wider movement for social revolution. Each fleet had its Party branch. The Lianjiang fleet alone was at one time handing seven thousand dollars a month to the Party's Lianjiang Committee, together with large quantities of supplies. Seaborne guerrillas also helped in more direct ways to develop the revolution on shore. They coordinated with land-based guerrillas to seize small settlements, broadcasting the seeds of agrarian revolt along a dozen maritime counties of Mindong and Minzhong. They set up secure bases on Xiyang and two smaller islands in the Bay of Sansha. They were careful to stay on good terms with merchants on these islands, protecting traders from attack and keeping the islanders supplied with firewood, salt, and pork. In return, the traders provided goods from the outside world when other sources failed.

Together, the guerrilla fleets and their merchant collaborators ensured that for most of the time, the Mindong Communists were spared one of the worst problems of the soviet years, namely the salt embargo. Between 1933 and mid-1935, Nationalist troops prevented salt from reaching most Communist bases in southern China. A similar blockade in Mindong largely failed, for Communists controlled the sea lanes and had good contacts among the coastal traders, who gave them both salt and intelligence. According to Ye Fei, the Communists even turned the tables on the government and enforced their own salt embargo on Nationalist areas.[58]

In the spring of 1935, the three fleets still employed more than six hundred guerrillas on a captured steamer and dozens of wooden junks. They disbanded a few months later during the repression of the Communist movement in Mindong, but not before they had helped guerrilla leaders from Lianjiang escape the siege and reestablish a base south of Fuzhou.[59]

## THE SHES

A second distinctive feature of the Communist movement in Mindong was its vital tie to one of China's so-called national minorities, the Shes. Studies on Chinese Communist policy toward minorities before 1949 suggest that early recruits to the Party from minority peoples came from the same class of urban intellectuals that produced the Han Communists[60] and that it was not until the Long March that the Party came to terms with non-Han peoples in western China and Tibet.[61] This suggestion is not entirely accurate. Even before the Long March, the Communists had contacts, sometimes close, with "tribespeople," including Miao and Tujia in parts of Hunan and Hubei, Li and Miao in the Wuzhi Mountains on Hainan Island, and Yao, Zhuang, Maonan, Mulao, and Jing in Guangxi.[62] If ethnicity is understood in its non-Marxist, anthropological sense, then the close links between Communists and Hakkas in Xianggan, Minxi, and elsewhere must also count as experience with minorities. Even so, the Mindong case was probably unique: only in Mindong were Red guerrillas continually and centrally dependent for support on one minority people over several years of almost complete isolation from the broader Party.

Shes differ in important ways from most of China's other recognized minorities. They live not in preponderantly minority areas but among Han Chinese. Most speak varieties of Chinese (though a few in Guangdong speak a language apparently related to Miao). Today, there are more than three hundred thousand Shes scattered across Fujian, Zhejiang, Guangdong, Jiangxi, and Anhui, but more than half live in the Tailao and Jiufeng Mountains of Mindong, where they call themselves the Shanmin, or "mountain people." The Shes of Mindong live in small dispersed settlements of between ten and one hundred households. There are few exclusively She villages in Mindong; most Shes have Han neighbors, and many mountain villages consist of mixed She and Han populations.[63]

Before 1949, the overwhelming majority of Shes were tenant farmers; others worked as long-term hired hands or seasonal laborers for Han Chinese or lived by gathering firewood. According to a 1952 survey of 8,122 She households in Fuan, only seven were landlords, and only twenty-five were rich peasants. In twenty-eight villages of Fuan, landlords—mainly Han—owned 33.5 percent of the land, rich peasants owned 8.5 percent, middle peasants owned 37 percent, and the remaining 70 percent of poor peasants and hired hands owned 21 percent between them.[64]

Communists could hardly miss the revolutionary potential of these people, who were crushed beneath "several layers of oppression." They first sent agitators in among them in 1927. The Shes regarded these Han missionaries with intense suspicion. Finally, a She called Zhong Aer was recruited to the Party, and within a short time many others had joined the guerrillas. In the spring of 1931, peasant associations spread like wildfire through the She villages of Fuan. In 1934, many She villages were sovietized. According to a study, "most She nationality areas were revolutionary bases, and in Mindong 70 percent of She areas were old soviets." Of 2,346 She "natural villages," 109 were "base villages" with a Party branch, a Communist administration, mass organizations, and revolutionary armed forces.[65]

Apart from harsh poverty and low status, the Shes had several other qualities that commended them to the Communists. They were fierce, hardy, and incomparably stubborn. Their communities were solid. They were masters of secrecy. Although most Shes speak Chinese, their dialect is a form of Hakka heavily interspersed with She words and with its own phonological and grammatical features, incomprehensible to outsiders but fairly standard among Shes in different places.[66] This language facilitated secret communication across great distances. Other non-Han peoples that the Communists bumped into on the Long March bore a grudge against Han Chinese and were impervious to Communist propaganda. The Shes of Mindong, though at first guarded and hostile, eventually became "of one heart with their Han class-brothers," apparently because they shared many settlements with Han Chinese and so did not automatically see them as enemies.[67]

She support was especially crucial in the Three-Year War. Over the centuries, the Shes had been driven higher and higher into the mountains by Han colonizers and invaders; so, too, were the Mindong Communists in the weeks after the fall of the soviet in early 1935. Shes and guerrillas came to share a habitat; the guerrillas were forced to adapt to their new hosts. "Their aid to the revolutionary struggle was greatest during the hardest years of 1935 to 1937," said Ye Fei. "We could only hold out in the mountains because we relied on She protection."[68]

The Shes provided the Communists with sites and sentries for their safe houses, hospitals, clothing factory, weapons-repair shop, and "*tuhao* factory" (for holding people they kidnapped). One hospital was split between two adjacent villages at the top of steep cliffs, each with a stretcher team ready to rush wounded guerrillas off to the other whenever the alert sounded. Guerrillas flowed constantly to and from the villages. A mobile sentry of Shes watched the passes day and night; teams of She women and children trailed the guerrillas up and down mountain paths, brushing away their tracks. Such pursuits were hard and dangerous. Between October 1936 and February 1937, Nationalist troops burned six She villages to the ground three times. Many villagers lost their lives.[69]

Shes also acted as couriers for the guerrillas. They delivered letters over long distances between Ye Fei and other leaders.[70] As in other areas, women played an important part in maintaining guerrilla communications in She areas. Males head She households, but the status of She women is higher than that of Han women: some She women have equal inheritance rights with men, and matrifocality is more common in She communities than in Han.[71] In periods of defeat and weakness like the Three-Year War, the role of women in the Communist movement grew. In She areas, women's status readily equipped them for this role. Mindong after 1934 was one of few places where the struggle to mobilize both women and a despised minority became central to Communist strategy. But in Mindong, in contrast to other regions, women were limited to a supporting role; the Mindong Communists had only one woman cadre, who was in charge of mimeography.[72] This difference shows that deep roots (as in Mindong) are not the same as radical depth (as in, say, Minxi).

Among the Shes, ethnicity and class coincided almost exactly. This combination, reinforced by common religious beliefs, explains the powerful sense of identity and loyalty that bound the Shes together. Once the Communists were accepted into these communities, their organization and ideology became a new focus and fiber of this loyalty. There was, of course, a tradeoff. The Communists brought trouble, but they also brought work, money, and reform to the She villages. Red Army doctors tended to ordinary Shes as well as to guerrillas.[73] The very presence of guerrillas condemned an entire village in Nationalist eyes, cementing the cohesion.

Red Belts, Seaborne Guerrillas, and Shes made the guerrilla movement in Mindong unique. In part, the three groups were linked. The Shes were a fervently religious people and ran many Red Belt altars after 1932. They were also fierce and warlike. In 1933, eleven of the 26 leaders of a Red Belt rising and even more of the ranks were Shes. Shes probably also played a key role in the guerrilla fleet. Many Shes live on the sea; She villages were active in the struggles that broke out along the Mindong coast in late 1933 against the hated salt-pan inspection posts.[74]

## THE FALL OF THE SOVIET

Because of the special impact on Mindong of the Fujian Rebellion, the passage through the region of the Anti-Japanese Expedition, and the success of the Red Belts, 1934 was the best year for the Communists there. Nationalist troops had briefly turned their attention to the Mindong Communists after the collapse of the Fujian Rebellion and had killed one hundred guerrillas, but the government's main target remained the Central Soviet, and its troops soon withdrew. While the Central Soviet was crumbling, the Mindong Soviet was at the height of its power. It easily recruited thousands of new supporters when the expedition marched through in August. But the Nanjing government came to see the Mindong Communists as a threat to the region, especially after the expedition's march on Fuzhou in August, and chose Mindong as a first target of the anti-Communist drive in Minzhewan'gan. The main phase of the campaign to "pacify" Mindong was begun by troops that arrived on the heels of the expedition. They were joined by the Nationalist New Tenth Division (originally based in Mindong), units of the navy, and other forces. They numbered between sixty and one hundred thousand men, half of them regular, half local.[75] By September, they had occupied Mindong's towns and river ports and many of its villages; by early November, they had occupied Boyang, the seat of the Communists' government.

The Red guerrillas were unprepared for the scale of the attack. They knew nothing of arrangements for the evacuation of the Central Soviet, and they were unaware of the approach of the main Nationalist force until it was just two days' march away. Their blindness to what lay in store for them is richly illustrated by an advertisement placed at about this time in Mindong's *Hongqi Bao* on behalf of the Workers and Peasants' Drama Troupe, a "tool in the class struggle," calling for actors willing to "expose the darkness of the old society."[76] They had only just set up soviets in their base. Their small and poorly equipped Red Army had no experience of opposing large-scale counterinsurgency waged by regulars. "Ideologically, organizationally, and militarily, we were underprepared," said Chen Ting. The Nationalist regulars, in contrast, were well versed in encircling and suppressing Communists, well armed, backed by warplanes, and many times stronger than the guerrillas.[77]

The Mindong Red Army was essentially a guerrilla force, but in the first few weeks of its counterencirclement campaign it massed instead of scattering and suffered heavy losses. In December 1934, the soviet leaders called on "every citizen" from sixteen to forty to enroll for service. They called for a big grain levy, an intensified purge of counterrevolutionaries, and a new land revolution.[78] For a while they "rushed out fiercely and fought fiercely"—a tactic that worked against poorly armed *mintuan* but not against experienced regulars.[79]

In January 1935, they at last understood that they faced defeat. They still knew nothing of the start of the Long March or even of the capture of Fang Zhimin.[80] At an important conference in the Yangmian Mountains, they discussed strategy and tactics. All those present were in their early or mid-twenties. Ye Fei was twenty; Ma Lifeng, soon to die, was the senior member at twenty-six.[81] The main debate at the conference was identical to those at numerous similar conferences in southern bases during this same period: to defend the soviet or to climb the mountains? But this debate was different in two important ways. In other such discussions, regular army officers tended to favor fighting by conventional means from fixed positions, while local guerrillas advocated taking to the hills. In Mindong, it was the other way round. Local guerrillas argued for the unconditional defense of the soviet, while regular soldiers left behind by the expedition opposed pitched or decisive battles. One explanation for this anomaly is that because the expedition's arrival in Mindong was unscheduled, its members had no specific instructions on what to do there and no reason to value the base (at first, the Ruijin leaders did not even know that it existed).[82] Another important difference lay in the resolution of the argument. Elsewhere, violent quarrels led to a polarization between "leftists" and the rest, but in Mindong, as a result of Ye Fei's mediation, the group reached a middle position.

Ye Fei was the Janus of the Mindong revolution. He understood and profoundly identified with the local movement, but he was a patriot with a far broader vision than his Mindong comrades. He knew next to nothing of military science, but one thing he had learned for sure: "Peasant movements need peasant armed forces—three years' experience had taught me that. An armed force is more important than a peasant movement." To that extent, he sided with the professionals who opposed a direct confrontation with the Nationalists. But at the same time, he sympathized with guerrillas who argued that to abandon the soviet without a fight would be betrayal. So he proposed a compromise: fight one last battle to hearten the Party's supporters in the villages and then go quickly to the hills. "Only if we fought this battle," said Ye Fei years later, "could we explain ourselves to the cadres and justify ourselves to the masses." The proposal was agreed to at dawn, after a violent argument that lasted a day and night.

The battle, fought around Fuan's Pengjia Mountains, went on for twenty-four hours and was the Mindong Red Army's largest ever. Its commanders, including some risen from the guerrilla ranks and inexperienced in their new role, fought bravely but recklessly. They destroyed up to one thousand enemy troops at the cost of about five hundred of their own men killed or wounded; they also used up almost all their ammunition.[83]

After this battle, Nationalist troops occupied all but three small pieces of Mindong. "The enemy swamped the entire base and almost drowned it," wrote Ye Fei.[84] During their purge of the region, they burned 133 villages, killed 2,159 "revolutionary cadres and masses," razed 34,911 houses, slaughtered 715 oxen, and caused nearly 30,000 people to die of hunger (according to Communist statistics). Landlords returned to the villages and nullified the Communist reforms. Because the Communists were forced to abandon their base abruptly and had no time to prepare their supporters for the new conditions, there were many costly defections and betrayals. Party networks collapsed, and the guerrillas were left without ammunition, food, or finance. For three months, local *mintuan* escorted troops into the mountains to hunt the guerrillas with trained dogs and set fire to great stretches of forest. By the end of the campaign, the Independent Division had lost most of its local leaders and was reduced to just two or three hundred men scattered far and wide in dozens of tiny units, many of them out of touch with Ye Fei's command.

But the period of retreat was relatively short. The Communists had vanished even more swiftly than they had come, but by May 1935, they were poised again for a period of growth. In April, Nationalist regulars, having crushed open resistance and restored landlord rule in the villages, deemed the region secure and gradually withdrew.[85] The Red Army, after its fleeting experiment with large-scale fighting, slipped back easily into its previous routine.

## MINZHONG

While remnants of Ye Fei's army were in hiding and in flight, a boatload of Communist leaders—including Chen Yunfei, who later wrote an account of his adventures—landed secretly on the coast of Fujian one hundred miles to the south, intent on founding a new base just outside the old soviet region of Minzhong. The story of how this expedition escaped the main Nationalist drive against Minzhong and survived to open up a tiny new front in the Daiyun Mountains is unique in the annals of the Three-Year War or even of the civil war, for the escapers took to the sea.

The story begins in late 1934, when ten thousand Nationalist troops, including regular infantry and marines, marched into Lianjiang near Fuzhou. Earlier, Lianjiang's Red Independent Regiment had gone to Ningde, where it was incorporated into the newly formed Mindong Division. In October 1934, Communist leaders in Lianjiang recruited five hundred supporters into a new regiment of five companies called Ma, Ke, Si, Lie, and Ning, syllables that together spell the names Marx and Lenin in Chinese. This Marx-Lenin Regiment withdrew, along with the Lianjiang Committee, to the coast to escape the Nationalists. They had played no part in Mindong's Yangmian Conference in January. They were out of radio contact with Mindong, which in those days was a month's journey away.[86]

In February, these fugitives sent emissaries to the small island of Xi-yang a few miles off the Fujian coast for talks with Ke Chenggui, leader of Mindong's Seaborne Guerrillas. Ke sent back word that the mainland-ers were welcome to take refuge on Xiyang and the neighboring island of Fuying. More than two hundred—the rest had melted away—put to sea in junks and hid around the islands. Their leaders were taken to an even tinier island off Xiyang and concealed in a cave at the foot of a cliff.

It was by then midwinter. The sea air was raw, and there were no sup-plies. Spotter planes circled the islands; naval patrols plied the nearby straits. At high water, vessels brought armed searchers to the islands who killed or rounded up many of the guerrillas. The twenty or so guerrilla leaders were luckier. Their cave was so small that they were permanently crouched, but when the tide rose and the searchers came, the mouth of the cave was hidden underwater.

They conferred on strategy. There was no going back to Lianjiang, and in Mindong, to the north, the soviet had collapsed. On the islands, the net was closing around them. The searchers had already picked up Ke Chenggui, who was later executed in Fuzhou.[87] His capture broke the link between the leaders' cave and the hideouts of their followers.

Chen Yunfei and his comrades decided that the best course was to brave the naval patrols and try to regain the mainland. Instead of head-ing straight for the nearest coast, where patrols were thickest, they headed out to sea, where they were hidden by high waves. They put into shore near the port of Haikou, some thirty miles south of Fuzhou.

The region around Haikou and nearby Fuqing and Putian was no Communist stronghold, but in 1930 and 1931 there had been antigov-ernment movements in some small towns, and Communist agitators had done their best to gain a foothold in the villages. In late 1934, a guerrilla detachment was set up at Fuqing, and another was operating between Putian and Xianyou to the south.[88] The authorities were expecting trou-ble and had prepared for it. Forts had been erected everywhere. Rich families had fortified their compound gates with metal strips, and the authorities had sealed off wells with barbed wire.

The Communist movement in Fuqing was represented by its secre-tary Huang Xiaomin, who had led a delegation to the Lianjiang Soviet and was known to the escapers, and by Chen Qinlin, an official of the Fuzhou Committee who had fled south after the crackdown in March 1934 and who now worked in a copper factory with other Communists. Huang and Chen explained to the escapers that the most pressing prob-lem was to find new sources of finance now that they could no longer rely on Fuzhou. They also proposed a solution: that Chen Yunfei seek out a base in the mountains.

Many of the highland regions to the west of Fuqing were bandit strongholds. One, Luohanli in Yongtai, was controlled by the bandit Liu Chunshui, who held out there with just a few hundred men. Luohanli was almost impregnable and had resources to support a population of one thousand. The slopes and valleys around it were thickly forested and knit by a tangle of confusing paths and goat tracks. These paths gave Liu's insiders access to five adjacent counties on which they preyed from their tiny well-connected kingdom. Chen Yunfei judged that Luohanli would make an excellent base from which to spread Party organization throughout Minzhong.

In March 1935, news reached Chen, in a nearby valley, that the authorities had killed Liu Chunshui and incorporated most of his followers into the Peace Preservation Corps. Chen saw that he should take immediate advantage of the interregnum in Luohanli. He went to the market town nearest the village and struck up a conversation with a peasant from Luohanli, who turned out to be childless. Chen talked this man into adopting him as his son; the two then went to Luohanli together. Normally, villagers would have chased Chen away or killed him, but in his newfound role he could enter the mountains freely. His adoptive father's wife turned out to be a cousin of the dead Liu Chunshui. Through her, Chen met Liu Chunshui's uncle, Liu Ahe, and told him how the Red Army "robbed the rich to help the poor." Chen used the following arguments in addressing Liu Ahe: Economic bandits like you have no future. First, because you go against the people's interest, so they oppose you. Second, because even though you may prosper now, your children and your children's children will be cursed as offspring of a bad ancestor. Third, because the Guomindang won't let you prosper. Didn't they kill your nephew Liu Chunshui? We Communists are not like the Guomindang, we do not cheat people. We are trustworthy and talk about policies. All you have to do is mend your ways and we will welcome you to cooperate with us. Then you will definitely have a future.

Chen had a weak hand but a winning tongue. After some thought, Liu Ahe put aside his opium pipe and agreed to an alliance, sealed by cock's blood in the village temple. "We had taken Luohanli without firing a shot," said Chen later. Very soon, a dozen or so survivors from Lianjiang arrived in the mountains to join an equal number of followers of Liu Ahe. A tiny army (the Minzhong First Guerrilla Detachment) was set up; Liu Ahe became its quartermaster (a telling comment on the role into which Chen Yunfei had talked him). In April 1935, Huang Xiaomin came to Luohanli with other local leaders. In May, a Minzhong Special Committee was formed there, through a merger of the Party's Putian and Fuqing committees. The new Minzhong Committee set up literacy classes in Luohanli, lectured about revolution to the villagers, organized attacks on powerholders in the region, and levied cash and grain on rich households. Later, it set up a Second Guerrilla Detachment at Changtai in Putian.[89]

From their two new bases, the Minzhong Communists waged sparrow warfare on nearby roads, darting down to snatch supplies and show the flag. On one occasion, in February 1936, they intercepted two army vehicles and captured thirty people, including three bigwigs: Governor Ch'en I's brother-in-law, a director of the Provincial Bank, and the Datian magistrate. They also captured two million dollars and much gold and silver. The authorities responded by sending several thousand troops to wipe out the base at Luohanli and wreak vengeance on Party supporters in the village. The Communists returned as soon as the occupiers had withdrawn.[90]

Chen Yunfei opened up Luohanli not by fighting his way in or agitating on social issues but by manipulating fictive kinship and appealing to Liu Ahe's sense of the continuum of descent, of ancestral responsibility, of personal and family honor, and of political pragmatism. Chen's story was, of course, exceptional. He had to achieve his end single-handed and empty-handed and to do so before the door that had magically swung open with the death of Liu Chunshui slammed shut again. Still, his tactics were not outside the norm for the Three-Year War but merely an extreme example, for guerrillas all over southern China mobilized every serviceable fiber of China's social and cultural tissue in their quest for friends after 1934.

## POLICY CHANGES IN 1935

Meanwhile, in Mindong to the north, guerrillas continued to hide out in the forests for most of 1935. Once the Nationalists had gone, they set about restoring their organization. The Mindong Committee had been reduced to just two members by the bloodletting of the spring, so in May a new political leadership was formed at Hanxi in Shouning under Ye Fei.[91] In August and September, the remnants of the Independent Division were reorganized into several independent columns; toward late 1935, a Mindong Military Subregion was formed to coordinate them.[92] By the end of the year, the guerrillas were said by sources in Fuzhou to number six hundred; clearly, they had made good some of their earlier losses.[93] Nor were they so glued to the peaks that their comrades in the Su-Liu Advance Division were unable to track them down when the Advance Division crossed Shouning in October and November 1935. They even formally merged with Su and Liu, though, for reasons explained earlier, this alliance collapsed.

The Party also regrouped. Between May 1935 and the winter of 1936, 265 Party branches were formed in Mindong with more than one thousand members. Soviets were set up in twenty counties, though at first the Party operated through revolutionary committees.[94] Before 1935, Mindong Communists had adopted what was later criticized as a "leftist" land policy. But they had protected traders in the region and had generally refrained from "interfering in the market." After 1934, they put even greater emphasis on "fair trade" and "let small traders from White areas come into the bases to do business, so that they stood to gain." Similar promises made by Communist stay-behinders in other places often rang hollow, but in Mindong the Communists had a tradition of conciliating "middle elements." Ye Fei's understanding with small traders, particularly salt traders, was crucial in helping him survive his isolation.[95]

Mindong Communists changed their policy toward landlords and *tuhao* in 1935. In the old days, they had stripped wealthy *tuhao* of their belongings and killed many, in some cases even after ransoms had been paid. Now they abandoned land revolution and lightened "fines and contributions." Instead of sweeping clean the granaries of the rich, they levied a grain tax on them according to the size of their holdings, to "stop contradictions intensifying." When enforcing loans on *tuhao*, they nominally aimed at 20 percent of movables, a less punitive rate than in other bases. The switch was not universal. More than three hundred "*tuhao* factories" were set up in the mountains in 1935 and 1936; ransoms were a main source of guerrilla finance. The grain tax that the guerrillas levied was steep: local people "voluntarily" gave up more than one-third of their harvest.[96]

The policy retreat was forced on the guerrillas by circumstance. Their supporters in most areas were so demoralized that they had voluntarily started paying rent again. Most mass organizations set up in the villages had collapsed. The guerrillas could preserve the changes brought about by land revolution in their strongholds, but not in most villages.[97] The Communists rarely left the mountains except for a few "Red *baojia* chiefs" whose "persons were in Cao Cao's camp but whose heart was with the Han."[98]

Among the new policies decided on by the Mindong Committee in May and June 1935 was one known as wave-like development. The gist of it was that new bases should be formed as wave-like extensions of existing bases and that in the course of this expansion, politics should prevail over the gun. The first step in setting up a base was to send in civilian cadres. Mindong veterans say that in this respect, the policy was unconventional. "It was different from other bases," said Chen Ting. "There it was often the Red Army that liberated places. Only later was the Party formed." In some cases, troops reached a new area first, but even so, their first task was to build a civilian political base; "only at the very last did they develop guns." In general, the rule in Mindong was that "local work should be to the fore and troop activities to the rear. . . . The Red Army only went where there was a certain mass base."[99]

Once guerrillas were established in such a base, they not only fought but also did political work in the villages. In the soviet period, different sorts of organizations had proliferated in Communist bases, but in Mindong after 1934, the old division between military and civilian cadres was largely abolished. Neighboring Minbei, in contrast, kept an unwieldy administration after 1934, and in Zhe'nan, according to Ye Fei, leaders of the Advance Division put too much emphasis on fighting and not enough on building bases.

The tactical differences between Liu Ying in Zhe'nan and Ye Fei in Mindong were an issue in the conflict that destroyed their cooperation. When Liu met Ye in December 1935, he criticized the Mindong Communists for their "conservatism." Su Yu, in contrast, was impressed by the ease with which Ye's guerrillas shook off their pursuers. He applied Ye's strategy in Zhe'nan; it was partly as a result that Su and Liu fell out.[100]

The Mindong guerrillas owed their elusiveness and agility to what Su Yu dubbed the "wily hare" trick: "a new luster that the Mindong Party added to Chairman Mao's thinking on bases and military affairs," a Mindong creation "commended by the proletarian revolutionary and outstanding military thinker Su Yu." This trick, which took its name from the proverb "A wily hare has three burrows," was an outgrowth of the strategy of wave-like development. With a minimum of three bases, the thinking went, the guerrillas would never need to retrace their steps while striving to shake off tails. They could move constantly forward, darting from base to base and diving from view among their supporters in the villages, leaving the enemy "lamenting his littleness before the vast ocean." The guerrillas built numerous small burrows in seventeen counties as well as four "consolidated bases" in Shouning, in Ningde, in Xiapu, and in Fuding and Pingyang, with four offices to coordinate them. Eventually, these four were linked into one.[101] They allocated an Independent Regiment to each base.

Within the bases, they restored an open or secret Communist administration, carried out mild reforms, and took measures to prevent the outflow of grain in order to ensure their own supplies. Their military intelligence was excellent: they almost always knew when the Nationalists were on the move, how strong they were, and where they were going. The wily hare trick worked best when the guerrillas were fighting in areas they knew well. As soon as they moved into unfamiliar territory, they became less mobile and secure. Most stayed in Mindong, though a few were transferred—never for long—to Minbei and Zhe'nan.[102]

Outside Mindong, language was the guerrillas' biggest problem. Different languages and dialects abounded in the Party's southern bases, and the resulting communication gap between the Red Army and the peasants on whom it depended for support has been largely ignored in studies of the Chinese Revolution. Mindong guerrillas sent to Zhejiang under Chen Ting in 1935 were able to talk with local peasants only through a specially formed team of interpreters.

Chen Ting's column had to march constantly through hostile and unfamiliar territory. Chen took extraordinary measures to win people's trust; he gave money to paupers he met along the road and even shot a quartermaster who helped himself to someone's melon. But by 1937, the guerrillas had become accepted in Zhejiang and had strongholds along the border where they could come and go at will.[103]

Though Ye Fei took great pride in the peculiarly local character of his guerrillas, he was open to proposals for regional cooperation. His alliance with the Advance Division fell apart, but he continued to seek wider links in the region. In early 1936, when he met with Huang Dao in the Donggong Mountains that marked the border between their bases, he agreed to set up a joint Min'gan Committee with him. But for most of the time Ye and Huang stayed out of touch and their cooperation was in name only.

Guerrillas in Mindong owed part of their success after 1934 to their peripatetic Red Army hospitals, which moved round a circuit of She villages high up in the mountains and changed their name almost as often as their site. Most Red Army stay-behinders in southern China ran mountain hospitals after 1934, but Mindong was different in that it had no long tradition of medical work to draw on. Before the second half of 1934, the guerrillas found it hard to recruit medical workers, and they either sent casualties home or treated them at the front. As the Red Army in Mindong grew, local leaders became more conscious of the need for an efficient medical system and began to found hospitals to cope with the growing number of casualties. At first, these hospitals were primitive. After the establishment of the Independent Division in September 1934, the Party took steps to improve them. Party leaders launched a campaign to recruit local doctors, and the Red Army kidnapped eight doctors during the attack on Luoyuan in August 1934. Others were left behind in Mindong by the Anti-Japanese Vanguard. The Mindong Division had seven or eight medical units and individual medical workers attached to its two regiments at the time of their founding. It never recruited a single professional nurse; nursing was the exclusive province of young women activists.

In the winter of 1934, many of these medical workers and their patients were killed by Nationalist troops. Newly founded hospitals like the

one at Lianjiang were destroyed, and methods of medical care in Mindong changed radically. Before the defeats of late 1934, the Mindong
Communists had found it relatively easy to get western medicines via sea
links, but high in the mountains, they had to fall back on local remedies.
They washed wounds in strong tea or treated them with pulverized
earthworms and the internal organs of freshly killed dogs and chickens
to reduce bleeding, pain, and inflammation. They switched their emphasis from cure to prevention. Plagues of rats, flies, mosquitoes, bed-
bugs, springtails, and other vermin posed serious health hazards. Cholera, plague, smallpox, typhoid, and malaria were endemic in the
villages; there were no vaccines, preventive medicines, or even mosquito
nets to halt their spread. Some contagious diseases, such as malaria and
scabies, infected nearly all guerrillas, but other ailments—including
cholera, plague, and smallpox—were kept in check by an emphasis on
hygiene. The guerrillas were also stricken by aches and pains brought on
by the humid and fickle climate of the coastal mountains. Backaches and
leg pains reduced their mobility. During engagements, these could be as
deadly as the plague. Hygiene workers taught the guerrillas to seek out
dry places when sleeping in the open and to put up straw fences to fend
off the damp sea winds.[104]

## THE MINDONG PURGES

Among the epidemics that the Mindong Communists failed to repel was
purge mania. Ye Fei and his fellow leaders successfully freed themselves
from the embrace of the Su-Liu Advance Division, but not before they
had succumbed to the new political plague from Ruijin. The Mindong
Party was cut off from the national Party in its founding years and
avoided many of its excesses. Being the last of the soviets had advantages, not least of which was that "it knew only traitors and counterrevolutionaries," not "AB's" or "Social Democrats," so its early purges were
less extreme than elsewhere.[105] The arrival of the Advance Division
changed all that. It led to fratricidal bloodshed on a scale that threatened the very existence of the Mindong base. To establish their ideological credentials and their superior authority, the envoys from Ruijin had
to convince Ye Fei that his movement was threatened by dark forces that
only they, as Marxist initiates, could name. In a bizarre confrontation,
they demanded of Ye Fei whether Social Democrats or "AB's" had been
detected in Mindong. Ye had never heard of either. Liu Ying demanded,
"There are 'AB's' in the Central Soviet even though it is so strong. How
then could there be none here?"

The question alarmed Ye Fei. He began to think that "perhaps we are
immature." On Liu Ying's instructions, a public security bureau, "like in

the Soviet Union," was set up in Mindong, under the personal direction of Liu Ying's emissaries. In March 1936, the purge started, taking as its target "cynics and grumblers." In just two days, 122 "AB's" were killed in Ningde alone after "confessions" had been extorted from them. Fan Shiren, chief of the newly formed security bureau, explained the technique: "You force him to confess, he confesses, you believe him, then you kill him; or he does not confess and you kill him."

The purge gained such momentum that the Mindong Communists took fright. To put things right, they started a second purge, directed against the officials who had carried out the first one. This main purge continued for half a year, during which, according to Ye Fei, "we killed our most loyal and steadfast people." "We murdered our cream," Fan Shiren concurred. Purges continued throughout the Three-Year War and claimed victims until the end. Fortunately for the Party's base in the villages, 99 percent of those purged were cadres and only 1 percent were "vacillating masses."

The purges were inevitably colored by local rivalries. In the summer of 1936, members of a Mindong guerrilla column sent to help the Red Army in Minbei became homesick and "started making cynical remarks"; all but a few were killed. At around the same time, Ye Fei ceded part of his territory to the Advance Division; two to three hundred people were subsequently killed there. The Mindong Communists themselves used purges to get rid of wounded soldiers left behind in August 1934 by the vanguard. All in all, nearly six hundred Communists were killed in purges in Mindong alone. "If you are a revolutionary," said survivors, "the Whites want to kill you; then again, you never know when the Reds might want to kill you."

Save for the purge, the Communist movement in Mindong might have emerged from the hills twice as strong in 1937. Chen Ting's column lost more troops in purges in February and March 1936 than in a whole year of fighting. The purges also caused a wave of desertions. "We could have avoided the mistakes committed in the purge if we had continued as an indigenous organization," said Ye Fei.[106]

## NEW OPENINGS, NEW DIRECTIONS

In 1936, Mindong guerrillas replenished their ranks somewhat as a result of repercussions in the region of the anti-Japanese movement in the cities, the main Red Army's Eastern Expedition of February 1936, and the Liang Guang Incident of June 1936.[107] In the winter, two events persuaded Ye Fei of the need for a change in policy. First, a platoon leader of the Nineteenth Route Army defected to him with a squad of troops. Unlike most defectors, this man had no history of sympathizing with the

Communists. Like many of his fellow officers, he was a fervent patriot; he had apparently been convinced by Communist leaflets about the threat from Japan. This incident suggested that the Communists could win support if they worked hard on the issue of Japanese aggression.[108] Second, Ye Fei received publications, including the August First (1935) Manifesto, from underground contacts in Fuzhou, Fuan, and Pingyang and got word from the Party's Southern Working Committee.[109] As a result of these two developments, he adopted even more moderate policies and began calling for unity against Japan. He gave "intellectuals" in soviet areas the rights to vote and to stand for office, and he promised added protection for "national bourgeois" and "enlightened gentry"—a concept that Mindong leaders claim to have developed independently. He also dropped the name "soviet" (though he never actually proclaimed its abolition) when he learned from Fuan that Communists in Minxi'nan were led by a Military and Administrative Committee, and he adopted a like title for his own region;[110] similarly, he began calling his guerrillas a People's rather than a Workers' and Peasants' Division.

Adopting Minxi'nan names and slogans did not immediately bring successes of the sort that Communists in Minxi'nan achieved. However, some of the policy changes worked to the Party's benefit and won new "social sympathizers" in the villages. The attitude of *baojia* chiefs and village gentry toward the Communists improved. "Intellectuals"—teachers and students—were now prepared to talk to them. When guerrillas turned up in White territory, they were no longer viewed with fear and hostility as they had been in the past. But government officials at first ignored Ye's unity proposals.[111] In January 1937, regular Nationalist divisions began a second major drive against the Mindong Communists that "according to incomplete statistics" killed 772 "Party members, revolutionary cadres, and members of the masses" and led to the razing of three thousand houses and seventy villages.[112] The campaign against the Communists in Mindong continued until late 1937.[113]

Ye Fei was better equipped for endgame than his fellow leaders elsewhere in the south. "The opposition between Red and White in the southern soviet regions was severe," said Ye Fei, " but Mindong had the advantage that it was the last of the soviets, so the opposition was less stark." Mindong Communists were more open than others to the idea of a united front "from above" in 1936, partly because of their experience in the Fujian Incident and perhaps also because they had not directly experienced the collapse of the first united front in 1927 (when their movement was barely formed and Ye Fei was a child of twelve).[114] Fuzhou was within relatively easy reach of Mindong; though the Party had been smashed in Fuzhou, the guerrillas still had tenuous ties to its underground supporters there. So Ye Fei learned early and in considerable detail of the national leadership's retreat from "leftism." Moreover, he first learned of the new policy in its traditional form, summarized in the slogan "Oppose Chiang and resist Japan"—a position familiar to Ye from the days of the revolutionary government in Fuzhou.

Through their Fuzhou link, the Mindong Communists also heard about the student demonstrations of December 9, 1935. This news, too, prepared them for the change in policy, which was smoother and more protracted in Mindong than in other southern bases. "The main thing is that it was a process," said Ye Fei. "We relied chiefly on ourselves to think the matter through to a conclusion. It was a turn not of 180 degrees but at most of sixty or eighty degrees."[115]

Had they first learned of the new policy in its later, more conciliatory form ("Ally with Chiang against Japan") they would have found it far harder to embrace. This new slogan startled and worried Ye when he first heard of it, so much so that he was unsure whether to believe it, especially when local Nationalists interpreted it to him as a surrender by the Communists to the Nanjing government.[116]

One of Ye's main sources of information in this period was the press, from which he learned news by raiding towns once every month or two. Because Mindong was near Fuzhou, newspapers from Hongkong and Shanghai were relatively easy to come by. Ye led a raid by two hundred guerrillas on the small coastal town of Badu in Ningde and scoured the place for newspapers to check the story about an alliance with Chiang. His haul convinced him that it was genuine. In August 1937, he approached the local authorities in Ningde, who obtained permission from the provincial government to start talks.[117]

### THE TALKS BEGIN

Over the next few months, representatives of the Party center, including Zhang Yunyi, made repeated attempts to contact Ye Fei. They failed, partly because of obstruction by Ch'en I, Fujian's provincial governor, who first denied that there were Communist guerrillas in Mindong and then said that they were always on the move and impossible to reach.[118] So Ye Fei had to make weighty decisions without consultation and advice. Between August and the year's end, three sets of negotiations took place; all failed. The Nationalists thought that if they kept Ye cut off from the outside world, they would be able to win him over and reorganize his forces under their own command.

Ye Fei, however, did not need a Central Committee directive to tell him the difference between a united front and an "offer of amnesty and enlistment to bandits." (He had read *The Water Margin*.) Armed clashes continued during the talks. Ye Fei refused to let the authorities issue him with finance and supplies, for he thought that accepting them would imply that he was being reorganized as part of the Nationalist Army rather than as an independent entity.[119] Far from slackening his military campaign, Ye stepped it up and ransomed several dozen *tuhao* for a hundred thousand dollars to wrest recognition from the authorities.

He entered the negotiations from a position of some strength. Even before they started, he had more than one thousand troops and six county committees in Mindong.[120] He was able to infiltrate coastal cities, where official and unofficial campaigns to resist Japan were underway.[121] Despite the armed clashes, local authorities could not afford to break off talks with him, for after the Battle of Shanghai in August 1937, all three regular Nationalist units were withdrawn from Fuzhou, and only local forces were left to hold the Communists in check. In December 1937, after a further intercession by Zhang Yunyi, Ye was finally called to Fuzhou for direct talks with Ch'en I.[122]

Governor Ch'en, expecting to meet a brigand, was taken aback by Ye Fei's refinement. "You are Ye Fei?" he asked. "But you look like a scholar." Men from the command of the Peace Preservation Corps were not so easily impressed. At a banquet given by Ch'en I, Ye was puzzled by the hostile glares they gave him. Later, he realized that it was because he was wearing the clothes of their chief of staff, whom he had recently killed.[123]

Ch'en I presented Ye with seven hundred army uniforms and five thousand dollars and let him publish a statement in *Fujian Ribao* in the name of the Mindong Special Committee.[124] He also agreed to let Ye choose his own name for the reorganized guerrillas. Ye did not yet know about the New Fourth Army, so he called them the Second Fujian Anti-Japanese Guerrilla Detachment after hearing that the Minxi guerrillas had used a similar name. The negotiators also agreed that fields distributed to the peasants in Mindong would not be restored to their original owners (though it is unlikely that the authorities kept to this agreement).[125]

Though the negotiations had started in August 1937, it was not until mid-February 1938 that the guerrillas finally left Mindong to join the New Fourth Army. The Mindong leaders took advantage of the intervening months to win and train three hundred new recruits to reinforce their 920 veterans (armed with five hundred rifles).[126] Four of the New Fourth Army's eight founding regiments came from Fujian. Of these four, the Sixth, formed by Mindong guerrillas, was the largest: 1,300 guerrillas were eventually reorganized, of whom 1,200 reached Wannan.[127] Guerrillas in Minbei, Xiang'egan, and elsewhere exaggerated their strength to get more supplies and then made good their claims by crash recruitment; the Mindong guerrillas did not. Though Communists in the region continued to recruit during the negotiations, they made no attempt to trick Ch'en I afterwards. "We reported the same number of people as we had," said Ye Fei. "We did not expand. Ultimately that was a mistake, a reflection of our immaturity." "We were too frank," said Fan Shiren. "Actually, we could have organized two regiments."[128]

Fan is right. If local forces are included, the Communists had influence over three to four thousand troops in Mindong. The experience of 1934 shows that they could grow at lightning speed once government troops withdrew.

The Mindong guerrillas were models of vigilance and defiance in the final stages of reorganization. They heard from supporters in Fuzhou about the Zhangpu Incident even before they had restored direct ties to the Central Committee; they drew their own conclusions. They resisted a Guomindang proposal that they assemble in the capital of Ningde and instead gathered their troops on a mountain near the city, which closed its gates for three days in panic. Eventually, they assembled in a village high in the Jiufeng Mountains and equally remote from all main centers of Nationalist power in Mindong, but not before the authorities had agreed to remove all troops from within a radius of thirty miles.[129] One guerrilla commander defected with thirty men to the Nationalists and got a local posting, but most (including many Shes) marched north despite their exclusively local provenance.[130]

The Communists did not withdraw completely; they left around one hundred armed men behind and did not uproot the basic organization of the Party, which in October 1937 had nine hundred members. So they avoided the two extremes of concentrating too little or too much of the Party's regional resources (though they left fewer men behind than Mao Zedong would have wished, and by 1939 their armed stay-behinders had been wiped out by Great Knives).[131]

## THE NEGOTIATIONS IN MINZHONG

In Minzhong, the course of negotiations was more troubled and resulted in an incident similar to that at Zhangpu in Minnan. The Minzhong leaders sent agents to Hongkong in the autumn of 1936 to contact the Party's Southern Committee. By December, they were receiving regular mailings of Party propaganda and had stopped military action against the Nationalists. For a while, they probably stayed hostile to the idea of a united front; when Mindong Communists sent a Fuzhou worker, nicknamed "Moscow," south to them with news of the new turn, they killed him.[132] By February 1937, they had apparently rethought their position, and they met to consider peace talks. Their meeting was betrayed, and all but Liu Tujun, who was absent, were caught by the Nationalists and executed four months later.

Liu, as sole survivor of the old committee, set up a new one and strove to mend the link to Hongkong. Some time after April 1937, he received new instructions from Hongkong through a second emissary. He was told to reorganize his guerrillas as Anti-Japanese Volunteers, choose a good time for talks with the authorities, and send a permanent representative to Hongkong. In August 1937, the Nationalists in Putian began publishing statements against Japan. At first, the Communists did not take them seriously; after all, just a few weeks earlier, the authorities in Fuzhou had killed the five Minzhong leaders seized in February. No doubt ill feeling on both sides increased the tension in Putian, where more than two hundred guerrillas assembled in a small village after negotiations in late August had led to an "agreement in principle."[133]

The authorities in Putian were worried that the Communists would launch mass movements in the region. The guerrillas, who were local people, created a stir when they marched down from the mountains. Though they had lost most of their main leaders, they were an unusually hardened bunch of fighters even by Red Army standards. To prevent them from causing trouble, the Nationalist command insisted that they leave Putian and go south to the city of Quanzhou on the coast, where they lacked natural bases of support and would be easier to control. In November 1937, Liu Tujun finally agreed. He was afraid that the Guomindang would cast doubt on his patriotism if he refused to move, and he was convinced by the argument that the southern front needed reinforcing. He also had his own reasons for wanting to go to Quanzhou. He believed that he could restore the Communist Party there, stiffen the urban resistance, and win new, educated cadres for his tiny and by now largely headless army. Apparently he had not heard of the disarming of the guerrillas under He Ming, who had tried with disastrous consequences to do the same at Zhangpu just a few months earlier.[134]

During negotiations, Liu had agreed to redesignate his followers as a unit of the locally based Eightieth Division of the Guomindang, even though he insisted that they remain independent and be allowed to join the New Fourth Army "at the necessary time." Communists elsewhere in southern China were generally wary of government attempts to incorporate guerrillas into existing forces. In Minzhong, as in other parts of Fujian, both north and south, the Communists would have preferred to fight the Japanese from their old haunts. This inclination may explain why they were prepared to accept an assignment (as part of the Eightieth Division) that they imagined would enable them to stay. Leaders higher up in the Party (though not Xiang Ying, who had the final say) also wanted guerrillas to stay put in the province. Minzhong Communist leaders had no reason to dissent; their troops, and they themselves, were natives of Fujian.

But joining the Eightieth Division turned out to be a grave mistake. The Nationalists had their own plans for Liu Tujun's guerrillas. After offering him a commission (which he turned down), they told him that his troops should quickly go to the Ningbo front in Zhejiang. Liu replied, "Our soldiers were born and bred here. They cannot even speak the national language properly. But their morale is high. If they stay in Minzhong to resist Japan, they can develop their forces and play an even greater role."

After this showdown, "friction and provocations" escalated. One reason for the trouble was that even as late as February 1938, higher bodies of the Communist Party had still not asked the Nationalist command to ratify the transfer of the Minzhong forces to the New Fourth Army. Again, they may have delayed because the Party generals wanted to maintain a presence in southern Fujian. Whatever the case, the effect was to leave Liu Tujun and his guerrillas, already isolated from other Communist concentrations, still more vulnerable to Nationalist reprisals. Liu did his best to persuade Communist leaders in Minxi to speed up his transfer to a Communist command, but to no avail.[135] Liu's dispute with the Nationalists dragged on until March 1938, when he and three other Communists were assassinated while on their way to Fuzhou to report to the New Fourth Army office there.

The day after the assassinations, the temple in Quanzhou where Liu's guerrillas were billeted was surrounded, and they were disarmed. Only ten days later, after protests by New Fourth Army leaders, were they released.[136] Between 110 and 160 guerrillas then went to Wannan and were reorganized as a special service battalion attached to the headquarters of the New Fourth Army.[137]

## COMMUNISTS OF A SPECIAL SORT

Veterans of the Gandongbei Soviet, writing in 1945, portray the Mindong Communist movement as especially prone to splits and violent disputes. They partly explain this fragmentation by the fact that the Mindong Communists were dispersed and out of touch with one another for months on end; their isolation enabled them to survive but made it hard for them to unite when conditions improved.[138] I have suggested other possible reasons for the problems that beset Ye Fei. His movement was young and inexperienced. It grew largely by skillful adjustment to the world of religious sectarianism. Ye's guerrillas, unlike the Su-Liu Advance Division in Zhe'nan and the regular Nationalist divisions that purged Mindong, were local people; they had no need for introductions or interpreters. But their special background inclined them at first to indiscipline, factionalism, and insularity. After the first upsurge of support for the Party in the villages of Mindong in the early 1930s, its founding leaders were joined in 1934 by refugees from the Fuzhou city branch and casualties left behind by the Anti-Japanese Vanguard. Before these three groups, with their different experiences and backgrounds, could thrash out their differences of opinion, agree to a redistribution of posts, and generally adapt to one another and unite, the soviet had fallen.

Despite these conflicts, the local component of the Mindong movement closed ranks around Ye Fei after 1934, partly because he was a strong and capable commander and partly because he came to represent its regional identity against the intruder Communists. According to one analysis, the Mindong Communists "held out best" of all the stay-behinders because they were not infected by Wang Ming-style "leftism." This view ignores the destructive purges carried out in Mindong, but otherwise it is largely true. The Communist movement in Mindong grew naturally from the region's social and political compost. It was invisible to the main Party centers and so escaped the imposition of policies and personnel. "Leftists" turned up in the region only at the last minute and by accident. When they tried to press their views on local Communists, they were stopped and crushed. So the Mindong Communist movement developed a different profile, and according to a different rhythm, from those of other Communist movements left behind in the south. It decided its policies independently, flexibly, and pragmatically, being largely unencumbered by dogma.

That both the Communists and their opponents were local people is another important difference between Mindong and other bases of the Three-Year War and a main reason for Ye Fei's success. Compared with those in other regions, the Nationalist garrison in Mindong was weak. Except during two short periods, it consisted entirely of local security forces and Great Knives. Consequently, the struggle in Mindong was often crueller and more intense, but the odds against Ye were shorter.[139]

The problems facing the refugees who assembled in the bandit stronghold of Luohanli in Minzhong in 1935 were more daunting. Though they, too, were local people, at first they had little or no following in Luohanli. They were tolerated only at the whim of their outlaw confederate until they succeeded in swinging the balance of support their way by importing comrades. During the Three-Year War, guerrillas either learned to compromise or went under. The Communists of Luohanli, dependent as they were on men like Liu Ahe, had to compromise more than most. When they marched to Quanzhou in late 1937, they had little strength to show for their years in the mountains. At least

160 of them had stayed behind because of old age, poor health, or lack of political conviction. The Party's local recruits were strongly attached to their villages: Liu Tujun found it hard to stop them returning home for New Year even in the middle of a critical phase of fighting.[140]

Perhaps Chen Yunfei and his comrades during their time in Changtai and Luohanli grew too trustful of unusual allies or too confident of their ability to sidestep trouble; or perhaps they were ignorant—because of their isolation from Party bureaus—of the dangers of an incident. Whatever the case, they had embraced the habit of compromise to excess; they recklessly exposed their guerrillas to the city and gambled away their independence by accepting reorganization as part of a Nationalist division. Partly as a result, Liu Tujun was killed, and the guerrillas were lucky to survive as an independent force.

However, 95 percent of those who eventually joined the New Fourth Army from Minzhong were Communist Party members, 60 percent were Communist Party or guerrilla veterans, and their average age (twenty-five) was the highest among all southern guerrilla units. In proportion to its size, the Minzhong Red Army contributed more in skills and leaders to the New Fourth Army than any other southern group. Natural selection contributed to this strength; the transfer to Quanzhou in November 1937 and the incident of March 1938 weeded out faint-hearts and montagnards recruited to the guerrillas by strictly local loyalties. Nearly forty Minzhong veterans (or one in four of the survivors) later held important posts in the New Fourth Army's Jiangnan and Jiangbei commands and in its First and Second Detachments.[141]

Of the three main bases in Minzhewan'gan, Mindong was strategically the best placed. Zhe'nan was too close for comfort to important concentrations of government power, while Minbei was too far from the coast to benefit from news of national political developments. The Communists in Mindong were attacked less often than their comrades to the north, in Zhe'nan, and they started calling for a united front several months earlier than their comrades to the west, in Minbei. Perhaps because of this foresight, they were able to present a relatively large contingent of guerrillas to the New Fourth Army. Today, the unit they formed is a crack unit of the People's Liberation Army.[142]

# Wanzhegan:
# Gathering the Fragments

◆　◆　◆

Wanzhegan is the name of the border region between the southern part of Anhui (Wan), the northern part of Zhejiang (Zhe), and the northeastern part of Jiangxi (Gan). It is the meeting point of four large mountain chains, the Huang, the Tianmu, the Huaiyu, and the Qianligang.[1] Communists were active here after 1934 in Fuliang, Wuyuan, Duchang, Leping, and other counties of Wannan, Zhexi, Gandongbei, Zhexibei, and Ganbei.[2] These tiny bases were mainly spawnings of the old soviet in Minzhegan (Gandongbei). Minzhegan after 1934 is best likened to the Central Soviet in the same period: in both places, the collapse of Communist power was almost total, the main difference being that in Minzhegan it happened sooner. None of the Communist units around Minzhegan established durable bases after this collapse; all emerged from the Three-Year War small and battered, particularly the Wanzhegan bases to the north and west of Minzhegan, which (unlike Minbei and Mindong) had seen little or no Communist presence before 1934. The failure of Communist movements to take root in Wanzhegan owed much to the problems of Minzhegan, where in 1934 conditions were chaotic and morale was poor.

Wanzhegan was strategically important for the Guomindang. The Zhegan railway runs through its southeastern region. Within striking distance to the north are major cities of the Chang Jiang region, and even closer are the potteries of Jingdezhen. The region is crossed by the Qingyang-Tunxi highway and by several rivers, including the Xin He, the Qingyi Jiang, and the Xin'an Jiang.

Wannan, the northern corner of the Wanzhegan triangle after 1934, was the intended destination of the Anti-Japanese Vanguard that marched north from Gandongbei under Fang Zhimin in the winter of

1934. It was also the intended site of bases from which the Communists planned to prick the heart of the government at Nanjing and so divert pressure from the main Red Army. Fang's expedition failed; the small bands of fugitives who fled the mountains never overcame their disarray. The fright raised in Nanjing was out of proportion to the threat. The authorities took every precaution to prevent the Communists from settling in Wanzhegan.

Communism was new to most of this region in 1934, but not to Wannan. Communists were active in Jingjingningxuan (comprising parts of Jingxian, Jingde, Ningguo, and Xuancheng) as early as 1930. At one point, a group of "revolutionary intellectuals" from the Dabie Mountains crossed the Chang Jiang to work as schoolteachers and carry out Party tasks both in Jingjingningxuan and in Guiqiudong's Gaoshan, near the Jiangxi border. Wannan was a promising target for Party activists. It was strategically valuable and had hills, high mountains, and fordable rivers, a combination good for both moving and hiding. It was richer than mountain regions to the south, and its population was more literate: newspapers (a main source of intelligence for the Communists) were available in all the bigger villages.[3]

Uprisings and disturbances in Wannan were widespread between 1929 and 1934. Though all failed, Party members had restored peasant associations in many mountain villages by early 1935.[4] Other early excursions into Wanzhegan and plans to open up the region miscarried. In late 1929 and early 1930, Communist forces from Gandongbei struck as far north as Jingdezhen and the region around Wuyuan in Wanzhegan, but they left no residue when they went back south. During the government's Third Encirclement of the Communists in 1931, when Nationalist troops massed along the Xin Jiang south of the Gandongbei Soviet to cut its links to the Central Soviet, indigenous Gandongbei leaders like Fang Zhimin and Shao Shiping again favored a sortie into Wanzhegan, which had as yet no lines of forts and few Nationalist regulars. But they were overridden by Zeng Hongyi, the Central Committee's representative in Gandongbei, who insisted that the main force in Gandongbei "fight its way through to the Central Soviet" in the south. In December 1933, with Fang Zhimin back in the saddle, the old strategy was reversed, and the New Tenth Red Army spread out to the north, where it set up a satellite soviet at Huawude, on the border between Jiangxi and Zhejiang, before heading toward Wannan. Several dozen cadres were detached to work for the Party around Jingdezhen and in White territory in Wannan. In 1934, expeditions penetrated deep into Wanzhegan, and Communist pockets briefly flourished along the Zhegan, Zhewan, and Wan'gan borders and in parts of Wannan, including Taiping and Jingxian.[5]

Ruijin leaders misrepresented these thrusts into Anhui as a "mass insurrection" and made them a pretext for the Northern Expedition by the Anti-Japanese Vanguard under Xun Huaizhou, who was told "to make propaganda for the resistance to Japan and come to the aid of Wannan." However, the real purpose of Xun's expedition was to threaten the Nationalist heartland, draw Nationalist troops away from the Central Soviet, and coordinate with the unannounced but secretly planned evacuation of the Central Soviet that was to culminate in the Long March. "Going to help Wannan" was a convenient pretense. Ruijin leaders knew soon after Xun's departure that the probes into Wannan had been defeated, but they did not tell Xun, who only learned of it at the end of September after reaching Duanxin in Wan'gan, close to his final goal.[6]

The Communist excursions into Wannan in 1934 alarmed Nanjing. Together with the northward progress of the Anti-Japanese Vanguard, these sorties drew more Nationalist troops into Wanzhegan. By the time Xun and Fang Zhimin marched into the Huang Mountains in the winter of 1934, a huge army had massed to block and rout them. Before fleeing toward Minbei in late December, Fang—having seen for himself how flimsily the Party was grounded in Wannan—told it to drop its soviet title and revert to guerrilla warfare. Apparently he did not expect to maintain contact with Wannan from his intended base in Minbei, for he told the Wannan Communists to look to Shanghai for future instructions.[7]

## WANZHEGAN AFTER THE DEFEAT OF FANG ZHIMIN

The shattering of the Fang Zhimin expedition rained debris on the whole of Wanzhegan. Only a small minority of marchers, some eight hundred, regrouped on the border between Dexing and Hengfeng under Su and Liu; of these, only half set out for Zhexi'nan. Just under three thousand marchers were taken prisoner; an unknown number died in the mountains. Probably several thousand soldiers of the Tenth Red Army Corps survived the expedition and went either home or into hiding. None of the host of guerrilla bases fastened along the mountains of Wanzhegan was strong enough to gather together the Communist fragments strewn across the region. The marchers' command was in ruins, unable to organize orderly retreats. Bands of fugitives blindly roamed the mountains, fighting, running, deserting, and defecting.[8]

In January 1935, the last few strongholds of the Gandongbei Soviet collapsed. The confusion increased as new groups of fugitives fled to the Wanzhe border.[9] By now, Communists of three sorts—local guerrillas from Wanzhegan, Tenth Red Army Corps escapers, and fugitives from

Gandongbei—were adrift in the mountains. Attempts to weld them together did not always work; according to one veteran, "sectarian" differences divided them. Like guerrillas in other parts of Minzhewan'gan, the guerrillas in Wanzhegan forged links to local outlaws and religious sects after 1934. In Fuliang, a "reformed" leader of the Red Gang became Party secretary.[10]

Among the bewildering profusion of guerrilla bases in Wanzhegan between 1935 and 1937, the best known were in Zhegan, Wan'gan, Wannan, Wanzhe, and Gandongbei (also called Minzhegan). This list is incomplete: alongside main bases under Guan Ying, Yu Hanchao, Yang Wenhan, Liu Yubiao, Wang Fengqing, and Li Buxin were numerous smaller ones under lesser leaders. Some fugitive bands from Gandongbei and remnants of the Tenth Red Army Corps were wiped out, others joined indigenous units, and still others held out independently until 1937.[11]

Even some individuals held out alone. Li Buxin, an early leader of the Party in Wannan's Huang Mountains and later a member of the Party's Eastern Bureau, spent much of the three years after 1934 among Wannan villagers, pretending to be mute in case his thick Jiangxi accent betrayed him in an area where "foreigners" were rare.[12] Another group of wounded survivors of the vanguard, eventually reduced to two, spent two winters in the mountains near Lake Poyang, fighting off wild animals with sticks at night.[13]

The history of the groups that ranged the mountains of Wanzhegan after 1934 is complex and scantily documented. The movements of just one unit illustrate the general pattern. In June 1934, guerrillas in an advance division under Wang Fengqing, Liu Zhenyu, and others slipped north into Wan'gan. At the beginning of winter, they spread west to Lake Poyang. En route, around Fuliang and Wuyuan, they rallied stragglers and fugitives of the Anti-Japanese Vanguard. At Lake Poyang, they set about organizing a soviet government. But within just a few weeks, they were driven away by a Nationalist attack. They marched north to the Chang Jiang, where they became active in the Guiqiudong area of Wannan. Here, in the Party's Gaoshan stronghold, they laid ambitious plans in April 1935 to carry out land revolution and turn Gaoshan into a "permanent base."

In July and August, 180 delegates met to set up a Jiangnan Soviet government, nominally covering the whole of the southern Chang Jiang delta. Liu Zhenyu stayed behind in Wan'gan, reinforced by units returning south from Guiqiudong. In Guiqiudong, Wang's division began to stage armed risings in the autumn of 1935 and soon controlled 1,500 troops. But because Wang "fought recklessly" and tried to defend Gaoshan from fixed positions, his base collapsed within six months, and he was forced to flee. Two hundred guerrillas were left behind on Gaoshan. Most were local people; all but a few deserted. This chaotic story of migrations, separations, fusions, retreats, remigrations, lightning growth, and sudden deathblows is characteristic of the Three-Year War in Wanzhegan.[14]

In 1935, stay-behinders of the Gandongbei Soviet in Dexing, Wuyuan, and other districts, having held out under Guan Ying for six months after the Nationalist reoccupation of the region, came under ever greater military pressure and lost several main leaders. Early in the year, Nationalist troops reduced the population of the old Hengfeng-Dexing Soviet from one hundred thousand to fifty thousand by terror and deportations. In the autumn, Guan Ying led remnants north toward Wannan; units that stayed behind in Gandongbei lost touch with one another and suffered heavy losses. The base was completely overrun, though a handful of guerrillas survived until 1937.[15]

Guan Ying wound up in the Zhanggong Mountains on the Wan'gan border between Wuyuan and Xiuning, where he found that the chaos in Gandongbei was not unique and that isolated groups throughout Wanzhegan were deep in crisis. He sent out people in all directions to reorganize these groups. Coincidentally, guerrilla leaders throughout Wanzhegan were abandoning their bases and seeking wider contacts because of losses through enemy action, defections, and a general lack of purpose. In January and February, various lost units gathered at Guan Ying's new headquarters in the Zhanggong Mountains; some found their own way there, others were collected. Among them were Wang Fengqing, at the head of a column of troops by then known as the Jiangnan guerrillas, and guerrillas fleeing Wannan's Jingjingningxuan, where efforts to found a base had come to grief after the defection of Wang Bi, left behind by Fang Zhimin to lead Wannan. After these defeats, "peasant movements in Anhui gradually stopped."[16]

## NEW DIRECTIONS

In April 1936, these leaders met under Guan Ying to decide on future action. They set up five special committees in the region, each with its own independent battalion, and pooled eight hundred guerrillas in a Wanzhegan Independent Regiment that operated from the Zhanggong Mountains. The new watchwords were discipline, education, and Party hegemony. In the villages, new methods were adopted, including the "red heart, white skin" tactic. In peacetime, a constant flow of traders climbed the mountains of Wanzhegan in search of goods to sell in the nearby towns and in markets overseas. The Communists did their best to restore this traffic. To mushroom traders, tea merchants, china-clay merchants, and transports of firewood for the pottery kilns, they allowed free passage through the areas they controlled. In exchange, they demanded books, newspapers, pens, ink, and medicine. Like guerrillas elsewhere in this period of retreat, they paid special attention to recruiting women to the Party and ran classes to teach local women the national language.[17]

New policies and the new system of regional coordination seemed to pay off. Within a few months, two thousand guerrillas had enlisted in Wanzhegan, bringing the Communists' total strength to nearly three thousand. But the growth was illusory and shallowly based; it vanished as quickly as it had come about. The decision of April 1936 to concentrate not just some but most groups of guerrillas led to disaster. Warfare became the main focus; political work in the villages was left unattended. Large forces were massed for suicide attacks on targets in Changhua, Kaihua, and Wuyuan after June. In July, guerrillas staged a sensational raid on the Kaihua jail to free twenty prisoners, including the wife of a Communist leader. In August, the Party "went public" in parts of Kaihua and prepared to divide the land. "We should not have waged armed struggle on such a large scale," concluded one veteran. "The enemy's main force had already withdrawn. Only the Peace Preservation Corps was left. We should therefore have done more mass work instead. We should have broadened our territory and done some relief work in the villages." Even where southern Communists could depend on a tradition of organization and support, they rarely concentrated their forces on such a scale after 1935. In Wanzhegan, soviets were practically unknown; even after the Zhanggong Conference, there were scarcely any places where Communists could gather in safety. To concentrate guerrillas in a region close to main government garrisons was suicidal folly and provoked devastating retribution.

The reckoning came in the wake of the Xi'an Incident of December 1936. The Wanzhegan leaders were unsure how to respond to the resulting political situation. They sent out a search party to find Liu Ying in Zhexi'nan (in fact he was in Zhe'nan), believing wrongly that he was still in radio contact with the Party center. They failed to foresee the offensive started by the Nationalists in Minzhewan'gan in early 1937, after the peaceful resolution of the Xi'an crisis. Worse still, Guan Ying led the entire Independent Regiment, representing 90 percent of his forces, east into Zhexi'nan to find Liu Ying just as the Nationalists were massing on the Zhegan border. Guan's regiment was surrounded and defeated at Kaihua in Zhejiang; its political commissar, Liu Yubiao, was taken prisoner.[18]

The guerrillas left behind to run the Party's bases in Wanzhegan fared equally badly. With only local forces to protect them, they too were unprepared for the extent of the Nationalist campaign. They remained optimistic about their chances even when the authorities began to reset-tle villagers away from "bandit-infested" areas. They refused to believe that the Nationalists would let the local economy collapse by preventing traffic from entering the mountains, for many local businessmen lived by selling mountain products. So they underestimated the extent and du-ration of the blockade.

Conditions for the Communists in Wanzhegan in the first half of 1937 were grim. Party branches, including that of Jingdezhen, collapsed one after the other as a result of killings, defections, and arrests. By March 1937, the Red Army was shattered, and Party organization in the vil-lages was destroyed. The Nationalists deployed sentries, snipers, spies, and trackers throughout the mountains; Communists holed up without supplies had to live off the land. When their matches ran out, they kindled moxa leaves. Eating wild roots and vegetables was fraught with risk. In one region, a "member of the masses" who had evaded re-settlement accompanied the guerrillas as food taster, trying out various plants to check whether they were poisonous. Several dozen guerrillas froze to death.[19]

### THE GUERRILLAS REORGANIZE

The blockade remained in place until the Japanese attack on Shanghai in August 1937, when Nationalist divisions began to withdraw from Min-zhewan'gan, still harassed by the Wanzhegan guerrillas. Before long, the authorities approached the Communists for talks. By then, the New Fourth Army had set up an office in Nanchang, and Xiang Ying and Chen Yi had published their "Open Letter to Southern Guerrillas." The letter was taken to Wanzhegan by Liu Yubiao, released from prison for this mission.

During the negotiations, the guerrillas refused to assemble in Jing-dezhen because they feared that their security would be endangered; Chen Yi praised them for their vigilance. After talks with Chen Yi in Nanchang, the Wanzhegan Communist leaders assembled nearly two hundred guerrillas, brought up to 350 by last-minute recruiting. They were reorganized as the First Detachment of the Jiangxi Anti-Japanese Volunteers. In early 1938, this detachment, by then five hundred strong, assembled at Yaoli in Jiangxi, near the Anhui border, and was redesig-nated as the Third Battalion of the Second Regiment of the First De-tachment of the New Fourth Army. Not all the guerrillas left the region; more than one hundred stayed behind to staff rear offices (later sup-pressed by the government) in Yaoli, Duchang, and Jingdezhen.[20]

Three units failed to reach Yaoli. One group of seventy guerrillas was ambushed and destroyed in Ningguo by the local magistrate, a Communist renegade. Two diehard units in Gandongbei saw the united front as a sellout and refused to give up the struggle. These recalcitrants called Mao Zedong a traitor and killed several Party representatives, including Guan Ying, who tried to talk them down from the mountains.[21] They, too, were eventually destroyed by Nationalists.[22] Gandongbei was not the only place where guerrillas held out against the united front, but it had more mutineers than most. This defiance probably stemmed from the local Party's failure to break with "leftism" after 1934, the fragmentation of guerrilla remnants in the region, and the immaturity of the movement in places outside the old Gandongbei Soviet. Treachery by the Guomindang stiffened the resistance to talks and unity. In December 1937, Qiu Laojin, leader of the Kaihua Soviet government set up in 1936, was lured down the mountains on the pretext of talks and was murdered.[23]

## PERSPECTIVES ON THE THREE-YEAR
## WAR IN WANZHEGAN

Wanzhegan was not a keystone of the Communist structure south of the Chang Jiang. It was not far north of the Gandongbei Soviet, which for a time had been one of the Party's biggest bases, but the main Communist troop movements from Gandongbei in the early 1930s were to the south, toward the Central Soviet, and to the east, into regions where indigenous Communist movements could feed on "warlord contradictions." Any incursion into Wanzhegan could be interpreted as a threat to Nanjing. Communists slipped into Wanzhegan in 1934 but failed to spread nets strong enough to catch the crumbling pieces of Fang Zhimin's defeated, demoralized, and divided Anti-Japanese Vanguard in the winter of 1934.

Prospects for the Communists fighting along the borders of Wanzhegan at the start of the Three-Year War were dim. The Wanzhegan bases were among the Party's newest, weakest, and least secure. Wanzhegan Communists fought with impetuous disregard for their own safety, choosing exposed targets and inviting catastrophic retribution. One example is the formation of the Independent Regiment in 1936 and its march east into Zhejiang. Another is Wang Fengqing's reckless attack, at the height of the Nationalist purge of Wanzhegan, on a British-owned coal mine in Leping; this episode led to Wang's capture and the rout of his guerrillas. In other respects, too, the switch from "leftist" policies was limited in Wanzhegan; killings of "comrades with ideological

defects" and "excessive killings" of landlords, local powerholders, and local officials still took place.[24]

The experience in Wanzhegan confirms that Communists—even
Communists without a real foothold in local society—could reorganize
their forces and surge up in supposedly "pacified" areas whenever the
pressure on them was relaxed after 1934. But the base established in
1936 barely survived the rigors of 1937, both because it was insufficiently
steeled and because its leaders were incautious. Chiang Kai-shek had no
qualms about letting Xiang Ying set up his headquarters in the Huang
Mountains of Wannan in early 1938. He would have felt less confident if
the Communists had built firm bases in Wanzhegan after 1934.

# Minzhewan'gan (II)

◆　◆　◆

These sketches of guerrilla struggles in five regions of Minzhewan'gan after 1934 show similarities as well as contrasts. Everywhere but Mindong, guerrillas ended up in places without much Communist tradition and with which they were largely or wholly unfamiliar. They had to build new bases under especially difficult circumstances: regionally and nationally, the revolution was in a deep trough; in Zhe'nan and Wanzhegan, stay-behind units were founded on the ruins of defeated armies. Unlike other regions where guerrillas fought after 1934, Minzhewan'gan adjoined strongholds of the Nanjing government.

The Three-Year War in Minzhewan'gan began with the arrival of the Anti-Japanese Vanguard under Xun Huaizhou, which enriched the Communist movement in Minzhewan'gan with anti-Japanese and patriotic themes. But it was impossible to whip up a campaign against Japan in the region, for unlike Minxi'nan in the south, it had not directly experienced Japanese political or economic pressure.[1]

The guerrilla units in Minzhewan'gan tried hard to overcome their isolation between 1934 and 1938. Su and Liu, inevitably, led the drive to unify the region. They saw themselves as plenipotentiaries of the Party center and had crossed the whole of Minzhewan'gan in late 1934 and 1935, so they had a uniquely broad view of it. Most guerrillas shared Su and Liu's goal of united action, but all attempts to achieve it foundered. The merger between Zhe'nan and Mindong came unstuck because of rivalry between the leaders of the two regions. Guan Ying's march east to join Liu Ying was blocked by a Nationalist army. Only the merger between Mindong and Minbei survived, but it was rarely more than nominal. Some units in Minzhewan'gan were rent internally by personal or factional rivalries.

Disunity is not uncommon in beleaguered political movements, but in Minzhewan'gan there were special reasons for the constant splits. Antagonisms arose between regulars and guerrillas and between outsider and local Communists thrown together after 1934. Close links to local bandits and religious sects in parts of Minzhewan'gan compromised some Communists, who began to act like their new-found friends. According to a later assessment of the movement in Minzhewan'gan, the slogan "Guarantee proletarian hegemony over the revolution" was used as a pretext to "usurp the Party and the [Communist Youth] League, to annex troops, . . . to cap, to beat, to kill, and to remove from office."[2]

Poisonous influences emanating from the Central Soviet were particularly powerful in new bases like those in Minzhewan'gan. In the depths of defeat and in the absence of big political movements, Party leaders found that the best way to win friends was through personal networks, but these also gave rise to increased personal friction. In Zhe'nan, friction between Liu Ying and Su Yu resulted in their parting company for a while. Minzhewan'gan lacked a diplomat like Chen Yi, who was sensitive to sources of friction in Ganyue and tried to lessen them. But the guerrillas of Minzhewan'gan were so widely scattered that even Chen's unifying gifts would have been hard put to overcome their rivalries and conflicts.

These tensions became an obstacle to unity in the New Fourth Army after 1937. Originally, Ye Fei's guerrillas were combined with survivors of the Su-Liu Advance Division into the New Fourth Army's Sixth Regiment, as part of the Third Detachment under Su Yu. Ye Fei protested and told army leaders about Su's role in the banquet incident. As a result, the Zhe'nan remnants were removed to another regiment. Su Yu was transferred to the Second Detachment, of which he became deputy commander, and the Mindong guerrillas became the sole component of the Sixth Regiment, whose brother regiment, the Fifth, was formed by Ye's old comrades from Minbei.[3]

In late 1937, the Central Committee paid tribute to the Minzhewan'gan Communists for having "stuck resolutely to the Party line, united with the broad masses, and flexibly employed guerrilla tactics," and it spoke of the "great significance" of their struggle after 1934.[4] The terms of this tribute were inflated. The switch to guerrilla warfare in Minzhewan'gan after 1934 was uneven: Communists in Minbei and Mindong, many of whom had never seen a regular Red Army soldier until the Anti-Japanese Vanguard marched by in 1934, accomplished it more smoothly than those in Zhe'nan and Wanzhegan. "The turn was not sufficiently clear and thorough," concluded veterans. "In some places premature insurrections and the repeat of past policy mistakes were a main cause of the new defeats in attempts to open up new areas."[5] The switch to united-front tactics happened sooner near the coast than in isolated inland regions.

Even so, Communists in the five main regions of Minzhewan'gan tied down large numbers of government troops after 1934;[6] they relieved pressure both on each other and on the Red Army main force during and after the Long March; and together they delivered more than three thousand recruits to the New Fourth Army in early 1938. Units in some parts of the region created an enduring tradition upon which southward-moving detachments of the New Fourth Army later built. After the fall of Wuhan in October 1938, thousands of Communists and their supporters were arrested in Gandongbei. Thousands more were arrested around the time of the Wannan Incident of January 1941, after which guerrillas once again became active in Minbei, Mindong, Zhe'nan, Zhexi'nan, Wan'gan, Wannan, and Gandongbei.[7]

# Eyuwan:
# The One-Armed General

◆   ◆   ◆

Eyuwan, in the Dabie Mountains where Hubei (E), Henan (Yu), and Anhui (Wan) join, was one the most important of the Chinese soviets. At
times it rivaled the Central Soviet in strength and size. It was the Red
Army's richest seedbed: according to statistics from the early 1950s, an
astonishing 70 percent of cadres at the divisional level and above in the
People's Liberation Army were natives of Eyuwan.[1] After 1934, Communists here were active in Jinzhai, Guangshan, Shangcheng (Chicheng), Taihu, Tongcheng, Xinyang, Huangchuan, and Xiaogan.[2] At its
peak, the Eyuwan Soviet had a population of 3.5 million, compared with
the Central Soviet's 2.5 million; but its surface area (40,000 square kilo-
metres) was slightly smaller and its Red Army (45,000) smaller by half.[3]
It was not only one of the two largest Communist bases in the early
1930s but also the best placed to disrupt the economy and communications of the Guomindang. It lay just to the west of the grain bins of the
Huai basin and the Chang Jiang floodplain; it was within striking distance of the tri-city of Wuhan, the Beijing-Hankou railway, and the
Chang Jiang; and of the great Communist bases, it had the best connections to the Party's nerve center in Shanghai before the Central Committee fled south to Ruijin in 1931 (map 8).[4]

Eyuwan might have played an even more central role in the history of
the Chinese Communist Party had the Shanghai leaders moved there
rather than to Gannan after the collapse of their work in the cities. But
its strategic location was as much a weakness as a strength. The Party's
base in Gannan was more isolated and better protected than that in Eyuwan and more properly a national center of the Party; while Eyuwan's
armies and leaders were overwhelmingly homegrown, Gannan's hailed
from all parts of China. According to Zhang Guotao, the Party's "ideal

hope" was to build a powerful base in Jiangxi from which other soviet zones south of the Chang Jiang could be unified and led.[5] There may have been a political as well as a strategic basis for the Shanghai leaders' choice of Ruijin: to curb Mao Zedong, who differed with them on how to run the movement.[6]

## THE STIGMATIZATION OF EYUWAN

It remains true that in the early 1930s Eyuwan was second only to the Central Soviet in scope and influence. "In waging armed struggle, carrying out land revolution, and establishing political power, it had its own creations and experiences," said one author. "It nurtured and trained a large number of outstanding leading cadres for the cause of the Chinese Revolution. . . . It deserves its own glorious position in the history of the Chinese Revolution."[7] From the point of view of this study, with its focus on Chinese Communism in collapse and the difficult transition between 1934 and 1938 from defeat to regrouping, the Communist movement in Eyuwan is even more relevant and important, for it survived the Three-Year War in the core areas of Wanxi (western Anhui) and Edong (eastern Hubei) better than other rearguard units. It yielded more troops for the New Fourth Army than any area save perhaps Minxi'nan, and after 1937 it continued as a key area of Communist recruitment and activity when most other bases of the Three-Year War had folded.

Until recently, however, only a few writings about the history of the Eyuwan base were published in China. The cause was not a lack of data. In 1958, researchers in Hubei, Henan, and Anhui began to cooperate on a vast study to reconstruct the history of the Eyuwan Soviet. Officials copied documents and materials running to some five million characters from the archives of the Party secretariat. Each province separately organized large teams of researchers to collect new materials, and a start was made on editing them. But before any could be published, the Cultural Revolution intervened. Not until the late 1970s was a "mass-style academic organization" set up to resume the project. Since then, a number of studies have been published, including a book-length history of Eyuwan from 1927 to 1937 and some reminiscences of the Three-Year War there.[8]

The reason for the previous neglect is not hard to divine. Eyuwan was not only physically isolated from Party strongholds in southern China by the Chang Jiang; it also developed its own distinct political identity and was led by men with little allegiance to any of the Party's central factions. According to a rare, early Western study of the Eyuwan Soviet, the base was more amenable than other soviets to control by the Shanghai-based anti-Mao leaders before 1931, so it lost scope for independence and

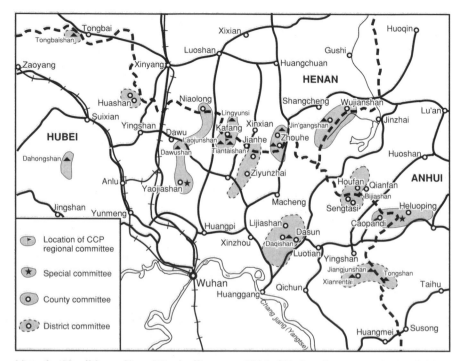

**Map 8. The Three-Year War in Eyuwan, 1934–37.** *Based on a map in Lin Wei-xian 1982.*

initiative and became a loyal base of Wang Ming's Returned Students in their struggle against the Maoists in Gannan.[9] But this view exaggerates the degree of central control over Eyuwan. In April 1931, the base was put under the direction of Zhang Guotao as representative of the Central Committee under Wang Ming; it is Eyuwan's association with the "traitor" Zhang Guotao that explains its long eclipse in histories of the revolution.

Zhang Guotao's assignment to Eyuwan was part of a wider effort by Shanghai leaders to put their central stamp on the Party's scattered rural bases. Some see his arrival in Eyuwan as an extension of the Wang Ming "leftist" line to the region; others see it the start of an "independent kingdom" there in competition with the Central Soviet in Jiangxi. Both views oversimplify. Zhang Guotao denies that he carried out Moscow's (i.e., Wang Ming's) line in Eyuwan or opposed "native Communists" in the region. Though he would be unlikely to admit otherwise, it is hard to see Zhang Guotao as anyone's willing tool. Before he went to Moscow for the second time in 1928, Zhang was known for his opposition to Moscow's policy of joining or allying with the Guomindang. In Moscow, he at first joined other Chinese in opposing the Russian, Pavel Mif, and Mif's Chinese protégé, Wang Ming. (Mif, who was associated with Sun Yat-sen University in Moscow, was the patron of the "Twenty-eight Bolsheviks," Moscow's most loyal supporters in the CCP.) However, three years in Moscow softened Zhang; by December 1930, Mif was prepared to withdraw an earlier criticism of Zhang, and in the meantime, Zhang had made friends among Wang Ming's Twenty-eight Bolsheviks. Still, Zhang insists that he only put down the cudgel against the Comintern to "get away from this cage [in Moscow] into the vast motherland."

His arrival in Eyuwan reaffirmed and strengthened its separate character while introducing to it the purge regime of the central leaders. When Mao called the First Soviet Congress in November 1931, some believe that Zhang Guotao found it convenient to stay away despite his appointment as one of the new soviet government's two vice chairs. On the day that the main congress met, Zhang called his own congress in Eyuwan: the "Second Congress of the Eyuwan Soviet Area."[10] But by then, communications between Eyuwan and Ruijin were so sporadic that Zhang was probably even unsure of the Central Committee's whereabouts.

## GAO JINGTING

Eyuwan's close association with the anti-Mao, anti-Comintern deviant Zhang Guotao is the main reason why its history was for so long suppressed, but Zhang's departure from the base in 1932 did not restore it to respectability. Between 1932 and 1934, it was run by the "leftist" Shen Zemin, who was one of the Twenty-eight Bolsheviks,[11] and after 1934, it became a fief of the local "leftist" Gao Jingting (also called Gao Junting). Gao was a towering figure in the movement in Eyuwan: a mixture of rebel and revolutionary, patriarch and mass fratricide, outlaw and commissar. His personality dominated Eyuwan's Three-Year War. He spent the whole of his Communist career shut off from the rest of the Party behind the mountains and rivers of central China. Unlike Zhang Guotao, who came to Eyuwan from Jiangxi (by way of Beijing, Shanghai, and Moscow), Gao was born and bred in the border region.[12] With Gao, the Party in Eyuwan was pared in 1934 to its irreducible core after shedding layer upon layer of broader-sighted leaders who marched off to found bases elsewhere.

In background and temperament, Gao was not unlike Xiang Ying, his distant neighbor in Ganyue during the Three-Year War and a native of Huangpi on the southwestern edge of Gao's Eyuwan base.[13] Gao also shared Xiang's plebeian origin: he was the son of a poor peasant, according to one biographer, and of a butcher, according to another. He was an avid reader, though not, apparently, of Marxist books. His favorite works included Sunzi's *Art of War* and *Romance of the Three Kingdoms.* The latter he carried with him always while fighting or marching, and he consulted it as a military manual between battles.[14] If the stories about him are true, he revered learning. According to one, when he discovered that a ransom victim, the small son of a rich landlord, was a pupil in a *sishu,* he arranged for a woman comrade to tutor the boy so that he would not fall behind in his studies.[15]

Like Xiang Ying, Gao "learned fighting from fighting." "He could not fight at all at first," said his comrade Lin Weixian. "But after the autumn of 1935 he often took the revolver team on inspection tours back and forth between Edong and Wanxi. Gradually he got some experience of combat."[16] Like Xiang Ying again, he was once grain commissioner (a post well suited to his talent for organized ruthlessness), and he was a savage purger.

Gao was renowned in the Communist movement for his brutality, both to his enemies and to friends he doubted. His cruelty can perhaps be explained by the harshness of his early life in war-torn southern Henan. Shortly after he became active in the revolution in 1927, his wife was killed by rich peasants. Later, his father was arrested and beaten to death after left-wing leaflets were discovered in his home. Gao's family house was burned to the ground, and his son vanished without trace. In manner and appearance, Gao was serious and even somber. Even when he was a young man, his face was lined, gaunt, and pale, but lit by piercingly brilliant eyes. He was a man of few words and of imposing presence. According to one veteran, "someone who did not know his background would think that he was not a soldier but an intellectual."[17]

Gao's first post in the Eyuwan Communist movement was as a lowly official in a frontline district committee frequently raided by White troops. After joining the Party in March 1929, he became chair of the district soviet and, in May 1930, of the Guangshan Soviet. In August 1930, he besieged a small township for 126 days and established his reputation as a slaughterer by killing forty "local tyrants and evil gentry" when the town fell. He soon rose to become a leader in Eyuwan and was made chair of its soviet on July 1, 1931.[18]

Some saw Gao as cold, severe, and inhuman; others say that he deeply loved his soldiers, who in their turn revered and awed him. Taciturn in private, he was a compelling speaker before crowds. He insisted on visiting wounded comrades in person during the Three-Year War. Despite his own poor health, he is said to have refused all privileges and to have given to his invalid comrades any special food presented him by subordinates.[19] Despite the fratricidal purges, Gao's Twenty-eighth Red Army was knit together, like other rearguard units, by ties of "care, trust, and sincerity." Gao clung tightly to his small troop even after its incorporation into the New Fourth Army in 1938; he was eventually shot by Commander Ye Ting as a mountaintoppist.[20] Here, too, he was a sort of Xiang Ying, but in miniature. Xiang Ying had pretensions to independent power over the New Fourth Army as a whole; the border patriarch Gao Jingting had pretensions to independent power over one of its detachments. Xiang Ying "clung to his small kingdom" in Wannan, Gao to his even smaller kingdom in the Dabie Mountains.

For forty years or so after Gao's execution in 1939, his name was not mentioned in public except to malign him. Among several unlikely charges, he was accused of following the "accommodationist" line of Wang Ming and Xiang Ying in central China after his guerrillas were reorganized in the New Fourth Army. In 1977, the General Political Department of the People's Liberation Army, acting on instructions left by the dying Mao, "rehabilitated Gao and made a factual assessment of the rights and wrongs of his life's achievements." The conclusion, shared by most of Gao's old comrades, was that though he had made mistakes, his contributions to the revolution were of value.[21] Even though the rehabilitation of Eyuwan Communist leaders has not extended to the "renegade" Zhang Guotao, the new spirit of truthfulness and objectivity in Chinese history-writing has freed Eyuwan, and its Three-Year War, from the factional clinch and has paved the way for a new look at its special features and its position in the broader movement.

## THE EARLY HISTORY OF THE BASE

Communists were active among peasants in Yudongnan (southeastern Henan) as early as 1923. In 1926 and 1927, warlord armies marched south into Eyuwan to block the Guomindang's Northern Expedition, but they scattered into the mountains as the Nationalist armies sliced through their lines. The Communist Party sent members into Eyuwan to organize the peasants into associations and resist these warlord stragglers. After the Nanchang Uprising of August 1, 1927, small batches of Communist insurgents arrived in Edong. In November 1927, Eyuwan's first soviet, called a peasants' government, was set up at Huang'an.[22] In these early years, the Communists mainly kept to Edongbei (northeastern Hubei), but in the summer of 1928, they switched their focus further north to the Chaishanbao region on the border between Hubei and Henan.

The early Communist movement in Huang'an and Chaishanbao could not compare even with the ragged bands of guerrillas that Mao Zedong and Zhu De took into the Jinggang Mountains in Xianggan in 1927. Zheng Weisan, a native of Huang'an and a founder of the Eyuwan Soviet, has commented on the special nature of the movement in Eyuwan and the differences between it and the movement in Gannan.[23] Zheng points out that among the several thousand fighters under Mao and Zhu were many experienced Party members from Wuhan and Hubei, including many with training in the army or the workers' armed picket. Others were survivors of Party-led uprisings in Jiangxi or Hunan or members of the Xiangnan Peasants' Self-Defense Army.[24] By the spring of 1928, this army had some ten thousand members. As newcomers to the region, Mao and Zhu at first had no choice but to ally with local bandits, but they dispensed with these allies once they were strong enough to act alone.

In Eyuwan, the revolutionaries were weaker than those south of the Chang Jiang, and counterrevolution was fiercer. In 1927, the Seventh Red Army was founded at Huang'an. For several months, it roamed the region northwest of Wuhan, spreading ideas and organization and laying the basis upon which the Eyuwan Communist movement was later built.[25] At first it was tiny, pitifully armed, overwhelmingly local in composition, and apolitical, having been assembled through ties of clan or friendship.[26] Its early leader, Xu Haidong, recruited Hubei's first "workers' and peasants' army" from among local pottery workers and peasants. "They numbered in the beginning only seventeen men," wrote Edgar Snow, "and they had only one revolver and eight bullets," Xu's own.[27] For the first few months of its existence, this army never grew beyond a few score recruits armed with a few dozen rifles—an army more in name than in fact.

According to Zheng Weisan, the Communists could have grown more quickly in Hubei than on the Chang Jiang if they had commanded a stronger armed force to serve as a magnet for fugitives from White terror. Mao's base in the Jinggang Mountains was an inspired strategic choice, physically screened from surrounding armies and equally remote from the two nearest provincial capitals. Hubei's early Red Army was chased from county to county by anti-Communist armed forces. Zheng Weisan claims that regions with large concentrations of intellectuals were its best recruiting grounds; educated sections of the local elite inclined toward the radical cause, so the gentry was split, its diehards were less influential, and local peasants were emboldened to join the revolution.[28] Eyuwan was such a region. It had more "revolutionary intellectuals," mainly the offspring of landlords and rich peasants, than other regions. The nucleus of the Eyuwan soviet movement, founded by students sent back there by the Party's urban cells, grew up in close dependence on the "long-gowned and broad-sleeved gentlemen" who in many of the border region's villages dominated the Red Spears and, later, the peasant associations. It was a long time before the Eyuwan Party became truly independent of such people. Its native roots distinguished it from the Communist movement in the Jinggang Mountains. Eyuwan's native Communists had social ties throughout society. Rich "class traitors" turned against their wealth and struck deep inside the enemy camp using ties of family, friendship, and their student days to sow chaos while running bookshops or teaching in local schools for legal cover.[29]

The decision of early 1928 to move into the Chaishanbao base on the Eyu border was strategically motivated but brought with it new problems that dogged the Communist movement in Eyuwan for ten years. Chaishanbao was a prosperous mountain area at the border of two provinces and three counties (Huang'an, Macheng, and Guangshan). Local powerholders had fled the region; for a time, lodges of the Red Spears had no choice but to tolerate the Communists. Local peasants had heard about land revolution in Edongbei; they, too, wanted land. Chaishanbao was also well placed for links to other Red pockets in Huang'an and Macheng.[30] But Communist influence in Chaishanbao had up to then been minimal, and the Party at first depended largely on its thousand unarmed peasant activists in Huang'an and Macheng for support.

In Jinggang, a leaven of Party outsiders brought the mountains into a lively ferment; in Chaishanbao, it was only in the course of building bases that the Party and the Red Army became strong. The advantage was that the backbone of four to five thousand Red cadres and soldiers stiffened together in the late 1920s was overwhelmingly a local product, formed by people who knew the Chaishanbao mountains intimately and had flesh-and-blood ties to local people. Because Communist outsiders in the base could communicate with these local cadres only through interpreters, it was not easy for them to become accepted.

The local Communists, however, knew little or nothing of Marxism. Most of the base's cadres and officials were in their late teens or early twenties. They had "few or no foreign dogmas," said Xu Xiangqian, "and some homegrown Marxism. Foreign dogmas would not have lasted a minute in that sort of setting." Few cadres had read any political writings. The Eyuwan Party Congress of 1931 was more like a peasant rally than a forum of leaders; according to Zhang Guotao, most delegates were illiterate and knew little about Communism or Party policies. The Party in Eyuwan recruited quickly—too quickly, according to Zheng Weisan—and for a long time, the great majority of its members had belonged for just a few weeks or months. Their "Party style" was poor, said Zheng; they were "immature" and "commandist." They made their decisions without reference to the masses, who were wholly in the dark about the Party's structure. "Very many were ignorant about the Party," wrote Xu Xiangqian. "They thought that those who took part in uprisings, attacked *tuhao*, and divided land were Communists 'belonging to the Party.' If they found out that the Party was organizing secret meetings, they would say angrily: 'Do you think I am reactionary? Why don't you invite me when you meet?' " Many, like peasants in other parts of China, thought that *suweiai* (soviet) was the name of a Party leader, Mr. Su. Links to Shanghai leaders were at first extremely thin; next to no instructions or guidelines arrived in Eyuwan. If a problem arose, a handful of Party and non-Party opinion leaders got together to discuss it.[31] Here lay the roots of Eyuwan's chronic "leftist" high-handedness and of the hostility to outsiders that was both its strength (being the basis of its solidarity) and, from the point of view of national goals, its weakness.

Between 1928 and 1930, Communists scattered along the border between Hubei, Henan, and Anhui staged a series of uprisings and gradually widened their territorial base. By mid-1929, the Party had twelve hundred members in Huang'an (its strongest base) and five hundred in nearby Macheng. In February 1930, the Party's Central Committee directed the leaders of bases in Yudongnan, along the Eyu border, and in Wanxi to join together in one big base, with a population of one million. The Eyuwan Special Committee was set up a few weeks later, and in June the First Congress of Eyuwan Workers and Peasants met to found the Eyuwan Soviet government.

The three divisions established in the three main bases in the previous two years were reorganized into the First Red Army, under Xu Jishen. This merger was intended to consolidate the new centralized base and overcome "local viewpoints" and "mountaintoppism," afflictions that troubled not only the Eyuwan Party as a whole but also its parts. Xu's new army soon grew from two thousand to five thousand. In 1930 and 1931, it drove back the Guomindang's First and Second Encirclements. In January 1931, it joined up with the Fifteenth Red Army, which had been operating in Edong, to form the Fourth Red Army. These twenty thousand troops operated in a base with 1,800,000 people where Red governments had been formed and land revolution had been carried out.[32]

## EYUWAN UNDER ZHANG GUOTAO

In April 1931, the Central Committee appointed Zhang Guotao as its representative in Eyuwan during a more general drive to assert control over Party bases and root out supporters of Li Lisan. Zhang Guotao is today accused of persecuting and killing thousands of people, including "founders and leaders" of the soviet, with the aim of imposing Wang Ming's "leftist" line on Eyuwan.[33] But Zhang says that the worst excesses of the Eyuwan purge happened without his knowledge and were anyway small in scope, thanks to his moderating influence. Many Eyuwan veterans died under Zhang. The bloodletting spread to the local Party organization, government, and mass associations. Yet the main targets were not "local veterans" but people like Xu Jishen, who had been sent by the Central Committee to lead the guerrilla struggle on the Yuwan border, and Zeng Zhongsheng, who had been sent by the Shanghai leaders to lead Eyuwan's Special Committee. Of the two, only Xu (whose relationship to Zhang Guotao was one of mutual hatred) died. Both Xu and Zheng had studied at Whampoa Military Academy; both were assigned to Eyuwan under Li Lisan.[34]

Though lists show that numerous Eyuwan veterans were among nearly ten thousand "cadres and masses" allegedly purged or killed under Zhang Guotao, many veterans continued to play a leading role in the Eyuwan Communist movement or its armies. Even if Zhang had wanted to replace the local leaders, he lacked enough outsiders to do so; only a score of trained cadres reached Eyuwan after the flight of the Central Committee from Shanghai in early 1931. So the purges left large parts of the Communist machine in Eyuwan intact; its local character was too deeply ingrained to be easily changed.

Zhang Guotao's rule only lasted for one and a half of the ten years of soviet government in Eyuwan. To a certain extent, as Chinese historians now admit, his influence was opposed and contained. Zhang used Wang Ming—style purges to strengthen his own hold on Eyuwan, in league with local leaders like Gao Jingting (appointed to Zhang's sub-bureau of the Central Committee), who were prepared to tolerate his domination.

There were no rebellions against the purges in Eyuwan of the sort that rocked the Central Soviet at Futian, for most of the ousted leaders were people sent by the Party center to take over from local Communists. The effect of the turbulence of 1931 and 1932 was not to assimilate Eyuwan to the Party center but rather to reinforce its tradition of ruthless authoritarianism. During the purges, people who knew each other well would not dare speak when they met for fear of being branded a secret organization. As a result, many feared to join the Party.[35]

In November 1931, at Qiliping in Hubei's Huang'an, Eyuwan's Red troops were reorganized into the Fourth Front Red Army under Xu Xiangqian. Under Xu, the Eyuwan Communists defeated the Nationalists' Third Encirclement of November 1931 to May 1932, and the Eyuwan Soviet expanded and prospered. Alarmed, Chiang Kai-shek launched his Fourth Encirclement in June 1932. He marshaled up to half a million troops to crush the Eyuwan Soviet, whose strategic position made it his priority target.[36] Xu Xiangqian's Fourth Front Red Army was no match for this onslaught; by late 1932, five-sixths of the Eyuwan base had fallen, and the soviet's population had dropped to seven hundred thousand. Today, the purges under Zhang Guotao are seen as the "main latent cause" of the failure to break the Fourth Encirclement.[37]

### THE TWO-YEAR WAR OF 1932–34

After this defeat, the core of the Fourth Front Red Army, twenty thousand strong, marched west into Sichuan under Zhang Guotao and Xu Xiangqian, but Xu Haidong and Shen Zemin stayed on in Eyuwan as guerrillas. Xu and Shen reorganized two remaining divisions of the Fourth Front Red Army, plus local forces and some wounded troops, into a new Twenty-fifth Red Army, with Gao Jingting as political commissar. To escape the worst Nationalist concentrations and retribution by returned landlords and *tuhao*, Gao and other leaders led retreats of the Party's "basic masses" to the mountains, where they set up huts.[38]

In the following period, known as the "two-year guerrilla war" in Eyuwan, the border region became the site of atrocities unparalleled in other defeated soviets.[39] "The savagery of the enemy's killing reached its greatest height in the Oyuwan [Eyuwan] region," wrote Zhang Guotao. "According to historical data that the CCP has now made public, two hundred thousand people were killed in that region, topping all other regions. . . . I have heard many accounts of enemy atrocities in the Soviet regions, including those perpetrated in the Soviet region in Northern Szechwan, where after our departure many '10,000-man pits' were constructed. Yet, compared with those in the Oyuwan region, they were Lilliputian beside Brobdingnagian."[40]

Though only five thousand Communist regulars, backed by some ten thousand local troops, stayed behind in Eyuwan, compared with the twenty thousand regulars who marched west, the Nationalists kept their main force in and around the base and used a smaller force to chase the marchers. For the next two years, they kept a minimum of fourteen divisions in Eyuwan, supported by tens of thousands of provincial security forces. Some two hundred thousand troops besieged the Communist rearguard in Eyuwan. These troops were reinforced by anti-Communist militias led by landlords who returned to the villages on the heels of the regular army.[41]

Nationalist garrisons in Eyuwan continued to carry out the policy formulated by the Hankou headquarters of the pacification drive in September 1932: that all able-bodied men in "bandit areas" should be "dealt with"; that all dwellings in "bandit areas" should be burned; and that all grain should be carted off or destroyed. In just twenty-nine *xiang* in Guangshan, 12,433 people died at the hands of Nationalist troops (excluding those killed on the battlefield), 12,325 houses were burned down, 203 households were wiped out, 439 villages were burned down, and 1,073 people went missing. Shanghai newspapers reported that more than one hundred thousand people were killed or starved to death in Hubei's Huang'an (Hongan) and eighty thousand in Henan's Xinxian; more than two hundred thousand people were forced to leave Edongbei. Tens of thousands of women and children, including many Red Army wives and offspring, were taken away and sold. Vast tracts of the Eyuwan countryside became no-man's-land where "pacifiers" shot on sight.[42]

Xu Haidong's small rearguard was unlikely to succeed where Xu Xiangqian's army had failed. It was stranded with few contacts or resources on shrinking territory, and its morale was low. Communications between Red units in Eyuwan were cut during the turmoil of the summer of 1932; many left behind in the base learned of the evacuation of the main body of the Fourth Front Red Army only after it had happened, when the Central Committee sent a message telling them not to expect Zhang Guotao to return. They saw the evacuation as evidence that the campaign to break the encirclement had failed.[43]

Still, Chiang Kai-shek was unable to achieve his aim of thoroughly purging Eyuwan by the end of January 1933, even though in December 1932 he announced the end of the offensive in Eyuwan and began the most active phase of the Fourth Encirclement against the Central Soviet to the south. By the following spring, the Eyuwan Communists had grown a little after the Nationalists withdrew even more forces to counter renewed Japanese military pressure in northern China. The worst of the crisis was over for the time being (as were the winter snows). In January 1933, a Twenty-eighth Red Army was formed from some three thousand troops left behind in Wanxibei (northwestern Anhui). In April, it merged with the Red Twenty-fifth, yielding a force of thirteen thousand. In July, Chiang Kai-shek, alarmed by this resurgence, began his Fifth Encirclement of Eyuwan.[44]

As the fortunes of the Communists in Eyuwan revived, so did their bad habits. Between May and October 1933, a new "left" line was adopted in the region. Border area leaders called for a policy of "winning back the towns," which was bound to fail when the Nationalists outnumbered the Communists by ten to one in Eyuwan, and the Party decreed a new campaign to root out "counterrevolutionaries" following the "great achievements" of the purges of 1931. Both policies were disastrous and led to a loss of most of the gains of the previous few months. In October 1933, the "left" line was slackened when the Eyuwan Provincial Committee, admitting that it had engaged in military "adventurism," switched to guerrilla tactics. Also in October, the Twenty-eighth Red Army was reformed in northeastern Anhui, this time under Xu Haidong, with 2,300 men and 1,200 rifles. Xu's army used flexible guerrilla tactics from the outset and won a string of small victories before its reincorporation in April 1934 into the Twenty-fifth Red Army, also under Xu.

By late June, the Party and its organizations were somewhat restored; the plainclothes groups of Communist civilians in White areas, which were to become a hallmark of the revolution in Eyuwan after October 1934, grew strongly. During this retreat from "leftism," Xu launched a major campaign to strengthen Communist troops politically and ideologically, to unite their ranks, and to instill in them the techniques of "mass work." He also adopted a milder policy toward local *mintuan* and *baojia* officials.[45]

Thus the transition to a new style of politics and fighting took place at least one year earlier in Eyuwan than in Communist bases south of the Chang Jiang. The Three-Year War in Eyuwan was in fact a four- or five-year war. The Nationalists were not yet experienced in mopping up the soviets, and they still faced a threat in southern and southeastern China. The Eyuwan guerrillas of 1933 were stronger, better equipped, and more experienced than in most other defeated soviets. They had more time and easier conditions in which to learn the tricks necessary for survival in defeat. Their strength stayed largely constant in 1933 and 1934.[46]

It was far harder to stop the purges in Eyuwan than to abandon the policy of attacking towns. In 1933 and 1934, Gao Jingting carried out four large purges. According to one source, Gao became political commissar of the Twenty-fifth Red Army after its reestablishment in November 1932, though another says that Wang Pingzhang held this post. In any case, Gao wielded great power in this army; at one point, he seized and killed more than one thousand members of its Seventy-fifth Division and disbanded the division's Party cell. In September 1934, the Eyuwan Committee sent Gao to investigate the movement in Wanxi, where he "chased the wind and clutched at shadows." "Wanxi work is in a great mess," Gao reported. "The leaders are all counterrevolutionaries."[47] Gao sacked the Party secretary in Wanxibei and liquidated many of the region's Communist leaders.

These purges, which continued even after 1934, are sometimes presented as a product of Gao's personal blood lust, but it is clear that the Eyuwan leadership shared responsibility for them. When the Provincial Committee cheered Gao on as a "purge expert," he began to hunt even more zealously for "class enemies." Others explain the purges as a result of the lingering influence of Zhang Guotao's "militaristic, sectarian style and 'leftist' errors."[48] Probably more important were the immaturity and cliquishness of the Eyuwan Communist movement, noted by Zheng Weisan,[49] and the exceptional ferocity of the civil war in Eyuwan, described by Edgar Snow as having "the intensity of religious wars." Most of Eyuwan's locally born Communists lost relatives through Nationalist atrocities; the Guomindang seems frequently to have wiped out the lineages of known Communists. Sixty-three members of Xu Haidong's clan were executed, including children and babies, and Xu's wife was sold as a concubine; of those killed, only three were Communists. Zheng Weisan's father died of illness after fleeing to the mountains; his mother died after eating poisonous roots; his first wife froze to death in a cave; and his baby daughter was carried from mountain to mountain by Zheng's guerrilla brother. Traumas such as these help explain the Eyuwan Communists' ruthless methods. According to Snow, "Their experiences had permanently marked the matrix of their minds with a class hatred ineradicable for life."[50]

These purges and the cumulative effect of military mistakes in the Eyuwan Committee's "adventurist" phase paralyzed the movement in some places. But the switch to more flexible tactics and the reforms in military organization overcame "past defects" in the army's functioning and enabled the Communists to hold their own and even prosper in a few mountain strongholds despite the three-month drive that Zhang Xueliang started against them in July 1934. Even so, the Eyuwan leaders knew that their chances of restoring a strong soviet and developing a big army were slight. Accordingly, they accepted the Central Committee's instructions, brought to them in September 1934 by Cheng Zihua, to organize a Fang Zhimin-style "Second Anti-Japanese Vanguard" and march off to found a new base where conditions were more favorable.[51]

On November 16, 1934, under the banner of anti-Japanese resistance, the Twenty-fifth Red Army broke out to the west, led by Cheng Zihua and Xu Haidong. Between two and three thousand troops left Eyuwan. Fewer than two thousand stayed behind, together with roughly one thousand officials and wounded soldiers.[52] Here is another difference between Eyuwan and soviets south of the Chang Jiang in late 1934. Whereas Communist power collapsed suddenly and almost completely in the Central Soviet and adjacent regions, in Eyuwan, a force of several thousand regulars held out against Nationalist encirclements after Zhang Guotao left in 1932; and the eventual retreat of that early rearguard was strategic and relatively orderly. After this 1934 retreat, the second of Eyuwan's long marches, the Nationalists left a larger force to garrison Eyuwan than in most other defeated soviets, experience having taught them that the soviet movement there was rooted and tenacious. But because it was the second retreat, Gao's rearguard troops were also better prepared for the purging of their villages.

## THE THREE-YEAR WAR BEGINS

The Communists' position in Eyuwan was already critical after the first long march from the region in October 1932; the prospects facing those left behind in late 1934 were even worse. Most stay-behinders had, at best, mixed feelings about their chances of holding out. Guerrillas with relatives in the region wondered whether it was right to expose them to yet more war and more reprisals.

Because of the fighting, flight of population, kidnappings, deportations, and Guomindang butchery, most soviet strongholds in the region were by now desolate, and Red troops could not maintain even the tiniest rearguard.

When Lin Weixian marched through Wanxibei in late autumn, the scenes that greeted him were like visions of hell. The roads were deserted and the wells poisoned. Crows flopped cawing to the ground among the felled trees. Wild grass choked the fields. Black smoke scarred the yellow walls of peasant houses; their roofs gaped. Village streets were littered with broken tiles, chicken feathers, and the rotting carcasses of pigs and cattle slaughtered by White troops. The ruins of the houses were littered with smashed pots and bowls. A wild dog sitting in the broken oven of one ruin ran off baring its teeth when Lin's guerrillas neared. Beyond one village, the ground was spongy underfoot; six inches below the surface were the corpses of three hundred villagers. Guomindang "killer squads" had carried out similar massacres in villages throughout the former soviet areas of Wanxibei, Yudongnan, and

Edongbei. Near one village in Jinzhai, 3,500 people were said to have been buried alive in just one night. One division reportedly collected seven hundred pounds of ears "to prove its merit."[53] Just as after the first long march in 1932, thousands of women and girls were raped and sold. Boys, too, were sold. "A considerable trade grew up," wrote Edgar Snow, "with middlemen buying the boys and women from Kuomintang officers. It became a very profitable business for a while, but threatened to corrupt the ranks of the army. Missionaries began talking about it, and Chiang Kai-shek was obliged to issue a stern order forbidding . . . the traffic." Snow thinks that the "singular savagery" of the Guomindang army in Eyuwan occurred because some of its leading generals were "natives of that region, sons of landlords who had lost their land to the Reds, and hence had an insatiable desire for revenge."[54]

Those who escaped slaughter or capture faced death in the mountains from cold or hunger, for winter clothes were scarce and most food had been removed. In the ice-sealed hills, even wild roots and leaves were hard to come by; leaves of the trumpet creeper formed the main "harvest" in late 1934. Many Communists died in caves or gullies, or along mountain paths. The Guomindang's policy of pitiless purge and slaughter left the survivors little choice but to stand firm. To beat the famine, stay-behinders in Wanxibei began a "winter production drive" high in the mountains, prising the frozen earth apart with wooden staves and broken pickax handles in place of the plows and oxen taken by the Whites. To feed themselves there and then, they roused a thousand-strong body of supporters armed with red-tasseled poles and marched down to "beat grain" out of returned landlords in the richer villages.[55]

The largest remaining base in Eyuwan after November 1934 was in the thickly forested mountains of Edongbei, along the northern border of Huang'an. This area had been the heartland of the soviet before the Fourth Encirclement, but it had since been purged and was by now largely uninhabited, save for Communists working under the Party's Edongbei Committee. These included a bodyguard of fifty that also ran communications and a plainclothes squad of fifty in charge of finding grain and funds. The Committee ran a hospital in which one hundred nurses and hospital workers tended two hundred Red Army invalids left behind by Xu Haidong; it also ran a small arsenal and sewing workshop staffed mainly by Red Army dependents. Between five and six hundred combat troops protected a "civilian" population of four to five hundred Party and government workers. Both groups outnumbered the four hundred "basic masses" who remained in the mountains.[56]

Eyuwan's repair shop had formerly employed more than three hundred workers who manufactured weapons from cannibalized parts. After Zhang Guotao left, its staff was reduced to a score, and it was able to carry out only simple repairs. By 1935, its tools and supplies were usually packed away in wooden crates humped across the mountains by its workers; whenever the guerrillas stopped to encamp or fight, these men set up their furnaces and worked. The clothing factory, founded in the winter of 1934 to 1935, also moved with the troops; whenever the marchers stopped, needles and scissors began to flick and clack; in just a few months, nearly one thousand items were produced from materials taken from *tuhao* to clothe the ragged guerrillas. In 1936, two guerrilla clothing factories merged. Their joint staff of twenty men and women reorganized and was soon producing up to thirty pieces of clothing a day on an expropriated sewing machine.[57]

In the northern Dabie Mountains of Wanxi, three small bases were left. The largest, in Chicheng, was only twenty miles long. Chicheng, or Shangcheng as it was known to the Guomindang, lay at the central junction of Eyuwan, "where a cock's crow could be heard in three provinces." Strategically, it was well chosen: a dozen roads ran through it, laced to nearby wooded slopes by hundreds of small paths along which guerrillas could mount attacks or take flight.[58] Before the Communist defeats, Chicheng had been densely populated by spinners, weavers, and papermakers. By late 1934, much of its old soviet core had been reduced to an ashy wilderness, relieved by a few dozen tiny settlements populated mainly by Party and Red Army dependents. These people were almost entirely without productive means; their tools had been taken or smashed, and their able-bodied sons had gone to join the guerrillas. Even soviet officials in the area were "old, weak, sick, or lame." Soviet dependents and cadres lived almost exclusively off the proceeds of grain raids by the Chicheng Committee's bodyguard and the two hundred local guerrillas.[59]

This part of the Dabie is cut by deep ravines and sheer cliff faces riddled with natural caves. During the Three-Year War, the seventy-two natural caves of Jin'gangtai became the home of the Chicheng Committee and the site of a labyrinthine hospital of scattered wards across which up to one hundred Red Army invalids were distributed. The stone-hewn beds and tables and the ash of fires on which the guerrillas cooked wild plants and animals can still be found there. Not far from the cave of the committee was the women's cave, whose forty denizens formed a special nurses' company that fought alongside the men whenever necessary. If the Nationalists searched one mountain, Red Army doctors and nurses carried the wounded to another or hid them under rotting vegetation among the trees, with just their eyes and noses left showing.

This hospital, like Red Army hospitals everywhere in rearguard areas after 1934, was desperately short of medicine. The usual makeshift remedies were adopted: nurses bathed wounds in boiled or salted water and plastered them with pumpkin pulp or wild pig fat when they festered or became maggoty. In the winters, including the winter of 1936, when the worst snows in living memory fell here, patients slept under thin sheets in the shrieking wind, forbidden to light fires or even cigarettes to avoid detection. As the blockade tightened, food became harder to find. At first, hospital guards continued to rob grain from *tuhao* in nearby villages, but when the *tuhao* fled, agents had to be sent on long and dangerous grain-buying missions, from which many never returned. Some wounded soldiers starved to death in the hospital caves, sometimes within earshot of enemy searchers who shouted that they would be helped if they surrendered.[60]

The main hospital of the Twenty-eighth Red Army was formed in February 1935 by medical personnel left behind by Xu Haidong. It could treat two hundred patients at a time and had three branch hospitals that could treat thirty patients each. Other parts of Eyuwan, too, had rear hospitals; each battalion had two or three peripatetic medical workers who went from mountain to mountain treating the wounded. Hospitals recruited apprentices to swell their tiny staff and taught them health care on the job. Their knowledge of the theory and practice of healing was minimal. They, too, lacked standard medicines and had to fall back on makeshift remedies.

Medical leaders put their main effort into preventive hygiene. Malaria was rife in the Dabie Mountains, so health workers taught the guerrillas to fumigate their shacks and caves with torches of straw and mugwort before sleeping in them. Though this step did not eliminate malaria, it kept the disease within manageable proportions. To prevent dysentery in the hot months, health workers taught the guerrillas food hygiene. To stem colds in the winter and the spring, they encouraged consumption of large quantities of pepper, ginger, and garlic. Teams of orderlies swept the guerrillas' mountain camp sites and dug latrines whenever possible.

The guerrillas' "essential asset" were their feet: because they were constantly on the march, their feet blistered easily, and blisters could be as deadly as bullets. Some guerrillas who fell behind because of blisters were killed. As a consequence, the army's medical team put great stress on foot care and hygiene. They explained the dangers of marching barefoot and taught guerrillas to wash their feet in hot water, to rub their legs to circulate the blood, and to prick blisters with sterilized needles whenever they pitched camp.

Because of the shortage of medical personnel and the decision to operate in tiny self-sufficient units, guerrillas were expected to treat their own minor wounds and illnesses. All could apply a splint or tourniquet and knew the essential rules of hygiene and first aid. No uncontrollable epidemics broke out among the Eyuwan guerrillas between 1934 and 1938 despite the harsh conditions. Sick or wounded guerrillas were cared for in caves like those at Jin'gangtai, in thatched shacks built to withstand the bitter weather of the Dabie Mountains, or in the houses of local sympathizers. "The masses became our hospital," said a Red Army doctor. "There were no hospitals and wards: everywhere was a hospital, everywhere was a ward."[61]

## EYU

The smallest and weakest of the Eyuwan bases in 1935 was Eyu, on the border between Hubei (E) and Henan (Yu), also known in studies as Yu'nan (southern Henan). Communists in Eyu after 1934 were active mainly in Queshan, Xinyang, and Nanyang.[62] The Party's Provincial Committee in Henan was repeatedly smashed between 1933 and 1935. In August 1935, the Communist leaders Zhou Junming, Wang Guohua, and Wang Guofu, recently returned to Henan from the Central Soviet, sought out Zhang Xingjiang, secretary of the Party's Eyu Working Committee. The four men decided to merge the Henan and Eyu Committees in a new Eyu Special Committee, also under Zhang. In the winter of 1934, leaders of the Twenty-fifth Red Army had passed briefly through Eyu and commissioned Zhang to "broadly develop guerrilla war, coordinate with the struggle in the Eyuwan Soviet, and build bases." Zhang's new committee set out to rebuild a base in Eyu's Tongbai Mountains. Throughout history, Eyu had been a cockpit of Chinese generals and warlords. Eyu's villages bristled with guns and commanders' flagpoles. In 1937, civilians held an estimated four hundred thousand firearms in parts of Eyu where Communists where active. Most of the guns were controlled by landlords, but some belonged to criminal gangs and bandits. Plebeian outlaws were by no means uniformly hostile to the Communists; the existence of a tradition of plebeian armed dissent in Eyu made it easier for the Communists to build strong bases there after 1934. So did the great poverty. The villagers lived mainly by cutting wood, burning charcoal, and gathering mountain fruit and fungi. Many young women lacked even a pair of trousers. The mountain nights were bitterly cold; fires were kept going twenty-four hours a day outside the cabin doors.

Base-building, Eyu-style, in 1935 combined elements of the native tradition of dissent with more orthodox forms of political mobilization adapted to the new conditions. "If bandits dare to take on the Guomindang and can develop in the mountains," said Zhang Xingjiang, "how much more so can we Communists, armed with Marxism-Leninism and organizational discipline?" In late August, Zhou Junming went to work gathering firewood in a small mountain village, where he sought protection in the home of his wife's uncle, a man called Wu Yuanchang. Zhou and his comrades chopped trees and sold firewood by day and made propaganda by night. At one point, they secretly set up a "carrying pole society" and organized a violent struggle against the firewood tax. This struggle spread swiftly through the mountains; Communist influence spread with it, at first along kinship lines.

Zhou's first convert was the son of his host Wu. In a nearby village lived a retired corporal, also Wu's relative, who had been caught and freed by the Red Army in Eyuwan and so thought highly of it. He, too, became a Communist after Zhou had "worked on him" and "awakened his class consciousness." Later Wu Renpu, the lineage schoolteacher, also joined the Party; more than one hundred others followed him. Different villages organized under different names; "active elements" in village organizations were drawn into the Party.

Communist military organization in Eyu grew more slowly. At first, the Communists had no guns at all. By late 1935, there were seven guerrillas in Eyu with one revolver, one rifle, and two bullets among them. By early 1936, they had grown to thirty, with fifteen rifles, after staging a series of armed robberies and attacking local strongmen attending an opera performance at a temple fair. A group of Party members who had gone underground in the capital of Suiping tracked down Wang Guohua in Yu'nan and decided to set up a liaison station under cover of a shop. Through this shop, the liaison workers rallied support for the Eyu Committee and put lost comrades in touch with it; the shop also served as a sanctuary for Party members on the run.

As the population of Wu Village grew, the Eyu Committee moved its headquarters there, taking with them a large team of Party workers, including invalids left behind by Xu Haidong's Twenty-fifth Red Army in 1934. At first, the guerrillas did everything they could to avoid notice, producing no written propaganda and saying nothing about agrarian reform. One of their main supports in the region was the bandit Gao Dianqing. Gao refused to join the guerrillas, saying, "As a bandit I am free." But he agreed to help them, partly because one of his followers had once been a Party member.

Later in 1936, the guerrillas became overconfident and suffered two serious defeats in which their main leader Zhang Xingjiang was killed and Party documents fell into the hands of the authorities. The Nationalists were alarmed to learn that the Red Army was active in the Tongbai and sent in a division to root out the guerrillas, who by then were down to eighteen men without funds or ammunition. The Communists pulled in their horns for a while to preserve their forces and regrouped into three six-man teams. One local Party leader took this retrenchment as a cue to send his guerrillas home and was relieved of his job as a consequence. Not until late 1937 did the Eyu guerrillas resume contact with Gao Jingting.[63]

## COUNTERREVOLUTION AND THE RESISTANCE

In November 1934, the Nationalists sent a large force after the Twenty-fifth Red Army but kept behind up to 170,000 regular troops of their Twenty-fifth Route Army and fifty-six regiments of the Northeastern (Manchurian) Army, together with twelve regiments of seasoned "bandit exterminators" from the Provincial Peace Preservation Corps, to search out and destroy the stay-behinders in Eyuwan.[64] The backbone of this force was the Thirty-second Division of Liang Guanying, the campaign's general commander. Liang aimed to trap the Communists in the mountains between lines of blockhouses and blockades, to destroy the forests that hid them, and to hunt them down: "to chop down all the trees and uncover the Red Army's roots." His troops caught dozens of Red Army invalids and more than thirty women nurses. He concentrated tens of thousands of villagers in "refugee centers"; Shangcheng (Chicheng) alone had four, each of which held several thousand people. Conditions in these camps were so primitive that at one point a hundred people a day were dying in them.[65]

The "pacifiers" rationed salt, food, and firewood in areas where Communists were active, and they poisoned unsupervised wells. Hunger and disease were universal in the mountains; for months on end the guerrillas ate no salt. Grain was often impossible to obtain, and even when it was available, it was dangerous to cook it over open fires. Sometimes the guerrillas ground it with a pestle and ate it raw, husks and all. Almost all of them suffered in some degree from malaria, and most were pocked with ringworm and other skin diseases.[66]

When Chiang Kai-shek personally put Liang Guanying in overall command of the pacification of Eyuwan, he told him to "make the destruction complete, so that there is never again distress; to make the eradication thorough, so that the meritorious task is finished"; and to do so within three months. At first Liang was confident that he could destroy the Communists within one month.[67] He was to eat his words.

Before quitting Eyuwan, the main political leaders of the soviet had left instructions for its further development. They told the rearguard that its main task was to "preserve the seeds" of revolution and that a small number of guerrillas should coordinate with civilian supporters to attack the *mintuan* but should avoid encounters with regular forces. For several weeks, Gao Jingting (in Wanxibei) was ignorant of this directive, but it was discussed and carried out by the Edongbei Committee the day after the Twenty-fifth Red Army left; the committee disrupted enemy communications to help the Twenty-fifth get free. An Edongbei Independent Regiment was formed from one hundred stay behind regulars (many were wounded) and four hundred new local recruits. This regiment then marched east to transmit the same directive to Gao Jingting.[68]

By the time the Hubei Communists met up with Gao in February 1935, he had already collected seven hundred troops in his Eighty-second Division. At Taihu, he and the Hubei forces merged in a revived Twenty-eighth Red Army under Gao and decided to fight guerrilla war and set up a new Eyuwan Committee. This was the Twenty-eighth's third resurrection (after December 1932 and October 1933).[69] With characteristic speed and resolution, Gao completed the reorganization in just one evening; within hours, he had broken camp.[70] Gao's new army had some 1,400 troops; it retained the system of political committees down to the battalion level, with Party branches in each company.[71]

Only a few of Gao's troops were regulars, and these included a battalion left behind accidentally by the retreating Twenty-fifth Army. "Most were peasants who lacked training," said Lin Weixian. "Some were fourteen- or fifteen-year-old little devils. They were shorter than their rifles. When you lined them up, they looked like a regiment of children. Eighty to 90 percent were orphans. They had one single goal: to avenge themselves by wiping out reactionaries."[72] It is unlikely that Gao's army could at first count on large numbers of local forces, for it was operating away from its original base (which the Nationalists had occupied). Local villages were under Nationalist control. Most villagers had been removed to camps. The Nationalists apparently believed at one point that there were twenty thousand armed men under the Communists in the Dabie Mountains at the start of the Three-Year War. Local forces in the region probably numbered between three and four hundred.[73]

When Liang Guanying learned that the Communists had once again set up an army in Eyuwan, he sent his Thirty-second Division in after them. The Communists suffered heavy casualties, though they did their best to avoid battle, and Liang's troops chased them for several weeks. In late April 1935, Liang transferred his headquarters from Wuhan to the Dabie Mountains. He divided Eyuwan into three heavily garrisoned defense zones and launched a new two-month drive against the Communists. "In checking bandit extermination along the Eyuwan border," Chiang Kai-shek told Liang, "I have repeatedly ordered their suppression. Now they are fleeing hither and thither just as before. Day by day they run rampant. If they are not quickly wiped out, seeds of disaster will be sown. Make new deployments to remove forever the root of future troubles. . . . Exterminate the bandit menace before the end of June or be charged with allowing them free range."[74]

In May 1935, to avoid destruction, leaders of the Twenty-eighth Red Army left Eyuwan and marched west. They ended up in Eyu's Tongbai Mountains, through which the Twenty-fifth Red Army had passed six months earlier. On the way, they fought various encounters, capturing nearly one thousand rifles, according to reports Gao sent to the Party's Shanghai Bureau, and absorbing several hundred new recruits.[75] They did not stay long in Eyu, for the Thirty-second Division was still chasing them. They were not familiar with the Tongbai Mountains and had little chance to influence local peasants, who spoke a barely intelligible dialect. Whenever the Communists approached, the peasants fled inside the *weizhai* or stockades that proliferated in this region.[76]

At one point, Gao considered marching across the plains to southern Shaanxi to join the Twenty-fifth Red Army. This idea disconcerted local leaders in Edongbei, who believed that their task was to hold out in Eyuwan. For various reasons, Gao decided against the plan. If the Reds abandoned Eyuwan, he said, the Nationalists would follow them, putting Xu Haidong at even greater risk. A scout from Xu's army told Gao that the plains were occupied by hostile forces, including several cavalry divisions. Gao himself was in no position to fight; he was seriously ill and had to be carried on a stretcher. By returning to Eyuwan and sticking to the Dabie Mountains, he could tie down enemy forces and put more pressure on Nanjing than by fleeing west. In June 1935, he was back in his old haunts.[77]

Over the next few months, the Twenty-eighth Red Army grew a little. At one time poorly armed, it was by now the best equipped of all the soviet stay-behind units: others fought mainly with clubs and spears, but Gao's guerrillas had 1,050 rifles or pistols and twenty-seven machine guns. According to a recent Party study, Gao's army did exceptionally well after 1934, scoring military successes "rare in the three-year struggle." Perhaps as a result, his troops stayed unusually loyal. "No soldiers of the Twenty-eighth Red Army defected in the three-year period," said Lin Weixian. "Lightly wounded men refused to leave the front. If soldiers got lost, one person could strike roots by himself. Generally, we did not lose our wounded soldiers."

In the summer of 1935, Communists in Wanxi even won the support of a prominent local opponent of Chiang Kai-shek, who set up an Anti-Japanese Army of National Salvation in collaboration with them; in six months, this force grew from just thirty to three hundred before it was finally crushed. In his message to the Central Committee, Gao urgently requested military cadres.[78] He had plenty of officers at the platoon level, but he was so short of higher-level officers that "a mere child," the seventeen-year old Fang Yongle, commanded his main division (the Eighty-second).[79]

After the failure of Liang Guanying's spring campaign, the Nationalists in Eyuwan developed a new "trinitarian" strategy to suppress the Communists. They added new forts to existing lines and increased the number of lines to three; they set up checkpoints throughout the mountains; and they stepped up their campaign to destroy the forests. The Communists developed various countermeasures, mobilizing their supporters to conceal or destroy tools and materials necessary to construct the forts. Where these efforts failed, they ordered *baojia* officials under their control to be especially helpful in building them so that they would be asked to man them when the regulars withdrew. Sometimes the guerrillas beat drums and gongs at captured checkpoints and attacked *mintuan* units that turned up in response; or they got their supporters appointed as sentries and used them to collect intelligence. The Communists also organized go-slows among peasants conscripted to destroy the forests. At one point, they won a respite by taking hostage three alleged foreign advisers of the Guomindang and threatening to kill them.[80]

These tactics worked. "Over the last few months, we have not inflicted heavy casualties on the bandits," Liang Guanying told Chiang Kai-shek. "Bandits returning east who are now within the area of our army are estimated to have reached one thousand. The deadline [of the two-month campaign] is about to expire. Thinking of my responsibilities, I am deeply anxious." Liang was right to worry. In August, Gao massacred a crowd of local bigwigs gathered to mourn the death of a "hegemon-landlord" in Macheng. Chiang Kai-shek punished Liang's officers for negligence and replaced Liang as chief of the Eyuwan campaign with Wei Lihuang. Wei was a deadlier threat to Gao than the ineffectual Liang; an earlier campaign by Wei against Communists in the Dabie had gone so well that Chiang Kai-shek named a county after him.[81]

## DEPOPULATING THE MOUNTAINS

Wei started his offensive in the autumn of 1935, declaring that he would clear the Dabie of Communists before the winter was out. Some village and district officials were secretly in league with the Communists or in their power; Wei did his best to replace them with loyal and reliable anti-Communists. He repaired the mountain forts and deployed troops—including specialists in mountain warfare from Yunnan and Guangxi—to cut off the Communists in Edongbei from those in Wanxi.[82] By this time, there were more than two hundred thousand Nationalist regulars in Eyuwan, backed by three hundred thousand *mintuan*.[83] As the winter wore on, Wei put less and less effort into searching the mountains and more and more into deporting people to the plains, presumably because resettlement was more effective than searching and destroying.

The Communists did their best to avoid head-on clashes with Wei's troops and tried instead to subvert the *mintuan*, who played a key role in Wei's strategy. They put their main effort into loosening Wei's grip on the Party's "basic masses" resettled in the nearby camps. Guomindang measures to depopulate "bandit areas" had reduced the Party all over Eyuwan to its professional apparatus, cutting its roots more or less cleanly away and leaving it in a state of suspension. Local Party leaders were afraid that unless they restored a base, their inverted pyramid might come down with a crash. The history of the Three-Year War in Eyuwan is in large part that of Communist efforts to forestall that collapse.

In Edongbei, the contest for population began almost immediately after the Twenty-fifth Red Army left. The local Party sent an agent to the town of Xuanhuadian, where he persuaded some "enlightened" *baojia* officials to act as guarantors for peasants deported from "bandit areas" so that they could return to the mountains. The authorities freed more than two hundred Party supporters. Back home, these people received money from Communist agents to rehabilitate their farms and enterprises.[84] Here is an instance, unorthodox for Marxists, of the Party creating its base rather than reflecting it.

Where possible, guerrillas prepared their supporters for deportation. They hid the remaining food around the mountains and destroyed everything in the villages before the occupiers came. Guerrillas were rarely in a position to lead people to resist resettlement, but by planning countermeasures and channeling money to supporters, they were able to ensure that some links and networks survived. At first, the Guomindang stockaded only the poorer peasants, so guerrillas could still appeal with social and kinship ties to the richer villagers who stayed behind. Later, when landlords and local gentry were also sent to the camps, the guerrillas' task became far harder. But even in the camps, they retained some influence.[85]

These camps, known as "Wood City" to the Communists, were built from bamboo carted down the mountains by deforestation teams. The camp regime was severe. Inmates were let out into the fields each morning but were guarded by *mintuan* and closely searched before leaving the stockade. They were reportedly subject to more than seventy sorts of tax, ranging from poll tax to taxes on ovens and grass sandals. Camp huts were flimsily built, without plaster; they offered little protection against the cold. Communist agents mobilized against conditions in the camps, combining uprisings from inside with guerrilla attacks from outside; according to one history, "most resettlement points had been destroyed" by late 1935, and guerrillas were able to escort people back to the villages. Again in early 1937, during the Nationalists' final drive against the Communists, Wood City was shaken by a stormy struggle for the right to go home. In Wanxi, Gao Jingting is said to have been too preoccupied with building his army to resist the campaign to isolate him, so the camps there were less easily dissolved; but eventually guerrillas seized a camp at gunpoint and called a meeting of its two thousand inmates. They shut up the landlords, *tuhao*, and gentry and shot "spies" pointed out to them by Red Army dependents and supporters. They distributed the property of the camp's rich to the camp's poor and freed the poor to their homes.[86]

These victories suggested that while Communists could not withstand the Guomindang in the mountains, they could survive and even win small victories "on the outer line." In late 1935 or early 1936, at a conference on a mountain in Hubei's Qichun, just outside the southern edge of the old Eyuwan base, Gao and other leaders of the Twenty-eighth Red Army drew the lessons of the winter campaign; they took decisions that marked the start of a new era in the Three-Year War in Eyuwan and of an even more decentralized, civilian style of politics and fighting. The Qichun conference shifted the Party's focus from the high ground to the plains, from the old soviets to the White areas, from the rifle to the pistol, and from the division to the battalion. Guerrillas organized in battalions slipped through the encirclement to operate independently behind enemy lines for days or weeks at a stretch. Ideally, they returned to general command at a prearranged time and place, but in practice they often stayed away for longer than planned. This strategy proved quite effective. On March 9, 1936, *Zhongyang Ribao* reported that "bandit leader Gao Jingting has slipped into the border area of Edong and split his forces into small bands that appear and disappear without pattern. . . . Important small towns are being attacked, with heavy losses."[87]

In March 1936, Wei Lihuang began a new campaign, strengthened by troops from six new divisions, to wipe out the "pestiferous Red bandits" in five months. Building on experience in Gannan after October 1934, he increased the main lines of forts in Eyuwan to eight, linked to a large number of new subsidiary lines, and manned them with new divisions.[88] He also devised ways to deal with Gao's tactic of "evading the enemy's spearhead and dispersing into his rear" and with his mobility. *Zhuijiao* (pursue and suppress) had two main forms: a specialist division (the Thirty-second) pursued the guerrillas day and night, even across provincial and sector boundaries; and troops garrisoning whichever sector the Communists tried to enter chased them in relays. *Weijiao* (encircle and suppress) was a familiar tactic in the art of "suppressing bandits," but Wei invested it with a new ingredient of stealth and deception

because of Gao's habit of "appearing and disappearing without pattern."
He surrounded guerrilla camps at night and destroyed them at first
light, or he concealed his men around likely "bandit haunts" so that they
could swiftly "rise from the grass" and suppress any guerrillas that
turned up in them. *Dujiao* (block and suppress) meant hemming the
guerrillas in by lines of forts, barbed wire, or even wooden fences. These
barriers were put up not only along main lines of communication but
also high in the mountains and across small paths. *Zhujiao* (garrison
and suppress) meant garrisoning a specific area and pursuing, encircling, or blocking guerrillas who entered it. *Qingjiao* (purge and suppress), another familiar tactic, meant establishing "basic villages"
guarded by Guomindang special activity forces that registered and reg-
ulated households.[89]

## THE PLAINCLOTHES GROUPS

The guerrillas' previous switch of tactics enabled them to survive Wei's
measures, though in March more than one hundred were killed in
Edong (eastern Hubei), and Gao Jingting's death was mistakenly reported in the press.[90] After slipping behind Wei's lines, the guerrillas coordinated with the Party's civilian pistol squads to strike at him from behind. "They took our mountains, we took their plains," said Lin
Weixian. "They took our base, we stole into their nest." The guerrillas
prepared for a long period of decentralization and "fighting on the
outer line."

The press carried alarming reports on the spread of "bandits" in the
early summer of 1936. The Communists suspended their political department and assigned its officials to guerrilla units or to the Party-run
sewing factories. This suspension of activity lasted for three months, until June, when units briefly reassembled at Macheng to reorganize before scattering again. In late August, Wei ended his unsuccessful, five-
month campaign in the central mountains of Eyuwan. By then, the
Twenty-eighth Red Army, though still small, was more widely spread
than ever, with a toehold in some forty counties. As Wei's regular troops
withdrew to the towns and plains, guerrillas destroyed *mintuan* units that
had taken over garrisoning the forts and even restored soviets here
and there.[91]

During this summer of growth and regroupment, Gao had a "joyous
reunion" with the Party's Shangnan Committee in Chicheng after reading in a newspaper that it was still active. The Shangnan Committee had
lost all ties to the Twenty-eighth Red Army after the spring of 1935; Gao
thought that it had been destroyed. At first, it had survived with the help
of a few isolated families high in the mountains who lived by digging

medicinal roots and collecting herbs. The women of these families acted as couriers, shoppers, and nurses for the committee. One by one, they were killed or deported to the plains. Cut off from the outside world, the Chicheng Communists lived in caves. They fed mainly on leaves, roots, and bark, which they cooked in cracked pans abandoned in the villages or in incense burners left behind in the temples. When ice sealed the mountains, they foraged for food by robbing or kidnapping *tuhao* or bought it in the villages. Often they ate nothing for days on end. To restore contact with the "broad masses," they divided their guerrillas into four plainclothes groups, each with a dozen members, and sent them down the mountains.[92]

These plainclothes groups, started by Zheng Weisan in 1933, were original to the Communist movement in Eyuwan. They were active everywhere along the border. In the interval between Eyuwan's first and second long marches, local Communists reported that plainclothes groups were "now the main movement, and the one with the greatest prospects for development."[93] After 1934, these groups came into their own, for they were ideally suited to conditions in Eyuwan after its second long march. They were on the agenda of each of the three conferences of the Eyuwan Party between 1934 and 1938.

Not all leaders of the Three-Year War in Eyuwan wanted civilian units of this sort, however. At the start, some people favored regrouping them into a new mobile force, but local leaders resisted this proposal. Leaders in Edongbei quietly ignored a similar attempt in early 1937. In conditions of extreme siege, said Zheng Weisan, normal distinctions between Party, soviet government, Red Army, and people no longer applied. Instead, all functions were merged in the plainclothes groups.

These groups were formed by local Party members, local supporters, and recuperating Red Army soldiers (who in Eyuwan were also local people) left behind by the long marchers. They dressed identically with the local people and lived in local people's homes, though they switched bases frequently. Each group had a dozen or so members armed with pistols and led by Party officials or people detached from the Twenty-eighth Red Army.[94] Group members worked in the fields or factories by day and for the Party after dark. Their main strengths were their flexibility and small size, their closeness to local society, their social relations with local strongmen, and their familiarity with local topography and conditions. "They grew by getting relatives to contact relatives and neighbors to join up with neighbors," wrote Lin Weixian. "Each spread outward from one point, across a whole area: from one village to several, from the mountains to the plains, from secret activity to . . . setting up Party organization; to controlling basic government; to opening 'mountain hospitals,' clothing factories, and repair shops; and to setting up relatively consolidated rear bases." Each group was a small family of the revolution, bound by ties of hardship, danger, and political belief.[95]

Originally, plainclothes groups had looked after wounded Red Army soldiers. But in the Three-Year War, their duties expanded to include suppressing "evil gentry," counterrevolutionaries, and "hegemon-landlords"; "consoling" and boosting the morale of Red Army dependents; spying and gathering intelligence; coordinating with or providing cover for regular units of the Twenty-eighth Red Army, for example by killing sentries or attacking patrols or lines of communication; restoring the Communist Party after the ravages of village purging; propagating Party policies; combating Nationalist propaganda; persuading local officials to work with the Communists; and rustling up new recruits, contributions, and supplies for the Red Army—anything from guns to toothpaste and umbrellas. To use a Party metaphor, the plainclothes groups and the Twenty-eighth Red Army formed the frame and pieces of a jigsaw puzzle.[96]

At first, they were restricted to the mountains, but after the conference of June 1936, all but a few moved to the plains, where they grew swiftly. Whenever Red Army regular units arrived in a new place, they detached two or three "politically resolute" guerrillas to found a plainclothes group there; these guerrillas trained new leaders and then returned to their units. One interested peasant was enough to set things going. Very soon, plainclothes groups were within a day's march of one another in more than forty counties of Eyuwan, all but a few well outside the old soviet base. At one point, there were eighty such groups with seven or eight hundred members, including groups in areas where there had never been guerrillas or even a Communist Party branch: wherever the Twenty-eighth Red Army fought, there was a plainclothes group to help it. "Not of imposing stature," notes one account, "but small and powerful, rooted among the masses, scattered like stars across the firmament."

As they accumulated members and support, the groups split and multiplied, and their tasks diversified. In some places, they formed "shadow soviets" or "soviets without signboards," with which local landlords consulted about rents and other issues. According to a 1937 Eyuwan report, plainclothes groups "upheld the soviet political program and laws" and restored a solid base for the Twenty-eighth Red Army. By September 1937, at the start of the Resistance War, they accounted for one-third of Communist armed forces in Eyuwan.[97]

Three main factors explain the great spread, unique in the Three-Year War, of civilian support groups in Eyuwan. Several writers have noted the exceptional degree of village unity and schooling in the art of collective self-defense in and around the Dabie Mountains.[98] The Reds of Eyuwan, including their main leaders, were from the start over-whelmingly local people. Through their local contacts and knowledge, they could tap this well of village solidarity. By 1934, they had become adept at converting to civilian forms of action. They were uniquely equipped to outwit the Nationalists, who put more and more emphasis on political and social measures in their campaign to crush the Communists.

The key to the Party's survival in Eyuwan was not firepower but pol-itics and flexibility. Under Shen Zemin and Xu Haidong, Communists in the border area had already switched to a milder line in dealing with the *mintuan* and the *baojia*. In Edongbei, shortly after Xu Haidong's march west, stay-behinders found that the peasants in Nationalist-controlled villages shunned them, some for fear of Guomindang reprisals, others because they believed the anti-Communist propaganda. The Commu-nists were themselves partly to blame: on grain raids, they often robbed indiscriminately from rich and poor alike. To overcome their isolation, they switched to a fairer system of grain levies, handing out receipts that theoretically absolved the holder from further requisitions. Plainclothes squads began to take half the rent directly from the tenant, who was given a receipt to show the landlord. They also put more effort—through slogans and leaflets—into countering the propaganda of the Nationalists. Gradually, they made new friends, including some *baojia* heads.[99]

## NEW POLICIES, NEW TACTICS

Gao Jingting found it harder to make the switch to new policies than many of his comrades. In August 1935, he staged a bloodbath, massa-cring local *tuhao*, landlords, and officials to "boost morale": the result was to bring down retribution on the heads of his supporters. However, he eventually abandoned the habit of "tickling the bums of *baojia* leaders [i.e., beating them] and not bothering to question [i.e., killing] the direc-tors of *baojia* federations." He spared the lives of officials who were friendly and not "evil"; after the initial excesses of 1935, he carried out fewer killings and "confiscations," and instead levied fines and "contri-butions." His policy toward the *mintuan* was to "both hit and pull." He sought out officials and small landlords who were prepared to collabo-rate with him, and kidnapped or threatened to kill those who refused. He dragged teachers, students, Guomindang officials, and "enlightened gentry" to his camps to "educate them in the righteous cause, eliminate their bad sides, point out the future to them, and cause them to serve" the Communists. He worked on other members of the local elite through their friends or relatives. One fiercely anti-Communist landlord in Shangcheng was eventually "turned into an enlightened personality" by his son, who had developed radical sympathies while a student. The Communists worked on the son and the son worked on the father, who became a reliable support of the guerrillas.

Powerholders won over in these ways collected intelligence and posted letters for the Communists; the village governments they controlled were Nationalist in name, soviet in fact. Members of plainclothes groups, wounded guerrillas, and women Communists and their children lived secretly in their houses, in one case for more than a year.[100]

In the early days after 1934, Gao usually freed prisoners and gave them "travel expenses." Later, he switched to a policy of welcoming them into his ranks to offset battle losses. Some prisoners became Red Army officers, bringing with them military expertise of the sort Gao lacked. Gao's policy on prisoners won the guerrillas friends among the Nationalists. Some fired into the air while searching. It was through a Guomindang military defector that Gao eventually got back in touch with the Party center.[101]

There were three main forms of Communist armed struggle in Eyuwan after 1934: guerrilla war waged across county and provincial boundaries by the Twenty-eighth Red Army; a more restricted form of guerrilla war carried out by local forces; and the secret underground struggle of the plainclothes groups, whose main job was "mass work and upholding the Soviet program and laws." The Eyuwan guerrillas developed special tactics to frustrate the Guomindang's strategy of "nets above and snares below" (i.e., tight encirclement). These tactics were later praised as "original creations . . . broadly in correspondence with the military thought of Mao Zedong."

Gao's basic precept was, "When the enemy climbs up the mountain, we climb down it; we split into many parts, and combine again into a whole." An article in *Shenbao* on June 28, 1936, described this strategy from a government point of view: "Gao Jingting's outlaw bands are all crack fighters. There are few more than one thousand of them. In the counties of the border area, they sometimes concentrate and sometimes disperse. . . . Sometimes they are a whole, sometimes they are parts. When infantry advances to quell them, they suddenly pop up behind it, so that when the army passes by, wherever it looks, there are no bandits."[102] On the mountains, Gao's guerrillas learned to climb like monkeys, scrambling up and down cliffs and darting through forests to shake off their pursuers. One popular training schedule was called "climbing the mountain to vie for the Red Flag." The flag was hung from a tree or an overhanging cliff. At a signal, the guerrillas raced for it; the prize was an extra round of ammunition.[103]

Among Gao's innovations was the set of rules known as "four times for fighting, four times for not fighting," that is, to fight only when they had a clear picture of what the enemy was doing, when their losses would be small, when their gains would be big, and when the terrain was advantageous; and not to fight when the situation was unclear, when they were in their bases, when they were weak and the enemy was strong, and when they lacked support from plainclothes groups. Gao's "flea tactic" involved leading a pursuer round in circles, hopping and jumping from forest to forest and from mountain to mountain, watching for a chance to bite, biting, and then making off. His "eagle-and-chicken tactic" was similar: tire out enemies by leading them on a long chase, take them by surprise, attack at the head or tail, destroy part of the force, and then leave. As both flea and eagle, Gao maintained the basic tactic of the "backward thrust," at which he excelled. To carry it out, the guerrillas feigned defeat, ran before their enemies, and then used natural conditions to open a "big sack" in which to occupy them and attack at close range with a small force, so that the rest could get away. In a variant on the same trick, they "gained mastery by striking only when struck."[104]

Gao's guerrillas were masters of disguise, a tactic born during the forced marches of early 1935, when the Reds were chased back and forth across three provinces. They extended the tactic greatly after moving to the plains in 1936. Huge numbers of government troops of many different designations, and an even greater variety of local forces, were stationed in Eyuwan. The guerrillas took advantage of this profusion of commands to move from sector to sector in stolen uniforms, pretending to be from different regiments or divisions. Individual guerrillas dressed up as *tuhao* or as Guomindang officials were able to pass through enemy checkpoints and enter fortified positions. As they became more mobile, they struck from unexpected quarters; in the winter of 1936, disguised troops and plainclothes fighters destroyed a dozen forts in a part of Lihuang in just one day.[105]

Gao Jingting was not a military theoretician. The talk about his innovations must be understood as part of the campaign to stress the neglected achievements of a wronged comrade. His military tags and maxims were drawn from the historical romances and adventure tales that he loved to read. Still, he was an outstanding practical guerrilla who developed effective measures against Wei Lihuang. "The policies to which the Twenty-eighth Red Army groped its way in the course of the struggle were excellent," said Zheng Weisan.[106]

Even before the start of the second long march from Eyuwan, local Communists had almost no communication with the Party center in

Gannan. In 1934, it took four and a half months for the Central Committee's directive of February 16 to reach Eyuwan, three months for the Central Committee's emissary Cheng Zihua to track down Zheng Weisan, and several more weeks for Cheng and Zheng to contact the provincial committee and the Twenty-fifth Red Army leaders (whom they finally reached in November 1934). One result was that Xu Haidong's Second Anti-Japanese Vanguard set out several months later than its better-known namesake under Fang Zhimin. After 1934, the Eyuwan Communists were completely cut off from the central Red Army. One report by Gao Jingting, dated July 16, 1935, reached the Central Committee, probably by way of Shanghai, but it is unlikely that any contacts passed the other way before 1937.[107] Gao fought the Three-Year War without help, working out his own policies and directions. In 1937, he took great pleasure in a letter written to the Central Committee by Zheng Weisan that said of Gao's lonely odyssey: "The heart asks the mouth, the mouth asks the heart; together they deliberate."[108]

Throughout the Three-Year War, Gao repeatedly tried to contact the Party center and showed no sign of the schismatism of which he was later accused. In September 1937, he told Party officials in Yan'an that he had "sent many liaison officials to establish links to upper levels and get instructions, but received no echo." (In fact, some emissaries did reach him, but Gao took them for enemy agents and had them killed.)[109]

Gao was anxious to maintain his image as representative in Eyuwan of a national political organization; he was also extremely sensitive, as his bodyguard Li Jiwen discovered, to the suggestion that he was a mere outlaw. One day, when Li was distributing grain to local villagers, someone asked where the grain was from. Li replied that it had been stolen from a landlord. Hearing this, Gao flew into a rage. "We are not bandits or Guomindang," he shouted. "We are returning to the masses what evil hegemon-landlords stole and exploited from them."[110]

Gao's lack of links to the Party center was paralleled within Eyuwan, where government troops blocked communication between the Party's various committees. In Wanxibei, around Hefei, Shouxian, and Shucheng, fewer than ten guerrillas were left at large after defeats in September and October 1934; after merging with guerrilla remnants from Wanbei (northern Anhui), they temporarily grew to more than one hundred, but this number was halved when they moved base. This group, under Sun Zhongde, managed to contact the Central Committee in late 1935 and was told to go to Eyuwan and seek out the Communists there. All they found were a few isolated stragglers; under enemy pressure, they returned to Hefei.[111] Even in central Eyuwan, the Shangcheng Committee lost contact with Gao after his excursion to the Tongbai Mountains in 1935; it was not until the summer of 1936 that

Gao restored ties to it, despite attempts by both sides to find one another. Even units directly under Gao operated independently of his day-to-day command for weeks and months on end after the decision of December 1935 to decentralize operations to the battalion level and to switch to plainclothes groups.

## GAO'S PURGES

An important thread in the history of the Twenty-eighth Red Army was Gao's obsession with "thought construction" and political purges. Purges were the bedrock of his Communism, and they scarcely stopped during the Three-Year War. Gao was suspicious, authoritarian, and violent. In 1934 and 1935, he was isolated for months on end from social contact. He became introspective, anxious to recreate in the Party's amputated "superstructure" the pure "class nature" of the workers and peasants to whom he lacked real ties. As the Party in Eyuwan became increasingly decentralized and fragmented after 1934, Gao became obsessed with cleaning away "class impurities." The purges, which came in three main waves, claimed fewer victims than those before November 1934, but their impact on Gao's tiny army was greater.

Typically, victims were accused of mistakes or shortcomings in ideology, work, or personal life. "Counterrevolutionary plots and sabotage" were discovered everywhere. Losing a rifle, writing an incorrect character in a slogan, failing to give sufficient care to wounded comrades, or saying the wrong thing at a conference typically resulted in the offender being branded as a "class enemy." A Party historian explained Gao's dictatorial regime: "Because the Twenty-eighth Red Army spent a long time in mountain areas scattered for guerrilla war and lost contact with the Central Committee, he consciously or unconsciously developed the style of a warlord and a mountaintopper. . . . He rarely listened to the views of others." In the purges of 1935 to 1937, Gao killed more than one hundred cadres and forced an even greater number to confess to being counterrevolutionaries and to "redeem themselves through good service."

These purges were, to some extent, a struggle for control over armed men. In the Three-Year War, leaders differed on the degree to which Communist forces in Eyuwan should "localize." Gao leaned toward centralization and incorporated into his Twenty-eighth Red Army forces belonging to "counterrevolutionaries" uncovered by the purges.

Eyuwan's first purge after the departure of the Twenty-fifth Red Army took place in the spring of 1935, after Nationalists had caught and killed the secretary of the Edongbei Committee. The purge started in the Committee's laundry team, where three workers were executed as counterrevolutionaries; it later claimed twenty or thirty further victims. In September 1935, Gao arrived in Edongbei and purged the two main instigators of the previous purge, including the political commissars of the army hospital, who were accused of killing wounded. Two more purges followed in 1936. One was triggered by the defection of Ding Shaoqing, Gao's chief of staff. Ding's defection created havoc in the local Party and plainclothes groups; Gao doubled the havoc by purging the army. The second purge came after the conference of June 1936, when Gao accused Xu Chengji, Fang Yongle, and Lin Weixian, leaders of the Twenty-eighth Red Army, of forming a counterrevolutionary "Reorganization Clique." Xu, afraid that Gao would liquidate him, fled to another place where he killed two supposed reactionaries and tried single-handedly to build a Red Army of his own before being caught and killed by *mintuan*. Fang, still not yet twenty, wrote a confession saying that he was a counterrevolutionary and then sacrificed himself in battle to show that he was not. The only survivor was Lin, who had once saved Gao's life.[112]

A recent Party assessment of Gao's role in the Three-Year War explains the purges of 1935 and 1936 in part as a product of Gao's personal insecurity and fear of competition. "After Gao Jingting joined the revolution," says the assessment, "within a very short time he rose from being an ordinary peasant to leader of the Eyuwan base. His cultural level was low and he lacked the necessary Marxist theoretical schooling, so he could not shake off the harmful influence of the old-style peasant feudal legacy. His thinking was therefore narrow. Fearing that the prestige of other leading cadres would surpass his own, he used purges as an excuse to attack them." The assessment concludes that Gao was isolated from the Party center for so long that he became a patriarch.[113] Gao's paranoia may also have had something to do with the high price—one hundred thousand dollars—that Wei Lihuang had put on his head.

In July 1935 or 1936, the Party's Eyushaan Committee (formed by leaders of the Twenty-fifth Red Army that had left Eyuwan in late 1934) made Gao secretary of the Eyuwan Committee. This appointment gave Gao supreme and uncontested authority over the army (of which he was already commander) and the Party and the soviet (which had by then fused).[114] This concentration of power in one person at a time of general purges and paranoia may also explain the violent and dictatorial nature of Gao's regime.

Party writers on Eyuwan differ in their views of the purges of the early 1930s. Some see them as manifestations of the "first Wang Ming line" in Eyuwan under Zhang Guotao; these authors condemn them out of hand, saying that all their victims should be rehabilitated. Others believe that they were necessary but went too far, punishing the innocent as well as the guilty.[115] Opinions on the purges after 1934 may be similarly divided, especially now that Gao has been rehabilitated. Gao's purges did not wreck his army; on the contrary, it grew quickest in the summer of 1936 following on two big purges, including that of Xu and Fang.[116]

Survival in the Three-Year War depended not only on ingenious and flexible tactics but on resoluteness of spirit. Gao's experience in the early 1930s had taught him resolution to the point of remorselessness. He never shirked from swift decisions in difficult circumstances. He joined his guerrillas to him with the solder of fear.[117] His purges sometimes turned Gao into a "one-armed general," for they wiped out a large part of his precious handful of good leaders and reduced the provincial committee to just two members, one of whom (He Yaobang) shortly became the object of yet another attempted purge.[118]

## TOWARD THE UNITED FRONT

In January 1937, Gao Jingting learned from a newspaper that Chiang Kai-shek had been taken prisoner at Xi'an and that Nationalist divisions in Eyuwan were mobilizing to assist him. Gao could get no detailed information on the incident, but he organized a short-lived attempt to harass and tie down these divisions.[119] While negotiating for a new united front after Xi'an, the Nanjing government laid secret plans to destroy the Red Army's southern guerrillas "in three months." The Twenty-eighth Red Army was a special target of this campaign. By then, Gao had restored some of his old base and posed a greater potential threat to the heartland of the Guomindang than most rearguard pockets south of the Chang Jiang. His guerrillas had destroyed or dispersed a dozen or so Nationalist battalions and numerous *mintuan* forces since early 1936 and were by now active in more than fifty counties. In March 1937, the Nationalists moved eight crack divisions into Eyuwan, and in April, Wei Lihuang began a huge drive against the Communists, reportedly carried out by an army of three hundred thousand regular and local forces organized in some two hundred regiments.

Gao learned of these plans from captured documents. At first, he took measures to avoid excessive losses, but he underestimated the threat to his position and massed his troops for a "decisive" campaign that he could not hope to win. In the middle of this crisis, he purged several top leaders of the Edongbei Committee. Wei Lihuang knocked out between six and seven hundred members of the Twenty-eighth Red Army, one in five of the plainclothes groups, and scores of their civilian supporters. He seized back most of the areas they controlled. The Communists' civilian network was severely damaged; the losses were the worst since

1934, though advocates of localization (including He Yaobang and others) prevented even greater losses by ignoring Gao's instruction to mobilize the plainclothes squads. Not until the summer did Gao decide to break through Guomindang lines into Wanxi rather than continue to pit his dwindling army against Wei Lihuang. The outbreak of all-out war with Japan on July 7, 1937, put an end to Wei's "three-month drive." Gao was saved by the bell.[120]

On July 13, 1937, the Central Committee in Yan'an told Gao to start talks with the Guomindang about putting an end to the fighting. Various stories about how this directive was brought to Gao's attention say much about how his comrades viewed his character and regime. Sometime in early 1937, a Guomindang corporal defected with twenty men to Communists operating independently along the Ewan (Hubei-Anhui) border. The leader of these Communists, He Yaobang, sent the defecting corporal to Shaanxi to search out the Twenty-fifth Red Army; eventually, he turned up at the Red Army liaison office in Xi'an. The Central Committee had often tried to contact Gao, but even when its agents penetrated the blockade, they had not always managed to track Gao down, and Gao shot as alleged enemy agents some that did. Through this Guomindang defector, the Central Committee sent He Yaobang a bundle of documents about the Xi'an Incident and the united front.

He's first problem was to meet Gao without being shot, for a new purge was under way and He was aware that he "had problems." To test Gao's mood, He and other suspect leaders sent emissaries to him. The emissaries reported that Gao was friendly. On July 13, He met up with Gao. He was uncertain how Gao would react to the documents. Would he dismiss them as forgeries and blame He for falling into a Guomindang trap? Others who had approached Gao with similar stories in the past had been killed.[121] To avoid that fate, He told Gao that he had captured the documents in battle and asked him to decide himself whether they were genuine. After shutting himself up for a night and a day to deliberate, Gao judged that they were. Gao approved of their injunction to "heighten vigilance and preserve independence in order to avoid mishaps" in negotiations with the Guomindang, and they seemed to confirm earlier remarks by prisoners. He decided that the time had come to propose a cease-fire.[122]

Events moved quickly. On July 15, a Communist agent dropped a letter from Gao to Wei Lihuang into an awning near a watchtower in Yuexi. This letter deliberately violated the conventions for communicating with officials: it ignored prescribed formulas and, as a sign of contempt, was written from left to right rather than from top to bottom. The letter proposed talks but added, "Our troops are here. Come up and take our guns if you can. Even if you destroy us, there are plenty more Twenty-eighth Red Army soldiers in Eyuwan." The Nationalists agreed the same day to talks. They had to take Gao seriously, for they did not yet know his real strength.[123] Now that war against Japan had been declared, they were urgently wanted at the front; they could hardly pull out before settling matters with Gao. At first, they surrounded Gao with four regiments and tried to talk him down from the mountains "with cash and the promise of office." On July 18, they gave up this attempt and started preliminary talks. On July 22, formal negotiations finally began between He Yaobang and a high-level representative of Wei Lihuang.[124]

He Yaobang was unhappy about conducting these talks alone. Fearing that his "low cultural level" would put him at a disadvantage, he hoped for help from the Party in Shanghai or Anqing. When no help came, he had to rely on his own judgment, reinforced by Party documents that he pored over night after night. The local Nationalists knew that the Eyuwan Communists were keen to restore links to the Party center and took steps to stop them doing so. They raided and wiped out the Party's underground cell in Qianshan, which was then handling ties to higher Party bodies.[125]

In the talks, He Yaobang asked that the villages between Qiliping and Xuanhuadian in Edongbei be assigned to the guerrillas, who would assemble there before the year's end. In 1933, the Communists had fought a bloody and famous battle at Qiliping, which was strategically located to the north of Wuhan, where the Party had its Chang Jiang Bureau. Qiliping was densely populated and had a revolutionary tradition, which would facilitate recruiting. To the north and northwest of it were mountain bases to which the guerrillas could retreat. He Yaobang demanded authority to "quell bandits and those disturbing the social order" around Qiliping, complete independence for Communist forces in Eyuwan, help in getting to the front, and the right to set up three offices in the border region. He raised the usual demands about democratic rights, political prisoners, army supplies, and Red Army dependents. He also raised the question of the fate of the tens of thousands of Eyuwan women sold as brides and prostitutes by the Nationalists, declaring that the local governments should help those women who wished to return to their original husbands and homes. After the talks, large crowds of people besieged the office of Wei Lihuang's representative in Qiliping: women whose husbands were in prison, men whose wives had been sold, mothers who had lost their sons, and families whose houses had been confiscated. The blockade, which was probably not spontaneous, was lifted only with the cooperation of He Yaobang.[126]

The Nationalist negotiators demanded an end to attacks on *tuhao*, sabotage, Communist poaching of government troops, and unauthorized expansion of the Twenty-eighth Red Army. They said that guerrillas would have to carry identity papers if their safety was to be guaranteed. They also called for the disbanding of the plainclothes network and threatened to suppress as bandits any plainclothes units that did not disband. It is unclear how many of these demands and conditions were mutually approved; some certainly were not. Still, the two sides reached an agreement that the Communists saw as favorable, and on July 28 Gao—in disguise and under an alias—climbed down the mountain to sign it.[127]

Gao spent most of August rallying his forces and explaining the united front to them. "It is not an end to revolution," he said; "still less is it a compromise or capitulation."[128] Gao had to contend with the hostility of many Guomindang officials to the Communists and with the even greater hostility of his own supporters to the Guomindang. Class war in the Dabie Mountains had been particularly cruel; the passions it had roused could not be stilled by mere talk of unity. As late as September 1937, seventy thousand Red Army dependents in Eyuwan were starving and freezing, according to a secret report by Dong Biwu.[129] Immediately after the negotiations, Gao called a conference at which he stressed the need for "class vigilance." But his chief preoccupation was with the "leftism" of his guerrillas, some of whom drew pistols when told of the united front.[130] "At this time of extreme national emergency," he said to them, "when the nation is threatened with extinction, all our troops wishing to resist Japan should go to Qiliping in Huang'an."

In August, Nationalist divisions began to quit Eyuwan for the front, leaving behind power vacuums into which the guerrillas rushed, sweeping away large numbers of *tuhao* despite Nationalist protests. To win these "leftists" to the united front, Gao told them that "the Red Army all over China is no longer fighting, so we too are no longer fighting." But he added that "even though we are cooperating with them, still we should not think that we and they are the same; we are still our old selves. We still maintain past class love and our past Red Army style."

"Make sure you do mass work," he added. "If [officials] interfere, win over the good ones but ignore the rest. Let these officials attend to their own affairs and us to ours. When necessary we can give them orders, for today we are their superiors. . . . Do not lightly come near other forces; never let them seize you. Do not let them cross our garrison areas. Close the town gates when they arrive, insist that they withdraw." But despite Gao's tough stand in favor of the united front, he did not entirely overcome resistance to it. Some plainclothes teams refused to leave the mountains even after Gao had talked to them.[131]

Gao's main concern was how best to mass a credible army. He was in no hurry to go to Qiliping, though a regiment of Wei Lihuang's forces in the town had been urgently summoned to the front and Wei wanted Gao to take the garrison over quickly. (One reason Wei had so readily agreed to let the Communists go there was—it is said—because he wanted them to quit his native Anhui as soon as possible.) Gao ignored three requests to go to Qiliping and directed all his efforts to swelling the ranks of his army. Though the region around Qiliping had a strong Communist tradition, the attacks of early 1937 had plunged the local Party deep into crisis. Whatever Wei Lihuang said, the Hubei provincial authorities were by no means certain to cede Qiliping to Gao. Along the roads to Qiliping and in and around the town, Nationalist units blocked Gao's passage, so he had to tough his way through their lines. His dream of massing a big army was in conflict with the need, felt most strongly by local leaders like He Yaobang, to "preserve revolutionary seeds" in Eyuwan. In the end, Gao agreed to He's proposal that plainclothes fighters be left in the villages unless they were known to the authorities. Thus the core of guerrillas reorganized into the New Fourth Army did not represent the Party's entire strength; an unknown number stayed behind in Eyuwan to do Party work.[132]

### THE COMMUNIST SURGE IN EYU

In August and September, Gao sent heavily armed units to the Tongbai Mountains in Eyu to contact Zhou Junming and Wang Guohua's guerrillas, who had grown from seven in 1935 to more than 1,300 (one of the New Fourth Army's largest contingents) by the time they left the mountains in March 1938.[133] Estimates of the number of guerrillas in Eyu in early 1937 vary. According to Lin Weixian, Zhou Junming at first had only seventy to eighty followers but recruited a further five hundred in just forty days once talks began. Of the 1,300 Tongbai guerrillas who massed at Henan's Zhugou to form the Eighth Regiment of the Fourth Detachment of the New Fourth Army, most were probably new recruits, including bandits and supporters rallied by Peng Xuefeng, who returned to work for the New Fourth Army in his native Eyu in early 1938 and mobilized his social contacts.[134]

There are several explanations for the quick growth of the guerrillas in Eyu after 1935. Their main area of operations, around Biyang in the Tongbai Mountains, was thinly garrisoned and thick with armed dissent. Through the Party shop in Suiping, they had been sent several new batches of recruits, including lost Party members. They had also received money and political intelligence through the shop after December 1936.[135] Because they had generally avoided attacking regular forces, "it was very difficult for the outside world to detect our presence." Thrown back completely on their own resources after the collapse of their link to the Party center, they were not compelled to apply the ideas of others. Partly because it was passed on by word of mouth, their propaganda was relevant to local issues and free of dogma and clichés. They developed their policies—for example, that of "broadly making friends," even among unrepentant bandits—on the basis of actual conditions rather than by abstract prescription. They recruited to the Party at least one opium addict, an official of the federated *baojia*. The Tongbai Mountains, once prosperous, had been depopulated by war and crisis and were almost wholly under the control of bandits, who operated in gangs ranging from a handful to thousands and even tens of thousands. The guerrillas needed a strategy for dealing with these bandits in order to retain a foothold in the mountains. They decided to infiltrate the larger groups and win their friendship; as for the smaller groups, they did their best to absorb them or, failing that, to drive them away.[136]

With little outside interference, the Party leaders in Eyu rarely disagreed; they usually reached their decisions unanimously. However, when they finally restored contact to national bodies of the Party with the help of the Suiping shop, they swung off course for a while and quickly weakened.[137] An official of the Party's Northern Bureau who was overzealously attached to the united front told them to stop attacking *tuhao* and even to disband and join the local *mintuan*. They did so, and as a result were soon without funds. All but fifty guerrillas were driven back home by hunger. In August or September 1937, they learned from Zhou Junming, who had returned to Eyu from Yan'an, that the Northern Bureau's directive was unauthorized and that they should continue to seize funds from reactionaries and expand their army to force the authorities to the negotiating table.

Strengthened by a battalion of Gao Jingting's Twenty-eighth Red Army, they expanded quickly. In just a few days, they seized a huge amount of grain and recruited more than three hundred guerrillas, including many bandits. Heartened by the rehabilitation of class struggle, they organized an uprising in the market town of Zhugou in November 1937 and executed the local strongman. They seized Zhugou and set up their headquarters there. (It became a key link between Communists in northern and central China after 1937.) By the time they reorganized in March 1938, they needed several villages to garrison their forces.[138]

One factor in the sudden growth of the Eyu guerrilla army was the arrival in Biyang in the spring of 1937 of units of Zhang Xueliang's Northeastern (Manchurian) Army, fresh from the events at Xi'an. At first, these units, under Zhou Fucheng, attacked guerrilla strongholds along the border, but soon officers at battalion and regimental level began cooperating with the Communists. They provided guerrillas with intelligence and guns and freed their own Communist prisoners. In the autumn of 1937, the Red Army in Eyu once again benefited from disaffection in the Nationalist camp when local forces under Zhang Zhoufang, discriminated against by Chiang Kai-shek, joined the Communists in a secret alliance. Personal ties played a role in this switch: one of the main leaders of these local forces was an ex-Communist and a friend of the guerrilla leader Zhou Junming.

Zhang Zhoufang's support for the Eyu guerrillas was not disinterested; he had been given a free hand by the Nationalists to recruit an army and had been promised supplies proportional to the size of it. He gave the Communists three thousand dollars' worth of supplies and more than one thousand uniforms. The guerrillas planned to amalgamate with Zhang, but Zhou Enlai in Wuhan had already assigned them to the New Fourth Army; Zhang reluctantly accepted this arrangement.[139] Communists under Gao Jingting in Eyuwan also benefited from splits in the Nationalist camp. Because Nationalist garrisons north of Wuhan were for various reasons less solidly behind the aims of the Nanjing government than those in guerrilla areas south of the Chang Jiang, the Eyu and Eyuwan guerrillas had this space in which to grow.

## MASSING AT QILIPING

Gao also sent word to other units scattered along the border. Among those who marched from the forests was a contingent of doctors, nurses, and a dozen wounded soldiers from the Red Army cave hospital in Shangcheng.[140] In the old guerrilla areas, Gao gave plundered silver and jade to the Party's "basic masses" who had cared for Red Army invalids and explained the new policy to them in simple terms. While Gao was reactivating links in Eyuwan and Eyu, batches of cadres came south from Yan'an to join him; later, Dong Biwu, Ye Jianying, and others visited Gao to instruct him in the new politics. As the scattered units marched in small groups and by small paths to Qiliping, they were helped and guided everywhere by plainclothes teams.[141]

By September, between 1,500 and 2,500 guerrillas had assembled.[142] Later, their number swelled to between three and five thousand, of which one-third were plainclothes fighters.[143] These people formed the Seventh and Ninth Regiments of the New Fourth Army's Fourth Detachment. Not all who went to Qiliping were veterans; at least three hundred, and probably many more, were new recruits.[144] But the proportion of veterans delivered to the New Fourth Army in Eyuwan was higher than in most other guerrilla areas. Having successfully gathered his people at Qiliping on October 17, Gao briefly put down his gun to marry the Communist Shi Yuqing.[145]

Communists in Eyuwan viewed Wei Lihuang and his negotiators with intense suspicion, but in reality the Nationalists in Eyuwan were split, and Wei's representatives were by no means as reactionary as the Communists imagined. Although Wei had served Chiang Kai-shek loyally, he

had never been a member of Chiang's inner circle. He had made his career by rising through the ranks rather than by graduating from the influential Whampoa Military Academy. Unlike many of Chiang's closest
allies, who were from China's eastern provinces, he was a native of
Anhui.[146]

Wei had more than once toyed with the idea of taking leave of Chiang
and setting up an independent army. This idea was supported by many
of his officers, who resented Chiang's weak stand against Japan and, as
Baoding graduates, Chiang's discrimination against officers who were
not part of his Whampoa clique. For Wei and men like Liu Gangfu (who
represented Wei in negotiations with the guerrillas in Eyuwan), Gao was
a "single flag" beyond Yan'an's control and an obvious candidate for the
independent army of which they dreamed.

Wei's secret interest in Gao explains the speed with which the two
reached agreement.[147] It also explains why Wei's negotiator Liu Gangfu
tried hiding from the Nanjing government what he thought to be Gao's
weakness. Liu Gangfu believed on the basis of intelligence reports that
Gao had only 108 guerrillas. (Here and at many other points, Gao's story
merges strikingly with that of Song Jiang, hero of *The Water Margin,* who
with his hand of 108 guerrilla *haohan*—a mixture, like Gao's, of gentry
dissidents and plebeian rebels—ruled the area around his Liangshan
lair with cunning, violence, and utter ruthlessness but in the end enlisted with the government.) To outsiders in Eyuwan, the difference between guerrillas and local people was hard to spot. Even a Communist
born and bred in Eyuwan found it difficult in late 1937 to round up
guerrillas, or even to track down their whereabouts, because of their
extreme secretiveness, vigilance, and suspicion. The estimate of Liu
Gangfu's informants, who claim to have counted the guerrillas through
a telescope, was almost certainly wrong. As we have seen, eventually
several thousand assembled at Qiliping. Liu, unaware of the latent support that Gao's men could mobilize, believed the lower figure and discreetly doubled it in his reports to Nanjing, thinking that he was doing
Gao a favor. So pay and supplies for Gao were set on the basis of two
hundred men.[148]

In Qiliping, the Nationalists tried one last time to prise Gao from the
Party center by playing on his vanity. In preliminary talks with He
Yaobang, they had proposed renaming the Twenty-eighth Red Army
"Gao's force"; He Yaobang said no. In the main negotiations with Gao,
they again offered to appoint him commander without consulting
Yan'an. Gao reportedly accepted, saying that if "the Central Committee's Red Army" could reorganize as the Eighth Route, then he too
had a right to organize his own division, having fought for several years
in Eyuwan.

The leaders in Yan'an saw this move as a challenge to their authority. The struggle in Yan'an between Mao and Zhang Guotao, who had patronized and promoted Gao in 1931, cannot have helped Gao, who was later denounced as "the last of the counterrevolutionary line of Zhang Guotao." Zheng Weisan, who had been sent down from Yan'an, was landed with the job of disenfeoffing Gao.

The story of how Zheng and He Yaobang outsmarted Gao and the Nationalist negotiator is a classic of the Three-Year War, a fable about the victory of morals, wits, and stamina over perfidy and greed. "We cannot use money, sex, or opium," He Yaobang told his comrades, out of Gao's hearing; "we can use only alcohol." He Yaobang was a moderate drinker, normally no match for his five-catty Guomindang adversary, and he was in poor health. But as the main Communist negotiator in Eyuwan, he was the only person who could drink with the Nationalist without raising his suspicion. "In the interests of the revolution," he declared, "I shall certainly fulfill the Party's task." Once the Nationalist was drunk enough, Zheng Weisan formally renounced Gao's appointment on the grounds that it violated the earlier agreement. Thus ended Gao's dream of an army of his own that would be independent of Yan'an. In his drunken stupor, He could hear Gao accusing him of selling out the Three-Year War by allying with people out to "seize power." The next day, Gao swallowed He's armed following. Fearing for his life, He fled with the help of Zheng Weisan to Wuhan, where he was put in charge of negotiating guerrilla reorganization north and south of the Chang Jiang.[149]

### GAO'S ACHIEVEMENT

To gauge Gao's extraordinary achievement in the Three-Year War, it is useful to compare it with that of stay-behinders in Minxi'nan, a base bigger and stronger than Eyuwan before the start of the Long March. The Minxi'nan guerrillas had a talented and cohesive leading team, whereas by 1935 all Eyuwan's outstanding leaders had left on the region's two long marches of 1932 and 1934. In Minxi'nan, the issue of Japanese aggression became important earlier than in other parts of China, especially isolated regions like Eyuwan. In Minxi'nan, as in most other places south of the Chang Jiang where guerrillas were active after 1934, the Liang Guang Incident of June 1936 gave Communists the chance to expand; in Eyuwan, they had no such advantage. Though Minxi'nan suffered under the repression, Eyuwan suffered worse, for the Nanjing government put greater effort into crushing the Communists there. The physical exhaustion of Eyuwan went deeper and began sooner, after the sudden decline of the base in late 1932. Still, the number of Gao's troops never dropped below one thousand, and eventually it topped three thousand.[150]

The guerrillas in Eyuwan may even have influenced Zhang Xueliang's fateful decision of 1936 to ally with the Communists in northwestern China and arrest Chiang Kai-shek. Zhang Xueliang was a "pacifier" in Eyuwan until his transfer to Xi'an in October 1935. Even in Eyuwan, he is said to have sympathized with the Communists. When he secretly met Zhou Enlai in April 1936, among the terms he agreed to was that "Communist armed forces in Jiangxi, Hainan, and the Dabie Mountains" should be reorganized together with the rest of the Red Army. As we have seen, Manchurian troops fraternized with guerrillas in Eyu in 1937.

In Eyuwan, Wei Lihuang had hopes of winning Gao to a new-style anti-Japanese army. His experience there may have helped incline him toward the Communists, with whom he cooperated both during and after the war against Japan.[151] Though Gao was far from the front against Japan before 1937 and could not exploit Japanese aggression as a central issue, he and his comrades in Eyu benefited from rivalries generated in the Nationalist camp by (among other things) differences on how to deal with the Japanese.

The deep local roots of the Communist movement in Eyuwan are the key to explaining the staying power of its guerrillas until their incorporation (long after Gao's death) into the Central Plains Liberated Area in the final stages of the Chinese Revolution. The Twenty-eighth Red Army was distinguished by its policy of selecting "brave peasants" to be its cadres. This policy began early in Eyuwan; by 1934, large numbers of Communist leaders in the region were of local, plebeian origin.[152] Though the Nationalists constantly cropped Gao's army, it just as constantly revived; during the Three-Year War, "according to incomplete statistics," more than two thousand local youths joined the Twenty-eighth Red Army.[153] Gao "preserved" 3,500 local forces in Eyuwan that backed up his army during operations and were an important source of its recruits.[154]

Another circumstance that helped Gao was the comparatively large number of veterans left behind in 1934 to serve as officers in the lower levels of his army, particularly its platoons.[155] By 1934, Communists in Eyuwan had already had two years' experience of countering the "pacifiers" under conditions that no longer held in other rearguard areas; in 1933, the Central Soviet could still absorb Chiang's main heat, and the Nationalists had not yet perfected their repressive methods.

The Communists in Eyuwan not only had the luxury of a rehearsal, but they also moved earlier than Communists elsewhere to guerrilla methods and policies despite some "leftist" lapses. After Eyuwan's second long march of 1934, there were few pitched battles of the sort fought in the Central Soviet at around the same time. Because the Communists in Eyuwan had no great state to dismantle and no illusions of statehood to drop, they were able to make a smoother transition than their comrades further south to tactics appropriate to the new conditions.

Gao's personal role was crucial throughout. He was resolute to the point of ruthlessness, quick to take decisions, good at acting independently, and adaptable to change.[156] His qualities were those of a self-made, homespun rebel: he embodied Eyuwan's intractable provincialism, which at times was a liability. In Eyuwan, it was only in the course of setting up the soviet that the Communist Party grew to be more than a handful of locally recruited intellectuals. The organization that grew up there with the revolution expanded far too quickly, according to Zheng Weisan; it was immature and had "bad style."[157] This rapid growth, together with the intensity of political conflict in the region, the harmful effects in Eyuwan of "leftism" in the late 1920s and early 1930s, Gao's constitutional brutality, and the region's general isolation, helps to explain the Eyuwan Party's chronic "warlordism," "commandism," "sectarianism," and purge mania.

These purges were intimately connected to the Party's and the Twenty-eighth Red Army's extreme decentralization after 1934, which called up its polar opposite in the Eyuwan command. The looser Gao's direct controls became, the greater his obsession with "thought construction" to stop people turning traitor. At some points in the Three-Year War, the Party in Eyuwan became so isolated by the blockades that it turned upon itself, waging an imaginary class struggle in its own ranks.

Gao's "warlordism," "mountaintoppism," and "hankering after an independent kingdom" became a problem after 1937. He seems at first to have disagreed with Mao's policy of moving swiftly east into territories occupied by the Japanese, so he procrastinated and missed some chances for the Party in northern Jiangsu and along the border between Jiangsu and Anhui. Later, relations between Gao and other Communist leaders in eastern China collapsed into crisis. "Separated from the main body of the New Fourth Army by the Yangtse [Chang Jiang] River," wrote Agnes Smedley in 1940 (in a passage that probably reflects the prejudices of her informants), Gao Jingting "soon developed into a local militarist. His head grew big with power, he took concubines, became corrupt, and arrested and killed anyone who opposed him. Medical supplies sent to him from general headquarters were sold to shopkeepers, but Commander [Gao] kept demanding more." In June 1939, Gao was shot after being tried before his own soldiers, who, says Smedley, "voted for his death."[158]

Despite his wish for a regime in Eyuwan more independent than Yan'an was prepared to stomach, Gao stayed true to his idea of the Party during his years of isolation. He even asked the Central Committee to send officers to help lead his forces.[159] His rehabilitation in 1977 suggests that many of the charges leveled against him in 1939 were exaggerated and perhaps invented outright. As a local revolutionary who barely set foot outside the region of his birth before 1938, Gao was parochial and introverted. But still he was a Communist, and his very narrowness precluded him from entertaining independent ambitions on any grand scale.

When the Resistance War began, peasants influenced by Gao formed an extensive network of plainclothes teams that "feared neither Japanese, nor Guomindang diehards, nor landlords." This network flourished to the north, the northwest, and the northeast of Wuhan after 1938. In Eyu, too, a Fifth Detachment of the New Fourth Army was formed after the fall of Wuhan in October 1938 from a handful of Red Army veterans and plainclothes groups; by late 1940, Communist-run militias had organized more than eighty thousand people, and by 1944 they had swollen to more than three hundred thousand. These networks, which survived until 1949, played a far more active role in supporting Communist armies in the war against Japan and the civil war than similar networks in other regions of the Three-Year War.[160] But their exceptional endurance also owed much to Eyuwan's proximity to the front and its position on a main line of communications between Yan'an and New Fourth Army units along the Chang Jiang.

# Xiang'egan:
## Persevering to the End

•   •   •

Xiang'egan is the name of the mountain region where Hunan (Xiang), Hubei (E), and Jiangxi (Gan) join (map 9). The Xiang'egan Soviet was once a main link in the chain of soviets fastened along the borders of China's central and southern provinces. To the north were Xiang'exi and Eyuwan, to the south Xianggan and the Central Soviet, and to the east the bases of Minzhewan'gan. Communist organizers highly valued this strategic border region, from which they hoped to threaten the nearby cities of Wuhan, Changsha, and Nanchang and the railways that marked the region's limits. Peasant movements flourished here between 1925 and 1927; in 1926, Communists organized supporters to greet and assist the Northern Expedition, which took Pingjiang on August 19. Starting in 1923, Communists agitated among the miners of Pingjiang, establishing a proletarian as well as a peasant base in Xiang'egan—one that was less completely crushed by the counterrevolution of 1927 than the Party's factory bases in the cities. After 1934, Communists in Xiang'-egan were active mainly in Liuyang, Pingjiang, Xiushui, Tonggu, and Yangxin.[1]

In the winter of 1927, the Party's Chang Jiang Bureau set up the Xiang'egan Special Committee. In March 1928, miners and peasants stormed the capital of Pingjiang under Communist leaders, and in July, Peng Dehuai and others led the famous Pingjiang Insurrection. From this rising was born Peng's Fifth Red Army, so called to distinguish it from Mao's Fourth Red Army in the nearby Jinggang Mountains. It was founded around insurgent sections of the warlord-dominated Hunan Army, which Peng had joined as a private in 1916. Its soldiers had no link to Pingjiang; they were unfamiliar with the region and its people. At first, not even Peng had ties to local Communists. To remedy this

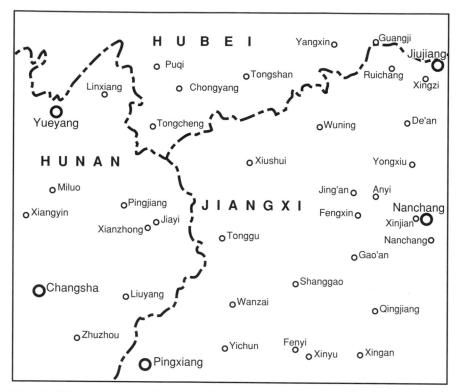

Map 9. Xiang'egan (the Hunan-Hubei-Jiangxi border region).

problem, and to replace insurgents who had deserted in later battles around Pingjiang, Peng's new army strengthened its ties to guerrillas in the region. In September 1928, the Xiang'egan Committee, which in the meantime had collapsed, was restored.[2] Rapid growth resulted, but the movement was set back by hotheads whose "wanton burning and killing" created a spiral of violence between Communists and local peasants. In late 1928, half the Communists' main force in Xiang'egan marched off under Peng to the Jinggang Mountains and then to Ruijin in Gannan; it did not return until a year later.

By then, the Xiang'egan guerrillas had grown a little, and "reckless action," though still a problem, was less common. Peng's army, with 3,100 soldiers, was below its strength of early 1928, and though it improved its ties to the villages by applying lessons learned in Xianggan, prisoners of war were apparently Peng's main source of new recruits. According to reports, "no serious effort was made to carry out land reform." Land had been divided in some parts of Pingjiang as early as December 1928, but less than a month later, the same places were retaken by the Nationalists. In 1928, the Xiang'egan Communist Party also held its first conference, representing just five counties. Although two-thirds of Pingjiang had been sovietized by 1930 and Pingjiang's First Soviet Congress was convened in July, it was not until March or April 1931 that the main round of land division was completed.[3]

The methods adopted were radical. Land was confiscated outright, rather than in part, and was sometimes farmed communally. These policies were derived from Central Committee directives, but studies claim that the basis for this extreme radicalism had been laid decades earlier by the rebel Taipings, whose Heavenly Kingdom (1851–64) extended into this area, and that communal farming under the Communists in Xiang'egan was almost identical to communal farming under the Taipings. Land policies in Xiang'egan were influenced by "economic determinism," that is, the view that small landholders automatically became counterrevolutionary even if they had been poor peasants or landless laborers before reform.[4]

By 1931, the Xiang'egan base was past its peak.[5] In 1930, Communists in Xiang'egan had sovietized parts of thirty-four counties and held fourteen county capitals, but after 1930, the soviet was reduced to "a narrow strip eight or nine hundred *li* long."[6] On September 23, 1931, 130 representatives from more than twenty counties met under the leadership of the newly proclaimed Xiang'egan Provincial Committee to set up the Xiang'egan Soviet government.[7] But its chances of taking root were slim.

The Communist movement in Xiang'egan after 1927 gained its initial impetus less from a local upsurge of support than from a switch of flags by warlord troops under Peng Dehuai. After that, the armed forces upon which it depended for survival were busier meeting the strategic needs of the main Red Army to the south than sinking roots in Xiang'-egan, whose strategic role was eventually downgraded. Even during the Fifth Encirclement of 1933–34, leaders of the Xiang'egan Red Army persisted in their plans to "develop toward the southeast" and surround Nanchang.[8] As a result, the revolution in Xiang'egan grew less vigorously than in soviet bases elsewhere. After the rising of August 1930, in which one hundred thousand Communist-led insurgents reportedly attacked Changsha, the capital of Hunan, Communist forces in the region suffered heavy losses. After the founding of the Xiang'egan Soviet in September 1931, the "purely military viewpoint" of local army leaders led to even greater losses and the collapse of the base.[9]

The Xiang'egan Communist movement still commanded strong pockets of support, especially around Pingjiang and Liuyang. Its leaders claim to have organized tens of millions of peasants around the time of the Changsha Uprising and to have set up Red defense squads throughout the border region.[10] But its main growth coincided with periods when the Guomindang was occupied elsewhere; the movement was too shallowly based to withstand the "bandit exterminators" who swept down on it after its first successes. Moreover, many of the problems of the Xiang'egan Communists were self-inflicted. More than ten thousand cadres and intellectuals were purged as alleged AB's, Reformists, or Third Party supporters after 1930. These purges, according to a recent study, caused "extremely great damage to the construction of the base."[11]

## THE START OF THE THREE-YEAR WAR

In the soviet's heyday, Xiang'egan's Red forces had acted as an outer defense of the Central Soviet, creating disturbances to divert Nationalist divisions when the Central Soviet was attacked.[12] The Three-Year War in Xiang'egan was largely waged by the Red Sixteenth Division, which started life in 1929 as the Xiang'egan Independent Regiment and was reorganized as a division and then as the Red Sixteenth Army in 1930. It grew swiftly in early 1933 and spawned a second army, the Red Eighteenth. In August 1933, both armies were reorganized as divisions of the Sixth Red Army Corps. During troop movements in 1934, this corps (under Xiao Ke) crossed and recrossed Xiang'egan, eventually replanting the Red Sixteenth Independent Division there.[13] Units of this division spent the next three years hiding out in densely wooded strongholds among the peaks and cliffs of the Luoxiao Mountains on the Xianggan border. They kept alive the embers of the revolution, and in late 1937, they stepped from the forests to join the New Fourth Army.[14]

In 1934 and early 1935, the ebb and flow of the Communist movement in Xiang'egan followed an opposite rhythm to that in Gannan. The Party's Xiang'egan headquarters and armed forces were practically wiped out in the Longmen Mountains in Ganxibei (northwestern Jiangxi) in the summer of 1934, when the Communist movement in Gannan was still buoyant. By the time Ruijin fell in late 1934 and the main Red Army marched off to the west, the Red Sixteenth had evaporated. It lost four thousand rifles and ten thousand men in 1934. By June, it had been reduced to one battalion and one thousand officials attached to the Xiang'egan Committee. The guerrilla struggle therefore began several months earlier in Xiang'egan than in the Central Soviet. After Xiang'egan's collapse in early 1934, most Nationalist units went south to join in attacking the main Red concentrations, so Communists in Xiang'egan were able to revive some of their military strength.[15]

The main leader of the Three-Year War in Xiang'egan, and typical of the core of Communists who sustained it, was Fu Qiutao, who in the ten years up to 1937 fought more than four hundred battles. Fu was born in a tiny mountain village in Pingjiang in 1907. At the age of ten, he became a cowherd. At fifteen, he began working in a shop. At eighteen he joined a farmhands' union and soon became its leader. In 1927, working as a bricklayer, he joined the workers' picket in Jiayi, which later became a soviet stronghold in Pingjiang, and in 1930 he became a Communist. He was illiterate when he first joined the Party, but as he began to take on political responsibilities, he set out to "raise his theoretical and particularly his cultural level" and asked an educated comrade to teach him characters. During the Three-Year War, he is said to have carried Lenin's *State and Revolution* and *Leftwing Communism* with him everywhere.[16]

In mid-1934, Fu, by then leader of the Xiang'egan Committee, and his deputy Tu Zhengkun were cut off from the Party center after their radio was destroyed in fighting. Within a few months, they had begun to revive the movement in Xiang'egan, sending out small teams to collect armed forces from surrounding areas.[17] In August 1934, Fu set out for Edongnan (southeastern Hubei) with just six men and as many pistols. Edongnan was a more likely place to restore Communist fortunes than the Longmen Mountains, for though Ganxibei had long known soviet government and had carried through land revolution, the Party was by then quite weak there. Landlords had returned to reclaim their fields, and the nearby plains were a convenient staging ground for Nationalist armies. To reach Edongnan, Fu and his men—reduced to three after a shoot-out in Tongcheng—skirted the towns and went by mountain roads, making contact along the way with Party committees. These committees had survived the repression and kept up a regional network and guerrilla nuclei, so Fu was met by a succession of local armed escorts as he slipped through the hills and mountains toward Hubei.

As he moved, he fought. In a few small battles, he captured one hundred rifles that he used to arm new recruits. His men attacked *tuhao* and local officials wherever they found them, seizing their food and weapons. By October, his column had grown to eleven hundred, joined by remnants of the scattered Sixteenth Division. In November, he sustained heavy losses, which he made good by recruiting in the old soviet areas around Pingjiang and across the border in Jiangxi. In the first few months of 1935, he enlisted 1500 new recruits in a "shock expansion campaign."[18] This success marked the start of a new high tide in Communist fortunes in Xiang'egan. But it was short-lived, and it blinded Fu to impending catastrophe.

In April, Fu's column, once more calling itself the Red Sixteenth Division, hit units of the Guomindang's Fiftieth Division at Dayuan near Xiushui, taking two hundred prisoners. The Nationalists, greatly alarmed, sent a company of the 105th Division to probe Fu's strength. As they marched through the wooded valleys, hidden eyes watched them from the nearby slopes. The men of the 105th Division were no mountain fighters. They moved slowly, using their rifle butts as walking sticks. In less than thirty minutes, practically the entire company fell to the Communists. They turned out to be Manchurians from Zhang Xueliang's army, many of whom resented Chiang Kai-shek's failure to stand up to the Japanese in northeastern China and had little interest in fighting the Communists. The Communist commander, Xu Yan'gang, told them that the Red Army also wanted to resist Japan and reassured them that they would be well treated. He had pigs slaughtered and sent the Manchurians back to their division after three days of eating, political lectures, and camaraderie. His hospitality had a big impact on the rest of the Manchurian division. (Several months later, Communist armies in northern China applied similar tactics with even greater success and with grave consequences for Chiang Kai-shek.)

The events in Xiang'egan were reported to the Guomindang's field headquarters in Wuhan. Before long, an official traveled south to investigate. He too was attacked and killed at a spot not far from the previous encounter. Four hundred of his men were captured; most were incorporated into the Red Sixteenth, which by then had grown to three regiments.[19]

Fu resumed his march toward Edongnan. While passing through Pingjiang, he scored another victory over two regiments of the Guomindang's Nineteenth Division. These regiments, part of a force calling itself the Ever-Victorious Army, had sworn to capture alive the men of the Red Sixteenth. Each Nationalist soldier carried a length of rope to bind the expected prisoners. Instead, five hundred Nationalist soldiers ended up bound by their own ropes after the Communists, acting on intelligence provided by supporters, ambushed them from the hills. By then, Fu's column was more than five thousand strong, backed by a growing network of local guerrillas.[20]

These were the best days of the Three-Year War in Xiang'egan. The Communists' morale, and that of their supporters, was high, and parts of the soviet (including all of the old Huangjin Soviet) had been restored.[21] The Communist threat was taken seriously by government officials, who reported that there were "ten thousand troops under Xu Yan'gang" in Xiang'egan. In May 1935, the United States Consul General at Hankou reported that "a band of Reds numbering 3,000" was massing to the southeast of Yuezhou and that American residents of Yuezhou had been told that their safety could not be guaranteed.[22] However, these successes were possible only because the Nationalists were putting their main effort in this period into mopping up soviets to the south and chasing the main Red Army. By June 1935, the Guomindang's "bandit suppressors" had finished purging the old Central Soviet and were ready to turn elsewhere.[23] He Jian, who had been in charge of "pacifying" Pingjiang, was secretly sacked for failing to wipe out the Reds, though publicly the Government continued to boast that they were a spent force.[24] Plans were laid for a thorough purging of Xiang'egan by more than one hundred thousand troops (including provincial security forces).[25]

## THE PURGING OF XIANG'EGAN

If the Xiang'egan leaders had been better prepared to meet these changes, they might have emerged less badly mauled from the fighting that was about to start. If they had known the fate of Communist forces elsewhere in southern China, they might have acted more cautiously. But their links to the main force of the Red Army and to rearguard remnants in Gannan were cut, and they had had little news of either. Their string of victories had weakened their vigilance. Though their morale was high, most of their troops were new to the Red Army and not tempered to battle. Xiang'egan Communists continued to concentrate their forces against the new, powerful enemy from the south. Only after devastating defeats did they scatter, rest, reorganize, and make the turn to guerrilla war. By then it was too late, and they were at the mercy of events.[26]

In June 1935, eleven Guomindang divisions under Tang Enbo and Fan Songfu moved up from Gannan into Xiang'egan.[27] Together with local forces, they set about repeating the tactics that had served them so well in Gannan. They formed a series of concentric circles, reinforced by innumerable blockhouses, around the Communists' main force, which did not respond to the buildup until it was already surrounded by an enemy many times its size. Nationalist troops then began transforming the topography within the circles, chopping down trees and setting up defense works and other obstacles along roads and paths. The Communists debated whether to flee or stand and fight. They decided to try to fight their way through to Ganxibei, whence they could slip south through the Luoxiao Mountains to the old Central Soviet area if the pressure became too great, or head north across the Chang Jiang into the Dabie Mountains.

After a week's preparation, they began their attempt to burst the circle, but they were thrown back into the mountains with heavy casualties. At night, star shells lit up their positions in the hills, sending waves of panic through Fu's new recruits. As losses mounted, the Communist leaders decided to abandon their attempt to reach Jiangxi and to try a northern route instead. Three columns of one regiment each marched out at night toward the line of forts. Two got through but were wiped out shortly afterwards. Of one, only sixteen men remained; of the other, fewer than seventy. The division's political headquarters was left behind amid the chaos but managed to find its way back to the remaining trapped column of some 1,700 troops.

These troops were pursued on the ground and from the air. Within the larger Nationalist circle, smaller circles closed around them as they fled from place to place. Party leaders sent out teams of agitators among the troops to stiffen their morale; those who still wavered, including some officers, were disarmed and put under guard. Spearheaded by a pistol squad, the column marched off unlit and in dead silence; most broke through. In less than one year, the Red Sixteenth had grown from a few hundred to five thousand; now it had shrunk back to just one thousand.[28] After analyzing the causes of their defeat, the Communists concluded that they had seen too late that the enemy would attack in such large numbers after the main Red Army left, so they had continued to fight ineffectively in large, regular formations.[29]

After cutting down the Communist forces in Xiang'egan by four-fifths in the summer, the new Nationalist commanders switched to intensive small-scale operations. They carved the border region into three large "bandit suppression zones," each with its own command, troops, and tasks. Each zone was further subdivided, garrisoned, and systematically scoured once, twice, or three times a month, for a week or more at a time. This strategy was called "prisoner's cage": the railways were its frame, the roads were its bars and chains, and the blockhouses were its locks. Line after line of pillboxes enmeshed the former soviet. All strategic lines of communication, mountain passes, towns, and villages were guarded by fortified points, which shot up like a stone forest. Within the larger system, lesser systems operated, with many smaller points clustered around one center. Villages of fewer than fifty households were directed to set up one pillbox, villages of between fifty and one hundred households two pillboxes, and so on. In just one part of Tonggu, not the most densely garrisoned place in Xiang'egan, there were 180 such pillboxes. Most were for army use, but nearly a third were garrisoned by civilian armed forces under local landlords.[30]

The different zones and subzones within Xiang'egan were in theory centrally coordinated across provincial, county, and village boundaries. In the past, the various authorities had been less tightly coordinated, and the Communists had easily exploited conflicts of interest and direction among them. Under the new, more centralized system, the Nationalists were able to avoid many of these conflicts, robbing the Communists of a major weapon. But the old divisions were by no means wholly overcome.

The reoccupying forces imposed a reign of terror on suspected Communists and their sympathizers. According to Fu Qiutao, people were burned, buried, or boiled alive, infants were torn in half, women were gang-raped and then killed, and whole families and villages were wiped out. This was not the impersonal killing of the battlefield but the venting of personal hatreds born of class war in the villages. The Lianyun Mountains in Pingjiang, once home to 120,000 people, were bared of population by the terror. The border region as a whole, where one million people had once lived, had a population of ten thousand by 1936, mostly women and children. At first, Nationalist soldiers took victims' heads as a tally of the killing. When the weight made carrying these trophies impracticable, they took ears instead, collecting them in large baskets. Houses, crops, tea plantations, timber forests, and bamboo groves were burned or chopped down.

The Nationalists called this tactic "draining the pond to catch the fish." If they could not sever the Communists' ties to society, then they would destroy society instead. They took away oxen, poultry, and clothes from the villages. They slaughtered the villagers' pigs, smashed their pots and stoves, and trampled their vegetables. They turned the former soviet into a wilderness. Reeds and small trees choked the paddy fields; wild pigs ran through the ruined villages; at night, wolves howled and tigers roared where once people had lived. As late as 1950, ruins and human bones were still scattered throughout the mountains.[31]

Most of those who survived "pacification" were expelled from the highlands and resettled away from the guerrillas in the towns or among clusters of fortified points along the roads. Merchants were forbidden to trade with the handful of people who escaped expulsion. Mountain people who had been resettled in the valleys and on the plains were allowed to buy only the minimum requirements of salt, oil, rice, cloth, medicine, and batteries. Agents mingled with them at the markets to check that they did not buy more than their ration; they were often searched on their way home.[32]

During the collapse of the soviet in Xiang'egan, large numbers of Communists deserted. Some simply went home; others switched their allegiance to the authorities, either voluntarily or under threat of force. These renegades were the Communists' worst enemies in Xiang'egan. They knew the Party's ways, the sites of its mountain hospitals, arsenals, and factories, and the identities of its leaders and undercover liaison workers. Nationalist authorities in Xiang'egan organized more than two hundred renegades into an "office for offering amnesty and enlistment to rebels." Part of their job was to persuade others to defect; they also spied and gathered information. Often small teams of them climbed the mountains to search areas through which they thought Communists might pass and to lay ambushes. Sometimes they dressed as hawkers or woodcutters and caught or killed any Communists they met. At other times, they disguised themselves as Red Army men and tricked Communist sympathizers into revealing themselves, or they turned villagers against the guerrillas by beating and robbing them. The Nationalists infiltrated women agents among dependents of the guerrillas to spy on them and undermine their morale. Some alleged women agents climbed the mountains to try to persuade the guerrillas to give up.[33]

## COMMUNIST TACTICS UNDER THE REPRESSION

But even in the relatively weak base of Xiang'egan, the Communists were able to maintain a marginal presence after 1934. The "soviet district" between 1934 and 1938 was no more than a thin line of disconnected guerrilla hideouts strung out along one hundred and fifty miles of mountain peaks.[34] Yet the Guomindang claim to have pacified the region was as much wishful thinking as the Communists' pretended soviet was.

One reason that the Communists in Xiang'egan survived pacification lay in the weaknesses of the Nationalist military system in the region. Though the government's military efforts were better coordinated now than before, its campaign along the border was waged from three provinces and chiefly by local troops after main-force units left following their victory over the Communists in June 1935. It was not in the nature of these local forces to forgo self-interest. Each tried to preserve itself at the expense of the rest. The resulting plots and feuds canceled out many of the advantages of central planning. When an offensive began, some held back, while others rushed forth. The Communists, with long experience of "exploiting the enemy's internal contradictions," skipped from one defense sector to the next, making the most of this disunity. "When the Jiangxi enemy attacked," said a veteran, "we fled to Hunan. When Hunan attacked, we fled to Jiangxi."

The pillbox strategy was itself an obstacle to flexible coordination, for though it allowed the Nationalists to garrison troops throughout the mountains, it meant that these troops were scattered over great distances and out of touch with one another. The Communists, in contrast, were organized in small, independent cells that could flit easily across enemy lines. And because the Nationalists had deliberately turned Xiang'egan into a wasteland, their soldiers could no longer provision themselves locally.[35]

Gradually, the guerrillas were able to take advantage of these shortcomings. By late 1935, they had begun to "restore and develop" their area of operations. This revival did not go unnoticed by the Guomindang. In the spring of 1936, Luo Lin, commander of the Xiang'egan pacification zone, announced a series of political measures to stem the Communists' advance. He ordered his officers to "get close to the popular masses and conscientiously lead them" in areas where Communists were reported, and he instructed each county magistrate to found a "roving headquarters" to crush the guerrillas. These small commands were to "extinguish bandit remnants, console refugees, readjust the *baojia* system, train the people . . . , and arrange important policies such as confessions by and conversions of [Communists] and all matters relating to pacifying villages and rehabilitation." At the same time, Luo Lin supervised the setting up of "anti-bandit groups" to infiltrate underground Communist organizations and "fight poison with poison."[36] In all, eleven divisions plus special commandos and local "Peace Preservers" were sent to Xiang'egan in March 1936. The guerrillas countered by splitting the region into four special districts, each with a committee combining political and military functions, and announced the restoration of the Red Sixteenth, which slipped from the mountains to harass the Nationalists in their strongholds.[37]

Fu Qiutao has explained the survival of his guerrillas by their "ties to the masses," as any orthodox Communist must.[38] The region in which Fu's Communists were active was the home of minority people renowned for their fierce spirit and independence. Because most local men were either dead or had left Xiang'egan, women became the guerrillas' mainstay in the Three-Year War. Among the tribespeople of the border area, women enjoyed higher status than in most other parts of China and were better equipped to play a political role after 1934.

Through them, the Party was able to maintain secret and sometimes open organizations in the old soviet heartland around Pingjiang. These women spied and carried goods for the Communists; their sons joined the guerrillas as soon as they reached their teens. "The women are more determined than the men that the government and the land system shall not revert to the old ways," said Deng Feng,[39] a Communist leader from the region, in 1937, "for they have their freedom now."[40] The guerrillas pooled the names of their friends and contacts, "found out who's good and who's bad, got one family to introduce us to the next," and established networks of support.[41] But Fu's talk of "mass ties" is greatly exaggerated, for though underground Communists on the plains risked their lives to transport goods and intelligence to the guerrillas, most people had been cleared from the mountains; the Communists lived for weeks and months on end without ever setting eyes on a worker or a peasant.

The main reason that a core of Communists survived intact after 1934 lay in their commitment to the Party and their spirit of self-sacrifice. They were from several walks of life (workers, peasants, intellectuals, and sons and daughters of the elite) and from different parts of China. They spent the three years before 1937 scattered across the mountains in small bands that acted independently for long periods. Yet they maintained their collective identity as Communists and withstood both arms and bribes at a time when they were out of touch with the world and saw no realistic prospect of an end to their isolation and apparent political futility. Even individuals who strayed from their units kept up the fight in ones and twos. A Xiang'egan Red Army bugler lost in the mountains fought alone for two years, leading villagers to hunt down *tuhao* and seize their property, before finding his way back to the guerrillas.[42]

The Communists in Xiang'egan responded to the shattering defeats of mid-1935 by making politics ever more central to their work. They fused the political, administrative, and military leadership of the revolution. The Party secretary and his committee now made policy, administered it, and fought guerrilla war, and the Xiang'egan Committee continued to proclaim on national political issues. To spread their message to the towns and cities, they held up postmen and slipped revolutionary propaganda into letters. The propaganda was written by hand, on bamboo paper; unlike guerrillas elsewhere, they had no mimeograph machine. They carved slogans like "The Communist Party still exists" and "The Red Army has not gone away" on trees or on bamboo stakes that they stuck in the ground at crossroads or at the entrances to villages.[43] This effort was as important for maintaining their own political self-image and self-respect as for carrying their message abroad.

To the Guomindang, these Communists were bandits. The Communists themselves believed that if they relaxed their vigilance, sheer pressure to survive might turn them into outlaws of the traditional sort, so they constantly reasserted their identity as part of a broader movement by pronouncing on national issues and trying to reestablish contact with the Party's national leaders. On different occasions, they sent people to Xianggan and to Exi (western Hubei), but it was not until mid-1937 that they restored direct contact with the Party center.[44]

Insofar as the Xiang'egan Communists kept up a shooting war after mid-1935, they switched entirely to guerrilla tactics. In March 1936, the committee reorganized its forces into ten independent battalions to facilitate the change.[45] When the enemy entered the mountains, they darted behind the lines to attack railways, roads, or unguarded towns. They fought only when they were sure of victory, avoiding all set patterns and routines. They marched by night over great distances and achieved as much through tricks and ruses as by force of arms. Normally, they avoided roads and moved along remote mountain paths or through forests. They became expert at tracking and at thwarting enemy trackers. Stalking through the trees, they constantly watched and listened for signs of human presence. The renegade teams did likewise. Their maxims were: "Listen for sounds, watch for smoke or fire, follow footprints, lay ambushes."

The guerrillas marched only at night so that the morning dew would not register their footprints. When it snowed, they brushed away their tracks or trod in footprints made by others. When crossing grass, they looked for lines of blades knotted by enemy trackers, retied the knots they had broken, and lifted flattened plants. Where possible, they walked in streams so that they would leave no trail. "Our two legs were our assets," wrote Fu Qiutao, "walking on them was our tactic." They mastered every aspect of the art of moving up, across, and down steep slopes, narrow ledges, sheer rock faces, muddy paths, snow, ice, and rushing water. They trained themselves to march for several days without sleep. Women, too, moved and fought in these columns. Some gave birth on the march, under a tree or by the wayside, with the help of neither medicine nor midwife. Once the baby was born, the mother wrapped it in a cloth and marched on.[46]

At times, searchers swamped the mountains in such large numbers that the guerrillas were pushed back into the remotest peaks and became almost wholly inactive. Then the Committee raised the slogan "Take work to the exterior lines, oppose the conservative ideology of standing siege on the mountain tops." Some cadres slipped secretly into the villages and towns, where they mingled with mountain evacuees. They agitated among local workers and, where possible, founded Party branches. One set up a pottery workers' union with more than one thousand members in Tongguan in Hunan's Yiyang. These White-area bases became an important link in the guerrillas' supply chain. Through them, they obtained newspapers and grain, which their contacts left in caves or hidden about the hills, and intelligence.[47]

If the Nationalists spread propaganda on "suppressing bandits" in such areas, the Communists tried to counter it. In one case, the authorities called a rally to denounce the "bandits." One thousand people attended, but they sat just outside the meeting place in response to a Communist instruction to show passive resistance. "The farmers took their big measures for holding grain and put them up in the trees so that the partisans could hide in them . . . in the daytime," said Deng Feng. "Then at night they led the partisans out to the places where they wanted them to arrest bad *t'uhao* and confiscate their goods."[48]

This move into the towns and villages led to important changes in policy and tactics. One main issue was how to deal with local people who, for various reasons, worked for the authorities. It was necessary to distinguish among them and to avoid indiscriminate "capping" or political stereotyping of these petty officials.

Only a few of these people were committed anti-Communists. Many were turncoats demoralized by the fall of the soviet, crushed by threats or torture, or enticed by the promise of some advantage. Not all had betrayed comrades or led search parties up the mountains. Some had made statements denouncing Communism; others had said or done nothing but had simply gone home and resumed their former lives. So the Communists began to differentiate between deserters and—where killing was an option—killed only the worst offenders.[49]

Lookout teams were another category of petty employees recruited mainly from the villages. Lookouts kept watch from pillboxes, at the entrances to villages, and at road junctions. The Communists worked hard to subvert them. Eventually, most lookouts secretly collaborated with the guerrillas and passed on only trivial intelligence to the authorities. When guerrillas came down to the villages to attack *tuhao* and take their property, some lookouts kept watch for them and raised the alarm only after they had gone.[50]

Communists subverted large parts of the *baojia* system, which was the cornerstone of Guomindang policing in Xiang'egan after 1935. Most *bao* officials were landlords or rich peasants, but not all were equally hostile to the Communists; most *jia* heads were ordinary villagers for whom the post was an inconvenience or an outright burden. Xiang'egan Communists used a mixture of blows and lures to soften up the *baojia* chiefs, killing some who refused to cooperate and befriending others who submitted to them. *Baojia* officials throughout Xiang'egan began working secretly for the Communists. They passed on intelligence, shielded the Communists when necessary, and supplied them with grain, medicine, and other daily needs. In return, the Communists promised not to attack them, seize their property, or expose them to the authorities. They even tried to bring some around to their way of thinking.

In some places, they had undermined the *baojia* system so thoroughly by 1936 that they controlled the appointment of its officers.[51] A Guomindang official reported from Pingjiang on *baojia* heads who had publicly vouched for a local Communist leader. He concluded:

> One can say that they have lost their powers of judgment. . . . Since they dare to pay bail for a notorious bandit, it is obvious that they must normally harbor, connive at, nurture, and aid bandits. . . . It is bad that troops engaged in bandit extermination rarely report bandits, and even worse that when they do catch them, many people come forward to bail them out. I am not complaining about the popular masses vouching for bandits, but I find it odious that *baojia* heads, who are the leaders of the popular masses, should do so. . . . It is not surprising that bandits abound in Pingjiang.[52]

The retreat from "leftism" in Xiang'egan was far from universal. Unlike other stay-behinders, the Communists in Liuyang and Pingjiang maintained the shell of a soviet government until September 1937, with a capital and a system of ministers and deputy ministers, and they continued to use their own names for the fifteen counties that they claimed to hold. But in reality their capital, Huangjintong, was a village, and their ministers either hid out in the mountains with the guerrillas or worked for their living under aliases in the towns and villages.[53]

## GUERRILLA LIFE

The crisis of 1935 resulted in big changes in the Xiang'egan Communists' internal regime. In the past, crises and defeats had led to bitter feuds and purges in the Party. But after the 1935 defeat, purges in Xiang'egan were no longer so bloody or sustained. The Party's ranks, including its leading ranks, were so depleted that most Communists realized that to purge them now would be suicidal. Amid the hardship, this small band of survivors knew a camaraderie foreign to larger, more complex bodies.

Under the early soviet, waverers or deviators were commonly silenced or reformed by violence or threats. During the Three-Year War in Xiang'egan, there were some killings during Party witch-hunts, but torture and slaughter were no longer the chief methods of Party discipline.[54] Survivors writing about this period in Xiang'egan stress the role of education and the purifying and unifying power of equality and democracy. These qualities, understood to mean communalism and participation, were an essential ingredient in the cement that held to a common purpose units scattered widely over the mountains of Xiang'egan and out of touch for long periods. Leaders like Tu Zhengkun spent much of their time between 1934 and 1938 climbing from mountain to mountain to talk doubters around and "help them resolve their ideological problems and material difficulties."[55]

Xiang'egan's Communist leaders met each season or half year, and more frequently when preparing big campaigns, to exchange views on how to maintain a stable "class standpoint" and Party loyalty; on how to find a way to the masses and to improve the guerrillas' well-being; and on how to eradicate "wrong thinking" and "bad style" through study. Reminiscences of this period place a strong emphasis on love and personal loyalty, for it was these qualities as much as political commitment that bound the guerrillas together in the face of adversity. "Ours was a hard and simple life, collectively democratic," wrote Fu Qiutao. "We lived a life of struggle, free and happy. We were all volunteers in the revolution." If there was food, all ate it, if there was a job to do, all joined in doing it. Cadres as well as soldiers took their turn at standing watch or scouting. When there was no action, they sat around swapping jokes and stories, enjoying the carefree life of the greenwood.

The guerrilla bands were families of the revolution, and there was something patriarchal about their society. "Comrades all greatly respected the senior cadre and the chief," wrote Fu Qiutao. "When there was a house to live in, it was reserved for the senior cadre. If you killed a pig while attacking *tuhao*, you sent the heart to the senior cadre. You loved and revered your senior cadre."[56]

Even in the darkest days, the Xiang'egan guerrillas ran a small mountain hospital, a clothing factory, and a portable arsenal. The arsenal was constantly moved around the mountain forests to avoid detection. It produced arms and ammunition for the guerrillas and kept going throughout the Three-Year War, however difficult the conditions. It employed some one hundred workers spread over eight departments (bullets, bombs, tool repair, ironwork, "technology," carpentry, materials, and storage).

Arsenal workers generally supplied their own daily needs by attacking *tuhao* and had their own guards and sentries. The authorities had banned the import of iron, steel, gold, sulfur, and saltpeter into the mountains to stop the Communists manufacturing explosives. Of the necessary materials, only charcoal was freely available, though the mountains had some metals, including gold. But it was usually possible to smuggle in scrap iron and copper from the nearby towns and villages.

Whenever the guerrillas fought, they were under strict orders to retrieve their own spent cartridge cases and, where possible, the enemy's.
Each used case could be recycled several times, producing generation
after generation of bullets that could be shot from Mausers and revolvers if they no longer worked in rifles. Merchants were paid to bring
saltpeter and sulfuric acid to secret collecting points, and sometimes
guerrillas slipped into the nearby towns to buy it in firecracker shops.

The arsenal had no big equipment or machines. Arsenal workers either acquired tools during raids or they improvised, for example by casting in mud rather than in iron. To keep their activities secret, they dug
tunnels that twisted sharply upward just beyond the mouth, trapping
noise and smoke. On the advice of a former medical student who remembered that the leaves and stem of bamboo are cooling agents, they
reduced the amount of smoke by using bamboo charcoal instead of
wood. Conditions in the fiery tunnels were hellish: arsenal men worked
masked and bare-chested. Besides small arms and explosives, they produced home-made trench mortars by using iron wire and hoops to
strengthen steel tubes salvaged from a disused gold mine and then coat-
ing them with rapeseed oil. They also produced the eight-catty shells
fired from these contraptions. They were even said to have turned out
light machine guns. Women and children made the bullets by hand; the
metal and repair work was done by men.[57]

After 1934, the guerrillas lived for months on end off wild grasses,
fruits, and nuts. They harvested what the mountains yielded: spring and
winter bamboo shoots, sweet potato leaves, hemp leaves, plantain stalks,
fir cones, arbutus berries, wild walnuts, wild melon pulp, wild lilies, glu-
tinous rice grass, and wild celery. Instead of salt, they used the sap of the
gallnut flower. When conditions allowed, they sent out rice-buying expeditions that slipped deep into Nationalist territory, moving at night and
lying low by day, running the gauntlet of enemy pillboxes and agents for
thirty miles or more. Whenever rice buyers were out, the guerrillas
stayed on red alert and posted "rice watches" on some high point to
watch for the buyers' return and check that they had picked up no tail.
If the buyers failed to return by an arranged time, the guerrillas struck
camp and moved on.

When they did manage to buy rice, their next problem was how to
cook it. The Nationalists had destroyed all pots and pans in the mountain villages, but most guerrillas had a jar, a tin, or a bowl in which they
not only washed their feet and faces but also boiled their food. When
vessels were not available, they cooked their rice by wrapping it in wet
cloth, encasing the cloth in mud, and covering it with a layer of loose
soil over which they lit a fire. The matches they used to light their fires
were exceedingly scarce and precious. In rainy weather, matches were

wrapped in oiled paper. When one was struck, a human circle formed around it to ward off gusts of air. Lighting fires was dangerous, for smoke and flames could attract attention; the guerrillas cooked in hidden gullies and depressions, using bone-dry wood to reduce the smoke or lighting their fires in mist and fog so that the smoke and fog merged. To reduce the risk still further, they cooked several meals at once, eating cold food on fireless days.[58]

Guerrillas' clothes came from many sources. The same person might wear a homburg, a rich man's silk padded jacket, a leather bandolier, ragged pyjamas, and a pair of handmade straw or bark sandals. Some clothes they seized from *tuhao;* others they stripped from the corpses of enemy soldiers. But most guerrillas wore unpadded clothing even in the depths of winter. As they fled before enemy searchers, their skin and clothes were constantly torn by thorns. Cloth soon became worn and tattered, but every guerrilla had a needle and thread and was adept at using it. Tu Zhengkun, a renowned needleworker, stitched in gold the characters "Persevere to the end" on a guerrilla flag.[59] Guerrillas made or repaired their own clothes from captured cloth: whenever they rested, they set about stitching, patching, and darning. "We wore old things, new things, long things, short things, things of all colors and all shapes," wrote Fu Qiutao. Some guerrillas made themselves quilts and palliasses; most slept on rice straw, branches, or wild grass, under a layer of broad leaves. In winter, they sought out hidden places and slept around small fires when the enemy was not about; otherwise, they huddled together for warmth under the leaves, waking constantly from cold.[60]

Since all houses, shrines, temples, and huts on the mountains had been burned down or blown up, the guerrillas used natural shelters or built shelters deep in the forest. Their "houses" came in a variety of styles. Sometimes they lived in rock caves with leaky roofs and uneven floors decked with moss or bat dung. In winter, these caves bristled with icicles; in summer, they were nicely cool. At other times, they made huts by laying reeds wigwam-style around a central pole or along a crossbeam suspended between two poles. These huts were warm in winter but easily caught fire, and fires were not only dangerous in themselves but could also alert searchers.

The guerrillas' "bamboo houses" were light and airy, and especially comfortable in summer. In winter, they could be reasonably well sealed. Their roofs were made by splitting equal lengths of bamboo down the middle and laying the split segments alternately face down and face up along a sloping bamboo frame, giving a corrugated, glazed-tile effect and good drainage. Splitting bamboo was dangerous, for it produces a report like a rifle shot. The guerrillas found that if they made a small cut at the base of the bamboo and wetted it thoroughly, it split less noisily.

"Cloth houses" were made by attaching weights to the corners of a square of cloth or tarpaulin and slinging it across the branches of trees or across wooden poles, like a stall at a temple fair. Because cloth houses were easily spotted from the air, they had to be camouflaged with leaves or branches. To make an "umbrella house," the guerrillas simply set up a giant umbrella and squatted under it, so that at least their heads were protected from the driving rain. If all else failed, they lived under "tree houses," which took no effort to build and offered some protection against the dew, the snow, and the rain. But trees were a favorite haunt of insects. To keep the ants, centipedes, and caterpillars from dropping down on them and to repel the mosquitoes, the guerrillas hung their trousers from the lowest branches and rested with their heads inside the trouser waists. Living under trees was risky, too: when the leaves rustled, enemy searchers could approach unheard, so the guerrillas posted lookouts in the highest branches. When housing in all its forms was vulnerable or unavailable, the guerrillas scythed away the grass and undergrowth and slept back to back under the stars.[61]

Lacking medicine, they invented their own cures and remedies. They ate chili soup to sweat out their colds and fevers. They healed their wounds as best they could with mountain herbs and salt water. But generally their health was poor. They became thin and sallow and were vulnerable to infections. On forced marches, some collapsed and died.[62]

They improvised everything. Their classroom was a spreading tree, their stools were rocks, their desks were their laps, and they wrote with twigs in the mud or dust. All guerrillas had food pouches in which they carried their rice, salt, chili, clothes, documents, and tools, and which they used as pillows or, when empty, as belts.[63]

Whenever Nationalists appeared in strength, they could inflict devastating defeats on the Communists in Xiang'egan, but once their backs were turned, the guerrillas started to revive. After their victories of mid-1935, the Nationalists withdrew their main-force divisions, so the Communists were able to reassemble scattered forces. In the summer of 1936, when the Nanjing government was briefly challenged by dissident forces in the south, the Communists in Xiang'egan surged up to destroy blockhouses along the border. "There were nine hundred blockhouses around Liuyang alone," said Deng Feng in 1937, "but now only twenty are left. The people, mainly women, carried wood into them and burned them." According to Deng Feng, 1936 was a good year for Communist recruiting in Xiang'egan: more than two thousand men from partisan areas spread over thirty counties came to the guerrillas "spontaneously in small groups of thirty or forty men together."[64] But these recruits were quickly lost, for this figure is twice as large as the entire complement of guerrillas assembled in Xiang'egan for the New Fourth Army.

## XIANG'EGAN AFTER THE XI'AN INCIDENT

In December 1936, Chiang Kai-shek was arrested in Xi'an and then freed. After that, he and the Communists' national leaders resumed their united front, directed now against Japan. The Communists in Xiang'egan read about these events in newspapers obtained by holding up the mail, but they could reconstruct only the broadest outlines of Party policy from them. Still, they could see that big changes were brewing, and they responded swiftly, seeking negotiations on their own account with the local Guomindang while sending people to Yan'an and elsewhere to restore contact with the Party center. Some were killed; others brought back documents. Tu Zhengkun acquired issues of the Party journal *Jiefang*. The provincial committee met several times to discuss their contents.[65]

They decided that in talks, they would offer to drop the Red Army name if the Guomindang agreed to release imprisoned Communists and to finance the guerrillas after reorganization. At a meeting in February 1937, they took the first step down this road when they renamed their guerrillas the Xiang'egan Field Army—a pretentious misnomer for their tiny band of irregulars—after Fu Qiutao and his bodyguard joined up again with the Red Sixteenth near Tongshan in Hubei. At around the same time, Tu took over from Fu as provincial secretary, and Fu appointed himself chair of the "Provincial Soviet"—which did not exist.[66] Their plan was to persuade the Nationalists to recognize Xiang'egan as a "special area," a term they had discovered in the Yan'an documents. This, too, was empty posturing, for they had only the flimsiest territorial base.

Fu and Tu called for the withdrawal of Guomindang troops from guerrilla areas; the ceding to the guerrillas of the small town of Jiayi in Pingjiang as a base from which to start negotiations and as an assembly point; and a Guomindang pledge of no arrests, killings, or "enticement" of guerrillas while they were concentrating and reorganizing.[67] The two sides agreed on these more modest demands, though in practice there were breaches.

Many guerrillas, and even some guerrilla chiefs, found it hard to swallow the idea of cooperating with the Guomindang after ten years of civil war. Their arguments against cooperation were emotional and practical. "We have gone from Jiangxi to Hubei to Hunan," said some, "we have suffered cold, hunger, and terrible ordeals, we have crossed mountains and braved countless dangers. Many comrades have shed their blood and given their precious lives. Many of our parents and wives have been slaughtered or raped. The people have suffered misery. Was all that in vain?" Others pointed out that the guerrillas would be at risk if they left their mountain strongholds. "Unity against Japan is good," they said, "we do not oppose that. But after ten years' civil war, how can we cooperate with Chiang Kai-shek? . . . It would be like sleeping with a wolf or walking with a tiger." But after many meetings, most guerrillas were won round to the united front.[68]

Between April and July 1937, the Nationalist leaders, while still negotiating with Yan'an, had one last try at wiping out the Communists in Xiang'egan. By this time, the guerrillas had again stepped up their attacks and widened their political influence after heavy losses in March and April, when they were reduced to two or three hundred men.[69] On May 15, Hunan's *Dagongbao* published the text of a telegram from Guomindang headquarters in Pingjiang to the "pacification office" in Xiang'egan manifesting exasperation and alarm: "Ever since 1927 there has not been a year free of Communist disturbances. . . . There are still frequent reports of their killing and robbing. They are increasingly active against banks and tea shops. Normally secure areas . . . have been robbed by Communists, with great losses. Vehicles and bridges only ten or even four or five *li* from the cities have been burned. The people are terrified, even in city suburbs and secure areas. Obviously the situation in bandit or semi-Communist areas is even worse. If you do not quickly dispatch a strong force . . . , the consequences will be disastrous."[70]

To fight this resurgence, the Nationalists once again applied a mixture of political and military measures. "County magistrates must regularly go on circuit," advised a security conference. "They must diligently seek out the masses' secrets, diminish the grounds upon which the bandits breed, and strictly prevent bandit organization."[71] The Fiftieth and Seventieth Divisions ran a "bandit-suppression campaign" in the Pingjiang-Liuyang area aimed at wiping out the guerrillas in three months. These were among the Communists' darkest days. Two of their main leaders defected, and others defected in the wake of a bitter quarrel of the sort that had so weakened the Party in the last years of the Central Soviet. The Red Sixteenth was reduced in just a few months from four hundred to one hundred. More than half of the thousand Party members in the region were lost in the repression. Women Communists were hit particularly hard: their numbers fell from several hundred to fewer than ten.[72] Where possible, the guerrillas avoided combat. They "changed guard" with the enemy: "When he enters the mountains, we leave the mountains; when he leaves, we go back in."[73]

But local Party leaders persevered with their preparations to reorganize their forces. They called for vigilance, ordering their scattered units not to assemble until they had received instructions from the provincial committee. They transferred exposed Communists in the towns and villages to the mountains and sent down others to replace them and join those whose cover was still intact. They told the guerrillas to mobilize former

Red Army men, recruit actively in guerrilla areas and White areas, and fight on until a cease-fire was negotiated. On April 22, they ordered attacks on Nationalist garrisons outside guerrilla areas. On May 15, they issued an appeal for unity against Japan. But they continued to call Nanjing "a government of traitors" and grandiosely announced that they would "direct the anti-Japanese activities of the people of the entire province and of all its armed forces." They sent out propaganda teams to paint slogans on walls and scatter leaflets, and they wrote letters to "democratic personages" setting out their new policies. To strengthen their links to the Party center, they sent more people to Yan'an between June and August. These people brought back new directives and personnel.[74]

## NEGOTIATIONS WITH THE GUOMINDANG

On July 13, the Communist Huang Yaonan held talks at Xianzhong in Pingjiang with two staff officers of the Guomindang's Wuhan Field Headquarters. Earlier, the guerrillas had refused to negotiate with two company commanders on the grounds that they were not senior enough. Two days later, these staff officers were joined by a regimental deputy commander of the Fiftieth Division. His appearance amounted to an admission that the campaign to wipe out the Communists had failed. The authorities had no choice but to recognize them. Later, Guomindang negotiators tried to impose their own officers on the reorganized guerrillas. According to one account, this effort failed; but more recent studies criticize Party leaders in Xiang'egan, in particular Fu Qiutao, for accepting this Guomindang condition.[75]

On August 20, the negotiations switched to Wuhan, where Dong Biwu, representing the Party's Central Committee, arranged for the Xiang'egan guerrillas to be reorganized as the First Regiment of the First Detachment of the New Fourth Army and to be sent east to fight the Japanese. In a belligerent statement, the Communists threatened to "severely repress and outlaw" those in Xiang'egan who tried to sabotage the "internal peace" or who said that the Red Army had "capitulated" or been "incorporated." The reorganization would probably have gone far less smoothly without Dong's intervention. In a secret message to Yan'an, Dong complained that the Xiang'egan comrades were immature, failed to understand Party policy, did not realize that there was more to an agreement than a mere cease-fire, and had become completely inactive in order to secure talks (despite their previous bravado). Dong revealed that the Nationalists had sent six officers to supervise the Xiang'egan Red Army, but he added that he was keeping them at arm's length by treating them as "honored guests."[76]

The agreement reached by Dong did not mean that the Communists were prepared to close shop in Xiang'egan, though the Guomindang clearly wanted them to. The Communists tried to deepen their political influence in the area and played up their new status as a unit of the national armed forces. Their August 20 statement hinted at the need for a continuing Communist presence in Xiang'egan, which "guards the middle reaches of the Chang Jiang, lies at the junction of three provinces, controls three railway lines, and occupies a position of great importance." They left behind 140 "revolutionary soldiers and dependents" in Xiang'egan, announced correspondence addresses, and set up liaison stations—soon closed by the authorities—in the border region. These stations made propaganda for the united front and worked for the release of imprisoned Communists.

In Jiayi, a village of one hundred households in Pingjiang, the Party opened a rear office to win recruits, protect Xiang'egan's Special Committee (as the provincial committee was now once again known), and support Red Army dependents and invalid guerrillas. This office coordinated the work of the local Party committees restored in eleven counties, and won more than one thousand new members to the Party. The committees recruited soldiers for the New Fourth Army, maintained contact between its fighters and their families, and arranged for the care of one hundred of its wounded.[77] The office and its director, Tu Zhengkun, became a thorn in the flesh of the Hunan authorities. In 1939, the office was attacked and Tu was killed in an incident that reflected the deterioration of relations between the two parties.

Negotiations started in July 1937 and produced an agreement on reorganization in August, but it was not until January 1938 that the last of the guerrillas quit the mountains and assembled at Jiayi. During those six months, the Hunan authorities tried hard to prise the Xiang'egan Communists free from the national Party and to stop them linking up with Yan'an. Communist negotiators in Xiang'egan were far from safe, even when their security was nominally guaranteed. In Hubei alone, twelve government bodies had powers of arrest, and factional rivalry among them was intense. Even as late as September, Nationalist officials were seizing Communists in the region and trying to incorporate the guerrillas into Government armies.[78] This pressure accounts in part for the Xiang'egan Communists' delay in completing their reorganization. But the guerrillas were also scattered far and wide, so calling them in inevitably took time. One group of fifty guerrillas who had held out independently in northeastern Xiang'egan recruited a further 150 men and joined up with the main Xiang'egan remnant in late 1937 after having been out of touch with it for three years.[79]

## THE GUERRILLAS DEPART

On January 4, 1938, more than 1,100 guerrillas and new recruits gathered in Jiayi's main square for a rally. In August and September, the Xiang'egan Communists had claimed a total of nearly four hundred guerrillas and five hundred political cadres. In the meantime, many cadres had been assigned to the towns and villages to run the regiment's offices and to restore the Party. Seven hundred new recruits had apparently been won since August. This spate of recruitment, too, helps explain the six-month delay between the start of negotiations and the guerrillas' final assembly. Many, perhaps most, of the recruits were fifteen- or sixteen-year-old boys. Some of those assembling in Jiayi wore the gray military uniform of the Guomindang; most wore peasant clothes or a colorful assortment of garments plundered from landlords. Mingling with the guerrillas were the regiment's new student recruits, wearing college uniforms, Sun Yat-sen jackets, long gowns, or Western-style suits. The regiment had just two hundred rifles and three light machine guns. Even some officers lacked weapons. Most guerrillas wore sabers, of which 730 had been newly cast, strapped to their backs; red tassels danced from the sable hafts as they wheeled into the square. Crowds of well-wishers, most of them relatives of the guerrillas, milled around the town, warming their hands on charcoal braziers and handing out straw sandals and cooked rice to the assembling troops.[80]

At one end of the square was a platform emblazoned with the slogan "Eastward to kill the enemy!" On it stood guerrilla leaders and local politicians, including the magistrate. Strings of firecrackers exploded as groups of civilians marched forward with banners reading "National Vanguard," which they presented to the regiment's commanders. Communist speakers praised the united front and urged guerrillas to master new fighting methods for the coming battles. The magistrate said: "You are going to the front to save the nation. Your dependents will be looked after by our local authorities." Eighteen months later, New Fourth Army workers under Tu Zhengkun were massacred in this town.

Fu Qiutao, by then deputy commander of the First Detachment, gave the main speech. He told the guerrillas:

> Today we eat red rice and vegetables. The government has no money, the people eat only hardship. But very soon you will eat good things. The enemy have much bread and milk. We will take it! The Japanese bandits wear leather shoes. They cannot climb mountains. . . . They do not know how to endure hardship. Most are petty traders and petty officials. At home they lead a life of ease. They were forced by the Japanese militarists to come and fight. They like to eat good things every day and to sleep in pleasant rooms. But comrades, we have eaten grass for a month, we have slept in the snowy mountains, we have gone without food for three days, and even

then we could still fight hand-to-hand! . . . You are good guerrilla fighters.
I do not know which of you is best. When you reach the front, you can
compete in killing the enemy. He who kills most is best![81]

Next day, the guerrillas set off through deep snow across the Jiuling
Mountains. Most walked; the entire column had only four horses. Guomindang officers had instructed them to go to the front by way of the cities of Changsha and Wuhan, but they preferred traveling through areas
free of government troops and with some Communist tradition. To
make doubly sure that they were not attacked, they marched mainly by
small paths, high above the valleys.

Ahead of them went teams of propagandists, mostly students, who explained to people along the route that the approaching column was a
unit of the New Fourth Army marching east to fight the Japanese. On
the walls of mountain towns and villages, they painted slogans partly directed at the troops and partly designed to reassure local people that
this was an army of a special sort, which they should trust and help: "Be
polite when talking to the masses! When you borrow things, return
them; when you break things, pay for them! Do not enter the bedrooms
of the people! Do not defecate or urinate just anywhere!" This propaganda worked. As the troops marched by, local people boiled water for
them. In the towns, welcoming firecrackers exploded, and crowds gathered to shout slogans.[82] In just four days, another four hundred recruits
joined the column.[83]

In Yichun, the marchers boarded a train for Shangrao, close to the
New Fourth Army's main staging ground at Yansi in Wannan. Most had
never seen a train, let alone ridden in one. A message from New Fourth
Army headquarters warned their leaders that along the line at Yuan-
zhou, two Nationalist regiments were waiting to destroy them. The
Communists took steps to defend themselves, mounting machine guns
on the locomotive and posting armed guards at the windows of each
compartment. They persuaded the engine crew to speed up at Yuan-
zhou and go through without stopping; if an ambush ever was intended,
it failed. At Yushan in Jiangxi, they left the train and marched on to
Kaihua in Zhejiang, where they were met by Chen Yi, their new commander. After a few days' rest, they marched north to Yansi, and their
three years of separation from the Party ended.[84]

## PERSPECTIVES ON THE THREE-YEAR
## WAR IN XIANG'EGAN

The Three-Year War in Xiang'egan was begun by a tiny handful of veterans who had survived the shattering defeats of the early summer of

1934. They were cut off from outside help and advice several months earlier than similar remnants elsewhere. At first, the Nationalists withdrew their main force to destroy the Central Soviet to the south; during this brief lull, Fu and Tu assembled five thousand new troops to make good their previous losses. But they could not withstand the suppression drive that began in June 1935. Within a few weeks, their army of raw recruits and captured soldiers had melted away as a result of the overconfidence and tactical errors of its leaders. After this second rout, the Communists in Xiang'egan scaled down their goals. They were pursued less often, less systematically, and by smaller numbers, so they were occasionally able to surge up again in old soviet strongholds.

Their campaign must be understood in the context of the earlier history of the Communist movement in Xiang'egan. The relationship between the 1928 Pingjiang Insurrection and the emergence of the Party's base in the surrounding countryside has been the subject of a scholarly debate in China. Before Peng Dehuai's disgrace, many saw the base as an outcome of the insurrection; after Peng's fall from power, most ignored the insurrection's role in the sovietization of Xiang'egan. Today, historians argue that though the insurrection played a "key and direct" role in creating the Xiang'egan base, the Party's long-term work in the region was crucial for the base's further survival, and they have begun to pay more attention to internal developments in the base after 1928.[85]

This new approach is more pragmatic and fruitful than earlier, politically motivated explanations. However, this new concern for balance should not blind us to the way in which the creation of the base affected its later evolution. The Xiang'egan Red Army was founded by professional outsiders and soon drawn off to fight in areas thought to be of more direct strategic value. The Party's roots in the Xiang'egan mountains were less deep and sturdy than in other regions. After the defeat of 1935, Communists retreated to the greenwood and were more preoccupied with preserving their own ranks than with developing strategic initiatives like the plainclothes movement in Eyuwan or the Minxi'nan campaign against Japan. Their retreat from "leftism" was incomplete: they kept the pretense and trappings of soviet government even in the forests. Still, within their own small circles, they developed a strong camaraderie and largely avoided the venomous purges that convulsed stay-behinder units elsewhere. Without the flinty resolve of Fu Qiutao, whose constant refrain was "Make a decision and stick to it," it is unlikely that they would have held out as successfully as they did.[86] In the end, they assembled a regiment for the New Fourth Army. But fewer than half of these soldiers had fought in the Three-Year War, and only a tiny handful were veterans of the soviet; most were recruited after the guerrillas came down the hills to join the united front.

# Xianggan:
# The Peasant Patriarch

◆　◆　◆

Xianggan is the abbreviated name of the border region between Hunan (Xiang) and Jiangxi (Gan) (map 10). It includes the site of the Jinggang base, the first of the Chinese Communist Party's independent armed regimes. Guerrillas in Xianggan after 1934 were active in Chaling, Yongxin, Lianhua, Fenyi, Anfu, Youxian, Anren, Ninggang, Pingxiang, and Yichun.[1]

Hills and mountains cover more than 85 percent of Xianggan and 90 percent of the old soviet areas of Ninggang and Lianhua. The Jinggang Mountains form part of the middle section of the Luoxiao range, which runs along the entire border, from Guangdong in the south to Hubei in the north. The Jinggang, "a huge natural fortress amid a cluster of loping ranges, an amoebic spill of rocks, crags, gullies,"[2] are typical of this central section of the border region. Their upper slopes, rising to more than six thousand feet, are cloaked in thick forests of pine and bamboo interspersed with camphor and the fiery red of the feng tree. These forests are the home of wild pigs, monkeys, and rare species of musk deer, game birds, and civets that sometimes ended up cooking in the guerrillas' oil drums or on their bamboo spits. Dangerous predators, including tigers and leopards, prowl among the trees. The mountain climate is generally mild and wet, though the seasons vary: winter brings snows and frost, summer sometimes oppressive heat. Rain falls two days out of three, storms alternating with light drizzle; between June and September, thunderstorms are common.

Because of the mild temperature and heavy rain, vegetation flourishes on the mountain slopes. Among the several thousand plant species in Xianggan are numerous medicinal herbs and roots that provide a living for collectors. Valleys and ravines overhung by steep cliffs, bristling

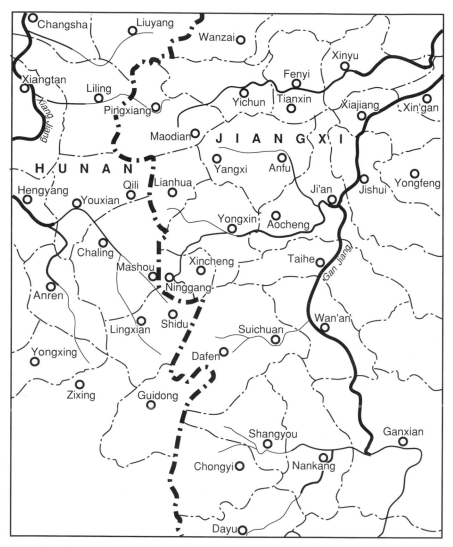

Map 10. The Xianggan Soviet and guerrilla area. *Based on a map in Hunan sheng caizheng ting, eds., 1986.*

with scrub and oily bushes, drive into the round hills and smaller mountains that flank the massive central peaks. Hidden among the cliffs are wells of flatter ground. These tiny enclosures cradle human settlements where mountain people wrest a scant harvest of rice, sweet potatoes, and pulse from the red earth, poorly watered despite abundant rain on the surrounding slopes.[3]

In October 1927, Mao led an army of one thousand Hanyang miners, peasant guards from northeastern Hunan, and Nationalist mutineers from Wuhan into the Jinggang gorges to set up a Red state. The local people, who lived in crushing poverty, suffered still more from the cordon thrown round Mao by government troops. These peasants husked their rice by hand with wooden pestles; they did not use the wheel, and they struck fire from stones. Their productivity was desperately low: just fifty kilograms of grain per *mu* in some villages, and rarely more than 150. At least 98 percent of people in the villages and market towns were illiterate or only semiliterate: for them, the Red Army, when it came, was not only a vehicle for class struggle but also a source of knowledge and instruction. In the weeks and months after October 1927, thousands more insurgents found their way to Mao, including three thousand under Zhu De in April 1928. This Zhu-Mao army could barely live off the region's tiny pockets of farmland; Mao strongly doubted that small Red regimes could last without a revolution throughout China.[4]

In a report written in November 1928, Mao explained why this middle tract of the Luoxiao, with its center at Ninggang, was "the most suitable [place] for our armed independent regime": its natural features and configuration were better suited to irregular warfare than the section to the north, which was in any case too close to the big political centers of the Guomindang; it had a better "mass base" than the southern section and was better placed for influencing Hunan and Jiangxi and, in particular, their lower river valleys.[5] The Jinggang Mountains commanded formidable natural defenses. The five passes to the central eminence were high and narrow: it is said that "one man can hold them against ten thousand." The long corridors linking the massif to the plains taper quickly among stout walls that are easy to defend and difficult to attack. Elsewhere, thin winding necks open unexpectedly into secluded valleys. Before 1949, there were no modern roads in these mountains. Transport through them was by foot or animal, along small roads, footways, and twisting goat paths.[6] For Mao, this seclusion had two advantages. It immured him against the Nationalists, and it screened him from orthodox hard-liners in his own Party who repudiated his innovations and wrote off his army as a "rifle movement."[7]

## THE PARTY AND THE HAKKAS

The mountains into which Mao fled, though poor, were no "blank page," and at first his ragged column of outsiders was in no position to scour them clean and paint the "newest, most beautiful pictures" on them. The villages of the central Jinggang massif, with their population of a few thousand souls, were territory of the Hakkas,[8] a people who, according to early observers of "the character of races," are "the cream of the Chinese," "a distinct and virile strain," fearless, self-reliant, and possessed of "military genius" and "the love of liberty which characterizes mountaineers the world over."[9] Several million Hakkas live along the Xianggan border. They are mainly descendants of northern Chinese who migrated into this region several centuries ago, during the Song and Ming dynasties. They are especially numerous in the counties around Jinggang. In Ninggang, two-fifths of the population, or fifteen thousand people, are Hakkas. However, because they constitute a smaller proportion of the overall population than Hakkas in more southerly counties of Jiangxi or northeastern Guangdong, they have suffered more from discrimination and exploitation.[10]

In the 1920s, the ethnic boundary between these *ke* (guest people) and the *tu* (native inhabitants) was razor-sharp. The Hakkas, as latecomers to southern China, generally live on the barren uplands and are excluded from the more fertile plains, which remain in *tu* hands. Hakkas were renowned as clannish, contentious, and unassimilable. They maintained their own customs, their own language, and a strong sense of ethnic solidarity.[11] In Xianggan, the *tu-ke* antagonism was particularly acute. "Their traditional feuds are deep-seated," wrote Mao in 1928, "and they sometimes erupt in violent clashes."[12] The government in Ninggang was controlled by *tu*. Hakka self-defense militias clashed bloodily and repeatedly with the government, and with other local *tu*, over control of land, forests, and schools.

The Communists in Xianggan became entangled in this ethnic conflict between highlanders and lowlanders. The Communist movement in Ninggang was originally led by young *tu* intellectuals like Long Chaoqing, who sought allies among the *ke* and persuaded the *ke* leader Yuan Wencai to come down from the mountains and join the revolution. In late 1926, Communist agitators exploited *ke* grievances in Ninggang to overthrow the *tu*-dominated local government. Shortly afterward, *tu* guides escorting White troops into Ninggang "once again stirred up the conflict between the native inhabitants and the settlers." At first, the Communists had managed to persuade *tu* peasants to band together with the *ke* against *tu* landlords, but when rumors spread that the *ke* were bent on murdering all *tu*, pro-Communist *tu* peasants defected to the

Whites; the Whites were routed, the *tu* fled, and the *ke* seized their property. The ethnic rift widened in 1927, when Nationalist forces swept down on *ke* strongholds in Xianggan.[13]

These ethnic squabbles spilled over into the Communist Party. Party leaders like Long Chaoqing, who were the kin of local powerholders, came under pressure to oppose *ke* "excesses." In the mountain villages, most of which were single-lineage settlements, branch meetings were often virtually indistinguishable from clan gatherings. The Red Army found it increasingly hard to shake off its *ke* identity and to wrest *tu* lineages from the grip of the power elite.[14] Worse still, having alienated many *tu*, they were soon to alienate the *ke*.

The Hakkas of the Jinggang were led by two bandit chiefs, Yuan Wencai and Wang Zuo, whose influence extended far beyond their mountain haunts. Yuan, who joined the Party in the autumn of 1926, was a graduate of middle school; Wang was an unlettered tailor. Both had several concubines and received monthly protection money from local landlords; both were born in 1898. According to Agnes Smedley, local peasants regarded Yuan and Wang as "friends and leaders who 'robbed the rich to give to the poor.' " Each commanded three hundred Hakka irregulars with "sixty rifles in bad repair."

After Mao arrived in Xianggan, Yuan and Wang brought him one thousand recruits who were incorporated wholesale into his "First Division of the First Peasants and Workers' Army." In May 1928, the "intellectual" Yuan was appointed chair of the Xianggan Workers, Peasants, and Soldiers' Government.[15] In June, land was divided, and local soviet governments were founded in the Jinggang base, now at its peak. In the following months, Nationalist armies in Hunan and Jiangxi combined in a series of drives against the Jinggang base; on January 14, 1929, it was evacuated by 3,600 troops of the Fourth Red Army under Mao, Zhu De, and Chen Yi, who went to Gannan and Minxi. At first, they intended to return to Xianggan after drawing off the Nationalists and replenishing supplies. But after learning of the fall of the Jinggang base and seeing for themselves that conditions were better in Gannan and Minxi, they decided on March 20, 1929, to abandon their old stronghold.[16]

Shortly before Mao and Zhu left, Peng Dehuai had joined them in the Jinggang Mountains with his Fifth Red Army. Mao and Zhu left Peng behind to defend the base when they withdrew, but Peng spent much of 1929 outside it, fleeing suppression drives and revisiting his old haunts in Xiang'egan.[17] (Later, Mao apologized to Peng for abandoning him; Peng refused to accept the apology.)[18] During these evacuations, civilians left behind in the base suffered terribly at the hands of the occupying troops. Among those who remained was Wang Zuo, the Hakka tailor.

The other Hakka leader, Yuan Wencai, had been induced to leave with Mao, who believed that Yuan's absence "would help reduce trouble in the Jinggang Mountains"; but Yuan deserted and returned to Xianggan "with ulterior motives."[19]

To keep the Hakkas loyal, the Communists needed to stay on good terms with Yuan and Wang, who "if it pleased their fancy . . . could lead the peasants against the Red Army." Without Yuan and Wang's cooperation, it was virtually impossible to enter the Jinggang Mountains. Under Mao, Hakka carriers "going in and out of the mountains, in and out of the plains surrounding the fortress heights, along paths known only to them and to salt smugglers, became an essential network and liaison." But the network depended on Yuan and Wang's goodwill.[20]

On February 23, 1930, Yuan and Wang were killed. In 1936, Mao attributed their deaths to peasants who had stopped being "faithful Communists" and had "returned to their bandit habits," but in reality, they died as a result of actions by the troops of Peng Dehuai.[21] Many Communists today deplore the killing of Yuan and Wang, who are seen as the innocent victims of a tragic error; both were rehabilitated as martyrs in the early 1950s.[22]

Why were the two men killed? At the time of their deaths, they were accused of opposing land revolution, opposing soviets, and colluding with the enemy, but these charges are groundless. At Mao's urging, Wang Zuo distributed more than one thousand *mu* of his paddy to peasants, and Yuan was chair of the Xianggan Red government. There is no evidence that either man colluded with the Nationalists; they were obeying orders to go to Yongxin when they died. Thirty years later, Peng Dehuai was accused of killing Yuan and Wang to get their troops. Today, Chinese scholars explain the Yuan-Wang incident as a combined result of the "left" line of the Sixth Congress, repercussions in the Party and Peng's Fifth Army of the antagonism between "settlers" and "natives" in Xianggan, and Yuan and Wang's indiscipline and "feudal" attitudes.

Yuan and Wang mistrusted the Communists after discovering that a paragraph in the resolution of the Party's Sixth Congress on "the need to win over the rank-and-file of bandit troops and isolate their chieftains" had been concealed from them. Many Communists in turn deeply mistrusted Yuan and Wang. Most of Yuan's Thirty-second Regiment was *ke;* almost all the members of the Party's Ninggang Committee were *tu*. In 1927, the idea took root in the Xianggan Communist movement that "the Party is *tu*, the gun is *ke*." ("A gun is a good thing," Wang told Mao. "You can get both food and revenge with it.") While Mao was in Xianggan, relations between *ke* and *tu* were tolerably good, but even so there were instances of friction, for example when *ke* braves torched a famous *tu* academy in Ninggang. Friction increased after Mao left Xianggan, for

Yuan was loyal to Mao rather than to the Party. "He believed only in individuals, not the masses," according to one of his 1929 critics, and he is
accused of saying "I only obey Commissioner Mao."[23]

This mutual mistrust ended in the confrontation in which the two
men died, whereupon some of their followers "broke through and went
back into the mountains." This incident greatly weakened the Red Army's influence in Xianggan. It "shook the confidence of some Jinggang
masses in the Party" and caused them to "form obstacles to the later construction of the base." Wang Zuo's older brother Wang Yunlong and
Yuan's company commander became sworn enemies of the Red Army.
They held out in different parts of the Jinggang Mountains in league
with other minor powerholders against repeated attempts by the Red
Army to dislodge them. Only a few of Yuan and Wang's supporters
found their way back to the ranks of the Red Army. Some Communist
supporters in the Jinggang villages were killed.[24]

Not until twenty years later, in 1949, were these bandit remnants
cleared from their Jinggang strongholds by the People's Liberation
Army, after the fall of Ji'an in July. The campaign to flush out the one
thousand "stubborn desperadoes" holed up in the Jinggang had many
features in common with the Nationalist campaign against the Communists in Xianggan after August 1934. But whereas the mop-up that
started in 1934 lasted on and off for three years and still failed, the mop-
up of 1949 succeeded in just weeks. In 1949, the Communists were able
to mobilize local communities to climb mountains, observe movements,
trail fugitives, and persuade the bandits to surrender.[25] Local people cooperated in the hope that these efforts would bring lasting peace. As for
the bandits, they could see no future in the mountains; they lacked the
unshakable optimism of the Communists in 1934.

The killing of the "forest outlaws" Yuan and Wang was more than a
regrettable mistake. It symbolized the start of the Red Army's transition
from a band of runaways to a complex, powerful machine capable of
centralizing and directing the revolution throughout China. It also announced the Party's declaration of independence from its base in the villages. In Gannan in 1929, Mao listed the "mistaken ideas" upon which
the Party must turn its back: individualism, the purely military viewpoint, a mercenary mentality, ultra-democracy, absolute egalitarianism,
subjectivism, and the ideology of roving rebel bands.[26] Mao's list of bad
habits reads like a character sketch of Yuan and Wang. The Party now
saw the Red Army as the revolution's essential and main instrument,
with the soviet as its disposable provider.

This vision was realized in its purest form in Gannan, but Xianggan
did not escape its implications, as the removal of Yuan and Wang
shows. By cutting out these self-willed middlemen, the Party simplified

its link to the villages, though at the cost of much goodwill. Thereafter, Xianggan figured at two levels in Party deliberations. For minor Party officials intent on making the base work, Xianggan was the sum of its villages and people, whose competing interests had to be sifted, weighed, and balanced by a combination of bureaucracy, violence, and persuasion. Far above the heads of these officials, the Party's central leaders treated Xianggan as an abstract symbol in a complicated power equation, as one square in a giant chess game between Reds and Whites. Where the needs of these two levels clashed, the higher took precedence: the Party purged those who thought differently (and who said so).

## XIANGGAN IN THE EARLY 1930S

The history of the Xianggan base after Mao's departure was largely dictated by events in the wider arena. Xianggan was no longer a vital focus of the Chinese Communist movement or a source of new ideas for it. In late 1929, Peng Dehuai's Fifth Red Army tried to link Xianggan with Xiang'egan and E'nan (southern Hubei) to the north into a single expanse of territory stretching from the Jinggang Mountains to the banks of the Chang Jiang. In January 1930, the Special Committees of Xianggan and Ganxi set up a new Ganxi'nan Committee. By the early summer of 1930, the Xianggan base was nearing the peak of its strength and had been successfully connected with Xiang'egan. But according to Peng Dehuai, "local work with the people . . . failed to keep up with the situation. Only some propaganda work was done." Instead, Red forces in the region were mobilized by the Central Committee to attack key cities like Wuchang and Changsha. Though Peng's Fifth Red Army was only seven thousand strong in June, it was ordered to grow to fifty thousand by August. Peng and others knew that these plans were unrealistic and "adventurist," but they loyally tried to implement them. Later in 1930, "localists" in Peng's army opposed marching east from Xianggan to create bases "in the vast expanse stretching from the Ganjiang River eastward to the seacoast" and proposed instead staying along the border to fight guerrilla war. But after an "intense ideological struggle" these objectors were "turned around."[27]

In October 1931, a Xianggan Soviet government was set up on Central Committee instructions under Wang Shoudao and Yuan Desheng. The base grew rapidly. At one point, it comprised parts of twelve counties, and its "administrative range" (including guerrilla areas) covered twenty-five counties with a population exceeding one million. By August 1932, Xianggan's newly formed Eighth Red Army, later to become the Red Seventeenth Division, had 13,700 men.

In the summer of 1933, the Xianggan Provincial Committee was dissolved because it was "right opportunist," and a new committee was set up under Ren Bishi. At the same time, Xianggan's Seventeenth Division was merged with Xiang'egan's Sixteenth Corps.[28] The resulting Sixth Red Army Corps was unable to stem the Nationalist advance during Chiang Kai-shek's Fifth Encirclement. The Xianggan base shrank rapidly in late 1933 and early 1934. In July 1934, the central base in Yongxin fell. A month later, Ren Bishi and Xiao Ke abandoned Xianggan on Central Committee instructions and set off at the head of an army of ten thousand to found a new base in Xiangzhong (central Hunan). (In fact, they ended up in eastern Guizhou, where they fused with He Long's Second Army Corps to form the Second Front Army.)[29]

The Jinggang Mountains were the cradle of the Chinese Red Army, of land revolution, and of Red power in China. Under the Mao cult, they were consecrated as a Party shrine to which busloads of revolutionary tourists sped along a new asphalt highway. Party hagiographers wrapped the Jinggang Mountains in a mystical nimbus and represented the early Jinggang Soviet as the armed struggle's sacred prologue, uncontaminated by degenerate lesser leaders, a period in which the prophet Mao had revelations that allowed him to break with the errors of the past and to bring in the millennium.

The hallowing of Jinggang was inevitable and even apt; it was, after all, a place where great inventions of the Chinese Revolution were made, tested, and refined by great early leaders of the Party. But the Jinggang legend served as much to obscure the truth as to dignify it. Because of it, Chinese historians were obliged either to ignore the further development of the Jinggang base and the mess left behind in it after the departure of the Zhu-Mao army or to make an ahistorical separation between the Jinggang and Xianggan periods and to gloss over the distinct origins of the Xianggan base by treating it as part of a wider system of bases, including Xiang'egan, Xiangnan, and Ganxi'nan. Few historians have analyzed the Xianggan base in independent terms, though the Xianggan Provincial Committee and Soviet Government never saw themselves as part of the Central Soviet, from which they were separated by the Gan Jiang.[30] Partly as a result of this retrospective conflation of Xianggan with other bases, research on it began later than research on other early sites of the revolution. For a time, comparatively little was published on its history since 1929, including the period between 1934 and 1937.

Because the distinction between the Jinggang and Xianggan bases is quite arbitrary, historians find it hard to agree on a date for the beginning of the Xianggan base. Possible dates include January 1929, when

Mao left; May 10, 1929, when the Fourth Extended Congress of the Xianggan Special Committee redrew the boundaries of the base and proposed moving to Yongxin; October 1929, when the move to Yongxin was completed; February 7, 1930, when the Special Committees of Xianggan, Ganxi, and Gannan merged; or August 1931, when the Xianggan Provincial Committee was provisionally established.[31] In reality, the Xianggan base was a continuation and development of the Jinggang base, and it is hard to say where one stopped and the other started.

The question of the relationship between the two bases is relevant in several ways to a study of the Three-Year War in Xianggan. Such a study must examine connections between the Jinggang and Xianggan periods of the revolution to explain the problems that beset the Party in the region. Jinggang's sacred prologue did not stand by itself but set themes for the main drama in Xianggan. During the Cultural Revolution, it was obligatory in China to blame Peng Dehuai for alienating Yuan and Wang, but it is now clear that Mao, too, mistrusted them (he thought that Yuan was "very sly and always up to something"). Mao publicly backed their eventual killing (though within the Party he is said to have criticized it, and, unlike Peng, he opposed killing them during the earlier discussion in Jinggang of the Sixth Congress resolution).[32]

The purging of Yuan and Wang foreshadowed the bloody purges in Xianggan in the early 1930s, first of the ranks and later of the leaders, that were a principal cause of the collapse of the base in 1934.[33] In the short term, alienation of Wang's Hakka irregulars bequeathed the Xianggan Communists with a minor nuisance. In late 1934, this minor nuisance became a major obstacle for the Communists when they were chased into the peaks. The prologue and the main acts of the Xianggan drama were intimately linked, and the epilogue (between 1934 and 1938) was staged in the same small section of the border as the prologue, after the base had shrunk back to its founding core; except that by then the Red guerrillas had forfeited their ties to the Jinggang Hakkas and lived—more so than Red Army remnants in other of the Party's former bases in southern China—as wild men, skulking in mountain hideouts. Elsewhere, strategic alliances sealed by stay-behinders with local outlaws were crucial to the Party's survival and eventual comeback after 1934, but in the Jinggang Mountains, the Red Army rearguard had no such links.

After Mao left the Jinggang Mountains, the drawing of Xianggan into a wider system of bases promoted the Party's abstraction from the villages. Xianggan occupied strategic ground between Gannan and Xiang'-egan and formed part of the western defenses of the Central Soviet. It played a crucial role in defeating the Fourth Encirclement, when the main body of Nationalist troops bore down on the Central Soviet from the west. Xianggan's sacrifices helped stave off the Central Soviet's collapse, but local Communists in Xianggan, not always convinced of the need for sacrifices, wanted more attention paid to the interests of the base itself. This division between localists and absolutists began with Mao, who unexpectedly abandoned the Jinggang base (taking with him the bothersome Yuan) after telling people that he would return to it.[34]

## THE LONG MARCH FROM XIANGGAN

The Central Committee's decision to evacuate Xianggan, two months before the main body of Long Marchers left the Central Soviet, was badly received by those left behind in the base. Even the graduating class of Xiao Ke's military academy—the future elite of Red Xianggan, selected for their "class awareness" and drilled in "revolutionary optimism"—were "full of doubts" when news of the decision reached the base; the same people were to lead the main force of the rearguard after August 1934.

Their misgivings about the evacuation were well founded. The notice of it from Ruijin was preposterously (though typically) short.[35] In the previous few months, military pressure on Xianggan had built up greatly as Nationalist concentrations blockaded the region to cut it off from Ruijin. All county capitals were now in Nationalist hands.[36] Some troops of the Xianggan Military District and the old Red Fifth Regiment were reorganized as part of the Sixth Red Army Corps and joined in the withdrawal. The only main-force unit left behind in the base was the new Red Fifth Regiment, formed around fresh graduates of the military school. This regiment had 1,500 troops; four other independent regiments had between three and four hundred soldiers each.[37] Elsewhere in the region were a further two to three thousand local guerrillas, "refugee guerrillas," and Party officials, making a total of up to five thousand Red troops in all.[38]

Party and soviet organization in Xianggan was still "rather healthy" at the time of the evacuation, and Tan Yubao, chair of the Xianggan Soviet and leader of the Three-Year War in Xianggan, forecast a period of quiet, thinking that the Nationalists would be drawn away by the Red Sixth. Others, however, thought that things were likely to get rough.[39] They were right. Most of the base collapsed soon after August 1934, and the local Party was plagued by defectors who betrayed its closest secrets to the Guomindang. Despite his public optimism, Tan Yubao had doubts about the future of the base. Three years later, during a famous confrontation with Chen Yi, he implied that the withdrawal was cowardly and "flightist."[40] Even today, some Communists believe that the Sixth Red Army Corps' move west was unnecessary and wrong. Most, however, defend it in terms of grand strategy, meaning the coordination of dispositions of strength on major and minor battlefields across the entire war theater. According to this view, Ren and Xiao's march west helped create the conditions to ensure the success of the Long March, just as the success of the Long March helped create the conditions for the survival of units on minor battlefields like Xianggan.[41] This reasoning rests on an erroneous equation of politics and warfare. But even in the terms of that equation, it can be faulted: the Long March, far from saving the Xianggan base, led to its collapse.

In the autumn of 1934, shortly after Ren and Xiao left Xianggan, Party officials converged on Niutian at the border between Yongxin, Wan'an, and Suichuan after destroying archives and freeing or killing captured Nationalist officers and other prisoners.[42] By October 1934, the whole of Yongxin was in White hands, and most of the Communist organization lay in ruins. Only a few tracts of mountain remained open to the guerrillas, mainly in the Wugong range in Anfu.[43]

The Nationalists withdrew their Hunan Army from Xianggan to chase Xiao Ke, but they left behind three to five strong divisions scattered across Ji'an, Anfu, Suichuan, and Taihe.[44] These divisions advanced on Communist positions from the north and east, guided through the mountains by local anti-Communists returning from exile in Ji'an, Ganzhou, and Changsha. The refugees, mainly landlords, formed restitution leagues that led efforts to mop up recaptured villages and took cruel revenge on their political opponents.[45]

In some parts of southern China, particularly in core areas of the old Minxi base, the Communists prevented the return of farmland to the landlords and the collection of rent and back rent after 1934. But in Xianggan, counterrevolution was radical and total. In Yongxin alone, 110,000 *mu* of land were taken back, and in just three districts of Yongxin, seventeen hundred tons of grain were seized as back rent.[46] Communists, former officials of the soviet, beneficiaries of land reform, and the families and lineages of these people were singled out for the harshest treatment. They had to pay big fines, including "surrender expenses," and were frequently pressed into "punitive coolie service." Their houses were easily recognizable: they were made to pin "moral renewal" certificates on their doors and to hang out red signs marked "special household." These households bore the brunt of the raids and searches.[47]

Together with regular troops, the returning legions split the former base into more than fifty small compartments that they combed "like a woman combs her hair, with numerous pulls," to remove all traces of the "Communist infestation." They evacuated all settlements of fewer than fifty households and forbade the inhabitants of these settlements to re-enter the mountains. They burned and killed wherever they met the least resistance.[48] A directive issued on May 29, 1935, by the authorities in Youxian and published in Hunan's *Dagongbao* gives some flavor of Nationalist methods during the "pacification" of Xianggan:

> [In this region] the forest is thick and the mountains are high. They are often used as hideouts by Communist bandits. There are many immigrants and outsiders here who are susceptible to manipulation by the bandits. To destroy the bandit lairs, first cleanse the area as follows: evacuate the people so that the Communists can no longer hide [among them] or secretly communicate [through them]; and throw a tight cordon round the area so that all salt, rice, and other necessary goods are blocked and communications are broken. Order local legions to carry out this directive to the letter. . . . If men or women are discovered [in the mountains] after the end of the month, troops must shoot them down as bandits, with absolutely no exceptions. All these points should be conveyed to district heads in the second and fourth district, who should instruct *baojia* heads in the villages to act accordingly.[49]

During this cleanup, the government invested massive resources in road-building in Hunan and Jiangxi to reduce their isolation from neighboring provinces and their vulnerability to Communist subversion. In Hunan, almost twice as much road (1,528 *li*) was laid in 1935 as in the previous three years combined. In the two years after 1934, four major highways were completed between Hunan and the provinces of Jiangxi, Guizhou, Guangxi, and Sichuan. The cost to human life and property was enormous. Six thousand people died building the road between Hunan and Sichuan. In June 1935, local people whose land had been taken over were waiting (in vain) for compensation totaling more than $714,000.[50]

## THE COMMUNISTS FLEE THROUGH
## THE MOUNTAINS

To escape the "pacifiers," Communists in Xianggan set out on a series of forced marches through the mountains. The movements of the various units on the loose in Xianggan were uncoordinated. Contact was lost between Xianggan and Xiao Ke soon after the provincial committee lost its radio in January 1935 (though not before the Xianggan leaders had received news of Xiao's merger with He Long). Contact among Xianggan remnants was also broken by the cordons and blockades.[51] In November 1934, central Party leaders ordered the Xianggan Soviet government and its core units, three thousand strong, to leave Xianggan and head south toward Guangdong, presumably to join the First Front Army on the Long March. But this plan to abandon Xianggan came to nothing, for their way was blocked and they were forced to return north.[52] The provincial committee moved to the Wugong Mountains, seeding the Yangmei Mountains along the way with guerrillas and picking up one hundred fugitives from the Central Soviet under Lu Wenxin.

The central peaks of the Wugong range rise to some six thousand feet. The mountain slopes are covered by forests so thick that visibility in some places is limited to four paces. They are warrened with natural caves, some big enough to hold fifty people.[53] Revolutionaries had been active in the Wugong region ever since 1928. When Communists first arrived in this old soviet base at the start of the Three-Year War, dozens of ancestral halls and one hundred or so monasteries, nunneries, and temples, some built in the Tang dynasty, adorned the cool lower slopes, where crowds of pilgrims from the surrounding provinces congregated each spring.[54] The region's natural defenses made it an ideal hiding place for the Xianggan leaders, who hoped to use it as a base from which to launch movements in the ten counties knit together by the mountains.[55]

But as enemy pressure and ill-advised Communist countertactics led to further losses and defeats, the guerrillas split into even smaller units and scattered over an even wider area to "narrow the target."[56] One group of a dozen headed for the Central Soviet to look for Xiang Ying and Chen Yi, but they were wiped out on the way.[57] Other tiny groups fled in disorder through the mountains, exhausted after an unsuccessful expedition, without maps or guides, in search of Fang Weixia and Cai Huiwen in Xiangnan. (Xiang Ying had sent Fang and Cai to Xiangnan to link up with the Xianggan Communists; a small party of Fang and Cai's men reached the Xianggan Provincial Committee in early 1935, but further contact was never established despite later missions.)[58] By the spring of 1935, fewer than one thousand of the original three thousand troops left in the base in the autumn of 1934 remained under arms. The Red Fifth had lost two-thirds of its complement, and the Red Third was down to a few dozen; worst hit was the Red First, which had just six survivors. Among those killed was Peng Huiming, the Red Fifth's commander.[59]

Later studies and reminiscences blame these losses on a combination of "flightism" and "left adventurism," including "seesaw battles fought from fixed positions."[60] True, various bad decisions contributed to the rout. At one point, two thousand troops of the Red Third and Fifth Regiments massed for a battle in which they suffered heavy losses (though in the course of that defeat they destroyed an enemy battalion).[61] But even a general of genius would have found it hard to hold out against such odds. By March 1935, the provincial committee had lost all but fifty of the eight hundred troops it had commanded just a month before.[62]

In some of the older soviets, crowds of Communist supporters and people incriminated by association with the Communists fled to the mountains to seek protection from the guerrillas. "Many basic cadres and basic masses escaped to us from enemy-occupied areas," wrote Tan Tangchi. "They could feel secure nowhere. They had no grain and ate wild plants instead. Sometimes, if children cried while crossing enemy lines after dark, their parents would stifle them to death so that they could reach us and make revolution."[63]

This trust and sacrifice often went unrewarded. Some guerrilla leaders saw camp followers as a burden and slipped away without informing them. Many of those thus abandoned were caught or shot on sight as they travailed through the mountains. Other guerrilla leaders besieged by refugees "educated" them to go home. "We told them that we would never forget them," said Liu Peishan, "and we gave them travel expenses." The end result was probably the same, as the refugees straggled back down into the valleys.

Civilians allowed to stay with the guerrillas could expect nothing but hardship. During the forced marches of the early months, they spent days on end without food or salt, bivouacking back-to-back in the mud under leaky umbrellas. Many women died of cold, hunger, wounds, disease, miscarriages, and grief. Back in the valleys, support for the Communists ebbed, partly because of fear but also because of disillusion: the events of 1934 had convinced even hardened optimists that the Party was unreliable. Guerrillas who ventured down the mountains found that they were no longer welcome in the villages.[64]

The defeats, the collapse of popular support, the news of the evacuation of the Central Soviet, and the harsh conditions shook the Party's courage and confidence. Memoirs suggest that proportionally more Communist leaders defected in Xianggan after 1934 than in other rearguard areas. Among the defectors were the original chief of staff, the original security chief, the original political commissar of the Fifth Red Regiment, the directors of the political and propaganda departments, and the replacement commander of the Red Fifth.[65] The most damaging defection was by Chen Hongshi, secretary of the Xianggan Committee, who went over to the Nationalists with twenty or thirty members and staff of his committee. Chen's defection came in the wake of a dispute on strategy in which he took the losing side. He believed that the Party had no future in the mountains and wanted to go to Anyuan in Pingxiang to organize the miners and the urban classes. (Chen was himself a Pingxiang man.) Tan Yubao, chair of the Xianggan Soviet, opposed Chen's proposal as "rightist" and won a majority for his views. The two men then split up to work in different places. Chen took advantage of Tan's absence to send members and officials of his committee, including his wife and Red Army doctors, to Pingxiang.

Shortly after this dispute, Chen was captured in battle and he recanted. He had with him secret codes, military maps, documents, and the provincial committee stamp.[66] He took the title of special recruitment officer and led Nationalist search parties through the mountains for the next six months, killing and capturing former comrades, forcing Party supporters down onto the plains, and spreading leaflets and posters carrying his declaration against Communism in an attempt to break the resolve of those still holding out.[67] When Chen defected, Tan Yubao was away in Xiangnan, so he was less informed than Chen of the whereabouts of other Party diehards. One unintended consequence of Chen's propaganda was to put Tan back in touch with Tan's fellow leader Liu Peishan. Tan used as signposts through the mountains the posters that Chen had pinned to trees in and around Liu's hangouts.[68]

Chen's defection created havoc in the Xianggan Party, particularly in its liaison networks.[69] In the crisis, others deserted or tried to desert. Everyone suspected everyone else. There were many killings as old and new doubts were put to rest and old scores were settled. When survivors of the main expedition to Xiangnan returned north after their defeat, they were greeted everywhere by Chen's posters. Their morale was already desperately low. Some were so weak from hunger that they sat down along the way and died. When the homecomers finally tracked Tan down, they hardly recognized him: his face was pale and bloodless, his eyes were deeply sunken (but still fiery), his matted hair hung down past his shoulders, and his gaunt frame was wrapped in a repeatedly patched gown. The expeditionaries, too, showed clear signs of starvation and distress. "An immense sadness descended on us," wrote Tan Tangchi; Duan Huanjing recalls that everyone wept.[70]

## THE QIPAN CONFERENCE OF JULY 1935

The Chen Hongshi incident was a key episode in shaping the character of the Three-Year War in Xianggan. The confrontation between Chen and Tan was one between flexibility and obstinacy, opportunism and dogmatism, irresolution and rock-like firmness. With Xiao Ke gone and the central Red Army disappearing west, the chances of quickly restoring the base in Xianggan were nil. Even before the evacuation of Ruijin, Xianggan was among the flattest of the fallen soviets. Within a day's march of Xianggan's embattled peaks were the colliery and shuntyards of Anyuan, China's first "Little Moscow," which had been the site of a main Party relay station after the establishment of the Jinggang base in 1927 and the source of thousands of recruits for the Red Army. Chen's idea of a strategic turn to this high, remote border town, with its unruly proletariat of miners, railwaymen, foundry workers, repairmen, machinists, papermakers, firecracker makers, linen makers, smugglers, and peddlers and its rows of gambling houses, opium dens, and brothels, made sense in many ways; but still it was rejected, for it violated discipline by departing from higher instructions.[71] Consequently, Tan Yubao won a majority of the band of survivors who gathered to decide on strategy for his line of drawing back and sitting tight.

Tan Yubao, a Chaling man, was born in 1899 and was twice the age of many of his guerrillas.[72] According to the writer Ding Yisan, who visited Tan sometime after 1949, he was poor and had had no schooling; for political education after 1934, he relied on a Party secretary who read aloud to him from *Lenin in Two Volumes;* what bits he grasped, he acted on.[73] Chen's defection confirmed Tan in his simple view that good conduct is identical with unflinching obedience to higher directives, and it fortified his resolve to hold out in the mountains. During the hunt triggered by the defection, incaution and negligence led repeatedly to catastrophe, so that resolution, mistrust, and vigilance became watchwords of the Communists in Xianggan. Tan, who personified these values, stepped forward to reorganize the guerrillas. Obstinacy and watchful suspicion kept him up the mountains after 1934, but in 1937 these same qualities made it hard for him to climb back down.

The meeting at which Chen and Tan argued about Anyuan merits no date in the official calendar of the Xianggan revolution. It belongs to the prehistory of the Three-Year War, before the so-called Qipan Conference of July 1935, which was held in the Qipan Mountains of Lianhua just south of the Wugong range. Tiny groups of Communist survivors converged on Qipan from all over Xianggan, summoned by envoys of Tan, who had just returned from his fruitless expedition to Xiangnan. Nationalist terror and the collapse of morale had virtually eliminated the Party in some counties; by the time the conference was held, fewer than two hundred Communist troops were left along the Xianggan border. Remnants of the Red Fifth, whittled down to fifty, had returned from their fruitless search for Fang Weixia and Cai Huiwen. An even tinier remnant of the Red Third Regiment arrived from the north, where it had been hiding in the forest caves of Mount Baike, the Wugong's highest peak. Individuals and small bands of fugitives representing local county committees and soviets also came in answer to Tan's call. The conference was attended by forty leaders of these various groups.[74]

Two issues formed its agenda: the expulsion of Chen Hongshi and the plotting of a course for the movement. The decision to expel Chen was, not surprisingly, unanimous, but still the conference resolved to wage a campaign in the Party and the army to "dispel his influence" and "prevent demoralization": this decision suggests that there was still support in the Party for Chen's views. Before planning future tasks, Tan and his comrades first had to deliver a sober reckoning of events in Xianggan in the ten months following Xiao Ke's flight west. Though the soviet in Xianggan was finished, they had not yet publicly admitted the fact or announced new policies for the new conditions. They had not even acknowledged to their supporters in the villages that the border region had been strategically downgraded (though only a fool could fail to realize it). To put matters right, they wrote a "Letter to the Masses" announcing that "the main Red Army has moved off to open up new areas." To reassure supporters, they added that "the Xianggan border region was founded by Chairman Mao himself and the Communist Party is indestructible"; the assertion must have rung hollow in villages abandoned to their fate by the Long Marchers. The most important decision of the conference was to wind up the Xianggan Soviet and Military Region and to merge their functions in a new Military and Administrative Committee (known as the Guerrilla Command) under Tan Yubao. With the pretense of power finally abandoned, the way was cleared for the Party to give up its extreme positions and for its supporters to make vital compromises with the occupying power. The conference chose a new provincial committee, also under Tan Yubao, to replace the old one smashed by Chen Hongshi (which by then preserved just three members), and it set up new county committees where old ones had collapsed. It reorganized its surviving troops into two detachments, each made up of three battalions; each battalion was subdivided into three ten-man platoons. This structure, because of its greater looseness, was better suited to guerrilla war.[75]

The Qipan Conference had a stabilizing and fortifying effect on the Xianggan survivors. It issued a new slogan for Party followers: "Don't fear death, don't waver, carry out Party policy, closely rely on the masses, persevere in the struggle to the end, and victory will be ours." With Chen Hongshi "exposed," the leadership in Xianggan spoke once again with one voice—literally so, for whereas power had previously been tripartite, with Party, army, and administration each led separately, now it was uniform, with all three functions concentrated in the person of Chairman Tan. To "overcome confused thought," the conference organized a two-week school for troops before sending them out to find lost comrades and spread the "spirit of Qipan."[76]

The conference also did its best to improve communications between the Party center and its local and military units. It directed local leaders to send fortnightly written reports to Tan Yubao and told battalion commanders to report to the provincial committee once a month in person, with or without troops, to confer and plan activities. It is unlikely that this system ever kept to schedule during the interminable emergencies of the years of quarantine. But it survived in part, for Tan Yubao kept a "cadres' training course" going right up until the end of 1937;[77] and when Chen Yi appeared unexpectedly in the mountains in October 1937, go-betweens had no difficulty in bringing him face to face with Tan.

The decision to decentralize military operations to the platoon level was a necessary response to the Nationalist swamping of the region, but it brought new problems. Few of the platoon commanders had much political experience. For a time, they alienated peasants by indiscriminate bullying. They lumped together rich peasants and middle peasants, labeled innocent people as *tuhao*, and massacred rich peasants and *baojia* officials. When these steps made them unpopular in the villages, they survived only by the use of even greater terror. By late 1935, however, most platoon leaders had turned over a new leaf. The distinctions they introduced were rough: someone with less than $500 ready cash was a rich peasant; someone with more was a *tuhao*. Now they "fined" rich peasants half their money instead of seizing or killing them, and they tried to placate local militias by leaving a share of the plunder outside their forts.[78]

### RIDING OUT THE STORMS

The steadying measures determined at Qipan enabled the guerrillas to ride out the storms of the summer of 1935, which for them was the most dangerous period of the Three-Year War. The Nationalists continued to employ Communist renegades to search the mountains. These search teams used a wide range of tricks to trail their quarry, from scattering ash at crossroads to weaving patterns in the grass so that it would register movements. The guerrillas developed countertactics to confuse the searchers, stamping the telltale ash in all directions, lifting the flattened grass, reweaving parted blades, and walking where possible off the beaten track, preferably in streams.[79] Most of the civilian population of the mountains had fled or been deported to the plains, but for a while, the temples and monasteries were left untouched, and guerrillas sometimes slept in them. Even after "a minority of reactionary monks" betrayed their presence to searchers, who stole up and attacked them, they were able to win the sympathy of the majority of monks and nuns with soothing words and propaganda; but within two months, Nationalist troops had torched the temples and killed or driven from the mountains several hundred monks and nuns. The guerrillas then moved to caves higher up the slopes, but when these too were discovered, for a time they slept among the trees in all weathers.[80]

For as long as their clothes held together, they wore them night and day in the cold months, huddling in groups for extra warmth when snow fell. Each guerrilla started out with an umbrella, a straw hat, unlined cotton clothes, a blanket, a provision bag, and a cup or bowl, but they had no padded garments, little salt, and no oil. It was too risky to light fires while searchers were about, so in cold months, the night chill was among their greatest enemies. In the daytime, they could keep warm by pounding their shoulders and moving about, but at night, the cold woke them repeatedly. They took to sleeping under leaves to defeat the frost. The layers of vegetation were heavy with damp; each morning, the guerrillas crawled out covered in fiery rashes. But these rashes were a lesser evil than the cold. During the spring rains, which fell for days and weeks on end, they slept back-to-back under their umbrellas.[81] The summer heat brought out swarms of insects and mosquitoes. "Our bodies were swollen all over with bites," wrote one veteran. "We itched unbearably and scratched running sores all over our bodies."[82] In the summer months, they ate pounds of bayberries to still their hunger; in the winter, pounds of bamboo shoots. Some guerrillas cooked and chewed skins stripped from temple drums for nourishment.[83]

Their clothes wore thin and ragged in the mountains, and they lacked needles and cloth to patch them. To replace them, the guerrillas stitched together *tong* leaves. They twisted stalks of grass into yarn and used it to thread and string the leaves into cloaks and skirts. *Tong* leaves are large, sturdy, and durable, and the garments made from them were windproof and waterproof; they also made first-rate camouflage. The leaf-clothes fashion spread rapidly through the guerrilla camps.[84]

By improvising, the Xianggan Communists were able to temper the worst rigors of cold and famine, but, without medicine and the security of a rear base, they could not hope to hold out for long. They changed their position every day and sometimes several times a day. The need to keep moving conflicted with their proclaimed intention to "forge links to the masses." They had no idea—even after Qipan—how long they could expect this hard life to last, or even of whether a Communist movement still existed outside the mountains. Already, weaker guerrillas were dying of malnutrition; many showed signs of starving, including abdominal distension.[85]

The quality they needed most was patience, in both its senses: physical and moral fortitude, and the calm abiding of the passage of time. Not all had this second kind. Silence and self-possession were as vital as courage during mountain searches. Some guerrillas who had worked as colliers in Pingxiang communicated noiselessly in a sign language invented by miners deafened in pit explosions.[86] But many hotheads gave themselves away by loud talking or impulsive behavior. Some guerrillas thought that it was better to fight to the death or burst through the cordon than to starve. Others countered that the main task was to fight hunger, not the Nationalists: "to stand firm and stay alive," and to tie down as many regiments as possible in order to lessen the pressure on Ren and Xiao on their march west.[87]

By late 1935, their patience was rewarded: not by the transfer of ever more enemy regiments into Xianggan, as Tan Yubao had once hoped, but by a gradual slackening of Nationalist military pressure on the Wugong Mountains and the withdrawal, for the time being, of Nationalist troops to the larger villages, the towns, and the main lines of communication. This respite gave the guerrillas the chance to rest, reorganize, and ponder the lessons of twelve months of repeated setbacks. The Nationalists withdrew from the mountains because they believed that the guerrillas had been destroyed by the summer mop-up and the three-month "encirclement and suppression" that ended in October. Broadly speaking, they were right. But they underestimated the guile and stamina of Tan Yubao, who at Qipan had directed the few remaining pockets of guerrillas not to press the enemy for the moment but rather to lie low and concentrate on sheer survival.[88] After October 1935, Tan fanned these tiny embers into new, small flames.

Throughout 1935, Tan Yubao made various attempts to restore his link to the outside world, but without success. A second expedition to Xiangnan under Wang Yongji, secretary of the Communist Youth League in Xianggan, lost touch forever with Tan Yubao but found Fang and Cai.[89] Shortly after Wang's arrival in Xianggan, however, he, Fang, and Cai died in an ambush, though some of his fellow expeditionaries survived.

Other expeditions to isolated outposts within Xianggan were more successful. In the summer of 1935, one party under Duan Huanjing and Tan Tangchi broke through into the Wugong Mountains, which the two men knew from an earlier visit in the spring. The soviet areas had been laid waste by Guomindang revanchists. Most villages had been burned to ash. There was no sign of the underground Party workers who had previously conducted Duan and Tan through the region. The two men climbed to the upper slopes to continue their search and found traces of human presence by the side of a stream. "We were as elated as if we had discovered a new continent," recalled Tan. They followed tracks to a point midway up the mountain where a hidden bluff fell steeply into a lake-filled valley. On the rocks below, they spied a crowd of several dozen men and women milling round the mouths of two caves. By the look of their pinched cheeks and ragged clothes, they were Party fugitives. Tan and Duan climbed down and announced themselves. After tearful embraces, they learned that these people were "basic cadres and basic masses." Hidden further out of reach was the local county committee, hollowed to a shell by losses. Beyond that, in an even more secret lurking place, were remnants of Liu Peishan's Third Regiment, from which the provincial committee had heard nothing for several months, and the regiment's lazaretto.[90] Another expedition to Lingxian in Xiangnan also netted a lost group of sixty stragglers; these returned to Xianggan, where they were reunited with the two main detachments.[91]

Groups like this holding out along the border took advantage of the relaxation after October 1935 to rebuild their commands, their regional networks, and their links to the villages. To boost morale after the Qipan Conference, some guerrillas staged an armed propaganda raid on a local government office, where they captured several dozen guns. Others later burned down more than one hundred forts in Yongxin. Similar raids, often sensationally (and usefully) exaggerated by the local press, kindled beacons along the border that drew a trickle of lost troops back to the ranks. These actions raised the Party's political standing in the region and led to the restoration of Party branches and even of some secret soviets.[92]

### THE GUERRILLAS REVIVE

As prospects brightened, the guerrillas shifted their emphasis from "safety first" to a more extroverted role. Before 1936, they had generally avoided combat unless cornered, and they had been content to play hide-and-seek with their enemies to tire them out and sap their morale.[93] Now they began to fight more often. The two detachments set up at Qipan fought independently but, wherever possible, in concert, from different sides of the provincial border: one under Tan Yubao in Chaling, Youxian, Lingxian, and Liling in Hunan, the other under Liu Peishan in Yongxin, Lianhua, Pingxiang, Anfu, and Yichun in the Jiangxi section of the Wugong Range. Other small groups of guerrillas sprang up here and there along the border.[94] At first, they lacked experience of guerrilla fighting and had little idea of how to go about it. In a marginal base like Xianggan, the crucible of Mao's guerrilla tactics, one might have expected graduates of the local Red Army school to possess at least one guerrilla handbook between them. They had none. When an old pamphlet on guerrilla warfare, printed in the Central Soviet, reached them through Fang and Cai, each guerrilla leader copied it, absorbed its contents, and tried to apply the prescribed tactics on the battlefield: the ambush, the lure, the feint, the night march, casting the net wide, drawing the net in, dodging the enemy's main force, striking where the enemy is weak. The Nationalists marched from their forts at dawn and marched back in again at dusk; the guerrillas stole from the forest at dusk and slipped back in again at dawn.[95]

By May 1936, the Party had set up or restored more than seventy branches in Xianggan. By the winter of 1936, the guerrillas were more active and better armed than at any time since 1934.[96] They no longer climbed down into the villages only after dark. They had restored bases of support, including peasant associations, in some villages, and they appointed small "aid teams" of five or six people to help peasants farm their land and defend themselves against press-gangs and tax collectors.[97] Communist women played a key role in setting up these links and in targeting *tuhao* for assassination. (Among the women activists was Tan Yubao's wife Yi Xiangsu, who ran the Party's propaganda department in the Chayoutian region; she was eventually arrested and imprisoned until after the start of the war against Japan.)[98] In 1936, a column of guerrillas under Liu Peishan marched from village to village along the border rounding up local landlords, *baojia* officials, and members of anti-Communist militias and lecturing them on Party policy. Some village heads worked for the guerrillas. Local strongmen who held out against the Communists were likely to end up dead or locked in *tuhao* cages high in the mountains, watched over by convalescing Red Army men or pro-Communist refugees.[99]

Stay-behinders in other parts of southern China put their main emphasis on sealing agreements and alliances with local powerholders and resorted to terror and assassination only when all else failed. This policy won them friends and space. Though Tan Yubao did not in principle oppose cooperating with enemy officials, his inclination was to confront them. The "white skin, red heart" tactic was not widely applied in Xianggan after 1934. Tan's speciality was assassination. Of the fourteen magistrates appointed to Ninggang between 1934 and 1949, nine were killed, three "took flight and ran," and two never dared go near the place.[100]

In the highlands, the guerrillas could by now come and go more or less at will. In December 1936, the two detachments formed at Qipan were merged into a Xianggan Red Independent Regiment under Liu Peishan and Duan Huanjing.[101] The guerrillas no longer dressed in leaves, for now there were secret conduits from the plains for supplies. They no longer slept under the stars, for they could now build huts in the forest glades. In some places, they came across dilapidated barracks built by guerrillas in the early days of land revolution, which they used for studying politics and military science. They leveled out parade grounds, playing fields, and running tracks around their settlements. By early 1937, their headquarters in the Jiulong Mountains had grown into a small town of wooden and bamboo houses, some with roofs of pine-bark "the spit and image of glazed tiles," others thatched with cogon grass. Narrow alleys and babbling streams wound between the rows of huts that followed the contours of the land, against a background of hills

bathed in a great sea of multicolored leaves. In this revolutionary arca-
dia—spoiled, if accounts are true, only by the mosquito swarms and
snakes—the guerrillas competed in sports, sang Red Army songs around
camp fires, laboriously penned their contributions to the Lenin Club
wall newspaper, and talked of war.[102]

The political thaw in Red Xianggan in late 1936 is symbolized in Party
literature by the wedding, performed by Tan Yubao "in full accordance
with soviet traditions" and registered on a marriage certificate from the
soviet period, between Duan Huanjing, the Xianggan chief of staff, and
the Anfu Communist Li Fagu. Chairman Tan told the couple that their
wedding was the first in two years under soviet law in the border region
and that it "illustrated the gradual turn for the better in the struggle."
The ceremony was followed by a feast, after which Li Fagu set off
through the snow to help abduct a *tuhao;* it was a year before the couple
met again.[103]

It is tempting to see the stay-behinders in southern China as soviet
fossils, kept by walls of rock from disintegrating or from keeping abreast
of change in the wider world. Generally speaking, this view is wrong. Political incidents and trends in China and abroad decisively affected the
guerrilla bases, whether or not the guerrillas knew about them at the
time. Leaders of the stay-behinders were conscious of their obligations
to the national movement and had been trained to see China as a single
battlefield. But these general propositions about the Three-Year War
apply less to Xianggan than to other regions. Tan Yubao was a stubborn
and parochial man, obsessed with secrecy, wary of change, and strongly
attached to the mountains around his native Chaling, and Xianggan was
too remote to be touched by changes important for reinvigorating Communist guerrillas elsewhere. Xianggan was severed from the wider
Party; veterans admit that most of the time, they knew nothing of outside events. Their relay stations were in ruins; their expeditions to other
regions invariably came to grief. They had heard vaguely of the Party's
Southern Committee, but they had no idea where it was, or even where
the Central Committee and the main Red Army were.[104] In the thousand days between January 1935 and October 1937, they received not
one directive from a higher Party body, so they made their own policy as
best they could. They were too far from the coast or cities to feel the impact of the demonstrations against Japan, and memoirs mention no repercussions in this region of the Liang Guang Incident of 1936 that
shook guerrilla bases elsewhere.

Nor does it seem that the Nationalists put half the effort into "pacifying" Xianggan after 1935 that they did in other regions. Not until the
spring of 1937 did the guerrillas learn of the Xi'an Incident of December 1936.[105] Sources suggest that it was only in the summer of 1937 that

ten thousand "peace preservers" pressed down on the region, in a short belated sequel to the main offensive launched against guerrillas in other parts of southern and central China in the immediate wake of the Incident.[106]

## FIRST MOVES TOWARD A CEASE-FIRE

In most other southern bases, the first steps to a cease-fire and peace talks were taken by the Communists, who learned of the united front through outside contacts. In Xianggan, the initiative was taken by the Nationalists. In the autumn of 1937, attacks on the guerrillas were suddenly suspended, and local authorities sent messengers into the mountains with letters proposing talks. One letter added ominously that "the [main] Communist army has already capitulated and been reorganized as the Eighteenth Army Corps."

The guerrilla leaders were unsure how to react to this unexpected overture. Some smelled a rat. Others suspected that things were happening at the national level of which they were unaware. They sent agents down the mountains to learn the truth and called in guerrillas from all over Xianggan for a crash training session in the Jiulong Mountains; they reorganized them "to prepare for an even fiercer attack or for whatever new high tide is on its way." Their spies struck gold. Among two hundred letters they stole from the post office in Ninggang were several from northern China and, by an astonishing coincidence, two from Yan'an that mentioned the united front and the Eighth Route Army.[107]

In September 1937, Tan Yubao issued a series of leaflets, some of which are preserved in the archives of the Intelligence Bureau in Taibei, setting terms for a cease-fire. At around the same time, the Nationalists renewed the pressure on Tan's Jiulong base by sending in the Nineteenth Regiment against him. Tan's declarations show how out of touch he was. He praised the "Zhu-Mao Red Army, actively advancing northward," and denounced Chiang Kai-shek's "false mask of anti-Japanese and anti-imperialist resistance" and his sending of the Twenty-ninth Army to "attack the Soviets and the Red Army." Tan's declarations contained ringing demands (which Mao would have favored) for fundamental economic and political reforms to break the landlords' monopoly of power in the villages. But for all their fiery tone and unorthodox formulations, the declarations showed that, under certain conditions, Tan Yubao was prepared to enter "an anti-imperialist joint front of all parties, factions, and armies without distinction (save traitors)." What he would not yet do was join a united front with the "national traitor" Chiang Kai-shek.[108] Just a few weeks later, Tan's unreconstructed loathing for Chiang almost landed him in the biggest trouble of his Communist career, when he came within an inch of liquidating as a turncoat the first Central Committee representative to reach Xianggan since the summer of 1934.

## CHEN YI ARRIVES IN THE MOUNTAINS

The events leading up to Chairman Tan's near-bungle began one October evening, when a Jiulong guerrilla sentry squatting in a tree spied two men carrying a bamboo sedan along a nearby road. At first, he paid little attention to the sedan, but he sat up with a start when it turned onto a small path and headed toward his tree. Shinning down to bar the way, he summoned a second man called Liu Biesheng. A face appeared from behind the curtains of the litter, that of a man wearing a scholar's cap (some remember it as a French beret) and a pair of gold-rimmed glasses. The stranger waved a walking stick in the direction of the sentry.

"Where have you come from?" asked the sentry, wide-eyed.

"Ji'an."

"Where are you heading for?"

The traveler climbed from the sedan, straightening his gown with one hand and leaning heavily on his stick with the other. He inspected the guerrillas. "I'm looking for your leader."

"Do you have a letter?" The traveler handed Liu a letter. Liu was barely literate; the characters defeated him. He suspected trickery: that bamboo chair, those clothes, that Sichuan accent. . . . Others shared Liu's suspicion that the traveler was a spy or traitor. Some thought he was a rich merchant or a scholar. Almost everyone had a theory. What no one at first believed was the traveler's own claim: that he was Chen Yi, supreme commander of the Jiangxi rearguard.

Chen Yi's visit to the Jiulong Mountains has been spun into a minor legend of Chinese Communism, which, as is the way with legends, crops up in an abundance of different forms. But in the various accounts of the episode by different actors in it, only the superficial details vary. Beneath a narrative surface disturbed by tricks of memory, differing perceptions, tactful omissions and amendments, poetic license, and other familiar obstacles to the smooth flow of truth in memoirs of the Chinese Revolution lies a common factual core that dramatizes a critical moment in the Three-Year War in Xianggan and in many other parts of southern and central China. I shall tell it here in full, though some of it has clearly been reconstructed after the event, and Chen Yi is portrayed at times in ways that seem too good to be true.[109]

Chen Yi had first heard about the guerrillas in Xianggan during his talks with the Guomindang in Nanchang, where he negotiated an agreement on behalf of all guerrillas to cooperate with the government in

Nanjing. After the negotiations, he and others traveled up and down southern China calling in the stay-behinders. Most climbed down the mountains; a few held out.

"The Communists talk of stopping the war," the Nationalists told Chen Yi, "but in Xianggan they have still not stopped. We will have to send in more troops to put them down."

"If you try to put them down, they'll continue fighting," said Chen Yi. "I'll go and talk to them."

So Chen Yi went to look for Tan Yubao. After his meeting with the sentry, he was taken up the hill to a village, where he lodged in a peasant's house. He dismissed his government-appointed bearers, both of them soldiers, with a handsome tip, generating fresh rumors about his great wealth. Then a surprising thing happened. This big shot, this rich merchant, this scholar, stripped off his long gown, rolled up his pants, hung his stick on the wall, and joined in the harvest. He explained to his hosts that he was a Communist, and he talked volubly about politics. "We were impressed by his fluent Marxism-Leninism," recalled a listener. When not cutting paddy or carrying water, he spoke in plain words and vivid phrases about the united front and the Long March. He became liked and trusted. But still the villagers stayed silent when he asked them who lived in the mountains. Then, one day, a stranger appeared in the village, winked furtively at Chen, and hurried off. Chen now knew for sure that he was near his goal.

Further up the mountain, Duan Huanjing and Liu Peishan pondered the letter Chen Yi had handed over. Signed by Xiang Ying, it said, "Comrade Chen Yi, the Communist Party's special envoy, has come to liaise with you." Neither Duan nor Liu had ever heard of Chen. They recalled bitterly that other so-called Party envoys had led search parties up the mountains after similar visits. The letter bore no stamp or seal, and though they knew who Xiang Ying was, neither they nor anyone else could verify his signature. Was the visitor a traitor? If so, by extension, they too were traitors. (Intentions mattered little; they were hard to prove and were pooh-poohed in Tan's two-volume *Lenin.*) Liu Peishan projected his anxiety onto Fu Yunfei, the undercover agent who had brought Chen's letter to him: "You've led a traitor up the mountain. When Chairman Tan hears this, he'll kill you."

Even so, he let Fu fetch Chen Yi. Fu and his fellow escort, Liu Biesheng, curious to see how the learned Mr. Chen would handle the hard climb, stole sideways looks at him. "In the late autumn," said Fu in a reminiscence, "the mountain nights are fearsome. The sky is inky. The cold wind invades you. On the dark, jagged, grotesquely shaped rocks, hideous faces loom up at you one after the other. The waterfalls gush down into the ravines like roaring tigers. In the distance will-o'-the-wisps flicker. Closer to, wolves and jackals howl." But Chen Yi, who had seen far worse, was troubled only by his limp.

The travelers reached the foot of a huge, jutting cliff with no visible way up. On top of it lived Duan and Liu. Nationalist troops had more than once searched this place but had never found a route up the cliff, so the hideaway remained a secret. Fu and Liu led Chen to the mouth of a cave hidden behind a spill of scree. The cave, spiraling steeply up through the rock, was the doorway to the clifftop lair. Once inside, Fu whistled. A rattan rope was lowered down the dripping shaft. The three men hauled themselves up it to the top.

As I have said, there are several different versions of Chen's journey to see Tan Yubao. In some, Chen is by now alone, save for his guerrilla escort; in others, he is attended during his meeting with Duan and Liu by a minor official of the local Guomindang. Shibboleths and minor embellishments apart, it is unusual for authors of historical texts in China to invent things; they are more likely to leave things out, in line with the Stalinist law of parsimony that no more causes or forces must be assumed than are necessary to keep out of trouble and explain the facts. Skating over the presence of Chen's Nationalist attendant avoids potentially embarrassing questions. Had Chen been wise to bring the man along? Were Duan and Liu wise to receive him? Having no axe to grind, I will accept the presence of this optional character on the clifftop and not ask how he got there.

Duan and Liu made no secret of their misgivings when Chen Yi arrived. Chen and his Guomindang companion were seized and bound, and Chen was thrown into a hut. When night fell, they started to interrogate him against a background of forest barks and screeches.

"You are a traitor."

"I have come to see Tan Yubao."

"Make a clean breast of things. How many troops do you control? Only if you are completely frank about your treason, your collusion with the enemy, and your plans to attack us will we show lenience."

"I negotiated with the enemy as representative of the Jiangxi base. I am no traitor."

"Where are your documents? Where is your proof?"

"I was given no documents."

"Why do you have no gun?"

"If I carried a gun, the local reactionaries, bandits, and returning legions would probably attack me to get it."

"How did you know our troops were here?"

"I read about you in the Nationalist press. When I went to Xingguo and Nanchang to negotiate with the Guomindang, they said we Communists were not sincere about the cease-fire and cooperation. I asked them why. They said that Tan Yubao's guerrillas in the Jiulong Mountains were still fighting. So I come here to liaise."

"If you are representing the Party, why are you alone?"

"That's what the organization decided. If higher levels tell me to come alone, I come alone. You're guerrilla leaders. Don't you recognize that principle?"

"Since we're talking about organizational principles, why did you come in broad daylight by main roads straight from Nationalist-held territory? Why didn't you come by forest paths through the mountains? Why didn't the Guomindang arrest you?"

While all this was going on, Chen Yi could hear bodyguards outside the hut savagely beating the Guomindang official. Suddenly one rushed in and said:

"You can stop pretending. He's told us everything. The way you're dressed, no one would take you for a Communist. The Guomindang even sent people to carry you. Confess. Tell us how you betrayed the Party."

"Comrades, your political level is too low. I have full power to parley with the Guomindang. I dress like this to do my work, to deal with the Nationalists. Why did I travel by sedan? To overawe the Nationalists, so that they would let me through their lines, and because I have a bad leg. Why did I come by the main road? Because it's quicker and safer."

"Look at the papers. Here it says that the Jiangxi Communist leader Chen Yi has surrendered."

"You believe the enemy press?"

"If you haven't capitulated, why is the enemy still attacking us?"

"It's you who are attacking them. The enemy wanted to launch a big offensive against you; we talked them out of it. It's not wrong in principle to fight the enemy or to attack local tyrants and evil gentry. But it's wrong now. It's politically wrong. In the north, Chairman Mao and Commander Zhu are cooperating with the Guomindang. If you continue fighting, you're out of step."

It did not seem to Chen that he had made much headway. He had already lost his hat, his watch, the lining of his coat, his fountain pen, and his leather shoes, which had been taken from him and distributed as "struggle fruits." Now he was convinced that he was about to lose his life. He was surprised and relieved when the next morning his captors announced that they would take him to see Tan.

Duan and Liu had passed the night in an agony of indecision. If Chen was a traitor, they could lose their heads for sparing him; if he was who he said he was, they could lose their heads for killing him. In the end, it was the chance of restoring links to the Party center that swayed them in Chen's favor. On balance, Chen seemed a good man. His courage—not a quality that Duan and Liu associated with renegades—impressed them. His message was hard to swallow and not the sort of thing that Chairman Tan said, but he had delivered it patiently and persuasively and had shown no rancor toward his inquisitors. Some of the guerrillas who had gathered to listen to his interrogation had recognized him as a Party big shot. In itself, this recognition meant little. After all, Chen Hongshi, another big shot, had still turned traitor. But seeds of trust had been sown in the minds of Duan and Liu, who, lacking power of decision in the matter, thought that they should grant Chen's wish to see Tan.

How to reach Tan's hideout? Chen Yi suggested that they go by the main road to save time; at once, the suspicions that Duan and Liu had with difficulty suppressed sprang back to life. Hastily, Chen withdrew his proposal and agreed to go by forest paths, though by now he was ill with dysentery and his time was precious. He and his escorts threaded their way through marshes, pushed their way through virgin forests, and scrambled up cliffs and down ravines. Their clothes were torn; their skin was cut and bleeding; the rain drenched them; the gusting wind turned their umbrellas inside out and snatched the bamboo hats from their heads. Two days later, they arrived at the Qipan Mountains in Lianhua where Tan Yubao had his headquarters.

### CHEN YI MEETS TAN YUBAO

Chairman Tan was secretly dismayed when he heard about Chen Yi. Just a few days earlier, a man had brought Tan a letter saying that Chen was on his way, but Tan had had the man beheaded even before reading it.[110] Tan was that sort of man: willful, mistrustful, arbitrary, and violent.[111]

"You've brought an opportunist," Tan told Liu Peishan, confirming Liu's worst fears. Tan hated traitors and opportunists from the bottom of his heart. They had wrought terrible destruction on the Party in Xianggan. His instinct was to liquidate Chen Yi on sight; doubt stayed him.

"You are a renegade," he said when Chen was brought before him. "I shall eat you. Tonight we shall chop your head off."

He fixed his eyes on Chen and tapped ash from his long-stemmed bamboo pipe. This was a sign for four armed men to seize Chen, bind him, and throw him into a bamboo clump, where he lay while his fate was being decided. Chen could hear every word of the discussion and of the decision: that he be killed.

"You're making a big mistake," he shouted. He added a few words about the need for a united front. "Chen Yi really can talk," recalled a participant in the scene. "Otherwise we would have killed him."

Tan Yubao knew about the reorganization of the Red Army in northern China, and he guessed that the Party center had changed its policy.

He was of two minds about Chen Yi. Instead of killing him there and then, he decided to give him a public trial before an audience of two hundred guerrillas and Party cadres.

Chairman Tan conducted his prosecution of Chen Yi with a Mauser at his waist and from behind dark glasses, as if to ward off Chen's inspection.

"Do you know who I am?" he asked.

"I know your name."

"I know you, from the Jinggang Mountains in 1928. You used to toss your head and spread your tail like a peacock. You would speak for hours on end without stopping. I had to sit and listen to you. Now you've forgotten all your grand words. Now you've become an opportunist. Now you're no longer a revolutionary. All this rubbish about cooperating with the Nationalists against Japan. What's wrong with class struggle? Only the soviet can save China. Why do you want to scrap the soviet?"

"Today the two main classes are cooperating. The national contradiction has eclipsed the domestic contradiction. You must subordinate yourself to the united front. Don't think only of yourself, think of the wider situation. You're a Communist; you should trust in the organization."

"We've only ever talked of class struggle. Now you're talking about class collaboration. You're Second International. You're a traitor. We've always said that only the soviet can save China. Now you want to abolish the soviet. That means you want to kill off China. You want to hand the people's army over to Chiang Kai-shek. If that's not treason, what is? I won't collaborate, even if people like you do. I will continue with the revolution. I'll always be for the peasants. I'm not like you intellectuals, who turn traitor as soon as things get tough."

Tan Yubao leaned over, hit Chen Yi hard on the head with his pipe, and cursed him.

"Stop that, you'll draw blood! Do you want to resist Japan?"

"I would this very minute if I could."

"It's easy enough."

"There's one condition. Chiang Kai-shek must first give back to me the eight counties of the Jinggang Mountains."

"Brother comrade, you lack depth. You are politically backward. We will win hegemony in the war against Japan and after victory all China will be ours, not just eight counties. All you can think about is your eight counties. You have a peasant consciousness. You are a peasant through and through."

"I suppose you're a bit right there."

"And you're a bit muddled."

Tan flared up again. "When you were talking to us in the Jinggang Mountains, you thought you were a big shot. Every other word was revolution. There I was listening to you, a spear across my shoulder. You spoke so well, and now you've turned traitor. I'll kill you!"

"What I said in 1928 was right. But this is 1937. We're at a different stage. We need new tactics. Your brain is too inflexible."

"Damned intellectuals, you're never short of arguments. But as soon as the enemy arrived, you took your troops and fled. I had to stay here and carry on the struggle. You lost the soviet and then you ditched us. You're all cowards. You left behind that traitor Chen Hongshi to lead us. You're an opportunist. You're a flightist."

"It was right for the Red Army to go north to mobilize against Japan. In any case, I myself stayed behind, like you."

"For three years you didn't send a single directive to Xianggan. Usually you never stop firing off directives."

"Aren't I bringing you a directive now? But you won't accept it. You just tie me up."

Again Tan hit Chen with his pipe. "Too many arguments, just like an intellectual."

"Why don't you send someone to see if I'm telling you the truth? If what I say is just my own idea, you can reject it. If it's Central Committee policy and you still disagree, you can discuss your criticisms with Party leaders. But you can't go on treating me like this—you'll injure me. I don't care about my own life. We revolutionaries must be prepared to die. But even dying has its value. Go to Ji'an, go to Nanchang—go to Yan'an and check for yourself. Ye Jianying is in Wuhan. Xiang Ying has just left Nanchang. . . ."

"Xiang Ying and Ye Jianying mean nothing to me. I'd arrest you even if Stalin and Mao Zedong had sent you."

Chen saw his chance.

"Chairman Tan has abandoned his class position," he shouted, appealing to the wider audience of guerrillas. "Shoot me if you wish, but stabilize your class position!"

"You are being insincere," protested Tan. "You are trying to squirm out of it. You are not allowed to speak. Shut up or I shall kill you."

Tan announced that the trial was over. He knew that he had gone too far and that his support might slip. Some people were even saying that Chen should be allowed to speak.

By now, Tan's fire was almost spent. Late at night on the fifth day of Chen's imprisonment, he went alone to where Chen was being held and whispered, "Confess all and I will say nothing."

"I have been here five days now. There's no point in reasoning with you. I can only lecture you. You preserved a guerrilla army. I approve of that, it's a glorious achievement. You're a peasant. It's great that you kept going. Your army will be an important asset in the struggle against Japan. But your views are unreasonable."

Tan called a meeting of his provincial committee to decide what to do with Chen. Four thought he was a traitor; five thought he was not. Tan secretly sent agents to Ji'an to check on Chen Yi's story, just after the Eighth Route Army won a famous victory in a surprise attack on the Japanese at Pingxingguan.

"The Communist Party is very strong," these people told Tan after their return from Ji'an, where they had met Zeng Shan. "Everyone is saying that Chiang Kai-shek is losing, the Communists are winning, and the world belongs to the Communists."

"And Chen Yi?"

"People say he is a good man."

Tan Yubao was no separatist or dissenter. His self-will should not be confused with self-interest or self-indulgence; his deference instantly overcame his obstinacy. His loyalty was tribal, not doctrinal. Beliefs were secondary; he would drop them and adopt new ones if his leaders told him that it was in the Party's interest for him to do so. After his agents had reported back to him, he again went to Chen Yi's hut.

"Now we shall speak as Communist to Communist," he began, straightening Chen's clothes to show respect. "I have treated you badly. I apologize. You are my superior. I shall open my heart to you. After you left the border region, things became hard for those of us left behind. We climbed the mountains, hid from the enemy, strengthened our forces. It was difficult to hold out here. All I know about is land revolution. I know little about Japan. If you were against Communism, I would kill you, but you are not. I want to learn from you. You should not be angry."

"I am not angry. I do not blame you. If I had followed procedures— if I had brought more than just one letter and not come alone—this might not have happened. You are very resolute, there's nothing wrong with that. I just wish you'd struck me less with your pipe. What about my arms and legs? I'm trussed like a pig. If you are contrite, you will untie me."

Tan loosened the ropes, weeping in remorse.

"Now you must accept the united front," said Chen. "Then people will know that we Communists keep our word."

It took Tan three days to complete his change of heart. It was not just a question of his own conscience; most of his guerrillas shared his scruples. To them, shut off from the world by mountains and blockades, Japanese imperialism was an abstraction. Chiang Kai-shek, on the other hand, was a known quantity and a constant threat. Many of Tan's guerrillas feared the plains and would rather have fought on in the mountains.[112]

After Tan's three days of reflection, Chen went down the mountain, and the cease-fire became universal throughout the south, save for a few tiny pockets of recusants. In November, Tan went to Chaling to negotiate an agreement with local magistrates. The Xianggan Provincial Committee issued a declaration saying that it would abandon hostile actions against the government, resist Japan, and hurry to the front. The declaration proudly added that Xianggan had "preserved a guerrilla base and a powerful force" during the years of isolation. It repeated demands contained in the September declaration, including the call for political and economic reform.[113]

Also in November, the guerrillas assembled at Longshan in Lianhua. Tan bore the marks of his three years in the wilderness, and he looked older than his thirty-eight years. Chen Yi, Xiang Ying, and Zeng Shan joined him to address a rally of several hundred guerrillas and their supporters. "We have won victory," Tan told the rally. "Today we cease our life as primitives."[114]

In January or February 1938, between three hundred and five hundred guerrillas marched north under Liu Peishan and Duan Huanjing to become the First Battalion of the Second Regiment of Chen Yi's First Detachment of the New Fourth Army. One-third of the region's 150 Communist officials were chosen to go to work for the New Fourth Army. The chief of staff of the Ji'an Peace Preservation Corps welcomed their withdrawal: "We are happy that Tan Yubao has come down the mountain. He fought well and caused us many problems." Not everyone left. Tan Yubao and others stayed behind, and a New Fourth Army office was opened in nearby Ji'an. After 1945, there were once again five hundred Communist guerrillas operating along the border.[115]

## PERSPECTIVES ON THE THREE-YEAR
## WAR IN XIANGGAN

Of the Party's main rearguard bases, Xianggan probably fared worst. It tied down fewer troops, it preserved only about a tenth of its original strength, and it supplied no future national leaders. Yet it had been the site of the Party's first independent regime and the Red Army's first safe haven, chosen by Mao for its political and strategic advantages and its excellent terrain. When the main force under Xiao Ke abandoned Xianggan in August 1934, several thousand regular and irregular troops stayed behind to defend the base. So why were Tan's guerrillas not more successful?

One reason was that by late 1934, the Party had lost most of its credibility and support in Xianggan. Party leaders had shown on several occasions that the base there was expendable. Mao wrote in 1928 that the border region "would at once suffer devastation . . . if the Red Army moved away . . . [;] the Party and our mass base would receive a crippling blow."[116] In fact, the Red Army moved away repeatedly, starting in August 1928.

The devastation was greatest in the Jinggang Mountains, which were largely lost to the Party after the alienation of the Hakka partisans. After 1928, the population of the Jinggang villages was more than halved. Every one of the region's 530 ploughing cattle and great quantities of tools were taken. Local villages were repeatedly burned (Xiajing was torched thirteen times) until they were abandoned. By 1949, just one hundred people lived in Dajing, one-eighth of the original population. In Chaling, more than twenty thousand people died as a result of the civil war. Ninggang and Yongxin also lost many thousands of people after 1928: according to some calculations, more than 150,000. Property losses went beyond houses, animals, and tools to great stretches of land that ran wild as a result of the depopulation: 18,000 *mu* went to seed in one part of Yongxin alone. Even as late as 1958, less than one-tenth of farmland had been reclaimed from the weeds in one part of the Jinggang Mountains.[117]

The Communists could do little to mitigate the effects of this counterrevolution, of which the civilian population bore the brunt. Xianggan after 1934 was a monument to Party failures in the early years of armed struggle, though Party hagiographers paint it as a monument to the Party's integrity, infallibility, and tenacity of purpose, a symbol of the unquenchable flame of revolution. By sacrificing the base to wider goals, the Party dissipated the trust and optimism its reforms had generated. At first, its support steadied again after 1929, but by 1935 the Xianggan base had been crushed.

After the Red Army evacuated Xianggan in 1934, Party morale collapsed for a time, symbolized by the defection of Chen Hongshi and a majority of the provincial committee. This incident dealt a great blow to the Xianggan rearguard, which was left without any leaders of real stature. The Party was unable to compensate by getting help from elsewhere. Its links to the outside world, including contact with Communist remnants in other parts of the south, were broken. The bases in Xiangnan, Gannan, and Xiang'egan, to which it had once been linked, were by now among the Party's weakest, concerned with little more than their own survival. Three months after the start of the Long March, 1,200 Red troops under Gong Chu, the newly appointed chief of staff of the Xiangyuegan Military Region, had marched west from the Central Soviet into Xiangnan, where Gong set up a base and a sub-bureau of the Central Committee. Had Gong's base survived, the rearguard in Xianggan might have rallied under its influence, for Gong was an intelligent and experienced Party leader. But when Gong defected to the Nationalists in May 1935, his base collapsed.[118]

The deaths of Fang Weixia and Cai Huiwen completed Tan Yubao's isolation. Had they lived, they might have brought the Xianggan Communists into contact with the Ganyue base, which was the main purpose of their mission to Hunan. In the event, there was no direct contact between Tan and the Fang-Cai group. However, Fang and Cai did manage to send Tan a handbook on guerrilla warfare that became Tan's Bible during the strategic turn of 1935. That even this slight link could have such a crucial impact on Tan shows that he was not closed to new ideas, though he found it hard to strike out in new directions. It also suggests that Tan's isolation from outside sources of knowledge and innovation was a principal cause of his conservatism and political stagnation.

The central peaks of Xianggan are high, secluded, and virtually invulnerable to direct assault. Tan Yubao's guerrillas slipped easily through the mountains after the withdrawal of the main Nationalist garrisons in 1935. But in a sense Tan, like other stay-behinders, became a victim of his own excellent security. Because his guerrillas were frequently on the run, they were unable to extend ties to the villages or to restore networks destroyed by Chen Hongshi. Instead, they became wild people, dressed in leaves and living as autarkists beyond the margins of society. In 1928, Mao predicted that if the Red Army left the Jinggang Mountains, only the "bandit mountaintops" would stay in Party hands.[119] This prediction was borne out in Xianggan in 1935. The Party was further paralyzed by the ancient rivalry, which it had been unable to transcend, between Hakkas and natives. Guerrillas in Fujian, Eyuwan, and elsewhere drew strength after 1934 from ties to local bandits, and in Mindong and Xiang'egan, the Communists allied with discriminated minorities. In Xianggan, such a strategy was impossible because of the bitterness created by the Yuan-Wang incident. Guerrilla bands in other parts of the south were shaken by important events on the national stage to which they responded—often with the help of Party representatives in the cities—by launching fresh political initiatives. The Communists of Xianggan, holed up in the mountains and dead to the outside world, were not directly touched by the Liang Guang Incident or by the growth of the movement against Japan. In the end, it was the Nationalists who brought the new issue of national unity to their notice.

It is tempting to explain the parochialism and inertia of the Xianggan Communists after 1934 by the character of Tan Yubao, though Tan probably reflected the mood of the Party after the defections as much as he created it. As one leader after the other died or deserted, Tan gathered more and more power into his hands. He was at least twice the age of most of his guerrillas and type-cast for the role of patriarch. He ran the Party like a fief; even his immediate subordinates lived in dread of him. He was an uneducated man who lacked the ability to think for himself. He was consumed by a single-minded class hatred for the Nationalists (who had his wife behind bars) and was incapable of devising new initiatives. "He was very resolute," said Chen Yi, "but he lacked direction; he feared deception, and it is true that he was in a difficult position, for he had experienced treachery."[120] However, it is to Tan's credit that he saved the movement from extinction after the betrayals, that he completed the switch to guerrilla tactics, that he stood fast for three years when all seemed lost, and that he meekly submitted to Chen Yi when he realized his mistake.

Chen Yi's arrival in Xianggan was crucial in saving Tan's guerrillas for the Party. Time was running out for Tan. Remnants elsewhere who missed the boat by rejecting the united front disappeared from the political map. Chen Yi was no less brave, steadfast, or cunning than Tan Yubao, and, unlike Tan, he was articulate and "fluent in Marxism-Leninism." He spoke clearly and rousingly; at times he was dauntingly blunt, but when necessary he showed tact and patience, for he sympathized with Tan as a veteran of the same Three-Year War. His trump card was to play on Tan's and the guerrillas' reverence for authority by jumping down Tan's throat when he spoke disrespectfully of Stalin and Mao. Had Chen not spoken up then, he might still have lost his head.

# Xiangnan

◆ ◆ ◆

Xiangnan, or southern Hunan, was the site of several small guerrilla bases connected for a time to the Xianggan Soviet to the north and to the fringe of the Jiangxi Soviet in Gannan to the east. In its broadest definition, the Xiangnan guerrilla region encompassed parts of Guangdong (Yue) and Jiangxi (Gan), so it is sometimes known as Xiangyue or Xiangyuegan. Between 1934 and 1938, groups of guerrillas, mostly tiny, were active along the borders of Yizhang, Lechang, Lianxian, Linwu, Yongxin, Leiyang, Changning, Anren, Chenxian, Shangyou, Chongyi, and Rucheng.[1]

The Communist movement in Xiangnan had its origins in the labor unrest that shook Hunan in 1922 and 1923. In December 1922, the Communists led a strike by miners at Shuikoushan in Changning. The Workers' Club at Shuikoushan was destroyed by troops a year later, but Communist influence persisted. In 1926, the club revived, and in 1927, three thousand miners and their supporters staged an unsuccessful attack on the Changning county seat.[2]

In January 1928, Zhu De, Chen Yi, and Lin Biao marched into Xiangnan at the head of two thousand rebel troops while retreating north after their rout at Shantou. They staged the "End-of-Year Insurrection," which led to the establishment of a short-lived soviet government at Yizhang. The insurrection was joined by nearly three thousand miners from Shuikoushan.[3] In March, the uprising was defeated, and in April, Zhu De led his army, enlarged to eight thousand in the fighting, to the nearby Jinggang Mountains, where they merged with troops under Mao Zedong.

Members of the Xiangnan Special Committee opposed this retreat and wanted to stay in Xiangnan and fight back against the Whites. They

414

were overruled by Chen Yi, who said that it was better to "preserve mil-itary forces and avoid decisive battles with the enemy when the circum-stances are unfavorable." A few did return to Xiangnan, where many of them lost their lives. During the Xiangnan Insurrection, local Commu-nists had gone on the rampage, burning and killing to create an atmo-sphere of Red terror that would force the "backward peasants" into class confrontation with the "evil gentry." The result was disastrous for the Communists. The violence, far from winning them support, drove local peasants further into the arms of the reactionaries.[4]

The Communist movement in Xiangnan never recovered from the defeat of 1928. In August, new probes into Xiangnan from Xianggan were defeated; another expedition in May 1929 soon returned to base. In 1931, the Xiangnan Working Committee set up two years earlier was elevated into a Special Committee supported by a guerrilla battalion. Party influence increased slightly, particularly in April 1934, when Xie Zhufeng set up a new body to run the Party in Leiyang, Anren, and Yongxing.[5]

The immediate causes of the Party's collapse in Xiangnan were the 1928 defeat, the retreat to Xianggan, and the bad name that the Com-munists had earned themselves during the insurrection. In any case, they would have found it hard to build a strong base in the region. They owed their success at Shuikoushan to special conditions that obtained nowhere else in Xiangnan. The Shuikoushan lead and zinc mine had been acquired by the Hunan provincial government in 1895 and was managed along lines that made its workers particularly susceptible to the Communist message. But this tiny raft of semimodern industry floated on a vast sea of conservatism that the Party proved powerless to influence.[6]

The mountains along the border with Guangdong are rich in coal de-posits and bamboo forests. Before 1949, the coal was mined and the bamboo harvested by self-employed "free artisans" who, according to a 1928 Party report, "found it difficult to develop a clear class conscious-ness, were rich in feudal thinking, and lived the lives of primitive trog-lodytes." In the 1920s, the Communists paid no attention to these "pitiful workers," even though they formed a majority in Yizhang and Leiyang. (Had the Communists heeded these workers, they might have been bet-ter prepared for the rigors of the Three-Year War, when they, too, lived as troglodytes.) Instead, they concentrated on organizing peasants on the plains around Anren. Here, too, "feudal" obstacles stood in the way of developing class struggle. The peasants were prosperous and heavily in awe of the "Confucian" powerholders. Xiangnan was territory of the Red Gang, who acted as bodyguards for the "evil gentry" who controlled the villages.[7]

## THE THREE-YEAR WAR BEGINS

The Three-Year War in Xiangnan began in August 1934, when the Sixth
Red Army crossed the region on its way west from Xianggan as part of
the general pattern of movements that preceded the start of the Long
March. It left behind an Independent Regiment in Xiangnan under Li
Zongbao. This regiment merged with local guerrillas under Peng
Linchang. On October 30, the front section of the Long March burst
through into Hunan, and on November 13, it occupied Yizhang and established a second soviet government there. On December 1, the marchers crossed the Xiang River into Guangxi. They suffered heavy casualties
fighting their way across Xiangnan and left several thousand wounded
behind. They also helped restore Party and guerrilla organizations in
the region.[8]

The Long March brought great commotion to Xiangnan. Nationalist
armies pursuing the marchers left behind a strong force to mop up
Communist remnants in the region. Three divisions of the Guangdong
Army and several regiments of the Peace Preservation Corps combed
the mountains along the border and removed people to strategic settlements in the valleys. They blocked the wells and sealed or burned the
houses in the empty villages. Elsewhere, they organized networks of
"widows, old people, the weak, and the halt" to spy on the Communists.
In November, Li Zongbao defected to the Nationalists, Peng Linchang
was killed by a traitor, the guerrillas were routed, and two thousand
wounded Red Army soldiers died. Finally, there were only six survivors
left, all of them wounded. Li Lin, a junior officer of the Communist regiment planted in Xiangnan in August, and Gu Ziyuan regrouped these
six survivors, together with two dozen stragglers from the Long March
who had turned up in the mountains and some troops sent south from
Xianggan. They then set up a new base on the border between Yizhang
and Pingshi in Guangdong.[9]

In early 1935, as part of the general retreat from Gannan after the
collapse of the Central Soviet, a regiment of 1,200 stay-behinders broke
through to the west and headed for Xiangnan. This regiment was
among the strongest of the dozen or so columns that tried to escape
Chiang's "metal bucket" in Gannan. Its leader, Gong Chu, chief of staff
of Xiang Ying's rearguard, had been commissioned to set up a new sub-
bureau of the Central Committee on the border between Hunan,
Guangdong, and Guangxi (Gui), to found a soviet government there,
and to round up scattered units of Long Marchers under a new general
command. Gong Chu's mission was seen at the time as vitally important
for the future of the Red Army in the south. Xiang Ying did not yet
know where the Long March would end, but he probably expected the
planned base in Xiangyuegui to serve as a key link between the Party
center and its southern branch around Gannan. This role probably ex-

plains why Gong's regiment was better provided than other columns, for example with telegraphic equipment and radio personnel. Gong was no stranger to Xiangnan; in August 1928, during a brief Red Army sortie into Xiangnan, Mao Zedong had left him behind at Zixing to reorganize the Xiangnan Committee.[10]

When Gong arrived in Xiangnan in early 1935, he made his way to Lianxian, on the Guangdong side of the Xiangyue border near Guangxi. Within two months, he had built a base connecting points all the way between Chenxian in the east and Lianxian in the west, more than 130 miles apart. News of his arrival spread swiftly; representatives of guerrilla bands active in various places on the Hunan border came to make contact with him. He had little difficulty in repelling attacks on his mountain stronghold by the Peace Preservation Corps. "The Communist armed forces developed rapidly in Xiangyuegui," he recalled. "By relying on these three adjacent provinces and the strategic and topographically variegated hills and mountains, we could advance to attack and retreat to maintain our position, so the situation stayed relatively stable." But Gong was disillusioned with Communism and no longer believed that the Party reflected popular interests. He also detected a changed attitude among local people. Five years earlier they had welcomed him; now they had an "unspeakable loathing" for the Red Army and "silently resisted" it.[11] Gong had been alienated by the execution of his friends in the Central Soviet for "wrong thought," "unsteady standpoint," and membership of the "counterrevolutionary landlord class," and he believed that he himself was under surveillance by Xiang Ying's agents. In May 1935, he defected, and the chance of a Party revival in Xiangnan vanished.

## THE XIANGNAN GUERRILLAS

There were at least four other guerrilla groups scattered around Xiangnan, although their relation to Gong's regiment is not clear. In Xiangyue, the group under Li Lin was shattered in 1936, but Li and two survivors held out in the Qitian Mountains around Yizhang. To the north, a dozen Communist diehards under Liu Xia and Xie Zhufeng fought along the borders of Leiyang, Anren, and Hengyang. Although the two groups were out of contact with one another throughout the Three-Year War, Li Lin heard reports of the Liu-Xie group and drew comfort from the thought of two tiny armies "working in tandem north and south."[12]

Further to the east, a group of seventy guerrillas, under Wang Zhi, held out between Lingxian and Guidong near the Jiangxi border. Wang Zhi, a Fujianese from Minxi, was just eighteen when he joined the Communist Party in 1934.[13] Wang's guerrillas bristled with bullets stuffed into their belts and bandoliers and appeared extremely fierce, but most of the bullets were made of wood. Each guerrilla carried a machete to cut trails through the forest and to clear bivouac sites. In the summer, they were bitten raw by mosquitoes, and their clothes were shredded by the brambly undergrowth. Their sole tailor could hardly produce uniforms for them all, so, to show that they were members of one army, each guerrilla sewed himself a five-cornered hat. To preserve discipline and morale, they kept to a strict military and political regime, with fixed times for training, listening to reports, discussions, and criticism and self-criticism. According to veterans, "this showed that we were Red guerrillas led by the Communist Party." Wang was principally bent on preserving forces; he made little attempt to win recruits.[14]

A fourth guerrilla band was active in Guidong and Rucheng near the border with Guangdong and Jiangxi. These Xiangyuegan guerrillas were remnants of the column under Cai Huiwen and Fang Weixia, who had led an expedition force of three hundred into the region in early 1935.[15] (See the chapter on Ganyue.) In Xiangnan, Cai and Fang linked up with one hundred guerrillas under the local Communist Zhou Li. Because Zhou Li's old base around Lingxian had been turned by Nationalist "pacifiers" into a wasteland inhabited by three people, the Cai-Fang column moved south to the Zhuguang Mountains between Guidong in Xiangnan and Shangyou in Gannan. In October 1935, Cai and Fang were killed when three Nationalist divisions swooped down on them.[16] Zhou Li fled with 160 survivors to the Mian Mountains "to preserve his forces."[17]

In 1937, these groups began to grow again. At one point, the detachment under Zhou Li had one thousand men under arms in two battalions. However, most chose to stay behind in the mountains rather than fight the Japanese.[18] Only three hundred of Zhou Li's Xiangyuegan guerrillas went to Wannan, where they joined the Third Battalion of the Second Regiment of the First Detachment of the New Fourth Army. In January 1938 Tan Yubao, leader of the Xianggan guerrillas, contacted Li Lin and Gu Ziyuan to tell them about the plans for reorganization. Between January and April 1938, Li Lin led three hundred guerrillas belonging to his own group and the Leiyang group to Chijiang in Ganyue, where they became part of the Special Services Battalion of New Fourth Army headquarters. Wang Zhi's group at first yielded only thirty men, but it too later expanded.[19]

In the end, groups active in and around Xiangnan presented the New Fourth Army with more than six hundred "living forces," but most were recruited in the last few months of 1937. The Communists in Xiangnan made no real headway after 1934. The several local guerrilla bands active in the region were small and out of touch with one another. The biggest group, under Zhou Li, originated outside Xiangnan, in neighboring Ganyue. Others had been sent south from Xianggan or west from Gannan. They, too, were outsiders to the region and found it difficult to strike roots. Their inability to coordinate their activities is one reason for their poor performance; another is the defection of Gong Chu, who knew Xiangnan and acted as a magnet for its Communists in early 1935. But even if Gong Chu had remained loyal and succeeded in unifying the scattered groups, it is doubtful whether he could have overcome the hostility and indifference of local people to the Communists.

# Min'gan

•  •  •

The Min'gan base and the Min'gan Provincial Committee set up to rule it were founded in April 1933 after the Red Army's victory over Chiang Kai-shek's Fourth Encirclement. Min'gan was formed from parts of three existing bases in Fujian (Min) and Jiangxi (Gan); its name is a compound of the abbreviated names of these two provinces (see map 5). At its peak, the Min'gan base had a population of one million in a triangle of territory stretching from Fuzhou in Jiangxi to Jianyang and Sanming in Fujian. The base occupied a strategic position linked in all directions to older soviets, and it was immensely important for the defense of the Central Soviet. Consequently, Chiang's generals started their Fifth Encirclement campaign in Min'gan. The base collapsed in a shambles after a series of bloody battles. In September 1933, its main bastion at Lichuan succumbed to the Nationalists, and its leaders fled south through the Wuyi Mountains, first to Jianning and then to Ninghua and Qingliu, while Huang Dao, Huang Ligui, and others were transferred to Minbei. By October 1934, the Nationalists controlled the entire base, save for a few pockets in the mountains. By May 1935, even these few pockets had been emptied.

Min'gan was one of only two regions (the other being Annanyongde) where the Communist movement was completely crushed in the Three-Year War. Today, the loss of the base is blamed on various "leftist" excesses that plagued the Min'gan Committee during its short life. Yang Daoming, a survivor of the Min'gan Soviet, has described them in a memoir. The Min'gan Committee had been brought into existence on the crest of a wave of "leftism" that engulfed most of the Party in early 1933. The Min'gan leaders launched their own miniature version of the struggle against the "Luo Ming line" that was laying waste the Party in Minxi and the Central Soviet.

When Yang arrived in Min'gan in August 1934, on the eve of the Three-Year War, the base was on the point of collapse. Its leaders, at a loss to understand the causes of the crisis, tried to stave off defeat by stepping up their campaign "to eliminate counterrevolutionaries." Most, perhaps all, of the victims were innocent of the charges laid against them. Yang gives the example of the head of the women's section, a young woman in her early twenties, who liked to amuse people by imitating leaders' voices. She was arrested on charges of "slander" and "making fun of people." Under torture, she "confessed" to a string of crimes and was executed. The killings demoralized Party members and alienated villagers. During land reform, "members of the masses" were wrongly classified as rich peasants and killed. Large numbers of people fled the region to escape the terror. "The flight of the masses became so serious," said Yang Daoming, "that how to get them to return became the provincial committee's number one concern."

The chaos in the base was increased when incompetents were promoted into leading positions. Able leaders were killed in purges or removed to make way for "base-level cadres and ordinary soldiers" in accordance with the theory of "the unique importance of class origins."

On October 26, 1934, Min'gan leaders declared that they would "fight independently to defend the Min'gan Soviet area" after receiving a directive from the Central Committee, which was about to set out on the Long March. They were slow to switch to guerrilla warfare as instructed. They continued to issue wildly inappropriate slogans like "Defend the towns," and they based their strategy on the assumption that the Red Army would soon swing around and march back to the Central Soviet. They can hardly be blamed for this misconception; Xiang Ying harbored the same illusion. But where Xiang had the skeptical Chen Yi to restrain him, in Min'gan no one dared question the "leftist" leaders.

In late 1934, the Min'gan Committee controlled more than one thousand troops and cadres. Instead of lying low in their old haunts or slipping into guerrilla areas like Minbei or Minxi, they bearded the Nationalists on their own ground. By early 1935, the Communists' numbers were down to six hundred. In March 1935, they received a message— probably from Xiang Ying—telling them "to continue the struggle independently and with the initiative in your hands; from now on the Central Committee can no longer maintain radio contact with you." Their leader, Zhong Xunren, told a meeting that it was now necessary to adopt guerrilla methods. Under the new conditions, leaders of the Min'gan

Red Army, under Xu Jianghan, lost heart; their lack of spirit in turn demoralized the ranks, which soon fell to pieces.

Xu Jianghan was a professional soldier who had come over to the Communists in December 1931 after serving as a junior officer in a Nationalist army. In the early months of the Three-Year War, people like Xu gave up the fight more easily than local Communists. In May 1935, Xu, surrounded in the Zi Mountains, defected at the head of several hundred troops. One hundred burst the circle and fled south to join Fang Fang's Red Ninth Regiment in Minxi. In the end, only seven remained in the mountains. Five returned to their homes in Jiangxi, and two, who had no homes to go to, shaved their heads and joined a monastery; one was Yang Daoming, who became head monk in the Anting Temple in Yongtai and a member of the Fujian People's Political Consultative Committee.

This defeat was not the end of the Min'gan Provincial Committee. In April 1936, leaders of guerrillas in Minbei and Mindong joined forces to resurrect it on a different part of the border further to the north. But the new committee never really got off the ground, and it was abolished in February 1938.

Why did the Min'gan Committee collapse so irretrievably in 1935? Communist writers say that it was because the committee's policies were extreme and its regime was tyrannous. This assessment is true, but it is not the whole truth. The Min'gan Committee was indeed born in a period of "leftism" and infected by the "leftist" virus. But not all the Party's younger bases infected by "leftist" maladies collapsed as a result after 1934. The Mindong base, born in early 1934, emerged in good health from the Three-Year War and presented the New Fourth Army with one of its best contingents. The difference between Min'gan and Mindong is that the Min'gan base did not arise independently from local conditions but was a military construct that sprang from the drawing boards of the Red Army high command. The ambitious young men and women sent to realize the drawing knew only the "leftist" politics of the Party's leading group. There was no strong local movement to check them if they went too far, no dissenting opinion of the sort that Luo Ming and the Maoists represented in Minxi and the Central Soviet. So the Min'gan pioneers were free to enact their gory drama through to its last futile scene. Their lack of familiarity with the region they were defending was another cause of their defeat. When the final crisis came in May 1935, they went over to the enemy in shoals. "They lacked a firm leading core," Fang Zhichun told Mao Zedong in November 1937.[1]

# Annanyongde

◆　◆　◆

Annanyongde, sometimes called Annanyong in Party literature, refers to that part of Fujian east of Minxi and to the southwest of Minzhong (see map 5). The name Annanyongde is a compound of the first syllables of Anxi, Nan'an, Yongchun, and Dehua, counties sixty or seventy miles north of Xiamen and around one hundred miles south of Fuzhou.

The Annanyongde region is mountainous and forested. The Communist base in Annanyongde was built in 1932 by infusions of people mainly from Xiamen, but also from Fuzhou and other cities; it was not until May 1933 that a small soviet was set up in the region. The Fujian Incident of December 1933 to January 1934 relieved pressure on the Communists in Annanyong, who in just a few weeks increased their armed forces from fewer than one hundred to more than five hundred. Among the new recruits were defectors (officers and men) from the rebel Nationalist Nineteenth Route Army responsible for the incident.

The Annanyongde Soviet grew throughout 1934. It was some time before the Nationalists managed to stabilize their military base in nearby Quanzhou in the wake of the incident. The Communists took advantage of the chaotic interlude to arm supporters, grab *tuhao* as hostages, organize rent resistance, divide land, and join the three counties of Annanyong into a single base. At the height of their campaign, they controlled one thousand Red Guards, whom they reorganized as Minnan Anti-Japanese Volunteers.

After the start of the Long March in October 1934, conditions in the base quickly deteriorated. In January 1935, more than twenty thousand Nationalist troops supported by *mintuan* and nearly ten thousand armed bandits bore down on Annanyong and began purging villages. The drive was spearheaded by six thousand troops belonging to a battalion of the

Ninth Division. The Annanyong Bandit Extermination Command was at first largely ineffectual, but in the early summer of 1935, it changed its strategy and began applying measures of the sort used to mop up the Central Soviet: "steady advance" through fortified rings combined with "collective recantations." The new tactics worked. "The masses took fright and did not dare approach us," recalled one veteran.

The guerrillas decided to burst through the encirclement and form new bases elsewhere. They headed south toward Zhangzhou, where they hoped to join up with Minnan's Red Third Regiment, but their way was blocked, and they were forced to return to Anxi. In August, a chain of defections by local Communists led to the collapse of the guerrillas and the destruction of the network of Party liaison stations in Annanyong. Some guerrillas who had "collectively betrayed" were reorganized as "eradicators of Communism." In October 1935, thirty survivors "scattered and hid" to preserve forces. Nearly half the survivors were Hainanese who were unfamiliar with the region and its language. These people were sent to Xiamen to get new assignments from the Party there. The rest hid in a cave, but they were betrayed to the Nationalists, surrounded, and forced to make a "collective recantation."

Today, Communists explain the collapse of the Party in Annanyongde by the Nationalists' greater military strength; the Communists' lack of arms, supplies, and experience in guerrilla warfare; the destruction of the Party's liaison network; the local Party's lack of resolve, reflected in a large number of desertions and defections; and ill effects of the "leftist" plague imported from nearby Xiamen. While these analyses are accurate and relevant, more attention should be given to political geography in accounting for the special weaknesses of the Annanyongde base. Like the base in Min'gan, it was founded chiefly by outsiders acting on instructions from the Party in Xiamen in January 1934. Communists had been active earlier in Annanyong, but the original base in the region had been practically wiped out in late 1933, when twelve Communist leaders were killed by bandits with whom they were trying to ally. Like Mindong, the base in Annanyong was strengthened by hundreds of new recruits during the crisis caused by the Fujian Incident. In Mindong, however, this sudden growth was securely rooted in local conditions; in Annanyong, it was not. The new leaders after 1933 continued to look to places outside Annanyong for security and direction, particularly to Xiamen and to the Red Third Regiment in Minnan. When the base was on the point of extinction in mid-1935, its main leader fled as if by instinct toward the Red Third's base around Xiamen. Ye Fei in Mindong did not have the same option in the crisis of 1935; even if he had, it is unlikely that he would have taken it.

So close was the relationship between Annanyong and Minnan, where the Red Third was mainly active, that the Annanyong guerrillas were known as the Second Detachment of the Minnan Guerrillas, though geographically they were part of Minzhong. When the base finally fell, a large minority of survivors, including all the non-Fujianese, sought refuge in Xiamen (a step for which they were later criticized). Because Annanyong was so close to Xiamen, Xiamen Communists could intervene in its affairs and infect it with the "leftism" that originated largely in the cities. Because of this meddling, the Annanyong Communists changed their Party secretary three times in six months and alienated rich peasants by ruthlessly attacking them. Just forty miles from the sea, Annanyong benefited more immediately than bases further inland from the ferment caused by the Fujian Incident in the coastal cities. But because of its lack of isolation, it also suffered at the hands of both its enemies in the Quanzhou garrison and its "friends" in the Party's Xiamen branch.[1]

# Hailufeng

•   ◆   •

In the winter of 1929, the Communist Party's Dong Jiang Special Committee organized armed peasants into the Red Forty-ninth Regiment under Peng Gui, who later set up a second regiment, the Forty-seventh. In 1934, the Dong Jiang guerrillas suffered heavy losses during a Nationalist drive against their base in the Da'nan Mountains north of Hailufeng. In early 1935, the Dong Jiang Committee reorganized them as the Red Second Regiment. In May 1935, they scattered to the plains in sixteen small teams and carried out guerrilla actions. Peng and other leaders were killed; by late 1935, the base had been destroyed.[1]

After this collapse, seventeen survivors fled to Dabu in eastern Guangdong, where they worked secretly for the Party. After 1937, Fang Fang recruited remnants of this group to the Dong Jiang Anti-Japanese Guerrillas.[2] These guerrillas had no direct ties to the New Fourth Army, but in late 1938, Ye Ting, commander of the New Fourth, visited Guangdong to try to set up a resistance base there. However, Ye Ting was soon sent away again by Chiang Kai-shek, and the two small units that stayed behind in the region were wiped out by the Guomindang in early 1940.[3]

# Wanxibei

❖   ❖   ❖

The Wanxibei, or northwestern Anhui, Committee was set up by the Party's Shanghai Executive Bureau in the autumn of 1934. By early 1935, it controlled one hundred guerrillas organized in three companies; by December 1935, it had nearly five hundred men under arms. These guerrillas were commanded by Sun Zhongde, an Anhui man who joined the Communist Party in 1934. In early 1936, Sun led some of his guerrillas to Eyuwan to reinforce Gao Jingting's Twenty-eighth Red Army. In the summer, he returned to Wanxibei with a small number of them. At first, Sun's guerrillas did not join the New Fourth Army but stayed in Wanxibei and fought the Japanese as an independent unit. In November 1938, by which time they had grown considerably, Zhang Yunyi incorporated them into the newly formed Jiangbei Guerrilla Column of the New Fourth Army.[1]

# Qiongya

$\bullet$  $\bullet$  $\bullet$

Qiongya is another name for Hainan, the large island off China's southern coast near Vietnam. The Qiongya Red Army was set up in 1927. At its peak in the summer of 1932, it had six to seven thousand men under arms and the support of twenty thousand armed irregulars. The Qiongya Soviet collapsed in the winter of 1932 as a result (according to Party historians) of "leftist" excesses. Twenty-six Red Army survivors fled to the Murui Mountains, where they held out under siege for ten months. In 1933, they regrouped in four guerrilla bands that scattered across the island. In May 1936, survivors set up the Qiongya Red Army Guerrilla Command with seven detachments. The following year, the Communists restored the Qiongya Soviet government along with governments in several counties. By late 1937, they had more than three hundred men under arms. These Qiongya guerrillas did not join the New Fourth Army, though they are often counted as participants in the Three-Year War.[1]

# The Three-Year War Ends, the Guerrillas Unite

•  •  •

The chapters on the Three-Year War in its various regions describe how each separate group of guerrillas received and responded to news of the united front, assembled, climbed down the mountains, and reorganized under the New Fourth Army flag (map 11). It remains to consider this same process from the point of view of the national leadership of the Communist Party, the Nationalist Government in Nanjing, and the New Fourth's central founders.

## YAN'AN, NANJING, AND THE GUERRILLAS

The Long Marchers' last radio contact with the rearguard in the Central Soviet was in the spring of 1935. Rearguards everywhere lost or abandoned their radios in late 1934 and early 1935. They also lost their "communication cadres": only one radio operator survived the Three-Year War as a revolutionary. After the founding of the New Fourth Army, one of the Yan'an leaders' first steps was to send south a batch of radio technicians.[1] Guerrillas in some regions had managed to renew links with urban comrades after 1935. One or two groups had indirectly contacted bureaus of the Party in Beijing and Shanghai. But it was not until late 1937 that they got back in touch with the Party center.

Communist leaders in Shaanbei continued to refer to the presence of Red forces in southern China throughout the period of their separation. "Our guerrilla forces there," said Mao in December 1935, two months after the end of the Long March, "have suffered some setbacks but have not been wiped out. In many places they are reasserting themselves, growing and expanding." Mao even claimed that guerrillas in old soviet areas were switching to the counteroffensive. In private, however, the

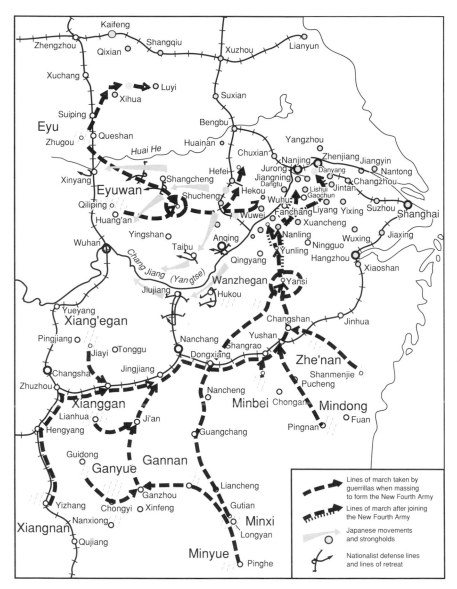

Map 11. The guerrillas march out to found the New Fourth Army and advance into Japanese-occupied areas (February–October 1938). *Based on a map in Junshi kexueyuan 1987, vol. 2.*

Communists in Shaanbei confessed that the fate of the rearguard was a mystery to them.[2] As late as June 23, 1937, Zhu De had no real idea of its strength. "We have partisan forces in a number of different areas," he told a visitor. "They exist in groups of from 1,000 to 3,000; it is hard to establish their exact total. Connections with some of these groups are still maintained, but not with all; at best they are none too good."[3] But despite the problems, Party leaders doggedly refused to give up the stay-behinders as lost.

On the Long March and in the first few months after their arrival in Shaanbei, Mao and his comrades had little idea of what was happening in other parts of China. But Communists in Beijing and the coastal cities with access to the press and to contacts in the provinces knew from reports that guerrillas were still active in some regions. In the winter of 1935, shortly after Chinese Communists in Moscow had revived the idea of a united front with the Guomindang, secret talks started between the Party's Northern Bureau (under Liu Shaoqi) and the Nationalist government in Nanjing.[4] The Northern Bureau was then almost certainly out of touch with the Central Committee in Shaanbei. In April 1936, the bureau's negotiator raised the question of the southern guerrillas in the last of six demands on the Guomindang. He called on the Nationalists to "settle an area in which the southern guerrillas can concentrate and reorganize, so that they can await the chance to go out and resist Japan."

Also in April, Zhou Enlai and Zhang Xueliang, setting terms for a new united front, mentioned the Communist armed forces "in Jiangxi, Hainan, and the Dabie Mountains [Eyuwan]," which "would also be subject to inspection and reorganization." In June or July, by which time Liu Shaoqi had probably restored ties to leaders in Shaanbei, the Party's negotiator again raised the question of the southern guerrillas. The Nationalists proposed that they "should have areas designated for them by the respective provinces in which to concentrate and should be reorganized as part of the National Revolutionary Army."

The Communists objected to this proposal, which they interpreted as a plan to incorporate the guerrillas into existing armies. The Nationalists then proposed "letting the guerrillas in the southern provinces go north to join up with the main Red Army." The Communists agreed, on condition that the guerrillas were guaranteed safe passage. In July and August 1936, the main negotiations moved to Yan'an, and it seems that the guerrillas disappeared for a while from the agenda.[5]

In later years, Nationalist historians tried to write off the guerrillas as a handful of desperadoes, but at the time, both Communists and Nationalists took them seriously enough to argue frequently over what to do with them. Events in northern China in 1936 showed that the Communists were by no means a spent force either on the battlefield or in the political arena. The Long March had given them a new sense of purpose and identity. A similar resurgence in the Party's old southern bases could not be ruled out, especially if the politics of patriotism that infected Beijing and Shanghai continued to spread through China's cities. The prospect of war with Japan gave Chiang Kai-shek another reason to look for a resolution of the problem of the guerrillas, He could not afford pockets of dissidence behind his lines. He tried various ways of removing these pockets during preparations to transfer his regular forces to northern China and the coast.

At first, Chiang tried to crush them by armed force. Clearly, he did not feel bound by the negotiations of the summer of 1936. There is no evidence that these talks had had official status in either Nanjing or Yan'an. The direct negotiations between the two capitals that started later did not apparently at first return to the issue of the guerrillas; more urgent questions, such as the future of the main Red Army and plans for the united front, had to be resolved.

Perhaps the omission was deliberate on both sides. For the Nationalists, the imminence of an agreement was a strong incentive for one last go at clearing up the south, before the guerrillas restored contact with the Communist center in Yan'an and forced their way back onto the agenda. For the Communists, the situation in the south was still a mystery, so they may have decided to shelve the issue of reorganization until they had more facts. It is quite likely that they were undecided about the Northern Bureau's earlier agreement to transfer the guerrillas north. They certainly intended to keep a southern foothold; they may have felt that discreet silence was the best way of retaining it.

On February 10, 1937, the Communists in Yan'an agreed to abandon revolutionary policies in return for a united front against Japan and to accept "special area" status for their Shaan'ganning base in the northwest. The February 10 statement made no specific provision for reorganizing the guerrillas.[6] This omission appeared to free Chiang's hands in the south, for by legalizing the Red Army in Shaan'ganning, it implicitly outlawed guerrillas in other parts of the country, rendering them fair game for a new military campaign.

The campaign started in early 1937, shortly after the resolution of the Xi'an Incident. Communists claim that it involved huge numbers of government troops; it was apparently planned at the highest levels. By April, more than a quarter of a million soldiers had reportedly been mobilized for the "final annihilation of all traces of the Red Army in Southeast China." This offensive resulted in massive losses for the guerrillas—as many as half, according to Ye Ting.

Once the attacks started, Communists in the north tried to ward them off by talks.[7] Guomindang representatives replied that the southern guerrillas were beneath attention. Nationalist politicians who had agreed, reluctantly, to talk with Yan'an drew a line at talking with the "false" Communists in the south and even suggested mischievously that it was because these Communists were "false" that the "true" Communists had abandoned them in 1934.[8] This feeling was not confined to leaders in the provinces troubled most by the "men in the mountains." Chiang Kai-shek made the same distinction when he raised the issue with Zhu De and Mao Zedong, who were in Yan'an. According to Chen Yi, he said, "We do not wish to talk with them. They are bandits who kill people and light fires. They have changed over the last three years. They are not like you."[9]

The first half of 1937 was the worst period of the Three-Year War for guerrillas in many regions.[10] However, the government's military measures were counteracted in part by new opportunities that opened up with the revival of the Communist Party in the cities and the broadening of the movement against Japan. The guerrillas emerged from battle once again bloodied but unbowed. "The [Nationalists] had united with the Eighth Route Army because they had no choice, while insisting that the drive to exterminate us would continue. But we held out and forced their collapse," said Chen Yi.[11]

## REORGANIZATION

On August 13, 1937, during final negotiations about reorganizing the Red Army in the north as the Eighth Route Army, Communist representatives proposed, and the Guomindang agreed, that the southern guerrillas, too, should be reorganized to fight behind Japanese lines, in central China.[12] By now, Party leaders had a clearer idea of the guerrillas' distribution and strength and of the likely course of the war.

Anti-Communist historians writing about this period see the Nationalists' acceptance of this proposal as a big mistake. It is easy to see why. By letting the Communists back into eastern China, the Guomindang contributed directly to its own eventual downfall. Within eight years of arriving there, the guerrillas had grown from several thousand to several hundred thousand and were poised to play a major role in overthrowing the Nationalist regime.

In early 1937, Chiang Kai-shek denounced the southern guerrillas as criminals; just a few months later, he invited them to form an army and to join in the resistance to Japan in Jiangnan, south of the lower Chang Jiang, the richest region in the whole of China and a haunt of the Communist Party in the 1920s. Supporters of the Guomindang suggest that Chiang Kai-shek was manipulated into this volte-face by a Communist mole who had infiltrated his military council. Another explanation of this "great mystery of modern history" is that the southern guerrillas were invited to reorganize as a sop to the Russians, who were providing Chiang with military supplies.[13] Both explanations are unconvincing. There is no evidence of a mole, and it is unlikely that Stalin would have been interested in the fate of a few thousand lost guerrillas when he had no scruples about sacrificing Yan'an's autonomy to placate the Guomindang. A third theory is that the Nationalists were deceived by Zhou Enlai's "smiling diplomacy."[14] All these theories premise the view that there were not enough guerrillas left in the south in 1937 to warrant authorizing a second Communist army and that it was only after entering Jiangnan that the Communists were able to win enough new recruits to fill the quota "generously" set for them at twelve thousand. This premise is unconvincing.

Communist writers, on the other hand, suggest that far from scorning the guerrillas, Chiang feared them; that far from being tricked into letting them into eastern China, he sent them deliberately to what he hoped would be their graveyard on one of China's most perilous battlefields. But they add that Chiang's plan to "borrow a knife" from the Japanese collapsed, and instead the New Fourth Army went from strength to strength.

My own view is that different groups wanted the New Fourth Army in Jiangnan for different reasons. Officially, the Guomindang argued that the southern Communists had skills that could be put to good use in central China. As guerrillas, they could harass the enemy behind the lines and coordinate with the government's regular armies at the front. Nationalist generals and politicians who believed in the united front hoped that the guerrillas would help tie down the Japanese; they did what they could to support the guerrillas, particularly in the Fifth War Zone in Anhui.[15] Some even believed that the New Fourth Army was more sincere about the united front than the Eighth Route Army in the north and that the trouble that later arose in central China was caused by "bandits sent down from Yan'an."[16]

Other Nationalist leaders, who were cynical about the guerrillas' good faith and combat skills, favored their reorganization for other reasons. In 1937, Communists in some parts of the south, particularly Minxi, were trying hard to forge alliances with Nationalist armies in the provinces "from above and below," with both officers and ranks. The patriotic wave sweeping China had stirred junior officers in many armies and made them receptive to such advances. Conservative generals may have feared a repeat performance of the drama that had led to the subversion of Nationalist armies sent to blockade the Reds in the north. A single agreement applicable to Communist remnants everywhere was preferable to a patchwork of separate regional agreements that conservatives would not necessarily control. Best of all would have been to remove the Communist threat to security in the south by military means, but they no longer had any realistic prospect of doing so. As a last resort, the conservatives were prepared to let "responsible" Communists call the guerrillas down the mountains and gather them together in one place alongside Nationalist armies in a position to keep them under watch and, if necessary, chasten them. The Nationalists were far better placed in the Chang Jiang delta than in the north to enforce restrictions on the Communists, who would in any case have their hands full dealing with the Japanese.

Opinion was analogously divided among the Communists. Xiang Ying and others believed in close cooperation with the Guomindang and did their best to avoid antagonizing the allied armies. Others in the New Fourth Army, notably Chen Yi, believed with Mao that the future of the New Fourth Army lay in independent development north of the Chang Jiang, and that to this end it should break from the restrictions imposed on it by the Nationalists and quit the Jiangnan death trap.[17]

## XIANG YING AND CHEN YI CALL IN THE GUERRILLAS

Even after Communists and Nationalists had agreed in principle that the southern guerrillas should combine into a single army, it was several weeks before direct communications were restored between Yan'an and the southern Communist leaders, including their nominal commander Xiang Ying. In some regions, the guerrillas first heard of reorganization through messages from government officials, requesting talks. Some guerrillas smelled a rat and rejected the approaches out of hand. These were the people later criticized as "left sectarians." Others—the so-called "rightists"— threw caution to the wind and ended up disarmed. Xiang Ying and Chen Yi had only a general idea of Party policy when they were first approached by local officials in Ganyue. They responded cautiously but constructively. "We could not go down the mountains to negotiate with the class enemy without instructions from the Central Committee," said Chen Yi in a memoir.

> But if we delayed too long, we risked missing a chance to develop. If the southern guerrillas in the various provinces linked up, they would become an important force; in order to link up, we should make full use of the chance for talks. We did so on the principle that we could agree to stopping armed clashes in guerrilla areas while the Nationalists should make every effort to facilitate communications, so that we could swiftly liaise with guerrillas in the different regions. The Central Committee was to be responsible for arrangements about political questions and future actions after armed clashes had stopped. The guerrillas had no authority to negotiate on that.[18]

Even after negotiations had started, the Nationalists at first refused to let Xiang Ying and Chen Yi speak on behalf of the southern guerrillas as a whole and were only prepared to discuss Gannan with them. Xiang and Chen reluctantly accepted this restriction, hoping that guerrillas in other regions would refuse to enter agreements that violated chains of authority in the Party. In all but one or two cases, their expectation was borne out, and the guerrillas left important decisions to Xiang's bureau or to Yan'an.[19] In September 1937, Xiang and Chen went to Ganzhou, where Chen signed a draft agreement on cooperation with Xiong Bin, chief of staff of the Jiangxi Peace Preservation Corps. In late September, Xiang Ying traveled on to Nanchang. There he talked with Xiong Shihui, governor of Jiangxi, and reached an oral agreement with Xiong Bin on three points: the Red Army guerrillas would be reorganized as Anti-Japanese Volunteers: "old and new debts" in villages in guerrilla areas would be canceled; and the Jiangxi Provincial Government would pay the cost of assembling the guerrillas. On September 29, while returning to Ganzhou, Xiang Ying addressed a letter to guerrillas everywhere telling them that "because of the urgent national crisis and in order to aid the country in its hour of need and to promote the independence and liberation of the Chinese nation, we have abolished past policies like the soviet movement and the violent seizure of land."[20]

Both before and after the start of negotiations, and especially after the general agreement in Nanchang, Xiang and Chen organized expeditions to restore links to guerrillas throughout the south. Many leaders of the Three-Year War, including Chen Yi, Deng Zihui, Zeng Shan, and Chen Pixian, took part in these searches. The expeditions were fraught with difficulty and danger. In the big cities, Communists and Nationalists were now for the most part on their best behavior, but in remote border areas, the united front often meant little to either side. Local powerholders could not be relied on to guarantee the safety of these Communist emissaries, and Communist diehards in the mountains often reacted violently when their suspicions were aroused. Eyeglasses and a scholar's hat might get a Party messenger safely past the local gentry, but they cut no ice with class-conscious guerrillas. Many Party representatives were threatened, and several were killed as traitors, by incredulous Communists, notably in Xianggan, Eyuwan, and Gandongbei.

The best way to track down guerrillas was through Party offices and liaison stations, but many liaison officials were wary of the searchers and obstructed them. In regions where Party networks were in ruins, the first problem was to find out where the guerrillas were hiding; the second was to make contact with them. The business of calling in guerrillas from eight provinces was complicated and arduous.[21] However, the great majority eventually came down the mountains after hearing about the united front. Most writers agree that the guerrillas' initial resistance stemmed not from a lack of loyalty or discipline but mainly from a lack of outside contacts and information.

Only a tiny minority, including a few "who were convinced at first but later changed their minds and went back up the mountains," chose to continue the class struggle and the guerrilla life. According to Chen Yi, these recusants became indistinguishable from bandits.[22] Others stayed behind for other reasons. Many were exhausted after three hard years in the mountains. Now that the heat was off, they wanted only to go home. Some whose wives had been sold or whose families had been destroyed were demoralized and could see no future for themselves or for the revolution. An unknown number took the chance to slip away and melt back into civilian life rather than march north under the dizzyingly abstract banner of resistance to imperialism. While mustering the troops, said Zhang Dingcheng, it was necessary to wage a two-pronged struggle: against sectarianism and against "a backward local viewpoint, family viewpoint, hankering after one's native place, and not wanting to go to the front."[23]

## YAN'AN'S PLANS FOR THE GUERRILLAS

In Party terms, Xiang and Chen were acting within their rights when they claimed to represent the southern guerrillas as a whole in talks with the Guomindang. But the Nationalists recognized only one Communist center in China. A brief period of confusion resulted, since Party leaders in Yan'an did not apparently intervene directly in the first stage of negotiations. Perhaps they felt that they lacked sufficient information to steer the talks to good effect. After all, they were out of touch with Xiang until late September, when he had already finished his main negotiations with the Nationalists. In any case, their hidden agenda for the south was better served by an outward show of laissez-faire.

Secretly, the Central Committee was extremely concerned to use the Communist presence in the south to the best possible strategic advantage. While Xiang and Chen were negotiating in Jiangxi, Party leaders in Yan'an several times put aside their own urgent business to consider the position of the southerners and draw up guidelines for them. Their directives stressed two main points: the need to maintain vigilance and a firm class line, and the need to leave behind an ample tail in the old southern bases.

A directive on August 1, 1937, stressed that though the time for soviets and land revolution was past, the fight for democracy and reforms to "improve the lives of the masses" was still on, and past gains of land revolution should be defended. Leaders in Yan'an knew from Fang

Fang, who had arrived from Minxi in June, that these issues were important in the old soviet areas. The Minxi Communists had campaigned with some success to prevent the overthrow of land reform. Their experience was probably a crucial influence on this directive, which instructed Communists in the south to maintain "absolute leadership" over their armed forces and to beware of plots to destroy them.

In the Nanjing negotiations of mid-1936, the Nationalists had agreed to drop demands for the absorption of guerrilla units into provincial armies. The Guomindang's refusal in mid-1937 to recognize Xiang Ying's right to speak for all guerrillas led to a "provincialization" of the negotiations. Nationalist leaders in the regions began once again to propose "provincial" solutions to the problem of reorganizing the guerrillas. In Minyue and Minzhong, guerrillas were subverted and disarmed. The new directive, meant as a warning against any more such incidents, instructed guerrillas to carry out changes, but only in inessential matters. The Party should give its armed forces new names to meet legal requirements and appoint commanders and deputy commanders in order to comply with the rules; but it should secretly continue to take all the main decisions. Communist guerrillas "not divorced from production" should, where possible, acquire legal status as *mintuan,* but even where they failed to do so, they should remain active and infiltrate existing militias. They should aim for funding by the government, but until they received official pay and supplies, they should finance their activities by demanding contributions from the rich and expropriating pro-Japanese traitors. When attacked, they should defend themselves. Whereas in the past they had tried to "dissolve" government armies by persuading troops to defect, they should now concentrate on making propaganda for the united front, though they should still try to "dissolve" hostile *mintuan.* The Party in the south should infiltrate its secret supporters everywhere, including the government. Moles should use their positions to protect the Party and to "democratize" the administration by spreading Communist influence in it.[24]

Publicly, the Communists in Yan'an were mouthing slogans that called for national reconciliation, cooperation, mutual trust, and compromise; privately, however, they intended to sacrifice not an ounce of independence in their rapprochement with the government. The August 1 directive was aimed at exporting this intransigent position to the south. But not all sections of the Party were promoting the same united front in mid-1937. Statements by Wang Ming in Moscow were sometimes at odds with statements from Yan'an. Party bureaus in the cities were in contact with both centers and could not always be relied on to follow Mao's line, for they were in close touch with Nationalist politicians and under pressure to follow a more conciliatory course of the sort favored by Wang Ming. Events later showed that Mao was right to be concerned about the politics of Xiang Ying's army, which became a bastion of right-wing "accommodationism" in the late 1930s.[25] Mao's message of August 1 got through to some southern groups but not to all, and a few suffered by compromising to excess.[26] However, even guerrillas who did not receive the instruction generally stayed vigilant and were wary of any agreement that might curtail their independence.

On September 30, Mao sent a second secret directive to the guerrillas. Sometime in late September, Xiang Ying had radioed Yan'an from Nanchang to ask his old comrades for their help. "During our long period of separation," he told them, "we have heard no sound and received no letter from one another. . . . Please send someone to liaise with me." The September 30 directive was probably Mao's response. It emphasized that the guerrillas should concentrate only three-fifths of their forces and leave the rest in place. A further message on October 1 explained the thinking behind this instruction:

> (1) The southern guerrilla areas will in days to come be strategic support points for the revolutionary movement in the south. They are the fruit of ten years' bloody war. They should be highly valued. (2) The Guomindang is trying to capture these strategic support points. After the Xi'an Incident, they did all they could to wrest them from us by slaughtering our people. When that failed, they started using the pretext of "resistance to Japan" in the hope of capturing them through Ye Ting.[27] The means may differ, but the end remains the same. (3) It would be very much against our interests to muster all the guerrilla forces in the different regions.

The directive specified precisely which areas the guerrillas should try to keep. Guerrillas should not refuse to concentrate their forces "on principle," it said, but none should move before a representative of the Central Committee had arrived to talk to them, which would take at least a few months. As for the units under Zhang Dingcheng (in Minxi), He Ming (in Minyue), and Liu Ying (in Minzhe), they should "stay in their original places, for the Japanese will invade Guangdong, Fujian, and Zhejiang. These three units should under no circumstances assemble and should ensure instead that they will be in a position to defend the guerrilla areas plus adjacent territory." It was probably because of their efforts—ultimately thwarted—to obey this directive that the guerrillas from Zhe'nan and Minxi'nan were the last of the big groups to go north (in March 1938).[28]

Mao and Wang had different views on how the war against Japan should be conducted and on the role that Communists should play in it. Wang strove to support the government and help build Chiang's armed forces. In the south, this policy meant abandoning policies and bases that threatened the united front. The Wangites had illusions about the durability and effectiveness of the alliance, and they were prepared to sacrifice other interests to support Chiang.[29]

The leaders in Yan'an, who had a more skeptical view of the agreement with the Guomindang, insisted on a strategy that combined unity with struggle. They saw the war as a chance to expand their armed forces and to strengthen their position in preparation for the future contest with the Guomindang for state power. The agreement on the guerrillas—and, later, on the New Fourth Army—was a precious opportunity to sow fertile new parts of China, including areas around the great cities of eastern China, with Communist armed forces. The opportunity should be seized, but not at the cost of abandoning older strongholds further south that would be of enormous strategic value in the coming civil war.

The directives of September 30 and October 1 show that Mao had not forgotten the old soviet bases in the south but rather had reserved a strategic place for them in his grand design for the war and for the revolution that he knew would follow. Earlier, I showed that Party leaders in Yan'an did not intervene directly and overtly in relations between the southern guerrillas and the Nationalists. I argued that they refrained partly because they were in the dark about conditions in the old southern bases. These directives suggest a second reason. In 1936, the Nationalists had proposed gathering the southern remnants together and sending them north to join the main Red Army. The Communist leaders in Yan'an apparently did nothing to implement that proposal; they probably saw it as the worst outcome short of the guerrillas' destruction. They were far more interested in maintaining their southern networks than in swelling their ranks in northern China with a few thousand more recruits. Moreover, Chiang Kai-shek had failed to remove the guerrillas from the south by force. He now hoped to remove them by pacific means. His generals were caught on numerous small guerrilla barbs that distracted their attention from bigger tasks. It was in Mao's interest to stay aloof and thus to imply that the guerrillas were an autonomous force that must be handled separately.

Xiang Ying had his own reason to play along; he feared losing control over his little army to the Communists in the north and was happy to negotiate in his own right with the authorities. Mao probably calculated that by emphasizing the guerrillas' autonomy, he would increase their chances of keeping a presence in the south. To retain that presence, he required Xiang's cooperation. As we shall see, Xiang gave a promise to cooperate but failed to keep it, so Mao's scheme miscarried.

The directives of August 1, September 30, and October 1 were in theory secret, but it is unlikely that they remained so for long, since they concerned a large number of small groups scattered across more than a dozen regions. When the directives eventually came to light, they must have confirmed the worst suspicions of conservative generals and politicians. Pro-Guomindang historians sometimes ask why the quota for the New Fourth Army was set at twelve thousand, a level that they imply was preposterously high. The quota was not in fact greatly inflated, but still the question is a good one, for quotas applying to Communist armies were generally the result of grudging compromises. Chiang's generosity probably had much to do with these directives. The message beamed south from Yan'an was a powerful incentive for him to clear as many guerrillas as possible from their strongholds before they dug back in and started causing trouble again. Through the quota, and the outlay on pay and weapons that it implied, Chiang hoped to thwart Mao by spurring Xiang to transfer all guerrillas to the assigned area, a strip of territory just fifty miles deep and one hundred and fifty miles long on the southern bank of the Chang Jiang. The ploy succeeded. Most guerrillas ended up in or around this region as a result of the efforts of Xiang, Chen Yi, and other leaders.

In Eyu and Eyuwan, north of the Chang Jiang, Xiang carried less clout. The guerrillas there belonged to a separate tradition led by local Communists and, earlier, by the Central Committee dissident Zhang Guotao. Both Xiang and the Nationalists would probably have liked these guerrillas to move south to Jiangnan, but instead, they followed an independent course. After some procrastination, they sent the bulk of their forces east toward northern Jiangsu, but they kept a strong presence in the mountains from which they had fought the Three-Year War. Early Nationalist accounts are strikingly silent about the presence of this Fourth Detachment of the New Fourth Army north of the Chang Jiang, though Communist accounts make no secret of it. Later, these Jiangbei guerrillas played an important role in helping the New Fourth Army's other detachments break out to the north. In the short term, Eyuwan's provincialism was valuable to Mao, for it enabled him to take decisions about Jiangbei independently of Xiang. The guerrillas in Eyuwan went furthest of any guerrilla group in the Three-Year War toward achieving Mao's dream of simultaneously developing new and old bases after 1937.

The August 1 directive advising vigilance was written after the He Ming Incident at Zhangpu in Minyue on July 16, 1937, when government troops disarmed several hundred guerrillas who had incautiously quit their mountain base. Minyue was not the only region where lapses of vigilance led to losses. "At that time," said Chen Yi, "the main political danger was rightism, moving toward capitalism. Because the situation [in the south] had changed suddenly, the guerrillas' thinking was insufficiently prepared, so they trusted the enemy excessively in the new conditions. They failed to distinguish between the enemy and us. They thought that cooperation meant that we were all one family. So they lost their political alertness and independence. . . . They lapsed into passivity."[30]

The Communists in the north had moved slowly and cautiously from class struggle to class collaboration. They had refined their position in the course of a muffled wrangle with Wang Ming in Moscow. The confrontation was sharp, though the distinctions were subtle. The guerrillas in the south did not enjoy the advantage of a gentle and controlled slide into the united front; instead, they were tipped into it at a time when most of them lacked access to information and to Party contacts who might have alerted them to hidden difficulties and dangers. The guerrilla strongholds were tiny Red islands in an ocean of White where powerholders had been waiting for ten years to avenge accumulated insults and injuries, and their vengeance took many forms. In some regions, they tried to crush the guerrillas on their staging grounds. In others, they tried to shatter the guerrillas' morale by harassing their families. Some conservatives tried to change the political complexion of guerrilla units by assassinating their leaders or "dissolving them with honeyed words."[31] "They thought that they would be able to split us and buy us over as we assembled," said Chen Yi. "They wanted to change the people's armed forces into their private slavish tool."[32]

The Yan'an directives were designed not to prevent friction but to prepare for it. They inevitably heightened the tension in the south; and, during the guerrillas' march north, provincial armies, local officials, and anti-Communist agitators raised obstacles and tried to provoke clashes. The guerrillas made long detours through the mountains to avoid these troublemakers. Agnes Smedley has described their difficult journey to the New Fourth Army assembly point in Wannan:

> Blockhouses were manned by local government troops or policemen, and trenches were thrown up along the routes of march. The guerrillas were under orders to fire no shot, but even as they marched against the Japanese, they stared into the muzzles of guns in the hands of their countrymen. Ragged, under-nourished, many of them sick or maimed, they continued to march, often changing their route and moving at night to avoid conflict. Many "Red Army families" went with them. As in the days of civil war, local landlords and officials spread rumours among the people that bandits were coming. Such incidents rankled in the hearts of the guerrillas.[33]

But despite bad communications, Nationalist harassment, and years of isolation in the mountains, most groups completed the move from their inaccessible mountain hideouts to the New Fourth Army staging point within just a few weeks of being called.

In isolation and on their own resources, the southern guerrillas were able to survive, but to fight their way back into the main political arena, they needed outside help. They were aware of the advantages of national and regional ties, which they had sought in different ways after 1934, for the most part unavailingly. In theory, it was the Central Committee's job to knit together the Party's disparate threads, but for most of the time, the southerners were out of touch with Communists elsewhere and were thrown back on their own resources. Not until they had formed their New Fourth Army were they able to restore formal ties with Party leaders in Yan'an and benefit from direction by a strong center. In the meantime, Mao and the others tried to identify suitable objectives for the guerrillas, determine strategies for achieving them, and communicate them to guerrilla leaders, first in secret directives and later through envoys and batches of Party cadres sent south.[34] Even before the guerrillas were plugged back into the central system, initiatives by regional bureaus and by individuals acting independently of the Party center crucially influenced the course of events in the southern bases. The most important of these initiatives was the maneuver that resulted in the appointment of Ye Ting, a secret supporter of the Communists, as commander of the New Fourth Army in late 1937.

## YE TING AND THE GUERRILLAS

Ye Ting was one of modern China's outstanding generals. He joined the Communist Party in 1925 in Moscow.[35] In 1926, he returned to China and commanded the famous Ironsides Regiment in the Northern Expedition. After the split with the Nationalists in 1927, he helped lead Communist uprisings in Nanchang and Guangzhou. He then went abroad, first to Moscow, where Wang Ming blamed him volubly (and unfairly) for the defeat in Guangzhou, and then to Germany, where he studied military science.[36] Some say he severed his connection to the Party, others that he was expelled from it.

Ye returned to China and went to live in the Portuguese colony of Macau sometime after the September 18 Incident of 1931, when the Japanese seized Shenyang. The Nationalists are said to have tried to win him over, but without success. Instead, he restored his ties to the Communists. In the autumn of 1935, Zhang Yunyi arrived in Macau "to hear his views and encourage him to return to his revolution." In July 1937, Zhou Enlai, fresh from his negotiations with Chiang Kai-shek at Lushan, sought out Ye Ting, who by then was in Shanghai. The two men agreed that Ye should approach the Guomindang and offer to bring the southern guerrillas into the war against Japan. Presumably Zhou Enlai's role in the matter was kept secret, for he advised Ye to raise the issue in his own name.

Until then, the Nationalists had intended appointing one of their own people—Chen Cheng and Zhang Fakui were candidates—to reorganize the guerrillas. But they knew that the Communists would resist such an appointment, so they were happy to accept Ye's offer. Ye appeared to stand aloof from party politics, and he was a soldier of enormous ability and prestige.[37] His friends in the Nationalist high command included the senior general Chen Cheng, with whom he had studied at the military academy.[38]

On September 28, the government proclaimed Ye's appointment without bothering to seek the Communists' formal assent. On October 2, the National Military Council, "granting a Communist request," issued an order "permitting collection and reorganization of scattered Communist guerrillas south of the Yangtze River [Chang Jiang] into the New Fourth Army of the National Revolutionary Forces." Four days later, the Government ordered "Red Army guerrillas of the five border regions" to reorganize under Ye Ting.[39] Chiang must have thought that he had worsted Yan'an by appointing Ye; in fact, he had caught a Tartar.[40]

At first, the Communists in Yan'an were unsure about Ye Ting, with whom they had had no dealings since 1927. It is unclear whether Zhang Yunyi was acting with their knowledge and consent when he visited Ye in Macau in late 1935; Zhou Enlai's talk with Ye was probably a private initiative. The Yan'an leaders had no reason to trust Ye, and they suspected that Chiang Kai-shek was out to trick them. They were not prepared to accept Ye's appointment merely on Chiang's say-so. First, they wanted to know how Ye felt about it. Was he willing to rejoin the Communist Party, or at least accept its leadership? Would he reject Nationalist interference? They therefore insisted that he first report to them in Yan'an; only then would they consider letting him reorganize the guerrillas. "If he completely agrees with the Central Committee's political and military principles he can go to Min'gan (or Minzhe) to take command of Zhang Dingcheng's (or Liu Ying's) troops and to expand them on that basis," they told Zhang Yunyi on October 1.

Ye Ting agreed to report to the Central Committee in Yan'an. The Yan'an leaders were reassured when they learned that Ye had approached the Guomindang on Zhou Enlai's advice and that he was prepared to resign if Yan'an refused to back his appointment. Ye left for Yan'an on October 23. Shortly before that, he and Ye Jianying clashed angrily with Chiang Kai-shek when Chiang tried to force them to agree to special conditions for the New Fourth Army muster. Chiang wanted a detailed inspection of the army—something he had been unable to impose on the Eighth Route in the north—and control over the appointment of its commanders at the divisional and brigade levels (or, presumably, at their New Fourth Army equivalents). Ye Ting retorted that the main goal was to get the guerrillas to the front; the issues that Chiang raised could best be resolved afterwards. Chiang replied belligerently that it was still not certain that the guerrillas would be allowed to leave for the front.

"With the guerrillas reorganized, the resistance to Japan will be strengthened. It will also help stabilize the rear," said Ye Ting.

Chiang Kai-shek reacted angrily to Ye's implied menace: "Let them cause trouble in the rear and I shall wipe them out. There is no question of you staying in the rear."[41]

Chiang and Ye Ting apparently parted company without settling their differences. But time was on Ye's side, for Chiang could do little to carry out his threat. He could not both keep the guerrillas from the front and ban them from the rear. In any case, his armies were too busy fighting the Japanese to take further military action against the Communists in the south. In the new mood of patriotic fervor, he could not impose his conditions on Ye Ting. Eventually, they struck a one-sided compromise. Chiang had his inspection, though it was outrageously rigged by the Communists; and the Communist Party nominated its own people to lead the detachments of the New Fourth Army, though the government formally appointed them.[42]

Ye Ting arrived in Yan'an on November 3. He received a warm welcome from Mao and others, who now agreed that he should reorganize the guerrillas in the eight southern provinces. In a speech, Ye revived his commitment to the Communist cause. "You can compare revolution to climbing a mountain," he told his welcomers. "Many comrades are not afraid of the height of the mountain and the difficulty of the route—they go straight on to the top. For a time, I climbed halfway up, but then I went back down again. Now I am going up with you and will follow the route indicated by the Party and Chairman Mao. I am determined to resist Japan to the end." However, Ye did not rejoin the Communist Party, even though Mao asked him if he wanted to.[43] After the war, in March 1946, Ye was accepted back into membership after his release from Guomindang detention, where he had spent the previous five years. He died in an air crash over Shaanxi on his way to Yan'an.[44]

## XIANG YING AND YE TING: THE SEEDS OF RANCOR

On November 7, Xiang Ying arrived in Yan'an and briefly discussed New Fourth Army business with Ye Ting before Ye left for Wuhan on November 9. In late September in Nanchang, Xiang had sent an urgent message asking the Central Committee to contact him. Until then, no one in Yan'an had known whether Xiang was alive or dead. Bo Gu, representing the Party in Nanjing, sent a messenger to find him. The messenger arrived in Nanchang after Xiang had left, but with the help of the authorities, he managed to track down Chen Yi in Ji'an. On October 11, he finally caught up with Xiang at Chijiang in Ganyue. The next day, Xiang left with him for Nanjing.

Xiang stopped frequently on his way north to hold discussions with comrades and arrange affairs; in Xingguo, he had a suit made. He arrived in Nanjing on October 23 and was reunited with Bo Gu and Ye Jianying. He reported to them on the "three-year guerrilla war in the south," probably using the term for the first time, and wrote an article about it that was published in Yan'an a week later. Bo and Ye told him about changes in Party policy.[45]

Xiang's arrival in Yan'an symbolized the return to the Party of the southern contingent. Other southerners, like Fang Fang, had made the journey to Yan'an earlier in the year, but the arrival of Xiang Ying was more important, for he was nominal leader of all the southern remnants. But in many ways, the reunion was more symbolic than real. Xiang's views differed from Mao's on several issues.[46]

In Yan'an, Xiang wrote a second report on the Three-Year War for the Central Committee and met his wife Suyun and his son Xuecheng for the first time since 1934. On December 13, the Party's Politburo adopted a resolution praising Xiang and other southern leaders for having "held out in a prolonged heroic guerrilla war and carrying out basically and correctly the Party line to fulfill the Party-assigned missions under extremely difficult circumstances," and for having preserved guerrilla areas in the south that "serve as major supporting bases for the Chinese people's war against Japan." The resolution added that Xiang and his comrades were models of spirit and willpower from whom the whole Party should learn. Similar expressions of gratitude and admiration were sent to guerrilla leaders in separate regions of the Three-Year War.[47]

In his report to the Politburo, Xiang replied that "each guerrilla unit's confidence in the Central Committee and the Zhu-Mao leadership is great." He went on to say that during reorganization "each guerrilla area should . . . leave behind one-third of its armed forces and do its best to leave behind even more. It should avoid absolute concentration." Xiang's report was acceptable to Mao, who praised it as "very good."[48] But Xiang went back almost immediately on his own undertaking to leave armed forces behind in the southern bases, causing the first of many differences between him and Mao. Despite the mutual back-slapping in Yan'an, their relationship quickly became troubled.[49] This rancor spread to and envenomed Xiang's dealings with Ye Ting.

The contrast between the political careers of Xiang and Ye was striking. Where Ye had "gone down the mountain" in 1928 and fled abroad to safety and comparative comfort, Xiang had climbed straight on into the peaks and stayed there against all odds and in the most appalling conditions. Ye's appointment created strains and cracks in the New Fourth Army that seriously weakened its command in later years. Xiang saw Ye as a threat to his position and authority. Xiang's hostility to Ye exasperated leaders in Yan'an. Ye had, after all, accepted Mao's proposals about the New Fourth Army and had agreed to model its internal organization on the Eighth Route Army.[50]

If Ye had been content to play second fiddle to Xiang, the ill feeling between them could have been avoided. But Ye could not be neutral. He had pledged his allegiance to Mao and needed Yan'an's support if he was to carry through his ambitious plans for the New Fourth Army, for unlike Xiang he had no networks among the reorganized guerrillas. He agreed with Mao's prescriptions for the war and supported Chen Yi's steps to realize them. In Moscow in 1928, he had locked horns with Wang Ming after Wang blamed him for the defeat at Guangzhou. This long-standing grudge probably prejudiced him not only against Wang but also against the Party leadership in central China in which Wang and Xiang worked together on policies criticized by Mao as rightist. To Xiang, Ye was a carpetbagger who stepped from the shadows at the last minute to commandeer the forces that Xiang and other southern leaders had preserved at such tremendous cost. Ye had been appointed commander behind Xiang's back and over his head; Ye had even been allowed to choose a name for the new army. The choice was highly personal; it harked back to the Fourth Army in which Ye had served as general in the Great Revolution of 1925–27.[51]

After Ye and Xiang's brief meeting in Yan'an, the New Fourth Army command moved to Wuhan, where Ye received Xiang on December 24. On January 6, 1938, the army leadership moved south to Nanchang and then east to Yansi in Wannan, close to its final destination at Yunling.[52] The New Fourth Army headquarters was inaugurated at Wuhan on December 25. The Yan'an leaders had apparently decided by October 30 to propose that Xiang Ying be appointed deputy commander of the New Fourth Army, but it was probably not until after his arrival in Wuhan that he was formally nominated. The Guomindang's Military Council subsequently approved the nomination. Xiang's post was equivalent to that of political commissioner, though for tactical reasons he used the more neutral military designation. During the last few days of December, Fu Qiutao, Gao Jingting, and other leaders of the Three-Year War arrived in Wuhan to be briefed.[53]

In Wuhan, Xiang Ying held further talks with representatives of the government and continued to plan the reorganization of the guerrillas. He also worked in the Central Committee's Chang Jiang Bureau in Wuhan under Wang Ming, his factional associate from the early 1930s.[54] In January 1938, this bureau set up a Southeastern Bureau under Xiang to run Party work in the New Fourth Army and in Minbei, Mindong, Minzhong, Zhejiang, Su'nan, and Wannan, the regions from which the New Fourth Army had come (save Minyuegan, which was allocated to the Chang Jiang Bureau) and the regions to which it had been assigned (save bases north of the Chang Jiang, including Eyuwan). Veterans of the Three-Year War were strongly represented in the Southeastern Bureau but not in the more powerful Chang Jiang Bureau. The New Fourth Army's close relationship with Wang's bureau had an important influence on its early evolution.[55]

## THE GUERRILLAS COME TO TOWN

In late 1937 and early 1938, two distinct streams of Chinese Communism flowed together in the New Fourth Army. From the south came veterans of the Three-Year War and their supporters, mountain people under local leaders. From the cities of central China and the Chang Jiang plain came students and workers who thronged the New Fourth Army offices to volunteer for service.[56] The two streams did not blend readily. The guerrillas from the south were not impressed by the credentials of their city cousins; and the new city recruits were driven by expectations about the revolution that often diverged from those of the montagnards. Many educated young men and women signed up in couples to escape marriages arranged for them by their parents. The veterans found this practice curious and even immoral; in the mountains, young men had joined the Red Army not to escape their families but with their families' blessing ("a mother sends her son," "a wife sends her husband," "a sister sends her brother").[57] This and other differences in outlook led to tensions and confrontations in the new army.

While Ye and Xiang were completing their preparations for the move to Yansi, units of veterans marched wide-eyed into the cities. "Weather-beaten, bare-footed, and bare-kneed," wrote Israel Epstein, ". . . they walked fast, with the swinging stride of the mountain warrior the world over. Their coolie-cloth uniforms bore no insignia. As they marched, they shouted slogans or sang."[58] Most had never seen a city. Everything was new to them, from trains to street lights. They squatted in groups to share long-stemmed pipes and discuss the mysteries of electricity and urban life. Some were shaken in their political resolve by the city lure. A few began to talk of "setting up with a wife, a home, and a job" and denounced the urban women comrades who spurned their marriage proposals. An unknown number deserted. Deng Zihui explained the desertions as the result of a loss of morale caused by the disruption of normal political routines. The old guerrilla regime of all-embracing intimacy and daily meetings collapsed in some units during the march north and was not restored until after the final muster at Yansi. In the cities, many of the guerrillas had things other than politics on their minds. Some had received money from relatives before leaving for the New Fourth Army. Chen Yi was puzzled when their smiles suddenly began to flash: it turned out that they had invested their relatives' capital in gold teeth.[59]

## YE TING STRIVES TO REGULARIZE THE GUERRILLAS

It was not easy at first for observers to take the guerrillas seriously as a fighting force. Detractors ridiculed them as "country bumpkins who have never seen the world." Even well-wishers despaired of the New Fourth Army's chances against the Japanese, for the guerrillas gave no impression of great strength. Many were armed with spears, broadswords, guns that jammed after one shot, and other primitive weapons. They included children in their early teens and veterans in their forties and fifties. Many were sick with scabies, chronic ulcers, malaria, pulmonary diseases, and other ailments, or hampered by badly set bones. But if Ye Ting had second thoughts, he hid them. He told the Nationalists, "In front of the Japanese, these people are tigers come down from the mountains."[60]

Ye Ting campaigned vigorously to recruit non-Communist military men, doctors, scholars, teachers, and writers for his army.[61] He also campaigned for a new regime: one more regular, more disciplined, and less personalized than that of guerrilla bands in the Three-Year War. Anecdotes about the early days in Jiangnan show why. Among the typical teething troubles were an anarchic disregard for rules and a cast of mind that put the interests of the gang above those of the army as a whole. Some troops regarded battle spoils as gang property and shared them out among themselves. One group ate a captured Japanese officer's horse; another cut up a captured leather coat and used the pieces to line their shoes.[62] For guerrillas who had never worn a uniform, marched in step, or greeted their leaders with anything other than a "hello," everything had suddenly changed, from the bugle call that woke them to lights-out, when all talking had to stop.[63]

The problem facing the New Fourth Army was the opposite of that facing the Eighth Route Army in the north. The Eighth Route had to relearn guerrilla methods after years of large-scale operations: the New Fourth had to temper its guerrilla style and gear up for mobile warfare.

Habits carried over from the Three-Year War created special difficulties in the more exacting conditions of the struggle against the Japanese. According to Ye Ting,

> Our men had for years been fighting in small detachments which were run on a purely democratic basis. Everyone knew everyone else, plans were discussed in common, and there was practically no formal discipline. In the New Fourth Army, the partisans had to recognise different degrees of authority in people they did not know and to obey their orders. Their daily life was subject to strict military routine, something they had not been accustomed to before. Most of them were peasants, to whom the whole conception of large-scale organisation was foreign. Among the old fighters, many were found who objected to these "infringements of democracy."[64]

Ye Ting's campaign to recruit qualified staff from the military schools, the universities, and the hospitals, to "overcome the psychology of the old partisan period," and to improve discipline and efficiency exacerbated tensions between him and Xiang.[65] Xiang was not opposed to regularizing his detachments; he did his best to promote new methods and routines. However, he was intensely suspicious of Ye's motives, partly because Ye was not a Communist, and he and his followers took exception to some of Ye's proposals.[66] In return, Ye found fault with Xiang on several issues. He took a dim view of Xiang's ragged appearance and ordered special green uniforms for all senior officers.[67] When Xiang and others arrived in Wuhan from Yan'an in December 1937, one of his first steps was to give them five dollars each for clothes, a visit to the bathhouse, and a haircut. There is no record of Xiang's response; it is easy to imagine that he took offense.

Ye Ting valued neatness, uniforms, and insignia; in that respect, he was a conventional military man. He held his first inspection of the New Fourth Army sporting a yellow serge uniform and the emblem of a lieutenant general. "Some people said that Commander Ye enjoyed reviewing troops," remarked the guerrilla Ye Fei. It is unlikely that Xiang, having lived for three years in caves and forests, shared Ye's preoccupation with form and appearance. Xiang probably also bridled when Ye Ting, who had once quit the revolution, told the guerrillas to "raise their political and military level" (though Ye thanked his fellow leaders in the New Fourth Army for the chance to learn from them and fight alongside them).[68]

Within a year or so, the differences between Xiang and Ye had escalated into general animosity. At one point, Ye left the New Fourth Army, fed up with Xiang's "despising and excluding" him. This kind of animosity was not confined to Xiang and Ye; it also infected relations between the army's newly recruited medical staff and veterans of the Three-Year War.[69]

The broader pattern, however, was one of successful integration of montagnards and city people, of the old, irregular tradition and the new drive for system and regularity, of the old class struggle and the new nationalism. Campaigns exhorted the troops to identify with the "excellent traditions" of the Red Army and to keep alive the guerrillas' resilient spirit. Ritual meals of brown rice and pumpkin soup symbolized the link to the past struggle in the mountains.[70] But as the army grew in size, complexity, and confidence, it slowly shed its irregular and anarchic ways. Informal procedures were replaced by formal ones; "direct democracy" gave way to a strict hierarchy; and small-scale guerrilla units were welded into large mobile forces belonging to "one united army." Gradually, the New Fourth came to look like the Eighth Route, an assimilation that was completed in the wake of the Wannan Incident of January 1941, when Xiang Ying was killed by a defector after the defeat of his forces, and command over the New Fourth passed into Maoist hands.[71]

In early 1938, the guerrillas, and their new recruits from the towns, debouched into the broad, flat, treeless, and watery eastern plains. These were linked by a vast web of canals, streams, and roads, studded by lakes and inland seas, and knit together by the broad channel of the Chang Jiang with its many tributaries. These plains were a far cry from the towering peaks and pathless forests of the south. Instinctively, the guerrillas made for the feature marked on their maps as the Mao Mountains; they were dismayed to find nothing but bald hills whose gentle slopes offered little obstacle to Japan's road-builders. The plains people, too, were of quite a different stamp from the simple people of the uplands. They were "urbane and sophisticated," said Xiang Ying, echoing a common prejudice about Jiangsu;[72] they were corrupted by "modern civilization and bad habits," including the "Seven Excesses" of mahjongg, teashops, public baths, Big Swords, bandits, the Green Gang, and double-dealers.[73] Here, with no mountains to control, the New Fourth Army leaders had to master the finer art of influencing people—something that Maoists like Chen Yi found easier than Xiang. At this point, a new chapter begins in the history of Chinese Communism in the south, and the story of the Three-Year War has run its course.

## THE NEW FOURTH ARMY

The New Fourth Army was organized into four detachments, known by the characters "unity," "forward," "daring," and "resistance," and one special battalion attached to general headquarters. The term "detachment," proposed by the Guomindang, was meant to show that the New Fourth Army was not entirely regular or independent. The New Fourth, said Xiang Ying in 1938, "has not so far acquired the legal status of a regular army. Our legal status is that of a special unit subordinated to the Chang Jiang front regular army," that is, to the Nationalists' Third War Zone. The Communists would have preferred to use the term "division," as in the Eighth Route Army, but to avoid conflict, they went along with the Nationalist proposal.[74]

The first three detachments, garrisoned south of the Chang Jiang, consisted of two regiments each; the Fourth Detachment, north of the Chang Jiang, had three regiments. This structure was expanded—illegally, according to the government—by the addition of new units.

The detachments were set up on a more or less geographic basis. The First Detachment was formed by guerrillas from the adjacent and at one time connected bases of Xiang'egan, Xianggan, Xiangnan, and Wannan, plus guerrillas from Ganyue; the Second by guerrillas from Minxi, Min'gan (Gannan), Minyue, and Zhe'nan, all on or near the Fujian border; the Third by guerrillas from the adjacent bases of Minbei, Mindong, and Minzhegan, in or around northern Fujian; and the Fourth by guerrillas from Eyuwan and Eyu, north of the Chang Jiang. The Headquarters Battalion was staffed by guerrillas from Xiangnan and Minzhong, plus some from Minxi.[75] The detachments were thus homogeneous enough to preserve regional identities. The only anomalies were small groups like those from Ganyue and Wannan and the Su-Liu division from Zhe'nan, which was transferred from the Third Detachment to the Second because of the bad blood between it and Ye Fei's Mindong guerrillas.[76]

Many guerrillas understood only their local variety of Chinese. The contingents from the fourteen bases were each bound by a strong collective spirit akin to ethnic feeling. By grouping the guerrillas regionally, New Fourth Army leaders probably aimed to elevate this loyalty in easy stages first to the regiments, which were regionally the most homogeneous of the army's larger units, then to the detachments, which recruited from clusters of adjacent regions, and finally to the army as a whole. The tactic did not always work, for sometimes small ethnic differences create deeper divisions than large ones: witness the feud at Yansi between the contingents from Zhe'nan and Mindong. On the whole, however, it helped ease the transition from small groups to big groups and from local dialect to national language, and it helped create an ever-broader sense of corporate identity in the army. The decision to tolerate some particularism in the early days of army-building, and not to rush through superseding old identities with new ones, was crucial for strengthening the guerrillas' moral fiber when great trials lay ahead of them. They were about to enter parts of China fraught with danger for them and foreign to them in almost every sense, from language to topography. To have mixed them too much at this early stage would have robbed them of a security that would help them find their bearings in the alien plains. The solidarity of the southerners in Jiangnan was especially intense. Far from their homes and from people they could understand, very few deserted.[77]

However, outsiders were implanted into strategic positions in the new army to fill certain gaps and at the same time to help contain "localism" and point the way toward fuller integration. Of the six early central leaders of the New Fourth Army, only Xiang Ying and Deng Zihui were veterans of the Three-Year War. Of the seven commanders and deputy commanders of the four detachments, all but Zhang Yunyi were Three-Year War veterans, but this is true of only two of the four chiefs of staff and of none of the three political directors that I could check (chart 1).[78] This pattern of appointments suggests that leaders in Yan'an thought that survivors of the Three-Year War lacked the skills and specialities necessary to build the New Fourth Army at the top levels. Southerners were only appointed to general leadership positions where their personal authority and prestige would strengthen solidarity. But they were usually balanced by newcomers imported from Yan'an to fill more specialized military roles and to hold the detachments on a firm political course.

At the regimental level, the great majority (eleven of the fourteen I could check) of the commanders and deputy commanders, but only three of the seven chiefs of staff, were veterans of the Three-Year War; this pattern is similar to that at the detachment level. However, all seven political directors in the regiments were southerners, whereas in the detachments, the political directors were all northerners. These appointments suggest that southern units were short of trained military men, an implication borne out by evidence from the separate regions. Many of the rearguard's professional soldiers had given up the struggle after 1934; those Communists who stayed the course became proficient at guerrilla war but lacked experience in other kinds of fighting. The Party leaders in Yan'an had more faith in the guerrillas' political competence than in their techniques on the battlefield. Wherever possible, they committed the guerrillas to trusted local men in order to maintain esprit de corps.

In some regiments, "outsiders" found it especially hard to gain acceptance. Ye Fei's Mindong regiment, the early New Fourth's least assimilated unit, was especially insular. "Mindong comrades from cadres to fighters did not trust outsider cadres," said Ye Fei, "and called them *lianggesheng* in dialect [i.e., people who speak only Mandarin]. They were all on their guard against such cadres." They had a special reason for their suspicions: the incidents between the Advance Division and Mindong guerrillas in the Three-Year War had intensified the prejudice against outsiders among Mindong Communists, who concluded that

Chart 1. The New Fourth Army Command, February 1938

|  |  |
|---|---|
| Commander: | Ye Ting |
| Deputy Commander: | Xiang Ying* |
| Chief of Staff: | Zhang Yunyi |
| Deputy Chief of Staff: | Zhou Zikun |
| Political Director: | Yuan Guoping |
| Deputy Political Director: | Deng Zihui* |

|  | First Detachment | Second Detachment | Third Detachment | Fourth Detachment |
|---|---|---|---|---|
| Commander: | Chen Yi* | Zhang Dingcheng* | Zhang Yunyi | Gao Jingting* |
| Deputy Commander: | Fu Qiutao* | Su Yu* | Tan Zhenlin* |  |
| Chief of Staff: | Hu Fajian | Luo Zhongyi* | Zhao Lingbo | Lin Weixian* |
| Political Director: | Liu Yan | Wang Jicheng | Hu Rong | Xiao Wangdong |

|  | 1st Regiment | 2d Regiment | 3d Regiment | 4th Regiment | 5th Regiment | 6th Regiment | 7th Regiment | 8th Regiment | 9th Regiment |
|---|---|---|---|---|---|---|---|---|---|
| C: | Fu Qiutao* | Zhang Zhengkun | Huang Huoxing* | Lu Sheng* | Rao Shoukun* | Ye Fei* | Yang Kezhi | Zhou Junming* | Gu Shiduo* |
| DC: | Jiang Weiqing* | Liu Peishan* | Qiu Jinsheng* | Ye Daoyun† | Zeng Zhaoming* | Wu Kun | Cao Yufu | Lin Kai | Gao Zhirong |
| CS: | Wang Huaisheng | Wang Bicheng | Xiong Menghui* | Wang Sheng* | Gui Pengzhou | Huang Yunyan | Lin Yingjian | Zhao Qimin | Tang Shaotian* |
| PD: | Zhong Qiguang* | Xiao Guosheng* | Zhong Guochu* | Liao Haitao* | Liu Wenxue* | Ruan Yingping* | Hu Jiting | Xu Xiangmao | Zheng Zhong* |

*Fought in Three-Year War.
†Did not arrive, so replaced by Zhou Guisheng.

Sources: Zhongguo renmin geming junshi bowuguan, eds., 1981:30; Yu Maoji et al. 1985:18–19; and Ma Hongcai, ed., 1985.

those who did not speak their dialect were unreliable. Some even warned Ye Fei that further incidents might happen of the sort that had nearly cost Ye's life.[79]

## THE SIZE OF THE NEW ARMY

The sources disagree on how many answered the summons to join the New Fourth Army in early 1938. The official figure of twelve thousand was set by the government. This figure was largely guesswork, for the guerrillas' actual strength was not known at the time. It was probably calculated on the basis of the army's planned structure: eight regiments (in fact nine were formed), each of 1,500 men. The conventional Communist estimate of the founding core of the New Fourth Army is 10,300 men armed with 6,200 rifles, but other early Communist estimates go as high as 19,000 and as low as 8,000 and even 5,000.[80] Nationalist estimates are on average far lower, at around 3,000 to 5,000, though Chiang Kai-shek gives the more generous estimate of 10,000.[81]

All these figures must be treated with great caution. The New Fourth was growing daily in early 1938, and different estimates do not necessarily refer to the same point in time. Both sides had a strong interest in rigging the statistics, for the size of the army determined the level of its pay and supplies. Nationalist historians have an added reason to keep the figure low. The existence of a strong New Fourth in early 1938 would be hard to reconcile with the idea that the Communists had been virtually wiped from the southern map after October 1934. The Communists, too, had an interest in concealing their true strength. For them, statistics were a legitimate and pliant weapon in the cause of resistance and expansion. At first, they exaggerated their number to reach the quota of twelve thousand in time for the inspection; later, they understated it to conceal unauthorized recruitment.[82]

On April 20, 1938, two days after the arrival of the last main batch of guerrillas on the staging ground at Yansi, the army assembled for inspection by government representatives. Some writers blame Xiang Ying for allowing this inspection rather than moving off at once to take up positions in the war.[83] This charge is just one of a number of accusations of opportunism leveled at Xiang Ying's actions, and it is probably unfair. As we have seen, Chiang Kai-shek insisted on an inspection in his confrontation with Ye Ting. For New Fourth Army leaders to have refused one would have constituted a provocation at a time when relations between the parties were better than they had been for eleven years. During earlier inspections in the separate regions, guerrilla leaders had adopted various ruses to swell their numbers at roll calls. At Yansi, too, Chen Yi took measures to outwit the Nationalist inspectors. He "fooled their eyes" by parading the same troops twice at different places and "stopped their mouths" with wine and food to give his men time to get their breath back and line up neatly after their rush from one parade ground to the next.[84]

Generals in old China traditionally peopled their armies with phantom soldiers so that they could embezzle the extra money. However, Chen Yi's purpose was not to line his pockets but to win time in which to reach the quota. The New Fourth Army kept no ghosts on its books. The subterfuge at Yansi, where two regiments were counted twice, probably overstated numbers by two thousand, but these two thousand phantoms soon materialized. The New Fourth Army doubled in size in 1938 and again in 1939 and in 1940, bettering the rate of growth of the Eighth Route Army in the same period.[85]

The estimates in earlier chapters of guerrilla strength in the separate regions at the end of the Three-Year War vary by a factor as high as three or four, partly because they refer to different types of guerrillas. A wartime Japanese study estimated that there were three thousand regular Red Army soldiers in the southern bases backed by seven thousand Red self-defense forces and twenty thousand irregulars.[86] Not all estimates distinguish between these categories. Table 2 shows that if the estimates for the individual regions are averaged, they more or less support the conventional figure of 10,300. Though perhaps a majority of irregulars stayed behind in the south after 1937, most guerrillas "divorced from production" left for the front. Not all arrived on time. Among volunteers who flocked to the New Fourth Army after it had joined the war were late batches of veterans from the south and scattered Red Army soldiers who reemerged from the villages, the road gangs, the wharfs, and the collieries in response to Xiang Ying and Chen Yi's "Return to the Army" drive.[87]

The New Fourth Army soon sank deep roots into the eastern plains. By early 1941, two-thirds of the officers of Tao Yong's Third Column were natives of Jiangsu. In 1939, by comparison, of twenty political workers Yuan Guoping listed as dead or wounded, nine were from Jiangxi, five from Hunan, four from Fujian, and one each from Zhejiang and Guangdong, all probably veterans of the Three-Year War.[88] But despite this rapid erosion of its core, the new units still accreted around this core and the New Fourth Army remained indelibly stamped by the experience in the south. In 1947, it was redesignated, along with troops from Shandong, as the Eastern Field Army. The stratification of this army, which swept down toward the Chang Jiang and across it into southern China in 1948 and 1949, reversing the movements of a decade earlier, reflected the early history of the New Fourth Army. It was led

TABLE 2    Numbers of Guerrillas Reorganized into the New
Fourth Army, Late 1937 to Early 1938

| Region | Estimate 1 | Estimate 2 | Estimate 3 |
|--------|-----------|-----------|-----------|
| Gannan | 300+ | 300+ | 350 |
| Ganyue | 300 | 300+ | 600 |
| Minxi | 1,200 | 1,500 | 2,000 |
| Minyue | | | 300 |
| Wanzhegan | 198 | 400 | 400 |
| Zhe'nan | 600 | 300 | 600 |
| Minbei | 600 | 600+ | 500 |
| Mindong | 920 | 1,000 | 1,200 |
| Minzhong | | | 150 |
| Xiang'egan | 1,100 | 400 | 1,000 |
| Xianggan | 335 | 1,000 | 400 |
| Xiangnan | 300 | 300+ | 600 |
| Eyuwan | 900 | 2,000+ | 2,000 |
| Eyu | 600 | 1,000 | 1,000 |
| Total | 8,000 | 9,500 | 11,100 |

SOURCES: Estimate 1 is based on Xinsijun canmouchu 1981 [1946]: 159. Estimate 2 is
based on Sheng Renxue and Zhang Junxiao, eds., 1987:192–200. Estimate 3 is based on
my own analysis.

mainly by veterans of the Three-Year War, while its ranks were drawn in
large part from Jiangsu and Anhui.[89]

## THE NEW FOURTH ARMY IN THE SENDING REGIONS

As we saw, not all guerrillas fighting in the south ended up in the New
Fourth Army. Some refused to leave the mountains because they saw the
united front as a surrender or betrayal. Others stayed behind in the villages because they feared for the safety of their families if the landlords
returned, or because after years of hard struggle they preferred to go
home rather than make the arduous journey north.[90]

A small number of Party officials stayed behind to staff the army's
rearguard offices. The agreement to set up the New Fourth Army made
provision for such offices in all the army's sending regions. In addition to
its central offices in the cities, the New Fourth Army ran liaison stations
and centers for secret work in many towns and villages in old guerrilla
areas.[91] These offices maintained links between New Fourth Army soldiers and their families, looked after army dependents, and recruited
troops. From the start, their functions also included reestablishing secret
Party networks, protecting peasants "by democratic means" against

campaigns to regain land and collect back rent, and setting up guerrilla organizations to fight the Japanese if the war moved far enough inland.

These offices, then, were not concerned only with providing for the needs of the New Fourth Army. They also had an independent role to play in Mao's grand strategy for the revolution. They harbored the seeds that, watered by favorable conditions, would sprout and grow into new areas of Communist control, continually extending the frontiers of Communist influence toward the south. Among their staff were important leaders of the Three-Year War such as Wang Guohua, Tu Zhengkun, Huang Dao, Yang Shangkui, Fang Fang, and Liu Ying.[92] They controlled both armed and unarmed personnel.

These Communist enclaves in Nationalist territory generated suspicion, friction, and outright conflict after 1937.[93] The local and national agreements under which they came into being, hastily drawn up at a time of national crisis, dealt with complex and thorny issues. Their vagueness, imprecision, and ambiguities were fruitful ground for conflict between the two parties, each of which interpreted them to its own best advantage as tensions grew. In 1939, two big incidents took place involving New Fourth Army liaison offices. These incidents were partly a reflection of mounting political tensions on the national stage; they were also a culmination of local conflicts between Communists and Nationalists carried over from the Three-Year War.[94]

The main task that Communist leaders in Yan'an assigned to the southern guerrillas in 1938 was to open up new bases for the Party in central China. As we saw, Party strategists at one point toyed with the idea of building a base against Japan along the Fujian coast, but they concentrated their main effort on the region west of Shanghai, where Chiang Kai-shek wanted the guerrillas. However, the Communists were no cat's-paws; they had their own reasons for accepting Chiang's assignment. From the beginning, Maoist leaders saw Jiangnan as a springboard into the Jiangbei region north of the Chang Jiang. Once the New Fourth Army had slipped Chiang's leash and ensconced itself in Jiangbei beyond his reach, the northern and southern branches of Communism could join, coordinate their activities, and prepare to strike back south from a firmer base.[95]

## MAO'S VIEW OF THE OLD SOUTHERN BASES

Mao had no intention of abandoning the southern bases altogether. He wanted to leave at least two-fifths of the guerrillas in the south, and in Minxi'nan and Zhe'nan he wanted all of them to stay. Xiang Ying disagreed, but not by much: he told the Politburo in Yan'an that at least one-third of the guerrillas should stay behind. Ideally, Party leaders would have given up none of their acquisitions in the south, but they were keener to retain some than others. Some had immediate strategic value, others would acquire strategic value as the war changed.

Party leaders probably had three main uses in mind for the old soviets. The Eyu and Eyuwan bases north of the Chang Jiang were southerly only in relation to Yan'an; the Eyu base in the Tongbai Mountains was the farthest north, within easy reach of Shaanbei and of garrisons of the Eighth Route Army. Strategic bases like Eyu were precious salvage of the Three-Year War that could be reconstructed into bridges and conduits to reunite the guerrillas physically with the Party center. A second category, which included all the Party's Fujian bases, was formed by bases south of the Chang Jiang that would fall if the Japanese continued their push into China. The Minzhewan'gan bases could serve as stepping stones between the New Fourth Army in central China and newly revived bases in Fujian. In more remote perspective, all southern bases were potential support points in the future contest for power with the Guomindang, a contest that the Communists expected to break out after the end of the war against Japan.

Xiang soon had second thoughts about his pledge to leave one-third of his guerrillas behind in the old bases. He reneged on his commitment to the Party center and left only handfuls. According to Xiang's critics, this was the first of a series of opportunistic retreats by Xiang in the early years of the Resistance War. It was not uncommon for the Red Army leaders to clash on the relative weight to be accorded army-building and movement-building. For example, it was only after a struggle that Gao Jingting was prevented from calling up the plainclothes squads in 1937 to swell his Twenty-eighth Red Army and impress the Guomindang. In Fujian, allegedly on Xiang's orders, far fewer than the prescribed two-fifths of Communist forces were left behind. Originally, one hundred cadres were left in Minyue and one company was left in each of Minxi'nan, Minbei, Mindong, and Minzhong, as were groups of people to staff the New Fourth Army offices in Fuzhou, Longyan, Chongan, and Mingde. But most were sent north to Yansi after Xiang's intervention, and only a few stayed.

Earlier, Xiang had played into the hands of the Fujian authorities by "very naively" agreeing to a time limit on the evacuation of Communist forces in a period when the Nationalists "only wished that [the guerrillas] would leave quickly." Local leaders argued that Xiang's directive was contrary to the earlier directive, but they obeyed it rather than challenge his authority. Fang Fang later called this acquiescence "the greatest mistake." Again, in May 1938, the Central Committee ordered the Chang Jiang Bureau (under Wang Ming) to send people to set up guerrilla bases along parts of the Fujian coast that looked likely to fall to the

Japanese; but because the instruction was allegedly blocked, they missed this and other chances to sink new roots around Fuzhou and Xiamen.[96]

Xiang wanted to empty the south of guerrillas partly to strengthen his army in the Chang Jiang delta and partly to placate the government by drawing this scatter of thorns from its side. He did not get his way everywhere. In some places, local activists ignored him, and in key areas north of the Chang Jiang, he lacked authority. Even in places where the overwhelming majority of guerrillas left at the end of the Three-Year War, the newly revived provincial committees—in Hunan, Jiangxi, Guangdong, and Fujian—saw to it that old networks were reestablished.[97]

In the first two years of the war against Japan, the most important of the old bases was Zhugou, a small town in the Tongbai Mountains in Eyu's Queshan. For ten years on and off, Zhugou had been a Red Army stronghold. It was strategically placed between Wuhan and the northern plains and between the New Fourth and the Eighth Route Armies. Zhugou was the launchpad of the New Fourth's Eighth Regiment in March 1938 and of two further batches of several hundred new recruits and cadres in May and October 1938. After 1937, Zhugou became the main relay station for Communists between Yan'an and the south, and it was called Yan'an Street or Little Shaanbei. According to Nationalist intelligence, more than seven hundred armed men stayed behind in Zhugou after the Eighth Regiment marched away.

On February 15, 1938, shortly before the regiment left, the Party's Eyu Committee put out a call for the armed defense of Henan and Wuhan and declared that the Tongbai region would play a key part in the war. After the Party's Sixth Plenum in Yan'an in late 1938, Zhugou became the home of Liu Shaoqi's Central Plains Bureau. Many hundreds of graduates of Mao's Resistance University in Yan'an filtered south through Zhugou. Two to three thousand young people from Zhengzhou, Kaifeng, Luoyang, Wuhan, and other cities flocked to this "pebble-sized piece of land" to study politics and prepare themselves for active service in the New Fourth Army. Altogether, more than five thousand people joined the New Fourth Army through Zhugou between the spring of 1938 and the winter of 1939, when Nationalists attacked the place and chased the Communists away.[98] Other regions, too, such as the Gan'e region on the border between Jiangxi and Hubei, were designated as "relay stations between the revolutionary movements north and south," but none developed as successfully as the Zhugou station.[99]

Zhugou had a strategic geographic position, and the Party in Yan'an invested major resources in it. The existence of this key junction was a main cause of the rapid assimilation of the New Fourth Army to Yan'-an's position on the war and of the isolation of Xiang Ying. By contrast, several bases of the Three-Year War that came under the jurisdiction of Xiang Ying and Wang Ming south of the Chang Jiang were obliterated after 1937. The main exceptions were bases in Fujian and on the border between Fujian and Guangdong. These provinces scarcely figured in the Communists' war against Japan,[100] but after 1945, guerrillas sprang up in several places in these rich seedbeds of the soviet as the civil war escalated, isolating the Nationalists even further and speeding Mao's final victory over Chiang.[101]

# The Three-Year War
# in Historical Perspective

◆　◆　◆

For more than half a century, Chinese Communism has been virtually synonymous with the Long March. Long Marchers or their surrogates hold the reins of state power in China; Long March rockets and satellites climb regularly into space above Xinjiang; policies and goods are sold to the public using Long March imagery; and today, the Long March has become a metaphor for China's economic march toward the year 2000.[1] Yet scholarly works on the Long March are scarce, in Chinese or in any language, and the light poured on it by popular accounts blinds more than it illuminates. This study permits us to look back on the Long March from the unfamiliar angle of the people it left behind. They included the vast majority of the Party's civilian followers in the south and a large minority of its leaders, officials, and armed forces. This fresh perspective yields startling new insights onto the place of the Long March in the Chinese Revolution, like an earthrise seen from the moon. It also reminds us that the Party existed in rich diversity outside the coalition that Mao accompanied north in 1935. Communist organization survived not only in the old southern bases but also in the cities: both the Party's southern guerrillas and its urban submarines saved forces that were to have a fundamental impact on its future.

## EVALUATIONS OF THE THREE-YEAR WAR

Chinese historians both sides of the Taiwan Strait see their task as apportioning praise and blame and edifying the public by "frightening the bad and encouraging the good."[2] The Three-Year War has suffered more than most periods in the history of the Chinese Revolution at the hands of government moralizers and apologists. On the mainland, it has

been dismissed as a backwater of the revolution polluted by its association with dissidents and traitors. Both in China and abroad, its history
was largely ignored until the 1980s.[3] It was rarely analyzed as an independent contribution to the Chinese Revolution but rather was depicted
at best as a moral support for the Long March or used as an algebraic
symbol of revolutionary continuity in the south.

Historians in Taiwan, as if on cue, award the Three-Year War a con-
temptible bit part in the drama of Communist perfidy. Nationalist military reports of the 1930s dealt mainly with the mop-up of Communist
remnants in Jiangxi in the first six months after the start of the Long
March. They claimed that "the task of extirpating Communists in the
twelve pacification zones" had been completed by April 1935, and that
thereafter the embers of Communism in the south had burned to ash.
According to Warren Kuo, Taibei's foremost historian of Chinese Communism, the guerrilla struggle in southern China amounted to "nothing more than the desperate flight of a handful of Communist remnants . . . subsisting at a near savage level in their mountain hideouts."
These remnant packs, said Kuo, were at most a few dozen strong but
mainly smaller, and by late 1937 they had "a strength of about 3,000
men."[4] They no longer even counted as true Communists; they had
abandoned their political ideals and become bandits. The Communist
movement in its southern strongholds had been smashed—like the
Communist movement in Nazi Germany just a few months earlier—into
a mass of bleeding flesh from which all life had been expelled, save for
residual signs like a corpse's hair and nails, which continue to grow for a
while even after death.[5]

Nationalist contempt for the "wild men" who "lurked and skulked in
the rugged mountains" is echoed in the abuse to which leaders of the
Three-Year War were subjected in Mao's Cultural Revolution. Their exploits were bound to be put in shadow by the Long March, which rescued China's Red Army from an impasse and brought Mao Zedong to
power. That success explains the general context in which veterans of
the Three-Year War could later become targets of vituperation. The
specific reason for their ostracism had to do with factional alignments
in the Party in the 1960s. By that time, Xiang Ying had been cast—
unfairly, as I shall show—as a domestic tool of the Moscow-educated
"traitor" Wang Ming.

But the denigration of the Three-Year War had less to do with the
"historical problems" of dead veterans like Xiang Ying than with those
of live ones like Chen Yi and Deng Zihui. Though Chen Yi had opposed
Xiang Ying on Maoist grounds between 1934 and 1938, his connection
to the traitor Xiang was a handy stick with which to beat him in the Cultural Revolution, when he was a source of trouble and annoyance to his

"radical" critics. So he and his comrades in the Three-Year War were maligned as "rightists" and worse. Their war against the Nationalists was ridiculed as "roaming without attacking," a wordplay (also used by Chiang Kai-shek about the New Fourth Army) on *youji* or "guerrilla war," meaning literally "to roam and attack." Minor veterans, especially those who had worked as Communist moles in the *baojia* or militia, were accused of betraying the Party and collaborating with the Guomindang. Indirectly, Liu Shaoqi and even Zhou Enlai were also targets of this campaign against Three-Year War veterans. Liu Shaoqi was closely connected with Chen Yi, Deng Zihui, and the New Fourth Army. Zhou Enlai's link to the New Fourth Army was weaker, but he had frequent dealings with veterans of the Three-Year War after he took over the Party's newly formed Southern Bureau in the autumn of 1938. The campaign by Lin Biao and the "Gang of Four" against the Three-Year War was not inspired by factional rancor alone: it stemmed from a totalitarian prejudice against any movement that followed its own lights, outside central control.

An opposite but similarly partisan view of the Three-Year War can be found in speeches and writings of Xiang Ying. In late 1937, when Xiang was trying to climb back to the top after his spell in the wilderness, he held up the Three-Year War as "a real model for the present War of Resistance, of exceptional importance for seizing final victory." He listed his forces' main achievements: they had preserved numerous foci of guerrilla war in the south; they had preserved a steeled army with ten years' experience of combat; they had tenaciously upheld the Party's proposals on resistance to Japan; and they had coordinated with the Long Marchers to propel the Chinese Revolution forward.[6]

Xiang attributed these successes to Party leadership and, most important, to reliance on "the masses." He believed that the achievements of the Three-Year War were greater than those of Zhu and Mao in the Jinggang Mountains, and he used them to support his campaign for recognition as a military genius and a leader of distinction. He said in his Yan'an report that though his guerrillas had been battling an enemy thirty to fifty times stronger than themselves, they had developed closer ties to the "broad masses" than Zhu and Mao in 1928; and the guerrillas had kept up a constant presence and struggle, whereas in the Jinggang Mountains under Zhu and Mao there had been "pauses in the continuity of the war." He concluded that "in the present resistance war we must include both the guerrilla warfare of the Jinggang period and that of the three-year period"; the latter was "especially important" now that the Japanese were seizing more and more territory in China.[7]

On December 13, 1937, the Party's Politburo endorsed parts of Xiang's report in a resolution praising him and other southern leaders for their heroic and loyal struggle and for having "preserved [guerrilla areas and guerrilla bands] until this day to serve as major supporting bases for the Chinese people's war against Japan." The resolution commended Xiang and the others as "apt models for our whole Party by virtue of their spirit in carrying through this struggle and their will-power in seeking resolute liberation of the Chinese people."[8]

This resolution was an encomium for long-lost friends who had miraculously reappeared, and due recognition of their achievement. It was designed to unite the Party and impress the public. Even so, it is a complex document that reflects issues and power struggles in the Chinese Communist Party of the day. The meeting at which it was adopted was the Party's first important meeting after the return from Moscow of Wang Ming, Xiang's factional leader in the early 1930s. The resolution singled out Xiang three times for special mention. The Party rarely gave a single individual such prominence; it is unlikely that Wang's return to China and Xiang's aggrandizement were unconnected. But the resolution stopped short of endorsing Xiang's specific claim to have invented a new and better sort of guerrilla war than Mao; it described the Three-Year War as a model only with reference to its "spirit" and "will-power," not to its guerrilla tactics. For Xiang was offending the Red Army's most experienced generals by trying to upstage them with his military "innovations," and in doing so he could not even count on the support of Wang, who was more interested in cooperating with Chiang Kai-shek's regular armies than in independent guerrilla warfare of any school.

More balanced views of the Three-Year War than those of Xiang and the Yan'an leaders or of the Guomindang can be found in three main places: memoirs written in the 1940s by Maoist leaders of the rearguard; early analyses made with a view to overcoming the weaknesses of the New Fourth Army and drawing on the guerrillas' special strengths; and confessional or rehabilitationist memoirs of the 1980s, written when veterans of the Three-Year War had finally been delivered from the threat of factional attacks. Both Chen Yi and Fang Fang ranked the Three-Year War on a par with the Long March for fortitude and daring. Both struggles, said Chen Yi, "proved that the Chinese Communist Party is a great and invincible revolutionary force."[9] Both were equally glorious, said Fang Fang in 1948. But neither they nor other veterans made any secret of the shortcomings of their little war, of its defensive character and limited aims. It was a struggle for survival after the revolution had met with a great defeat, said Fang Fang, so it was neither comparable to Zhu and Mao's war in the Jinggang Mountains nor a model for the liberation war. "For people to take it entirely uncritically as a guide for guerrilla warfare now is to make a mistake of principle," he added.

For Fang Fang, the war's significance was the success of the stay-behinders in holding out for three years despite harsh repression, in cramped retreats, when the masses had little fight left in them, with Party members defecting constantly, and cut off from news, communications, and outside help, "in a situation where Mao Zedong thought had been stifled and not developed into the line for the whole Party." Fang Fang gave four reasons why they had managed to hold firm: they had followed the instruction received in late 1934 to switch to guerrilla war; they were able to depend on the support of peasants who had acquired land in the revolution; they successfully "localized" their cadre, that is, they persuaded Party outsiders to study local conditions and identify with local people; and they maintained their position and isolated the enemy during the offensive against them in 1937. Fang Fang concluded by listing the main shortcomings of the guerrillas: they had not moderated their land policies or tried to win the middle classes soon enough; they did not switch to guerrilla warfare quickly or smoothly enough; and they punished deviants by "organizational means" instead of giving them "ideological help."[10]

Xiang Ying's fight for a definition of the Three-Year War that played up its achievements, disregarded its imperfections, and would therefore raise his standing in the Party to equality with Mao was unlikely to succeed; it was too blatantly self-advertising and inaccurate. Xiang made little secret of his ambitions. His supporters in Yan'an told Helen Snow that he "ranks with Mao Tse-tung as a combination of military and political genius, and in the councils of the Communist Party is inferior only to Mao Tse-tung." Xiang the worker looked down on Mao for his "peasant mentality"; Xiang presented himself to journalists as an authentic proletarian and joined Wang Ming's call for the urgent "proletarianization" of the Party.[11]

Neither Wang nor Xiang had enough authority to challenge Mao alone. However, Xiang's stature as a leader with laurels earned in Jiangxi, not Moscow, and his control of an army must have impressed Wang, who had neither, while Wang's status as a Marxist theoretician and Comintern plenipotentiary undoubtedly impressed Xiang Ying. Even so, Xiang's base was still weak, and Wang's Comintern ties did not stop Stalin coming down on Mao's side in 1938.

Xiang's attempt to capitalize on the Three-Year War was thus checked at an early stage, and he had to settle for a less flattering definition. In July and August 1939, the First Congress of the Communist Party in the New Fourth Army summed up the legacy of the rearguard struggle. It agreed with the Politburo that the Three-Year War was a model for the whole Party and urged guerrillas everywhere to study its lessons. It concluded that Party unity, a mass base, guerrilla warfare, and flexible leadership had been the main keys to "victory" in the Three-Year War. But the experience had bequeathed the New Fourth Army with ills as well as blessings. True, fighting for so long in isolation and against great odds had sifted the paladins from the cravens. The units of the New Fourth Army were steeled against hardship and good at acting independently. On the other hand, they were unused to central direction, poorly organized, and smitten with the disease of "individual heroism," which inclined them to wage "adventurist pitched battles without regard to objective or subjective circumstances."

The Congress instructed the New Fourth Army urgently to "sweep away the various bad tendencies" that had resulted from the Three-Year War. It voiced doubts about the political purity of southern veterans and said that during their isolation from the Party leadership, some had been influenced by non-Party outsiders and "neglected the overall situation"; a few had even discarded politics and "changed qualitatively" into bandits. It concluded that the New Fourth Army should strengthen its political leadership and "progress toward enlarging the main force," for guerrilla methods were good for attacking the enemy but insufficient to defeat the enemy.[12]

This new and discriminating evaluation of the Three-Year War owed its origins to several factors. By 1939, it was clear to New Fourth Army leaders, including newcomers from Yan'an, that reforms were urgently needed if the army was to fulfill the Party center's expectations. These expectations, set out in various directives, required new attitudes and structures.[13] In the longer term, the New Fourth's strategic realignment required changes in its command, in particular the transfer of power from Xiang Ying to Liu Shaoqi, Chen Yi, and others. But that is a subject for a separate study.

### THE GUERRILLAS' STRENGTHS AND
### WEAKNESSES RECONSIDERED

For the purposes of this book, I have distilled a set of propositions about the Three-Year War from evaluations of it by Communist leaders. These serve as loose cues for my own reflections on the guerrillas' strengths and achievements, and on their weaknesses and failures. Early Communist accounts of the war are more or less agreed on several points; it was only later that the consensus collapsed and some leaders began to throw doubt on the very idea of it as a discrete movement or counterpoint in the symphony of the revolution and implied instead (with the Nationalists) that it was nothing more than a largely inaudible held note. The early view, however, was that the southern guerrillas preserved strategic fulcrums (as opposed to bases) and armed forces for the revolution; that they upheld Party policy; that they acted in remote but effective concert with the Long March; and that they held firm because of Party leadership and mass support. These claims provide the starting point and framework for my conclusions. But first let us remind ourselves of the constraints within which the guerrillas waged their war and of their aims in it.

Achievements can be measured against either goals set or odds met. When goals are set rationally in full knowledge of the odds, the two measures should not conflict. But when the Party leaders abandoned the Central Soviet without a proper accounting to those they left behind, they set the central rearguard in Gannan tasks that it could not hope to carry out, like defending the soviet borders, restoring fallen soviets, and founding new soviets. For Xiang Ying, the tasks quickly became part of the odds against him. Rearguards outside Gannan were only nominally under Xiang's control; in reality, they heard little or nothing from him. Tasks and objectives differed greatly from place to place, but some general aims were common to all groups. Their main task, especially after the spring of 1935, was to preserve resources rather than add to them. By keeping up an armed presence, they would tie down enemy forces that might otherwise be used against the main Red Army; thus they would chime in on a third front with the Party's other two main fronts: on the Long March (and later in Shaanbei) and in the cities. At the same time, they would preserve footholds for use in the revolution's next "high tide."[14]

Measured against the columns that marched west in October 1934, the rearguard under Xiang Ying was a puny remnant, but it was bigger than the Zhu-Mao army that opened up Gannan and Minxi for the Communists in 1929 and three times as big as the New Fourth Army in early 1938. Even so, it could not hope to repeat the successes of the late 1920s or anticipate those of the late 1930s. Communist accounts of the Three-Year War blame Xiang's early defeat on misguided policy; they claim that the right people at the helm could have contained the defeat. Hypothetical history is contentious history, and doubly so when the hypotheses are informed by malice and pronounced true by presumption. Whatever Xiang's mistakes, it is hard to see how anyone else could have done much better. The odds were stacked too high against him. Rearguard units everywhere were hampered by tight blockades and cankered by the irresolute. A good half of the units were active in places where disillusion with the Party was by then commonplace. Seasoned troops had gone off on the Long March; many of those who remained were young and inexperienced.

Communist writers describe a vast scything of human life in old soviet bases between 1934 and 1937. The Party had suffered its worst defeat ever. Whole regions previously under its control were laid waste. According to one estimate, eight hundred thousand people were killed in Jiangxi and Minxi.[15] In Fujian, at least 350,000 people are said to have been killed during the Three-Year War or to have died because of it. The same incomplete statistics say that 2,564 villages in Fujian were destroyed, 86,319 households wiped out, 430,000 homes destroyed, fifty thousand head of cattle seized, and two million *mu* of land devastated.[16] Figures for emigration and deportation are unavailable, but government measures to depopulate regions of Communist influence were highly effective. For example, Xiang'egan's original population of 120,000 was removed almost completely.[17] By "strengthening the walls and cleaning up the countryside," Chiang's generals deprived the Communists of moral support, intelligence, supplies, and cover.

Despite the odds, the rearguard's achievement, in numerical terms, easily matches that of the Long Marchers, though this fact is rarely acknowledged publicly in China. In late 1934, forty-two thousand troops were left behind in central and southern China, representing about one-sixth of the Red Army's total strength.[18] Three years later, this ratio had barely changed. When the Eighth Route Army was set up by Mao and the Long Marchers in August 1937 on the basis of remnants of the two hundred thousand marchers and northern partisans, it claimed a total of forty-seven thousand troops, compared with the ten thousand who joined the New Fourth Army.[19]

The two main evacuations from southern China in 1934 were from the central Soviet and Xianggan. Almost as many troops were left behind in these two regions as in all the other regions put together; proportionally, far fewer of them survived. If the Central Soviet and Xianggan are omitted from our calculation, the proportion of survivors in the Three-Year War is almost twice that of the Long Marchers over the entire three-year period. The ten thousand guerrillas who joined the New Fourth represented about one-quarter of the original rearguard. The main Red Army lost a far greater proportion of its people during the Long March: of the eighty-six thousand who set out from Gannan in late 1934, a scant four thousand reached Shaanbei in late 1935.[20]

After the Xi'an Incident, the Nationalists sent large numbers of troops south in a last attempt to wipe out the guerrillas, but they were eventually forced to let Ye Ting reorganize the guerrillas instead. The Nationalists agreed to negotiate with the southern guerrillas only as a last resort. They could not afford pockets of subversion and instability behind their lines at a time of rising tension. The negotiations were partly the result of intervention by Communist leaders in Yan'an, but guerrillas in several regions had begun talking with local authorities even before restoring ties to the Party center; Communists in Minxi'nan were especially active in campaigning for unity against Japan.[21] The Guomindang's late drive on the guerrillas and its readiness to negotiate, make concessions, and let them set up a new army in the south make nonsense of Nationalist attempts to portray the stay-behinders as a desperate, degenerate rabble.

Losses had been extremely heavy in all rearguard areas; perhaps half of those who joined the New Fourth at the end of the Three-Year War were new recruits (but so were more than half of those who formed the Eighth Route Army in the north). However, many Communists in the south who had lost contact with the Party after the fall of the soviet took heart after the Party's political successes in 1937 and rejoined the ranks. Probably only a minority of New Fourth Army recruits were complete novices. All but a few of the officers were old Red Army men. "Those who remained were seasoned veterans of scores of battles," said Xiang Ying. "They were hardened warriors, but they were disciplined and iron-willed revolutionaries. Our ordeals had cleared out the faint-hearted and the traitors. Nearly every man was capable of leading others in battle."[22] These same men provided a large part of the Third Field Army elite after 1949, as well as a fair share of the early leadership of the People's Republic.

By holding out until the end of 1934, the rearguard in Gannan pinned down Nationalist divisions that could otherwise have joined in chasing the Long March. After the final collapse, a minority proposed ending the armed struggle, at least for the time being, and tried to win support for a strategy of burrowing deep and lying low. Others wanted to leave the mountains and do underground work in large population centers. But the majority stoutly resisted these proposals. Instead, they fought their way back from the depths of defeat in 1935 to reestablish themselves as a tiny but incontrovertible armed nuisance. In time, the nuisance grew, and the authorities were forced to rebuild their garrisons in the south.

The southern Communists' refusal to put down the gun was neither a case of unthinking routine nor a reckless and romantic gesture. The stay-behinders were rational actors in the Party cause: their main reason for persevering in the guerrilla struggle after 1934 was that they saw their role in a far wider context. This vision is evidenced by their constant (and generally fruitless) search for links with the Party center and other guerrilla units in the south and by the inspiration they drew from news of Communist activities along nearby borders and rare reports of the victorious progress of the Long March. China was a chessboard; their own role was to command as many squares as possible to limit the options of the Guomindang. "Every square is a partial flag, every flag influences the whole."[23]

Later, the concept of three battlefields was developed to describe Communist deployments during the last three years of the civil war after 1934, with the main front on the Long March and in the north and ancillary fronts in the Nationalist-controlled cities and in guerrilla regions in the south. In this triptych of mutually supporting panels, the main concert was between the Party's two military arms in the north and south. But they were out of direct contact with one another and unable to work together tactically; their coordination was strictly strategic. The southern guerrillas benefited from the successes on the Long March and in the northwest. These Red Army campaigns lessened the pressure on the southern bases and left some parts of eastern China practically empty of government troops for long periods. The southern guerrillas were scattered over a vast area, and the various pockets of resistance were also in strategic coordination among themselves, though they were too widely spread for concentrated efforts.[24] Pictured from the angle of the Three-Year War, southern China was a bank of doors: as the Nationalists rushed to slam one shut, another two banged open behind them.

In keeping up their little war, the southern guerrillas were trying to hold down Chiang Kai-shek's forces and to deplete his resources in accordance with Party instructions. The northerners and southerners in the Party's triangle of forces were largely ignorant of each other's doings, and most southerners knew little about political developments in the cities. For the northerners, this lack of contact was of no real account, for by 1936, their forces and their political options were increasing rapidly. For the southerners, the isolation was a test of faith. By standing firm, they helped relieve pressure on the main force.

The repeated resurgence of Communist guerrillas in the old Red bases and their appearance in places previously untroubled by insurgents helped wear down the Nationalists morally and materially. The government's campaign against the southern Communists was a big drain on its resources. In 1935, a single campaign lasting no more than a few months cost the provincial governments of Minzhewan'gan 2.5 million yuan.[25] It did not take much to alarm the authorities; just a flicker of agitation by two or three Communist fugitives could trigger off a big campaign of suppression.[26]

It is not easy to estimate the number of government troops tied down by the Three-Year War, for the campaign against the guerrillas was discontinuous and employed forces of many different sorts. One Communist study claims that over the whole three-year period, the southern guerrillas tied down 180 divisions and thirty brigades, but it does not specify for how long.[27] Another study says that the Nationalists used thirty-two regiments in their first campaign against the Communists in Zhe'nan and forty-three in their second; one division, two brigades, and four regiments in their first campaign in Mindong and five divisions in their second; three divisions in Xiangyuegan in October 1935; sixty regiments in Xiang'egan in June 1935 and eleven divisions, plus units of the Peace Preservation Corps from three provinces, in March 1936; and nine divisions in Eyuwan in 1936 and thirty-eight regiments in April 1937. The same study claims that they waged five large-scale campaigns against the Communists in Minxi, using at one point as many as six divisions.[28] According to Edgar Snow's informants, Nanjing mobilized more than a quarter of a million troops in thirty-odd divisions in April 1937 for the "final annihilation of all traces of the Red Army in Southeast [sic] China."[29]

All these statistics are of questionable value. Most of them are described as incomplete, and they have inevitably been distorted by various interested parties: Communists anxious to exaggerate their own importance, Nationalist commanders out for funds and supplies, and so on. But even if we allow for a margin of exaggeration, the figures are a tribute to the impact of the Three-Year War, which cannot be measured only by the number of troops salvaged for the New Fourth Army. The guerrillas won because they did not lose; the government lost because it did not win.

The southern guerrillas acted their part under far tougher conditions than the forces in Shaanbei, where the Long March halted. Shaanbei provided "a haven and a home," built in the early 1930s by local Communists, where the Long Marchers could rest and reorganize.[30] Peasants in northwestern China were receptive to the Party. The Nationalist armies in the region were outraged more by Japanese imperialists than by Chinese Communists, and, from the government's point of view, these Nationalist armies were unreliable and ineffective. The main Red Army could not be pinned down and isolated as easily as the southern remnants. Though its new base in the northwest was desperately poor, it was free to launch big expeditions to the west and east for supplies and recruits and to spread its political message.

The southerners, in contrast, were mostly under siege in places socially and economically devastated by war. They were confronted during the main drive against them by a strong and relatively united army; all the provinces in which they fought (including Guangdong by late 1936) were controlled by Chiang Kai-shek. For a while, they were deeply demoralized and disorganized. The resolve of the Long Marchers, on the other hand, was fortified by the emergence of a new collective leadership at Zunyi. The Long March itself was a unifying experience that generated optimism and confidence among those who stayed the course. "The Communists apparently believed," wrote Edgar Snow, "that they were advancing toward an anti-Japanese front, and this was a psychological factor of great importance. It helped them turn what might have been a demoralized retreat into a spirited march of victory."[31] It represented a branching out into new politics as well as new geography. It made anti-imperialism, previously abstract, suddenly real. It reestablished the Communist Party as a main force in national political life and became an instant legend, one of the great legends of the century.

The condition of the stay-behinders could hardly have been more different. They were physically scattered in dozens of mainly unconnected fragments and cut off from the outside world for three years. For a time their leaders were imprisoned within useless and discredited dogmas. They lacked an overview of the political processes in China and were often unaware of major crises until after the event.

## THEORIES ABOUT HOW THE GUERRILLAS SURVIVED

As we saw earlier, orthodox Communists cite three main reasons why the southern guerrillas survived the hardships and why the Three-Year War can be considered a success. First, the guerrillas upheld the principle of Party leadership; second, they upheld Party policies; third, they established roots among the local masses. To many, these arguments will seem more like dogma-mongering than explanation, but the theses appear more rational when their terms are specified. I will try to make clear the limitations of the orthodox Communist view and to advance alternative explanations on the basis of my criticism.

## THE GUERRILLAS AND THE PARTY

Xiang Ying and other rearguard leaders had good reason to insist loudly that they had kept Party structures essentially intact during their three years in the wilderness. According to the Guomindang, they had sunk into apolitical banditry after 1934 and had forfeited the right to political status. They were degenerate mutants who "killed people and lit fires."[32] These charges outraged Xiang, but many probably believed them. Not all Xiang's comrades in the south had stayed true to the cause; a minority became outlaws.[33] Even veterans of the Three-Year War referred to themselves half-jokingly as wild men who lived like animals. Rearguard remnants all over southern and central China were chased from the villages into the forests and the jungles, where they lived as nomads and troglodytes. But though the stone-age analogy is vivid and suggestive, it reveals little of the essence of the Three-Year War. The cave and forest dwellers who darted about the mountains saw themselves not as savages but as the vanguard of human society's most advanced form: Communist society, the "negation of the negation" of primitive communalism.

Their "three treasures" were the rifle, the umbrella (including the giant umbrella, under which several guerrillas could squat together), and the safety match.[34] The rifle was the tool of their trade, replaced more often than not by the shotgun, the knife, the spear, the hammer, the pitchfork, the club, or a pair of scissors. The umbrella, more recently associated with Mao's self-depiction as a lonely monk, offered practical protection against the sun and rain, but it also symbolized their isolation and self-reliance. (Dogmatists disliked the image; when one guerrilla drew a cartoon of a Red Army man climbing a mountain in a violent storm clutching a leaky umbrella, he was tortured for being a "Social Democrat" and for "sabotaging the revolution.")[35] The match was both a precious resource and a favorite symbol in the memoirs of southern guerrillas. It stood for science, industry, and enlightenment; it accorded with the guerrillas' self-symbolizing as "fire-seeds" of the revolution; and it represented the cauterizing power of the Party that would one day set the plains alight, just as counterrevolutionaries after 1934 had set fire to the mountains. Books, too, were precious. The printed page represented Marxist learning and the long-term view. Match and book were treasured objects in the Three-Year War; to carry them and protect them against the elements was a duty and a privilege.

The Party was an organizing principle of guerrilla life. In the Three-Year War, it often took wayward and unconventional forms, but local leaders rarely strayed far enough from the right path to disqualify themselves altogether as Marxist-Leninists. Aberrations generally resulted from a combination of inexperience and adaptation to circumstance, and they were easily righted once conditions improved. Most regions of the Three-Year War have their sacred calendar of conferences at which old policies were overthrown and new paths charted, and most boasted miniature versions of the main conferences of the Long Marchers in this period: Zunyi, Maoergai, Wayaobao, and Luochuan. Several regions retained at least some Party organization at the county, district, and detachment levels. Xiang Ying and Chen Yi conferred irregularly from their separate hideouts. Like guerrilla leaders in Minxi'nan, they reacted with statements and manifestos to all major crises in China after 1934. These pronouncements had little impact on events, but they strengthened the leaders' claim to political status, if only in their own eyes.

Party organization in the Three-Year War was characterized by the concentration of power in one or a few individuals and by violent factional struggles on a variety of issues. In some regions, groups of people schooled in Marxist thinking and organizational techniques tried to form collective leaderships. The best example is Minxi'nan's Military and Administrative Committee, which produced a torrent of policies and directives as well as several of the Party's main later leaders. But many guerrilla bands were under the spell of a single powerful individual who dressed and ate better than the rest and was better protected. This retreat into patriarchy was helped by the streamlining of functions and the unification of the army and the Party that happened everywhere in the crisis after the start of the Long March.

This concentration of power was partly a result of the extreme shortage of trained leaders in many rearguard areas, but a strong collective leadership was rare even where no such shortage existed. Sometimes the presence of more than one talented leader led to disagreements and either to a separation of ways or to competition for control over armed forces, followed by purges. Other leaders split up so as to offer a less compact target to the Nationalists. Communist patriarchs often turned their tiny fiefs into families of the revolution where widows, orphans, and dependents of Red Army fighters lived in separate caves alongside the guerrillas. These divisions of the Party were to be a troublesome legacy of the Three-Year War.

Many losers in factional fights after 1934 had no scruples about joining the counterrevolution. These renegades were the Communists' worst enemy, for they knew the guerrillas' ways and were thirsty for revenge. Where possible, guerrilla leaders staunched the defections by vigilance, discipline, and terror. Hunger and exhaustion tried the resolve of many guerrillas, but defection was also a risky business, for the Nationalists put defectors to the test by pressing them into dangerous missions against their old comrades.

Factional quarrels developed on all sorts of grounds, between proponents of rival strategies and between different generations of guerrillas. For example, some who joined the revolution during the Three-Year War purged veterans who had "passed the gate" in "easier" days.[36] Regional differences became especially important. Many of those in charge of the guerrillas at the start of the Three-Year War were outsiders appointed by higher Party authorities. These included regular Nationalist army officers who had defected to the Communists during encirclement campaigns. Many of them found it difficult to switch to guerrilla warfare. Local Communists on the Party's lower rungs resented these central plants and frequently turned on them when the balance of power swung to the villages after the start of the Long March. These purges were not aberrations unique to the Three-Year War but rather tiny imitations of the purges of the early 1930s.

Party leaders encouraged the ranks mainly by the promotion of group solidarity and the use of terror against dissidents, but education also played a crucial role in motivating the guerrillas to look beyond their present misery. The guerrillas were scattered along the borders of eight provinces, often ignorant of events and trends and of changes in

Party policy and under frequent enemy attack. What is surprising is not that they sometimes took wrong decisions but that the overwhelming majority of them accepted the united front when it was eventually sprung on them. One of the main reasons they held out for so long after 1934 and complied so swiftly with the new policy in 1937 was the schooling they received in the mountains. Their situation was analogous to that of Communists in jail in the cities, who turned their cells into studies and used their enforced idleness to catch up on the learning for which they had lacked time in the world outside.[37] The southern guerrillas were in some ways worse off than these prisoners, who sometimes had access to books and who had much knowledge to pool and impart. Up in the mountains, books were scarce, and few guerrillas could read. But some of the guerrilla leaders were educated and resourceful people who had earlier taught for a living. During periods of quiet after 1934, men like Chen Yi, Huang Dao, Zhang Dingcheng, and Gao Jingting wrote literacy textbooks and ran classes in politics and Marxism.[38]

Probably most survivors of the initial hecatomb continued to identify with the Party. They were aware of the advantages of national and regional ties and sought them in different ways, for the most part unavailingly. Chen Yi wrote to Mao Dun and Lu Xun in an unsuccessful attempt to reach the Central Committee. Guerrillas everywhere closely scanned the local press for news of the Party and even fought battles to get newspapers. The news of Chiang Kai-shek's release at Xi'an in December 1936 and the adoption of new moderate policies at first angered many guerrilla leaders, but most of them loyally adjusted to the new line.

In 1937, the Yan'an leaders sent messengers south with secret directives for the guerrillas and assigned cadres to beef them up ideologically. Despite bad communications, continuing harassment, and years of isolation, the guerrillas finished assembling at New Fourth Army staging areas in Wannan within just four months of being called, leaving a tiny handful of recusants and rejectionists behind in the mountains.

## POLICY CHANGES AFTER 1934

It has always been dangerous in the Chinese Communist Party to confess to consulting expediency above principle. In the real world, Party activists constantly improvised and fell back on old remedies, especially after the defeat in the towns in 1927. But in their reports, they rarely admitted to such practices, instead dressing up impromptu unorthodoxies in conformist garb to escape charges of opportunism, accommodationism, feudal mentality, or worse. During the early stages of the rearguard action, unreflecting "leftism" and failure to adjust military tactics to the

new mood and conditions often led to the pursuit of wildly inappropriate political goals. The facade of soviet government, even at the provincial level, was maintained in some regions up to and even beyond the
summer of 1935. *Baojia* heads were sometimes killed in large numbers,
with the inevitable result that the authorities stepped up their drives
against the Communists. But political retreat was as indispensable as
military retreat if the stay-behinders were to survive the new conditions.

After 1934, the southern guerrillas extemporized on an unprecedented scale and dropped central policies and slogans, but still they
prided themselves, with some justification, on having stuck by Party proposals. They could point to three main ways in which they loyally maintained the Party program, even though they stopped trying to divide the
land or to set up soviets. First, they clung to basic Party principles. Policy
was never sacrosanct in the Chinese Communist movement. Most southern Communists dropped impractical slogans, but they secretly kept the
soviet "signboard" and were firmly resolved to start dividing the land
again as soon as the new "high tide" came. (They were not, of course,
alone in changing names and policies. Even in Shaanbei, the Party's
strongest base at the end of the Long March, land revolution was first
modified and then suspended after 1935. In this sense, policy evolution
in the southern enclaves was a rough and unheard overture, in a wild
flourish of instruments, to the main drama that was to start in Shaanbei
in 1936.) Second, most southern Communists promoted the Party's policy on resistance to Japan. This policy, settled by the Central Committee
before the start of the Long March, was used as a justification for the
Long March and in particular for the Fang Zhimin expedition that had
such a seminal impact on the Three-Year War. Anti-Japanese resistance
was a main weapon in the guerrillas' political arsenal; many used it
extensively, especially in Minxi'nan. Third, the policy switches made in
the south after 1934 were legitimized by the directives sent back by
the Long Marchers from Zunyi. These ordered a turn to policies "appropriate to guerrilla areas," thus absolving the rearguard from impossible
obligations.

Not all stay-behinders received these directives, and those who did
were not always unanimous about their meaning. In the Chinese Communist movement, to switch policies without precise instructions was a
gamble that could cost one's head (though failing to switch could also be
fatal). Those left behind in the south had little tradition of independent
policymaking; the Stalinist crackdown on independent thinking in Communist parties outside Russia was probably more effective in China than
anywhere else, for China was the only place besides Russia and Mongolia
where Communists held state power (albeit only in the mountains).
In late 1937, survivors of the Three-Year War reported in fear and

trembling on their policy innovations, and it was with great relief that they learned that in the main they had done right. Each guerrilla band received its own congratulatory message from Yan'an, separate from the general encomium delivered in the presence of Xiang Ying at the Politburo in December 1937.

Changes in Party policy after 1934 were largely restricted to public policy, and the Party's internal structures and behavior changed less, except insofar as they were simplified. Guerrillas kept up not only Party cells and committees wherever possible but also the system of purges. In some places, the greater the crisis, the fiercer the purge. Purges probably thinned the ranks after the spring of 1935 more than any other factor, including enemy attacks. For the obedient core, the Three-Year War was a period of intense emotional and political bonding, but for dissenters it was generally a sentence of death or of banishment from the ranks of the revolution. Under conditions of siege, even minor differences of opinion or habit were often viewed as intolerable; without a soviet state or economy to stabilize loyalties, the only tactic that remained was terror.

Military policy entered a period of experimentation and innovation. In former core areas of the soviet and core units of the Red Army, the change in military tactics was sudden and more or less outright. In the first few months after the start of the Long March, many such units stuck rather rigidly to old tactics, but in early 1935, they gave up "pitched battles" and turned to guerrilla warfare. Some units, for example the Su-Liu Advance Division in Zhe'nan, continued to mass their forces against enemy targets, but these efforts usually proved suicidal. Some regions had never developed beyond the guerrilla stage and did not need to change. The guerrilla tactics used in the Three-Year War were not new, despite Xiang Ying's claim that the stay-behinders developed "new tactical principles" uniquely instructive for the wider movement and a necessary supplementation of earlier guerrilla tactics.[39] Xiang's principles added nothing to those that Mao and others had formulated in the late 1920s.

In other areas of policy, leaders of the Three-Year War can claim with greater justification to have perfected useful tactics. The adoption of new methods in the Party's "external work" was neither swift nor uniform.[40] Some changes happened earlier than others; some regions changed sooner than the rest.

The new policies and tactics were a long-overdue recognition of the Party's crushing defeat in late 1934. They were characterized by greater flexibility, greater sensitivity to local pressures, and a new awareness of the Party's limitations. The change in political direction was sometimes accompanied by power struggles and further defections by the defeated party. Rearguard leaders faced two urgent challenges. They had to re-define their relationship to the outside world now that their organization in the villages was smashed; and they had to devise a milder polit-ical program. These two requirements were complementary: a strong organization can afford aggressive policies, but a weak, exhausted one must trim according to expediency.

## WHITE SKIN, RED HEART

The guerrillas needed new networks of support to replace the ones that had been destroyed. All but a few of their liaison stations had been closed down, and those that remained were in constant danger of dis-covery or betrayal by renegades or aggrieved victims of the Party. But without a supporting base in the villages, the guerrillas were cut off from intelligence and supplies. Their solution was to subvert existing networks rather than try to set up new ones (though in some regions they preserved their own independent arrangements). At first, they tried to smash the *baojia* and kill its officials. Later, they developed a "double-edged" policy of isolating reactionaries by winning over those *baojia* officials who occupied "middle" political positions or turning them into double-dealers.

As long as the guerrillas were too weak to restore the soviet, they would strive to "turn the *baojia* into a Red joint defense organization." They rebuilt their networks parasitically and even extended their tenta-cles into the *lianbao* that linked the *baojia* above village level. At the same time, they sapped the foundations of the village militias set up against them; in many areas, they either controlled these militias or struck se-cret pacts with them. Forming such bonds was not difficult, for holding local office was dangerous and unpopular. Those pressed into it were of-ten local people of no great wealth, social standing, or political commit-ment. They were on the front line of the struggle against Communism, but they were isolated and vulnerable except during main drives against the guerrillas, when government troops flooded in. Many local officials were related to Communists by ties of kinship, schooling, or (like the Hakkas, She, and Tujia) ethnicity. Many had themselves been Commu-nists or Red Army troops in the past and were susceptible to political pressure, especially after the guerrillas softened their stance toward those who had fallen away from the Party. Through a judicious mixture of terror, blackmail, and social manipulation, the guerrillas won over many such leaders, or at least fixed them on a neutral course. In some cases, they infiltrated Party members into office. Converts or Party agents were called inverted radishes or sweet potatoes: people with white skins and red hearts.[41] "Double-dealers" were called "agents of an

intermediate color," and the territory they controlled was called gray or
yellow. The old dichromic opposition between Red and White gave way
to a polychrome through which the chameleon-like guerrillas could
move with greater freedom. In some mountain districts, almost the entire *baojia* system was under Communist control by 1937, and in some
villages, Communists paraded openly with guns.

Government bodies like the *baojia* were not the only targets of this political offensive. In some regions, the guerrillas worked through Associations of Fellow Townspeople or Fellow Provincials and exploited distant
kinship ties of their supporters in the mountains. Guerrillas in most
places formed alliances with marginal or dissident social groups, including bandits (especially "social" bandits), Daoist sectarians, and even
monks, all of whom they had tried to destroy in the past. Now they
adopted a more discriminating approach, striking pacts wherever possible and avoiding conflict except where absolutely necessary.

Sipping blood with bandits and "spirit soldiers" was profitable in several ways: it increased the guerrillas' security, opened new networks to
them in the villages, and even opened channels to Nationalist politicians
with criminal or sect ties. But such alliances were also risky. Some bandits
and sect leaders fell out with the Communists and attacked them, and
some Communists "changed color" through contamination, though
most kept a safe political distance from their so-called allies.

In addition to overcoming their isolation and reestablishing contacts
in the villages, the Communists also took steps to adjust more generally
to their loss of power and contacts. In the past, "outsider" Communists—usually people from the towns and cities or Red Army professionals—had tended to lord it over the country bumpkins who supported
the Party in the villages. After 1934, the balance of power swung the
other way. In some regions, rearguard leaders tried to engineer a
change of attitude by calling for the "localization of cadres" and for outsiders to learn from natives. In other regions, the problem was resolved
by violence in which local Communists almost invariably worsted the
cosmopolitans.

The guerrillas had to devise new policies to replace those superseded
by the fall of the soviet and to accord with the new strategy of subversion
and alliance, of maximum advantage with minimum friction. Their campaigns were designed to contain the counterrevolution, to win support
in "intermediate" classes that the Party had previously attacked, and to
restore the Party's human base in the mountains by reversing the government's depopulation measures. The guerrillas were powerless to roll
back Chiang's Thermidor, but they tried to retrieve some popularity by
campaigning to mitigate its least popular consequences. In Minxi, they
campaigned with some success to sustain land reform; elsewhere, they

tried to win support by campaigning for lower rents and interest, by seizing grain and secretly distributing it to the peasants, and by opposing government conscription. They were highly successful in combining legal, semilegal, and illegal actions in support of their campaigns. The Nationalists' continuing drive against the guerrillas independently created new issues on which the Party could campaign. Communists in Minxi campaigned vigorously for an end to government drives against them, on the grounds that setting fire to mountain forests destroyed capitalist industry and put workers out of jobs.

Depopulation was the Nationalists' most effective weapon against the guerrillas. Without a popular base, the Communists lacked moral support, intelligence, material supplies, and cover. The guerrillas' main concern was to reconstruct a civilian base by mobilizing deportees to petition for the right to return home to the mountains. They also tried to befriend any itinerant and seasonal traffickers who slipped through the blockade. Communists in many regions stepped forward as champions of the hucksters, hawkers, barbers, mushroomers, paper makers, charcoal burners, and other sojourners and itinerants whose livelihood had suffered as a result of the mountain sieges.

The most powerful issue upon which guerrillas could win support from among the educated classes was resistance to Japan, though this issue was not everywhere equally resonant. However, even where it was not yet a burning political issue, guerrillas often used it as an excuse to squeeze money from the rich. Many guerrillas eventually gave up "fines," outright robbery, and ransoming as ways of raising funds and switched instead to a system of "contributions," often collected on the pretext of furthering the anti-Japanese resistance. Most of them scaled down their financial demands on *tuhao* to "prevent contradictions intensifying."[42]

## THE SOURCES OF THE NEW POLICIES

What were the origins of the policies adopted after 1934? Memoirs of the Three-Year War in its many regions suggest that the switch was remarkably uniform all over southern and central China. This uniformity is partly an invention. Memoirs in the People's Republic of China have a didactic purpose that encourages the creation of edifying stereotypes, and they are written in a climate that rewards conformity and punishes deviance. So some of the uniformity was probably concocted retroactively by local leaders bent on showing how orthodox they were. Such hindsight is especially likely now that "the three-year guerrilla struggle" has not only been rehabilitated but is officially equated with "restoring Mao Zedong's line in the Party."[43] Even so, the evidence in this book shows that policy evolved along broadly similar lines in most areas of the Three-Year War. The question is, Why?

The Chinese answer would probably be framed—like most such answers—in terms of the two-line struggle between Mao and the "left" opportunists. Most Chinese historians writing about the Three-Year War today describe it as a victory of Mao supporters over Wang Ming–style "leftists," matching Mao's own supposed victory over the "leftists" at Zunyi. Mao supporters could defeat the "leftists" because the fall of the soviet had convinced the Party ranks of the bankruptcy of "leftism." So the uniformity of the switch can be explained as a result of the rise to power of Mao supporters.

This explanation should not be dismissed entirely. Mao favored a more pragmatic and flexible approach than the ruling "leftists" in Ruijin, and Mao's friends formed a majority in some bases during the Three-Year War. Most stay-behinders who received news of the Zunyi decisions probably realized that Zunyi represented a defeat for the policies of the Comintern-appointed leaders. But an explanation based on factional rivalries meets serious objections. Xiang Ying, chief of the stay-behinders, was an old supporter of the "leftist" Wang Ming. Stay-behinders in many bases committed "leftist" excesses whenever the pressure on them lifted, for example during the Liang Guang Incident of 1936; at other times, their milder policies had more in common with Wang Ming's "second right opportunist line" than with Mao's views. Neither a strictly "Maoist" line nor a disciplined faction of Mao supporters existed in the 1930s. In Mindong, one of the most successful and archetypically Maoist regions of the Three-Year War, guerrilla leaders like Ye Fei had "only a vague idea of Chairman Mao, even of his name."[44] At best, there was a general current of feeling that one could anachronistically label Maoist, broad enough to admit all sorts of discordancies and inconsistencies.

We can therefore reject the idea of a Maoist orchestration of the Three-Year War, though we should remain sensitive to the historical link between Mao and some rearguard leaders. How, then, can we account for the striking similarities between different regions? Many of the shared innovations were simply a commonsense adaptation to identical circumstances. The Party had never before suffered a defeat like that in 1934. For the first time, Party leaders were faced with huge numbers of people who had once worked for the revolution but were now collaborating—often halfheartedly, sometimes unwillingly—with the enemy. In a few places, guerrillas isolated themselves by failing to seek an understanding with these turncoats, but most stowed away their grudges and made deals. Other widely adopted policies were the results of diffusion. The Zunyi directives that Xiang Ying transmitted to some bases legitimated the switch in tactics. Likewise, the proposals for a united front against Japan were diffused from the cities to some of the more easily reached bases and thence to other bases. But the transmission was by megaphone, not telephone, and generally it conveyed only the main drift of the message; nuances had to be reinvented on the spot. Finally, some widespread policies and tactics were the product of a shared past and a common conceptual framework. What seemed at first to be innovations were not innovations at all but retreats by Communists in unconnected bases along identical pathways in the revolution's collective memory.

Most of the people left behind in 1934 were local Communists with strong ties to the provincial towns and the villages, pragmatic men and women ill at ease with dogma. They were the bedrock of provincial Communism from which by 1935 most surface deposits had been washed. One tradition to which they turned as if by instinct was the old guerrilla tradition epitomized by people like Luo Ming in Minxi. By 1935, the local people were probably used to switching policies, having done so many times as the balance of power seesawed from Red to White in disputed areas. So it was a practiced retreat, well rehearsed and expertly performed.

Some of the apparent innovations were ingenious adaptations to rural life of tactics developed a decade or so before to serve the movement in the cities. Among tactics borrowed from an urban repertoire of tricks were the united front from above, the united front from below, the secret infiltration of organizations through which the rich controlled the poor, the "amphibian" combination of legal and illegal methods, the planting of moles, the creation of double-dealers, and winning support by minor reforms when revolutionary measures were impossible. The rent and interest cuts promoted after 1934 had been Communist policy before 1927.

Communists in peripheral soviets and guerrilla areas had generally tolerated and benefited from their links to itinerants and traffickers; after 1934, it became even more important to win the cooperation of such people. The "yellow village" idea was derived from the "yellow unions" that Party activists secretly infiltrated in the cities. The origin of the term "white skin, red heart" is more obscure. Some veterans of the Three-Year War first heard it only after 1949.[45] Others say that it was a peasant coinage of the late 1920s, when it referred to Communists working in Nationalist areas.[46] It may have been a playful metaplasm, originally used for "red-skinned" conservatives under the soviet. In Hongan in Eyuwan there is a special sort of water radish with white skin and red flesh, "extremely succulent, sweet and peppery, good for quenching the thirst."[47] But this usage does not explain the appearance of the term in memoirs from other regions.

We know so little about Communist activities in peripheral bases before 1934 that it is hard to say when these adaptations first evolved. Some were perhaps original achievements of the Three-Year War; most were probably not. The spotlight was almost always on the Party bigwigs in Ruijin; and innovations in the smaller soviets often went unreported because they were unauthorized. They were the truest form of the "nationalization" of Marxism after 1927, but they were never advertised as such by their authors, who in reports tended to present their heretical activities in orthodox terms to avoid criticism. But whether they were born of the Three-Year War or carried over from before, such tactics are certainly characteristic of the Three-Year War, when stealth, subterfuge, dissimulation, trickery, and double-dealing of all sorts were more important than force of arms for survival.

## THE GUERRILLAS AND THE PEOPLE

The proudest boast of veterans of the Three-Year War is that they survived because of the "selfless support" of the masses. "We changed all our struggles into struggles of us and the masses," said Xiang Ying. "The masses became our ears, our eyes, our hands, our feet."[48] Although Ye Ting and Xiang disagreed on many things, they were agreed that the secret of the guerrillas' survival was that "under all circumstances they have known how to retain their close link to the people."[49]

This claim is usually echoed by mainland historians. It is not entirely disingenuous, for the term "masses" has a special meaning in this context. But the evidence in this book speaks loudly against it in all its customary senses. Some guerrilla bands, particularly those in parts of Fujian, were less isolated than others, but even in periods of "stabilization," most of them spent months on end flitting between mountain tops in isolation from society, only occasionally descending to attack traffic on the roads, kill local reactionaries, or collect "contributions."

The Xianggan case is particularly instructive here. According to Xiang Ying, the Three-Year War had a stronger mass base than the Zhu-Mao struggle in Xianggan's Jinggang Mountains in the late 1920s.[50] But by 1934, the Jinggang Mountains were barred to Communist guerrillas, not by Nationalists but by the Hakka irregulars who had previously backed Mao. Mountain people may have held Xiang Ying's guerrillas in awe, but many also held them at arm's length, for they saw the Communists as "fire spirits" who either torched the villages themselves or brought Nationalist fire-raisers down onto them. The guerrillas were "constantly moving and . . . unable to build a base anywhere," admitted Xiang Ying in a candid moment; they made their beds in the caves and forests.[51] The flags they raised were not banners of mass support but markers of territory that they had all but lost, for Xiang's war was a defensive one, fought on the remotest borders of provinces and counties.

How, then, did the guerrillas manage to survive? At times, they lived almost exclusively off the land and their own resources. Subsistence was easier in some seasons and some places than in others. Whenever conditions allowed, they tried to "localize" their organization and outlook. To do so, they first had to drop the pretense that they represented a national soviet state. They had to educate themselves to respect local cadres, learn from local people, study local customs, and regard the local area as their home.

"Localization," even where it was successful, cannot be equated with restoring a mass base. The latter term implies a close identity and mutual dependence between the Party and a community or social class that wants social change and is mobilized and organized to bring it about. Only a small minority of guerrillas, mainly in Minxi and Mindong, achieved ties to society (in tiny and secluded mountain villages) that met these criteria, even by their minimal definition. The great majority, including those in Minxi and Mindong for much of the time, were not based on organized mass followings whose interests they represented, defended, and elevated into political programs. Instead, they lived on society's margins, stretching out tendrils into it, learning its ways, and studying its social arrangements not to change it but to strike deals with it. Their targets were generally not whole communities but individual powerholders, strategically placed networks, and marginal groups. The guerrillas gained food, protection, and intelligence from such deals; the targets won promises of immunity from molestation or of support against their enemies. These deals created a vicious circle: they resulted from the guerrillas' lack of popular support, and they made campaigning for such support on radical grounds unnecessary and even undesirable.

Because China in the 1930s was a kinship-based society, it is not surprising that kin ties were a main target of Communist manipulation. Many guerrilla leaders were descended from the powerful lineages that stretched like membranes across the provincial backlands. The Nationalists killed relatives of the Communists to intimidate these lineages, but they were rarely able to destroy such ties altogether. Guerrilla leaders were also able to knit other sorts of ties into networks of support. Most had grown up with men who now enjoyed influence in local society. Ever since Chiang Kai-shek's victory in 1927, relations between the rural elite and the new Nationalist administration had been tense and troubled. In the late 1920s, the Communists had tried to profit from these tensions by infiltrating conservative militias in the villages, and they had exploited family and social connections to do so.[52]

At first, their radicalism alienated many of these potential allies. But by 1935, the Communists no longer represented a revolutionary threat to the established order in the villages. Moreover, new targets for them had emerged among the many lapsed and defected Communists who had become officials in the villages and counties. These people were "historically" unreliable from a Party point of view, but they were also vulnerable to extortion and appeals. Sometimes the guerrillas created networks by armed force, kidnapping people or holding their relatives to ransom to force them to cooperate. Afterwards, the victims, having become the guerrillas' accessories, had little choice but to become their partners.

Secret networks and links of this sort were far more important to the guerrillas' survival than economic mobilization on class grounds. Official historians describe the Chinese Revolution as a revolution against "feudalism" as well as against capitalism and imperialism. But the links mobilized by stay-behinders after 1934 were in many ways strikingly feudal, just as the bonds between Communist partriarchs and their guerrilla followers were bonds of feudal loyalty. The strong "feudal" flavor of Communism in the Three-Year War contrasted markedly with the bureaucratic-centralist character of the Party in the north, and this contrast explains some of the tensions that arose between the two traditions after 1937 and prevented their smooth reintegration.

Although most border dwellers had learned to fear the Communists, some continued to hope and believe that the "Red Army will return" and were prepared to risk their lives to help the guerrillas prepare for that day. These people were the true "masses" or *qunzhong* of the Three-Year War; but in this case, "masses" meant no more than tiny nests of civilian supporters, which is why Communist writers on the Three-Year War are not embarrassed to record the support that "one *qunzhong*" or "a handful of *qunzhong*" gave to the guerrillas. These masses included young people who had been brought up under the soviet and indoctrinated in its ideology, older people with sons in the Red Army, and women. The boys joined the guerrillas as they reached their teens. Wives of the main leaders of the Long March and the rearguard had quit the soviet, but wives of men in the lower ranks had stayed. In some regions, many were raped and sold to brothels.

Young women played a crucial role in obtaining intelligence and supplies for the guerrillas, carrying messages for them, healing and tending them, and—occasionally—fighting. In Tingrui, some 15 percent of Party activists after 1934 were women, compared with something like one in two thousand on the Long March.[53] Many young women who had become confident and "politically aware" under the soviet cherished the rights they had gained through the revolution. Women were therefore more conspicuous in the Party in Gannan, Minbei, and Minxi than in Mindong, where there had been no Long March (and thus no shortage of young men) and no strong and rooted soviet to run night schools for young women. Women could move around more freely than men after the worst of the repression was over. Women activists provided an important element of continuity after 1934 and again after 1937: when the majority of men left Tingrui to join the New Fourth Army in 1938, all the women activists stayed behind.

If enough individuals, especially important individuals, started working for the Communists in a remote or isolated village or chain of villages, the "color" of the place eventually changed, and the Communists hoisted a secret flag over it. In this case, the people were under pressure not to avoid the Communists but to collaborate with them. Just as it was easy to be branded a Communist under the Whites, so it was easy to be labeled a counterrevolutionary under the Reds. Once a village had changed sides, support for the Communists became involuntary and automatic. The Party was then able to move from secret presence in a place to an open impact on it and from surreptitious control of its administration to an open parade of armed force.

If the Long March led to a feminization of the Party in the old soviet bases, it also propelled into the front line other classes of people previously on the margins of political life. These groups included outlaws, solitary traders, religious dissidents, and the like: people whom in the past the Party had ignored, scorned, or liquidated. The Long March took the Red Army—almost for the first time—clean out of Han society and into contact with "tribal" peoples in the remote west. The southern Communists' three-year trek through the wilderness similarly brought some of them into close contact with non-Han peoples on China's internal frontiers in the provincial uplands. The most striking example was in Mindong, where the Party founded some of its strongest open bases in villages inhabited by She people.

Until recently, the strong connection between the Communists and the She in Mindong was apparently not considered fit for public mention, perhaps because it was exceptional and therefore possibly wrong or because it suggested that ethnicity may have sustained the movement more than class. Not until the more open climate of the 1980s was attention focused on the She contribution to the Three-Year War; even then, a great and far from convincing stress was laid on the unity of Han and She in the Mindong revolution. The Shes, with their tightly knit communities, strong ethnic identity, and thick mesh of kinship ties, were an ideal ally for Ye Fei's guerrillas. Once a She village had turned Red, it became an unshakable bastion of the Party. But She assistance to the Red Army was not selfless. A Red village perched high in the mountains was unlikely to be troubled by rent collectors, tax collectors, or the press-gang. The Mindong guerrillas brought the villagers work, a trickle of loot, a few services (including that of a Red Army doctor), and the chiliastic promise of a society without classes and the state.[54] Here the Party did not so much represent an economic interest as create one.

### THE UPS AND DOWNS OF THE THREE-YEAR WAR

But though a few guerrillas were able to call on tiny "mass bases" after 1934, most never controlled more than thin strings and occasional loose knots of support. Xiang Ying's claim that the struggle in the south was uninterrupted and unremitting, and therefore exceptional in the history of guerrilla warfare in the Chinese Revolution, is also quite unfounded. Chinese historians conventionally distinguish three main stages in the Three-Year War: a period of crushing defeats in the last quarter of 1934 and the first quarter of 1935; a period of "consolidation and development" from mid-1935 to late 1936; and a period in 1937 when the guerrillas resolutely fought back against the Nationalists' final onslaught and victoriously negotiated to become the New Fourth Army.[55] These distinctions are too general to be of much use and too obviously designed to fit the Three-Year War into the general scheme of Party history for the mid-1930s (the defeat of "leftism," the rise of Mao-Marxism, and the campaign for a united front).

No tidy chronology of the Three-Year War can get around the fact that the war was fought in many different regions by an even larger number of unconnected guerrilla units. The war's very name is inexact, for some units switched to guerrilla fighting well before the start of the main Long March and kept it up for four or five years. (Others fought for less than three years. Chen Yi's war in Ganyue lasted "a thousand days and nights," or two years and eight months.)[56] What is certain is that the course of the war was not a single sustained movement on an upward line, as Xiang Ying and others imply, but a jagged, twisting line, full of sharp turns, loops, gaps, and breaks. Sometimes, however, rudiments of a pattern show through. Guerrillas in most regions were at their nadir in early 1935, when some forces fizzled out altogether and others made strategic turns. Many in the south surged up during the Liang Guang Incident in the summer of 1936, and guerrillas nearly everywhere were hit extremely hard in early 1937, when the Nationalists destroyed almost all of the support, amounting to half of all southern

Communist forces, that the guerrillas had captured during their earlier uprising in Ganyue, Fujian, and Zhe'nan.[57]

If the guerrillas had their ups and downs, so did the government campaign against them. Chiang's generals knew from experience that it was not enough to defeat the Communists on one battlefield and then leave for the next. They had to "catch their chiefs" and destroy their support at the root to prevent it from recovering. Even so, they lacked the diligence and the perseverance—and probably the means—to eradicate the Communists on the spot. Their campaign to deport mountain people to the plains, seal off the guerrilla haunts, destroy houses and villages, lay the fields waste, and burn the mountainsides within the blockade was successful for as long as it lasted: it isolated the Communists and forced them into the wild. But forest fires are generally ineffective against even the shallowest root stocks, which start to produce new growth as soon as the flames have swept over them. As long as the Nationalists stayed in the mountains in force, they held the guerrillas down. But on several occasions, starting in the summer of 1935, they withdrew after concluding that the Communists had been smashed. The guerrilla survivors then had the chance to rest from forced marches, reorganize, reassess, readjust, and eventually revive. Guerrilla pockets were scattered across a vast area; the government could not attend to all of them simultaneously. Periods of harsh repression alternated with longer periods of respite. National emergencies in the north (caused by the main Red Army or the Japanese) and in the south (caused by dissident generals in Guangdong and Guangxi) helped relieve the pressure on the old soviet bases. The guerrillas did not resist continuously, and the government did not pursue them continuously; the Three-Year War was marked by alternating periods of calm and tension. During the respites, stubborn handfuls of Communists invariably bounced back. Their rise and fall correlated almost exactly with the absence or presence of strong Nationalist garrisons (though there were regions where the movement ceased).

## A COMPARATIVE ECOLOGY OF THE THREE-YEAR WAR

Seas of ink have been spent explaining what causes revolutions and what determines their success. Such explanations are often an exercise in comparison. The scale of comparison is often vast—revolutions in general, revolutions in the Third World, revolutions in Asia—and the results are correspondingly crude.[58] This book permits a more minute comparison of the ecology of revolution in the context of the Three-Year War. It deals with Communist movements grappling with similar problems in different regions over a similar span of time, and these common features alleviate some of the problems that bedevil broader studies.

None of these movements escaped the general repression, but some bounced back higher than others. A crude measure of their resilience is the size of the contingent that each delivered to the New Fourth Army in early 1938, effectively the differential survival rate. One might object that this indicator concerns only military forces and that it is based on a fleeting moment and says little about success or failure over the war as a whole. But while the numbers that came down the mountains are not a perfect index, they are the most obvious and reliable quantitative measure available. Moreover, they reflect the close relationship in the Chinese Revolution between military success and political organization. One might further object that my comparison takes little account of the different starting sizes of the different rearguards, but this omission is broadly justifiable: by 1935, rearguards everywhere had been cut down to roughly the same size.

Veterans of the Three-Year War and Chinese Communist historians have advanced various theories about why the guerrillas succeeded in outwitting their pursuers. These propositions are asserted rather than argued, and they are cast at a level that is mostly too general to be useful. They have not been tested empirically, for example by measuring their ability to predict regional variance in success. Instead, they are imposed on events and proclaimed incontrovertible. Such an approach is only to be expected, since Party history in China embodies general "truths" not subject to empirical investigation. Even so, it is interesting to examine these explanations for clues about the conditions that led to success or failure in the Three-Year War. Here I present and test a collection of hypotheses formulated by Chinese Communist observers. These are not hypotheses entertained by Marxist theoreticians but rather post hoc explanations by Party activists (though of course these two categories overlap). I use them more as a framework of cues on which to hang my own reflections than because I necessarily take them seriously as sociological explanations.

This analysis reveals little or nothing about the origins of the Chinese Revolution, for the Three-Year War was a period of massive revolutionary retreat. Many of its findings are specific to the Three-Year War, which was a unique interlude in the Chinese Revolution. But there are important parallels between the position of guerrillas in the Three-Year War and that of the fringes of the Party in southern China during the War of Resistance and the civil war of 1946–49 (whose southern campaigns are often called the second Three-Year War in Party literature), so any conclusions about the former may also be applicable to the latter.[59] Insofar as my reflections show why some rearguards failed, they will throw light on causes of the Communist defeat in 1934. Insofar as they show why some rearguards succeeded, they will throw general light on ways in which mature Communist movements can best secure support when under pressure.

Naturally, these findings are not relevant to all parts of the Chinese Communist movement. The conditions in secure bases in the northwest after 1935 were quite different from those of the tiny groups of stay-behinders battling against all odds in the old soviet bases. However, guerrilla efforts to reestablish support in areas where the revolution had been repelled in 1934 have parallels with the New Fourth Army's venture into parts of eastern China behind Japanese lines after 1937, and the same people led both endeavors.

Is it legitimate to treat the Three-Year War as a single and integral episode? The answer must be yes. The course of the war in its main bases was broadly uniform. Most guerrilla units had a common origin in the decisions of 1934, and all but a few eventually came together in the New Fourth Army. All the guerrillas were isolated from the Party center for very long periods; their bases were invaded and broken up into pieces; they lacked ties to guerrillas in other areas; and their links to local society were tenuous at best. Even so, there are striking and important differences between the guerrilla regions in environmental constraints and opportunities and in the strategic choices made by local leaders. Until just a few years ago, the dearth of data ruled out a systematic study of individual regions and thus a comparison between regions. Even now, the flow of information is slow and shallow, but enough has accrued to allow a variable analysis of sorts.

One source of this new knowledge is provincial Party journals. In the past, local historians took pains to stress the orthodox character of movements led by local Party people, but in the 1980s, they were just as likely to dwell on the "special nature" and "special achievements" of local movements. In the 1970s, the Three-Year War was described in a monotone. Today, it is revealed as a richly varied episode in Party history. Some of its leaders were pragmatists; others were dogmatists, hide-aways, or adventurists. Some bases were old, others were young, and a few were new; some were flattened, others contracted. Some guerrillas were active in regions where the soviet had been weak, others where it had been strong. Some movements were homegrown and others transplanted before the start of the Long March; still others pulled up their roots after 1934 and sought new sanctuaries. Some stay-behinders had always been guerrillas; others had been regular units of the Red Army (and are aggrieved by the failure of historians to note this fact).[60] Some units shrank to a few dozen people or even to a handful, others set up independent regiments, and still others died away altogether. The differences were eventually to be ironed out by the New Fourth Army and Mao's Rectification Campaign of 1942–44, but in the Three-Year War they were paramount.

The geography of the bases varied hugely from north to south and from east to west. These differences bore centrally on guerrilla ecology, as many memoirs attest. Guerrillas fought mainly in the wild, with little shelter, medicine, or equipment; the weather had a direct impact on everyday life in their bivouacs. The climate differs markedly between Minxi, Minnan, and Ganyue on one hand and the bases further north and further inland on the other. Winter in Hubei, Hunan, Jiangxi, and the Dabie Mountains' "world of wind and snow" can be extremely harsh and lasts for three to four months; in Minxi, Minnan, and Ganyue the winter is raw and damp but less cold.[61] Guerrillas often lived "like kings" in the gentle mountain climate of the south. Inland, however, in the bases to the north of Ganyue where nature was less clement, they paid a heavy toll in health and life to snow, rain, strong winds, and cloying fogs. Even in Minbei, some guerrillas froze to death.[62] Climate strongly affected morale. It was better to sleep rough on a southern mountain than on a northern mountain, and it was easier to find food in the evergreen forests of the subtropical south than in the deciduous forests further north.

The fourteen bases of the Three-Year War can be grouped conveniently into three main regions: the bases of the coastal provinces (including the Zhe, Min, and Yue bases); those in and around Jiangxi and north of Ganyue; and those north of the Chang Jiang. Political differences between these regions were significant, and national events affected the regions in different ways. The 1936 Liang Guang Incident in southern China had important consequences for guerrillas in the coastal provinces. The commotion provided a big opening for guerrillas in Ganyue, Minxi, Zhe'nan, and elsewhere. Though they soon lost most of the ground they had won in the crisis, they changed their policies as a result of it, and in Minxi, they eventually made up their losses. The Eyu and Eyuwan bases in the north were not directly affected by the Liang Guang Incident, but because of their northerly position, they caught reverberations of the Xi'an Incident of December 1936, in the form of overtures by disaffected militarists, sooner than their comrades in the south. The Jiangxi bases—partly for geopolitical reasons—were not directly affected by either incident.[63]

The bases in the coastal provinces had special advantages for the guerrillas. Armed religious sects proliferated in the villages of Fujian and Zhejiang, and in Fujian, some allied with the Communists. Fujian is divided up by mountains, and in the 1930s its settlements were scattered and disunited. It was not a normal region of Nationalist control. All these factors benefited the guerrillas. The bases north of the Chang Jiang, too, were able to draw on a heritage of organized dissent and disaffection in the villages. Historically, they had enjoyed greater autonomy from the Party center than bases south of the river, particularly those in Jiangxi. This independence was a blessing in the Three-Year War, when local roots became all-important. As for Jiangxi, in late 1934 it was a prize and symbol for Chiang Kai-shek and therefore a special target of his purges. Southern Jiangxi (Gannan) was a political symbol for the Communists and therefore the focus of Xiang Ying's defensive efforts. The bases of the Three-Year War north of the Chang Jiang and near the Fujian coast were unique in the Chinese Revolution; they were both old soviet areas and close to the Japanese forward lines after 1937. They remained bases of the revolution from the late 1920s until the end of the civil war in 1949.

Most theories about why revolutions happen focus on origins rather than on what keeps revolutions going after the first surge of enthusiasm has ebbed. These theories are of little direct relevance to the Three-Year War, which was primarily defensive. However, propositions abound about the causes of Xiang's "precious victory" in the south. Few try to explain it solely in economic terms, but the theory that class conflict is the ultimate "moving power" of all history is so routine in Chinese social science that it is an obvious starting point in any search for hypotheses. Most other Communist explanations of the "victory" look to political, organizational, and strategical factors rather than to the usual social and economic ones.

One common assumption is that places where the Communist movement was strongest before October 1934 would more readily support a guerrilla movement, for "mass consciousness" would be highest there. Another is that since the Three-Year War was a defensive war, the further the guerrillas moved from concentrations of Nationalist power and the deeper they ensconced themselves in the rugged mountains and remote forests, the better their chances of survival and revival. They could improve their prospects still further by seeking out regions where the enemy was split and there were "contradictions" to exploit.

According to a further proposition, even more important for success in the Three-Year War than these "objective" factors were "subjective" factors like quality of leadership, strength of organization, and degree of internal unity. Only experienced and politically "correct" leaders could consolidate the ranks, "strengthen thought," invent new policies to meet new circumstances, and think out new, flexible fighting tactics.[64] In this view, the most important "subjective" requirements were organizational discipline and the ability to act independently and in isolation; but links—however faint—to a Party center or Party bureaus in the cities were (so the theory goes) the surest way of avoiding "subjectivist" mistakes. Class struggle, a revolutionary tradition, geographic isolation, splits in the enemy camp, resourceful leaders, and a line to the Central Committee or the cities—these, then, are the factors to which Communist writers attribute the southern triumph. I shall now examine their ability, singly and in combinations, to account for the varying fortunes of guerrillas in selected regions.

## THE THREE-YEAR WAR AND THE CLASS STRUGGLE

Since none of the guerrillas enjoyed broad support after 1934, the proposition that success in the Three-Year War correlated with the intensity of class struggle must be false. That assertion does not mean that the Communists failed completely to stimulate class struggle or that they did not occasionally benefit from it. In their three strongest bases (Minxi, Mindong, and Eyuwan) they connected a few isolated settlements with a healthy tissue of Communist organization. They mounted spasmodic campaigns on economic issues in all regions of the Three-Year War. In Minxi, they even succeeded in preventing the return of land to the landlords in many villages where the fields had been divided. Elsewhere, they waged campaigns against rent, tax, conscription, and other banes of peasant life and gave to the poor grain and property taken from the rich. But these campaigns were often started against the wishes of the masses and without their cooperation. Many peasants had had enough of class struggle and its repercussions under the soviet, and they feared the consequences if they went along with the Communist "fire gods" for a second time.

Eventually, the guerrillas worked out ways of binding these people with them in complicity. However, these campaigns were a case not of class struggle producing revolution but of revolution producing class struggle. Class struggle became progressively less conspicuous during the Three-Year War as guerrillas switched their attention to the more lucrative business of forging links with local powerholders. But all the guerrillas kept economic demands in their program and are generally credited with avoiding the pitfall of "rightist accommodationism," if only abstractly, in their paper proclamations. The correlation between class struggle and Party strength in Minxi did not hold in Mindong or Eyuwan, where the Party stayed relatively strong even though land revolution was overthrown.

## A TYPOLOGY OF REVOLUTIONARY BASES

The second proposition is that guerrillas held out best in areas that had boasted a strong revolutionary tradition before 1935, for there the masses were politically aware, Communist organization was firmly rooted, and the Party derived prestige from previous success. This hypothesis is more promising than the abstract class-struggle theory, for it concedes that the Communists after 1934 dwelt in a world that they themselves had shaped, and it directs attention to the previous impact of the Party on the bases of the Three-Year War. Though the proposition as framed is too sweeping, it has much potential to explain events once finer distinctions are introduced.

It is easy to show that the mere presence of a revolutionary tradition in a region could not in itself guarantee success after 1934. In China in the 1930s, several sorts of revolutionary tradition coexisted, ranging from the highly centralized and absolutist to the parochial and down-to-earth. It is far from true that the stronger the tradition, the firmer the resistance. On the contrary, deep Red bases like the Central Soviet fell almost completely to the Nationalists, while newer ones under obscure provincial leaders like Ye Fei prospered.

To understand the Three-Year War, it is useful to divide both bases and leaders into classes and to see how the resulting typologies interact. I distinguish five types of base and four types of leader. These typologies are intended mainly to help explain developments in the Three-Year War, but they are also of wider relevance.

There are two sorts of base that we can call local. A local base was remote from the Party's central authority. Soviet power in local bases was limited, compromised, and generally responsive to local conditions. The characteristic military style in these bases was irregular, though their guerrillas were frequently required to contribute levies of men to the Party's regular armies elsewhere. The degree of central meddling in such bases is the criterion for a further distinction between autonomous and subordinate local bases.

A good example of an autonomous local base is Mindong, which flourished in relative obscurity and suffered minimal interference from above. Xianggan, Xiang'egan, and the main Minzhegan base are examples of subordinate local bases that were subjected to a great deal of intervention by the central leaders, who imposed personnel on them and taxed them for soldiers and supplies. For example, local Communists in the Minbei leadership were removed from power and replaced by Jiangxi people, whereas in neighboring Mindong, practically the entire leadership was made up of Mindong natives.[65] Subordinate local bases were sometimes evacuated for a while if they could be preserved only at the cost of more important places. Communist presence in an autonomous local base tended in contrast to be continuous. The Eyuwan case lies somewhere between these two extremes. Eyuwan's leader, the dissident Zhang Guotao, was appointed by the Party center, but he went partly "native" and left the base's layer of indigenous leaders largely intact. The Eyuwan Communist movement, like Communist movements in autonomous local bases, was indigenous. Subordinate local bases like Xiang'egan, Xianggan, and Xiangnan were created largely by outsiders, who imposed Red power at gunpoint. The Eyuwan base, like Mindong and Minxi, was native born and bred.

The Gannan and Minxi bases before October 1934 formed interrelated categories that can be described as central and peripheral. The Gannan base contained the capital of the Chinese Soviet Republic and was the hub of soviet economic and military life in the early 1930s. Soviet power here was least constrained, mobilization of human and material resources was most radical, and the Communist elite's local ties were slightest. The Communist movement in Gannan was not, however, purely a foreign import. Indigenous revolutionaries had played an important role in paving the way for the soviet. But centralizers quickly won the upper hand after the arrival in Gannan of the Zhu-Mao army in 1929; indigenous leaders were neutralized or engulfed, especially after the Futian Incident of 1930.

Ruijin, the soviet capital, was different from other parts of Gannan. In Ruijin, the Party had few indigenous roots before 1929, and the Red Army took power there by force of arms. The Minxi base was physically joined to Gannan and was nominally reckoned as part of the Central Soviet, but its origins, character, and function were distinct. Minxi Communists set up their own guerrilla units on the basis of eight armed uprisings in advance of the arrival of the Zhu-Mao army in Minxi, and they independently developed their own radical land-reform plan, unlike their more conservative and parochial cousins across the border in Gannan.[66]

The Communist movement in Minxi kept its local character throughout the soviet period. The people who set up the Party in the 1920s remained in charge until the end of the Three-Year War. Minxi was never as secure a bastion of the soviet as Gannan; it functioned as an eastern outpost. Minxi Communists generally tried to steer clear of the extreme "commandist" style of the regime in Ruijin. Their approach had more in common with that of indigenous Communists in the local bases: they tended to adjust their policies pragmatically to local conditions, and their military commanders preferred to fight by guerrilla means. But because Minxi was close to Ruijin, its leaders were inevitably drawn into the affairs and debates of the capital. This involvement diminished their autonomy, but it broadened their political horizons and their range of expertise and skills. Over the years, the Communist movement in Minxi evolved into a sort of hybrid between the Central Soviet and local movements to the north and west of Gannan.

Not all bases of the Three-Year War had a revolutionary tradition. Some regions, including Zhe'nan and, to a lesser extent, Xiangnan, were relatively blank pages, save for brief bloodbaths in the 1920s, and Zhe-xi'nan was altogether blank. All three bases were created by outsiders after the start of the Long March. These new bases form my fifth category. They permit a negative test of the proposition that Communists held out in the Three-Year War because they were able to build on past achievements.

## A TYPOLOGY OF REVOLUTIONARY LEADERS

Most analyses of Chinese Communist politics in the 1930s distinguish between two classes of leaders: the so-called Returned Students, a Russian-influenced faction that favored the centralization of power and an orthodox class-line approach; and a "mass-line" group around Mao that was less centralist, more responsive to local issues, and more closely tied to local society. Recently, this distinction between class-line and mass-line leaders has been challenged by several writers, and it is true that Mao and the Returned Students shared some aims and beliefs.[67] The main difference between them is that Mao saw the Red Army as the key to victory in the revolution, whereas the Returned Students had a more conventionally Marxist expectation of victory through proletarian action. Mao's greater realism and his indifference in the early 1930s to ideological shibboleths made it easier for him than for his theorist rivals to adjust to practical reality. Mao and his supporters were pragmatic centralists who kept their ears close to the ground; the Returned Students were dogmatic centralists who put theory above practice.

Some writers have associated the pragmatic centralists around Mao with local leaders in the smaller and peripheral soviets, but one must distinguish between them.[68] Local Communists connected by ties of kinship, friendship, schooling, and obligation to native places had a different outlook on life from those in the Party's self-directing center. Many of them despaired at the exactions and ukases rained down on their bases by Party commissioners. They resented the centralists who were planted among them, and they were dismayed by the decampments of Red Army garrisons that culminated in the Long March. But though they tried hard to protect the interests of their constituents, in the end they were usually swayed by "Party spirit" to sacrifice them to the "greater good." Not all of these local leaders were pragmatists; some degenerated into local despots. At their best, however, they were sensitive to local configurations of power and good at settling terms with the people who embodied it. The Minxi leaders form a category on their own—our fourth—that combines elements of pragmatic centralism with a strong local identity and understanding.

The formal affinities between the typology of bases and the typology of leaders did not necessarily hold in practice. Not all local bases were led by local leaders in the Three-Year War, and the central base was no longer led by central leaders. Central leaders were scattered across most regions by the reassignments of 1934 and the chaotic evacuation of the Central Soviet. The Three-Year War in Gannan—the engine-room of centralization before October 1934—was led exclusively by local Communists after Xiang Ying left for Ganyue.

### CENTRALISM AND LOCALISM
### IN THE THREE-YEAR WAR

The two regions that salvaged the most "living forces" for the New Fourth Army were Minxi and Eyuwan. The Mindong guerrillas also emerged exceptionally strong from the war, especially considering how few they were at the start. Because of poor communications, Communists in Eyuwan and Mindong had never been closely tied to the Party center and had long been used to acting and deciding independently. The Minxi Party, too, was a local product, led by local people whose exposure to the wider movement had not completely estranged them from their roots. Local bases like Xianggan and Xiang'egan, founded by outsiders and treated as dispensable auxiliaries by the central leaders, emerged less creditably from the Three-Year War, as did locally founded bases like Minbei, in which Communist outsiders from Jiangxi had strongly intervened. In Xianggan, this failure probably had much to do with the character of Tan Yubao, who wielded absolute power over the base but had little idea how to use it flexibly and imaginatively. The Minzhegan (or Gandongbei) base, founded by local Communists under Fang Zhimin, collapsed entirely after 1934, partly because it had been ruthlessly milked by Ruijin and then crushed by the defeat of Fang Zhimin's expedition into Wannan. Among the weakest bases by 1937 was that in Ganyue under Xiang Ying and Chen Yi. Ganyue was a local base, but it abutted on the Central Soviet and lacked strong and willful local leaders. After the death of Li Letian, its main early leader, in 1936, power over the Ganyue guerrillas passed even more surely into the hands of Xiang and Chen, both central leaders, one a dogmatist, the other a pragmatist.

New bases founded by outsiders in 1934 and 1935, during or after the events that culminated in the Long March, either collapsed entirely (in Min'gan and Annanyongde) or only just survived (in Xiangnan, Wanzhegan, and Zhe'nan). In early 1935, the Xiangnan base under Gong Chu expanded quickly, and in 1936, the bases in Zhe'nan and Wanzhegan seemed to represent a real threat to the government. It appears that in regions with little experience of civil war and soviet power, the Communists could achieve quick breakthroughs but not translate them into lasting gains. Guerrillas in the old central base in Gannan did about as well as guerrillas in the new base in Xiangnan, but less well than the Advance Division in Zhe'nan.

Minxi apart, the bases that fared best after 1934 were local bases founded by local people and subject to the least central interference. Next best were local bases founded by outsiders and subject before 1935 only to indirect control by the Party center. The bases that fared worst were new bases and bases previously under direct central control. Minxi was a special case. Although it physically adjoined the central system of bases, its origins and early history were distinct. Its proximity to Ruijin attuned its leaders to the danger of "leftist" imports and raised barriers that reduced their damage.

Why did local Communists in local bases fare best in the Three-Year War? Psychologically, politically, and on the battlefield, their leaders were better prepared for the conditions that governed the war than were officers and officials from stable soviets. They were intuitive adepts of guerrilla warfare and of Minxi's "Luo Ming Line," the "heresy" that sought an end to blanket ordinances and called instead for a sensitive response to local moods and issues. Despite Ruijin's bull of condemnation against Luo Ming, many opponents of extreme centralism in the Party continued to follow this approach. Unlike the regular Red Army men scattered across the south after 1934, who could only address local people through interpreters, these Communists could speak local languages.[69] Languages were especially important in the Three-Year War, when local militias were used in pacification drives and even a wrongly pronounced syllable could betray a guerrilla.[70]

Communists in local and peripheral bases had more experience than those in central bases and regular Red Army units of conciliating their opponents, and they were thus better prepared for a period in which they could no longer play the lord. They also had more ties to the market towns and villages, so they could more easily strike alliances with malcontents. Daoist sects had their lodges throughout the mountains of Fujian and Zhejiang, but it was mainly in Fujian that the Party succeeded in winning their support because most guerrillas in the Min bases were local people with local ties. The guerrillas in Zhejiang were not only outsiders but were also led by regular Red Army officers who had a more orthodox and conventional view of revolution. The alliances in Fujian were crucial to the success of the Min guerrillas. The Daoists were at first a threat to the Communists' security, but once their confidence had been gained, their cooperation became invaluable. They knew the mountains intimately, they were powerful in the villages, they had channels down into the valleys, and they were fearless, thinking themselves indestructible.

Because "leftism" had been less extreme in local guerrilla bases in the early 1930s, villagers there were less likely to be disillusioned with Communism and alienated from the Party than the "basic masses" in the old soviet heartland. In old "leftist" areas, said the Minxi Communist Lin Jian, the Party's erstwhile supporters had become apathetic or downright hostile to the Communists. "But in Yanyonghang [in Minxi] and in other old soviet bases where the 'leftist' line had ruled for a comparatively short period, the masses were not only highly aware but had a rich experience of struggle and understood how to apply different methods of struggle in contending with the enemy."[71]

Xiang Ying's last-ditch stand in Gannan was a final blow to the Party's support there. Xiang, a dogmatic centralist, temporized for several months before yielding to the pragmatic Chen Yi, who had favored an early switch to guerrilla warfare. Most local bases, including parts of Minxi, had made the switch well in advance of the start of the Long March. This tactic paid off, for the Nationalists put most resources into quelling the most obvious trouble spots.[72] Xiang and Chen continued to argue about policy even after fleeing to Ganyue in March 1935. As a result, the Ganyue leadership was disunited. For all Chen Yi's talk of "localizing," the Communists in Ganyue remained isolated.

The proposition that regions with a strong revolutionary tradition stood up best in the Three-Year War holds only if important qualifications are admitted. A centralist revolutionary tradition like that in Gannan spelt disaster after the start of the Long March. In areas where soviet power had been most extensive, counterrevolution was most complete, partly because the Nationalists scoured out these areas with particular thoroughness, and partly because disillusion with Communism after 1934 developed in direct proportion to how closely people had experienced the effects of central Party rule. Economic crisis caused by war and the commandeering of countless men, animals, and tons of grain, extensive purges, and the final disillusion caused by the Long March and the collapse of the rearguard destroyed popular morale. Even though the Communist movement in Gannan reverted to indigenous leadership after 1934, the damage had been done. Regions like Minxi, Mindong, and Eyuwan with an indigenous revolutionary tradition in some degree resistant to central meddling weathered the storms with most success and yielded the richest harvests. Local bases like Xianggan, Xiang'egan, Minbei, and Minzhegan, founded by outsiders or subjected to excessive central interference, slumped in 1935 and marked time for the rest of the war. New bases without a revolutionary tradition either collapsed entirely or just scraped through. Mindong is an exception. The difference between Mindong and Zhe'nan, the newest base in the Three-Year War, is that Mindong was founded a year earlier than Zhe'nan and by indigenous leaders, whereas the Zhe'nan base was founded by high-ranking Red Army regulars.

## POLITICAL GEOGRAPHY

Three of the four remaining propositions about the causes of success in the Three-Year War are best treated collectively, for they are all rooted in political geography. One is that physical isolation was the key to survival after 1934. Another is that guerrillas benefited from links to urban Communists and Party centers. Finally, there is the proposition that guerrillas survived best where they could exploit splits among their enemies.

The Three-Year War was a defensive war, fought mainly within enemy encirclements by tiny, isolated nuclei of Red Army guerrillas. All guerrilla units sought out fastnesses in the mountains after 1934, but though their natural environments were at first sight broadly similar, there were important differences, which resulted from circumstance and choice. Some regions to which units were assigned in 1934 had more strategic potential than others, and whether this potential was used depended on the strategists.

The assumption that, for stay-behinders, safety lay in maximum seclusion behind rock walls and in thick forests is false. Some insulation was indispensable; too much was suffocating. Guerrillas far away from Nationalist garrisons were unlikely to be caught off guard, but they were also unlikely to light on new political opportunities early enough to make good use of them. Strategy is often defined as the art of calculated risk. In the Three-Year War, preoccupation with secrecy and security was just as harmful as reckless belligerence. Guerrilla leaders had to strike a balance between hiding and flaunting themselves, between "passive skulking" and "blind activism."

Xianggan and Ganyue, where the guerrillas were most obsessed with security, were among the weakest of the bases that did not actually collapse. Xianggan was, anyway, physically remote from the scenes of important political events, and Tan Yubao's paranoid introversion sealed it even more tightly against influences from outside. The Communists in Ganyue were at the hub of several different guerrilla bases and on the border between forces of Chiang Kai-shek and of Chiang's militarist rival Chen Jitang, but they kept themselves largely invisible. Xiang Ying and Chen Yi both set greater store by preserving old forces for the Party than by developing new ones. Some bases were too secluded or remote; others were not secluded or remote enough. The bases in

Minzhewan'gan, particularly the Zhe'nan base, were close to the political and economic heartland of the Guomindang and to the birthplaces of Chiang Kai-shek and Chen Cheng, so they were more likely to become targets of government repression.

Not all bases of the Three-Year War were stuck on the Guomindang's doorstep or stranded in the outer wilderness. Some bases were sufficiently insulated to be secure while still keeping tiny windows on the outside world. These openings let in news of major political events on the national stage such as the Liang Guang Incident, the Xi'an Incident, and the steps toward a second united front. This news enabled guerrillas to seize new opportunities and stopped them from stagnating or dissolving into their surroundings. On rare occasions, these secret vents and spyholes also allowed the transmission of Party messages. The guerrillas thereby learned of new directions in Party policy. They were also heartened by the knowledge that Communism still survived in the cities and in the north.

The outlying soviets had been at the end of the communication chain before 1935. When the Central Soviet fell and intelligence lines from the cities petered out well short of Xiang's headquarters in Ganyue, these former fringe regions became first rather than last stops on the new, shortened lines of correspondence. Some bases in Fujian and the new base in Zhe'nan were best placed to receive these contacts. Fujian and Zhejiang are coastal provinces with sea links to Shanghai and Hongkong. Bases in these provinces had secret lines to the big ports: Zhe'nan to Wenzhou, Mindong to Fuzhou, Minyue to Shantou, Minxi to Zhangzhou and Xiamen. Along these lines flowed crucial information, such as news of the August First Manifesto issued in Moscow in 1935. Such contacts were particularly important in Zhe'nan and Mindong, which had barely got wind of the decisions taken at Zunyi before all radio contact was lost.[73]

The networks run by Fujian bases were quite different in character from those further inland. Guerrilla leaders in Ganyue, Xianggan, and Xiang'egan were lucky if they stayed in touch with their own units, let alone ran lines to the cities or to other bases. But bases in Fujian were linked not only to the ports, which gave them people, provisions, and Party publications, but also to one another; each reinforced the other's growth in a dialectic of regional cooperation. The Communists in Minxi also used existing networks created by emigration to spread their political message. For example, they made an impact far beyond the mountains by writing to Fellow Provincials' Associations in the cities about their proposals for a united front in 1937. Such propaganda was much easier to spread in Minxi than in bases further inland, where patterns of migration also probably differed. The division between Red uplands and

White lowlands was clearer cut where "leftism" had been strong than in the old guerrilla areas of Fujian. Communist leaders in Ganyue also took advantage of such lineage ties to send feelers down onto the nearby plains, but they made little headway.

Accounts differ about the importance of outside Party links in shaping the innovations made by leaders of the Three-Year War. Some say the changes were made in response to directives issued by the Party center, for example at Zunyi in early 1935. Others suggest that the guerrillas worked them out independently, without waiting for instructions. These differences arise partly because some guerrillas received news of the directives from Zunyi while others did not, but they also have a political explanation. Rearguard veterans like Chen Yi, who supported Mao and welcomed the directives, say that they were crucial; others, like Xiang Ying, caught out by Zunyi, imply that continuity and "native" adjustment were the keys to success. In the 1980s, leaders like Ye Fei also began to claim that they adopted new policies independently after 1934, in accordance with local conditions. Such claims were in part a bid for glory by old men in the twilight of their lives; they were also consonant with the new spirit of the 1980s, which valued independent initiative and "seeking truth from the facts."

Because remoteness was just as likely as accessibility to inhibit Communist success, the best formula for a strong movement was a middle position. The distance between safety and extreme hazard could be a matter of a few miles. The Annanyongde base, close to Minxi, collapsed early in the Three-Year War because it was too near to the Nationalist garrison at Quanzhou. It was probably also too near for its own good to the Party office in Xiamen, whose proximity left an easy way out for Party fainthearts and an easy way in for "leftist" fallacies.

The Eyu, Eyuwan, and Mindong bases were all historically and physically remote from main Party centers. Communists from these places say that this remoteness was to their advantage: it forced them to seek their own solutions to their own problems.[74]

In most cases, it is a tautology to say that the strength of a base was determined mainly by the size of the campaign against it, for the size of the campaign generally varied with the size of the threat that the base posed. Chiang Kai-shek put most of his effort into pacifying Gannan after the start of the Long March partly because Xiang Ying continued to fight large-scale engagements there and refused to concede. Small, inactive bases like Tan Yubao's in Xianggan were less likely to attract attention than large, active bases.

Revolutionaries generate their own oppositions by their choice of grounds and tactics. Some bases managed to grow by playing possum. For example, by working secretly and avoiding armed clashes with

regular forces, the relatively successful base in Eyu largely escaped notice in 1936.[75] All guerrilla leaders sought to minimize opposition and to
maximize their own chances of survival by retiring to border areas between counties, provinces, and military cliques and by exploiting contradictions among their enemies. How much did these tactics contribute to
their success?

The sort of contradictions that the guerrillas tried to play on or to
open up ranged from minor strains and tensions in village administra-
tions to important conflicts of interest among Nationalist armies or between those armies and local elites. These conflicts had a variety of
sources: social, economic, political, ethnic, generational, religious, and
military. Guerrillas everywhere wiggled the blade of discord in the
cracks of rural life and exploited the power vacuum along political borders. But few had the chance to take advantage of bigger schisms. Major
contradictions were few during the Three-Year War; Chiang Kai-shek's
campaign against the soviets had not only swept away the Communists
but had also extensively undermined Chiang's other regional rivals. After the Liang Guang Incident of 1936, Chiang's grip on southern China
tightened. The two regions where contradictions gave the Communists
an advantage after 1934 were Eyuwan and Minxi. These were also the
regions that preserved the most forces for the Party.

In Eyu, Manchurian troops fraternized with Communist guerrillas in
1937, and leaders of regional forces who believed that Chiang Kai-shek
had victimized them slipped the Communists money and supplies.[76] In
Eyuwan, too, the Communists profited from divisions in the Nationalist
camp. In Minxi, the Communists had various contradictions to exploit.
Before the Liang Guang Incident, they tried to play on anti-Japanese
and anti-Chiang sentiment in Minxi's Fujianese garrison. But whatever
progress they made was brought to naught by the transfer of these Fujianese to Guangdong after the incident (and by the guerrillas' accompanying lurch into "leftism"). The Cantonese who took over the garrison in Minxi were no well-wishers of Chiang Kai-shek, and they, too,
were susceptible to anti-Japanese agitation. Minxi Communists planted
a cell in the Guangdong Army and influenced some of its middle officers
and ranks, but their efforts had nowhere near as much effect as that of
Communists in Shaanbei on Zhang Xueliang's divisions.

Minxi Communists did not aim only at army targets. The Minxi base
was in easy reach of one of southeastern China's main economic centers,
around Xiamen and Zhangzhou. Through the local elite ran rich seams
of disaffection at which Communist quarriers hacked and blasted in
1936 and 1937. One conflict was between local capitalists and the Guangdong Army, which destroyed profitable bamboo groves in its campaign
against the Communists. Another was between local patriots and busi-

nessmen on the one hand and Japanese soldiers, traders, and carpetbaggers, together with the local or Taiwanese riffraff who acted as their henchmen, on the other. Because Fujian is across the strait from Taiwan, then occupied by the Japanese, it was especially vulnerable to Japanese pressure. This weakness provided the Minxi Communists with ample opportunities. Though they never achieved a breakthrough of the sort made in the north, their campaign against the Japanese won them regard and prepared them better than other guerrillas in the south for the new united front.

## THE QUALITY OF LEADERSHIP

Subjective factors, such as quality of leadership—which according to our final proposition was even more important for victory than external or objective conditions in the different regions—are harder to define and appraise. The Chinese Communist definition of good leadership has changed radically over the years. The old belief in forceful and highly centralized leadership has given way to a more relaxed prescription. Today, a good leader is expected to derive power from esteem rather than from unquestioning obedience. Such a leader prefers rewards to penalties and persuasion to coercion, promotes solidarity over conflict, and consults through established channels before making decisions.[77] Most leaders of the Three-Year War embodied very few of these attributes.

Only a minority were experienced captains of the Party with practical and theoretical training in the art of revolution. Most leaders had little grounding in theory, and their practical experience was confined to minor posts in provincial and county soviets or committees. Zhe'nan, Ganyue, and Minxi, which were led by teams of experienced leaders, were exceptions. But of the three, only Minxi prospered. One might even conclude that strong leadership fragmented the group, for in Zhe'nan, and to a lesser extent in Ganyue, the leadership fell apart amid accusations and counteraccusations. Leaders elsewhere with less experience—for example Ye Fei in Mindong and Gao Jingting in Eyuwan—emerged far stronger from the Three-Year War.

If tolerance is a second subjective measure of good leadership, the results are again inconclusive. Guerrilla leaders everywhere jettisoned their more extreme public policies after 1934, but only a handful relaxed their internal regimes. Most guerrilla units were split by struggles between different factions and classes of Communists after the start of the Long March. Almost all of the winners in these conflicts dealt with the losers by "administrative" means, namely by purges and attacks. Some victims deserted or defected; others died. Confrontations pitted natives against outsiders, guerrillas against Red Army regulars, Communists from one region against those from another, "defeatists" against "adventurists," "opportunists" against "leftists," and old Communists against new Communists. Many of these feuds probably involved settling some scores that had little to do with politics.

In Ganyue, Chen Yi strove to prevent feuds by urging newcomers to respect local Communists and to learn from them. He also took a lenient view of waverers, arguing that it was better to let them go than to hold them in the mountains against their will. His measures were important for morale. By 1937, the Ganyue remnant was rich in the quality of its fighters (many of its veterans were to have a great influence on China) but poor in numbers.

Most guerrilla leaders, successful and unsuccessful, purged remorselessly after 1934. Two of the bloodiest purgers were Ye Fei and Gao Jingting, who also ran two of the best campaigns of the war. Even the Minxi Communists purged each other. Purges resulted in comparatively large losses, but, measured in terms of the number of guerrillas preserved region by region for the New Fourth Army, the purges were apparently a stronger cement than the mildness and flexibility advocated by Chen Yi. Some purges coincided with or preceded periods of growth.

According to sociologists, a leader can more easily gain ascendancy over people by courting them than by beating them, for violence and punishments drive followers away. Machiavelli writes that a cruel and arbitrary leader engenders a feeling of paranoia, and the leader is likely to be killed by subordinates. However, a leader must first gain a following before trying to earn its esteem. Chen Yi's authority in Ganyue was unimpeachable: as a distinguished revolutionary and an adopted son of Ganyue, where he had spent three years after 1928, he was respected and could afford to be magnanimous. Leaders in other regions, who felt less secure, mobilized followers by displaying brute force against their rivals.

The new circumstances after 1934 required new policies; often, the switch involved violent struggles leading to schismogenesis, which the anthropologist Gregory Bateson defined in another context as a process in which "oppositions are continually and dialectically heightened once begun." Terror welded the survivors of these schisms to the winners. Some people stayed in the mountains because they could see nowhere else to go. "One reason they didn't surrender," said Ye Fei, "was the massacre policy of Chiang Kai-shek and especially of local reactionary landlords. We should be warmly thankful to Chiang Kai-shek for that. They even killed many [Communist] traitors, so that people had no choice but to continue along the revolutionary road."[78] Would-be defectors also feared the long arm of the Party, which they had been given to believe stretched everywhere. Though terror may not persuade when it can be avoided, ineluctable terror apparently works only too well. But despite its bonding power, terror devoured talents that the guerrillas sorely needed. It was effective in the short term, but in the long term, Chen Yi's volunteers probably contributed more to the Party than the cowed retinues of Gao Jingting or Tan Yubao.

The relative size and complexity of Party organization is a third measure of the quality of leadership. The Party was best organized in Minxi, where the rearguard's strongest leading team sometimes had logistic help from coastal cities. The Minxi'nan Military and Administrative Committee became a model for guerrillas in other nearby bases. The Minxi Communists maintained an extensive system of branches and committees and published a steady flow of leaflets, pamphlets, and journals. In Ganyue, too, Xiang Ying and Chen Yi did their best to maintain Party organization in the counties, districts, and guerrilla detachments, though to less effect.[79] However, other bases—particularly those in Mindong, Eyuwan, and Xianggan—were virtual monocracies. Neither the collectives nor the one-man shows had a monopoly on success or failure in the Three-Year War. Neither strong Party organization nor leaders' experience and tolerance seems to have been the determining factor in the fate of a base. Leaders functioned within a complex overall environment in which a whole range of factors operated. Some situations rewarded impetuosity and terror; others collapsed because of it.

## QUANTITATIVE AND QUALITATIVE SUCCESS

So far, I have measured success only by numbers, but if we use other criteria, the picture changes. In purely quantitative terms, Gao Jingting in Eyuwan matched and even surpassed the achievement of the Minxi Communists. But Gao's movement was parochial and self-contained, whereas the Minxi Communists had a broader vision. In 1938, Minxi veterans shot to the top of the New Fourth Army and played key roles in the Party's rise to power. Eyuwan veterans of the Three-Year War furnished few figures of any note in Party history. Of course, this obscurity may be due partly to prejudice against them, for Gao and his guerrillas were tainted by their association with the "traitor" Zhang Guotao, but prejudice was not the only issue. In the first few months of 1938, when guerrillas from the southern bases were loyally marching to the front, Gao held back for a while and was criticized as selfish and a "mountaintoppist." The conflict between Gao and the New Fourth Army command was not resolved even when Gao eventually headed east; and in June 1939, Ye Ting shot him as a "warlord."

The Party center mistrusted local loyalties, especially when they were translated into personal loyalties of the sort Gao craved. The Eyuwan leaders after 1934 were more than regional introverts; they were soldiers first and only then politicians. They were less motivated than the Minxi leaders to see the revolution through to the end at the national level after 1937. In many bases of the Three-Year War, natives and outsiders fought civil wars within the civil war; the two sides continued to mistrust each other even after 1937. The best prescription for a loyal, competent, and durable movement was neither one-sided "localism" nor a Party of cosmopolitans; it was a leadership like that in Minxi, formed by people who were native to the region they were fighting in but who were knowledgeable about the wider political scene because of their long association with the national Party. In a leadership of this sort, the distinction between natives and professionals was less relevant.

I began by formulating some propositions on the basis—such as it is—of Chinese Communist theory about the Three-Year War, and I went on to see how far they held good for different regions. The bases that failed were typically those where the Party center had previously had the greatest influence, where revolution had been imported by the army, where centralists led the rearguard, or where the Party had previously been inactive. The bases that survived best were those founded and led by local revolutionary pragmatists, defended by guerrillas, neither too secluded nor too exposed, but open to outside influences and opportunities and at the same time secure. There is no consistent correlation between leadership experience and leadership success. Experienced leaders in Ganyue did not do well, whereas experienced leaders in Minxi did extremely well; the most successful campaigns were led by people who made up for their lack of experience by the strength of their local ties and knowledge. These findings are consistent with my earlier conclusion: that the Three-Year War involved a switch from the general to the particular, from the center to the periphery, from the valleys to the mountains, from the limelight to the twilight, from being "host" to being "guest."

## IMPLICATIONS FOR THE NEW FOURTH ARMY

The Three-Year War bequeathed the New Fourth Army with all manner of afflictions and bad habits but also with some strengths and virtues. Most southern veterans were poorly armed; many were diseased and malnourished.[80] The guerrillas were individualistic, clannish, and poorly disciplined. They hankered after the mountains and feared the lakes and plains.[81] They lacked modern technical military skills. For a long time, they showed little sympathy for the New Fourth Army's campaign to formalize and standardize procedures in the units. Even so, at the end of the Three-Year War they marched to the resistance front almost without pausing: they had little or no time to rest, recuperate, train, or remedy their failings after their reorganization in early 1938.[82] But they were inured to hardship, and they put their outstanding knowledge and experience of guerrilla fighting to effective use in the awesomely difficult conditions of eastern China. Moreover, unlike some of the newer Communist units in the north, they were not afraid to take the initiative. Yet, apart from this practical legacy, the Three-Year War bequeathed parts of the New Fourth Army with an identity and a style that brought them into conflict with the Maoists in Yan'an. To disentangle the complexities of this friction, we must look briefly beyond the New Fourth Army to the wider factional struggle in the Chinese Communist Party.

### XIANG YING AND THE NEW FOURTH ARMY

For Chinese Communist historians of the Resistance War, the New Fourth Army under Xiang Ying was a hotbed of rightist deviations. In the early part of the war, Xiang frowned on radical measures and reforms that might provoke the Guomindang. His policy was best typified by the slogan "Everything through the united front," which was closely associated with Wang Ming and was criticized by Mao and Liu Shaoqi as opportunist. Xiang Ying was probably the last Chinese Communist leader to use this slogan in public. Xiang's critics later took his reluctance to "match unity with struggle" in his relations with the Guomindang as evidence that he supported the "second Wang Ming line" of "rightist accommodationism," which had its origins in Stalin's Moscow. After all, Xiang had belonged to Wang Ming's "Internationalist" faction under the Jiangxi Soviet, and in 1938, his Southeastern Bureau came under Wang's direction. But it is hard to picture a home-grown, steeled revolutionary like Xiang, who could "make waves where there was no wind," as a client of the bureaucrat Wang Ming, especially now that Communist writers admit that the differences between Xiang and his Mao-Marxist critics were less straightforward than was once claimed.[83] Instead, it is worth looking for an explanation of Xiang's behavior in his own ambitions and experience.

The simplest explanation of Xiang's new desire to conciliate the Nationalists is that his base in Wannan after 1937 was close to important Nationalist concentrations. To carry out a more radical program, he would have had to march east or north into areas less susceptible to Guomindang control. He would not do so for three main reasons. First, he believed strongly in cooperating with the Guomindang and feared that going north would split the united front and strain his resources. Second, the Three-Year War had lit the fire of independence in him. He had a proprietary view of the New Fourth Army, which he saw as the product of a separate tradition in the Party and the main guarantee of his own political autonomy. He was not prepared to relinquish control over it. Chen Yi, Xiang's comrade in the Three-Year War and a commander of the New Fourth Army under him, had been associated with Mao since the early 1930s. When the time came in 1938 to strike deep behind Japanese lines to the east and north and to pursue that combination of social reform and shifting class alliance that was Mao's policy in the war, it was Chen Yi who answered Mao's call. Xiang preferred to stay behind in Wannan and "preside over his little court at Yunling." He feared that if he crossed the river northward, "the Central Committee might transfer him away from his troops and divest him of responsibility for the New Fourth Army." His love of independence was more important than his commitment to the united front. He stayed in Wannan even when Chiang Kai-shek, for reasons of his own, told him to leave.[84]

The third reason that Xiang clung to the mountains of Wannan rather than venture down onto the watery, teeming plains of eastern China was that he was a man of habit, unlike the more adaptable Chen Yi. Xiang Ying can best be described as a Party elitist; despite his lip service to "the masses," experience had convinced him that the key to victory rested with the chosen few.

Before the Long March, Xiang was a member of the Party's centralist, bureaucratic elite. He headed various government departments and rarely traveled into the villages. After the start of the Long March, he and Chen Yi darted between mountain tops for three years and made their homes in the wild. Only rarely could they mobilize local people in struggle and organize them in associations, and never on a scale remotely approaching that in other places. In extreme circumstances, their guerrillas gave up fighting altogether and took jobs as laborers or set up mountain industries. They adapted to local conditions so completely that they became indistinguishable from ordinary mountain people.

Unlike the Long Marchers in northwestern China, Xiang and Chen had no experience of mass-based politics between 1934 and 1938. They no longer shaped society but instead lived on its margins and in its cracks. They adapted more or less passively to the power structure in the villages rather than try to change it. Well in advance of the Long Marchers, they developed an ability to compromise with and manipulate local officials, militia commanders, bandit chiefs, gentry leaders, and others with power and authority; without these compromises, they would probably have been wiped from the political map. Their survival rested on contradictory principles: a resolute refusal to submit to Nationalist blandishments or pressure and an ability to pull secret strings and bend with the wind.

This experience was particularly important for Xiang Ying, who had never known any other kind of guerrilla war. It helped shape Xiang's idea of warfare until his death in 1941. Chen Yi, in contrast, had fought in the villages since 1927 and knew how to rouse the peasants on class lines and to create strong bases. Xiang's love of the mountains, his "fear of the plains," and his failure to see the need for deep, broad social mobilization of a sort possible only behind Japanese lines, where the Guomindang's writ no longer ran, resulted partly from the style and outlook he formed after the Long March. He had learned then that nimbleness, quick wits, pliancy, and patience could preserve even a tiny handful of people against vast armies. He had become convinced of his own indestructibility, like the Daoist "magic armies" courted by guerrillas in Fujian in 1935. After 1937, he believed for a long time that the Nationalist garrisons around his base in Wannan would not attack him, and that even if they did, his troops could slip away unhurt. "During the three-year guerrilla struggle the Nationalists could never touch us," Xiang's adjutant Yuan Guoping (not himself a veteran of the Three-Year War) told Zhou Enlai in late 1940, on the eve of Xiang's death. "Now we have tens of thousands of troops."[85]

Xiang's Maoist critics see a pattern in Xiang's political evolution: first he supported an offensive against the Nationalists under the "leftist" Wang Ming leadership of the early 1930s, then he "snuggled up" to the Nationalists during the second "rightist" Wang Ming line of the late 1930s. Both "deviations" stemmed from the solipsistic fallacy, which "slights the enemy" and sees the world exclusively in terms of one's own mission. If all else failed, Xiang's last shift would be to "take the officers, leave the men, scatter for guerrilla war." He is accused of raising this slogan in the Wannan Incident of January 1941, "with the illusion of repeating the experience of the three-year guerrilla war." This stratagem—the famous "thirty-sixth trick" in the folk warfare manual, called "it is best to leave"—had worked in early 1935, but in the different circumstances of 1941, it failed. Shortly after absconding, Xiang was murdered by a Communist defector.[86]

Xiang's experience in the Three-Year War helps explain his affinity with Wang Ming after 1937. Wang was far readier than Mao to tone down policies for the sake of unity with the Guomindang. During the negotiations with the Nationalists, Wang was in Moscow, where Stalin's voice rang louder than that of the peasants who formed the Party's social base in northwestern China. Mao, in contrast, was faced daily with the urgent need to win the peasants. Xiang in the Three-Year War was not constrained in the same way as Mao in Shaanbei. He had no real social base and no prospect of building one while under siege in the south. He had moderated his policies before Mao and took part in only the last stages of the debate on how to integrate national unity and class struggle. Consequently, he had more in common with Wang Ming than a past factional link; it is facile to reduce his leadership of the New Fourth Army to an emanation of the "Wang Ming line."

## A LEGACY OF DISUNITY AND DIVISION

Another legacy of the Three-Year War was factionalism and disunity. After years of dispersal, the guerrillas who came together under Xiang lacked discipline and cohesion. The main Red Army operated in large divisions under a unified command; the southern guerrillas were splintered into many unconnected fragments, "orphaned and helpless."[87] The Central Committee Sub-Bureau set up under Xiang in October 1934 was never much more than a name. It commanded no binding loyalty over the southern Communists. One task of the early New Fourth Army was to "gather the fragments into a whole," said Chen Yi in January 1938.[88]

Having skillfully exploited regional divisions and factional affiliations in the Nationalist armies, the Communists were on their guard against similar divisions in their own ranks. In the long run, New Fourth Army leaders overcame this legacy of fragmentation; in the short run, it worked to Yan'an's advantage by thwarting Xiang's plan to run his army as an "independent kingdom." For though Xiang aspired to independence, he lacked the means to realize it. His efforts to build on the separate identity of the New Fourth Army foundered on its lack of solidarity. Many units under Xiang were not prepared to defer, with him, to the Guomindang. Friction and incidents at regional staging points and on the way to Wannan had inclined the guerrillas to distrust the Nationalists. The New Fourth's lack of a strong overarching sense of identity proved useful to the Maoists in their campaign to entice Xiang's detachments to cross the Chang Jiang. By 1940 at the latest, a Maoist faction had coalesced from the New Fourth's shifting currents, sealing Xiang's fate.

Communists under Chen Yi thrust boldly into areas where the Guomindang was weak and divided and where the Japanese presence was slight. When Chen first arrived behind Japanese lines in Jiangnan, he trod lightly and refrained from radical campaigns. During this early period, his subversive experience in the Three-Year War helped him greatly. But when the time was ripe, he started a program of military expansion and social and political reform inspired by the idea of base-building as Mao preached it. Xiang generally opposed Chen's move north, but its logic exposed him to increasing danger. Chen left mainly to avoid future friction with the Guomindang, but in the short term, going north made friction inevitable. By staying close to Nationalist lines,

Xiang unwittingly set himself up as the chief victim of this friction. After Xiang's defeat, the assimilation of the New Fourth Army to orthodox Maoist positions was soon completed.[89]

## THE MOBILIZATION OF ALL FACTORS

The Three-Year War was an exceptional period in the history of the Chinese Revolution; it would be unwise to try to draw too many general conclusions from it. I shall confine myself to just a few comments on the war's broader context.

The southern campaign brings into sharp focus the Chinese Communists' concern in planning their revolution for wider dimensions of time and space. Strategy, the art of marshaling forces over large areas and long periods, is called grand or higher strategy when it correlates closely with national political and other goals. Grand strategy is a good name for the Chinese Red Army's disposition of military means over many regions in the mid- to late 1930s. In the three years after 1934, the Red Army command achieved little or no central coordination and even less operational management across its scattered war theaters, but the particular spread of forces in that period was the product of strategic judgment. The strategy depended partly on political and psychological objectives: to signal Nationalist impotence and the invincibility of the revolution, and to drive home the Communist claim to represent all China.

We have long been used to fitting the Chinese Revolution into geographical slots: the Jiangxi period and the Yan'an period have become so fixed in historical imagination that some even speak of southern and northern phases of the struggle.[90] This view is too simple. Both the Three-Year War and the New Fourth Army show that Communist presence in a region was rarely erased even after great defeats. Once the Party had sunk roots, it proved remarkably hard to weed out. Nearly everywhere, it left some secret marker as evidence for a future claim. The southern bases of the Party helped in a small way to relieve pressure on the main Red Army and were the springboards from which Communists vaulted into eastern China in early 1938. Some of these bases, particularly those in Eyuwan and Minyue, remained active throughout the Resistance War and the subsequent civil war.

This concern to "mobilize all factors" in a grand design is an early example of what later became the hallmark of Maoist development strategy. By the mid-1930s, Chinese Communists had trekked from the cities to the mountains and from Gannan to Shaanbei. They were loath at each turning point to relinquish any gain, however small. They were constrained by political considerations to integrate more and more lost battlefields into a "dialectical totality," as they proclaimed each defeat to be a victory and each retreat to be an advance. The increasingly military character of the revolution eventually infused strategy into this hop-scotch: old bases became subsidiary fronts or future support points in the war.

After 1937, the Eighth Route Army in the north and the New Fourth Army in the east were linked strategically, but the southern leg of the Party's strategic tripod bore little weight because too few forces had been left behind in 1934 or 1937, the two turning points in the southern struggle. The Three-Year War bestowed the Communist high command with a notion of grand strategy and with the troops, regrouped as the New Fourth Army, to realize it. By 1938, the Japanese had created the conditions in central and eastern China for a second Communist army to grow apace, beyond reach of the Guomindang.

In earlier years, plans for subsidiary fronts to take the heat off the main Red Army had not come to much, mainly because the Communists were unable to commit enough resources to them. They had a far smaller recruiting base than the Guomindang, and they also had to contend with a strong centralist bias. In the early 1930s and at the start of the Long March, the transfer of troops from peripheral bases to support concentrated efforts in the main war theaters alienated Party supporters in abandoned regions. It even alienated Party cadres, who, according to Ye Fei, "persevered not for Communism but for the local revolution."[91]

Communist studies conventionally blame tensions between "localist" Party branches and the Red Army on the "petit bourgeois revolutionary impetuosity and petit bourgeois conservatism" of the local Party and rarely on the army.[92] Strategists justified the "nationalization" of regional forces by pointing to the interaction between main and ancillary battlefields and the inevitability of defeat at the edges if the center fell,[93] just as Party leaders after 1949 justified all-out concentration on steel or grain with the maxim "Once the headrope is pulled up, the meshes of the net will open." But the strategic argument can have convinced few Party supporters left behind in the villages, for the headrope was raised too high and the meshes closed.[94]

In late 1937, Mao planned to leave two-fifths of the southern guerril-las behind in the old bases, but he was thwarted by Xiang Ying, who wanted them at the front, where he thought he could control them. This case is just one of many in which Party leaders—Mao included—strengthened the main force by sacrificing the periphery. As a result, almost all the southern bases fell dormant in the war against Japan, thus failing to fulfill the hopes of Mao and others. But bases of the Three-Year War in central and eastern China played an important role in the expansion of the New Fourth Army.

The stripping of the Party's "subsidiary battlefields" in 1937 and 1938 left local people disillusioned and embittered. The stripping of large parts of southern, central, and eastern China by the New Fourth Army in 1945 provoked a similar reaction, which the Party tried to stem by propaganda. It is not true, said Party leaders in November 1945, that "the Communist Party's New Fourth Army looks on people as mere trifles, that they take them when they need them and cast them aside when they don't."[95] The propaganda apparently did not have much success. In 1949, peasants in the South looked on in stony silence as the Communists returned to "liberate" them. By then, central Party leaders positively disapproved of autonomous movements in the regions and preferred to extend their power over the south by military conquest. In provinces like Fujian, where small indigenous guerrilla movements continued to flourish after 1937, local Communists became thorns in the flesh of the bureaucracy imposed by the People's Liberation Army in 1949 and were a focus of dissent in the Cultural Revolution.

The whittling down of the Communist movement in the old soviets by the evacuations of 1934 and 1937 weakened or destroyed robust regional traditions of Communism and stifled diversity in the Party. Communists in bases outside the Red Army's main former garrisons were more likely than those in central bases to moderate their demands on the villages, handle local issues sensitively, and achieve a reciprocal and harmonious relationship with local society. Their transfer north freed them from local constraints and changed their relationship to the villages. On the positive side, it flung the cliques and patriarchs of regional Communism into the New Fourth Army melting pot.

According to one theory, the Communist Party's Long March was "dictated by the mandate of political history." The south was too exhausted, physically and mentally, to produce a second revolution; the Communists' historic mission lay in the restless north.[96] This theory, if correct, would justify the abandonment of the south in 1934 and the final withdrawal in 1937. But the record of events after 1934 scarcely bears out this apocalyptic view. Parts of southern and central China were still piled high with explosive charge after the main Red Army left. Communists in Fujian and Eyuwan, in particular, preserved thousands of recruits for the New Fourth Army despite their relative inexperience, disarray, and isolation, and despite the departure of most of their officers and seasoned troops in support of the Long March. The New Fourth Army, far from flocking north after 1937, fought on both banks of the Chang Jiang and by 1945 had penetrated much further south. The decision in the late 1930s to concentrate the main New Fourth Army detachments north of the Chang Jiang was dictated by military strategy, not historical inevitability. Similarly, it was strategic considerations that resolved Chen Yi to strike back south again after setting up a secure base in Jiangbei in 1940.

## THE THREE-YEAR WAR TODAY

The angle from which Chinese historians view the Three-Year War has changed many times over the last half-century. Much of what passes for history in the People's Republic of China is important less for itself than for the light it sheds on extrinsic matters of contemporary interest. The Party-controlled press devotes huge resources to manufacturing new traditions and updating old ones to match the government's changing goals. Since 1979, the Three-Year War has been spun into a minor legend of the Chinese Revolution that blends bowdlerized fact and significant fiction, with the aim of producing "pious wonderment and burning ambition" in the Chinese people.[97] Myths and legends are recited to show how things allegedly come to be the way they are and to help keep them so. The expurgated epic of the Three-Year War plays only a humble role in the Chinese Communist body of myths and legends, chief among which is the Long March. Some of the virtues celebrated by the major and minor legends—optimism, perseverance, courage, self-sacrifice—are the same. Others, including "heroism in defeat," keeping faith with the masses, and education as an antidote to hard times, are associated mainly with the Three-Year War.

A mythologized Three-Year War has many more potential uses in China now as a counterpoint to the quite different import of the legend of the Long March. Each campaign illustrates an opposite set of aims and values. The Long March symbolizes centralism, homogeneity, and the rise to power of the Party's historic leader; the Three-Year War represents polycentrism and regional diversity. The march is celebrated as a new turn after a wrong start; the war exemplifies continuity and loyalty to the victims of Party failures. The march was primarily a feat of arms performed by men; the war combined military and civilian forms of struggle and enlisted secret armies of women. The march united the Party and brought its different factions into one political line; the war required the creative adjustment of policy to varied circumstance, compromise, improvisation, flexibility, and independent initiative. The march exemplifies urgency and haste, and, as a forced march to safety, has become a symbol of China's hopes for rapid progress toward wealth and power; the war is the tortoise to Mao's hare, the hedgehog to his fox, a symbol of patience and stoical endurance. The march is hailed as an act of immense will that miraculously snatched the Red Army from the jaws of ruin; the virtues of the war were tact, brains, moderation, and its human scale.

# APPENDIX:
# LEADERS OF REARGUARDS
# AND OF THE THREE-YEAR WAR

Listed here in alphabetical order, grouped by region, are the main political and military leaders of the Three-Year War, with the various regions introduced in the same order as in the book. The lists are not necessarily comprehensive. They do not distinguish between those who survived the Three-Year War as revolutionaries and those who died, deserted, or defected. Sources include Zhongguo renim geming junshi bowuguan, eds., 1981: 28; Hao Mengbi and Duan Haoran, eds., 1980: 180; Xu Zhanquan 1987: 587–609; Zhang Yangui and Yuan Wei 1987; Wang Jianying 1986a; and the foregoing chapters of this book.

## CENTRAL COMMITTEE SUB-BUREAU

Chen Tanqiu, Chen Yi, Deng Zihui, He Chang, Li Cailian, Liang Botai, Mao Zetan, Qu Qiubai, Tan Zhenlin, Wang Jinxiang, Xiang Ying, Zeng Shan, Zhang Dingcheng.

## GANNAN

Guo Qingyi, Hu Rongjia, Lai Changzuo, Liu Guoxing, Liu Lianbiao, Liu Tingfei, Luo Mengwen, Peng Hu, Peng Shengbiao, Qiu Lesheng, Song Yongquan, Yang Shizhu, Zhang Kaijing, Zhong Desheng, Zhong Min, Zhong Xunren, Zhou Guisheng.

## GANYUE

Chen Pixian, Chen Yi, He Changlin, Huang Chengze, Li Guoxing, Li Letian, Liu Xinchao, Xiang Xianglin, Xiang Ying, Yang Shangkui, Zeng Biao, Zhang Riqing.

## MINXI

Chen Deqing, Chen Liangjun, Deng Zihui, Fan Lechun, Fang Fang, Guo Yiwei, Lai Rongchuan, Li Chibiao, Liu Han, Liu Shang, Liu Yongsheng, Luo Zhongyi, Qiu Jinsheng, Qiu Lisheng, Qiu Zhiyun, Qu Shangcong, Ruan Wensong, Tan Zhenlin, Wan Yongcheng, Wang Rongchun, Wei Jinshui, Wen Hanzhen, Wu Hongxiang, Wu Mengyun, Wu Sheng, Wu Zaiyun, Wu Zhangtan, Xie Yucai, Xiong Menghui, You Heshun, Zhang Dingcheng, Zhong Guochu, Zhu Sen.

## MINYUE

He Jun, He Ming, Huang Huicong, Lu Sheng, Peng Deqing, Wu Jin, Yin Linping, Yin Yidong, Zhang Changshui, Zhang Min.

## ZHE'NAN

Chen Yicheng, Hong Jiayun, Huang Fuwu, Liu Dayun, Liu Han, Liu Ying, Lu Daying, Luo Liansheng, Su Yu, Wang Luli, Wang Weixin, Wang Wenrui, Wang Yisan, Xu Xinkun, Yao Abao, Zhou Lianqing.

## MINBEI

Chen Yi, Huang Dao, Huang Huairen, Huang Ligui, Li Desheng, Liu Wenxue, Lu Wenqing, Rao Shoukun, Wang Zhu, Wu Xianxi, Zeng Jingbing.

## MINDONG

Chen Ting, Fan Beicheng, Fan Shiren, Feng Pintai, Lai Jinbiao, Ma Lifeng, Ruan Yingping, Shen Guanguo, Yang Ying, Ye Xiufan, Ye Fei.

## MINZHONG

Chen Yunfei, Ke Chenggui, Huang Xiaomin, Liu Tujun.

## WANZHEGAN

Cheng Boqian, Guan Ying, He Ying, Jiang Tianhui, Kuang Longhai, Li Buxin, Liu Yubiao, Liu Zhenwu, Liu Zhibiao, Shao Changhe, Tang Zaigang, Wang Fengqing, Xiong Gang, Yu Hanchao, Yu Jinde, Zhao Lisheng, Zhou Chenglong.

## EYUWAN

Chen Mingjiang, Chen Shouxin, Chen Xitang, Fang Yongle, Gao Jingting, Gao Kewen, Gu Shiduo, He Yaobang, Hong Yiwan, Hu Jiting, Huang Renting, Li

Shihuai, Li Yuanming, Liang Congxue, Lin Weixian, Liu Yuanchen, Lu Congju, Luo Chengyun, Luo Zuofan, Shi Yutian, Sun Zhongde, Wang Fuming, Xiong Dahai, Xiong Xianchun, Xu Chengji, Xu Jiancai, Yang Kezhi, Zhan Huayu, Zhang Shengxian, Zheng Weixiao, Zhou Shijue.

## EYU

Tong Zhongyu, Wang Guofu, Wang Guohua, Zhang Wangwu, Zhang Xinjiang, Zhou Junming.

## XIANG'EGAN

Cao Maobo, Chen Shoucheng, Deng Hong, Fang Buzhou, Fu Qiutao, Gao Yongsheng, Gao Ziming, Huang Jiagao, Jiang Weiqing, Li Xiangtao, Liu Yutang, Lü Jianzhang, Ming Anlou, Qian Lin, Qin Hualong, Tan Fengming, Tan Qilong, Tu Zhengkun, Wei Ping, Wu Yongxiang, Xu Yan'gang, Yan Tuge, Yuan Hongguo, Zeng Guoqi, Zhang Fan, Zhao Duanzhong, Zhao Jianxin, Zhao Long, Zhong Qiguang.

## XIANGGAN

Chen Hongshi, Chen Yonghui, Duan Huanjing, Guo Meng, Huang Xiyuan, Kuang Zhuquan, Lin Shaopu, Liu Baolu, Liu Biesheng, Liu Fayun, Liu Peishan, Liu Ri, Luo Weidao, Peng Huiming, Qiu Renbiao, Tan Fuying, Tan Tangchi, Tan Yubao, Wang Xuanchun, Wang Yongji, Wang Zhigu, Xu Defu, Zeng Kaifu, Zhou Jie, Zhu Yongsheng.

## XIANGNAN

Cai Huiwen, Fang Weixia, Gong Chu, Li Lin, Li Shoubao, Li Zongbao, Liu Xia, Peng Linchang, Xie Zhufeng.

## QIONGYA

Chen Meishen, Chen Ying, Feng Baiju, Huang Dayou, Li Ming, Lin Tiande, Lin Tiangui, Liu Qiuju, Wang Bolun, Wang Yongxin, Xiao Huanhui, Zhu Keping.

# NOTES

## PREFACE

1. For this and other special terms—geographic, political, and administrative—used in this book, see the "Note on Terms."

2. Wen Yangchun 1985:72.

3. Ye Cao 1948:ii.

4. Benton 1986.

5. Benton 1975. For a more up-to-date discussion, see Shum 1988 and Garver 1988a and 1988b.

6. See the section "Terms."

7. Benton 1989 is an amended version of that chapter.

8. Two of the better researched regions are Minxi and Eyu. Probably more middle-ranking leaders of the Minxi base survive than of any other base of the Three-Year War. The guerrilla war in Eyu lasted less than two years; it proceeded more smoothly than in other regions, with fewer setbacks or abrupt changes; there is a relatively large body of materials relating to it; and a relatively large number of its veterans are still alive. So these two regions are among the easiest to research, and studies on them are intended in China to serve as models for historians of the dozen or so other regions in which the Three-Year War was fought. (See Zhu Yunqian 1987.)

9. To borrow a sentence from Kahn and Feuerwerker 1968:1.

10. Spurgeon 1935:12.

11. Garraghan 1946:244–45.

12. Garraghan 1946:239 and 283; Elton 1970:80–82; Barzun and Graff 1970:99–102.

13. The parallel with Taiwan is striking. In 1959, Taiwan's Academia Sinica inaugurated an oral-history project to help older Nationalist revolutionaries record their experiences. The advantages of the project, says Winston Hsieh (1975:72), are that "some scholarly discipline is brought to bear on the selection and compilation of information"; and that "the subjects may feel a greater sense

of security and freedom in expressing their views, since the records will not be published until a date that has been fixed in accordance with their wish." I do not know whether memoirs in the People's Republic are collected on the same condition, but the official nature of the project is in itself a guarantee of sorts.

14. Garraghan 1946:291.

15. Elton 1970:74.

16. Writing about the Soviet Union and quoted in Mazour (1971:22).

17. Heffernan 1988:4–19.

18. I am mainly referring to oral and local historians. Official histories of the national Communist movement, general histories, histories of science and philosophy, economic histories, and the like have still not shaken off the habit, imported from the Soviet Union, of *tsitatnevsko* or "quotism."

19. Hsieh 1975:13.

20. Belden 1939:6.

21. In Beijing in September 1989, I spotted a huge volume titled *Nanfang sannian youji zhanzheng* ("The three-year guerrilla war in the south") in the window of the People's Liberation Army Bookshop on Ping'anli. It turned out to be an advertiser's mock-up, full of hundreds and hundreds of blank pages; no publication date had been announced.

22. Zhu Yunqian 1987.

23. Elton 1970:158.

24. China has too often been used to illustrate general theories by people "viewing flowers from horseback." See Lyman P. Van Slyke's foreword in Yung-fa Chen 1985; and Chen and Benton 1986.


### A NOTE ON TERMS

1. Wang Fuyi 1987a:95–96.

2. Zhongguo geming bowuguan 1982:297–98.

3. For the sake of completeness, this book includes a short note on Qiongya at the time of the Three-Year War.

4. My comments on Ganyue, Minyue, Wanzhegan, Eyu, Minxi, Zhe'nan, Minbei, Xiangnan, and Minzhong are based partly or wholly on Yan Jingtang 1986.

5. Xiong Shihui, quoted in William Wei 1989:36.

6. William Wei 1989:46.


### THE SOVIET FALLS, THE THREE-YEAR WAR BEGINS

1. Snow 1941, vol. 1: 125 and 127.

2. Benton 1979:278.

3. Elton 1970:162.

4. Smedley 1956:311; Cai Xiaoqian 1970:208–9.

5. Yuan Chen Yi tongzhi 1977:191.

6. Smedley 1956:310–11; Chen Chang-feng 1972:21–26; Salisbury 1985: 51; Wu Jiqing 1979:222; Cheng Fangwu 1977:17–21.

7. Snow 1968:205.

8. Zhonggong zhongyang dangshi ziliao zhengji weiyuanhui, zhongyang dang'anguan, eds., 1985:32.

9. Mao Tse-tung 1961–1965, vol. 1:160.

10. Braun 1973:115.

11. Chen Yi 1981 [1957]: 541.

12. Smedley 1956:309; Cao Boyi 1969:567; Ma Wenbin et al. 1986:519.

13. Smedley 1956:308–11; Cai Xiaoqian 1970:208–10; Braun 1973:117; Chen Yi 1981 [1957]: 543.

14. Trotsky 1969:118.

15. Knei-Paz 1978:253–69.

16. Trotsky 1969:100.

17. Liu Zhengming 1982:20; Smedley 1956:309; Zeng Zhi, ed., 1986, vol. 1:203 and 344. But two thousand women are said to have marched with Zhang Guotao's Fourth Front Army, which left Eyuwan in 1932 (Salisbury 1985:72).

18. Smedley 1956:310; Cao Juru 1981:375.

19. Lu Dingyi 1983:11–12.

20. Smedley 1956:311; Braun 1973:122; Ma Wenbin et al. 1986:521.

21. Chen Pixian 1982:2–3; Guofangbu 1967, vol. 3:437 and vol. 5:797; Ganyuemin'exiang 1968 [1937], vol. 1, appendix 4; Chen Yi 1980 [1959]: 3 and 1986 [1940]: 115; Dai Xiangqing et al. 1986:682.

22. Gong Chu in *Mingbao yuekan* 97:99–101 and 98:90.

23. Chen Pixian 1979:105 and 1982:2–3; Kong Yongsong and Lin Tianyi 1982:311; Dai Xiangqing et al. 1986:682; Hao Mengbi and Duan Haoran, eds., 1984, vol. 2:179.

24. Smedley 1956:309; Chen Yi 1980 [1959]: 3 and 1986 [1940]: 115; Chen Pixian 1979:111; Junshi kexueyuan 1987, vol. 1:296.

25. Braun 1973:109.

26. Guofangbu 1967, vol. 3:437–39 and vol. 5:797; Ganyuemin'exiang 1968 [1937], vol. 1, appendix 4; Wang Duonian 1982, vol. 5:115–19.

27. See Bingzhang Yang 1986:128.

28. Zong Zhidi 1980 [1952]:137; Junshi kexueyuan 1987, vol. 1:296.

29. Ganyuemin'exiang 1968 [1937], vol. 1:509–14; Guofangbu 1967, vol. 5:811; S. Y. Chi 1935:252.

30. See table 1.

31. Smedley 1956:308; Braun 1973:109–19. Chen Pixian 1982:2; Hao Mengbi and Duan Haoran, eds., 1984, vol. 1:179.

32. Kuo (1968–71, vol. 3:2–3) substitutes Ruan Xiaoxian and Zeng Shan for Qu Qiubai and Chen Tanqiu. Zeng was political commissar of the Jiangxi Military Region and Ruan commissar of the Gannan Military Region. It is unlikely that they were in daily touch with Xiang, though Ruan later joined Xiang at Renfeng.

33. Yan Jingtang 1986:42–43; Hao Mengbi and Duan Haoran, eds., 1984, vol. 1:179; Chen Pixian 1982:2; Zhong ge junwei 1986 [1934]:45.

34. Benton 1979; William Wei 1985:118.

35. Cai Xiaoqian 1969, pt. 7:102–3.

36. Gong Chu 1954:410–14; Song Wei 1987:48.

37. Cao Juru 1981:375; Song Wei 1987:48; William Wei 1985:119. Most of the banknotes that piled up in the soviet in this period were destroyed after 1934, but the new currency issued by the People's Republic in 1955 could be exchanged one for one with soviet currency.

38. Kuo 1968–71, vol. 2:616–17; Huang Liangcheng 1979:10; Braun 1973:119.

39. Cai Xiaoqian 1969, pt. 7:102–21; Dai Xiangqing et al. 1986:635.

40. Song Wei 1987:48–49.

41. Chen Yi 1981 [1957]: 541; Cheng Fangwu 1977:17.

42. Braun 1973:119; Gong Chu 1954:409–14 and in *Mingbao yuekan* 98:90; Whang 1934:122; Benton 1979:16.

43. Donovan 1976:105; Cai Xiaoqian 1969, pt. 7:119; Gong Chu 1954:411–14; Kuo 1968–71, vol. 2:614–16; William Wei 1985:141.

44. Chen Yi 1981 [1957]: 552.

45. *Hongse Zhonghua,* October 3, 1934.

46. Sun Tzu 1963:108.

47. Gittings 1967:65–66.

48. Chen Yi 1981 [1957]: 542–44.

49. Chen Yi 1980 [1959]: 1–2.

50. Yin Zixian 1987:33.

51. But according to Yin Zixian (1987:36), even Zhu De learned of the plan to evacuate the Central Soviet only at the last moment.

52. Wang Jianying 1986b:32–34; Li Weihan 1986.

53. Wang Jianying 1986b:32–36; Chen Yi 1981 [1957]: 542; Bingzhang Yang 1986:159–61; Wang Tingke 1985:2–3; Gong Chu 1954:404 and in *Mingbao yue-kan* 97:100 (1974), *See also* the chapter on Xianggan.

54. Braun 1973:121–22; Wales 1952:105–6.

55. Smedley 1956:310.

56. Many were given tasseled spears (Cheng Fangwu 1977:19). According to Braun (1973:114), the Long Marchers had more than forty thousand rifles and one thousand machine guns. According to a researcher quoted by Salisbury (1985:92), they had 32,243 rifles and other guns.

57. Smedley 1956:310; Cai Xiaoqian 1969, pt. 7:120–21 and 1970:209; Kuo 1968–71, vol. 2:616–18; Zeng Zhi, ed., 1986, vol. 1:25; Chen Chang-feng 1972:24; Cheng Fangwu 1977:19; Yuan Guang 1982:92.

58. Wilson 1971:66; Chen Yi 1981 [1957]: 543–44; Nie Rongzhen 1983:216.

59. Bingzhang Yang 1986:165.

60. Smedley 1956:308; Braun 1973:110; Wang Jianying 1986b:32–36; Cai Xiaoqian 1970:201; Chen Changfeng 1986:105–15.

61. Tso-liang Hsiao 1961, vol. 1:299–300; Zhang Wentian 1934; Kuo 1968–71, vol. 2:636–38.

62. Wales 1952:64–65; Bingzhang Yang 1986:131.

63. Wang Jianying 1986b:34; Zhang Tianrong 1986:27.

64. However, as part of an internal debate, Zhou Enlai, writing in *Hongxing bao* [Red star] on August 8, 1934, called for a thrust deep behind enemy lines in order to "create a new situation and not to return to this old soviet again" (quoted in Bingzhang Yang 1986:130).

65. Tso-liang Hsiao 1961, vol. 1:301.

66. Chen Yi 1981 [1957]: 543; Cai Xiaoqian 1970–71, pt. 1:106.

67. Chen Yi 1981 [1957]: 543; Chen Pixian 1979:106; Zhu Dongsheng 1983:133.

68. Smedley 1956:309–10; Xiao Feng 1979:1–5; Huang Liangcheng 1979:5–8; Yuan Guang 1982:92–93; Cheng Fangwu 1977:17–19; Wang Jianying 1986b:36; Chen Changfeng 1986:115; Dai Xiangqing 1985:189.

69. Smedley 1956:310–11; Cai Xiaoqian 1970:209; Wales 1952:65.

70. Zhang Tianrong 1986:31; Wales 1952:65; Li Anbao 1986a:48.

71. Yuan Xuezu 1980:35–36; Chen Pixian 1982:5.

72. Yang Zhihong 1981:469; Cheng Fangwu 1977:20–21; Li Anbao, ed., 1978:8.

73. Benton 1979:17.

74. Braun 1973:110; Zhang Tianrong 1986:34–35.

75. Wu Gu 1979: seventh trick.

76. Sun Tzu 1963:41.

77. Wu Gu 1979: twenty-first trick.

78. Wu Gu 1979: eleventh trick.

79. Zhang Tianrong 1986:32.

80. Cf. Chen Pixian 1982:5.

81. Wu Gu 1979: seventh trick.

82. Chen Yi 1981 [1957]: 543.

83. He Shishan and He Shisi 1982.

84. Dai Xiangqing 1985:189.

85. Wilson 1971:63; Cai Xiaoqian 1969, pt. 7:107; Salisbury 1985:10.

86. Li Ang 1954:134; Klein and Clark 1971:323; Harrison 1972:242 and 569.

87. Salisbury 1985:10.

88. Harrison 1972:227–37; Litten 1988:67; Braun 1973:100–101.

89. Smedley 1956:309; Cao Juru 1981:375; Klein and Clark 1971:675 and 697.

90. Salisbury 1985:10.

91. Kuo 1968–71, vol. 2:209 and 564–65; Chen Wenxiu et al. 1983:243–45.

92. Salisbury 1985:46 and 68–69.

93. Salisbury 1985:296.

94. Chen Yi 1980 [1959]: 6.

95. Snow 1941, vol. 1:125.

96. Chen Yi 1981 [1957]: 544.

97. Braun 1973:119; Zeng Shan 1980:10.

98. He Shishan and He Shisi 1982:37; Cao Xiaoqian 1970–71, pt. 1:108.

99. Chen Yi 1981 [1957]: 544.

100. Chen Gang et al. 1985:304–5.

101. Zhu Dongsheng 1983:133.

102. Chen Yi 1981 [1957]: 543–47; Dai Xiangqing 1985:189.

103. Smedley 1956:309; He Shishan and He Shisi 1982.

104. Kuo 1968–71, vol. 3:63.

105. Smedley 1956:309; Hunan sheng bowuguan 1981:137; Chen Yi 1981 [1957]: 546; Jiang Xinli 1978:345–47. Chen Yi apparently had a different view.

He proposed sending out Qu and two other leaders ill with tuberculosis to fight guerrilla war.

106. Salisbury 1985:208.

107. Huang Liangcheng 1979:10.

108. Smedley 1956:309; Chen Yi 1986 [1940]: 118.

109. Whitson 1973:206–7.

110. Kuo 1968–71, vol. 3:4.

111. Braun 1973:69.

112. Zhang Dingcheng 1982:66; Tan Zhenlin et al. 1983:24.

113. Gong Chu 1954:435–38 and in *Mingbao yuekan* 98:87; Kuo 1968–71, vol. 2:620–21.

114. Smedley 1956:308.

115. Kuo 1968–71, vol. 3:2–4.

116. Xiao Feng 1979:1.

117. Braun 1973:114; Salisbury 1985:92.

118. Braun 1973:109; Gong Chu in *Mingbao yuekan* 98:90; S. Y. Chi 1935:251; Guofangbu 1967, vol. 5:800 and 810–11; Ganyuemin'exiang 1968 [1937], vol. 1:509ff.

119. Smedley 1956:309; Braun 1973:117.

120. Snow 1941, vol. 1:126.

121. Braun 1973:107–8.

122. Snow 1941, vol. 1:127; Chen Yi 1980 [1959]: 3 and 1981 [1957]: 548–50.

123. Gong Chu 1954:443; Guofangbu 1967, vol. 3:438 and vol. 5:798–834; Ganyuemin'exiang 1968 [1937], vol. 1:487–527; Chen Pixian 1982:3.

124. Bingzhang Yang 1986:97; S. Y. Chi 1934:27; Hunan shengzhi 1959, vol. 1:640–41; Guofangbu 1967, vol. 3:437–38; *China Weekly Review,* November 3 and December 22, 1934 and April 6, 1935; Ganyuemin'exiang 1968 [1937], vol. 1:490–514.

125. Guofangbu 1967, vol. 3:439–41 and vol. 5:798–834; Ganyuemin'exiang 1968 [1937], vol. 1: appendix 4.

126. Military History Office 1966:36; Wang Jianming 1965, vol. 2:623.

127. William Wei 1985:137ff.; *China Weekly Review,* February 2 and 22, 1935.

128. Tien 1972:111–12; William Wei 1985:102ff.

129. Tien 1972:110–12; William Wei 1985:140.

130. Taylor 1935:309–10.

131. T. L. Lin 1935:362–63; *China Weekly Review,* April 6, 1935.

132. Xin Hunan bao 1950; Thomson 1969:113, 119, and 222. William Wei 1985:147; Abend and Billingham 1936:239.

133. Thomson 1969:113–15 and 212; Tien 1972:100.

134. Tien 1972:100.

135. Thomson 1969:158.

136. Tien 1972:158.

137. William Wei 1985; Taylor 1935:306–10; Ganyuemin'exiang 1968 [1937], vol. 1:489.

138. Tien 1972:98–102.

139. Wei 1985:141–50.

140. Mo Xiong 1985:11; Guofangbu 1967, vol. 5:800; Taylor 1935:308.

141. Chen Yi 1981 [1957]: 548.

142. Benton 1979:22–23; *China Weekly Review,* April 6, 1935; *Times* (London), January 18, 1935.

143. Chen Yi 1981 [1957]: 550.

144. Benton 1986:709.

145. Feng Ding 1979:408.

146. Chen Yi 1981 [1957]: 551; Shi Yan and Wu Kebin 1983:65–66.

147. For example, Yang Shangkui 1977.

148. Carlson 1940:280.

149. Quoted in Klein and Clark 1971:324.

150. Xu Xingzhi 1983 [1941]: 554.

151. Wang Fuyi 1984a:445–46; Bian Xiezu 1982:89–90.

152. Chen Yi 1981 [1963]:29.

153. The Four Books are *The Great Learning, The Doctrine of the Mean, The Analects of Confucius,* and *Mencius.*

154. Someone who passed examinations at the county level in the Qing dynasty.

155. Chen Yi 1981 [1963]:29.

156. Chen Yi 1981 [1952]:18.

157. Lois Wheeler Snow 1981:213; Chen Yi 1981 [1942], 1981 [1952], and 1981 [1963]; Zhang Yingpo and Wang Zhongyuan 1986.

158. Bian Xiezu 1982:89–90; Wang Fuyi 1984a:445–49.

159. Chen Yi 1973:410–11, 1981 [1942], 1981 [1952], and 1981 [1963].

160. Snow 1941, vol. 1:126.

161. Haitian chubanshe 1935, vol. 3:339–40.

162. Ibid: 339–41; Bian Xiezu 1982:90–91; Wang Fuyi 1984a:445–57; Li Zurong and Guang Zhai 1983:163–65.

163. Chen Yi 1981 [1952]: 24.

164. Chen Yi 1981 [1957]: 544–55.

165. Chen Yi 1981 [1957]: 554.

166. Smedley 1944:181.

167. Chen Pixian 1986:45.

168. Xu Xingzhi 1983 [1941]: 556. Zhu Zhongli 1985:66. However, according to Jacques Guillermaz (1989:280), Chen Yi's French was nil, and he had probably never seriously studied it.

169. Chen Yi 1973:413; Tong Huaizhou 1980.

170. He Li 1980:116.

171. Xu Xingzhi 1983 [1941]: 555; Shi Yan and Wu Kebing 1983:130; Ding Qiusheng 1983:24.

172. Ye Chao 1980:140–47.

173. Ding Qiusheng 1983:23–24.

174. Tan Chen-lin and Su Yu 1978:124–25; Zhu Dongsheng 1983:121–33; Klein and Clark 1971:104–13 and 320–25; Bianco and Chevrier 1985:140–43 and 673–76.

175. Luo Mengwen 1962:1–2; Dai Xiangqing et al. 1986:691–92; Ye Juyun 1981; Zhong Guang 1981; Guo Guangbei 1981; Zhou Aimin 1981b; Zhong Liangpei 1981; Lin Jianshu 1981.

176. The phrase is taken from George Bernanos.

177. *Hongse Zhonghua,* October 20, 1934.

178. Chen Yi 1981 [1957]: 544–45; Wang Fuyi 1984b:97–98; Chen Pixian 1979:106 and 1982:4.

179. Wang Fuyi 1987b:41; Dai Xiangqing et al. 1986:696

180. Chen Yi 1980 [1959]: 3 and 1981 [1957]: 546; Yan Jingtang 1986:43.

181. Chen Yi 1981 [1957]: 546; Xia Honggen and Zhang Kechang 1987: 226–27. *Hongse Zhonghua* 264, perhaps the last issue, is displayed in Ruijin's Memorial Hall of the Revolution. It carries a stirring editorial titled "The Lesson of Lenin" that calls on revolutionaries to stand in the front line in times of crisis and setbacks.

182. Chen Pixian 1979:106–9; Chen Yi 1980 [1959]: 4 and 1981 [1957]: 547; Bian Xiezu 1982:91; Chen Chun'e 1986; Dai Xiangqing et al. 1986:697–98. See Zhongguo dier lishi dang'anguan 1987, vol. 1:224 for a contemporaneous report of this battle.

183. Wang Fuyi 1984a:457–58.

184. Chen Pixian 1979:106–7; Kong Yongsong and Lin Tianyi 1982:313; Chen Yi 1980 [1959]: 3 and 1981 [1957]: 546.

185. Chen Yi 1980 [1959]: 2–3 and 1981 [1957]: 545–46.

186. Chen Yi 1980 [1959]: 2–3 and 1981 [1957]: 545–46.

187. Braun 1973:119; Gong Chu 1954:409–10.

188. Wang Fuyi 1984a:457–58.

189. *Hongse Zhonghua,* October 3, 1934.

190. Mo Xiong 1985:10.

191. Chen Yi 1981 [1957]: 546–47.

192. Salisbury 1985:66–67.

193. Guofangbu 1967, vol. 3:437.

194. Wang Duonian 1982, vol. 4:138.

195. Zhongguo dier lishi dang'anguan 1987, vol. 1:59, 166, 209–10, 238, and 240.

196. Braun 1973:111–12; Bingzhang Yang 1986:131 and 380.

197. Ma Wenbin et al. 1986:520; Yan Jingtang and Jiang Tingyu 1989:63. According to Zhu De (Smedley 1956:309), perhaps twenty full divisions (i.e., around two hundred thousand troops) stayed behind. Another source says that four hundred thousand Nationalists remained in and around the old Central Soviet (Zhou Aimin 1981b:535), and yet another that a majority stayed (Chen Chun'e 1986:79).

198. Guofangbu 1967, vol. 3:437; Ganyuemin'exiang 1968 [1937], vol. 1:493; Gong Chu 1954:443.

199. Chen Yi 1981 [1957]: 547.

200. Hatano Ken'ichi 1961, vol. 4:407–8. But Nationalist generals knew that Mao had gone. See Zhongguo dier lishi dang'anguan 1987, vol. 1:137 and 240.

201. Chen Yi 1980 [1959]: 3.

202. Guofangbu 1967, vol. 3:437; Chen Yi 1980 [1959]: 7.

203. Chen Yi 1980 [1959]: 4 and 1981 [1957]: 547; Chen Pixian 1979:109; Yang Shangkui 1977:33.

204. Wang Duonian 1982, vol. 5:92.

205. Chen Pixian 1979:106–9.

206. Jiang Fengbo and Xu Zhanquan 1989:431.

207. Dai Xiangqing 1985:191–92.

208. Guofangbu 1967, vol. 5:804–6; Dai Xiangqing et al. 1986:697–98; Li Tianrong 1987.

209. Chen Yi 1980 [1959]: 2–4 and 1981 [1957]: 547–49.

210. Chen Pixian 1979:109; Chen Chun'e 1986:81–82; Dai Xiangqing 1985:191; Chen Yi 1980 [1959]: 4 and 1981 [1957]: 548–49.

211. Chen Yi 1986 [1940]: 116–17.

212. Chen Yi 1980 [1959]: 1; Gong Chu in *Mingbao yuekan* 97:103.

213. Nihon kokusai mondai kenkyujo 1970–75, vol. 7:411.

214. Chen Yi and Liang Botai 1986 [1934].

215. Guo Guangbei 1981.

216. Cf. Qu Qiubai, writing from a Guomindang prison in Changting in May 1935, a month before his execution, who said that in the end, having lost faith in his own qualifications as a revolutionary, he had felt that he was playing in a comedy (Kuo 1968–71, vol. 3:58).

217. Tang Jiaqing 1982:85–86; Yuan Xuezu 1980:35–43; Chen Pixian 1982:5; Zong Zhidi 1980 [1952]: 142.

218. Smedley 1956:309; Chen Pixian 1979:111; Chen Yi 1980 [1959]: 4–5 and 1981 [1957]: 547; Dai Xiangqing 1985:192; Junshi kexueyuan 1987, vol. 1:296.

219. This calculation is problematic. It does not take account of soldiers who deserted or were captured. The figure for casualties is cumulative, whereas that for able-bodied troops refers to a fixed point in time. However, there is no reason to suppose that the Red Army was bigger in the summer of 1934 than in October. Moreover, the ratio of dead to wounded in the Red Army was probably higher than 1:3. Such a high casualty rate is not unprecedented in modern warfare. Between July and October 1916, the British Armies in France lost 450,000 men (out of 1.4 million) during the battles of the Somme (Guinn 1965:132–55). But the Big Push of 1916 was an offensive action aiming at swift victory by one stunning blow, whereas the Chinese Red Army in late 1934 was fighting a defensive war. Moreover, the British High Command could still count on huge resources of new manpower to replace its casualties, whereas the Chinese Communists were stranded on a shrinking and exhausted base.

220. Smedley 1956:309; Snow 1968:189.

221. Smedley 1956:309.

222. Salisbury 1985:204.

223. Gong Chu in *Mingbao yuekan* 98:90.

224. Chen Yi 1981 [1957]: 545.

225. Zhong ge junwei 1986 [1934]: 45; Chen Pixian 1979:111; Chen Yi 1981 [1957]: 547; Zhang Kai 1980:114.

226. Chen Pixian 1979:111; Zong Zhidi 1980 [1952]: 142–43; Chen Yi 1980 [1959]: 4–5 and 1981 [1957]: 547; Dai Xiangqing 1985:192–93; Yuan Xuezu 1980:37.

227. Chen Pixian 1979:111; Zong Zhidi 1980 [1952]: 142–43; Chen Yi 1980 [1959]: 4–5 and 1981 [1957]: 547; Chen Wenxiu et al. 1983:245. This speech and the next are reconstructed from more than one source.

228. Chen Yi 1980 [1959]: 5 and 1981 [1957]: 550.

229. Dai Xiangqing et al. 1986:695.

230. Chen Yi 1981 [1957]: 550.

231. *China Weekly Review,* May 11, 1935.

232. Zhang Kai 1980:116.

233. Chen Yi 1980 [1959]: 3 and 1981 [1957]: 548–49; Chen Chun'e 1986:80–81; Chen Pixian 1982:5.

234. Zeng Shan 1980:10.

235. Guofangbu 1967, vol. 5:804–6 and 811; *China Weekly Review,* April 20, 1935.

236. Qiu Zhizhuo et al., eds., 1986:423.

237. Guofangbu 1967, vol. 5: 798–867; *China Weekly Review,* April 20, 1935; Dai Xiangqing et al. 1986:691–92; Ye Juyun 1981; Zhong Guang 1981; Zhou Aimin 1981b; Lin Jianshu 1981; Zhang Qi 1981.

238. Chen Pixian 1979:109; Chen Yi 1981 [1957]: 551; Yan Jingtang and Jiang Tingyu 1989:65.

239. Chen Chun'e 1986:82.

240. Zhonggong zhongyang 1986 [1935]; Dai Xiangqing 1985:191; Zheng Xueqiu 1986.

241. One source (Zheng Xueqiu 1986) says several hundred.

242. Dai Xingqing 1985:191–92; Dai Xiangqing et al. 1986:699–700; Zheng Xueqiu 1986; Chen Yi 1981 [1957]: 551. Other sources (e.g., Bian Xiezu 1982:91 and Chen Wenxiu et al. 1983:245) give different dates for these directives. On February 28, the Central Committee radioed other field armies and Xiang Ying's Central Military Region to tell them about the Zunyi decisions, criticizing the retreat from the Central Soviet as "a flight and a house removal," and directing Communists in the Central Soviet and in Xianggan to "persevere in guerrilla warfare" (Zhonggong zhongyang dangshi, eds., 1985). It is not clear whether this message reached Xiang Ying. On January 20, the Central Committee sent a small team of soldiers back east with a letter for Xiang and Chen about Zunyi. A member of the team arrived in Ganyue two months later and found Chen Yi—thin, sunburned, and bearded, his hair down to his shoulders, his clothes in tatters—on a lonely mountain (Chai Rongsheng 1985).

243. Zheng Xueqiu 1986; Dai Xiangqing et al. 1986:699–712; Chen Yi 1981 [1957]: 551–52.

244. Chen Pixian 1979:111; Dai Xiangqing 1985:192; Chen Yi 1980 [1959]: 5 and 1981 [1957]: 551–52.

245. Zhong ge junwei 1986 [1934]; Zhongyang junqu Xiang Ying 1986 [1935].

246. Zhongyang junqu Xiang Ying 1986 [1935].

247. Gong Chu 1954:443–44 and in *Mingbao yuekan* 98:90; Wang Jianming 1965, vol. 2:623. Unfortunately, Gong Chu gives no date for this plan.

248. Chen Yi 1981 [1957]: 552–53.

249. Zhongyang junqu Xiang Ying 1986 [1935]; Dai Xiangqing et al. 1986:700–701; Chen Pixian 1979:112 and 1982:9–10; Chen Yi 1980 [1959]: 5 and 1981 [1957]: 553–55; Liang Guang 1981; Chen Maohui 1981; Gong Chu 1954:444–45 and in *Mingbao yuekan* 98:90. Not all the routes and troop numbers mentioned in these sources tally.

250. Zhongyang junqu Xiang Ying 1986 [1935].

251. Ibid. Wufu is written with *wu* "martial" rather than *wu* "five"; I assume that it refers to Wufuting in Jiangxi.

252. Chen Yi 1980 [1959]: 5.

253. Chen Pixian 1982:8.

254. Zong Zhidi 1980 [1952]: 138–39; Chen Yi 1980 [1959]: 5.

255. Guofangbu 1967, vol. 5:811; *China Weekly Review,* April 20, 1935.

256. Chen Pixian 1979:112; Chen Yi 1980 [1959]: 5 and 1981 [1957]: 554; Chen Wenxiu et al. 1983:246.

257. Chen Pixian 1982:11.

258. Chen Pixian 1979:112–14; Chen Yi 1980 [1959]: 5–6. Chen Yi wanted to stay on around Ruijin, but Xiang Ying would not let him (Chen Yi 1981 [1957]: 553–54). According to Yan Jingtang and Jiang Tingyu (1989:66), Xiang and Chen's original destination was Changting in Fujian.

259. Zhongyang junqu Xiang Ying 1986 [1935].

260. Guofangbu 1967, vol. 5:809–10; Chen Pixian 1979:114; Tan Yunxiang and Liu Puqing 1985:323.

261. Chen Pixian 1979:112–14; Chen Yi 1981 [1957]: 554–55; Chen Wenxiu et al. 1983:246.

262. Yang Shangkui 1977:34; Chen Pixian 1979:114–15 and 1982:23; Zong Zhidi 1980 [1952]: 140; Chen Yi 1980 [1959]: 6 and 1981 [1957]: 555.

263. Zong Zhidi 1980 [1952]: 142; Chen Yi 1980 [1959]: 5.

264. Chen Pixian 1979:140–41; Chen Yi 1981 [1957]: 555–56.

265. Chen Pixian 1979:115; Chen Yi 1981 [1957]: 556; Zong Zhidi 1980 [1952]: 141–43.

266. Benton 1986:706.

267. Zong Zhidi 1980 [1952]: 144–48; Chen Yi 1981 [1957]: 557–62.

268. Zong Zhidi 1980 [1952]: 162; Chen Yi 1981 [1957]: 561; Chen Pixian 1979:129.

269. Zong Zhidi 1980 [1952]: 144–48; Chen Yi 1981 [1957]: 557–62.

270. Wu Gu 1979:107.

271. Chen Pixian 1979:151.

272. Chen Chun'e 1986:82.

273. Yu Maoji et al. 1985:7.

274. Kuo 1968–71, vol. 3:36–40.

275. See next chapter.

## GANNAN: SEEDS OF FIRE

1. Renmin chubanshe 1953 [1945]:53; Zhongguo geming bowuguan 1982:298. These names refer to counties. I give similar lists near the start of the chapters on each of the different regions in which the Three-Year War was fought.

2. Zeng Shan 1980:3–4; Xia Daohan 1986:52–53.

3. These paragraphs on the early Communist movement in Gannan draw on Averill 1987.

4. Xia Daohan 1986:52–53; Ma Wenbin et al. 1986:62.

5. Xiao Ke 1981:131.
6. Smedley 1934:369.
7. Qiu Linzhong 1983.
8. Zheng Weisan 1982 [1941]: 135–36.
9. Ye Fei 1983a, pt. 1:13–14.
10. Xie Huiying 1963:127–29.
11. Huang Changjiao 1963:56–57 and 1981:74–75; Liu Huishan, interview, Ruijin, November 1986.
12. Xie Huiying 1963:127–29; Huang Changjiao 1963 and 1981:75; Peng Xueying 1985; Zhang Zhaodi 1983.
13. Luo Mengwen n.d., 1962:1ff., and 1981:41–43; Zhou Aimin 1981b; Dai Xiangqing et al. 1986:691–92.
14. Luo Mengwen 1962:144ff.
15. Xie Huiying 1963; Dai Xiangqing et al. 1986:692; Zhou Aimin 1981a:444; "Xianggan geming" 1982:143.
16. Xu Zhanquan 1987:591.
17. Chen Yi 1980 [1959]: 4 and 1981 [1957]: 548.
18. Xi Hong 1958; Qiu Zhizhuo et al. 1986:118; Deng Haishan 1981:72.
19. Peng Shengbiao 1958:69.
20. Peng Shengbiao 1958:70–72 and 1984:3–4; Zhang Zhaodi 1983; Dai Xiangqing et al. 1986:726.
21. Deng Haishan 1981:69.
22. One source calls them the Tingruihui Guerrillas, that is, the guerrillas of Changting, Ruijin, and Huichang (Xu Zhanquan 1987:591).
23. Peng Shengbiao 1958:70–72; Yu Boliu 1985:63; Kong Yongsong et al. 1985:464–65; Xu Zhanquan 1987:591; Zhang Zhaodi 1983:63–65; Wang Jianying 1986a:402–3; Dai Xiangqing et al. 1986:726.
24. Zhang Zhaodi 1983:62; Luo Mengwen 1962:147.
25. Tan Yannian 1981:592.
26. Peng Shengbiao 1958:69–70.
27. Liu Huishan, interview, Ruijin, November 1986.
28. Peng Shengbiao 1958:70–72; Zhang Zhaodi 1983:55–63; Deng Haishan 1981:69.
29. Peng Shengbiao 1958 and 1984; Xi Hong 1958:234–37; Yang Shangk'uei 1961:86; Zhang Zhaodi 1983:59–63; Fu Yongdao 1963:92–94; Xu Zhanquan 1987:592.
30. Xi Hong 1958:234–36.
31. Peng Shengbiao 1958:73–76.
32. Peng Shengbiao 1984:4–5. A similar incident—perhaps the same one—is said by Xie Yongcong (1979) to have happened in 1938. Xie says that the guerrillas in Ruijin were not recognized until July 1939. He may refer to a separate, maverick group.
33. Peng Shengbiao 1958:78–80; Peng Xueying 1985; Zeng Shan 1982:248; Shi Yan et al. 1981:10–11; Chen Pixian 1982:132–33; Zhang Zhaodi 1983: 64–65.
34. Peng Xueying 1985:50; Peng Shengbiao 1984:5–7; Liang Guobin 1981: 67–68.

35. Yu Boliu 1985:63–64; Wang Jianying 1986a:403; Peng Shengbiao 1958:75–80 and 1984:5–7; Xu Zhanquan 1987:592; Peng Xueying 1985:50.

36. Yu Boliu 1983:135; Dai Xiangqing et al. 1986:741; Huang Changjiao 1981:75; Huang Zhaosong and Liu Hanqing 1986; Zhang Zhaodi 1983:65; Lu Yongli and Liu Zijian 1983:340. Kuo (1968–71, vol. 3:353) wrongly reports that Liu Guoxing refused to join the New Fourth Army because he thought that the united front was a surrender to the Guomindang.

37. Zhang Zhaodi 1983:64; Peng Xueying 1985:51; Deng Haishan 1981:72.

38. Dai Xiangqing et al. 1986:685; Xi Hong 1958:236; Chen Pixian 1982:6; Yu Maoji et al. 1985:6.


## GANYUE: HEROES IN DEFEAT

1. Renmin chubanshe 1953 [1945]: 53; Zhongguo geming bowuguan 1982:298.

2. Zheng Tianbao 1983.

3. Yang Shangkui 1977:36.

4. Zhang Riqing 1982:1 and 26; Wu Kebin 1986:35.

5. Song Shengfa 1978:1.

6. Liu Jianhua 1982:3–4.

7. Zhang Riqing 1982:3; Chen Yi 1981 [1957]:553–54; Zhu Dongsheng 1983:121–31.

8. Cai Xiaoqian 1970, pt. 4:86–87.

9. Zheng Tianbao 1983:43ff.

10. Zong Zhidi 1980 [1952]: 138; Chen Yi 1980 [1959]: 6; Liu Jianhua 1982:2.

11. Zong Zhidi 1980 [1952]: 148–49.

12. Chen Yi 1986 [1940]: 113.

13. Chen Yi 1981 [1957]: 554; Zhang Riqing 1982:5.

14. Zong Zhidi 1980 [1952]: 138.

15. Ibid:148.

16. Song Shengfa 1978:3–4; Zhang Riqing 1982:1–2; Dai Xiangqing et al. 1986:693–700; Liu Jianhua 1982:2; Yang Shang-k'uei 1961:1–2; Jiang Fengbo and Xu Zhanquan 1989:432.

17. Yang Shang-k'uei 1961:23; Yang Shangkui 1961:169–70, 1977:36, and 1980:8; Chen Pixian 1979:115–16; Tan Yunxiang and Liu Puqing 1985:323–24; Chen Yi 1980 [1959]: 6–7 and 1981 [1957]: 561–62; Zhang Riqing 1982:12; Zong Zhidi 1980 [1952]: 149; Cai Xiaoqian 1970–71, pt. 2:86–87.

18. Zhang Riqing 1982:4–5.

19. Yang Shangkui 1977:37.

20. Zhang Riqing 1982:5–10.

21. Ibid:7–12.

22. Yang Shangkui 1977:38.

23. Yang Shangkui 1961:170–71 and 1977:37–39; Yang Shang-k'uei 1961:27; Zhang Riqing 1982:13–14 and 77–78; Chen Pixian 1979:120; Chen Yi 1980 [1959]: 9–10, 1981 [1957]: 564–66, and 1986 [1940]: 117–18; Wu Kebin 1986:36.

24. Yang Shangkui 1961:170–71 and 1977:37–39.

25. Yang Shangkui 1961:170–71 and 1977:38; Liu Jianhua 1982:7–12; Zhang Riqing 1982:17.

26. Yang Shangkui 1977:39; Yang Shang-k'uei 1961:27; Chen Yi 1981 [1957]: 573; Liu Jianhua 1982:20; Zhang Riqing 1982:16–18.

27. Mu Qing 1950:20–22; Zong Zhidi 1980 [1952]: 149; Chen Pixian 1979:118–20; Zhang Riqing 1982:16–17; Tan Yunxiang and Liu Puqing 1985:328–34.

28. Yang Shang-k'uei 1961:76–77.

29. Xiao Zili 1981:85–86.

30. Zhang Riqing 1982; Xiao Zili 1981.

31. Chen Pixian 1979:117; Song Shengfa 1978:25; Liu Jianhua 1982:12.

32. Yang Shangkui 1977:44; Chen Pixian 1979:117–18; Zong Zhidi 1980 [1952]: 155–56; Chen Yi 1980 [1959]: 7–8, 1981 [1957]: 563–65, and 1986 [1940]: 119.

33. Song Shengfa 1978:26; Chen Yi 1981 [1957]: 565.

34. Zhang Riqing 1982:157; Song Shengfa 1978:25; Chen Yi 1980 [1959]: 7–8, 1981 [1957]: 563–64, and 1986 [1940]: 119.

35. Zong Zhidi 1980 [1952]: 158.

36. Snow 1941, vol. 1:129.

37. Chen Yi 1981 [1957]: 550; Yang Shang-k'uei 1961:14.

38. Chen Yi 1980 [1959]: 14–15 and 1981 [1957]: 573.

39. Chen Yi 1986 [1940]: 118.

40. Chen Pixian 1979:123; Zong Zhidi 1980 [1952]: 160; Chen Yi 1980 [1959]: 8–14 and 1981 [1957]: 564–65 and 573–75.

41. Song Shengfa 1978:59; Yang Shangkui 1980:33; Yang Shang-k'uei 1961:62; Chen Yi 1981 [1957]: 572–73.

42. Chen Pixian 1979:131.

43. Wang Fuyi 1984b:101.

44. Xiao Zili 1981:94.

45. Snow 1941, vol. 1:129.

46. Zong Zhidi 1980 [1952]: 159–60; Chen Pixian 1979:128–29; Yang Shang-k'uei 1961:115; Chen Yi 1981 [1957]: 573.

47. Chen Yi 1980 [1959]: 14 and 1981 [1957]: 580.

48. Chen Yi 1986 [1940]: 116.

49. Wales 1945:217.

50. Yang Shang-k'uei 1961:91.

51. Ibid:74.

52. Chen Pixian 1980 and 1982:59–60.

53. Chen Yi 1980 [1959]: 8–9 and 16–17 and 1981 [1957]: 568–72; Yang Shangkui 1978a:39; Yang Shang-k'uei 1961:36; Zong Zhidi 1980 [1952]: 149; Chen Pixian 1979:127–28.

54. Chen Pixian 1979:129 and 1982:68–78; Tan Yannian 1981; Yang Shang-k'uei 1961:36–38; Liu Jianhua 1982:10.

55. Zong Zhidi 1980 [1952]: 156; Chen Pixian 1979:121–23; Chen Yi 1980 [1959]: 17.

56. Zong Zhidi 1980 [1952]: 155; Song Shengfa 1978:37; Yang Shang-k'uei 1961:71; Yang Shangkui 1978a:37–38; Chen Yi 1980 [1959]:16.

57. Zong Zhidi 1980 [1952]: 152; Chen Pixian 1979:123; Chen Yi 1981 [1957]: 568–69 and 583; Yang Shangkui 1977:42.

58. Zong Zhidi 1980 [1952]: 150. Some people may dispute my contention that the Chinese Communists suffered a worse defeat in 1934 than in 1927. However, probably less than a tenth as many died in 1927 (when, of course, the Party had far less to lose) than in 1934; and whereas in 1927 the urban Party survived, at least in the underground, by the mid–1930s it had (according to Liu Shaoqi's report to the Party's Eighth Congress in 1945) been nearly 100 percent destroyed.

59. Song Shengfa 1978:30.

60. Chen Yi 1981 [1957]: 580–81.

61. Chen Pixian 1979:127.

62. Zong Zhidi 1980 [1952]: 151; Song Shengfa 1978:30.

63. The concept of yellow (and gray) villages will be discussed below.

64. Chen Yi 1980 [1959]: 11–12. See also Chen Yi 1981 [1957]: 581. See Tan Yannian 1981:595–96 on desertions motivated by "leftism."

65. Song Shengfa 1978:26 and 30; Chen Pixian 1979:124–25; Chen Yi 1981 [1957]: 575–76; Tan Yannian 1981:595; Junshi kexueyuan 1987, vol. 1:298.

66. Zhang Riqing 1982:77–78.

67. Chen Yi 1981 [1957]: 571–78; Chen Pixian 1979:124–25; Snow 1941, vol. 1:129.

68. Chen Yi 1980 [1959]: 12 and 1981 [1957]: 582.

69. Shi Yan and Wu Kebin 1983:11.

70. Ding Shanghuai 1979:158; Yang Shang-k'uei 1961:122; Chen Pixian 1982:86; Liu Jianhua 1982:16.

71. Chen Pixian 1982:86–87.

72. Yang Shang-k'uei 1961:123.

73. Chen Yi 1981 [1957]: 582–83; Liu Jianhua 1982:11.

74. Zong Zhidi 1980 [1952]: 153; Chen Yi 1980 [1959]: 8 and 1981 [1957]: 570; Yang Shangkui 1977:44 and 1978a:31.

75. Zong Zhidi 1980 [1952]: 149; Song Shengfa 1978:70.

76. Xiao Zili 1981:94.

77. Chen Yi 1980 [1959]: 8–9, 1981 [1957]: 570–71, and 1986 [1940]: 119; Zong Zhidi 1980 [1952]: 154; Yang Shang-k'uei 1961:64.

78. Ding Zhihui 1981:46; Zhang Riqing 1982:23; Zong Zhidi 1980 [1952]: 161; Dan Jiang 1981:52; Zhou Lan 1981:599; Yang Shang-k'uei 1961:113.

79. Yang Shangkui 1961:185–87 and 1977:42; Yang Shang-k'uei 1961:97 and 116; Chen Yi 1981 [1957]: 567.

80. Chen Yi 1981 [1957]: 567; Chen Pixian 1979:133–34; Bian Xiezu 1982:91; Yang Shang-k'uei 1961:96–97.

81. Chen Pixian 1979:133–38; Chen Yi 1980 [1959]: 13; Yang Shang-k'uei 1961:98–102.

82. Yang Shangkui 1977:42; Yang Shang-k'uei 1961:99–101; Chen Pixian 1979:133–34 and 1982:83–86; Song Shengfa 1978:42.

83. Chen Yi 1981 [1957]: 567; Chen Pixian 1979:138–39, 1980:47, and 1982:86; Yang Shang-k'uei 1961:102–3; Bian Xiezu 1982:91.

84. Chen Yi 1980 [1959]: 16–19.

85. Chen Pixian 1979:139.

86. Chen Yi 1980 [1959]: 13–14 and 1981 [1957]: 578–79; Chen Pixian 1980:47–50 and 1982:89–95; Yang Shangkui 1977:42–43; Yang Shang-k'uei 1961:80–95.

87. Zong Zhidi 1980 [1952]: 159; Song Shengfa 1978:66; Chen Yi 1980 [1959]: 13–14 and 1981 [1957]:578–79; Zhao Zengyan 1986:81–82; Liu Jianhua 1982:17.

88. Yang Shangkui 1961:181–82; Zhao Zengyan 1986; Chen Yi 1986 [1940]: 118.

89. Yang Shangkui 1961:182; Chen Pixian 1979:122ff., 1980:47, and 1982: 59, 85, and 98; Chen Yi 1980 [1959]: 13 and 1981 [1957]: 579; Liu Jianhua 1982:18.

90. Chen Si et al. 1982:85–86.

91. Zeng Shiwen 1983.

92. Chen Yi 1980 [1959]: 14 and 1981 [1957]: 579.

93. Yang Shang-k'uei 1961:131–32; Li Fengmin 1969:337; Wales 1945:218; Yang Shangkui 1961:187; Dai Xiangqing et al. 1986:722; Yan Jingtang and Jiang Tingyu 1989:69.

94. Zong Zhidi 1980 [1952]: 168.

95. Chen Yi 1981 [1957]: 584.

96. Song Shengfa 1958:90; Dai Xiangqing et al. 1986:722; Chen Yi 1980 [1959]:6; Yang Shang-k'uei 1961:104–5; Yang Shangkui 1980.

97. Chen Pixian 1979:147; Chen Yi 1980 [1959]: 17–18 and 1981 [1957]: 569–70 and 579; Liu Jianhua 1982:23.

98. Bian Xiezu 1982:91; Wales 1945:218–19; Chen Yi 1981 [1957]: 584; Yu Boliu 1983:132–33; Wang Fuyi 1987b:37–38; Dai Xiangqing et al. 1986:730–31.

99. Chen Yi 1980 [1959]: 18–19 and 1981 [1957]: 585–86; Chen Pixian 1979:148–49; Yang Shang-k'uei 1961:129–34.

100. Wang Fuyi 1987b:37–38.

101. Lai Zhigang 1982.

102. Chen Pixian 1979:149–50.

103. Zhongguo gongchandang Ganyue bian weiyuanhui 1937.

104. Chen Pixian 1979:149–50 and 1982:119ff; Wang Fuyi 1987b:37; Yu Boliu 1983:132–33.

105. Central Committee resolution, January 15, 1941, in Zhonggong zhongyang dangxiao chubanshe 1982:266–68 and Anhui sheng wenwuju 1981:264–67.

106. Cao Yanhang and Gan Guozhi 1983:42. According to a recent article (Yan Jingtang and Jiang Tingyu 1989:70–72), Xiang Ying wrote in July 1937 that the Communists should "not neglect independence" in the new united front. The same article adds that Xiang Ying's "small errors" arose from his lack of information and that it is untrue that he "fell into the Guomindang's trap." The article quotes a report dated October 26 by Bo Gu and Ye Jianying that says: "Because the situation is not clear, Xiang and Chen sometimes acted un-

soundly in the talks, but their general direction was right" (Yan Jingtang and Jiang Tingyu 1989:72).

107. Song Shengfa 1978:93; Wang Fuyi 1987b:38.
108. Yang Shang-k'uei 1961:153–54.
109. Lai Zhigang 1982:40.
110. Xiao Zili 1981:93; Liu Jianhua 1982:23.
111. Yang Shang-k'uei 1961:155.
112. Ge Demao 1983:133; Benton 1979:60.
113. Yang Shangkui 1977:61; Liu Jianhua 1982:24; Lai Zhigang 1982:40.
114. Wang Zuoyao 1983b:138–49; Liu Jianhua 1985:3–14.
115. Liu Mianyu 1984:217.
116. Tan Chen-lin and Su Yu 1978:125.
117. Liu Jianhua 1982:25–27.
118. Ibid:11–12.
119. Snow 1941, vol. 1:129.
120. Chen Yi 1986 [1940]: 118.
121. I translated "Guerrilla Fighting" from Zhongguo renmin geming junshi bowuguan, eds., 1986:111–12 and adapted "Three Stanzas Written at Meiling" from *Chinese Literature* (Beijing) 1977:7. I translated all the other poems from Chen Yi 1977.

## MINXI'NAN: MOUNTAIN MARXISTS

1. Meskill 1979:17–18.
2. Shaw 1914; Andrews 1920; Fortune 1949 [1847].
3. Renmin chubanshe 1953 [1945]: 53; Zhongguo geming bowuguan 1982: 302.
4. Fortune 1979 [1847]: 8.
5. Xue Moucheng and Zheng Quanbei 1980:54.
6. Fang Qingqiu 1983:105–7; Shen Jiawu 1983:124–26; Xue Moucheng et al. 1983:176–79; Fujian sheng dang'anguan, eds., 1984:147–52; Lu Sheng 1984:227–28 and 1985a:18.
7. Dong Huanran 1937:82.
8. Xiao Xuexin 1984.
9. Huang Huicong 1936; "Jiajin" 1937; Kong Li 1979:134.
10. Zhang Dingcheng 1982:1–2; Sun Ching-chih 1962 [1959]: 360–62; Kao Yun-lan 1959:iii and 52; Zhang Dingcheng et al. 1983.
11. Kerr 1965:55.
12. Kao Yun-lan 1959:86–87; Yi Linping 1983:157.
13. Chen Yafang 1986:45.
14. Tan Zhenlin et al. 1983:21–22; Kong Yongsong and Lin Tianyi 1982:1–19; Jordan 1976:95; Ye Fei 1983b:9; Liao Kaizhu, ed., 1986:7. See Qiu Linzhong et al. 1983 for a general source on the early transmission of Marxism to Minxi.
15. Xiamen daxue 1978:1–4; Kong Yongsong and Lin Tianyi 1982:19–20; *Minxi dangshi ziliao tongxun*, January 5, 1983, no. 1, 26.
16. Ma Wenbin et al. 1986:62.

17. Qiu Linzhong 1983:43; Ma Wenbin et al. 1986:55–69; Sheng Renxue and Zhang Junxiao 1987:26–27; Liao Kaizhu, ed., 1986:4 and 15–17; Zhang Guangxin and Yang Shuzhen, eds., 1985:53; Chen Yi et al. 1981:13. See Chen Yi et al. 1981 on Gannan.

18. Xiamen daxue 1978:4–7; Kong Yongsong and Lin Tianyi 1982:71–125; Sheng Renxue and Zhang Junxiao 1987:27–35; Jiang Boying 1987a:120.

19. Lin Jian 1985b:18.

20. Kong Yongsong and Lin Tianyi 1982:139–59; Tan Zhenlin et al. 1983:23–24; Wei Jinshui 1983b:36; Harrison 1972:174ff; Griffin 1976:31–32.

21. Tan Zhenlin et al. 1983:23–24; Kong Yongsong and Lin Tianyi 1982:156–203; Lian Yin 1982:34; Zhonggong Fujian shengwei dangshi ziliao zhengji weiyuanhui 1986. Some authors (Harrison 1972:204, Kuo 1968–71, vol. 2:489) do not see Deng Fa's removal as a demotion.

22. Donovan 1976:108; Kuo 1968–71, vol. 2:489.

23. Kong Yongsong and Lin Tianyi 1982:263–68; Sima Lu, ed., 1982:102–3; Lian Yin 1982:34; Wen Yangchun 1987:195; Zhonggong Longyan diwei 1987: 204–5.

24. Kong Yongsong and Lin Tianyi 1982:265–77; Tan Zhenlin et al. 1983:24; Lian Yin 1982:34; Zhang Dingcheng and Tan Zhenlin 1981:15; Lu Yongli and Liu Zijian 1983:332–33. Luo Ming took part in the early stages of the Long March but was left behind in Guizhou in April 1935. Hostile sources say that he was captured by the Nationalists and released after recanting (Kuo 1968–71, vol. 2:490). After 1949, he returned to China from Southeast Asia and became vice-principal of Guangzhou's Southern University. In the 1980s he was still active. I met him in Xiamen in November 1986.

25. Kuo 1968–71, vol. 2:480 and 563.

26. Bingzhang Yang 1986:100.

27. Xiamen daxue 1978:8; Kong Yongsong and Lin Tianyi 1982:261–63; Lu Yongli and Liu Zijian 1983:332–33.

28. Zhang Dingcheng 1982:63–64; Kong Yongsong and Lin Tianyi 1982: 263–65; Xia Daohan 1983:285.

29. Lin Jian 1985b:21.

30. Zhang Dingcheng 1982:80.

31. Fawubu diaochaju, eds., 1982, Zhonggong "nongmin yundong," 135–36.

32. Minxi dangshi ziliao tongxun, January 5, 1983, no. 1, 7.

33. Kong Yongsong and Lin Tianyi 1982:312–18; Lu Yongli and Liu Zijian 1983:333–34.

34. Kong Yongsong and Lin Tianyi 1982:315–16; Zhang Dingcheng 1982:66; Zhang Dingcheng and Tan Zhenlin 1981:17; Xie Bizhen 1984:76–77; Lin Jian 1985b:18–20.

35. Wu Hongxiang 1986, pt. 1:20.

36. Zhang Dingcheng and Tan Zhenlin 1981:17; Wang Sheng 1983:126–27; Wu Hongxiang 1986, pt. 1:13–15.

37. Kong Yongsong and Lin Tianyi 1982:315–16; Chen Maohui 1983:134–36; Wu Hongxiang 1986, pt. 1:19ff.; Liao Kaizhu, ed., 1986:123; Zhang Dingcheng et al. 1984:51.

38. Zhang Dingcheng and Tan Zhenlin 1981:17–18; Kong Yongsong and Lin Tianyi 1982:315–17. Chen Maohui 1983:133–34; Zhang Dingcheng 1982:66; Lu Dingyi 1983:11; Lin Jian 1985b:18–19.

39. Ye Cao 1948:3–6 and 12–20; Kong Yongsong and Lin Tianyi 1982:317–18; Wu Hongxiang 1986, pt. 1:13.

40. Zhang Dingcheng and Tan Zhenlin 1981:18; Lian Yin 1982:34–35; Chen Maohui 1983:134; Yu Boliu 1985:60; Liao Kaizhu, ed., 1986:122; Dai Xiangqing et al. 1986:682.

41. He Shisi 1986; Salisbury 1985:205; Klein and Clark 1971:307.

42. Zhang Dingcheng and Tan Zhenlin 1981:18; Kong Yongsong and Lin Tianyi 1982:320–23; Jiang Boying et al. 1983:330–31.

43. Zhang Dingcheng and Tan Zhenlin 1981:18–19; Ye Cao 1948:22–25; Kong Yongsong and Lin Tianyi 1982:318; Lu Yongli and Liu Zijian 1983:335.

44. Shen Zhongwen 1982; Kong Yongsong and Lin Tianyi 1982:318; Lu Sheng 1984:224–26; Yin Linping 1983:151–53.

45. Lu Sheng 1983c:20–22, 1984:227–29, and 1985a:19; Jiti 1982:17; Lin Tianyi 1985:52.

46. Ye Cao 1948:26; Kong Yongsong and Lin Tianyi 1982:318; Lu Yongli and Liu Zijian 1983:336; Kuo 1968–71, vol. 2:553 and 588–89; Klein and Clark 1971:137–38; Hu Yunqiu et al. 1981:70; Hu Liangzhong 1987a:499–500.

47. Xie Yucai 1985:26–27.

48. Ye Cao 1948:27–29; Zhang Dingcheng and Tan Zhenlin 1981:18; Lu Yongli and Liu Zijian 1983:336.

49. Kong Yongsong and Lin Tianyi 1982:326; Zhang Dingcheng and Tan Zhenlin 1981:19; Xie Yucai 1985:29–32; Lin Jian 1985b:26–27.

50. Ye Cao 1948:27–29.

51. Zhang Dingcheng and Tan Zhenlin 1981:18; Kong Yongsong and Lin Tianyi 1982:325–26.

52. Benjamin Yang 1986:235.

53. Chen Maohui 1984.

54. Zheng Xueqiu 1986; Lin Jian 1985b:22–23; Hu Yunqiu et al. 1981:70.

55. Qiu Linzhong et al. 1983:16; Lin Jian 1985b:22; Wang Wei 1985:25.

56. Zhonggong Huanggang 1981:107–17; Hu Yunqiu et al. 1981:70.

57. Jiang Maosheng 1982:125–27; Ye Cao 1948:57–58.

58. Ye Cao 1948:24–28; Zhang Dingcheng and Tan Zhenlin 1981:19; Xiamen daxue 1978:145–46; Zheng Guiqing 1984:12–13; Liao Kaizhu, ed., 1986:117–31; Lin Jian 1985b:22–24.

59. Wei Jinshui 1983b:33–40 and 1983c:175; Yanyongjing xianwei 1936; Zhao Zengyan 1986:79–80.

60. Zhao Zengyan 1986:83.

61. Yanyongjing xianwei 1936; "Zenyang zuzhi" 1936; He Ming 1935; Hu Liangzhong 1987a; Zhang Dingcheng et al. 1984:58.

62. Zhang Dingcheng et al. 1984:57; Liao Kaizhu, ed., 1986:200; Wei Jinshui 1983c:172–73.

63. Zhang Dingcheng et al. 1984:51; Lin Jian 1985b:26–27; Zhang Dingcheng and Tan Zhenlin 1981:19.

64. Wu Hongxiang 1986, pt. 2:27; Zhang Dingcheng and Tan Zhenlin 1981:19; Chen Maohui 1983:141; Fang Fang 1936.

65. Zhang Dingcheng and Tan Zhenlin 1981:19; Ye Cao 1948:32; Lin Jian 1985b:28; Wu Hongxiang 1986, pt. 2:20.

66. Lu Yongli and Liu Zijian 1983:336; Ye Cao 1948:32; Jiang Maosheng 1982:126–28; He Ming 1935; Xing Yinyuan 1936; Zheng Guiqing 1984:13.

67. Lu Yongli and Liu Zijian 1983:327; Jiang Boying 1986:164; Zheng Guiqing 1984:13–14; Lin Huicai 1983:42.

68. Minxi'nan junzhengwei n.d.

69. Kong Yongsong and Lin Tianyi 1982:333; Ye Cao 1948:46; Chen Maohui 1983:138–40.

70. Zhang Dingcheng and Tan Zhenlin 1981:20.

71. Jiang Boying 1986:163–64; Lin Huicai 1983:44; Zheng Guiqing 1984:13–14; Lin Jian 1985b:25.

72. Jiang Maosheng 1982:128–47.

73. Minxi'nan junzheng weiyuanhui 1982? [1936].

74. Chen Maohui 1983:136–37; Wang Shaojie 1982:256–57.

75. Jiang Boying 1986:161–67; Zhang Dingcheng et al. 1984:46–58; Zheng Guiqing 1984:15.

76. Zhong ge junwei 1986 [1934]: 45.

77. Ye Cao 1948:7–60; Lu Yongli and Liu Zijian 1983:337–38; Zheng Guiqing 1984:15.

78. Lu Yongli and Liu Zijian 1983:337; Ye Cao 1948:35–53.

79. Wu Hongxiang 1986, pt. 2:27.

80. Ye Cao 1948:60; Wei Jinshui 1982:40.

81. Zhang Dingcheng and Tan Zhenlin 1981:20; Zhang Dingcheng et al. 1984:61; Jiang Boying 1986:169; Lin Jian 1985b:28–29; Wu Hongxiang 1986, pt. 2:30.

82. Zhonghua suweiai gongheguo Minxi'nan junzheng weiyuanhui 1979 [1936]; Lin Jian 1985b:29.

83. Huang Huicong 1935.

84. Kong Yongsong and Lin Tianyi 1982:339–40; Jiang Boying et al. 1983:334–35; Zhonghua suweiai gongheguo Minxi'nan junzheng weiyuanhui 1979 [1936].

85. Wei Jinshui 1983c:173–74; Hu Liangzhong 1987a:502.

86. Zhonghua suweiai gongheguo Minxi'nan junzheng weiyuanhui 1979 [1936]; Kong Yongsong and Lin Tianyi 1982:339–41; Jiang Boying et al. 1983:334–35; Liao Kaizhu, ed., 1986:141; Lin Jian 1985b:29.

87. Huang Huicong 1935; Deng Zihui 1936d; Zhonghua suweiai gongheguo Minxi'nan junzheng weiyuanhui 1979 [1936]; Kong Yongsong and Lin Tianyi 1982:340–41.

88. Ye Cao 1948:54–60; Xiamen daxue 1978:146–47; Lian Yin 1982:35.

89. Jiang Boying 1986:173–74.

90. Ye Cao 1948:2–25; Kong Yongsong and Lin Tianyi 1982:241; Xiamen daxue 1978:146–47; Zhongyang zuzhibu, eds., 1936.

91. Kong Yongsong and Lin Tianyi 1982:341–43; Zhang Dingcheng and Tan Zhenlin 1981:20.

92. Zhang Dingcheng et al. 1984:62–66.
93. "Xinci baijun" 1936; Sanfenqu 1936; Minxi'nan junzheng weiyuanhui zhengzhibu 1936.
94. Minxi'nan junzheng weiyuanhui zhengzhibu 1936.
95. Ibid; "Xinci baijun" 1936; Sanfenqu 1936.
96. Mao Tse-tung 1978 [1937]: 20.
97. Hong Zhong 1984.
98. "Xinci baijun" 1936.
99. Chen Bolin 1986:47.
100. Deng Zihui 1936d; Jiang Boying et al. 1983:335.
101. Deng Zihui 1936a.
102. Deng Zihui 1936b.
103. Lin Jian 1985b:30.
104. Zhang Dingcheng et al. 1984:67; Zheng Guiqing 1984:16; Wang Sheng 1983:132.
105. Zhang Dingcheng 1936; "Kengxiaxiang" 1936; Liao Kaizhu, ed., 1986:143 and 197.
106. Ye Cao 1948:64; Zhang Dingcheng et al. 1984:69.
107. Ye Cao 1948:66–67; Chen Bolin 1986:47–48; Zhang Dingcheng et al. 1984:69.
108. Lin Huicai 1983:40–41.
109. Minxi'nan junzheng weiyuanhui zhengzhibu 1936.
110. Zhongguo gongchandang Minxi'nan junzheng weiyuanhui 1936; Zai Tian 1936; "Gei Li Hua" 1936.
111. Jiang Boying 1986:179.
112. Jiang Maosheng 1982:147.
113. Chen Bolin 1986:49.
114. Dai Xiangqing et al. 1986:717.
115. Renmin chubanshe 1953 [1945]: 53; Zhongguo geming bowuguan 1982:302.
116. Huang Jianlan 1986.
117. Lu Sheng 1984:232 and 1985a; Yin Linping 1983:156–57; Qiu Song-qing 1985:56–57.
118. Wang Yifan 1985:49; Lin Tianyi 1985:53; Huang Jianlan 1985:19; Lu Dao 1985; Lu Sheng 1985a; Liao Kaizhu, ed., 1986:158–59; Wang Bingnan 1987:114.
119. Li Xikai 1985:37–38; Huang Jianlan 1986.
120. Lu Sheng 1985a:22; Wang Yifan 1985:46; Huang Huicong 1935; Lin Tianyi 1985:55–56; Lu Dao 1985:23.
121. Lu Dao 1985:22–23; Wang Yifan 1985:45–48.
122. Huang Jianlan 1986; Ye Fei 1983b:9; Lu Sheng 1985a:27.
123. Wang Yifan 1985:44–45; Lin Tianyi 1985:54; Huang Jianlan 1986; Chen Yafang 1986:45.
124. Yin Linping 1983:156–57; Lu Sheng 1985a:19–21; Wu Yunlin 1985:63–64; Lin Tianyi 1985:56.
125. Huang Jianlan 1985:18 and 1986; Wang Yifan 1985; Lin Tianyi 1985:55–56; Wang Bingnan 1985:18; Li Xikai 1985:40–41.

126. Huang Jianlan 1986; Lu Sheng 1985a:27; Wang Yifan 1985; Wang Wei 1985:24–27; Lu Dao 1985:23; Lin Tianyi 1985:56; Liao Kaizhu, ed., 1986:159.

127. Lu Sheng 1985a:24.

128. Wang Yifan 1985:50–51; Lin Tianyi 1985:56; Wang Wei 1985:26; Liao Kaizhu, ed., 1986:161.

129. Yin Linping 1983:157; Anonymous 1985:45; Wang Yifan 1985:51.

130. Zhonghua suweiai gongheguo Minxi'nan junzheng weiyuanhui 1936b.

131. Ye Cao 1948:67; Minxi'nan junzheng weiyuanhui zhengzhibu 1936; Zai Tian 1936.

132. Zhonghua suweiai gongheguo Minxi'nan junzheng weiyuanhui 1936a and 1936b; Zhongguo gongchandang Minxi'nan weiyuanhui jiguan bao, *Hongqi*, December 1, 1936, no. 9, editorial comment; Ye Cao 1948:68–69; Zhonghua renmin suweiai gongheguo Minxi'nan junzheng weiyuanhui 1937c.

133. Jiang Maosheng 1982:138–47.

134. Minxi'nan junzheng weiyuanhui zhengzhibu 1936.

135. Minxi'nan junzhengwei junshibu 1937.

136. Minxi'nan junzheng weiyuanhui fenhui 1937; Minxi'nan junzhengwei junshibu 1937.

137. Minxi'nan junzheng weiyuanhui fenhui 1937.

138. Minxi'nan junzhengwei junshibu 1937.

139. Wang Ming 1974 [1935].

140. Minxi'nan junzheng weiyuanhui fenhui 1937; Minxi'nan junzhengwei junshibu 1937.

141. Lu Sheng 1983c:22–24.

142. Wei Jinshui 1983a:39.

143. Xiamen daxue 1978:147–48; Kong Yongsong and Lin Tianyi 1982:345; Lu Yongli and Liu Zijian 1983:339; Ye Cao 1948:71–79; Wen Yangchun 1985:66–67; Zhao Zengyan 1986:82–83.

144. Ye Cao 1948:74–75.

145. Kong Yongsong and Lin Tianyi 1982:346; Lu Yongli and Liu Zijian 1983:339.

146. Kong Yongsong and Lin Tianyi 1982:346–47; Jiang Boying et al. 1983:339–40.

147. Zhongyao tongxun 1937.

148. Zhang Dingcheng et al. 1937?

149. Minxi'nan junzheng weiyuanhui 1937.

150. Wei Jinshui 1983a:40.

151. Minxi'nan junzhengwei 1986 [1937]: 21–24.

152. Minxi'nan junzhengwei 1986 [1937]; Minxi'nan junzheng weiyuanhui zhengzhibu 1937.

153. Minxi'nan junzhengwei 1986 [1937]: 23; Zhonghua suweiai gongheguo Minxi'nan junzheng weiyuanhui 1937a, 1937b, 1937d, and 1937f; Minxi'nan junzheng weiyuanhui zhengzhibu 1937; Minxi'nan junzheng weiyuanhui 1937.

154. Minxi'nan junzhengwei 1986 [1937]: 24.

155. Wei Jinshui 1983a:39–40.

156. Chen Bolin 1986:47–48.

157. Kong Yongsong and Lin Tianyi 1982:348.

158. Minxi'nan junzhengwei 1986 [1937]: 25–26; Ye Cao 1948:79; Zhang Dingcheng 1982:83.

159. Minxi'nan junzheng weiyuanhui zhengzhibu 1937.

160. Zhonghua renmin suweiai gongheguo Minxi'nan junzheng weiyuanhui 1937a, 1937d, and 1937f; Minxi'nan junzheng weiyuanhui 1937.

161. Kong Yongsong and Lin Tianyi 1982:349; Jiang Boying et al. 1983:338–40; Jiang Maosheng 1982:160–61.

162. Liang Guobin 1981:61.

163. Qiu Linzhong and Su Juncai 1985:43–45; Wei Jinshui 1983a:39–40; Jiang Boying 1986:186; Jiang Boying et al. 1983:339; Ye Cao 1948:81–83; Kong Yongsong and Lin Tianyi 1982:351.

164. Ke Sheng 1937.

165. Zhonggong Minyue bianqu tewei 1937b.

166. Yan wei 1937.

167. Jiang Maosheng 1984:64.

168. Wei Jinshui 1985:24–25.

169. Mao Tse-tung 1961–65, vol. 2:67–68; Ye Cao 1948:81; S. K. 1937; Jiang Boying et al. 1983:338–39; Liang Guobin 1981:59.

170. S. K. 1937; Lu Sheng 1983b:134; Wang Bingnan 1985:18.

171. Zhang Dingcheng et al. 1937?

172. Zhonggong Minyue bianqu tewei 1937a; Lu Sheng 1983b:138–43; Shi Yan et al. 1982:18–21; S. K. 1937; Tang Bin 1984:58.

173. Lu Sheng 1985a:21.

174. S. K. 1937.

175. Zhonggong Minyue bianqu tewei 1937b; Lu Sheng 1983b:143; Kong Yongsong and Lin Tianyi 1982:351; Zhonggong Minyue bianqu 1937.

176. S. K. 1937; Lu Sheng 1983a:179, 1983b:142, and 1985a:26; Shi Yan et al. 1981:20–21.

177. Xie Yucai 1985:34; Liang Guobin 1981:71.

178. Tang Bin 1984:57.

179. Xie Yucai 1985:33–34; Lin Yinping 1983:159–60; Zhang Zaoxun 1982:46–47; Lin Tianyi 1985:58.

180. Lu Sheng 1983b; Kong Yongsong and Lin Tianyi 1982:350, n. 2.

181. Wang Bingnan 1985.

182. S. K. 1937.

183. Zhang Zaoxun 1985.

184. Lin Tianyi 1985:57; Lu Sheng 1985b:53–54.

185. Chen Gaoshun 1982:28; Yin Linping 1983:158; Lu Sheng 1985a:25–26; Tang Bin 1984:60.

186. Yin Linping 1983:159; Lin Jian 1985a:21–22; Wang Datong et al. 1984:44.

187. Chen Bolin 1986:51.

188. Yin Linping 1983:159.

189. Chen Bolin 1986:49–52; Zhang Zaoxun 1982:46; Wang Wei 1985:27; Cai Xinsheng 1984:68; Wang Datong et al. 1984:45–46; Lin Tianyi 1985:58; Chen Gaoshun 1982:30.

190. Liao Kaizhu, ed., 1986:162.

191. S. K. 1937.
192. Zhang Dingcheng et al. 1937?; Zhonggong Minyue bianqu 1937:4.
193. Zhang Dingcheng 1982:87.
194. S. K. 1937.
195. Wang Bingnan 1985:25.
196. S. K. 1937.
197. Minyue bianqu tewei 1938:8.
198. Ibid:7.
199. Ibid:10.
200. Ye Cao 1948:83.
201. Zhongguo gongchandang Minyuegan sheng weiyuanhui 1937; Zhong-guo gongchandang Minyuegan bian sheng weiyuanhui 1937; "Jiajin baowei Hua'nan" 1937.
202. Kong Yongsong and Lin Tianyi 1982:351.
203. Wen Yangchun 1985:72.
204. Kong Yongsong and Lin Tianyi 1982:351–52; Ye Cao 1948:81–83; Zhongguo gongchandang Minyuegan bian sheng weiyuanhui 1937; Lin Jian 1985a:21; Liang Guobin 1981:63–64; Zheng Guiqing 1984:20.
205. Cao Yanhang and Gan Guozhi 1983:42.
206. Ye Cao 1948:84.
207. Kong Yongsong and Lin Tianyi 1982:351–53; Ye Cao 1948:84; Zeng Shan 1982:248; Liang Guobin 1981:61–62; Xiamen daxue 1978:148.
208. Zheng Guiqing 1984:20.
209. Kong Yongsong and Lin Tianyi 1982:353; Xiamen daxue 1978:147.
210. Zhongyang diaocha tongjiju 1940:9; Xinsijun canmouchu 1981 [1946]: 159; Lian Yin 1982:35.
211. Qiu Linzhong and Su Juncai 1985:45.
212. Zhonggong Minyue bianqu 1937:11.
213. Minyue bianqu tewei 1938:8.
214. Zhang Dingcheng 1982:87.
215. Ye Cao 1948:84; Kong Yongsong and Lin Tianyi 1982:354; Ge Demao 1983:133; Xiamen daxue 1978:148; Liang Guobin 1981:70–73.
216. Wang Zhi 1985:105–8.
217. Minyue bianqu tewei 1938:8.
218. Xinsijun canmouchu 1981 [1946]: 160.
219. Wei Jinshui 1983b:42–43; Li Jumin 1983:77; Lu Sheng 1985a:17; Zeng Meisheng 1985:56–57; Wu Yunlin 1983:6; Xie Bizhen 1985:35.
220. Xie Bizhen 1984:79–80 and 1985:35–37; Ye Cao 1948:84; Kong Yong-song and Lin Tianyi 1982:354–55; Lu Yongli and Liu Zijian 1983:343; Zeng Meisheng 1985:56–58; Lin Jian 1985a:22–23.
221. Zhonggong Minyue bianqu 1937:9–14.
222. Liu Yongsheng 1980:115–16.
223. Minyue bianqu tewei 1938:13–19; Xie Bizhen 1984:80; Lu Yongli and Liu Zijian 1983:342.
224. Zeng Meisheng 1985:57–58; Lin Jian 1985a:22–23.
225. Lu Yongli and Liu Zijian 1983:340–42; Liu Yongsheng 1980:116.
226. Zeng Meisheng 1985:57–58.

227. Lu Yongli and Liu Zijian 1983:342.
228. Zhongyang diaocha tongjiju 1940:10.
229. Lu Yongli and Liu Zijian 1983:343.
230. Tu Jianchen 1944.
231. Wei Jinshui 1983b:33–34; Liu Yongsheng 1980:132; Zhao Zengyan 1986:83; Zheng Xueqiu 1982:46.
232. Wei Jinshui 1983b:40–57; Deng Zihui 1983:36.
233. Lin Jian 1985a:24.
234. Zhongguo gongchandang Zhangzhou zhongxin xian weiyuanhui 1940a, 1940b, and 1940c; Liu Yongsheng 1980:116–17.
235. Zhongguo gongchandang Zhangzhou zhongxin xian weiyuanhui 1940a.
236. Liu Yongsheng 1980:116–18; Lu Yongli and Liu Zijian 1983:344–46; Xie Bizhen 1984:80 and 1985:35–36.
237. Zhonggong nanfangju 1941? 1942?
238. Liu Yongsheng 1980:117–24; Lu Yongli and Liu Zijian 1983:341–44.
239. Zhang Dingcheng and Tan Zhenlin 1981:22; Huang Keyong 1981.
240. Esherick 1975:214–15.
241. Ibid:xviii.
242. Liu Yongsheng 1980:124–30.
243. Lin Jian 1985b:25.
244. Liu Yongsheng 1980:130–32.
245. Huang Jianlan 1986:43.
246. Hu Liangzhong 1987a:505.
247. Lu Sheng 1985a:27.
248. Liu Yongsheng 1980:131.

## MINZHEWAN'GAN (I)

1. Fang Zhichun 1980:1.
2. Ibid:3–7; Shao Shiping et al. 1983 [1945]: 11–12.
3. Shao Shiping et al. 1983 [1945]: 12–13.
4. Zhongguo geming bowuguan 1982:226–29; Fang Zhichun 1980:11–39; Shao Shiping et al. 1983 [1945]: 13–22; Sheng Renxue and Zhang Junxiao 1987:117.
5. Shao Shiping et al. 1983 [1945]: 32–33.
6. Zhongguo geming bowuguan 1982:230–32; Sheng Renxue and Zhang Junxiao 1987:120–23.
7. Fang Zhichun 1980:90–91 and 1981a:163–65; Shao Shiping et al. 1983 [1945]: 34.
8. Shao Shiping et el. 1983 [1945]: 31–35; Zhongguo geming bowuguan 1982:232.
9. Fang Zhichun 1980:90–93; Zhongguo geming bowuguan 1982:233; Gong Chu in *Mingbao yuekan* 99; Huang Zhizhen 1979:308.
10. Fang Zhichun 1981a:173–77; Shao Shiping et al. 1983 [1945]: 33.
11. Shao Shiping et al. 1983 [1945]: 30–31.
12. Su Yu 1982:2–4; Fang Zhichun 1980:93–94; Tu Tongjin 1982:93; Huang Huoqing 1985; Dai Xiangqing et al. 1986:643–44.

13. Liu Ying 1983 [1940]: 191–93; Su Yu 1982:2–4 and 23; Dai Xiangqing et al. 1986:643.

14. Bingzhang Yang 1986:120–21.

15. Su Yu 1982:5–9 and 18–24; Liu Ying 1983 [1940]: 206.

16. In 1973, Zhu De told the Military Academy that the expedition should have gone not north but south (Su Yu 1982:22).

17. Su Yu 1982:3–6 and 13; Tu Tongjin 1982:95; Dai Xiangqing et al. 1986:644–45; Zhonggong Ningde diwei dangshi zhengbianwei 1986:38–39; Cheng Meixing 1982:26.

18. Su Yu 1982:6–8; Chen Ting 1983b:27–28; Zhonggong Ningde diwei dangshi zhengbianwei 1986:38–39.

19. Xue Zongyao and Wang Nianzu 1985:47–48.

20. Yue Shaohua 1983:265.

21. Zhonggong Ningde diwei dangshi zhengbianwei 1986:44–48; Chen Ting 1983b:27–30.

22. Yue Shaohua 1983:265; Su Yu 1982:8–9; Chen Ting 1983b:29–31.

23. Su Yu 1982:8–9; Xue Zongyao and Wang Nianzu 1985:48–49.

24. Ye Fei 1987a:326.

25. Yue Shaohua 1983:272; Su Yu 1982:3–15.

26. Gong Chu in *Mingbao yuekan* 99; Yang Ziyao 1986, pt. 2:49; Wang Jianying 1986a:71.

27. Su Yu 1982:15–16; Fang Zhichun 1980:94–95; Xu Zhanquan 1987:597–98.

28. Bingzhang Yang 1986:118–20; Wang Jianming 1965, pt. 2:623–24; Miao Min 1958:83–89; Miao Chuhuang 1954:85–86; Shao Jiang and Qiao Xinming 1958:113–15; Su Yu 1982:18–19; Fang Zhichun 1980:95.

29. Miao Min 1958:83–89; Wang Jianming 1965, pt. 2:623–24; Miao Chuhuang 1954:85–86; Su Yu 1982:19–21; Li Buxin et al. 1981:192; Liu Xiangyun 1954:81.

30. Benton 1985 and 1986.

31. Ye Fei 1983a, pt. 2:3.

32. H. 1936:68–71.

33. Shao Jiang and Qiao Xinming 1958:119–20; H. 1936:68–71; "Fang Zhimin zhuan" 1982:266–77; Fang Zhichun 1980:96.

34. Long Yue 1984:51.


ZHE'NAN: WALKING ON TWO LEGS

1. Gong Chu in *Mingbao yuekan* 99.

2. Su Yu 1982:16.

3. Wu Kebin 1984:167 says February 4. Liu Xiangyun 1954:81–82; Su Yu 1984:2–3; Zhang Wenbi 1981:2; Jiti mantan 1981:153; Xuan Enjin 1983:530.

4. Zhejiang sheng junqu dangshi ziliao zhengji bangongshi 1987:230.

5. Huang Shumeng and Zhang Jichang 1984:268–69.

6. Liu Ying 1983 [1940]: 208; Zhang Wenbi 1981:5; Li Ziping 1983:68.

7. Wu Kebin 1984:168–78.

8. Xuan Enjin 1983:531; Huang Zhizhen 1983:426; Su Yu 1984:2–3; Jiti mantan 1981:155.

9. Wu Kebin 1984:182–83; Yu Longgui 1979:32.

10. Liu Xiangyun 1954:82; Wu Kebin 1984:169–70 and 183; Zhang Wenbi 1981:7–8; Long Yue et al. 1983:162–63; Xuan Enjin 1983:530; Su Yu 1984:2–9.

11. Cheng Meixing 1984:262; Yu Longgui 1979:33 and 39 and 1984:109–10; Wu Kebin 1984:168–69.

12. Liu Ying 1983 [1940]: 214; Yu Longgui 1984:108–13; Cheng Meixing 1984:262.

13. Liu Ying 1983 [1940]: 214; Wu Kebin 1984:182–84; Zhejiang sheng junqu dangshi ziliao zhengji lingdao xiaozu 1984:2–4; Su Yu 1984:7–9; Xuan Enjin 1983:532.

14. Cheng Meixing 1982:31.

15. Su Yu 1984:9–11; Hatano Ken'ichi 1961, vol. 5:44; Wu Kebin 1984: 183–84.

16. Huang Shaoxiong 1945:297–98; Zhang Wenbi 1981:8.

17. Wu Kebin 1984:189–90; Su Yu 1984:2; Huang Shumeng and Zhang Jichang 1984:269; Jiti mantan 1981:153.

18. Liu Ying 1983 [1940]: 220; Wu Kebin 1984:170–72; Su Yu 1984:9–11.

19. Wang Fan-hsi 1980:118.

20. Su Yu 1984:9–12; Zhejiang sheng junqu dangshi ziliao zhengji lingdao xiaozu 1984:4; Wu Kebin 1984:171–72; Xuan Enjin 1983:535–37; Yu Longgui 1979:56; Zhou Yijin 1986:2.

21. Wu Kebin 1984:170–74 and 184; Su Yu 1984:12–14; Zhang Wenbi 1981:7–9; Xuan Enjin 1983:537; Zhejiang sheng junqu dangshi ziliao zhengji bangongshi 1987:236; Huang Shumeng and Zhang Jichang 1984:270.

22. Liu Ying 1983 [1940]: 227; Long Yue et al. 1983:163; Su Yu 1984:13–14; Wu Kebin 1984:172–73; Zhang Wenbi 1981:8–9; Jiti mantan 1981:153–54.

23. Wu Kebin 1984:173–74; Su Yu 1984:13–14; Xuan Enjin 1983:533–39.

24. Liu Ying 1983 [1940]: 220; Ye Fei 1987a:337; Xuan Enjin 1983:537–40; Su Yu 1988:165.

25. Xuan Enjin 1983:543–52; Su Yu 1984:14–16.

26. Zhang Renyuan 1958:195–201.

27. Liu Xiangyun 1954:83; Xuan Enjin 1983:545; Wu Kebin 1984:174–75.

28. Long Yue 1984:47–48.

29. Wu Kebin 1984:175; Jiti mantan 1981:154.

30. Long Yue et al. 1983:163; Su Yu 1984:26.

31. Wu Kebin 1984:173; Su Yu 1984:16; Zhang Wenbi 1981:9.

32. Su Yu 1984:17; Ye Fei 1987a:338; Ye Dabing 1982:1–6 and 136; Wu Kebin 1984:186; Junshi kexueyuan 1987, vol. 1:70–71.

33. Renmin chubanshe 1953 [1945]: 53; Zhongguo geming bowuguan 1982:301.

34. Wu Kebin 1984:166 and 181.

35. Long Yue 1984:44; Liu Ying 1983 [1940]: 253.

36. Zhejiang sheng junqu dangshi ziliao zhengji lingdao xiaozu 1984:2; Wu Kebin 1984:182.

37. Su Yu 1984:17.

38. Wu Kebin 1984:174–75.

39. Huang Shumeng and Zhang Jichang 1984:272–73; Lin Huishan 1979:58–59; Huang Xianhe 1979:73.

40. Su Yu 1984:17–18.

41. Zhang Wenbi 1981:17.

42. Wu Kebin 1984:191.

43. Wu Kebin 1984:187–89; Su Yu 1984:20–25; Liu Ying 1983 [1940]: 256; Jiti mantan 1981:154; Zhejiang sheng junqu dangshi ziliao zhengji bangongshi 1987:240–42.

44. Mei Jiasheng and Peng Deqing 1986:154.

45. Su Yu 1984:19; Zhang Wenbi 1981:13; Wu Kebin 1984:175.

46. Su Yu 1984:20–25; Long Yue 1984:53; Ni Guozhen 1984?:122–23; Ye Fei 1987a:338.

47. Liu Ying 1983 [1940]: 234; Long Yue 1984:54; Su Yu 1984:19–26; Mei Jiasheng and Peng Deqing 1986:154; Zhejiang sheng junqu dangshi ziliao zhengji bangongshi 1987:244.

48. Long Yue 1984:45–51; Wu Kebin 1984:189; Liu Xian 1987:26.

49. Lin Huishan 1979:62.

50. Huang Xianhe 1979:69; Yang Jin 1981:44–48.

51. Wu Kebin 1984:175–76; Long Yue 1984:46–53; Zhou Yijin 1986:3–4.

52. Wu Kebin 1984:173 and 193–94; Liao Kaizhu, ed., 1986:180; Ye Fei 1987a:337–38.

53. Liu Xiao 1983:54–55; Ye Fei 1984 [1957]: 5–6 and 1987a:339–40.

54. Wu Kebin 1984:193–94; Su Yu 1984:18; Huang Shumeng and Zhang Jichang 1984:275.

55. Wu Kebin 1984:193–94.

56. Ni Guozhen 1982:39–43 and 1984?:82 and 125; Su Yu 1984:18 and 1988:168–69; Liu Ying 1983 [1940]: 220–33; Wu Kebin 1984:193–94; Ye Fei 1987a:337–41.

57. Shao Shiping et al. 1983 [1945]: 41. News of Ye Fei's arrest created a wave of anger back in Mindong. Some Mindong guerrillas wanted to launch an armed attack on the Advance Division. Fortunately for both sides, Ye Fei managed to talk them out of it (Ye Fei 1988:77).

58. Ni Guozhen 1982:42–43; Ye Fei 1984 [1957]: 94–95 and 1987a:337; Su Yu 1988; Mei Jiasheng and Peng Deqing 1986:153; Huang Shumeng and Zhang Jichang 1984:261. According to Klein and Clark (1971:774), Bartke (1981), and others, Su was a native of Fujian, though he spent his childhood in Hunan. If true, this fact might explain Su's inclination to side with Fujian Communists like Ye Fei when they clashed with Liu Ying. But according to Su Yu himself (1988:1), he was born in Huitong in western Hunan; this apparently autobiographical source does not mention any early connection between Su Yu or his family and Fujian, so these reports should probably be discounted.

59. Su Yu 1988:170.

60. Liu Ying 1983 [1940]; Su Yu 1983:25 n.

61. Wu Kebin 1984:193–94; Su Yu 1984:18.

62. Wu Kebin 1984:176; Su Yu 1984:27; Long Yue 1984:54; Li Ziping 1983:72; Yu Longgui 1979:43.

63. Su Yu 1988:181. For a discussion of the "CC Clique," see Pepper 1978:47 n 8.

64. Zhang Wenbi 1981:13–14.

65. Su Yu 1984:23–24 and 28–29; Long Yue 1984:67; Wu Kebin 1984:176–77.

66. Wu Kebin 1984:191–92; Shao Shiping et al. 1983 [1945]: 40; Liu Ying 1983 [1940]: 235.

67. Zhang Wenbi 1981:14–15; Wu Kebin 1984:177; Liu Ying 1983 [1940]: 239 and 251.

68. Su Yu 1984:28–36; Long Yue 1984:57–59; Wu Kebin 1984:178; Long Yue and Wu Yu 1986 [1937]: 18.

69. Su Yu 1988:186.

70. Su Yu 1984:28–35.

71. Long Yue 1984:67.

72. Su Yu 1984:28–34 and 1988:183–84; Long Yue 1984:55–56.

73. Wu Kebin 1984:177; Su Yu 1984:37–38; Yang Jin 1981:46–48; Liu Ying 1983 [1940]: 240; Ye Bingnan 1987:4.

74. Wu Kebin 1984:177–78; Long Yue 1984:60–61; Liu Ying 1983 [1940]: 240.

75. Long Yue and Wu Yu 1986 [1937]: 17–18; Wu Kebin 1984:178; Huang Shumeng and Zhang Jichang 1984:276; Ye Bingnan 1987:4.

76. Huang Shumeng and Zhang Jichang 1984:278.

77. Wu Kebin 1984:178; Long Yue 1984:60–62; cf. Liu Ying 1983 [1940]: 241.

78. Long Yue 1984:63; Wu Kebin 1984:178; Su Yu 1984:37–39.

79. Yu Longgui 1979:47; Su Yu 1984:39.

80. Long Yue 1984:64; Li Ziping 1983:73; Su Yu 1984:39; Wu Kebin 1984:178–79.

81. Huang Shaoxiong 1945:413 and 1987:36–37.

82. Wu Kebin 1984:179; Qiu Qinghua 1984.

83. Shao Shiping et al. 1983 [1945]: 42; Long Yue 1984:65; Su Yu 1984:39–40; Wu Kebin 1984:185; Zhongyang shujichu 1985 [1937].

84. Li Ziping 1983:73–75 and 1984:250–53; Wu Kebin 1984:179 and 185.

85. Shao Shiping et al. 1983 [1945]: 38.

86. Wu Kebin 1984:191.

87. Zhejiang sheng junqu dangshi ziliao zhengji bangongshi 1987:252.

88. Su Yu 1984:41.

89. Wu Kebin 1984:184; Long Yue 1984:66.

90. Liu Ying 1983 [1940]: 254–55.


## MINBEI: THE PARTY AND THE DAO

1. For example, Huang Zhizhen 1983:426.

2. Huang Zhizhen 1983:421; Shao Shiping et al. 1983 [1945]: 21–24.

3. In May 1930, the so-called Northern Coalition of Yan Xishan and Feng Yuxiang went to war against Chiang Kai-shek.

4. Tong Huizhen 1983:109; Chen Qunzhe 1983:123.

5. Shao Shiping et al. 1983 [1945]: 25; Zeng Jingbing 1984 [1958]: 245; Ye Fei 1983a, pt. 1:13; Xue Zizheng 1983b:335.

6. Xue Zizheng 1983b:333; Chen Xueming et al. 1983; Zeng Jingbing 1984 [1958]: 245.

7. Shao Shiping et al. 1983 [1945]: 34; Chen Xueming et al. 1983:285–86.

8. Huang Zhizhen 1979:308; Chen Xueming et al. 1983:285; Chen Renhong 1983b:148.

9. Xue Zizheng 1983b:336; Shao Shiping et al. 1983 [1945]: 34; Huang Zhizhen 1979:309; Tong Huizhen 1983:113–14; Huang Ying 1983:457.

10. Jiti mantan 1981:145; Chen Qunzhe 1983:136–37; Huang Zhizhen 1979:309; Yang Jinfu 1983:518–20; Chen Xueming et al. 1983:287; Tong Huizhen 1983:113.

11. Renmin chubanshe 1953 [1945]: 53; Zhongguo geming bowuguan 1982:301.

12. Huang Ying 1983:456; Chen Renhong 1985a:43.

13. Tong Huizhen 1983:114; Chen Renhong 1983a:20 and 1985a:42–44; Sheng Renxue and Zhang Junxiao 1987:124–25.

14. Liao Kaizhu, ed., 1986:164; Jiti mantan 1981:145; Chen Renhong 1983a:21, 1983b:152–66, and 1985a:44–45.

15. Huang Zhizhen 1983:426; Liu Ying 1983 [1940]: 208; Zhang Wenbi 1981:5.

16. Chen Renhong 1985a:48–49.

17. Huang Zhizhen 1979:309; Jiti mantan 1981:145–46; Long Yue et al. 1983:156.

18. Guofangbu 1967, vol. 3:438; Wang Jianying 1986a:406; Chen Renhong 1985a:52–53; Liu Xiao 1981:2; Liao Kaizhu, ed., 1986:165.

19. Chen Renhong 1985a:49.

20. Jiti mantan 1981:146; Long Yue et al. 1983:157; Ma Changyan 1983:514; Yang Jinfu 1983:520–21; Chen Qunzhe 1983:137; Tong Huizhen 1983:115.

21. Chen Qunzhe 1983:138; Yang Jinfu 1983:520; Zeng Jingbing 1983a:432–33 and 1984 [1958]: 253.

22. Huang Zhizhen 1959:110.

23. Chen Renhong 1985a:51–56.

24. Rao Shoukun 1980:52 and 1983:489–90; Jiti mantan 1981:147; Long Yue et al. 1983:157.

25. Fan Shiren 1984 [1959]: 128; Ye Fei 1983a, pt. 6:22.

26. Liu Xiao 1981:4–5.

27. Jiti mantan 1981:147–50; Chen Qunzhe 1983:140; Chen Xueming et al. 1983:288–89.

28. Zeng Jingbing 1983a:434 and 1984 [1958]: 250.

29. Liu Xiao 1981:5; Chen Renhong 1985a:119–21.

30. Xuan Jintang 1982:38–41; Zhang Liren and Ye Jianzhong 1983:40–44; Huang Ying 1983:454–55; Ni Guozhen 1982:39.

31. Chen Renhong 1985a:106–36.

32. Jiti mantan 1981:149; Xuan Jintang 1983:517; Chen Qunzhe 1983:139.

33. Rao Shoukun 1980:52–53 and 1983:490–91.

34. Rao Shoukun 1980:52–53; Chen Renhong 1985a:99.

35. Chen Xueming et al. 1983:283; Zhang Liren and Ye Jianzhong 1983:41 42; Chen Renhong 1985a:99.

36. Huang Zhizhen 1959:116–18; Rao Shoukun 1980 and 1983; Xuan Jintang 1983:517–18; Chen Qunzhe 1983:139–40; Jiti mantan 1981:149–50.

37. *North China Herald,* January 26, 1936.

38. Rao Shoukun 1980:55–56; Jiti mantan 1981:149 50; Xuan Jintang 1983:518; Chen Qunzhe 1983:139–40.

39. Zeng Jingbing 1983a:430–32 and 1984 [1958]: 256; Huang Ying 1983:457.

40. Chen Renhong 1983a:20.

41. Tong Huizhen 1983:116.

42. Chen Qunzhe 1983; Huang Zhizhen 1979:310; Tong Huizhen 1983: 117–18.

43. Jiti mantan 1981:147.

44. Long Yue et al. 1983:157; Yang Jinfu 1983:521; Zeng Jingbing 1983a:429–30 and 1983b:515; Zhonggong Jianyang 1985:69; Wu Huayou 1982:197–98.

45. Chen Qunzhe 1983:140.

46. Jiti mantan 1981:148.

47. Zeng Jingbing 1983a:432 and 1984 [1958]: 255–57; Chen Renhong 1985a:76.

48. Huang Zhizhen 1979:309–10; Jiti mantan 1981:149; Wu Huayou 1982:198; Chen Qunzhe 1983:139.

49. Zeng Jingbing 1983b.

50. Zheng Fulong 1983:47–49; Liu Xiao 1983:54–55; Chen Renhong 1985a:101.

51. Long Yue et al. 1983:160; Huang Zhizhen 1983:426; Liao Kaizhu, ed., 1986:172.

52. Chen Xueming et al. 1983:291; Jiti mantan 1981:151–52; Long Yue 1983:160–61.

53. *North China Herald,* May 26, 1937.

54. I am indebted to John S. Service for this information about the *North China Herald.*

55. Chen Qunzhe 1983:141; Shao Shiping et al. 1983 [1945]: 40; Rao Shoukun 1980:56–57 and 1983:497–99.

56. Rao Shoukun 1980:56–57 and 1983:498–99; Chen Xueming et al. 1983:292.

57. Long Yue et al. 1983:164; Zeng Jingbing 1983a:435; Chen Qunzhe 1983:141; Tong Huizhen 1983:118.

58. Chen Renhong 1985a:127.

59. Rao Shoukun 1983:498–99.

60. Jiti mantan 1981:155; Wu Huayou 1982:197–205; Long Yue et al. 1983:164.

61. Chen Qunzhe 1983:141–42.

62. Jiti mantan 1981:155–56; Chen Renhong 1985a:127–28.
63. Zeng Jingbing 1983a:435; Wang Wenbo 1983:452; Shao Shiping et al. 1983 [1945]: 40; Kong Yongsong 1986:73.
64. Zeng Jingbing 1983a:436 and 1984 [1958]: 258–59; Wang Wenbo 1983:451.
65. Shao Shiping et al. 1983 [1945]: 40; Zeng Jingbing 1984 [1958]: 259.
66. Zeng Jingbing 1983a:437 and 1984 [1958]: 259; Wang Wenbo 1983:452.
67. Zeng Jingbing 1983a:430.
68. Rao Shoukun 1980:58.
69. Wang Wenbo 1983:451–52.
70. Rao Shoukun 1980:57–58 and 1983:499–500; Chen Xueming et al. 1983:292–93.
71. Liu Xiao 1981:9; Chen Renhong 1985a:130–32.
72. Shao Shiping et al. 1983 [1945]: 40; Ye Fei 1983a, pt. 6:20–21; Huang Zhizhen 1983:427; Zeng Jingbing 1983a:436; Chen Renhong 1985a:133–34 and 1985b:61–62.
73. Huang Zhizhen 1979:311–12.
74. Chen Renhong 1985b:61.
75. See the chapter on Eyuwan.
76. Fan Shiren 1984 [1959]: 128.
77. Huang Ying 1983:457.


## MINDONG: THE WILY HARE

1. Ye Fei 1983c:2 and 1986a, pt. 1.
2. Lan Jiongxi et al. 1984:5; Ye Fei 1988:28.
3. Renmin chubanshe 1953 [1945]: 53; Zhongguo geming bowuguan 1982:302.
4. Shao Shiping et al. 1983 [1945]: 36; Ye Fei 1987a:307.
5. Zheng Chuyun 1984:97.
6. Klein and Clark (1971:1009) wrongly report that Ye Fei helped organize a guerrilla base in Mindong in 1926 (when he would have been twelve years old).
7. Lan Jiongxi et al. 1984:12.
8. Jiti mantan 1981:147–48; Shao Shiping et al. 1983 [1945]: 37–38; Long Yue et al. 1983:158; "Fujian geming jishi" 1985, pt. 3:56–60; Ye Fei 1986a:2–3.
9. Ye Fei 1983a, pt. 1:12 and pts. 4–5:12–14; Lan Jiongxi et al. 1984:19.
10. Zheng Chuyun 1984:98.
11. Dai Xuanzhi 1973:136–37.
12. Zeng Zhi 1982:1.
13. Ye Fei 1986a, pt. 1:4.
14. Ye Fei 1987a:316–18 and 1988:42. The name "Red Belts" was not new; sects went by it even before the arrival of Ye and Fan.
15. Zeng Zhi 1982:1.
16. Chen Ting 1982a:22–24 and 1984:169–70.
17. Ye Fei 1986a, pt. 1:4; Zeng Zhi 1982:1; Chen Ting 1982b:5 and 1984:141.
18. Ni Guozhen 1982:31; Ye Fei 1987a:317; Zeng Zhi 1982:1.

19. Fan Shiren 1982:64–73; Ni Guozhen 1982:26 and 1984?:34–35; Chen Songqing 1986:51; Chen Ting 1984:142; Lan Jiongxi et al. 1984:15.

20. Chen Ting 1984:141; Ye Fei 1987a.

21. Ye Fei 1987a:316.

22. Yue Shaohua 1983:265; Ni Guozhen 1984?:82.

23. Fan Shiren 1984 [1959]: 99.

24. Ye Fei 1986a, pt. 1:2–3.

25. Shao Shiping et al. 1983 [1945]: 38; Chen Yunfei 1983:45. In the winter of 1934, the Mindong Special Committee sent Su Da to Shanghai to establish links to the Party center, but he failed to return (Ye Fei 1988:53).

26. Shao Shiping et al. 1983 [1945]: 38.

27. Ye Fei 1986a, pt. 1:5–6, 1987a:307, and 1988:49–56; Chen Songqing 1986:51; Ni Guozhen 1982:26; Deng Jiakun et al. 1984:40–44; Lan Jiongxi et al. 1984:30.

28. Zhonggong Ningde diwei dangshi zhengbianwei 1986:44.

29. Shao Shiping et al. 1983 [1945]: 38; Ye Fei 1986a, pt. 1:6; Xue Zongyao and Wang Nianzu 1985:48.

30. Fan Shiren 1982:73; Shao Shiping et al. 1983 [1945]: 38; Chen Ting 1983b:32; Han Shirui and Hu Guhua 1986:40; Wang Jianying 1986a:409; Ni Guozhen 1982:26.

31. Ye Fei 1986a, pt. 2:11.

32. Xue Zongyao and Wang Nianzu 1985:47–48.

33. Zhonggong Ningde diwei dangshi zhengbianwei 1986:45.

34. Fan Shiren 1984 [1959]: 197.

35. Ye Fei 1987a:326 says one hundred.

36. Lan Jiongxi et al. 1984:38; Yang Caiheng 1982:84; Xue Zongyao and Wang Nianzu 1985:48.

37. Shao Shiping et al. 1983 [1945]: 37–38; Chen Yunfei 1983:42–45; Yang Caiheng 1983:133; Deng Jiakun et al. 1984:44.

38. Ye Fei 1984b:1–2 and 1984 [1957]: 92.

39. Cheng Meixing 1982:27; Zheng Danpu 1983:65.

40. Fan Shiren 1984 [1959]: 107.

41. Ye Fei 1984b:7–8 and 1983a, pt. 2:6–11 and pt. 3:13; Lan Jiongxi et al. 1984:72; Ni Guozhen 1984?: 112; Fan Shiren 1984 [1959]: 119; Han Shirui and Hu Guhua 1986:42.

42. Chen Ting 1983a:5 and 1984:158; Ye Fei 1986a, pt. 2:14.

43. Ye Fei 1984b:6; Qiu Jiming 1984:8. Ye Fei's opinion of Ma Lifeng is less flattering than that held by Ma's official biographers. According to Ye, Ma had prestige but little ability; his main strengths were modesty and obedience to the Party (Ye Fei 1983a, pt. 1:8–9).

44. Qiu Jiming 1985:279–80; Liao Kaizhu, ed., 1986:178.

45. Chen Ting 1982a:22; Fan Shiren 1984 [1959]: 103.

46. Even natives of Mindong who left the region to study rarely traveled any further than Fuzhou (Ye Fei 1988:29).

47. Ye Fei 1983a, pt. 6:17 and 1988:1–7.

48. Chen Ting 1982a:24 and 1984:171.

49. Ye Fei 1986a, pt. 2:11; Chen Songqing 1986:49–50; Ni Guozhen 1984:31.

50. Zhuo Hongpo et al. 1986:43–44.
51. Ye Fei 1983a, pt. 1:14 and 1983c:3.
52. Chen Ting 1982a:22.
53. Selden 1971:40 and 69ff.
54. Ye Fei 1983c:2, 1984b:1–2 and 1987a:306–7; Yang Ziyao 1986, pt. 1:63.
55. Ye Fei 1984b:1.
56. Ye Fei 1987a:307; Chen Ting 1982a:24.
57. Ye Fei 1983a, pt. 2:11–12.
58. Ye Fei 1983b:17; Fan Shiren 1984 [1959]: 105–6; Lan Jiongxi et al. 1984:36.
59. Lin Jian 1986:64–65; Liao Kaizhu, ed., 1986:182; Zhonggong Lianjiang 1986; Shi Yan 1986:122; Fan Shiren 1984 [1959]: 105–6.
60. For example, Dreyer 1976:63–92.
61. Cf. Fei Hsiao Tong 1981:22.
62. Guojia minwei 1981:12, 454, and 555–56.
63. "Shezu jianshi" 1980:1; Ye Fei 1986a, pt. 3:18 and 1987a:343. According to the 1982 census, 80 percent of Fujian's 168,176 Shes live in Mindong.
64. Miao Cichao 1983:32; "Shezu jianshi" 1980:54–55.
65. Miao Cichao 1983:33; Ye Fei 1984 [1957]: 95 and 1986a:18; Zhongyang minzu 1974:23; "Shezu jianshi" 1980:63–68.
66. Shi Lianzhu 1987:18–19; Luo Meizhen 1987:314.
67. Miao Cichao 1983:33.
68. Ye Fei 1986a:18.
69. Ye Fei 1986a:18; Zhong Chenkun 1982:86–88; Li Jipeng et al. 1982:37; "Shezu jianshi" 1980:72–74.
70. Zhong Chenkun 1982:87–88.
71. Guojia minwei 1981:567; "Shezu jianshi" 1980:74–75 and 97.
72. Fan Shiren 1984 [1959]: 128.
73. Zhong Chenkun 1982:87.
74. Guojia minwei 1981:571; "Shezu jianshi" 1980:66 and 104–5; Miao Cichao 1983:34.
75. Ye Fei 1986a, pt. 1:5 and pt. 2:12; Han Shirui and Hu Guhua 1986:40; "Fujian geming" 1985, pt. 5:61; Sun Liming 1984:40.
76. Ye Fei 1984b:2 and 1986a, pt. 2:12; Ni Guozhen 1984?: 106.
77. Chen Ting 1983a:4 and 1983b:32; Ye Fei 1984b:2; Lan Jiongxi et al. 1984:54–55.
78. Ni Guozhen 1982:31; Lan Jiongxi et al. 1984:59–60.
79. Chen Ting 1983a:4.
80. Ye Fei 1987a:327–28.
81. Lan Jiongxi et al. 1984:63.
82. Zhonggong Ningde diwei dangshi zhengbianwei 1986:38–39; Ye Fei 1983c:2.
83. Ye Fei 1984b:1–6, 1984 [1957]: 93, and 1986a, pt. 2:12–13; Ni Guozhen 1982:31; Li Jipeng et al. 1982:32; "Fujian geming" 1985, pt. 5:61; Chen Ting 1984:154.
84. Chen Ting 1984:157; Ye Fei 1987a:330.
85. Li Jipeng et al. 1982:33–34; Chen Ting 1983a:5, 1983b:33–36, and 1984:155–58; Ye Fei 1984b:6–7 and 1986a, pt. 2:14; Ni Guozhen 1982:33.

86. Ye Fei 1983a, pt. 3:4.

87. Lin Jian 1986:64–65.

88. Chen Zhengfang and Zhang Ruizhe 1984:131–36; Yan Jingtang 1986:47–49; "Fujian geming" 1985, pt. 3:57–60.

89. Chen Yunfei 1983; Yang Caiheng 1983:133; Yan Jingtang 1986:48–49; Lan Jiongxi et al. 1984:70–71; Ni Guozhen 1982:33.

90. Liao Kaizhu, ed., 1986:188–89; "Fujian geming" 1985, pt. 5:63; Jiang Fengbo and Xu Zhanquan 1989:536.

91. Liao Kaizhu, ed., 1986:179; Lan Jiongxi et al. 1984:77; Ye Fei 1986a, pt. 2:14.

92. Ye Fei 1986a, pt. 2:14 and 1987a:332–33; Chen Ting 1983a:7–8 and 1984:161; Ni Guozhen 1982:37.

93. *North China Herald,* January 29, 1936.

94. Liao Kaizhu, ed., 1986:182; Li Jipeng et al. 1982:36; Ye Fei 1987a:336; Fan Shiren 1984 [1959]: 116.

95. Ni Guozhen 1984:35; Fan Shiren 1984 [1959]: 104–17.

96. Chen Ting 1983a:9–11; Fan Shiren 1984 [1959]: 116; Lan Jiongxi et al. 1984:77 and 82; Sun Liming 1984:45; Liao Kaizhu, ed., 1986:179; Ye Fei 1987a:336.

97. Sun Liming 1984: 44–45; Ni Guozhen 1984:35.

98. Ni Guozhen 1982:35–36; Fan Shiren 1984 [1959]: 117.

99. Ni Guozhen 1982:35; Chen Ting 1982a:23–24 and 1984:171; Li Jipeng et al. 1982:35.

100. Fan Shiren 1984 [1959]: 127; Ye Fei 1984 [1957]: 94.

101. After 1935, Ye Fei ceded Fuding (in Fujian) and Pingyang (in Zhejiang) to the Liu-Su Advance Division (Ye Fei 1987a:338).

102. Ye Fei 1983a, pts. 4–5:19 and 1987a:333–39; Ni Guozhen 1984:35 and 1984?: 122–23; Chen Ting 1982a:24 and 1984:171.

103. Chen Ting 1983a:8–9.

104. Han Shirui and Hu Guhua 1986; Zhong Chenkun 1982:86–87.

105. Ni Guozhen 1982:39 and 1984?: 82 and 126.

106. Liao Kaizhu, ed., 1986:178 and 183; Lan Jiongxi et al. 1984:92–94; Ni Guozhen 1982:39; Ye Fei 1984b:7–8 and 1984 [1957]: 95; Fan Shiren 1984 [1959]: 115–19.

107. Shao Shiping et al. 1983 [1945]: 40.

108. Sheng Renxue and Zhang Junxiao 1987; Ye Fei 1984a:3 and 1987a:346.

109. Fan Shiren 1983:167; Liao Kaizhu, ed., 1986:184; Ni Guozhen 1982:42; Ye Fei 1984a:1–3; Zeng Jingbing 1983a:435.

110. Liao Kaizhu, ed., 1986:184–86; Ni Guozhen 1984:35 (which wrongly says that the August First Manifesto reached Mindong in the winter of 1935); Ye Fei 1984a:3 and 1987a:345.

111. Ye Fei 1984a:3–4, 1984 [1957]: 96, and 1987a:346.

112. Liao Kaizhu, ed., 1986:183; Ni Guozhen 1982:41.

113. Fan Shiren 1983:168; Jiti mantan 1981:155; Ye Fei 1986a:18; Ni Guozhen 1982:44–45.

114. Ye Fei 1983a, pts. 4–5:3.

115. Ye Fei 1984a.

116. Chen Ting 1983a:11; Ye Fei 1984a:4.

117. Ye Fei 1984a:5–6.

118. Ibid; Anonymous 1986b:63; Ni Guozhen 1982:45.

119. Kong Yongsong 1986:73; Ye Fei 1983a, pt. 6:11–13 and 1984a:5–7.

120. Anonymous 1986b:63; Fan Shiren 1984 [1959]: 122; Ni Guozhen 1984:34.

121. Ni Guozhen 1982:45; Liao Kaizhu, ed., 1986:185; Zhuo Hongpo 1986:43–44; Ye Fei 1984 [1957]: 96.

122. Ye Fei 1984a:9 and 1987a:347; Ni Guozhen 1982:44–45.

123. Ye Fei 1983a, pt. 6:14, 1986a, pt. 3:21, and 1987a:351.

124. Fan Shiren 1983:172–73; Ye Fei 1987a:350.

125. Ye Fei 1984a:9 and 1987a:348–50; Ni Guozhen 1982:44–46; Kong Yongsong 1986:73.

126. Ni Guozhen 1984?: 147; Wang Jianying 1986a:410.

127. Ye Fei 1983a, pt. 1:14 and 1983c:3; Fan Shiren 1983:173.

128. Ye Fei 1983a, pt. 6:21, 1984 [1957]: 97, and 1987a:350; Zhou Xiaojun 1982:50; Fan Shiren 1984 [1959]: 125–26.

129. Fan Shiren 1983:173; Ye Fei 1984a:9–10 and 1987a:350; Zhuo Hongpo 1986:42.

130. Ye Fei 1984 [1957]: 95; Huang Chuiming 1986:11.

131. Ye Fei 1984 [1957]: 97; Ni Guozhen 1984?: 142; Huang Chuiming 1986:15.

132. Ye Fei 1984a:1–2.

133. Yang Caiheng 1985a:59–62; Jiang Weidan 1985:41–43.

134. Yang Caiheng 1985a:61–62; Jiang Weidan 1985:43–44; Lin Jian 1985a:21.

135. Jiang Weidan 1985:43–44.

136. Kong Yongsong 1986:71.

137. Yang Caiheng 1983:134–38; Liu Jimin and Song Enfu 1985:349; Liao Kaizhu, ed., 1986:217.

138. Shao Shiping et al. 1983 [1945]: 38.

139. Chen Ting 1982a:23–24 and 1984:171; Ye Fei 1984 [1957]: 97.

140. Yang Caiheng 1983:134.

141. Yang Caiheng 1985b:17–18.

142. Lan Jiongxi et al. 1984:1–3.


## WANZHEGAN: GATHERING THE FRAGMENTS

1. Li Buxin et al. 1981:188; Xu Zhanquan 1987:596.

2. Renmin chubanshe 1953 [1945]: 53; Zhongguo geming bowuguan 1982:301.

3. Li Buxin et al. 1983:463–73; Ni Nanshan 1980:81–85; Su Yu 1982:12.

4. Ni Nanshan 1980:85–87.

5. Shao Shiping et al. 1983 [1945]; 26–35; Nie Hongjun 1983:345; Li Buxin et al. 1983:468–69.

6. Su Yu 1982:3–12.

7. Li Buxin et al. 1983:469; Nie Hongjun 1983:346.

8. Jiti mantan 1981:142–44; Long Yue et al. 1983:154.

9. Jiti mantan 1981:143; Li Buxin et al. 1983:469–70.

10. Zou Zhicheng 1983:527–29.

11. Long Yue et al. 1983:153–54; Li Buxin et al. 1981:193–94; Zhang Yangui and Yuan Wei 1987:401–3; Fang Zhichun 1980:97.

12. Guan Jie, ed., 1980.

13. Fu Xueyuan 1958:184–94.

14. Li Buxin et al. 1983:468–72; Long Yue et al. 1983:154; Jiti mantan 1981:143–44; Ni Nanshan 1980; Zhonggong Anhui 1987:148.

15. Jiti mantan 1981:142–43; Li Buxin et al. 1983:467–68; Zhang Yangui and Yuan Wei 1987:401–3; Huang Ying 1985:3.

16. Jiti mantan 1981:143–44; Sheng Renxue and Zhang Junxiao 1987:194; Li Buxin et al. 1983:469–76; Zhang Yangui and Yuan Wei 1987:401–3; Long Yue et al. 1983:154; Zhonggong Anhui 1987:148.

17. Li Buxin et al. 1981:188 and 205–11; Long Yue et al. 1983:154–55; Ni Nanshan 1983:522; Xu Zhanquan 1987:598.

18. Li Buxin et al. 1983:480–85; Xu Zhanquan 1987:598; Ni Nanshan 1982:15–16 and 1983:525–26; Hong Da 1986:22–24; Zou Zhicheng 1983:527.

19. Li Buxin et al. 1983:484–86; Ni Nanshan 1982:16 and 1983:525; Zhang Hai 1986:22.

20. Shao Shiping et al. 1983 [1945]: 40; Zou Zhicheng 1983:527–28; Ni Nanshan 1982:25; Liu Jimin and Song Enfu 1985:345; Li Buxin et al. 1983:486–88.

21. According to Yu Longgui (1979:48), Guan Ying also refused to negotiate and killed Party representatives who tried to persuade him to do so.

22. Ni Nanshan 1982:22–24; Yu Maoji et al. 1985:15; Chen Yi 1986 [1940]: 122.

23. Hong Da 1986:25–26.

24. Ni Nanshan 1983:525–26; Zou Zhicheng 1983:527.

## MINZHEWAN'GAN (II)

1. Su Yu 1982:23.

2. Shao Shiping et al. 1983 [1945]: 43.

3. Ye Fei 1987a:342.

4. Zhonggong Minzhegan 1937.

5. Shao Shiping et al. 1983 [1945]: 38–41.

6. The Nationalist General Liu Jianxu was still planning campaigns of re-settlement and pacification in Minzhewan'gan as late as June 1937 (Jiang Fengbo and Xu Zhanquan 1989:645).

7. Jiti mantan 1981:158–59.

## EYUWAN: THE ONE-ARMED GENERAL

1. Hubei "Eyuwan" 1987:172.

2. Renmin chubanshe 1953 [1945]: 53; Zhongguo geming bowuguan 1982:301.

3. Zhongguo geming bowuguan 1982:192, 197, and 214.

4. McColl 1967.

5. Chang Kuo-t'ao 1971, vol. 2:170–71.

6. McColl 1967:41.

7. Guo Buyun 1980:11.

8. Guo Buyun 1980:11; "Eyuwan suqu" 1983:4; Guo Yuzhong and Xu Li 1984:31–33.

9. McColl 1967:41–60.

10. Yu Ji'nan 1982:100–110; Chang Kuo-t'ao 1971, vol. 2:131–32 and 226–28; Guo Yuzhong and Xu Li 1984:31; Klein and Clark 1971:39–41.

11. "Eyuwan suqu" 1983:233ff.

12. Lin Weixian 1982:15–16; Jiang Kangmei 1983:73; Hou Zhiying et al. 1982:49; Li Yongchun and Heng Xueming 1985:407; He Shijie and Peng Xing 1986:21.

13. Haitian chubanshe, eds., 1935, vol. 3:338–43.

14. He Shijie and Peng Xing 1986:21; Hou Zhiying et al. 1982:49; Lin Weixian 1982:15–16.

15. When the child's father paid the ransom, the boy asked to be allowed to stay on with the Red Army. At first Gao refused, but he eventually gave in. The boy spied for the Reds before he was finally caught and killed.

16. Lin Weixian 1979?: 223 and 1982:16; Wu Xiuying et al. 1984:47; Jiang Kangmei 1983:73.

17. Hou Zhiying et al. 1982:49; Lin Weixian 1982:16; He Shijie and Peng Xing 1986:21; Li Jiwen 1983:18.

18. Hou Zhiying et al. 1982:50; Guangshan 1983:2.

19. Guangshan 1983:7; Li Jiwen 1983:18–19; Li Shian et al. 1982:75; Luo Yingchen 1984:60; Lin Weixian 1984b:75.

20. See the section "Terms."

21. Hou Zhiying et al. 1982:49; Lin Weixian 1982:273–76.

22. "Eyuwan suqu" 1983:134; Mei Shaoqing 1982a:2–3.

23. Klein and Clark 1971:158–59.

24. Ni Zhongwen 1983:9.

25. "Eyuwan suqu" 1983:14–38.

26. For example, Zhang Lin 1982:38ff.

27. Snow 1968:297.

28. Ni Zhongwen 1983:8–10.

29. Isaacs 1961:222, quoted in McColl 1967:47; Guo Yuzhong and Xu Li 1984:32–34.

30. "Eyuwan suqu" 1983:33.

31. Xu Xiangqian 1984:73–78; Chang Kuo-t'ao 1971, vol. 2:240–41; Ni Zhongwen 1983:9–10.

32. Mei Shaoqing 1982a:3–9; Xu Xiangqian 1984:73–115; Zhongguo geming bowuguan 1982:211–16; "Eyuwan suqu" 1983:72ff.

33. "Eyuwan suqu" 1983:160ff.; Zhongguo geming bowuguan 1982:213–14.

34. Yu Ji'nan 1982:133–46; Chang Kuo-t'ao 1971, vol. 2:201, 219, and 256–57; Mei Shaoqing 1982a:9; Xu Xiangqian 1984:155–57; Kuo 1968–71, vol. 2:428; Tan Kesheng and Ouyang Zhiliang, eds., 1987:217ff.

35. Xu Xiangqian 1984:159–60; Hou Zhiying et al. 1982:50; Guo Yuzhong and Xu Li 1984:34; Hubei "Eyuwan" 1987:173–75; Bingzhang Yang 1986:73.

36. Zhongguo geming bowuguan 1982:214–15; Chang Kuo-t'ao 1971, vol. 2:277ff.; "Eyuwan suqu" 1983:171ff.

37. "Eyuwan suqu" 1983:215ff.; Mei Shaoqing 1982a:15–16; Yu Ji'nan 1982:169; Guo Yuzhong and Xu Li 1984:34.

38. Mei Shaoqing 1982a:16–17; Hou Zhiying et al. 1982:50; Yu Ji'nan 1982:167; Liu Huaqing 1982:38; Zhongguo geming bowuguan 1982:215; "Eyuwan suqu" 1983:231ff.

39. Liu Huaqing 1982.

40. Chang Kuo-t'ao 1971, vol. 2:464.

41. "Eyuwan suqu" 1983:233; Mei Shaoqing 1982a:16; Liu Huaqing 1982:38.

42. "Eyuwan suqu" 1983:232; Yu Ji'nan 1982:169; Mei Shaoqing 1982a:19; Hubei "Eyuwan" 1987:176.

43. Mei Shaoqing 1982a:16.

44. "Eyuwan suqu" 1983:239–50; Whitson 1973:277; Hou Zhiying et al. 1982:50.

45. "Eyuwan suqu" 1983:244–80.

46. Hatano Ken'ichi 1961, vol. 4:407–8.

47. Hou Zhiying et al. 1982:51.

48. "Eyuwan suqu" 1983:238–47; Hou Zhiying et al. 1982:50–51.

49. Ni Zhongwen 1983:9.

50. Snow 1968:298–303; He Yaobang 1959:221; Li Zhaochun 1985:97.

51. "Eyuwan suqu" 1983:272–86.

52. Ibid:287; Zhang Lin 1982:154; Snow 1968:298; Lin Weixian 1984a:1.

53. Wang Shaochuan 1984:159; Ni Zhongwen 1983:11–12; Yu Ge 1980:7; Lin Weixian 1982:7–12.

54. Snow 1968:300–301; Hou Zhiying et al. 1982:51.

55. Lin Weixian 1982:18–20; "Eyuwan suqu" 1983:291.

56. "Eyuwan suqu" 1983:288–89.

57. Tang Yuewu 1984; Li Zhengqing 1984.

58. Yu Ge 1980:8; Xu Qichang 1981:218–19.

59. "Eyuwan suqu" 1983:289.

60. Shi Yuqing 1981:277–88; Yu Ge 1980:8; Zhonggong Shangcheng 1981:84–86; "Eyuwan suqu" 1983:289; Chen Xiang 1980:151–52.

61. Gao Enxian 1987:117–19; Wang Hao 1984.

62. Renmin chubanshe 1953 [1945]: 53.

63. Kang Jian 1985; Niu Desheng 1983:36; Zhou Junming 1983; Li Zijian 1986; Wuhan yexiao n.d.:25; Quan Zhongyu 1985; Shi Yan et al. 1981:75–78; Hou Zhiying et al. 1982:58–59.

64. Sun Baosheng 1986:58; Xu Zhanquan 1987:606; Lin Weixian 1984a:1.

65. Xu Qichang 1981:219; "Eyuwan suqu" 1983:290–91.

66. Xu Qichang 1981:219–21; "Eyuwan suqu" 1983:291; He Yaobang 1959:76ff.; Chen Xiang 1980:150.

67. Hou Zhiying et al. 1982:51.

68. Mei Shaoqing 1982a:24; "Eyuwan suqu" 1983:292–93.

69. Sun Baosheng 1986:58; "Eyuwan suqu" 1983:297–98; Jiang Kangmei 1983:74.

70. He Shijie and Peng Xing 1986:23; Mei Shaoqing 1982a:24–25.

71. Lin Weixian 1984a:4; Hou Zhiying et al. 1982:51–52; "Eyuwan suqu" 1983:298.

72. Chen Xiang 1980:148–49; Lin Weixian 1987:489.

73. "Eyuwan suqu" 1983:297–98; Zhongyang diaocha tongjiju 1940:2.

74. Mei Shaoqing 1982a:25–26; "Eyuwan suqu" 1983:299–301; Hou Zhiying et al. 1982:52.

75. "Eyuwan suqu" 1983:301–2; Hou Zhiying et al. 1982:52.

76. Zhan Huayu 1984:95; Mei Shaoqing 1982a:26–28.

77. He Yaobang 1959:71–74; Lin Weixian 1982:90; Jiang Kangmei 1983:75; Zhan Huayu 1984:95:"Eyuwan suqu" 1983:302–4; Mei Shaoqing 1982a:28.

78. Sun Baosheng 1986:59; Lin Weixian 1979?: 224; Zhu Guodong 1984:148.

79. Mei Shaoqing 1982a:31; He Yaobang 1959:71.

80. "Eyuwan suqu" 1983:309–14.

81. Tan Kesheng and Ouyang Zhiliang, eds., 1987:532; Hou Zhiying et al. 1982:53; Lin Weixian 1982:149–50; Boorman and Howard 1967–71, vol. 3:405.

82. He Shijie and Peng Xing 1986:24.

83. Mei Shaoqing 1982a:29 and 1987:484.

84. "Eyuwan suqu" 1983:293.

85. Wu Xiuying et al. 1984:51-52; He Yaobang 1959:211ff. and 262–96.

86. Wang Zhongyan 1984:196–202; He Yaobang 1959:269–303; "Eyuwan suqu" 1983:318–21.

87. Hou Zhiying et al. 1982:53.

88. Xu Zhanquan 1987:607; *China Weekly Review,* April 4, 1936; "Eyuwan suqu" 1983:323–27.

89. "Eyuwan suqu" 1983:324; Hou Zhiying et al. 1982:53.

90. *China Weekly Review,* April 4, 1936.

91. Tan Kesheng and Ouyang Zhiliang, eds., 1987:523ff.; Hou Zhiying et al. 1982:53; Lin Weixian 1982:226; "Eyuwan suqu" 1983:324–28; Jiang Kangmei 1983:76; Zhonggong Lu'an 1987:262.

92. Xu Qichang 1981:220–31; Yu Ge 1980:8.

93. Tan Kesheng and Ouyang Zhiliang, eds., 1987:443; Lin Weixian 1984a:10–11; Li Zhaochun 1985:98.

94. Jiang Kangmei 1983:78; Hou Zhiying et al. 1982:55–56; He Yaobang 1959:71 and 326; Ni Zhongwen 1983:12.

95. Lin Weixian 1982:114 and 1984a:12.

96. Tan Kesheng and Ouyang Zhiliang, eds., 1987:561–68; "Eyuwan suqu" 1983:304–6 and 328–30; Lin Weixian 1982:113 and 1984a:10–12; Xu Qichang 1981:226; Hou Zhiying et al. 1982:55–56; Yu Ge 1980:8; Zhonggong Lu'an 1987:245–48 and 258–62; Hongan xian 1987:290–94.

97. Zheng Weisan 1982 [1941]: 136; Lin Weixian 1982:115 and 1984a:10–12; Jiang Kangmei 1983:78; Hou Zhiying et al. 1982:55–56; "Eyuwan suqu" 1983:328–30; Tan Kesheng and Ouyang Zhiliang, eds., 1987:555ff.

98. Strong 1965:132–33; Smedley 1944:330; Perry 1980:208; Junshi kexue-yuan 1987, vol. 1:51.

99. "Eyuwan suqu" 1983:276–96; Lin Weixian 1984a:13–14.

100. Jiang Kangmei 1983:79; Hou Zhiying et al. 1982:53–56; Li Shian et al. 1982:69–70; Yu Ge 1980:8; Xu Qichang 1981:227–28; Wu Xiuying et al. 1984:47–48; Lin Weixian 1979?: 224; Sun Baosheng 1986:61.

101. Li Shian et al. 1982:70–71; Lin Weixian 1984a:15.

102. Li Shian et al. 1982:59–60; Lin Weixian 1984a:11; Hou Zhiying et al. 1982:54.

103. Li Shian and Zhang Guoan 1984:86.

104. Hou Zhiying et al. 1982:54–55; Li Shian et al. 1982:60–65; "Eyuwan suqu" 1983:317; Lin Weixian 1984a:7–8; Guangshan 1983:10.

105. Hou Zhiying et al. 1982:54–55; "Eyuwan suqu" 1983:314–25; Li Shian et al. 1982:61; Lin Weixian 1984a:9.

106. Ni Zhongwen 1983:12.

107. "Eyuwan suqu" 1983:281–82; Hou Zhiying et al. 1982:52.

108. Ni Zhongwen 1983:56.

109. Jiang Kangmei 1983:77; He Yaobang 1959:342–44.

110. Li Jiwen 1983:19.

111. "Eyuwan suqu" 1983:307–8.

112. Lin Weixian 1982:205–6; Zhu Guodong 1984:149; Li Shian and Zhang Guoan 1984:93; Hou Zhiying et al. 1982:56–57; He Yaobang 1959:271–91; "Eyuwan suqu" 1983:316 and 326.

113. Sun Baosheng 1986:62.

114. Liu Gangfu 1983:9; He Shijie and Peng Xing 1986:24; Guangshan 1983:2–4.

115. Zhang Xiangbing 1981:38; Sun Baosheng 1986:62.

116. "Eyuwan suqu" 1983:326.

117. Lin Weixian 1982:16; Ni Zhongwen 1983:12.

118. He Yaobang 1959:353–96.

119. Hou Zhiying et al. 1982:57; Mei Shaoqing 1982a:31; He Yaobang 1959:316–17.

120. Hou Zhiying et al. 1982:53; "Eyuwan suqu" 1983:332–37; He Yaobang 1959:316–34; Xu Zhanquan 1987:607–8; Tan Kesheng and Ouyang Zhiliang, eds., 1987:571–76; Hongan xian 1987:294–98.

121. He Yaobang 1959:272 and 341–53; Lin Weixian 1982:270–71.

122. Luo Yingchen 1984:57; Shi Yan et al. 1981:11–16; Hou Zhiying et al. 1982:57; "Eyuwan suqu" 1983:337–38.

123. Wang Gongying and Jin Xiaoguang 1984:372; Hou Zhiying et al. 1982:57; "Eyuwan suqu" 1983:338–39.

124. He Yaobang 1959:360–67; Hou Zhiying et al. 1982:57; Jiang Kangmei 1983:76.

125. He Yaobang 1959:343–77.

126. Hou Zhiying et al. 1982:57–58; Li Shian et al. 1982:77–78; "Eyuwan suqu" 1983:339; Liu Gangfu 1983:19–20.

127. Hou Zhiying et al. 1982:58; "Eyuwan suqu" 1983:340.

128. Luo Yingchen 1984:57.

129. Dong Biwu 1986 [1937]: 15.

130. Li Shiyan 1984:398–99.

131. Hou Zhiying et al. 1982:58–59; "Eyuwan suqu" 1983:340.

132. He Yaobang 1959:380–83; Liu Gangfu 1983:19.
133. Kang Jian 1985:198–99; Shi Yan et al. 1981:37.
134. Lin Weixian 1979?: 222; Xinsijun canmouchu 1981 [1946]: 161; Li Zijian 1982:31; Liu Guangming 1985:48.
135. Li Zijian 1986:167–69.
136. Kang Jian 1985:125–59.
137. Li Zijian 1986:170.
138. Liu Zihou et al. 1985:204; Wang Jianying 1986a:413–15; Kang Jian 1985:171–99.
139. Liu Zihou et al. 1985:213–16; Li Zijian 1982:28–30.
140. Xu Qichang 1981:233; Chen Zigan 1981:90.
141. Hou Zhiying et al. 1982:58–59; Li Shian et al. 1982:78.
142. Hou Zhiying et al. 1982:58; Wang Jianying 1986a:413; Tan Kesheng and Ouyang Zhiliang, eds., 1987:584; Hongan xian 1987:300.
143. Hou Zhiying et al. 1982:56–59; "Eyuwan suqu" 1983:341; He Yaobang 1959:394; Liu Gangfu 1983:23; Liu Guangming 1985:48; Lin Weixian 1979?: 222.
144. Xinsijun canmouchu 1981 [1946]: 160; Lin Weixian 1979?: 222.
145. Luo Yingchen 1984:58; Zheng Zhong 1987:117–18.
146. Boorman and Howard 1967–71, vol. 3:405–6; Liu Gangfu 1983:9–10.
147. Zhao Rongsheng 1985:15.
148. Liu Gangfu 1983:12–19; Shi Yutian 1980:212–22.
149. He Yaobang 1959:374–97; cf. He Yaobang 1983; Li Zhaochun 1985:100. This story, which is omitted from later editions of He's memoirs, is not necessarily or wholly true.
150. Hou Zhiying et al. 1982:53; Sun Baosheng 1986:60.
151. Li Yunhan 1981, pt. 1:11; Zhao Rongsheng 1985:9 and 15; Zhai Zuojun 1985:32; Boorman and Howard 1967–71, vol. 3:405–6.
152. Ni Zhongwen 1983:12 and 56.
153. Lin Weixian 1984a:17.
154. Sun Baosheng 1986:60.
155. Ni Zhongwen 1983:12.
156. Ni Zhongwen 1983:12 and 56.
157. Ni Zhongwen 1983:9–12.
158. Zhu Yunqian 1987:58; Smedley 1944:222.
159. Hou Zhiying et al. 1982:52.
160. Zheng Weisan 1982 [1941]: 135–36; Li Zhaochun 1985:98; Smedley 1944:330; Zhonggong Jinzhai 1980:245ff; Ren Zhibin 1985:33; Jin Ge 1985:217–20.

## XIANG'EGAN: PERSEVERING TO THE END

1. Ling Hui and He Xiaoji 1984:259–60; Wu Dingbang 1985:2; Fu Qiutao 1979 [1959]: 1; Renmin chubanshe 1953 [1945]: 53.
2. Fu Qiutao 1979 [1959]: 10–11; Wu Dingbang 1985:2; Peng Dehuai 1984:189 and 211; Huang Keyun 1985:31.

3. Pcng Dchuai 1984:222–66; Ling Hui and He Xiaoji 1984:262–64.

4. Huang Keyun 1985:31–32.

5. Ye Husheng 1956:105; Zhongguo geming bowuguan 1982:209.

6. Wales 1952:108.

7. Ling Hui and He Xiaoji 1984:265; Wu Dingbang 1985:3.

8. Huang Keyun 1985:28.

9. Zhongguo geming bowuguan 1982:210.

10. Fu Qiutao 1979 [1959]: 10–11.

11. Huang Keyun 1985:28.

12. Fu Qiutao 1979 [1959]: 2.

13. Hunan shengzhi 1959, vol. 1:651; Wales 1952:105; Wu Dingbang 1985: 2–3.

14. Fu Qiutao 1979 [1959]: 60.

15. Ling Hui and He Xiaoji 1984:266; Hunan sheng shehui kexueyuan 1982:230–33; Wu Dingbang 1985:3; Fu Qiutao 1979 [1959]: 23.

16. Zi Qin 1938:6; Guo Jidong and Fang Lieshu 1984:297–300 and 1986:391ff.

17. Hunan sheng shehui kexueyuan 1982:232; Ling Hui 1979:52; Guo Jidong and Fang Lieshu 1984:300–301.

18. Fu Qiutao 1979 [1959]: 15–19.

19. Ibid:19–20; Wu Dingbang 1985:3; Liu Yutang 1986:225; Yang Jianxin 1986.

20. Guo Jidong and Fang Lieshu 1984:301–2.

21. Hunan shengzhi 1959, vol. 1:653.

22. Hatano Ken'ichi 1961, vol. 5:43–44; Department of State 1953, vol. 3:684.

23. Fu Qiutao 1979 [1959]: 20–23.

24. *Meizhou* 1935.

25. Guo Jidong and Fang Lieshu 1984:306.

26. Fu Qiutao 1979 [1959]: 30–31.

27. Hunan shengzhi 1959, vol. 1:652.

28. Fu Qiutao 1979 [1959]: 24–30 and 37; Liu Yutang 1986:226.

29. Fu Qiutao 1979 [1959]: 30–31.

30. Ibid:3–4 and 31.

31. Wales 1952:102 and 107–8; Wuhan yexiao n.d.: 263; Fu Qiutao 1979 [1959]: 4–6.

32. Fu Qiutao 1979 [1959]: 6–7.

33. Ibid:8 and 32–34; Ling Hui 1979:53–54.

34. Wales 1952:108.

35. Fu Qiutao 1979 [1959]: 13–14; Hunan shengzhi 1959, vol. 1:652–53; Zhong Qiguang 1987:411.

36. Hunan shengzhi 1959, vol. 1:653.

37. Zhonggong Hunan shengwei dangshi 1986:114.

38. Fu Qiutao 1979 [1959]: 62–63.

39. Probably Deng Hong (see Dong Biwu 1986 [1937]:14 and Guo Jidong and Fang Lieshu 1986:404), but hereafter still referred to as Deng Feng, following the original source.

40. Wales 1952:104–7.

41. Zhong Qiguang 1987:410–11.

42. Fu Qiutao 1979 [1959]: 13.

43. Zhong Qiguang 1987:411–12; Wu Jiamin 1986:274.

44. Fu Qiutao 1979 [1959]: 35–36.

45. Guo Jidong and Fang Lieshu 1986:401.

46. Fu Qiutao 1979 [1959]: 35–38 and 51–52.

47. Ibid: 41; Hunan sheng shehui kexueyuan 1982:264.

48. Wales 1952:106–7.

49. Fu Qiutao 1979 [1959]: 40–41.

50. Ibid:42.

51. Ibid:42–43.

52. Hunan shengzhi 1959, vol. 1:654.

53. Wales 1952:104–9.

54. Ling Hui 1979:57.

55. Ling Hui and He Xiaoji 1984:268.

56. Fu Qiutao 1979 [1959]: 43–44 and 52–53.

57. Ibid:43–45; Kong Qiaofan 1979:47–51; Wales 1952:107.

58. Fu Qiutao 1979 [1959]: 46–48 and 52; Kong Qiaofan 1979:52.

59. Kong Qiaofan 1979:52; Ling Hui and He Xiaoji 1984:268.

60. Fu Qiutao 1979 [1959]: 48–49; Kong Qiaofan 1979:52.

61. Fu Qiutao 1979 [1959]: 49–50.

62. Kong Qiaofan 1979:52; Dong Biwu 1986 [1937]: 15.

63. Fu Qiutao 1979 [1959]: 52.

64. Wales 1952:105 and 109; Liu Yutang 1986:228.

65. Guo Jidong and Fang Lieshu 1984:306; Hunan sheng shehui kexueyuan 1982:265; Ling Hui and He Xiaoji 1984:269–70.

66. Guo Jidong and Fang Lieshu 1986:401–3; Zhonggong Hunan shengwei dangshi 1986:114.

67. Fu Qiutao 1979 [1959]: 54–55.

68. Ibid:55–56.

69. Zhonggong Hunan shengwei dangshi 1986:115.

70. Hunan shengzhi 1959, vol. 1:655.

71. Hunan shengzhi 1959, vol. 1:655.

72. Ling Hui 1979:57–58; Dong Biwu 1986 [1937]: 14.

73. Zhong Qiguang 1987:410.

74. Fu Qiutao 1979 [1959]: 56–57; Hunan sheng shehui kexueyuan 1982:268–69; Zhonghua junwei Xiang'egan junqu 1985 [1937]; Huang Yaonan 1985:185; Gao Jidong and Fang Lieshu 1986:404.

75. Fu Qiutao 1979 [1959]: 57–58; Huang Yaonan 1985:182–83; Gong Gujin and Tang Peiji, eds., 1983, vol. 1:263; Guo Jidong and Fang Lieshu 1984:311.

76. Fu Qiutao 1979 [1959]: 59–60; Ling Hui 1979:60; Shi Yan et al. 1981:16–18; Zhonghua junwei Xiang'egan renmin 1985 [1937]: 48–49; Huang Yaonan 1985:186; Dong Biwu 1986 [1937]: 13.

77. Hunan shengzhi 1959, vol. 1:695; Ling Hui and He Xiaoji 1984:271–77; Wu Dingbang 1985:7; Zhongguo gongchandang Xiang'egan 1985 [1937]: 46.

78. Fu Qiutao 1979 [1959]: 60–61; Ling Hui 1979:60; Dong Biwu 1986 [1937]: 13–14.

79. Wu Jiamin 1986:286–90.

80. Fu Qiutao 1979 [1959]: 60–61; Hunan sheng shehui kexueyuan 1982:273–76; Zi Qin 1938; Xinsijun canmouchu 1981 [1946]: 159; Ling Hui 1979:62–63; Dong Biwu 1986 [1937]: 14; Luo Qixun 1985:192; Ye Fei 1983a, pt. 6:20.

81. Zi Qin 1938:6–8.

82. Zi Qin 1938.

83. Fu Qiutao 1979 [1959]: 61; Hunan sheng shehui kexueyuan 1982:276; Liu Guangming 1985:49.

84. Fu Qiutao 1979 [1959]: 61; Zi Qin 1938:37ff.

85. Huang Keyun 1985:31.

86. Zhong Qiguang 1987:412.

## XIANGGAN: THE PEASANT PATRIARCH

1. Renmin chubanshe 1953 [1945]: 53; Zhongguo geming bowuguan 1982:300.

2. Han Suyin 1976, vol. 1:230.

3. Gui Yulin 1986a:2–4; Guillermaz 1972:166; Li Shi 1977: 18–24.

4. Mao Tse-tung 1961–65, vol. 1:89–93; Han Suyin 1976, vol. 1:230; Gui Yulin 1986a:4–5.

5. Mao Tse-tung 1961–65, vol. 1:99; Chen Fu 1985:23.

6. Li Shi 1977:21–22.

7. Snow 1968:167.

8. Smedley 1934:105; Han Suyin 1976, vol. 1:230.

9. Quoted in Shih 1967:304–6.

10. Qiu Zhizhuo 1985:41–42; Alley 1973:323.

11. Shih 1967:304–19; Jen Yu-wen 1973:10–11.

12. Mao Tse-tung 1961–65, vol. 1:93.

13. Xu Chunhua et al. 1984:458; Qiu Zhizhuo 1985:42–44; Jinggangshan geming bowuguan 1985:123; Mao Tse-tung 1961–65, vol. 1:93–94.

14. Xu Chunhua et al. 1984:465–66; Gui Yulin 1986a:1; Mao Tse-tung 1961–65, vol. 1:93–94.

15. Gui Yulin 1986a:47; Smedley 1934:101–17; Alley 1973:323; Peng Dehuai 1984:275–78; Snow 1968:165; Huang Zhongfang 1987:3; Mao Tse-tung 1961–65, vol. 1:74.

16. Zhongguo geming bowuguan 1982:173–76; Gui Yulin 1986b:4.

17. Zhongguo geming bowuguan 1982:176.

18. Bingzhang Yang 1986:37.

19. Peng Dehuai 1984:254–78.

20. Smedley 1934:101; Xu Chunhua et al. 1984:460; Han Suyin 1976, vol. 1:240.

21. Snow 1968:167; Peng Dehuai 1984:274ff; Qiu Zhizhuo 1985:48.

22. Xu Chunhua et al. 1984:469; Chen Fu 1985:25–27. Yuan's widow has been well looked after by the Party (Alley 1973:323); in 1965, Mao posed for a photo with the families of Yuan and Wang while on a visit to Xianggan (Huang Zhongfang 1987:18).

23. Xu Chunhua et al. 1984:455–67; Peng Dehuai 1984:231 and 278; Li Shouxuan 1984;73; Jinggangshan geming bowuguan 1985:123, 188, and 191; Qiu Zhizhuo 1985:44–48; Huang Zhongfang 1987:9; Gui Yulin 1986a:246–47; "Xianggan geming" 1982:21–22.

24. Peng Dehuai 1984:276; Li Shouxuan 1984:72–74; Chen Fu 1985:27; Xu Chunhua et al. 1984:457; Jinggangshan geming bowuguan 1985:191; Gui Yulin 1986a:248.

25. Li Li 1983:90.

26. Mao Tse-tung 1961–65, vol. 1:105–15.

27. Peng Dehuai 1984:264–307; Zhongguo geming bowuguan 1982:177.

28. Chen Fu 1985:24 and 31; Tan Yunxiang and Liu Puqing 1985:319.

29. Zhang Yangui and Yuan Wei 1987:204; Zhongguo geming bowuguan 1982:178–79; Tan Tangchi 1980:123.

30. Chen Fu 1985:25–31.

31. Gui Yulin 1986a:4–5; Chen Fu 1985:31.

32. Xu Chunhua et al. 1984:463–69; Peng Dehuai 1984:277; Snow 1968: 167.

33. Chen Fu 1985:26–28.

34. Ibid:25; Gui Yulin 1986b:4.

35. Duan Huanjing 1979:358–59.

36. Tan Yubao n.d.: 245–46.

37. Peng Jiazhu 1984:507–11; Tan Tangchi 1980:122.

38. Tan Tangchi 1980:123; Duan Huanjing 1983:80; Hunan sheng caizhengting, eds., 1986:101; Tan Yubao n.d.: 245; "Xianggan geming" 1982: 137.

39. Tan Tangchi 1980:121–23; Duan Huanjing 1979:360.

40. Chen Yi 1979 [1962]: 43.

41. Chen Fu 1985:30.

42. Liu Peishan 1958:188; Peng Jiazhu 1984:508; Tan Tangchi 1980:12.

43. Peng Bo 1982:55–56.

44. Wang Shoudao 1951:54; Tan Tangchi 1980:124; Duan Huanjing 1980:97; Hunan shengzhi 1959, vol. 1:647; "Xianggan geming" 1982:137.

45. Peng Jiazhu 1984:509–10; Tan Yubao n.d.:250.

46. Li Wei 1956:39.

47. Shixue shuangzhoukan she 1956:74–75.

48. Duan Huanjing 1980:97; Wang Shoudao 1951:54; Hunan shengzhi 1959, vol. 1:647–48; Tan Tangchi 1980:124; Peng Bo 1982:57; Peng Jiazhu 1984:512.

49. Hunan shengzhi 1959, vol. 1:648.

50. Ibid:640–41.

51. Tan Tangchi 1980:123–25; Liu Peishan 1958:188–89; Wang Shoudao 1951:54–55.

52. Peng Bo 1982:55.

53. Peng Jiazhu 1984:509.

54. Duan Huanjing 1979:360; Smedley 1934:119; Peng Bo 1982:56; "Xianggan geming" 1982:140.

55. Hunan sheng caizhengting, eds., 1986:97.

56. Tan Tangchi 1980:125.
57. Liu Peishan 1958:189.
58. Tan Tangchi 1980:125; Lu Wenxin 1979:26–27; Duan Huanjing 1975:381 and 1979:364–65; Peng Jiazhu 1984:512.
59. Huang Bingguang 1983:97; Peng Jiazhu 1984:512; Duan Huanjing 1975:380.
60. Tan Yubao n.d.: 246–48; Tan Tangchi 1980:125.
61. Peng Jiazhu 1984:511.
62. Wang Shoudao 1951:53–55; Tan Yubao n.d.: 245–46.
63. Tan Tangchi 1980:124.
64. Ibid:124; Peng Jiazhu 1984:513–17; Liu Peishan 1958:191; Wu Xing 1958.
65. Tan Tangchi 1980:122–29; Hunan sheng caizhengting, eds., 1986:94; Liu Peishan 1958:189–91; Hunan shengzhi 1959, vol. 1:649.
66. Fu Yunfei 1979:21; Peng Jiazhu 1984:513; Tan Tangchi 1980:126; Zhonggong Anfu 1987:261; "Xianggan geming" 1982:143.
67. Peng Jiazhu 1984:513; Tan Tangchi 1980:127; Tan Yubao n.d.: 246–48; Wang Shoudao 1951:55–56; Liu Peishan 1958:189–91; Hunan shengzhi 1959, vol. 1:648–49.
68. Luo Weidao 1982:44.
69. Duan Huanjing 1980:98.
70. Tan Tangchi 1980:128–29; Luo Weidao 1982:42; Duan Huanjing 1979:364–71 and 1983:80.
71. Shaffer 1982, ch. 4; Li Jui 1977:199ff.
72. Qiu Zhizhuo et al. 1986:463.
73. Ding Yisan 1979:110.
74. Wang Shoudao 1951:55–56; Tan Tangchi 1980:127–34; Peng Jiazhu 1984:515; Peng Bo 1982:56; Duan Huanjing 1979:370–71.
75. Tan Tangchi 1980:129–37; Tan Yubao n.d.: 55–58; Duan Huanjing 1975:384 and 1980:98; Hunan shengzhi 1959, vol. 1:649–50; Peng Bo 1982:56. Cf. Peng Jiazhu (1984:514–15), who says that not six but three battalions were formed, and Zhonggong Hunan shengwei dangshi (1986:111), which says that first four and later six battalions were formed.
76. Tan Tangchi 1980:130–31; Duan Huanjing 1979:374; Hunan sheng caizhengting, eds., 1986:91–92; "Xianggan geming" 1982:145.
77. Tan Yubao n.d.: 246–48; Duan Huanjing 1983:80.
78. Hunan sheng caizhengting, eds., 1986:96.
79. Lu Wenxin 1979:27–29; Tan Tangchi 1980:133–35.
80. Peng Bo 1982:56–58.
81. Peng Bo 1982:58–59.
82. Peng Jiazhu 1984:517.
83. Tan Tangchi 1980:135.
84. Peng Bo 1982:59.
85. Ibid:58–60; Duan Huanjing 1980:98–99; Wuhan yexiao n.d.: 246; Peng Jiazhu 1984:517.
86. Smedley 1934:111.
87. Peng Bo 1982:57–61.

88. Tan Tangchi 1980:137; Peng Bo 1982:61–62; Lu Wenxin 1979:32–33; Liu Peishan 1958:189–91.

89. Tan Tangchi 1980:130–31; Hunan shengzhi 1959, vol. 1:649–50.

90. Peng Jiazhu 1984:516; Tan Tangchi 1980:131–33.

91. Hunan sheng caizhengting, eds., 1986:92.

92. Tan Yubao n.d.:249–50; Wang Shoudao 1951:57–58; Hunan shengzhi 1959, vol. 1:650–52; "Xianggan geming" 1982:147.

93. Jiangxi sheng funü 1963:40.

94. Liu Peishan 1958:189–93; Hunan sheng caizhengting, eds., 1986:103.

95. Huang Bingguang 1983:97; Tan Tangchi 1980:137–38.

96. Liu Peishan 1958:192–93; Duan Huanjing 1979:382; Zhonggong Hunan shengwei dangshi 1986:114; "Xianggan geming" 1982:147.

97. Wang Shoudao 1951:56–57; Peng Bo 1982:61–62.

98. Jiangxi sheng funü 1963; Wu Xing 1958; Hunan shengzhi 1959, vol. 1:521–22.

99. Peng Bo 1982:62–63; Lu Wenxin 1979:33–36; Li Shan 1979:387.

100. Li Wei 1956:40.

101. Zhonggong Hunan shengwei dangshi 1986:114.

102. Lu Wenxin 1979:32; Liu Peishan 1958:188–95; Duan Huanjing 1979:382–83; Peng Jiazhu 1984:523.

103. Duan Huanjing 1979:376–77; Jiangxi sheng funü 1963:34; Wu Xing 1958.

104. Lu Wenxin 1979:40; Ding Yisan 1979:110; Jiangxi sheng funü 1963:43; Zhonggong Anfu 1987:267.

105. Lu Wenxin 1979:40.

106. Jiangxi sheng funü 1963:43.

107. Lu Wenxin 1979:41–43; Duan Huanjing 1980:99.

108. Xianggan bian hongjun 1937a and 1937b.

109. This account of Chen Yi's visit to Xianggan draws on several partly conflicting sources. I have taken what is common to them and, where choice was necessary, chosen the version that struck me as most authentic. The sources are Ding Yisan 1979:110, Tan Tangchi 1980:139–40, Duan Huanjing 1979:383–96 and 1980:99–108, Shi Yan et al. 1981:3–4, Chen Yi 1979 [1962]: 40–46 and 1981 [1957]: 586–89, Fu Yunfei 1979, and Huang Bingguang 1983:97–101. I wrote the dialogue by combining numerous fragments of direct speech contained in various reminiscences. I added nothing of substance to these passages, but I tried to smoothe the conversation and edit out repetition. Needless to say, the dialogue cannot be taken as an accurate record of what was said, even in the sources I draw on.

110. This man, Cao Shuliang, was a Red Army guerrilla from Xiangnan. Both he and his bodyguard were killed. When Cao's comrades learned of his death during their reorganization as part of the New Fourth Army, they wanted revenge. Chen Yi calmed them down by telling them about his own experience with Tan. In 1982, Cao was declared a martyr (Xie Youcai 1984, letter).

111. After 1949, Tan's talent for punishing and coercing earned him appointment to the Hunan Party's discipline committee (Qiu Zhizhuo et al. 1986:463).

112. Duan Huanjing 1980:101–2; Jiangxi sheng funü 1963:43.

113. Hunan shengzhi 1959, vol. 1:694–95; Zhonggong Xianggan sheng weiyuanhui 1937.

114. Lu Wenxin 1979:44.

115. Hunan shengzhi 1959, vol. 1:694–95; Li Li 1983:88–89; Li Jiaquan 1985:19; Lu Wenxin 1979:44; Peng Jiazhu 1984:526; Chen Yi 1981 [1957]: 589; Fu Yunfei 1979:25; Tan Yubao n.d.: 250; "Xianggan geming" 1982: 152.

116. Mao Tse-tung 1961–65, vol. 1:101.

117. Li Li 1983:91; Shixue shuangzhoukan she 1956:73–74; Li Wei 1956:36–39; Alley 1962:16–17.

118. Liu Puqing and Tan Yunxiang 1987:549; Wang Duonian, ed., 1982, vol. 4:115; Gong Chu 1954:446–48.

119. Mao Zedong 1970–72, vol. 2:63.

120. Chen Yi 1981 [1957]: 589.


XIANGNAN

1. Wang Jianying 1986a:395; Renmin chubanshe 1953 [1945]: 53; Zhongguo geming bowuguan 1982:299; Yan Jingtang 1986:47.

2. Shaffer 1982:164–203.

3. Smedley 1934:24ff.

4. Zhang Guangxin and Yang Shuzhen, eds., 1985:47; Gui Yulin 1986a:82–91; Jinggangshan geming bowuguan 1985:61–63; Xiao Chaoran et al. 1986, vol. 1:362; Zhonggong Hunan shengwei dangshi 1986:67ff.; Zhonggong Chenzhou 1986.

5. Hunan sheng caizhengting, eds., 1986:25–26; Zhonggong Hunan shengwei dangshi 1986:73ff.

6. Shaffer 1982:197.

7. Xu Lin 1986 [1928]: 22–23.

8. Zhonggong Hunan shengwei dangshi 1986:106.

9. Hunan shengzhi 1959, vol. 1:695; Gu Ziyuan n.d.; Mu Qing 1950:20–21; Zhonggong Hunan shengwei dangshi 1986:110; Wang Jianying 1986a:395; Xu Zhanquan 1987:605–6.

10. Gong Chu 1954; Zhonggong Hunan shengwei dangshi 1986:72.

11. Gong Chu 1954:443–48; Wang Duonian 1982, vol. 4:115.

12. Xu Zhanquan 1987:606; Wang Jianying 1986a:396; Zhang Yangui and Yuan Wei 1987:401; Gu Ziyuan n.d.: 257.

13. Ma Hongcai 1985, vol. 1:20.

14. Hunan sheng caizhengting, eds., 1986:92–93.

15. Wang Jianying 1986a:395; Tan Yunxiang and Liu Puqing 1985:329; Sheng Renxue and Zhang Junxiao 1987:191.

16. Qiu Zhizhuo et al. 1986:459–60; Zhang Hai 1986:21.

17. Zhonggong Hunan shengwei dangshi 1986:111–14; Mu Qing 1950:20–22; Wang Jianying 1986a:396.

18. Mu Qing 1950:20–22.

19. Zhonggong Hunan shengwei dangshi 1986:120; Hunan shengzhi 1959, vol. 1:695; Wang Jianying 1986a:396; Zhang Yangui and Yuan Wei 1987:401; Hunan sheng caizhengting, eds., 1986:93; Xie Zhufeng 1987:160–62.

## MIN'GAN

1. Sources on Min'gan include Lei Jianming 1984, Liao Kaizhu, ed., 1986:193–95, Yang Daoming 1986, and Min'gan genjudi 1985.

## ANNANYONGDE

1. Zhonggong Anxi 1982:35–36; Yin Linping 1984; Liao Kaizhu, ed., 1986:75–76 and 154–55.

## HAILUFENG

1. According to Zhonggong Guangdong shengwei dangshi yanjiu weiyuanhui bangongshi et al. 1986, no. 2:273, Peng Gui died not in 1935 but in 1933.
2. Sheng Renxue and Zhang Junxiao 1987:65; Wang Jianying 1986a:416–17; Zhongguo geming bowuguan 1982:202; Li Ruxiang 1987:384.
3. Benton 1986:691.

## WANXIBEI

1. Wang Jianying 1986a:420; Ma Hongcai 1985, vol. 1:118.

## QIONGYA

1. Zhang Yangui and Yuan Wei 1987:415–20; Wang Jianying 1986a:415–16; Xu Zhanquan 1987:609.

## THE THREE-YEAR WAR ENDS, THE GUERRILLAS UNITE

1. Shi Yan et al. 1981:139.
2. Mao Tse-tung 1961–65, vol. 1:161; Mao Zedong 1970–72, vol. 5:21; Snow 1941, vol. 1:127. P. Miff's publication commemorating the fifteenth anniversary of the founding of the Chinese Communist Party contains not a single reference to the fate of the Red Army's southern columns (Miff 1937).
3. Bisson 1973:39.
4. Benton 1975.
5. Zhang Xueliang 1989 [1968]: 70; Lü Zhenyu 1980:162–66.
6. Benton 1975:72–73; Kuo 1968–71, vol. 3:273–75.
7. Snow 1941, vol. 1:130; Bisson 1973:45.

8. Zong Zhidi 1980 [1952]: 168.
9. Chen Yi 1986 [1940]: 120.
10. Zong Zhidi 1980 [1952]: 168; Xinsijun canmouchu 1981 [1946]: 158.
11. Chen Yi 1986 [1940]: 120.
12. Zhou Luo 1977:44; Yu Maoji et al. 1985:13.
13. Yan Jingwen 1974:247.
14. Ibid:247–50; Yue Qian 1972, pt. 2:52.
15. Zhongyang diaocha tongjiju 1939a; Smedley 1944:234ff.
16. Zhou Luo 1977:44 and 50.
17. Benton 1986.
18. Chen Yi 1980 [1959]: 18.
19. Chen Yi 1986 [1940]: 121.
20. Benton 1979:76; Wang Fuyi 1987b:37–38.
21. Wang Fuyi 1984a:462–63; Chen Pixian 1982:131–32.
22. Zhang Dingcheng 1984:176–77; Yu Boliu 1983:135; Zhang Yunlong 1984:52; Chen Yi 1986 [1940]: 122.
23. Zhang Dingcheng 1982 [1940]: 121 and 1984:176–77.
24. Zhongyang 1982 [1937].
25. Benton 1975 and 1986.
26. For example, Zhang Dingcheng et al. 1937?
27. A non-Communist and founding commander of the New Fourth Army. See below.
28. Wang Fuyi 1987b:39; Wei Pu and Yang Wenlong 1987:30–31; Zhongyang shujichu 1985 [1937].
29. Benton 1975, 1977, 1980, and 1986.
30. Chen Yi 1980 [1959]: 19.
31. Zhang Dingcheng 1982 [1940]: 116–17 and 1984:176–77.
32. Xinsijun zhengzhibu 1943:1–2.
33. Smedley 1944:178–79.
34. Yue Xia 1980:200; Zhang Yunlong 1984:49.
35. Benton 1985b:321.
36. Qiu Zhizhuo et al. 1986:65.
37. Zhexuexi 1977, pt. 2:39 and pt. 3:51; Theoretical Group 1978:154; Wei Pu and Yang Wenlong 1987:29–31; Chen Guangxiang 1988:58. According to Yung-fa Chen (1986:28), Chiang Kai-shek called Ye to Luoyang in 1936 and established a rapport with him. I have no evidence to confirm this story.
38. Yue Qian 1972, pt. 2:52.
39. Wei Pu and Yang Wenlong 1987:30; Lü Dianyun et al. 1986; Lu Quan and Xuan Qianhong 1987:135–36; Kuo 1968–71, vol. 3:351–52; Chen Guangxiang 1988:57.
40. According to information displayed in Maoshan's New Fourth Army Exhibition Hall, Nationalists and Communists agreed on October 2 to reorganize the southern guerrillas, and the Nationalists announced the decision on October 12. This account usefully reconciles the many studies that give either one or the other of these dates.
41. Wei Pu and Yang Wenlong 1987:30–33.
42. Wang Fuyi 1987b:44.

43. Lü Dianyun et al. 1986; Wei Pu and Yang Wenlong 1987:32; Theoretical Group 1978:155–56; Chen Guangxiang 1988:59.

44. Leng Xin 1967:85; Wang Yuanjian 1978:6–10.

45. Wei Pu and Yang Wenlong 1987:33; Wang Fuyi 1987b:40–41; Xiang Ying 1937.

46. See below and Benton 1986.

47. Wang Fuyi 1987b:41–42; Kuo 1968–71, vol. 3:365.

48. Wang Fuyi 1987b:42.

49. Benton 1986. Ye Ting's role in the evacuation of the southern bases remains to be elucidated. It is easy to imagine that he, too, favored gathering together in one place as many of the guerrillas as possible.

50. Chang Kuo-t'ao 1971, vol. 2:555; Zhang Guotao in *Mingbao yuekan* 60:87.

51. Zhexuexi 1977, pt. 3:51; Ye Jianmei and Wang Chunjiang 1982:40.

52. Wei Pu and Yang Wenlong 1987:33–34.

53. Wang Fuyi 1984a:464 and 1987b:43–44; "Xinsijun" shiliao 1986:43–44; Chen Guangxiang 1988:60–61; Lü Dianyun et al. 1986. According to Chen Wen (1987), the inauguration of the New Fourth Army headquarters was not an event but a process that extended over more than six months.

54. Wang Fuyi 1987b:44.

55. Zeng Meisheng 1985:53; Benton 1979 and 1986; *see* Kuo 1968–71, vol. 3:348–50 for the staff of these and other bureaus.

56. Huang Zhizhen 1958:322–23.

57. Zhang Yunlong 1984:54.

58. Epstein 1939:262.

59. Zi Qin 1938:37ff.; Xu Xingzhi 1983 [1941]: 557; Sun Keji 1984:31.

60. Xu Xingzhi 1983 [1941]: 557; Dan Jiang 1981:52; Zhexuexi 1977, pt. 3:53; Zhang Yunlong 1984:49–55.

61. Zhexuexi 1977, pt. 3:53; Wei Pu and Yang Wenlong 1987:34.

62. Xu Xingzhi 1983 [1941]: 559.

63. Ye Fei 1988:99–100.

64. Epstein 1939:264–65.

65. Ibid:265.

66. Zhu Yujin 1982:139.

67. Lin Zhifu 1978 [1946]: 92–93. Partly because of their distinctive dress, only a small handful of officers—Xiang among them—escaped during the Wannan Incident of January 1941.

68. Wei Pu and Yang Wenlong 1987:34–35; Theoretical Group 1978:156; Ye Fei 1988:102.

69. Benton 1979:115ff. and 1986:692–94; Wang Yuxian 1983:61.

70. Ling Lihua and Zhu Jianying 1981:28.

71. Epstein 1939:264ff.; Benton 1986.

72. See Long-chang Young 1988:36–37.

73. Xiang Ying 1939:43–44.

74. Epstein 1939:268; Xiatikesi 1941:96; Shi Yan et al. 1981:124–25.

75. Zhang Yunlong 1984:48–49; Xinsijun canmouchu 1981 [1946]: 160; Yu Maoji et al. 1985:18–19.

76. Ye Fei 1987a:342.

77. Ye Fei 1983a, pt. 2:18.
78. Ma Hongcai 1985, 2 vols. See chart 1.
79. Ye Fei 1983a, pt. 6:16–17 and 1988:101.
80. Lu Feng 1947:29; Zhang Yunlong 1984:49; Xinsijun canmouchu 1981 [1946]: 159; Epstein 1939:260–61; Ye Ting 1938:14 and 29.
81. Chiang Kai-shek 1969:89.
82. Benton 1979:156–57.
83. Xinsijun canmouchu 1981 [1946]: 160; Huang Kaiyuan et al. 1981:23.
84. Zhang Yunlong 1984:53–54.
85. Benton 1979:156–57.
86. Yung-fa Chen 1986:29.
87. Zhongyang diaocha tongjiju 1940:7.
88. Benton 1979:277–78; Shi Yan et al. 1981:51–52.
89. Whitson 1973:202ff.
90. Chen Jun 1939:46; Kuo 1968–71, vol. 3:353.
91. Huang Zhizhen 1958:321–23; Chen Lisheng et al. 1982:307; Benton 1979:89–90; Yang Shang-k'uei 1961:156ff.
92. Benton 1979:214–17; Kuo 1968–71, vol. 3:349–50.
93. Zhongyang diaocha tongjiju 1939c:45.
94. Benton 1979:90–91 and 214–17.
95. Benton 1986.
96. Zeng Meisheng 1985:54–58; Xie Bizhen 1985:35; Ye Cao 1948:84.
97. Lin Jian 1985a:22–23; Lü Zhenyu 1982; Chen Si et al. 1982; Li Lianpo and Yang Xiaogang 1980; Huang Zhizhen 1958.
98. Niu Desheng et al. 1983:53–54; Queshan Zhugou 1980:1; Zhongyang diaocha tongjiju 1939b; Zhonggong Eyu 1938; Yue Xia 1980:201–2; Qi Guang 1984.
99. Jiangxi sheng diaocha shi 1941?
100. Liang Shan 1984; Lin Jian 1985a:24–25.
101. Mao Tse-tung 1961–65, vol. 4:271; Mei Feng 1986.

## THE THREE-YEAR WAR IN
## HISTORICAL PERSPECTIVE

1. Bingzhang Yang 1986:1–2; Salisbury 1985:346–48.
2. Van der Loon 1961:25.
3. Ye Fei 1983a, pt. 2:4.
4. Kuo 1968–71, vol. 3:36–40 and 352.
5. The image is from Koestler 1964:31.
6. Xiatikesi 1941:95–96; Xiang Ying 1937.
7. Xiang Ying 1937.
8. Kuo 1968–71, vol. 3:365.
9. Chen Yi 1977:363.
10. Ye Cao 1948:86–89.
11. *China Weekly Review,* August 20, 1938, 391; Kuo 1968–71, vol. 4:274; Benton 1979:114.
12. Anonymous 1986a:54; Wang Fuyi and Xue Wenhao 1985.

13. Benton 1986.
14. Dai Xiangqing et al. 1986:682; Wu Kebin 1984:180–81.
15. Hubei sheng "Zhongguo gongchandang" 1982, vol. 1:106.
16. Kong Yongsong 1986:69; "Fujian geming jishi" 1986, no. 7:54.
17. Yu Maoji et al. 1985:6.
18. In late 1934, the Red Army, excluding rearguards, was nearly 200,000 strong. This figure includes 86,000 under Zhu De, between 7,000 and 20,000 under Ren Bishi and He Long (Bingzhang Yang 1986:126 and Braun 1973:117), between 2,000 and 7,000 under Xu Haidong (see relevant chapter; Bingzhang Yang 1986:126; and Braun 1973:117), between 60,000 and 80,000 under Zhang Guotao (Kuo 1968–71, vol. 3:69–71 and Braun 1973:118), and several thousand miscellaneous troops in other parts of western and northern China.
19. Hao Mengbi and Duan Haoran, eds., 1984:212.
20. Salisbury 1985:296–97.
21. Xu Jin 1986:25; Ye Fei 1986c:41.
22. Snow 1941, vol. 1:130.
23. Wu Kebin 1984:193.
24. Ibid:185.
25. Ibid:184.
26. For example, Fu Xueyuan 1958.
27. Xu Jin 1986:21.
28. Zhang Hai 1986:21.
29. Snow 1941, vol. 1:130.
30. Selden 1971.
31. Snow 1968:205.
32. Chen Yi 1986 [1940]: 120.
33. Wang Fuyi and Xue Wenhao 1985:67.
34. Zheng Guiqing 1984:14.
35. Lu Dao 1985:23.
36. Zhang Liren and Ye Jianzhong 1983:43.
37. Wang Fan-hsi 1980:170–71.
38. Lei Lirong and Yi Shaolin 1986:37–38.
39. Xiang Ying 1937.
40. Cf. Ristaino 1987, where the distinction between the Party's external and internal work is usefully analyzed.
41. Jiti mantan 1981:114–16.
42. Sun Liming 1984:44–45.
43. Qiu Linzhong et al. 1983:16.
44. Ye Fei 1983c:3.
45. Liu Huishan, interview, Ruijin, November 1986.
46. Jiti mantan 1981:114–16; Fan Shiren 1984 [1959]: 117.
47. Zheng Zhong 1987:27.
48. Xiang Ying 1937.
49. Quoted in Epstein 1939:261.
50. Xiang Ying 1937.
51. Wales 1945:217.
52. Averill 1987:291; William Wei 1985.
53. Liu Huishan, interview, Ruijin, November 1986.

54. Zhong Chenkun 1982:87.

55. Sheng Renxue and Zhang Junxiao 1987:189–200; Liao Guoliang and Tian Yuanle 1987:237.

56. Chen Yi 1986 [1940]: 113; Chen Pixian 1982:iii.

57. Snow 1941, vol. 1:130.

58. See Hofheinz 1969 and 1977, ch. 7.

59. Cf. Ni Nanshan 1985.

60. Wang Fuyi 1987a:95–96.

61. Zhonggong Jinzhai 1980:151.

62. Chen Qunzhe 1983:137.

63. Excluding Ganyue.

64. Lei Lirong and Yi Shaolin 1986:35–40.

65. Ye Fei 1983c:2.

66. Liao Kaizhu, ed., 1986:15–17; Sheng Renxue and Zhang Junxiao 1987:26–28; Zheng Weisan 1982 [1941]: 135–36.

67. For example, Ristaino 1987:216 and Bingzhang Yang 1986:39ff.

68. For example, Ristaino 1987.

69. Wu Kebin 1984:182.

70. Chen Yi 1981 [1957]: 564.

71. Lin Jian 1985b:21.

72. Chen Yi 1986 [1940]: 117.

73. Wu Kebin 1984:189–90.

74. Li Zijian 1982:31–32; Ye Fei 1983c:3.

75. Ibid:32.

76. Ibid:28–30.

77. Cf. Lei Lirong and Yi Shaolin 1986:37–38.

78. Ye Fei 1983a, pt. 2:5.

79. Liu Jianhua 1982:25.

80. Dan Jiang 1981:52.

81. Lin Zhifu 1978 [1946]: 54.

82. Chen Yi 1942 [1941]: 43, 1982a [1939]: 106, 1982b [1939]: 46, and 1986 [1940]: 122; Ye Ting 1981 [1939]: 201–3; Sun Keji 1984:31.

83. Benton 1986:683–84.

84. Ibid:684.

85. Zhu Yujin 1982:139.

86. Benton 1986:706–9.

87. Ye Fei 1983a, pt. 2:4.

88. Zhang Yunlong 1984:50.

89. Benton 1986.

90. For example, Bingzhang Yang 1986:339–41.

91. Ye Fei 1983a, pt. 2:5.

92. For example, Chen Ronghua 1987 [1985]: 158.

93. Chen Fu 1985:30.

94. As also happened in 1959, the event to which Wang Ruoshui (1986:52–53) was referring when he developed this metaphor.

95. Jiangnan xinsijun 1982 [1945]: 103.

96. Bingzhang Yang 1986:349–52.

97. This description of the aim of myths is Erik Erikson's.

# BIBLIOGRAPHY

Abend, Hallet, and Anthony J. Billingham. 1936. *Can China Survive?* New York: Ives Washburn.

Alley, Rewi. 1962. *Land and Folk in Kiangsi: A Chinese Province in 1961.* Beijing: New World Press.

—————. 1973. *Travels in China, 1966–1971.* Beijing: New World Press.

Andrews, Roy Chapman, and Yvette Borup Andrews. 1920. *Camps and Trails in China: A Narrative of Exploration, Adventure, and Sport in Little-Known China.* New York: D. Appleton and Company.

Anhui sheng junqu, eds. 1982. *Xinsijun zai Anhui* [The New Fourth Army in Anhui]. Hefei: Anhui renmin chubanshe.

Anhui sheng wenwuju xinsijun wenshi zhengjizu, eds. 1981. *Wannan shibian ziliaoxuan* [Materials on the Wannan Incident]. Hefei: Anhui renmin chubanshe.

Anhui sheng Wuhu shi wenlian. 1980. *Wannan yi ye* [Wannan chapter]. Shanghai wenyi chubanshe.

Anonymous. 1985. "Huang Huicong." *Minnan geming shi yanjiu* 1:42–45.

Anonymous. 1986a. "Xinsijun diyici dang daibiao dahui" [The New Fourth Army's First Party Congress]. *Dangshi ziliao yu yanjiu* (Fuzhou) 1:54.

Anonymous. 1986b. "Xinsijun sanzhidui gaibian qianhou" [Around the time of the reorganization of the New Fourth Army's Third Detachment]. *Dangshi ziliao yu yanjiu* (Fuzhou) 3:63.

Averill, Stephen C. 1987. "Party, Society and Local Elite in the Jiangxi Communist Movement." *Journal of Asian Studies* 46 (2): 279–303.

Bartke, Wolfgang. 1981. *Who's Who in the People's Republic of China.* Brighton: Harvester.

Barzun, Jacques, and Henry F. Graff. 1970. *The Modern Researcher.* Rev. ed. New York: Harcourt, Brace, and World.

NOTE: I have indicated the file numbers of documents kept in the archive of the Guomindang's Bureau of Investigations in Taibei.

Belden, Jack. 1939. *The New Fourth Army*. Reprinted from a series of articles in Shanghai's *Evening Post and Mercury*. Shanghai.

Benton, Gregor. 1975. "The Second Wang Ming Line, 1935–38." *China Quarterly* 61:61–94.

———. 1977. "The 'Second Wang Ming Line (1935–38)': A Reply." *China Quarterly* 69:145–54.

———. 1979. "The Origins and Early Growth of the New Fourth Army, 1934–1941." Ph.D. Thesis. University of Leeds.

———. 1980. "Xiang Ying and the New Fourth Army: Nation and Class in Chinese Communist Strategy, 1938–1941." *Symposion: Tijdschrift voor Maatschappijwetenschap* (Amsterdam) 2 (1): 103–16.

———. 1984. "China and Democracy." *New Left Review* 148:57–73.

———. 1985a. "Lun Wannan shibian" [On the Wannan Incident]. In Nankai daxue lishixi, eds. *Zhongguo kangRi genjudi shi guoji xueshu taolunhui lunwenji*. Beijing: Dang'an chubanshe.

———. 1985b. "Two Purged Leaders of Early Chinese Communism." *China Quarterly* 102:317–28.

———. 1986. "The South Anhui Incident." *Journal of Asian Studies* 45 (4): 681–720.

———. 1989. "Communist Guerrilla Bases in Southeast China after the Start of the Long March." In Hartford and Goldstein, 62–91.

Bian Xiezu. 1982. "Xiang Ying zhuanlüe" [Biographical sketch of Xiang Ying]. *Fudan xuebao (shehui kexue ban)* 3:89–93.

Bianco, Lucien, and Yves Chevrier, eds. 1985. *Dictionnaire biographique du mouvement ouvrier international. La Chine*. Paris: Editions Ouvrières.

Bisson, Thomas Arthur. 1973. *Yenan in 1937: Talks with the Communist Leaders*. Berkeley: Center for Chinese Studies.

Boorman, Howard L., and Richard C. Howard, eds. 1967–1979. *Biographical Dictionary of Republican China*. 5 vols. New York: Columbia University Press.

Braun, Otto. 1973. *Chinesische Aufzeichnungen (1932–1939)*. Berlin: Dietz Verlag.

Cai Xiaoqian. 1969. "Jiangxi suqu huiyi pianduan" [Recollections of the Central Soviet]. 11 parts. *Feiqing yanjiu* 3 (2–12).

———. 1970. *Jiangxi suqu: Hongjun xicuan huiyi* [The Jiangxi Soviet: Reminiscences of the Red Army's flight west]. Taibei: Zhonggong yanjiu zazhi she.

———. 1970–1971. "Hongjun xicuan huiyi" [Recollections of the Red Army fleeing west]. 12 parts. *Zhonggong yanjiu* 4 (2)–5 (3).

Cai Xinsheng. 1984. "Minzhu geming shiqi Minnan dang lingdao jigoude yan'ge" [The evolution of Party-led organs in Minnan during the democratic revolution]. *Dangshi ziliao yu yanjiu* (Fujian) 2:65–71.

Cao Boyi. 1969. *Suweiaizhi jianli ji qi bengkui, 1931–1934* [The founding and collapse of the soviet, 1931–1934]. Taibei: Guoli zhengzhi daxue dong Ya yanjiusuo.

Cao Juru. 1981. "Zhonghua suweiai gongheguo guojia yinhang gongzuode bufen qingkuang" [Aspects of state banking in the Chinese Soviet Republic]. In Chen Yi et al. 1981, 369–75.

Cao Yanhang and Cai Tingguang. 1982. "Wannan shibian shimo" [The whole story of the Wannan Incident]. *Dangshi yanjiu* 1:2–18.

Cao Yanhang and Gan Guozhi. 1983. "Guanyu Wannan shibianqian xinsijun fazhan fangzhende jige wenti" [On some questions about the New Fourth Army's direction of development during the Wannan Incident]. *Dangshi yanjiu* 5:41–49.

Carlson, Evans Fordyce. 1940. *Twin Stars of China*. New York: Dodd, Mead, and Coy.

Chai Rongsheng. 1985. "Chen Yi tongzhi shi ruhe zhi Zunyi huiyi qingkuangde?" [How did Comrade Chen Yi find out about the Zunyi Conference?]. *Dangshi tongxun* 3:46.

Chang Kuo-t'ao. 1971. *The Rise of the Chinese Communist Party, 1921–1927. An Autobiography of Chang Kuo-t'ao*. 2 vols. Lawrence: University Press of Kansas.

Chen Bolin. 1986. "Yuejun yiwuqi shi zhu Min 'jiaogong' shilüe" [The Guangdong Army's 157th Division "eradicates Communists" in Fujian]. *Fujian dangshi tongxun* 3:47–56.

Chen Chang-feng. 1972. *On the Long March with Chairman Mao*. Beijing: Foreign Languages Press.

Chen Changfeng. 1986. *Gensui Mao zhuxi changzheng* [Following Chairman Mao on the Long March]. Rev. ed. Beijing: Jiefangjun wenyi chubanshe.

Chen Chun'e. 1986. "Cong 'baowei zhongyang suqu' dao quanmian kaizhan youjizhanzhengde zhuanbian" [The turn from "defending the Central Soviet" to developing all-round guerrilla war]. *Jiangxi shifan daxue xuebao (zhexue shehui kexue ban)* 2:79–83.

Chen Fu. 1985. "Xianggan geming genjudi shi yanjiu zongshu" [Survey of research on the history of the Xianggan revolutionary base]. *Dangshi tongxun* 3:23–31.

Chen Gang et al. 1985. "Liang Botai." *Zhonggong dangshi renwu zhuan* 22: 281–307.

Chen Gaoshun. 1982. "Huiyi 'Zhangpu shibian' " [Recalling the "Zhangpu Incident"]. *Wenshi shiliao xuanji* (Zhangzhou) 3:27–35.

Chen Guangxiang. 1988. "Xinsijun zaoqi lingdaoren shi zenyang bei quedingde?" [How were the New Fourth Army's early leaders determined?] *Geming shi ziliao* 9:56–62.

Chen Jun. 1939. *Xinsijun manji* [Random notes on the New Fourth Army]. Shanghai?: Tongyi chubanshe.

Chen Lisheng et al. 1982. "Zhanbuduande dixia jiaotongxian" [An indestructible underground liaison network]. In Anhui sheng junqu, 307–9.

Chen Maohui. 1981. "Husong Chen Tanqiu tongzhi guo baiqu" [Escorting Comrade Chen Tanqiu into White territory]. In Zhonggong Huanggang xianwei hui, 109–10.

———. 1983. "Huainian Liao Haitao lieshi" [In memory of the martyr Liao Haitao]. *Fengzhan hongqi* 2:133–47.

———. 1984. "Tan Minxi dangshi jige wenti" [Some questions in Minxi Party history]. *Minxi dangshi ziliao tongxun* 3:1–2.

Chen Pixian. 1979. "Mitian fenghuo ju hongqi: Huiyi Chen Yi tongzhi lingdaode nanfang sannian youjizhanzheng" [Holding high the Red Flag as war signals fill the sky: Memories of Comrade Chen Yi leading the three-year guerrilla war in the south]. In Shanghai renmin chubanshe, 104–51.

————. 1980. "Youshan jiaoxia" [At the foot of Youshan]. *Xinghuo liaoyuan congkan* 1:44–50.

————. 1982. *Gannan sannian youjizhanzheng* [The three-year guerrilla war in Gannan]. Beijing: Renmin chubanshe.

————. 1986. "Tan dui Xiang Yingde pingjia wenti" [On the assessment of Xiang Ying]. *Dangshi tongxun* 1:45.

Chen Qunzhe. 1983. "Huang Dao." *Zhonggong dangshi renwu zhuan* 7:123–49.

Chen Renhong. 1983a. "Chechu Minbei hongse shoufu Da'anjie" [Retreating from Minbei's Red capital Da'anjie]. *Dangshi ziliao yu yanjiu* (Fujian) 10:18–22.

————. 1983b. "Min'gan bian sannian youjizhanzheng xumu" [Prelude to the three-year guerrilla war on the Min'gan border]. *Fengzhan hongqi* 2:148–66.

————. 1985a. *Cong Minbei dao Wannan* [From Minbei to Wannan]. Fuzhou: Fujian renmin chubanshe.

————. 1985b. "Shitang zhengbian" [Reorganizing at Shitang]. *Dangshi ziliao yu yanjiu* (Fujian) 4:55–64.

Chen Ronghua. 1987 [1985]. "Difang dang yu hongjunde xingdong xianghe pai wenti chutan" [Preliminary investigations into the unity of the local Party and the Red Army]. In *Zhonggong dangshi wenzhai niankan (1985 nian)*, ed. Liao Gailong. Beijing: Zhonggong dangshi ziliao chubanshe.

Chen Si et al. 1982. "Guangdong qingnian kangRi xianfengduide zhandou licheng" [The course of the struggle of the anti-Japanese vanguard of Guangdong youth]. *Xueshu yanjiu* 3:85–93.

Chen Songqing. 1986. " 'Minbian' yu Mindong geming jueqi" [The Fujian Incident and the rise of the Mindong revolution]. *Fujian dangshi tongxun* 2:49–52.

Chen Ting. 1982a. "Guanyu erzhan shiqi Mindong geming douzhengde yixie tedian" [Some special features of the revolutionary struggle in Mindong during the second civil war]. *Dangshi ziliao yu yanjiu* (Fujian) 12:22–24.

————. 1982b. "Tan Mindong hongjunde chengzhang" [On the growing to maturity of the Mindong Red Army]. *Dangshi ziliao yu yanjiu* (Fujian) 8:1–12.

————. 1983a. "Huiyi Mindong sannian youjizhanzheng" [Recalling Mindong's three-year guerrilla war]. *Dangshi ziliao yu yanjiu* (Fujian) 1:1–12.

————. 1983b. "Mindong fenghuo" [Mindong beacon]. *Fengzhan hongqi* 3:27–41.

————. 1984. "Huiyi Mindong hongjun douzheng lishi" [Recalling the Mindong Red Army's history of struggle]. *Fujian dangshi ziliao* 3:135–71.

Chen Weike. 1984. "Fang Zhimin." *Jiefang jiangling zhuan* 1:3–52.

Chen Wen. 1987. "Ye tan xinsijun junbu chenglide shijian, didian" [Again on the time and place of the establishment of the New Fourth Army headquarters]. *Junshi shilin* 3:43–45.

Chen Wenxiu et al. 1983. "He Chang." *Zhonggong dangshi renwu zhuan* 12:217–47.

Chen Xiang. 1980. "Sannian youjizhanzhengde qidian" [The starting point of the three-year guerrilla war]. In Zhonggong Jinzhai, 148–55.

————. 1984. "Jiannande licheng" [Arduous course]. In Wanxi geming, 20–42.

Chen Xiaocen. 1982. "Xi'an shibianqian guogong liangdang tanpande pianduan huiyi" [Recollections of Nationalist-Communist talks before the Xi'an Incident]. *Dangshi yanjiu ziliao* 3:567–78.

Chen Xueming et al. 1983. "Huang Ligui." *Zhonggong dangshi renwu zhuan* 11:281–93.

Chen Yafang. 1986. "Minnan dangde zaoqi huodong" [The early activities of the Minnan Party]. *Dangshi ziliao yu yanjiu* (Fujian) 4:45–47.

Chen Yi. 1942 [1941]. "Lun jianjun gongzuo" [On army building]. In Qishi zhengzhibu yiyin, *Lilun (Chen Yi), dangnei jiaocaizhi si.* July. Mimeo. 052.1 577 16655 N 3,4.

———. 1973. "Wo zhege waijiao buzhang" [I, Foreign Affairs Minister]. In "Zhonggong yanjiu," 410–13.

———. 1977. *Shici xuanji* [Collected poems]. Beijing: Renmin wenxue chubanshe.

———. 1979 [1962]. "Zai quanguo huaju, geju, ertongju chuangzuo zuotan-huishangde jianghua" [Speech at national seminar on the creation of plays, musicals, and children's drama]. *Wenyi bao* 8:40–45.

———. 1980 [1959]. "Yi sannian youjizhanzheng" [Remembering the three-year guerrilla war]. *Jindai shi yanjiu* 2:1–19.

———. 1981 [1942]. "Gei Luo Shengte tongzhide xin" [Letter to Comrade Luo Shengte]. In Nie Yuansu et al., 9–11.

———. 1981 [1952]. "Zaonian huiyi" [Early reminiscences]. In Nie Yuansu et al., 12–26.

———. 1981 [1957]. "Yi jiankude sannian youjizhanzheng" [Remembering the harsh three-year guerrilla war]. In Chen Yi et al. 1981, 541–90.

———. 1981 [1963]. "Xuanze gemingde daolu" [Choosing the revolutionary road]. In Nie Yuansu et al., 27–40.

———. 1982a [1939]. "Guanyu xuexi" [On study]. In Zhenjiang diqu, 105–15.

———. 1982b [1939]. "Maoshan yinian—Jiangnan youjiqu" [One year in Mao-shan: Jiangnan's guerrilla area]. In Zhenjiang diqu, 25–51.

———. 1986 [1940]. "Nanfang sannian youjizhanzheng" [The three-year guer-rilla war in the south]. In Zhongguo renmin geming junshi bowuguan, 113–22.

Chen Yi and Liang Botai. 1986 [1934]. "Zhongyang zhengfu banshichu jinji ming-ling" [Urgent order of the Central Government Office]. December 20. In Zhongguo renmin geming junshi bowuguan, 108–10.

Chen Yi et al. 1980. *Kangzhanzhi chun* [Spring in the Resistance War]. Rugao: Jiangsu renmin chubanshe.

———. 1981. *Huiyi zhongyang suqu* [Memories of the Central Soviet]. Nanchang: Jiangxi renmin chubanshe.

Chen Yunfei. 1983. "Luohanli bo huozhong" [Scattering embers at Luohanli]. *Fengzhan hongqi* 3:42–54.

Chen, Yung-fa. 1986. *Making Revolution: The Communist Movement in Eastern and Central China, 1937–1945.* Berkeley: University of California Press.

Chen Yung-fa and Gregor Benton. 1986. *Moral Economy and the Chinese Revolu-tion: A Critique.* Amsterdam: ZZOA Publications, University of Amsterdam.

Chen Zhengfang and Zhang Ruizhe. 1984. "Yi Fuqing Long-Gao nongmin qiyi" [Recalling Fuqing's Longgao peasant uprising]. *Fengzhan hongqi* 4:131–36.

Chen Zigan. 1981. "Milin huozhong" [Live cinders in the deepest forest]. In Zhonggong Shangcheng xianweihui, 84–90.

Cheng Fangwu. 1977. *Changzheng huiyilu* [Memories of the Long March]. Beijing: Renmin chubanshe.

Cheng Meixing. 1982. "Huiyi lusui Liu Ying tongzhi zhandoude suiyue" [Reminiscences of fighting under Comrade Liu Ying in difficult times]. *Jiangxi wenshi ziliao xuanji* 3:26–34.

———. 1984. "Zai Liu Ying tongzhide shenbian" [At Comrade Liu Ying's side]. In Zhejiang sheng junqu, 254–70.

Chi, S. Y. 1934. "Noteworthy Reconstruction in Kiangsi Province." *China Weekly Review,* November 3.

———. 1935. "Further Details on How General Chiang Drove the Communists from Kiangsi." *China Weekly Review,* April 20.

Chiang Kai-shek. 1969. *Soviet Russia in China.* Taibei: China Publishing Company.

Chongqing xiandai geming shi ziliao congshu bianweihui, eds. 1983. *Huiyi nanfangju* [Recalling the Southern Bureau]. Chongqing: Chongqing chubanshe.

Cui Yitian, ed. 1983. *Baiyi zhanshi yi Chen zong* [White-coated soldiers remember Commander Chen]. Shanghai: Renmin chubanshe.

Dai Xiangqing. 1985. "Lun Chen Yi sannian youjizhanzhengzhongde diwei he zuoyong" [Chen Yi's position and role in the three-year guerrilla war]. *Zhongguo xiandai shi yuekan* 11:189–95.

Dai Xiangqing et al. 1986. *Zhongyang geming genjudi shigao* [Draft history of the central revolutionary base]. Shanghai: Shanghai renmin chubanshe.

Dai Xuanzhi. 1973. *Hongqianghui (1916–1949)* [The Red Spears (1916–1949)]. Taibei: Shihuo chubanshe.

Dan Jiang. 1981. "Chizizhi xin" [Utter innocence]. In Renmin chubanshe, 50–56.

Deng Haishan. 1981. "Huiyi Ting, Rui diqu sannian youjizhanzheng" [Recalling the three-year guerrilla war in the Tingrui area]. *Jiangxi wenshi ziliao xuanji* 7:68–73.

Deng Jiakun et al. 1984. "Mindong suweiai zhengquande chuangjian yu fazhan" [The creation and development of soviet regimes in Mindong]. *Dangshi ziliao yu yanjiu* (Fujian) 5:37–45.

[Deng] Zihui. 1936a. "Xi'nan shibian yu Zhongguo geming" [The Southwestern Incident and the Chinese Revolution]. In Zhongguo gongchandang Minxi'nan weiyuanhui jiguan bao, *Hongqi* 3. July 9. Mimeo. 052.1 813 15523 N 9–11.

———. 1936b. "Zai fangongzhong dangde celüe kouhaode zhuanbian" [Changes in the Party's tactical slogans during the counteroffensive]. In Zhongguo gongchandang Minxi'nan weiyuanhui jiguan bao, *Hongqi.* August 25. Mimeo. 052.1 813 15521 N 5.

———. 1936c. "Zai fentian douzhengzhongde jingyan yu jiaoxun" [Experiences and lessons in the struggle to divide the land]. In Zhongguo gongchandang Minxi'nan weiyuanhui jiguan bao, *Hongqi* 6. September 10. Mimeo. 052.1 813 15521 N 5.

———. 1936d. "Zai tongyi zhanxianzhong jige cuowu qingkuang" [Some mistakes in the united front]. In Zhongguo gongchandang Minxi'nan weiyuanhui jiguan bao, *Hongqi* 2. June 12. Mimeo. 052.1 813 15523 N 9–11.

———. 1982. "Wode zizhuan" [My autobiography]. *Geming shi ziliao* 8:1–22.

————. 1983. "Longyan renmin geming douzheng huiyilu" [Memoirs of the Longyan people's revolutionary struggle]. *Fujian dangshi ziliao* 2:1–45.

————. 1985 [1937]. "Zai wei heping ei douzhengde liangge yuezhong" [Two months of struggle for peace]. In Zhonggong Fujian shengwei, 12–17.

Department of State, Division of Publications, Office of Public Affairs. 1953. *Foreign Relations of the United States, Diplomatic Papers, 1935. Vol. 3. The Far East.* Washington: United States Government Printing Office.

Ding Qiusheng. 1983. "Lülun Chen Yi tongzhi zhihui yishude tese" [Special features of Comrade Chen Yi's art of command]. *Dangshi tongxun* 13:23–24.

Ding Shanghuai. 1979. "Cha yigan hongqi zai shanshang" [Planting a red flag on the mountain]. In Shanghai renmin chubanshe, 152–64.

Ding Yisan. 1979. "Chen Yi chu shan" [Chen Yi leaves the mountains]. *Xinhua yuebao (wenzhai ban)* 3:110–31.

————. 1980. *Chen Yi chu shan* [Chen Yi leaves the mountains]. Beijing: Zhongguo xiju chubanshe.

Ding Zhihui. 1981. "Chen Yi tongzhi kanwang shangbingyuan" [Comrade Chen Yi visits the sick and wounded]. *Xinghuo liaoyuan congkan* 3:46.

Dong Biwu. 1986 [1937]. "Guanyu Xiang'egan suqu budui gaibian wenti gei zhongyang xin" [Letter to the Central Committee about reforming the troops of the Xiang'egan Soviet]. *Geming shi ziliao* 3:13–16.

Dong Huanran. 1937. "Minbei nongcunde yizhong shenmi jieshe" [A mysterious society in the Minbei villages]. *Zhongguo nongcun* 3 (2): 81–86.

Donovan, Peter Williams. 1976. *The Red Army in Kiangsi, 1931–1934.* Cornell University East Asia Papers, no. 10.

Dreyer, June Teufel. 1976. *China's Forty Millions: Minority Nationalities and National Integration in the People's Republic of China.* Cambridge: Harvard University Press.

Duan Huanjing. 1975. "Jianchi zai Xianggan bianqu" [Holding out in Xianggan]. In *Jinian hongjun changzheng shengli sishi zhounian,* ed. Jiangxi daxue lishi yanjiushi, Yiyang: N.p., 380–91.

————. 1979. "Jianchi zai Xianggan bianqu" [Holding out in Xianggan]. In *Geming douzheng huiyilu.* 2 vols. Jiangxi renmin chubanshe. Vol. 2, 358–86.

————. 1980. "Gensui Chen Yi tongzhi chushan kangRi" [Following Comrade Chen Yi from the mountains to resist Japan]. In Renmin chubanshe, 96–112.

————. 1983. "Mitian fenghuo ju hongqi" [The Red Flag fills the sky]. *Xinghuo liaoyuan* 4:82–85.

Elton, G. R. 1970. *Political History: Principles and Practice.* London: Allen Lane.

Epstein, Israel. 1939. *The People's War.* London: Victor Gollancz.

Esherick, Joseph W. 1975. *Lost Chance in China: The World War Two Despatches of John S. Service.* New York: Vintage Books.

Eyu bianqu geming shi bianjibu, eds. 1985. *Xinsijun diwushi kangzhan licheng* [The New Fourth Army's Fifth Division in the anti-Japanese resistance]. Hubei: Renmin chubanshe.

"Eyuwan suqu lishi jianbian" bianxiezu, eds. 1983. *Eyuwan suqu lishi jianbian* [Introduction to the history of the Eyuwan Soviet]. Xiangyang: Hubei renmin chubanshe.

Fan Shiren. 1982. "Hong shiliuliande dansheng" [The birthday of the Red Sixteenth Company.] *Fengzhan hongqi* 1:64–74.

———. 1983. "Mindong hetan qianhou" [Around the time of the Mindong peace talks]. *Fengzhan hongqi* 2:167–74.

———. 1984 [1959]. "Huiyi Mindong dangde douzheng lishi" [Recalling the Mindong Party's history of struggle]. *Fujian dangshi ziliao* 3:98–134.

Fang Fang. 1936. "Muqian Longlianning biande douzheng jumian" [The present struggle in the Longlianning border area]. In Zhongguo gongchandang Minxi'nan weiyuanhui jiguan bao, *Hongqi* 6. September 10. Mimeo. 052.1 813 15521 N 5.

———. 1979. "Sannian youjizhanzheng" [The three-year guerrilla struggle]. *Hongqi piaopiao* 18:74–148.

Fang Qingqiu. 1983. "Fujian shibian shulun" [On the Fujian Incident]. *Lishi dang'an* 1:103–10.

Fang Zhichun. 1980. *Gandongbei suweiai chuanglide lishi* [The history of the founding of the Gandongbei Soviet]. Beijing: Renmin chubanshe.

———. 1981a. "Daolu shi quzhede: Yi Min'gan douzheng wunian" [The path is tortuous: Memories of five years of struggle of Min'gan]. In Fang Zhimin et al. 1981, 163–86.

———. 1981b. "Shi qiong jie nai xian" [Courage in extreme adversity]. In Zhonggong Huanggang xianwei hui, 162–71.

———. 1983. "Yi Min'gan douzheng wunian" [Recalling five years' struggle in Min'gan]. In Fang Zhimin et al. 1983, 171–90.

Fang Zhimin. 1980. *Wo congshi geming douzhengde lüeshu* [An outline of my service in the revolutionary struggle]. Beijing: Renmin chubanshe.

Fang Zhimin et al. 1981. *Huiyi Minzhewan'gande geming douzheng* [Remembering the revolutionary struggle in Minzhewan'gan]. Nanchang: Jiangxi renmin chubanshe.

———. 1983. *Huiyi Minzhewan'gan suqu* [Recalling Minzhewan'gan's soviet areas]. Nanchang: Jiangxi renmin chubanshe.

"Fang Zhimin zhuan" bianxiezu. 1982. *Fang Zhimin zhuan* [Biography of Fang Zhimin]. Nanchang: Jiangxi renmin chubanshe.

Fawubu diaochaju, eds. 1982a. *Zhonggong "nongmin yundong" yuanshi wenjian huibian* [Original documents of the Chinese Communists' "peasant movement"]. Taiwan: Fawubu diaochaju.

———. 1982b. *Zhonggong "dangde jianshe" yuanshi wenjian huibian* [Original documents of the Chinese Communists' "Party Construction"]. Taiwan: Fawubu diaochaju.

Fei Hsiao Tong [Fei Xiaotong]. 1981. *Toward a People's Anthropology.* Beijing: New World Press.

Feng Ding. 1979. "Yipian danxin zhao Hanqi" [A loyal heart shines on the Chinese flag]. In Shanghai renmin chubanshe, 402–16.

———. 1983. "Guanyu kangda wufenxiao yiduan lishide huiyi" [Memoirs of the fifth branch of Resistance University]. In Yancheng shi, 482–83.

Foreign Languages Press, eds. 1978. *Fifty Years of the Chinese People's Liberation Army.* Beijing: Foreign Languages Press.

Fortune, Robert. 1979 [1847]. *Three Years' Wandering in the Northern Provinces of China.* Reprint of the original edition published by J. Murray, London. New York and London: Garland.

Fu Qiutao. 1979 [1959]. *Gaoju hongqi jianchi douzheng: Xiang'egan bianqu sannian youjizhanzhengde huiyi (1934–1937)* [Holding high the Red Flag and persevering with the struggle: Recollections of the three-year guerrilla struggle in the Xiang'egan border area (1934–1937)]. Nanchang: Jiangxi renmin chubanshe.

Fu Xueyuan. 1958. "Kaoyan" [Tests and trials]. *Hongse fengbao* 2:184–94.

Fu Yongdao. 1963. "Youjiduide 'liangzhan' " [The guerrillas' "grain station"]. In Jiangxi sheng funü lianhehui, 92–97.

Fu Yunfei. 1979. "Chen Yi tongzhi xunzhao Xianggan youjidui" [Comrade Chen Yi seeks out the Xianggan guerrillas]. *Zhengrong suiyue* 1:11–25.

"Fujian geming jishi" bianxiezu, eds. 1985. "Fujian geming jishi" [Chronicle of the Fujian revolution]. Pts. 3 and 5. *Fujian dangshi tongxun* 5:55–63 and 7:53–64.

Fujian sheng dang'anguan, eds. 1984. *Fujian shibian dang'an ziliao* [Archive materials on the Fujian Incident]. Fuzhou: Fujian renmin chubanshe.

Ganyuemin'exiang beilu jiaofeijun disan lujun zongzhihuibu canmouchu. 1968 [1937]. *Wuci weijiao zhanshi* [Five encirclements]. 2 vols. Taibei: Zhonghua minguo kaiguo wushinian wenxuan weiyuanhui.

Gao Enxian. 1987. *Zhongguo gongnong hongjun weisheng gongzuo lishi jianbian* [History of health work in the Chinese Red Army]. Beijing: Renmin junyi chubanshe.

Garraghan, Gilbert J. 1946. *A Guide to Historical Method.* Edited by Jean Delanglez. New York: Fordham University Press.

Garver, John W. 1988a. *Chinese-Soviet Relations, 1937–1945.* New York: Oxford University Press.

———. 1988b. "The Origins of the Second United Front: The Comintern and the Chinese Communist Party." *China Quarterly* 113:29–59.

Ge Demao. 1983. "Guanyu xinsijun chengli shide guogong tanpan, budui jizhong yu jianzhi" [Nationalist-Communist talks, concentration of troops, and the organizational system of the New Fourth Army at the time of its establishment]. *Zhongguo xiandai shi yuekan* 5:129–34.

"Gei Li Hua tongzhide xin" [Letter to Comrade Li Hua]. 1936. December 13. In Zhongguo gongchandang Minxi'nan weiyuanhui jiguan bao, *Hongqi* 10. Mimeo. 052.1 813 15523 N 9–11.

Gittings, John. 1967. *The Role of the Chinese Army.* London: Oxford University Press.

Gong Chu. 1954. *Wo yu hongjun* [I and the Red Army]. Hongkong: Nanfeng chubanshe.

———. 1971–74. "Canjia Zhonggong wuzhuang douzheng jishi" [Record of taking part in the Chinese Communists' armed struggle]. *Mingbao yuekan,* nos. 63–98.

Gong Gujin and Tang Peiji, eds. 1983. *Zhongguo kangRi zhanzheng shigao* [Draft history of China's anti-Japanese war]. 2 vols. Hubei: Renmin chubanshe.

Griffin, Patricia E. 1976. *The Chinese Communist Treatment of Counterrevolutionaries.* Princeton: Princeton University Press.

Gu Ziyuan. N.d. "Huiyi Xiangnan renmin jianku yingyongde wuzhuang douzheng" [Recalling the bitter and heroic armed struggle of the Xiangnan people]. In Wuhan yexiao.

Guan Jie, ed. 1980. "Huanghualing xia youqing" [Friendship in the Huanghua Mountains]. In Anhui sheng Wuhu shi, 155–67.

Guangshan xian difang dangshi bianzuan bangongshi, eds. 1983. "Chicheng Eyuwan, gongzhao Dabieshan" [Gallop to Eyuwan to win achievements in the Dabie Mountains]. In Henan sheng minzhengting, vol. 4, 1–13.

Guangzhou shi zhengxie wenshi ziliao yanjiu weiyuanhui, eds. 1987. *Nantian suiyue: Chen Jitang zhu Yue shiqi jianwen shilu* [Years in the south: Record of experiences during Chen Jitang's governorship of Guangdong]. *Guangzhou wenshi ziliao*, no. 37. Guangdong renmin chubanshe.

Gui Yulin. 1986a. *Jinggangshan geming douzheng shi* [History of the revolutionary struggle in the Jinggang Mountains]. Beijing: Jiefangjun chubanshe.

———. 1986b. "Jinggangshan geming genjudi shi jige wentide yanjiu zongshu" [Research into several questions concerning the history of the Jinggang Mountains revolutionary base]. *Jiangxi geming wenwu* 2:1–5.

Guillermaz, Jacques. 1972. *A History of the Chinese Communist Party, 1921–1949.* Trans. Anne Destenay. London: Methuen.

Guillermaz, Jacques. 1989. *Une vie pour la Chine: Mémoires, 1937–1989.* Paris: Robert Laffont.

Guinn, Paul. 1965. *British Strategy and Politics, 1914 to 1918.* Oxford: Clarendon Press.

Guo Buyun. 1980. "Renzhen yanjiu Eyuwan suqu geming shi" [Conscientiously research the history of the soviet revolution in Eyuwan]. *Jianghan luntan* 3:11–13.

Guo Guangbei. 1981. "He Shuheng tongzhi zhaoji women kai zuotanhui" [Comrade He Shuheng calls us together for a discussion]. In Chen Yi et al. 1981, 532–33.

Guo Jidong and Fang Lieshu. 1984. "Fu Qiutao." *Zhonggong dangshi renwu zhuan* 18:297–334.

———. 1986. "Fu Qiutao." *Jiefangjun jiangling zhuan* 3:391–424.

Guo Yuzhong and Xu Li. 1984. "Eyuwan geming genjudi shi yanjiu zongshu" [General survey of historical research on the Eyuwan revolutionary base]. *Dangshi tongxun* 11:31–38.

Guofangbu, shizhengju. 1967. *Jiaofei zhanshi* [The wars to exterminate the bandits]. 6 vols. Taibei: Zhonghua da dian bianyinhui.

Guojia minwei minzu wenti wuzhong congshu bianji weiyuanhui. 1981. *Zhongguo shaoshu minzu* [China's minority nationalities]. Beijing: Renmin chubanshe.

H. 1936. "Fan Chi-min—Hero of the Chinese People." *China at Bay* (January) 68–71.

Haitian chubanshe, eds. 1935. *Xiandai shiliao* [Contemporary historical materials]. 4 vols. N.p.: Haitian chubanshe.

Han Shirui and Hu Guhua. 1986. "Mindong youjiqude weisheng gongzuo" [Health work in the Mindong guerrilla area]. *Dangshi ziliao yu yanjiu* (Fuzhou) 2:40–43.

Han Suyin. 1976. *The Morning Deluge: Mao Tsetung and the Chinese Revolution. Vol. 1: 1893–1935.* Frogmore: Panther.

Hao Mengbi and Duan Haoran, eds. 1984. *Zhongguo gongchandang liushinian* [Sixty years of the Chinese Communist Party]. 2 vols. Beijing: Jiefangjun chubanshe.

Harrison, James P. 1972. *The Long March to Power: A History of the Communist Party, 1921–72.* London: Macmillan.

Hartford, Kathleen, and Steven M. Goldstein, eds. 1989. *Single Sparks: China's Rural Revolutions.* Armonk and New York: M. E. Sharpe and the East Asian Institute of Columbia University.

Hatano Ken'ichi. 1961. *Chugoku kyosantoshi* [History of the Chinese Communist Party]. 7 vols. Tokyo: Jiji tsushin sha.

He Li. 1980. "Wannan shibian" [The Wannan Incident]. *Jindai shi yanjiu* 3:96–119.

He Ming. 1935. "Zenmo qu fadong nianguan douzheng" [How to develop the end-of-year struggle]. In Zhonggong Minyue bianqu tewei jiguan bao, *Zhandou* 2. December 30. 052.1 813 16356 N 2.

He Shijie and Peng Xing. 1986. "Gao Jingting zhuanlüe" [Brief biography of Gao Jingting]. *Dangshi ziliao zhengji tongxun* 2:21–25.

He Shisan and He Shisi. 1982. "He Shuheng tongzhi zai zhongyang suqu" [Comrade He Shuheng in the Central Soviet]. *Geming huiyilu* 5:31–40.

He Shisi. 1986. "He Shuheng tongzhi shi zai tuweizhong bei dijun shahaide" [Comrade He Shuheng was killed by enemy troops while breaking through the encirclement]. *Dangshi ziliao zhengji tongxun* 2:19–20.

He Yaobang. 1959. *Dabieshanshang hongqi piao* [The Red Flag flutters in the Dabie Mountains]. Beijing: Zhongguo qingnian chubanshe.

———. 1983. *Dabieshanshang hongqi piao* [The Red Flag flutters in the Dabie Mountains]. Rev. ed. Beijing: Zhongguo qingnian chubanshe.

Heffernan, Thomas J. 1988. *Sacred Biography: Saints and Their Biographers in the Middle Ages.* New York: Oxford University Press.

Henan sheng minzhengting, eds. 1983. *Lieshi yongsheng* [Immortal martyrs]. Vol. 4. Henan renmin chubanshe.

Hofheinz, Roy, Jr. 1969. "The Ecology of Chinese Communist Success." In *Chinese Communist Politics in Action,* ed. A. D. Barnett, Seattle: University of Washington Press, 3–77.

———. 1977. *The Broken Wave: The Chinese Communist Peasant Movement, 1922–1928.* Cambridge: Harvard University Press.

Hong Da. 1986. "Tuoqi changhong, yong fang guangcai" [Hold up the rainbow, it will be eternally bright]. *Kaihua wenshi ziliao* 1:19–26.

Hong Zhong. 1984. "Kangzhan qianhou Riben dui Xiamende junshi qinlüe" [Japan's military aggression against Xiamen at around the time of the Resistance War]. *Xiamen fangzhi tongxun* 3:19.

Hongan xian geming shi bianxie bangongshi, eds. 1987. *Hongan xian geming shi* [Revolutionary history of Hongan county]. Wuhan: Wuhan daxue chubanshe.

Hou Zhiying et al. 1982. "Hong ershiba jun zhengwei Gao Jingting" [Commissar Gao Jingting of the Twenty-eighth Red Army]. *Henan shida xuebao (Shehui kexue ban)* 6:49–61.

———. 1983. "Gao Jingting." *Zhonggong dangshi renwu zhuan* 8:254–84.

Hsiao, Tso-liang. 1961. *Power Relations within the Chinese Communist Movement, 1930–1934: A Study of Documents.* 2 vols. Seattle: University of Washington Press.

Hsieh, Winston. 1975. *Chinese Historiography on the Revolution of 1911*. Stanford: Hoover Institute Press.

Hu Liangzhong. 1987a. "Tan Zhenlin." *Jiefangjun jiangling zhuan* 4:471–521.

———. 1987b. "Tan Zhenlin." *Zhonggong dangshi renwu zhuan* 31:25–104.

Hu Yunqiu et al. 1981. "Chen Tanqiu shengping huodong nianbiao" [A chronology of Chen Tanqiu]. *Zhongguo xiandai shi* 18:65–72.

Huang Bingguang. 1983. "Husong Chen Yi shangshan ji" [Escorting Chen Yi up the mountain]. *Fengzhan hongqi* 3:96–102.

Huang Changjiao. 1963. "Buqude zhandou" [Unyielding fight]. In Jiangxi sheng funü, 55–67.

———. 1981. "Wo suo zhidaode Tingrui youjidui pianduan" [Recollections of the Tingrui Guerrillas as I knew them]. *Jiangxi wenshi ziliao xuanji* 7: 74–76.

Huang Chuiming. 1986. "Wo suo jinglide banian kangzhan" [My experience of eight years of the Resistance War]. *Fujian dangshi tongxun* 2:11–16.

Huang Guozhang. 1986. " 'Quanzhou shibian' qianhou" [Around the time of the "Quanzhou Incident"]. *Fujian dangshi ziliao* 4:101–5.

[Huang] Huicong. 1935. "Jianjuede weizhe kaizhan fanRi tongyi zhanxian yu chuangzao fanJiangde tongyi zhanxian er douzheng" [Struggle to develop the anti-Japanese united front and to create an anti-Chiang [Kai-shek] united front]. In Zhonggong Minyue bianqu tewei jiguanbao, *Zhandou* 2. December 30. 052.1 813 16356 N 2.

———. 1936. "Fujiande weiji yu dang muqiande jinji renwu" [The Fujian crisis and the Party's present urgent tasks]. In Zhonggong Minyue bianqu tewei jiguan bao, *Zhandou* 4, April 15. 052.1 813 1357 N 4.

———. 1985 [1937]. "Zhonggong Minyue bianqu tewei shuji Huang Huicong gei zhongyangde zonghe baogao" [Report by Huang Huicong, secretary of the Minyue Special Committee, to the Central Committee]. April 20. In Zhonggong Fujian sheng Longxi, vol. 1, 205–46.

———. 1985. "Hongjiu juntuan husong hongqi juntuan duguo Min Jiang beishang kangRi jingguo" [The Red Ninth Army Group escorts the Red Seventh Army Group north across the Min Jiang to resist Japan]. *Fujian dangshi tongxun* 7:8.

Huang Jianlan. 1985. "Minyue bianqu sannian youjizhanzheng" [The three-year guerrilla war in Minyue]. Pt. 1. *Minnan geming shi yanjiu* 1:11–22.

———. 1986. "Minyue bianqu sannian youjizhanzheng xueshu taolunhui jianjie" [Academic symposium on the three-year guerrilla war in Minyue]. *Dangshi tongxun* 1:43–44.

Huang Kaiyuan et al. 1981. "Wannan shibian ji qi lishi jiaoxun" [The Wannan Incident and its historical lessons]. *Anhui shida xuebao* 3:16–25.

Huang Keyong. 1981. "Zhandou zai Minyuegan bianqu" [The armed struggle on the Minyuegan border]. In Zhang Dingcheng et al., *Hongqi yueguo Ting Jiang*. Fuzhou: Fujian renmin chubanshe.

Huang Keyun. 1985. "Xiang'egan geming genjudi shi yanjiu zongshu" [Survey of historical research on the Xiang'egan revolutionary base]. *Dangshi tongxun* 2:28–32.

Huang Liangcheng. 1979. *Yi changzheng* [Recalling the Long March]. Shenyang: Chunfeng wenyi chubanshe.

Huang Shaoxiong. 1945. *Wushi huiyi* [Memoirs at fifty]. 2 pts. Shanghai.

———. 1987. "Zai zhanhuozhong zhu Zhe banian" [Eight years of governing Zhejiang amid war fires]. In Zhejiang sheng zhengxie, 33–44.

Huang Shumeng and Zhang Jichang. 1984. "Liu Ying." *Zhonggong dangshi renwu zhuan* 20:261–91.

Huang Xianhe. 1979. "Minzhe linshi shengwei zhaodao zhongyang jingguo" [How the Minzhe Provisional Provincial Committee found the Party's Central Committee]. *Zhejiang wenshi ziliao xuanji* 14:69–85.

Huang Yaonan. 1985. "Guanyu Xiang'egan diqu hezuo tanpan ji 'Pingjiang can'an' jingguo qingkuangde huiyi" [Memoirs of the Xiang'egan peace talks and the "Pingjiang massacre"]. In Zhonggong Pingjiang xianwei, 181–91.

Huang Ying. 1983. "Guanyu Minbei geming douzheng jige wenti" [Some questions about the revolutionary struggle in Minbei]. In Fang Zhimin et al. 1983, 453–58.

———. 1985. "Yi Gandongbei sannian youjizhanzheng pianduan" [Recalling scenes from the three-year guerrilla war in Gandongbei]. *Shangrao shi wenshi ziliao* 4:1–6.

Huang Zhaosong and Liu Hanqing. 1986. "Tingrui youjidui shuping" [The Tingrui Guerrillas]. *Fujian dangshi tongxun* 9:69–73.

Huang Zhizhen. 1958. "Xinsijun banshichu zai Nanchangde kangRi jiuwang yundong" [The Nanchang New Fourth Army office's movement to resist Japan and save China]. In Jiangxi renmin chubanshe, 321–24.

———. 1959. "Minbei sannian" [Three years in Minbei]. *Hongqi piaopiao* 11:109–20.

———. 1979. "Huainian Huang Dao tongzhi" [In memory of Comrade Huang Dao]. In *Geming douzheng huiyilu*. 2 vols. Jiangxi renmin chubanshe, vol. 2, 304–12.

———. 1983. "Yi Minbeide youjizhanzheng" [Recalling Minbei's guerrilla war]. In Fang Zhimin et al. 1983, 421–27.

Huang Zhongfang. 1987. "Wang Zuo." *Jiefangjun jiangling zhuan* 5:3–18.

Hubei "Eyuwan suqu lishi jianbian" bianxiezu. 1987. "Eyuwan geming genjudide lishi diwei ji zuoyong" [The historical position and role of the Eyuwan revolutionary base]. In Quanguo Zhonggong dangshi yanjiuhui, 163–77.

Hubei sheng junqu zhengzhi bu. 1987. *Dabieshande erzi* [Sons of the Dabie Mountains]. Beijing: Jiefangjun chubanshe.

Hubei sheng "Zhongguo gongchandang lishi jiangyi" bianxiezu. 1982. *Zhongguo gongchandang lishi jiangyi* [Teaching materials on Chinese Communist Party history]. 2 vols. 2d rev. ed. N.p.: Hubei renmin chubanshe.

Hunan renmin chubanshe, eds. 1980. *Huainian Liu Shaoqi tongzhi* [In commemoration of Comrade Liu Shaoqi]. Changsha: Hunan renmin chubanshe.

Hunan sheng bowuguan, eds. 1981. *Hunan geming lieshi shizi shuxin xuan* [An anthology of poems and letters by revolutionary martyrs of Hunan]. Changsha: Hunan renmin chubanshe.

Hunan sheng caizhengting, eds. 1986. *Xianggan geming genjudi caizheng jingji shiliao zhaibian* [Materials relating to the finances and economy of the Xianggan revolutionary base]. Changsha: Hunan renmin chubanshe.

Hunan sheng jiaotongting, eds. 1988. *Hunan gonglu shi* [A history of Hunan roads]. Vol. 1. Beijing: Renmin jiaotong chubanshe.

Hunan sheng shehui kexue yuan, Wuhan shifan xueyuan lishixi, eds. 1982. *Xiang'egan suqu shigao* [Draft history of the Xiang'egan Soviet]. Changsha: Hunan renmin chubanshe.

Hunan shengzhi bianzuan weiyuanhui. 1959. *Hunan shengzhi* [Hunan provincial annals]. 2 vols. Changsha: Hunan renmin chubanshe.

Isaacs, Harold R. 1961. *The Tragedy of the Chinese Revolution*. Stanford: Stanford University Press.

Jen Yu-wen. 1973. *The Taiping Revolutionary Movement*. New Haven: Yale University Press.

"Jiajin baowei Hua'nan" [Urgently defend southern China]. 1937. *Dalu* 6, September 30.

Jiang Boying. 1986. *Deng Zihui zhuan* [Biography of Deng Zihui]. Shanghai: Renmin chubanshe.

———. 1987a. "Minxi geming genjudide chuangli yu fazhan" [The creation and development of the Minxi revolutionary base]. In Quanguo Zhonggong dangshi yanjiuhui, 118–32.

———. 1987b. *Minxi geming genjudi shi* [A history of the Minxi revolutionary base]. Fuzhou: Fujian renmin chubanshe.

Jiang Boying et al. 1983. "Deng Zihui." *Zhonggong dangshi renwu zhuan* 7:296–380.

Jiang Fengbo and Xu Zhanquan. 1989. *Tudi geming zhanzheng jishi* [A chronology of the revolutionary land war]. Beijing: Jiefangjun chubanshe.

Jiang Kangmei. 1983. "Eyuwan sannian youjizhanzhengde zhouyue lingdaozhe Gao Jingting" [Gao Jingting, an outstanding leader of the three-year guerrilla struggle in Eyuwan]. *Huazhong shiyuan xuebao* 1:73–79.

Jiang Maosheng. 1982. "Qiebuduande jiaotongxian" [Unbreakable communication line]. *Fengzhan hongqi* 1:124–63.

———. 1984. "Xionghuai daju, yanyu lüji—huiyi Zhang Dingcheng tongzhi" [Breadth of vision and strict self-discipline—remembering Comrade Zhang Dingcheng]. *Fengzhan hongqi* 4:64–71.

Jiang Weidan. 1985. "Mindong diqu guogong hetan yu 'Quanzhou shibian'" [Nationalist-Communist peace talks in Mindong and the "Quanzhou Incident"]. *Fujian dangshi tongxun* 7:41–45.

Jiang Xinli. 1978. *Qu Qiubaide beiju* [The tragedy of Qu Qiubai]. Taibei: Guoli zhengzhi daxue dongya yanjiusuo.

Jiangnan xinsijun. 1982 [1945]. "Jiangnan xinsijun beiyi gaobie minzhong shu" [The Jiangnan New Fourth Army's farewell message to the masses on the occasion of its transfer north]. In Zhenjiang diqu, 102–4.

Jiangxi renmin chubanshe. 1958. *Zhongguo gongchandang zai Jiangxi diqu lingdao geming douzhengde ziliao* [Materials on the revolutionary struggle led by the Chinese Communist Party in the Jiangxi region]. Nanchang: Jiangxi renmin chubanshe.

Jiangxi sheng diaocha shi, eds. 1941? *Zhonggong zai Gan zhi celüe yinmou* [The Chinese Communists' tactics and plots in Jiangxi]. N.p.

Jiangxi sheng funü lianhehui. 1963. *Jiangxi funü geming douzheng gushi* [Stories of Jiangxi women's revolutionary struggle]. Beijing.

Jin Ge. 1985. "Eyu bianqude minbing jianshe" [Militia construction in the Eyu border region]. In Eyu bianqu, 216–29.

Jinggangshan geming bowuguan. 1985. *Jinggangshan douzheng dashi jieshao* [Introduction to important events in the struggle in the Jinggang Mountains]. Beijing: Jiefangjun chubanshe.

Jiti. 1982. "Hongsantuande wuzhuang douzheng" [The Red Third Regiment's armed struggle]. *Zhangpu wenshi ziliao* (new series) 2:14–19.

Jiti mantan. 1981. "Mantan Minzhegan lao genjudi" [Informal discussion on the old Minzhegan base]. In Fang Zhimin et al. 1981, 106–62.

Jordan, Donald A. 1976. *The Northern Expedition: China's National Revolution of 1926–1928.* Honolulu: University Press of Hawaii.

Junbo "Nanfang sannian youjizhanzheng" yanjiu xiaozu, eds. 1986. "Nanfang sannian youjizhanzheng lishi wenxian yizu" [A set of historical documents relating to the three-year guerrilla war in the south]. *Junshi shilin* 4:14 and 45–46.

Junshi kexueyuan junshi lishi yanjiubu, eds. 1987. *Zhongguo renmin jiefangjun zhanshi* [Battle history of the Chinese People's Liberation Army]. 3 vols. Beijing.

Kahn, Harold, and Albert Feuerwerker. 1968. "The Ideology of Scholarship: China's New Historiography." In *History in Communist China,* ed. Albert Feuerwerker, 1–13. Cambridge: Massachusetts Institute of Technology Press.

Kang Jian. 1985. "Hengdao lima Tongboshan" [A forest of swords in the Tongbo Mountains]. In Zhou Weisong, 115–202.

Kao Yun-lan. 1959. *Annals of a Provincial Town.* Beijing: Foreign Languages Press.

Ke Sheng. 1937. "Heping gaocheng yihou" [After the peace talks]. In Zhongguo gongchandang Minxi'nan weiyuanhui jiguan bao, *Hongqi* 19. August 5. Mimeo. 052.1 813 15526 N 19.

"Kengxiaxiang fentian jingguo" [Dividing the land in Kengxiaxiang]. 1936. In Zhongguo gongchandang Minxi'nan weiyuanhui jiguan bao, *Hongqi.* August 25. Mimeo. 052.1 813 15521 N 5.

Kerr, George H. 1965. *Formosa Betrayed.* Boston: Houghton Mifflin.

Klein, Donald, and Anne Clark. 1971. *Biographical Dictionary of Chinese Communism.* 2 vols. Cambridge: Harvard University Press.

Knei-Paz, Baruch. 1978. *The Social and Political Thought of Leon Trotsky.* Oxford: Clarendon Press.

Koestler, Arthur. 1964. *Darkness at Noon.* Harmondsworth: Penguin Books.

Kong Li. 1979. *Xiamen shihua* [Narrative history of Xiamen]. Shanghai: Renmin chubanshe.

Kong Qiaofan. 1979. "Jiankude sannian youjizhanzheng shenghuo" [Life during the harsh three-year guerrilla war]. *Zhengrong suiyue* 1:45–53.

Kong Yongsong. 1986. "Kangzhan chuqi Fujian guogong hezuo kangRi tanpande guocheng ji qi jingyan" [The talks about a joint Nationalist-Communist resistance in Fujian in the early part of the Resistance War and their outcome]. *Zhongguo xiandai shi yuekan* 1:67–75.

Kong Yongsong and Lin Tianyi. 1982. *Min'gan lu qianli* [Min'gan's thousand-mile journey]. Shanghai: Shanghai renmin chubanshe.

Kong Yongsong et al. 1985. *Zhongyang geming genjudi shiyao* [History of the central revolutionary base]. Nanchang: Jiangxi renmin chubanshe.

Kong Yuan. 1981. "Chen Tanqiu tongzhi zai Mosike" [Comrade Chen Tanqiu in Moscow]. In Zhonggong Huanggang xianwei hui, 111–14.

Kuo, Warren. 1968–71. *Analytical History of the Chinese Communist Party.* 4 vols. Taibei: Institute of International Relations.

Lai Zhigang. 1982. "Chen Yi xiashan ceji" [Sidelight on Chen Yi coming down the mountain]. *Jiangxi wenshi ziliao xuanji* 2:35–41.

Lan Jiongxi et al. 1984. *Zhongguo gongnong hongjun Mindong duli shi* [The Chinese Red Army's Mindong Independent Division]. Ningde: Jianyang diqu dangshi ziliao bangongshi.

Lan Zhougen. 1987. "Shezu you zijide yuyan" [The She have their own language]. In Shi Lianzhu, 334–40.

Lei Jianming. 1984. "Min'gan geming genjudide jianli ji qi douzheng jianshu" [The establishment of the Min'gan revolutionary base and its struggle]. *Dangshi ziliao yu yanjiu* (Fujian) 4:27–32.

Lei Lirong and Yi Shaolin. 1986. "Shilun nanfang sannian youjizhanzheng nenggou jianchide yuanyin" [Why the three-year guerrilla war in the south was able to persist]. *Jiangxi daxue xuebao (Zhexue shehui kexue ban)* 1:35–41.

Lei Weihe and Fu Xinyu. 1981. "Chanchu pantu Zhang Deshan" [Rooting out the traitor Zhang Deshan]. In Zhonggong Shangcheng xianweihui, 347–53.

Leng Xin. 1967. *Cong canjia kangzhan dao mudu Rijun touxiang* [From participating in the Resistance War to witnessing Japan's surrender]. Taibei: Zhuanji wenxue chubanshe.

Li Anbao. 1986a. *Changzheng shi* [History of the Long March]. Beijing: Zhongguo qingnian chubanshe.

———. 1986b. "Guanyu hongjun changzheng yanjiuzhongde yixie wenti" [Some questions in research concerning the Red Army's Long March]. *Dangshi yanjiu ziliao* 10:2–8.

Li Anbao, ed. 1978. *Changzheng shihua* [Narrative history of the Long March]. Beijing: Zhongguo qingnian chubanshe.

Li Ang. 1954. *Hongse wutai* [Red stage]. Taibei.

Li Buxin et al. 1981. "Wanzhegan bianqu sannian youjizhanzheng gaikuang" [Three years of guerrilla warfare in the Wanzhegan border area]. In Fang Zhimin et al. 1981, 187–218.

Li Buxin et al. 1983. "Wanzhegan bianqu sannian youjizhanzheng gaikuang" [The three-year guerrilla struggle in Wanzhegan]. In Fang Zhimin et al. 1983, 462–88.

Li Dean. 1982. "Nanwangde suiyue" [Unforgettable years]. *Fengzhan hongqi* 1:96–107.

Li Fengmin. 1969. *Zhonggong shouyao shilüe huibian* [A short sketch of the Chinese Communist Party]. Taibei.

Li Jiaquan. 1985. "Xinsijun zhu Jitong tongxunchu" [The New Fourth Army's communications stantion at Jitong]. *Dangshi yanjiu ziliao* 7:19–21.

Li Jipeng et al. 1982. "Mindong sannian youjizhanzheng" [The three-year guerrilla war in Mindong]. *Dangshi yanjiu cankao ziliao* (Fujian) 6:31–44.

Li Jiwen. 1983. "Zai Gao Jingting junzhang shenbian gongzuode shihou" [Working alongside Commander Gao Jingting]. In Henan sheng minzhengting, vol. 4, 14–24.

Li Jui. 1977. *The Early Revolutionary Activities of Comrade Mao Tse-tung.* Trans. Anthony W. Sariti, ed. James C. Hsiung, introduced by Stuart R. Schram. White Plains, New York: M. E. Sharpe.

Li Jumin. 1983. "Piyao" [Refuting a rumor]. *Fengzhan hongqi* 3:77–82.

Li Li. 1983. *Geming yaolan Jinggangshan* [The Jinggang Mountains, cradle of the revolution]. Beijing: Renmin chubanshe.

Li Lianpo and Yang Xiaogang. 1980. "Xu Teli tongzhi kangzhan qi zai Hunan" [Comrade Xu Teli in Hunan during the War of Resistance]. *Geming wenwu* 2:12–18.

Li Ruxiang. 1987. "Duershi Da'nanshan hongse genjudide 'weijiao' " ["Encircling and exterminating" by the Independent Second Division in the Da'nanshan Red base]. In Guangzhou shi zhengxie, 379–81.

Li Shan. 1979. "Liangshi" [Grain]. In *Geming douzheng huiyilu.* 2 vols. Jiangxi renmin chubanshe, vol. 1, 387–99.

Li Shi. 1977. *Zhongguo geming jinian di* [Places where the Chinese Revolution is commemorated]. Hongkong: Chaoyang chubanshe.

Li Shian and Zhang Guoan. 1984. "Huainian 'xiao shi zhengwei' Fang Yongle" [Recalling the "young divisional political commissioner" Fang Yongle]. In Wanxi geming, 84–94.

Li Shian et al. 1982. "Dabieshanqude sannian youjizhan he Gao Jingting tongzhi" [The three-year guerrilla war in the Dabie Mountains and Comrade Gao Jingting]. *Geming huiyilu* 7:55–81.

Li Shiyan. 1984. "Zai lishi zhuanzhe guantou" [A key turning point in history]. In Wanxi geming, 385–401.

Li Shouxuan. 1984. "Huiyi Yuan Wencai, Wang Zuo shijian" [Recalling the Yuan Wencai and Wang Zuo incident]. *Zhengrong suiyue* 5:69–74.

Li Tianrong. 1987. "Niulingzhi zhan" [Battle at Niuling]. In Guangzhou shi zhengxie, 440–44.

Li Wei. 1956. *Jinggangshan.* Shanghai: Xin zhishi chubanshe.

Li Weihan. 1986. "Zai zhongyang suqu" [In the Central Soviet]. *Dangshi tongxun* 1:11–14.

Li Xikai. 1985. "Xuexi, fayang Minyue bianqu sannian youjizhanzhengde geming jingsheng" [Study and promote the revolutionary spirit of Minyue's three-year guerrilla war]. *Minnan geming shi yanjiu* 5:36–42.

Li Yongchun and Heng Xueming. 1985. "Gao Jingting." *Jiefangjun jiangling zhuan* 2:407–47.

Li Yunhan, 1981. "Xi'an shibiande qianyin yu jingguo" [The causes and course of the Xi'an Incident]. *Zhuanji wenxue* 235, vol. 39, no. 6 (December), 10–23 (pt. 1) and no. 238, vol. 40, no. 3 (March), 107–9 (pt. 4).

Li Zhaochun. 1984. "Su Yude shengping" [Su Yu's life]. *Gongdang wenti yanjiu* 10 (3): 99–103.

———. 1985. "Changqi baobing you cao pohai siwangde Zheng Weisan" [Zheng Weisan, who was long ill and persecuted to death]. *Gongdang wenti yanjiu* 9:97–101.

Li Zhengqing. 1984. "Hong ershibajun beifuchang" [The Red Twenty-eighth Army's clothing factory]. In Wanxi geming, 125–32.

Li Zijian. 1982. "Zhonggong Eyu bian dang jianku niandai chuangye jishi" [Record of the Chinese Communist Party's years of hardship and pioneering on the Eyu border]. Geming shi ziliao 9:17–33.

———. 1986. "Eyu bianqu Zhuping lianluozhan: Sifang shangdian" [The Zhuping liaison station in Eyu: Sifang Shop]. Geming huiyilu 20:165–72.

Li Ziping. 1983. "Zai tingjinshide rizili" [With the Advance Division]. Fengzhan hongqi 3:67–76.

———. 1984. "Tingjinshi ersan shi" [Some facts about the Advance Division]. In Zhejiang sheng junqu, 243–53.

Li Zurong and Guang Zhai. 1983. "Xiang Ying zai zhongyang suqu ersan shi" [Some facts about Xiang Ying in the Central Soviet]. Zhongguo xiandai shi yuekan 5:162–66.

Lian Yin. 1982. "Mianhuai Zhang Dingcheng tongzhi zai Fujian geming douzhengzhongde gongji" [Cherishing the memory of Comrade Zhang Dingcheng's achievements in Fujian's revolutionary struggle]. Fujian luntan 2:30–35.

Liang Guang. 1981. "Cong Jiangxi tuwei dao zhuanfu Mosike" [Breaking through the encirclement in Jiangxi and transferring to Moscow]. In Zhonggong Huanggang xianwei hui, 107–8.

Liang Guobin. 1981. "KangRi zhanzheng shiqide pianduan huiyi" [Recalling the war against Japan]. In Longyan diqu wenhuaju et al., eds., Minxi geming shi lunwen ziliao, Longyan: N.p., 59–89.

———. 1985. "KangRi zhanzheng shiqide pianduan huiyi" [Recalling the war against Japan]. In Zhonggong Fujian shengwei, 77–99.

Liang Shan. 1984. Hua'nan kangRi genjudi gaikuang [Anti-Japanese bases in southern China]. Paper at International Symposium on Chinese Anti-Japanese Bases in World War II. Nankai University. August.

Liao Gailong, ed. 1987. Zhonggong dangshi wenzhai niankan (1984 nian) [Abstract of articles on the history of the Chinese Communist Party (1984)]. Beijing: Zhonggong dangshi ziliao chubanshe.

Liao Guoliang and Tian Yuanle. 1987. Zhongguo gongnong hongjun shijian renwu lu [Record of events and people in the Chinese Red Army]. Shanghai: Renmin chubanshe.

Liao Kaizhu, ed. 1986. Fujian geming zhanzheng shigao [Draft history of Fujian's revolutionary war]. Fuzhou: Fujian renmin chubanshe.

Lin Huicai. 1983. "Hongbatuan youjizhan shi" [A history of the Red Eighth Regiment's guerrilla warfare]. Longyan wenshi ziliao 7:35–46.

Lin Huishan. 1979. "Yi Liu Ying tongzhi" [Recalling Comrade Liu Ying]. Zhejiang wenshi ziliao xuanji 14:52–68.

Lin Jian. 1985a. "Lun 'duli zizhu' ji qita" [On "independence and initiative" and other things]. Fujian dangshi tongxun 9:20–28.

———. 1985b. "Lusui Zhang Dingcheng tongzhi da youji" [Fighting guerrilla war alongside Comrade Zhang Dingcheng]. Fujian dangshi tongxun 7:18–30.

———. 1986. "Mindong jixing" [Mindong travel notes]. Fujian dangshi tongxun 2:61–68.

Lin Jianshu. 1981. "Yi 'Xinglongxun'an xian geming weiyuanhui'de chengli" [Recalling the setting up of the Xinglongxun'an Revolutionary Committee]. In Chen Yi et al. 1981, 538–40.

Lin, T. L. 1935. "The Rise and Fall of Communism in Fukien." *China Weekly Review*. May 11, 362–63.

Lin Tianyi. 1985. "Minyue bianqu sannian youjizhanzheng pinglun" [A review of the three-year guerrilla war in Minyue]. *Fujian dangshi tongxun* 9:52–59.

Lin Weixian. 1979? "Eyuwan sannian youjizhanzheng qingkuang" [The three-year guerrilla war in Eyuwan]. In *Eyuwan suqu geming shi ziliaobian*, ed. Huazhong shiyuan lishixi, Zhongguo jindaishi jiaoyanshi, vol. 2, 214–27. 2 vols. N.p.

———. 1982. *Dihou sannian* [Three years behind enemy lines]. Ed. Lu Yu. Hangzhou: Zhejiang renmin chubanshe.

———. 1984a. "Hongqi yong budao" [The Red Flag never falls]. In Wanxi geming, 1–19.

———. 1984b. "Zhanyou qing" [Affection between comrades in arms]. In Wanxi geming, 75–83.

———. 1987. "Taoshuling chuang zhangong" [Outstanding military exploits at Taoshuling]. In Wu Zaowen, 489–99.

Lin Zhifu. 1978 [1946]. "Wo zai xinsijun qinli he jianwen" [My experiences and perceptions of the New Fourth Army]. *Guangdong wenshi ziliao* 22:38–124.

Ling Hui. 1979. *Tu Zhengkun lieshi zhuanlüe* [A brief biography of the martyr Tu Zhengkun]. Changsha: Hunan renmin chubanshe.

Ling Hui and He Xiaoji. 1984. "Tu Zhengkun." *Zhonggong dangshi renwu zhuan* 18:258–79.

Ling Lihua and Zhu Jianying. 1981. "Xinsijun zai Yansi" [The New Fourth Army at Yansi]. *Anhui shida xuebao* 3:26–30.

Litten, Freddy. 1988. *Otto Brauns frühes Wirken in China*. Munich: Osteuropa Institut München.

Liu Gangfu. 1983. "Huiyi dierci guogong hezuo shiqi wo he Gao Jingting tanpan dacheng xieyide jingguo" [Recalling how I and Gao Jingting reached agreement in talks during the period of the second Nationalist-Communist cooperation]. *Jiangsu wenshi ziliao xuanji* 11:8–24.

Liu Guangming. 1985. "Kangzhan chuqi Eyu bianqude tongyi zhanxian gongzuo" [United front work in Eyu in the early period of the Resistance War]. *Dangshi yanjiu* 5:42–49.

Liu Guoliang. 1981. "Deng Zihui tongzhide zaoqi geming huodong" [Comrade Deng Zihui's early revolutionary activities]. *Liaoyuan: Geming chuantong jiaoyu congkan* 4:139–65.

Liu Huaqing. 1982. "Edongbei daowei lingdaoxiade liangnian youjizhanzheng" [The two-year guerrilla war under the leadership of the Edongbei Committee]. *Geming huiyilu* 7:34–54.

Liu Jianhua. 1982. "Ganyue bianqu sannian youjizhanzhengde huiyi" [Recalling the three-year guerrilla war in Ganyue]. *Jiangxi wenshi ziliao xuanji* 4:1–29.

———. 1985. "Gannan zhidui chengli qianhoude zhandou licheng" [The struggle before and after setting up the Gannan detachment]. *Jiangxi wenshi ziliao* 15:1–22.

Liu Jimin and Song Enfu. 1985. "Xinsijunde zujian he jijie" [The organization and concentration of the New Fourth Army]. *Dangshi yanjiu ziliao* 6:342–54.

Liu Mianyu. 1984. "Xiang Ying zai nanfang sannian youjizhanzhengzhongde diwei yu zuoyong" [Xiang Ying's position and role in the three-year guerrilla war in the south]. *Zhongguo xiandai shi yuekan* 1:211–17.

Liu Peishan. 1958. "Huiyi Xianggan bianqude sannian youjizhanzheng" [Recalling the three-year guerrilla war in Xianggan]. In Jiangxi renmin chubanshe, 188–96.

Liu Puqing and Tan Yunxiang. 1987. "Cai Huiwen." *Jiefangjun jiangling zhuan* 4:525–51.

Liu Xian. 1987. "Wei guogong liangdang zai Zhejiang shixian dierci hezuo zuo zhongda gongxiande Liu Ying tongzhi" [Comrade Liu Ying, who made a great contribution to the realization of the second Nationalist-Communist cooperation in Zhejiang]. In Zhejiang sheng zhengxie, 26–32.

Liu Xiangyun. 1954. "Yi hongshijunde douzheng" [Recalling the Red Tenth Army's struggle]. In Zhongguo qingnian chubanshe, 81–84.

Liu Xiao. 1981. "Minbei sannian youjizhanzheng" [The three-year guerrilla war in Minbei]. *Dangshi yanjiu cankao ziliao* (Fujian) 8:1–10.

———. 1983. "Min'gan shengwei chengli wenti wo jian" [My experience of the setting up of the Min'gan Provincial Committee]. In *Dangshi ziliao yu yanjiu* 11:52–56.

Liu Ying. 1983 [1940]. "Beishang kangRi yu jianchi sannian douzhengde huiyi" [Recalling the march north to resist Japan and the three-year struggle]. In Fang Zhimin et al. 1983, 191–261.

Liu Yongsheng. 1980. "Minyuegan bianqu renminde geming wuzhuang douzheng" [The revolutionary armed struggle of the people in the Minyue border area]. *Geming huiyilu* 2:115–36.

Liu Yutang. 1986. "Yi Xiang'egan suqude jianku douzheng" [Recalling the hard struggle in the Xiang'egan Soviet area]. In Xiang'egan geming genjudi wenxian ziliao bianxuanzu, 219–30.

Liu Zhengming. 1982. "Huiyi hongjun yiyuande ruogan qingkuang" [Recalling the Red Army hospital]. *Jiangxi wenshi ziliao* 1:16–25.

Liu Zihou et al. 1985. "Huoxian tanpan" [Talks at the battle front]. In Zhou Weisong, 203–19.

Long Yue. 1983. "Jianchi Zhe'nan shiwunian douzhengde huiyi" [Memoirs of persisting in the struggle in Zhe'nan for fifteen years]. *Zhe'nan geming douzheng shi ziliao* 18:14–26.

———. 1984. "Huiyi Zhe'nan youji genjudide douzheng" [Recalling the struggle in the Zhe'nan guerrilla bases]. In Zhejiang sheng junqu, 43–67.

Long Yue and Wu Yu. 1986 [1937]. "Guanyu Minzhe bianqu hongjun lici yu guomindang tanpan jingguode baogao" [Report on the Minzhe Red Army's series of talks with the Guomindang]. *Geming shi ziliao* 3:17–20.

Long Yue et al. 1983. "Mantan Minzhegan lao genjudi" [Talking about the old Minzhegan base]. In Fang Zhimin et al. 1983, 121–70.

Lu Dao. 1985. "Minyue bianqu sannian youjizhanzhengde zhanlüe diwei" [The strategic position of Minyue's three-year guerrilla war]. *Minnan geming shi yanjiu* 5:19–23.

Lü Dianyun et al. 1986. "Guanyu xinsijun junbu chengli wentide kaozheng" [Textual research on the question of the setting up of the New Fourth Army headquarters]. *Dangshi tongxun* 6:35–36.

Lu Dingyi. 1983. "Guanyu Tang Yizhen lieshide huiyi" [Memories of the martyr Tang Yizhen]. *Fangzhan hongqi* 2:1–15.

Lu Feng. 1947. *Gangtiede duiwu* [Steel ranks]. Hongkong: Yangzi chubanshe.

Lu Quan and Xuan Qianhong. 1987. *Ye Ting zhuan* [Biography of Ye Ting]. Henan renmin chubanshe.

Lu Sheng. 1983a. "Chongjian Mindong hongsantuan" [Rebuilding Mindong's Red Third Regiment]. *Fengzhan hongqi* 2:175–80.

———. 1983b. " 'He Ming weixian'de fasheng ji qi jiaoxun" [The 'He Ming danger' and its lessons]. *Geming huiyilu* 9:134–44.

———. 1983c. "Huoyue Minyue biande hongsantuan he duliying" [The Red Third Regiment and the Independent Battalion invigorate Minyue]. *Fengzhan hongqi* 3:19–26.

———. 1984. "Huigu hongsantuan zai Minnande zhandou licheng" [Recalling the Red Third Regiment's battles in Minnan]. *Fujian dangshi ziliao* 3:224–44.

———. 1985a. "Minyue bianqu sannian youjizhanzheng ji qi lishi zuoyong" [The three-year guerrilla war in Minyue and its historical function]. *Fujian dangshi tongxun* 11:18–29 and 17.

———. 1985b. " 'Zhangpu shijian' qianhou" [Around the time of the "Zhangpu Incident"]. In Zhonggong Fujian shengwei, 51–58.

Lu Wenxin. 1979. "Nanwangde zhandou licheng" [Unforgettable struggle]. *Zhengrong suiyue* 1:26–44.

Lu Yongli and Liu Zijian. 1983. "Fang Fang." *Zhonggong dangshi renwu zhuan* 11:323–68.

Lü Zhenyu. 1980. "Shaoqi tongzhi he Nanjing tanpan" [Comrade [Liu] Shaoqi and the Nanjing talks]. In Hunan renmin chubanshe, 159–67.

Lü Zhenyu. 1982. "Ji Hunan wenhua jie kangdi houyuan hui" [Memories of the Hunan Association of Cultural Circles in Support of the Resistance]. *Geming huiyilu* 4:116–26.

Luo Mengwen. 1962. *Douzheng zai Yanggan hongqu yu baiqu* [The struggle in Yanggan's Red and White areas]. Beijing: Zuojia chubanshe.

Luo Mengwen. 1981. "Nanwangde yige dongtian" [An unforgettable winter]. *Jiangxi wenshi ziliao xuanji* 5:41–53.

———. N.d. "Zhenxi, gonggu yu guangda da geming shengli" [Treasure, consolidate, and widen the revolution's great victory]. In Wuhan yexiao.

Luo Meizhen. 1987. "Shezu suo shuode Kejiahua" [The Hakka spoken by the She]. In Shi Lianzhu, ed., 314–33.

Luo Qixun. 1985. "Guanyu 'Pingjiang can'an' qianhou Xiang'egan tewei zuzhi he huodong qingkuangde huiyi" [Recalling the Xiang'egan Special Committee's organization and activity at around the time of the "Pingjiang massacre"]. In Zhonggong Pingjiang xianwei, 192–205.

Luo Weidao. 1982. "Ta shi geming qiangzhong qiang" [He is the rock of the revolution]. *Xinghuo liaoyuan* 1:42–45.

Luo Yingchen. 1984. "Huiyi Gao Jingting tongzhi ersan shi" [Some reminiscences of Comrade Gao Jingting]. In Wanxi geming, 55–60.

Ma Changyan. 1983. "Minbei hongjunde douzheng" [The Red Army's struggle in Minbei]. In Fang Zhimin et al. 1983, 512–14.

Ma Hongcai. 1985. *Xinsijun renwu zhi* [Figures in the New Fourth Army]. 2 vols. Zhenjiang: Jiangsu renmin chubanshe.

Ma Wenbin et al. 1986. *Zhongyang geming genjudi shi* [History of the central revolutionary base]. Beijing: Renmin chubanshe.

Mao Tse-tung [Mao Zedong]. 1961–65. *Selected Works.* 4 vols. Beijing: Foreign Languages Press.

———. 1978 [1937]. *On Guerrilla Warfare.* Trans. Samuel B. Griffith II. New York: Anchor Press.

Mao Zedong. 1970–72. *Mao Zedong ji* [Collected writings of Mao Zedong]. 10 vols. Tokyo: Hokubosha.

McColl, Robert W. 1967. "The Eyuwan Soviet Area." *Journal of Asian Studies* 27 (1): 41–60.

Mazour, Anatole G. 1971. *The Writing of History in the Soviet Union.* Stanford: Hoover Institute Press.

Mei Feng. 1986. "Disanci guonei geming zhanzheng shiqide nanfang renmin youjizhanzheng" [The southern people's guerrilla war during the third revolutionary civil war]. *Jindai shi yanjiu* 2:237–47.

Mei Jiasheng and Peng Deqing. 1986. "Yi Su Yu tongzhi" [Recalling Comrade Su Yu]. *Geming huiyilu* 7:1–33.

Mei Shaoqing. 1982a. "Eyuwan diqu shinian douzheng gaikuang" [Ten years of struggle in Eyuwan]. *Geming huiyilu* 20:153–64.

———. 1982b. "Huiyi Eyuwan bianqude douzheng" [Recalling the struggle on the Eyuwan border]. *Geming shi ziliao* 9:33–62.

———. 1987. "Huiyi Eyuwan bianqude douzheng (jiexuan)" [Recalling the struggle in Eyuwan (abridged)]. In Wu Zaowen, 479–88.

*Meizhou qingbao zhaiyao. Difang ji dangpai xiaoxi* [Weekly intelligence digest. Local and party news]. 1935. June 7–13, no. 15. 276 820 8272 N 15.

Meskill, Johanna Menzel. 1979. *A Chinese Pioneer Family: The Lins of Wu-feng, Taiwan, 1729–1895.* Princeton: Princeton University Press.

Miao Chuhuang. 1954. "Zhongguo gongnong hongjun changzheng gaishu" [The Chinese Red Army's Long March]. *Lishi yanjiu* 2:85–96.

Miao Cichao. 1983. "Lüeshu Mindong Shezu geming douzhengde fazhen ji tedian" [The development and special features of the revolutionary struggle of Mindong's She]. *Dangshi ziliao yu yanjiu* (Fujian) 9:32–41.

Miao Min. 1958. *Fang Zhimin zhandoude yisheng* [Fang Zhimin's life of struggle]. Beijing.

Miff, P. 1937. *Heroic China: Fifteen Years of the Communist Party of China.* New York: Workers' Library.

Military History Office. 1966. *Military Campaigns in China, 1924–1950.* Taibei.

Min'gan genjudi zhuanti xiezuo xiaozu. 1985. "Min'gan geming genjudide jianli ji qi douzheng" [The establishment of the Min'gan revolutionary base and its struggle]. *Fujian dangshi tongxun* 12:31–40 and 53.

Minxi'nan junzhengwei. N.d. *Dirende zhanshu yu womende duice* [The enemy's tactics and our countertactics]. March 10. Mimeo. 292.94 743 15086.

Minxi'nan junzhengwei. 1986 [1937]. "Minxi'nan heping tanpan yu dongyuan gongzuo baogao" [Report on peace talks and mobilization work in Minxi'-nan]. *Geming shi ziliao* 3:21–28.

Minxi'nan junzheng wei junshibu. 1937. *Dui ge hongse budui gongzuode jiancha he jinhou jige gongzuode zhishi* [Investigation of Red Army work and some future directives on work]. March 7. Mimeo. 590.8 743 15084.

Minxi'nan junzheng weiyuanhui. 1937. *Wei dui nei heping lianhe kangRi gei ge hongse budui yifeng zhishi xin* [A letter with directives to all Red troops calling for internal peace and an alliance against Japan]. June 1. Mimeo. 590.8 743 4543.

———. 1982? [1936]. "Guanyu funü gongzuode jueding" [Resolution on women's work]. *Fujian sheng funü yundong shiliao huibian* 1:85–91.

Minxi'nan junzheng weiyuanhui fenhui. 1937. *Yannanzhangde yanzhong jumian yu Li Hua tongzhide jihuizhuyi* [The serious situation in Yannanzhang and Comrade Li Hua's opportunism]. March 5. Mimeo 256.1 813 7326.

Minxi'nan junzheng weiyuanhui zhengzhibu. 1936. *Zhengqu Yuejun gongzuo* [Winning over the Guangdong army]. November 5. N.p. Mimeo. 596.872 743 4342.

———. 1937. *Wei shixian tingzhi neizhan yizhi kangRi gei ge zhengzhibu zhengzhichude gongzuo zhishi xin* [Directive to all political departments on realizing an end to civil war and a consistent resistance to Japan]. June 5. N.p. Mimeo. 596.872 743 4401.

Minyue bianqu tewei. 1938. *Zhonggong Minyue bianqu tewei dierci guangda huide jueyi* [Resolution of the first extended conference of the Chinese Communist Party's Minyue border area special committee]. April 11. Mimeo. 255.31 814 2508.

Mo Xiong. 1985. "Wo yu Zhongguo gongchandang hezuode huiyi" [My recollections of cooperating with the Chinese Communist Party]. *Geming shi ziliao* 15:1–33.

Mou Guangqin. 1984. "Shitan 'erzhan shiqi' Mindong suqude wuzhuang douzheng" [The armed struggle in the Mindong Soviet during the "second civil war"]. *Dangshi ziliao yu yanjiu* (Fujian) 4:11–17.

Mu Qing. 1950. *Xiangzhongde hongqi* [Red Flag in central Hunan]. N.p.

Ni Guozhen. 1982. *Mindong geming genjudi shi dashi nianbiao (chugao)* [Chronicle of important events in the history of Mindong's revolutionary base (draft)]. Ningde: N.p.

———. 1984. "Mindong geming genjudi shi zenyang fazhanlaide" [How the Mindong revolutionary base started to develop]. *Dangshi ziliao yu yanjiu* (Fujian) 5:29–36.

———. 1984? *Mindong geming genjudi shi dashi nianbiao, 1919–1938* [Chronicle of events in the history of the Mindong revolutionary base, 1919–1938]. Ningde: Zhonggong Fujian sheng Ningde diwei dangshi bangongshi.

Ni Nanshan. 1980. "Gaoshan geming genjudide douzheng" [The struggle for the Gaoshan revolutionary base]. *Jiangxi wenshi ziliao xuanji* 3:81–100.

———. 1982. "Wanzhegan bianqude sannian youjizhanzheng" [Wanzhegan's three-year guerrilla war]. *Jiangxi wenshi ziliao xuanji* 3:14–25.

————. 1983. "Huiyi sannian youjizhanzheng" [Recalling the three-year guerrilla war]. In Fang Zhimin et al. 1983, 522–26.

————. 1985. "Jianchi Jiangnan dierci sannian youjizhanzheng" [Persevering in the second three-year guerrilla war in Jiangnan]. *Jiangxi wenshi ziliao* 15:23–29.

Ni Zhongwen. 1983. "Huiyi Zheng Weisan tongzhi tan Eyuwan suqu lishizhongde jige zhongda wenti" [Recalling Comrade Zheng Weisan's comments on some important questions in the history of the Eyuwan Soviet]. *Wuhan daxue xuebao (shehui kexue ban)* 3:8–12 and 56.

Nie Hongjun. 1983. "Dui Gandongbei sinian douzhengde huiyi" [Recalling four years of struggle in Gandongbei]. In Fang Zhimin et al. 1983, 343–46.

Nie Rongzhen. 1983. *Huiyilu* [Memoirs]. Beijing: Zhanshi chubanshe.

Nie Yuansu et al. 1981. *Chen Yi zaoniande huiyi he wengao* [Chen Yi's early recollections and texts]. Chengdu: Sichuan renmin chubanshe.

Nihon kokusai mondai kenkyujo, Chugoku bu kai. 1970–75. *Chugoku kyosanto shi shiriyo shu* [Materials on Chinese Communist Party history]. 12 vols. Tokyo: Keiso shobo.

Niu Desheng. 1983. "Yi Eyu bianqu shengwei shuji Zhang Xingjiang" [Recalling Eyu Provincial Committee secretary Zhang Xingjiang]. In Henan sheng minzhengting, vol. 4, 35–40.

Niu Desheng et al. 1983. "Xiao Yan'an—Zhugou zhen" [Little Yan'an: The town of Zhugou]. *Xinghuo liaoyuan* 4:53–55.

Peng Bo. 1982. "Nanwangde Wugongshan zhandou" [Unforgettable battles in the Wugong Mountains]. *Jiangxi wenshi ziliao xuanji* 3:55–63.

Peng Dehuai. 1984. *Memoirs of a Chinese Marshal: The Autobiographical Notes of Peng Dehuai (1898–1974)*. Trans. Zheng Longpu. Beijing: Foreign Languages Press.

Peng Deqing. 1986. "Annanyong youjidui houqi qingkuangde huigu" [Recalling the later period of the Annanyong guerrillas]. *Fujian dangshi ziliao* 4:73–80.

Peng Jiazhu. 1984. "Xianggan bianqu sannian youjizhanzheng pianduan huiyi" [Reminiscences of the three-year southern guerrilla war in Xianggan]. *Jiangxi dangshi tongxun 1981–1984 hedingben* 2:507–27.

Peng Shengbiao. 1958. "Jianchi zhongyang suqu sannian" [Holding out for three years in the Central Soviet]. *Hongse fengbao* 3:69–80.

————. 1984. "Tingrui youjidui gaibian wei xinsijun erzhidui qingkuang" [The transformation of the Tingrui Guerrillas into the Second Detachment]. *Minxi dangshi ziliao tongxun* 3:3–7.

Peng Xueying. 1985. "Huiyi Tingrui youjidui chengli qianhoude rizili" [Before and after the setting up of the Tingrui Guerrillas]. *Minxi dangshi ziliao tongxun* 2:46–51.

Pepper, Suzanne. 1978. *Civil War in China*. Berkeley: University of California Press.

Perry, Elizabeth J. 1980. *Rebels and Revolutionaries in North China, 1845–1945*. Stanford: Stanford University Press.

Qi Guang. 1984. "Zhugou can'an" [Zhugou massacre]. *Geming huiyilu* 11:6–75.

Qiu Jiming. 1984. "Ma Lifeng zhuan" [Biography of Ma Lifeng]. *Dangshi ziliao yu yanjiu* (Fujian) 2:8–23.

Qiu Jiming. 1985. "Ma Lifeng." *Zhonggong dangshi renwu zhuan* 22:270–80.

Qiu Linzhong. 1983. "Jianli Gannan, Minxi geming genjudi fangzhende zhiding yu shijian" [Deciding and realizing the policy of setting up revolutionary bases in Gannan and Minxi]. *Longyan wenshi ziliao* 8:42–50.

Qiu Linzhong and Su Juncai. 1985. "Minxi dierci guogong hezuode xingcheng" [The steps toward the second Nationalist-Communist cooperation in Minxi]. *Fujian dangshi tongxun* 10:42–45.

Qiu Linzhong et al. 1983. "Makesizhuyi zai Minxide chuanbo yu shijian" [The transmission and realization of Marxism in Minxi]. *Zhongguo xiandai shi yuekan* 10:7–19.

Qiu Qinghua. 1984. "Huiyi Minzhe bian kangRi jiuwang ganbu dangxiao" [Recalling the anti-Japanese national salvation Party cadre school in Minzhe]. In Zhejiang sheng junqu, 235–42.

Qiu Songqing. 1985. "Lüelun Minyue bianqu 'sufan' yundong" [Minyue's movement to "suppress counterrevolutionaries"]. *Minnan geming shi yanjiu* 5:56–59.

Qiu Zhizhuo. 1985. "Shilun Jinggangshan geming genjudide tukeji maodun wenti" [On the clashes between natives and settlers in the revolutionary base in the Jinggang Mountains]. *Zhongguo xiandai shi yuekan* 2:41–48.

Qiu Zhizhuo et al., eds. 1986. *Zhonggong dangshi renming lu* [Figures in Chinese Communist Party history]. Chongqing: Chongqing chubanshe.

Quan Zhongyu. 1985. "Zhonggong Eyu bianqu dangshi jianshu" [Introduction to Chinese Communist Party history in Eyu]. *Henan wenshi ziliao* 2:1–6.

Quanguo Zhonggong dangshi yanjiuhui, eds. 1987. *Tudi geming zhanzheng shiqi genjudi yanjiu* [Research on bases during the period of the revolutionary land war]. Ji'nan: Shandong renmin chubanshe.

Queshan Zhugou geming jinianguan. 1980. "Yonghengde jinian: Liu Shaoqi tongzhi zai Zhugou guanghuide geming shiji" [Eternal commemoration: Comrade Liu Shaoqi's glorious revolutionary deeds at Zhugou]. *Henan wenbo tongxun* 2:1–2.

Rao Shoukun. 1980. "Mindongbeide youji zhanhuo" [Flames of guerrilla war in Mindongbei]. *Xinghuo liaoyuan congkan* 1:51–58.

———. 1983. "Kaibi Mindongbei youjiqu" [Opening up the Mindongbei guerrilla area]. In Fang Zhimin et al. 1983, 489–500.

Ren Zhibin. 1985. "Xinsijun diwushide kangzhan licheng jiqi shijian jingyan" [The New Fourth Army's Fifth Division in the Resistance War and its practical experiences]. In Eyu bianqu, 31–67.

Renmin chubanshe, eds. 1953 [1945]. *KangRi zhanzheng shiqide Zhongguo renmin jiefangjun* [The Chinese People's Liberation Army in the Resistance War]. Beijing: Renmin chubanshe.

———. 1980. *Huiyi Chen Yi* [Recalling Chen Yi]. Beijing: Renmin chubanshe.

———. 1981. *Huiyi Ye Ting* [Recalling Ye Ting]. Beijing: Renmin chubanshe.

Renmin tiyu chubanshe, eds. 1977a. *Huainian jing'aide Zhu De weiyuanzhang he Chen Yi, He Long tongzhi* [In commemoration of respected and beloved committee chairman Zhu De and Comrades Chen Yi and He Long]. Beijing: Renmin tiyu chubanshe.

———. 1977b. *Jing'aide Zhou zongli, women yongyuan huainian ni* [Respected and beloved Premier Zhou, we will commemorate you forever]. Beijing: Renmin tiyu chubanshe.

Ristaino, Marcia R. 1987. *China's Art of Revolution: The Mobilization of Discontent, 1927 and 1928*. Durham: Duke University Press.

S. K. 1937. "Guanyu He Ming shijiande jiaoxun" [On the lessons of the He Ming Incident]. In Zhongguo gongchandang Minxi'nan weiyuanhui jiguan bao, *Hongqi* 19. August 5. Mimeo. 052.1 813 15526 N 19.

Salisbury, Harrison. 1985. *The Long March: The Untold Story*. New York: Harper and Row.

Sanfenqu tongxun. 1936. "Dui baijun shibing hanhuade jingyan" [Shouting propaganda at White troops]. In Zhongguo gongchandang Minxi'nan weiyuanhui jiguan bao, *Hongqi* 2, June 12. Mimeo. 052.1 813 15523 N 9–11.

Selden, Mark. 1971. *The Yenan Way in Revolutionary China*. Cambridge: Harvard University Press.

Shaffer, Lynda. 1982. *Mao and the Workers: The Hunan Labor Movement, 1920–1923*. Armonk, N.Y.: M. E. Sharpe.

Shanghai renmin chubanshe. 1979. *Renminde zhongcheng zhanshi: Mianhuai Chen Yi tongzhi* [People's loyal fighter: In memory of Comrade Chen Yi]. Shanghai: Renmin chubanshe.

Shanghai renmin chubanshe. 1982. *Xinsijun he Huazhong kangRi genjudi shiliaoxuan, 1937–1940* [Historical materials on the New Fourth Army and the anti-Japanese bases in central China, 1937–1940]. Vol. 1. Shanghai: Shanghai renmin chubanshe.

Shao Jiang and Qiao Xinming. 1958. "Huiyi Fang Zhimin tongzhi" [Recalling Comrade Fang Zhimin]. *Hongse fengbao* 1:113–23.

Shao Shiping et al. 1983 [1945]. "Minzhewan'gan (Gandongbei) dangshi" [Party history of Minzhewan'gan (Gandongbei)]. In Fang Zhimin et al. 1983, 10–44.

Shaw, Norman. 1914. *Chinese Forest Trees and Timber Supply*. London: T. Fisher Unwin.

Shen Jiawu. 1983. "Shilun Fujian renmin geming zhengfu shibaide yuanyin ji qi yingxiang" [On the causes and effects of the defeat of Fujian's revolutionary government]. *Lishi dang'an* 3:124–28.

Shen Zhongwen. 1982. "Gongke Zhangzhou" [Capturing Zhangzhou]. *Fengzhan hongqi* 1:86–95.

Sheng Renxue and Zhang Junxiao. 1987. *Zhongguo gongnong hongjun ge geming genjudi jianjie* [Introduction to the Chinese Red Army's bases]. Beijing: Jiefangjun chubanshe.

"Shezu jianshi" bianxiezu. 1980. *Shezu jianshi* [A short history of the She]. Fuzhou: Fujian renmin chubanshe.

Shi Feng, ed. 1975. *Fang Zhimin*. Shanghai: Renmin chubanshe.

Shi Lianzhu. 1987. "Jiefang yilai Shezu yanjiu zongshu" [Review of research on the She since liberation]. In Shi Lianzhu, ed., 6–19.

Shi Lianzhu, ed. 1987. *Shezu yanjiu lunwenji* [Essays on the She]. N.p.: Minzu chubanshe.

Shi Yan. 1986. "Wo qu dangshi yanjiu gongzuode xin jinzhan" [New developments in research into Party history in our region]. *Mindong dangshi* 2:119–23.

Shi Yan and Wu Kebin. 1983. *Chen Yi beidu* [Chen Yi crosses north]. Beijing: Zhanshi chubanshe.

Shi Yan et al. 1981. *Xinsijun gushiji* [Collection of stories about the New Fourth Army]. Yangzhou: Jiangsu renmin chubanshe.

Shi Yuqing. 1981. "Jin'gangtaishang funüpai" [The women's platoon on Jin'-gangtai]. In Zhonggong Shangcheng xianweihui, 277–92.

Shi Yutian. 1980. "Zhandou zai Wanxi" [Fighting in Wanxi]. In Zhonggong Jin-zhai, 212–22.

Shih, Vincent Y. C. 1967. *The Taiping Ideology: Its Sources, Interpretations, and Influences.* Seattle: University of Washington Press.

Shixue shuangzhoukan she. 1956. *Dierci guonei geming zhanzheng shiqi shishi luncong* [The period of the second revolutionary civil war]. Beijing: Sanlian shu-dian chubanshe.

Shum Kui Kwong. 1988. *The Chinese Communists' Road to Power: The Anti-Japanese National United Front (1935–1945).* New York: Oxford University Press.

Sima Lu, ed. 1982. *Zhonggong suqude baoweizhan* [The Chinese Communists' battle to defend the soviet]. Hongkong: Zilian chubanshe.

Smedley, Agnes. 1934. *Red Flood over China.* Moscow: Cooperative Publishing Society of Foreign Workers in the USSR.

———. 1944. *Battle Hymn of China.* London: Victor Gollancz.

———. 1956. *The Great Road: The Life and Times of Chu Teh.* New York: Monthly Review Press.

Snow, Edgar. 1941. *Scorched Earth.* 2 vols. London: Gollancz.

———. 1968. *Red Star over China.* Rev. ed. New York: Grove Press.

Snow, Lois Wheeler. 1981. *Edgar Snow's China: A Personal Account of the Chinese Revolution Compiled from the Writings of Edgar Snow.* London: Orbis.

Song Shengfa. 1958. "Dayulingshang lixianji" [Adventures on the Dayuling]. *Hongse fengbao* 1:88–95.

———. 1978. *Gensui Chen Yi tongzhi da youji* [Fighting guerrilla war alongside Comrade Chen Yi]. Beijing: Jiefangjun wenyishe.

Song Wei. 1987. "Hongjun yu liangshi" [The Red Army and grain]. *Junshi shilin* 6:47–50.

Spurgeon, Caroline F. E. 1935. *Shakespeare's Imagery, and What It Tells Us.* Cambridge: Cambridge University Press.

Strong, Anna Louise. 1965. *China's Millions.* Beijing: New World Press.

Su Yu. 1982. "Huigu hongjun beishang kangRi xianqiandui" [Recalling the Red Army's expedition to the north to resist Japan]. *Fengzhan hongqi* 1:1–28.

———. 1983. "Huiyi Zhe'nan sannian youjizhanzheng" [Recalling the three-year guerrilla war in Zhe'nan]. *Dangshi tongxun* 15–16:3–25.

———. 1984. "Huiyi Zhe'nan sannian youjizhanzheng" [Recalling the three-year guerrilla war in Zhe'nan]. In Zhejiang sheng junqu, 1–42.

———. 1988. *Zhanzheng huiyilu* [War memoirs]. Beijing: Jiefangjun chubanshe.

Sun Baosheng. 1986. "Gao Jingting zai Eyuwan sannian youjizhanzheng shiqi pinglun" [Gao Jingting during the three-year guerrilla war in Eyuwan]. *Dangshi yanjiu* 5:58–62.

Sun Ching-chih. 1962 [1959]. *Economic Geography of South China (Kwangtung, Kwangsi, Fukien).* Joint Publications Research Service (JPRS) 14954.

Sun Keji. 1984. "Yi Chen Yi tongzhi gei liangtuan yifeng xin" [Recalling Comrade Chen Yi's letter to the Fine Regiment]. *Fengzhan hongqi* 4:30–36.

Sun Liming. 1984. "Jianlun sannian youjizhanzheng shiqi Minbei Mindong gen-
judide jige zhengce yu celüe wenti" [On some policies and tactics used in the
Minbei and Mindong bases during the three-year guerrilla war]. *Dangshi zi-
liao yu yanjiu* (Fujian) 1:39–47.
Sun Tzu [Sunzi]. 1963. *The Art of War.* Trans. Samuel B. Griffith. Oxford: Oxford
University Press.
T. P. 1937. "Wei He Ming shijian er xie" [Written concerning the He Ming In-
cident]. In Zhongguo gongchandang Minxi'nan weiyuanhui jiguan bao, *Hon-
gqi* 19, August 5. Mimeo. 052.1 813 15526 N 19.
Tan Chen-lin [Tan Zhenlin] and Su Yu. 1978. "A Man Open and Above Board,
a Revolutionary All His Life: In Memory of Comrade Chen Yi." In Foreign
Languages Press, eds., 120–40.
Tan Kesheng and Ouyang Zhiliang, eds. 1987. *Eyuwan geming genjudi douzheng
shi* [History of the struggle in the Eyuwan revolutionary base]. Beijing:
Jiefangjun chubanshe.
Tan Tangchi. 1980. "Ji Xianggan bianqu sannian youjizhanzheng" [Memories of
the three-year guerrilla war in Xianggan]. In *Geming shi ziliao*, ed. Zhongguo
renmin zhengzhi xieshang huiyi quanguo weiyuanhui wenshi ziliao yanjiu
weiyuanhui. Beijing: Wenshi ziliao chubanshe, vol. 1, 121–41.
Tan Yannian. 1981. "Yikao qunzhong jianchi youjizhanzheng" [Persisting in
guerrilla war by relying on the masses]. In Chen Yi et al. 1981, 591–96.
Tan Yubao. N.d. "Jianchi zai Xianggan bianqu" [Holding out on the Xianggan
border]. In Wuhan yexiao, 245–50.
Tan Yunxiang and Liu Puqing. 1985. "Cai Huiwen." *Zhonggong dangshi renwu
zhuan* 22:308–35.
Tan Zhenlin et al. 1983. "Dang he renminde zhongcheng zhanshi" [A loyal
fighter for the Party and the people]. *Fengzhan hongqi* 2:21–28.
Tang Bin. 1984. " 'Zhangpu shijian' yu He Ming cuowu" [The "Zhangpu Inci-
dent" and He Ming's mistakes]. *Dangshi ziliao yu yanjiu* (Fujian) 1:57–62.
Tang Jiaqing. 1982. "Suqu shiqide zhongyang jutuan" [The central theater
corps in the soviet period]. *Jiangxi wenshi ziliao xuanji* 2:81–86.
Tang Yuewu. 1984. "Jianbangshangde xiuxiesuo" [Shouldered repair shop]. In
Wanxi geming, 122–24.
Tao Yong et al. 1981. *Jianghai fengyun* [Storms over the rivers and seas]. Zhen-
jiang: Jiangsu renmin chubanshe.
Taylor, G. E. 1935. "Reconstruction after Revolution: Kiangsi Province and the
Chinese Nation." *Pacific Affairs* 8, no. 3 (September).
Theoretical Group of the Academy of Military Science of the Chinese People's
Liberation Army. 1978. "Comrade Yeh [Ye] Ting: Indomitable People's
Fighter." In Foreign Languages Press, eds., 151–61.
Thomson, James C., Jr. 1969. *While China Faced West: American Reformers in Na-
tionalist China, 1928–1937.* Cambridge: Harvard University Press.
Tien, Hung-mao. 1972. *Government and Politics in Kuomintang China, 1927–1937.*
Stanford: Stanford University Press.
Tong Huaizhou. 1980. "Shuang zhong se yu nong" [At his best in adversity]. In
Renmin chubanshe, 220–53.
Tong Huizhen. 1983. "Nanwangde jiaohui" [Unforgettable teaching]. *Fengzhan
hongqi* 3:109–19.

Tong Zhiqiang. 1982. "Gao Jingting gongguo shuping" [An evaluation of Gao Jingting's merits and demerits]. *Dangshi ziliao congkan* 1:137–44.

Trotsky, Leon. 1969. *Marxism and Military Affairs*. Colombo, Ceylon: Suriya.

Tu Jianchen. 1944. *Longyanzhi tudi wenti* [The land problem in Longyan]. N.p.

Tu Ke. 1982. "Xinsijun meishu huodong diandi" [New Fourth Army art activity]. In Yang Han, ed., 11–14.

Tu Tongjin. 1982. "Hong jiu juntuan husong kangRi xianqiandui beishang kangRi" [The Ninth Red Army Group escorts the Anti-Japanese Vanguard on its way north to resist Japan]. *Geming huiyilu* 4:91–105.

Van der Loon, P. 1961. "The Ancient Chinese Chronicles and the Growth of Historical Ideas." In *Historians of China and Japan*, ed. W. G. Beasley and E. G. Pulleyblank. London: Oxford University Press.

Wales, Nym. 1945. *The Chinese Labor Movement*. New York: John Day Company.

———. 1952. *Red Dust*. Stanford: Stanford University Press.

Wang Bingnan. 1985. " 'He Ming shijian'de zhenxiang he qishi" [The truth about the "He Ming Incident"]. *Minnan geming shi yanjiu* 3–4:18–27.

———. 1987. "Minnan geming genjudi xingcheng yu fazhan" [The formation and development of the Minnan revolutionary base]. In Quanguo Zhonggong dangshi yanjiuhui, 102–17.

Wang Datong et al. 1984. "Qian tan 'Zhangpu shijian'de jige wenti" [Some comments on questions relating to the "Zhangpu Incident"]. *Dangshi ziliao yu yanjiu* (Fujian) 2:40–48.

Wang Duonian, ed. 1982. *Fangong zhanluan* [The chaos caused by the wars against the Communists]. 5 vols. Taibei: Liming wenhua shiye gongsi.

Wang Fan-hsi [Wang Fanxi]. 1980. *Chinese Revolutionary, Memoirs, 1919–1949*. Trans. Gregor Benton. Oxford: Oxford University Press.

Wang Fuyi. 1984a. "Xiang Ying." *Jiefang jiangling zhuan* 1:445–70.

———. 1984b. "Xiang Ying yu nanfang sannian youjizhanzheng" [Xiang Ying and the three-year guerrilla war in the south]. *Dangshi ziliao congkan* 3:97–105.

———. 1987a. "Guanyu xinsijun lishi ruogan wentide kaozheng" [Investigations into some questions concerning New Fourth Army history]. *Geming shi ziliao* 5:95–104.

———. 1987b. "Xiang Ying cong Gannan dao Wannan" [Xiang Ying goes from Gannan to Wannan]. *Geming shi ziliao* 6:36–45.

Wang Fuyi and Xue Wenhao. 1985. "Xinsijun diyici dang daibiao dahui" [The New Fourth Army's First Party Congress]. *Dangshi ziliao congkan* 3:64–68.

Wang Gongying and Jin Xiaoguang. 1984. "Tanpan shimo" [Negotiations]. In Wanxi geming, 371–84.

Wang Hao. 1984. "Shanlin youji yiyuan" [Guerrilla hospital in the mountain forest]. In Wanxi geming, 133–42.

Wang Jianming. 1965. *Zhongguo gongchandang shigao* [Draft history of the Chinese Communist Party]. 3 vols. Taibei: N.p.

Wang Jianying. 1986a. *Zhongguo gongnong hongjun fazhan shi jianbian (1927–1937)* [Introduction to the history of the development of the Chinese Red Army (1927–1937)]. Beijing: Jiefangjun chubanshe.

———. 1986b. "Zhongyang hongjun changzhengqiande yunniang he zhunbei" [The central Red Army's informal discussions and preparations before the Long March]. *Dangshi ziliao zhengji tongxun* 8:32–37.

Wang Jinchen. 1984. "Mimi jiaotongzhan" [Secret liaison office]. In Wanxi ge-
    ming, 364–70.
Wang Ming. 1974 [1935]. "Lun fandi tongyi zhanxian wenti" [On the question of
    the anti-imperialist united front]. In *Wang Ming xuanji*, vol. 4, 179–302.
Wang Quanying. 1984. "Jinggangshan daolu yu Eyuwan suqude chuangjian"
    [The Jinggang Mountains road and the creation of the Eyuwan Soviet].
    *Zhongguo xiandaishi yuekan* 1:75–80.
Wang Ruoshui. 1986. *Wei rendaozhuyi bianhu* [In defense of humanism]. Beijing:
    Sanlian shudian.
Wang Shaochuan. 1984. "Wanxi diyizhi bianyidui" [The Wanxi First Detach-
    ment's plainclothes squad]. In Wanxi geming, 157–63.
Wang Shaojie. 1982. "Xuexi Luo Zhongyi, Liao Haitao liang tongzhi" [Learn
    from Comrades Luo Zhongyi and Liao Haitao]. In Zhenjiang diqu, 253–59.
Wang Sheng. 1983. "Qiu Jinsheng yu hongbatuan" [Qiu Jinsheng and the Red
    Eighth Regiment]. *Fenzhan hongqi* 2:126–32.
Wang Shoudao. 1951. *Zhongguo gongchandang lingdao Hunan renmin yingyong
    douzhengde sanshinian* [Thirty years of Chinese Communist Party leadership
    of the Hunan people's heroic struggle]. Changsha.
Wang Tingke. 1985. *Hongjun changzheng yanjiu* [Research on the Red Army's
    Long March]. Chengdu: Sichuan sheng shehui kexueyuan chubanshe.
Wang Wei. 1985. "Minyue bianqu sannian youjizhanzhengde weida shengli ji qi
    yiyi" [The great victory and significance of Minyue's three-year guerrilla war].
    *Minnan geming shi yanjiu* 5:24–29.
Wang Wenbo. 1983. "Dui Minbei geming douzheng qingkuangde huiyi" [Recall-
    ing the revolutionary struggle in Minbei]. In Fang Zhimin et al. 1983,
    439–52.
Wang Yifan. 1985. "Luntan Minyue bianqu sannian youjizhanzhengde jiben te-
    dian yu zhuyao jingyan" [On some special features and important experi-
    ences of the three-year guerrilla war in Minyue]. *Fujian dangshi tongxun*
    9:44–51.
Wang Yuanjian. 1978. "Zai liehuo he rexue yongsheng" [Immortal in the raging
    flames and hot blood]. *Geming wenwu* 4:6–11.
Wang Yuxian. 1983. "Shenshende huainian" [Deep memories]. In Cui Yitian
    1983, 56–61.
Wang Zhi. 1985. "Wan gong she Ri, chicheng Jiangnan" [Bend the bow against
    Japan, gallop to Jiangnan]. In Zhonggong Fujian shengwei, 105–15.
Wang Zhongyan. 1984. "Muchenglide douzheng" [The struggle in Wood City].
    In Wanxi geming, 195–202.
Wang Zongli. 1986. "Dui kangzhan chuqi Chang Jiang ju gongzuode pingjia"
    [Assessment of the Chang Jiang Bureau in the early period of the Resistance
    War]. *Dangshi tongxun* 2:44.
Wang Zuoyao. 1983a. *Dongzong yiye* [A chapter in the story of the Dong Jiang col-
    umn]. Shaoguan: Guangdong renmin chubanshe.
———. 1983b. "Tingjin Yuebei" [Advancing into Yuebei]. In Zeng Sheng et al.,
    138–54.
Wanxi geming douzheng shi bianxiezu, eds. 1984. *Wanxi geming huiyilu* [Memoirs
    of the Wanxi revolution]. Hefei: Huangshan shushe.

Wei Hongyun, ed. 1981. *Zhongguo xiandai shigao* [Draft contemporary history of China]. 2 vols. Harbin: Heilongjiang renmin chubanshe.

Wei Jinshui. 1983a. "Longyan dangde zuzhi wuzhuang douzheng ji tongyi zhanxiande gaikuang" [The Longyan Party organizes armed struggle and the united front]. *Longyan wenshi ziliao* 8:37–41.

———. 1983b. "Qiji cong he er lai" [Where do miracles come from?] *Fengzhan hongqi* 2:33–58.

———. 1983c. "Zhandou zai diren houfang" [Fighting behind enemy lines]. *Fujian dangshi ziliao* 2:161–76.

Wei Jinshui. 1985. "Tanpan zhuoshangde douzheng" [Struggle at the negotiating table]. In Zhonggong Fujian shengwei, 18–29.

Wei Pu and Yang Wenlong. 1987. "Ye Ting cong Aomen dao Wannan" [Ye Ting goes from Macao to Wannan]. *Geming shi ziliao* 6:29–35.

Wei, William. 1985. *Counterrevolution in China: The Nationalists in Jiangxi during the Soviet Period.* Ann Arbor: University of Michigan Press.

———. 1989. "Law and Order: The Role of the Guomindang Security Forces in the Suppression of the Communist Bases during the Soviet Period." In Hartford and Goldstein, 34–61.

Wen Yangchun. 1941. "Xinsijun yu Jiangnan minzhong" [The New Fourth Army and the Jiangnan masses]. *Jianghuai*, February 15, 4:6–9. 052.4 806 16257 N 4 5 6.

———. 1985. "Beishang kangRi qianhoude douzheng" [The struggle at around the time of going north to resist Japan]. In Zhonggong Fujian shengwei, 66–76.

———. 1987. "Fan Luo Ming luxiande zhenxiang" [The true story of the struggle against Luo Ming]. In Liao Gailong, 194–96.

Weng Chengjin. 1986. "Tudi geming zhanzheng shiqi Annanyongde geming douzheng yishu" [Recalling the revolutionary struggle in Annanyongde during the land revolution]. *Fujian dangshi ziliao* 4:50–62.

Whang, Paul K. 1934. "Rehabilitation of Red-Devastated Areas: A Call to Shanghai Bankers." *China Weekly Review,* December 22.

Whitson, William W., with Chen-hsia Huang. 1973. *The Chinese High Command: A History of Communist Military Politics, 1927–1971.* London: Macmillan.

Wilson, Dick. 1971. *The Long March, 1935: The Epic of Chinese Communism's Survival.* London: Hamilton.

Wu Dingbang. 1985. "Pingjiang can'an shimo" [The whole story of the "Pingjiang massacre"]. In Zhonggong Pingjiang xianwei, 1–42.

Wu Gu. 1979. *Sanshiliu ji* [Thirty-six tricks]. Changchun: Jilin renmin chubanshe.

Wu Hongxiang. 1986. "Jianchi Minxi sannian youjizhanzhengde hongbatuan" [The Red Eighth Regiment upholds the three-year guerrilla war in Minxi]. 2 parts. *Fujian dangshi tongxun* 3:13–24 and 4:18–30.

Wu Huayou. 1982. "Qianli song wenjian" [Sending documents over one thousand *li*]. *Fengzhan hongqi* 1:197–206.

Wu Jiamin. 1986. "Jianding bishengde xinnian" [Strengthening the will to win]. In Xiang'egan geming genjudi wenxian ziliao bianxuanzu, 268–90.

Wu Jiqing. 1979. "Gaobie suqu" [Taking leave of the soviet]. In *Geming douzheng huiyilu.* 2 vols. Jiangxi renmin chubanshe. Vol. 2, 216–29.

Wu Kebin. 1984. "Guanyu Zhe'nan sannian youjizhanzheng" [On the three-year guerrilla war in Zhe'nan]. *Jindai shi yanjiu* 4:166–94.

———. 1986. "Chen Yi zai sannian youjizhanzheng" [Chen Yi in the three-year guerrilla war]. *Junshi shilin* 4:35–38.

Wu Xing. 1958. "Yige hongjun nü youjidui" [A Red Army women's guerrilla unit]. *Hongse fengbao* 3:125–63.

Wu Xiuying et al. 1984. "Gao Jingting yu Yaoluoping renmin" [Gao Jingting and the people of Yaoluoping]. In Wanxi geming, 43–54.

Wu Yunlin. 1983. "Xiaomie tufei he dizhu wuzhuang, gonggu Houdong genjudi" [Destroying bandits and landlord forces, consolidating the Houdong base]. *Zhangpu wenshi ziliao* (new series) 3:1–6.

———. 1985. "Minyue bianqu sannian youjizhanzheng shiqi jiaotong gongzuo qingkuang" [Liaison work in Minyue during the three-year guerrilla war]. *Minnan geming shi yanjiu* 3–4:63–66.

Wu Zaowen, ed. 1987. *Yi nanfang sannian youjizhanzheng* [Memoirs of the three-year guerrilla war in the south]. Shanghai: Shanghai renmin chubanshe.

Wuhan yexiao. N.d. *Zhongguo gongchandang zai zhongnan diqu lingdao geming douzheng lishi ziliao* [Historical materials on the revolutionary struggle led by the Chinese Communist Party in central-southern China]. N.p.: Zhongnan renmin chubanshe.

Xi Hong. 1958. "Hongdu youjidui" [Red capital guerrillas]. In Jiangxi renmin chubanshe, 232–37.

Xia Daohan. 1983. "Gu Bo." *Zhonggong dangshi renwu zhuan* 12:273–92.

———. 1986. "Jiangxi suweiai zhengfu ji qi lishi zuoyong" [The Jiangxi Soviet government and its historical function]. *Jiangxi daxue xuebao (zhexue shehui kexue ban)* 2:52–57.

Xia Honggen and Zhang Kechang. 1987. "Liu Bojian." *Jiefang jiangling zhuan* 5:201–36.

Xiamen daxue lishixi Zhonggong dangshi jiaoyanzu. 1978. *Minxi geming genjudi* [The Minxi revolutionary base]. Shanghai: Renmin chubanshe.

Xiang Ying. 1937. "Nanfang sannian youjizhanzheng jingyan yu dangqian kangzhande jiaoxun" [The experience of the three-year guerrilla war in the south and its lessons for the present Resistance War]. *Jiefang zhoukan* (Yan'an). October 30.

———. 1939. "Xin jieduanzhong xinsijun zai Jiangnan kangzhande renwu" [The New Fourth Army's tasks in the Jiangnan Resistance War in the new stage]. In *Shilun congkan* 3:31–53.

Xiang'egan geming genjudi wenxian ziliao bianxuanzu, eds. 1986. *Xiang'egan geming genjudi huiyilu* [Memoirs of the Xiang'egan revolutionary base]. Beijing.

Xianggan bian hongjun junzheng weiyuanhui. 1937a. *Wei Lugouqiao gao qunzhong shu* [Letter to the masses about Lugouqiao]. September 27. Mimeo. 590.807 742 13089.

———. 1937b. *Wei Lugouqiao shibian gao qunzhong shu* [Letter to the masses about the Lugouqiao Incident]. Signed by Tan Yubao. September. Mimeo. 255.35 824.

"Xianggan geming genjudi douzhcng shi" bianxiezu, eds. 1982. *Xianggan geming genjudi douzheng shi* [History of the struggle in the Xianggan revolutionary base]. Nanchang: Jiangxi renmin chubanshe.

Xiao Chaoran et al. 1986. *Zhonggong dangshi jianming cidian* [Concise dictionary of Chinese Communist Party history]. 2 vols. Beijing: Jiefangjun chubanshe.

Xiao Feng. 1979. *Changzheng riji* [Diary of the Long March]. Shanghai: Shanghai renmin chubanshe.

Xiao Ke. 1981. "Xiang Gannan, Minxi jinjun he diyici fan 'weijiao' " [Advancing into Gannan and Minxi and countering the First Encirclement campaign]. In Chen Yi et al. 1981, 129–37.

Xiao Xuexin. 1984. " 'Jiuyiba' shibianhou Fujian xueshengde fanRi aiguo douzheng" [The Fujian students' patriotic struggle against Japan after the "September 18" Incident]. *Dangshi ziliao yu yanjiu* [Fujian] 4:33–40.

Xiao Zili. 1981. "Sannan youji fenghuo" [Guerrilla beacon in Sannan]. *Jiangxi wenshi ziliao xuanji* 5:83–100.

Xiatikesi [Asiaticus]. 1941. "Ye Xiang liang jiangjun fangwen ji" [Account of a visit to Generals Ye and Xiang]. In Beierdeng [Jack Belden], *Chengwei shiju zhongxinde xinsijun,* Shanghai? 80–97.

Xie Bizhen. 1984. "Liu Yongsheng zhandou zai Minyuegan bianqu" [Liu Yongsheng's struggle in the Minyuegan border region]. *Fengzhan hongqi* 4:72–92.

———. 1985. "Kangzhan shiqi Minyuegan bianqu dangshi xuyao tanlunde liangge wenti" [Two questions that need to be researched in Minyuegan history during the Resistance War]. *Fujian dangshi tongxun* 7:35–37.

Xie Huiying. 1963. "Yu bai gouzi zuo douzheng" [Battling with the White dogs]. In Jiangxi sheng funü, 127–31.

Xie Yongcong. 1979. "Dade diren chengrenle" [To gain the enemy's recognition by fighting]. In *Geming douzheng huiyilu.* 2 vols. Jiangxi renmin chubanshe. Vol. 2, 355–57.

Xie Youcai. 1984. Letter. *Zhengrong suiyue* 5:335–36.

Xie Yucai. 1985. "Guanyu Zhangpu shijian ji hongjiutuan" [On the Zhangpu Incident and the Red Ninth Regiment]. *Minxi dangshi ziliao tongxun* 2:26–36.

Xie Zanju. 1982. "Baipi hongxin" [White skin, red heart]. *Fengzhan hongqi* 1:222–45.

Xie Zhufeng. 1987. *Chang ye kudou ji* [Record of a hard struggle in the long night]. Changsha: Hunan renmin chubanshe.

Xin Hunan bao. 1950. *Hunan nongcun diaocha baogao* [Report of investigations in Hunan villages]. Changsha.

"Xinci baijun shibing baodong jingguo" [The uprising of the Xinci White troops]. 1936. In Zhongguo gongchandang Minxi'nan weiyuanhui jiguan bao, *Hongqi* 2, June 12. Mimeo. 052.1 813 15523 N 9–11.

Xing Yinyuan. 1936. "Zai gongzuozhong suo gei wode jingyan yu jiaoxun" [Experiences and lessons gained in work]. In Zhonggong Minyue bianqu tewei jiguan bao, *Zhandou* 4, April 15. 052.1 813 16357 N 4.

Xinsijun canmouchu. 1981 [1946]. "Xinsijunde qianshen ji qi zucheng yu fazhan jingguo gaikuang" [The origins of the New Fourth Army and its formation and development]. In Anhui sheng wenwuju, 157–77.

"Xinsijun" shiliao congshu wenxian bianjizu. 1986. "Xinsijun junbu chenglide shijian, didian" [The time and place of the setting up of the New Fourth Army headquarters]. *Wenxian yu yanjiu* 3:43–44.

Xinsijun zhengzhibu, eds. 1943. *Xinsijun xunguo xianlie jinian ce* [In commemoration of New Fourth Army martyrs]. N.p. 299.35 735 3973 c.l.

Xu Chunhua et al. 1984. "Yuan Wencai, Wang Zuo bei sha shi cuowu" [Killing Yuan Wencai and Wang Zuo was a mistake]. *Jiangxi dangshi tongxun 1981–1984 hedingben* 1:455–69.

Xu Jin. 1986. "Weidade dier zhanchang" [The great second battleground]. *Dangshi tongxun* 9:20–26.

Xu Lin. 1986. [1928]. "Guanyu Xiangnan baodong jingguode baogao" [On the course of the Xiangnan Uprising]. In Hunan sheng caizhengting, 22–23.

Xu Qichang. 1981. "Xue ran zhanqi qi geng hong: Jin'gangtai youjizhan huigu" [Blood dyes the battle standard even redder: Looking back on the guerrilla war on Jin'gangtai]. In Zhonggong Shangcheng xianweihui, 217–33.

Xu Xiangqian. 1984. *Lishide huigu* [Looking back on history]. Beijing: Jiefangjun chubanshe.

Xu Xingzhi. 1983 [1941]. "Jiangjun miaoyu jue renjian" [The general's witticisms are the best in human history]. In Yancheng shi, 554–64.

Xu Zhanquan. 1987. "Nanfang basheng sannian youjizhanzheng gaikuang" [The three-year guerrilla war in eight southern provinces]. In Wu Zaowen, 587–609.

Xuan Enjin. 1983. "Guanyu tingjinshi dier zongdui jianchi Zhexi'nan geming douzhengde qingkuang" [On the revolutionary struggle waged by the Advance Division's Second Column in Zhexi'nan]. In Fang Zhimin et al. 1983, 530–59.

Xuan Jintang. 1982. "Wo suo zhidaode Minzhegan suqu sufan qingkuang" [My experience of suppressing counterrevolutionaries in the Minzhegan Soviet]. *Jiangxi wenshi ziliao xuanji* 3:38–41.

———. 1983. "Shoubian dadaohui" [Absorbing the Great Knives]. In Fang Zhimin et al. 1983, 517–18.

Xue Moucheng and Zheng Quanbei. 1980. "Fujian renmin geming zhengfude chengli he shibai" [The establishment and defeat of the Fujian People's Revolutionary Government]. *Xiamen daxue xuebao (zhexue shehui kexue ban)* 1:42–54.

Xue Moucheng et al. 1983. *"Fujian shibian" ziliao xuanbian* [Materials on the "Fujian Incident"]. Nanchang: Jiangxi renmin chubanshe.

Xue Zizheng. 1983a. "Guanyu nanfangju junshi zu he Nanyue youji ganbu xunlianbande bufen qingkuang" [On the Southern Bureau's military group and the Nanyue guerrilla cadres' training class]. In Chongqing xiandai gemingshi, 23–38.

———. 1983b. "Youguan Gandongbei, Minbeide bufen qingkuang" [Some facts about Gandongbei and Minbei]. In Fang Zhimin et al. 1983, 328–42.

Xue Zongyao and Wang Nianzu. 1985. "Hongjun beishang kangRi xianqiandui zai Min huodong gaishu" [The activities in Fujian of the Red Army's anti-Japanese Northern Expedition]. *Fujian dangshi tongxun* 5:43–49.

Yan Jingtang. 1986. "Guanyu 'nanfang sannian youjizhanzheng'de jige wenti" [Some questions relating to the "three-year guerrilla war in the south"]. *Dangshi yanjiu* 2:42–49.

Yan Jingtang and Jiang Tingyu. 1989. "Xiang Ying zai nanfang sannian youjizhanzhengzhongde gongxian" [Xiang Ying's contribution in the three-year guerrilla war in the south]. *Zhonggong dangshi yanjiu* 1:62–72.

Yan Jingwen. 1974. *Zhou Enlai pingzhuan* [A critical biography of Zhou Enlai]. Hongkong: Bowen shuju.

Yan wei. 1937. "Dui Baitu shouzutuan huren qiangpo jiaozu yijian shu" [Views on the Baitu rent-collectors' forcing rent payment]. In Zhongguo gongchandang Minxi'nan weiyuanhui jiguan bao, *Hongqi* 19. August 5. Mimeo. 052.1 8813 15526 N 19.

Yancheng shi "Xinsijun chongjian junbu yihou" bianxuanzu, eds. 1983. *Xinsijun chongjian junbu yihou* [After the restoration of the New Fourth Army headquarters]. Yancheng: Jiangsu renmin chubanshe.

Yang, Benjamin [Yang, Bingzhang]. 1986. "The Zunyi Conference as One Step in Mao's Rise to Power: A Survey of Historical Studies of the Chinese Communist Party." *China Quarterly* 106:235–71.

Yang, Bingzhang. 1986. "From Revolution to Politics: The Long March and the Rise of Mao." Ph.D. Thesis. Harvard University.

Yang Caiheng. 1982. "Xun Huaizhou tongzhi huozai women xinzhong" [Comrade Xun Huaizhou lives in our hearts]. *Fengzhan hongqi* 1:80–85.

———. 1983. "Liu Tujun tongzhide douzheng fengmao" [Comrade Liu Tujun's style of struggle]. *Fengzhan hongqi* 3:130–38.

———. 1985a. "Minzhong guogong tanpan ji 'Quanzhou shijian' shimo" [The whole story behind the Mindong talks between Nationalists and Communists and the "Quanzhou Incident"]. In Zhonggong Fujian shengwei, 59–65.

———. 1985b. "Minzhong youjidui beishang yihou" [After the Minzhong guerrillas marched north]. *Fujian dangshi tongxun* 9:17–18.

Yang Daoming. 1986. "Huiyi Min'gan sheng houqide douzheng" [Recalling the later period of the Min'gan struggle]. *Fujian dangshi tongxun* 9:31–34.

Yang Han, ed. 1982. *Xinsijun meishu gongzuo huiyilu* [Memoirs of New Fourth Army art activity]. Shanghai: Shanghai renmin chubanshe.

Yang Jianxin. 1986. "Hongqiao jiandi" [Wiping out the enemy at Hongqiao]. In Xiang'egan geming genjudi wenxian ziliao bianxuanzu, 257–61.

Yang Jin. 1981. "Zhe'nan hongjun youjidui he Shanghai dang zuzhi lianxide jingguo" [The liaison between the Zhe'nan Red Army guerrillas and the Shanghai Party organization]. *Dangshi ziliao congkan* 3:44–48.

Yang Jinfu. 1983. "Zai jiankude suiyueli" [Difficult years]. In Fang Zhimin et al. 1983, 519–21.

Yang Shang-k'uei [Yang Shangkui]. 1961. *The Red Kiangsi-Kwangtung Border Region*. Beijing: Foreign Languages Press.

Yang Shangkui. 1961. "Jiannande suiyue" [Hard years]. *Xinghuo liaoyuan* 4:169–93.

———. 1977. "Chuangye jiannan bai zhan duo" [An enterprise that is difficult and requires more than one hundred battles]. *Lishi yanjiu* 6:32–61.

————. 1978a. "Chongdu 'Gannan youji ci' " [On rereading the poem "Guerrilla War in Gannan"]. *Geming wenwu* 1:30–40.

————. 1978b. *Chen Yi zai Gannan* [Chen Yi in Gannan]. Beijing: Zhongguo shaonian ertong chubanshe.

————. 1980. "Chongdu Chen Yi tongzhi shi 'Meiling sanzhang' " [On rereading Comrade Chen Yi's "Three Stanzas at Meiling"]. *Geming wenwu* 2:8–11.

————. 1981. *Chen Yi and the Jiangxi-Guangdong Base Area.* Beijing: Foreign Languages Press.

Yang Zhihong. 1981. "Dui zhongyang suqude pianduan huiyi" [Fragments of reminiscences about the Central Soviet]. In Chen Yi et al. 1981, 457–72.

Yang Ziyao. 1986. "Zhongguo gongnong hongjun beishang kangRi xianqiandui dashiji" [Chronicle of the Chinese Red Army's anti-Japanese Northern Expedition]. 2 parts. *Junshi shilin* 4:61–63 and 5:48–51.

Yanyongjing xianwei jueyi. 1936. "Guanyu ban suqu limian zai qiushou douzhengzhongde gongzuo fangshi" [On work methods during the autumn harvest struggle in semi-soviet areas]. In Zhongguo gongchandang Minxi'nan weiyuanhui jiguan bao, *Hongqi.* August 2. Mimeo. 052.1 813 15521 N 5.

Ye Bingnan. 1987. "Dierci guogong hezuo zai Zhejiangde lishi gaikuang" [The history of the second Nationalist-Communist cooperation in Zhejiang]. In Zhejiang sheng zhengxie, 3–17.

Ye Cao [Fang Fang]. 1948. *Sannian youjizhanzheng* [Three-year guerrilla war]. Hongkong: Zhengbao chubanshe.

Ye Chao. 1980. "Chicheng dajiangnanbei jian qigong" [Performing outstanding service while galloping north and south of the Chang Jiang]. In Renmin chubanshe, 140–52.

Ye Dabing. 1982. *Zhe'nan nongmin baodong he hong shisan jun* [Peasant insurrection in Zhe'nan and the Thirteenth Red Army]. Hangzhou: Zhejiang renmin chubanshe.

Ye Fei. 1983a. "Huiyi Mindong geming douzheng" [Recalling the revolutionary struggle in Mindong]. 6 parts. *Mindong dangshi ziliao yu yanjiu* 1:3–15, 2:1–12, 3:1–13, 4–5?:1–21?, and 6:11–22.

————. 1983b. "Tan erzhan shiqi Mindong dang zuzhi gaikuang" [On the general situation of Party organization in Mindong during the second civil war]. *Dangshi ziliao yu yanjiu* (Fujian) 10:9–17.

————. 1983c. "Zai jiejian Mindong dangshi gongzuozhe shide yici jianghua" [Talk on receiving some Mindong Party history workers]. *Dangshi ziliao yu yanjiu* (Fujian) 8:1–3.

————. 1984a. "Tan Mindong guogong hezuo kangRi tanpan wenti" [On the talks between Nationalists and Communists in Mindong about cooperation against Japan]. *Dangshi ziliao yu yanjiu* (Fujian) 4:1–10.

————. 1984b. "Tan Mindong sannian youjizhanzheng gaikuang ji suqing AB tuan wenti" [On the three-year guerrilla war in Mindong and the purge of the AB's]. *Dangshi ziliao yu yanjiu* (Fujian) 2:1–8.

————. 1984 [1957]. "Guanyu Mindong dangde douzheng lishide huiyi" [Recalling the Mindong Party's history of struggle]. *Fujian dangshi ziliao* 3:85–97.

————. 1986a. "Mindong—zuihou jianlide suqu" [Mindong: The last soviet to be set up]. 3 parts. *Zongheng* 3:2–7, 4:11–15, and 5:18–21.

————. 1986b. "Tan dui bianxie xinsijun shiliao congshude yijian" [Views on collection of New Fourth Army materials]. *Dangshi tongxun* 4:44.

————. 1986c. "Tan xinsijun douzheng lishide tedian" [On special features in the New Fourth Army's history of struggle]. *Dangshi ziliao zhengji tongxun* 9:41–42.

————. 1987a. "Mindong suqude chuangjian he sannian youjizhanzheng" [The founding of the Mindong Soviet and the three-year guerrilla war]. In Wu Zaowen, 306–51.

————. 1987b. "Zou xiang kangRi qianxiande lu" [Going toward the front of resistance to Japan]. *Dajiang nanbei* 5:3–7.

————. 1988. *Huiyilu* [Memoirs]. Beijing: Jiefangjun chubanshe.

Ye Husheng. 1956. *Jinggangshande hongqi* [Red Flag in the Jinggang Mountains]. Beijing: Gongren chubanshe.

Ye Jianmei and Wang Chunjiang. 1982. "Ye Ting jiangjun zai Wannan" [General Ye Ting in Wannan]. In Anhui sheng junqu, 40–45.

Ye Juyun. 1981. "Yi Mao Zedong tongzhi zai Yudude yici jianghua" [Remembering a speech by Comrade Mao Zedong at Yudu]. In Chen Yi et al. 1981, 528–29.

Ye Ting. 1938. "The New Fourth Army's First Year." *New China Information Bulletin* (Chongqing) 10.

————. 1981 [1939]. "Xiandai zhanzhengde xingzhi tedian yu zhihui" [Special characteristics of the nature of contemporary warfare and command]. In Renmin chubanshe, 191–204.

Yin Lidong. 1986. "Zai Annanyongde diqude geming douzheng" [The revolutionary struggle in the Annanyongde region]. *Fujian dangshi ziliao* 4:63–72.

Yin Linping. 1983. "Hongsantuande wuzhuang douzheng" [The Red Third Regiment's armed struggle]. *Fujian dangshi ziliao* 2:151–60.

————. 1984. "Guanyu Annanyongde diqu geming douzheng" [On the revolutionary struggle in the Annanyongde region]. *Dangshi ziliao yu yanjiu* (Fujian) 5:21–29.

Yin Zixian. 1987. "Shilun zhongyang pai qijuntuan beishang, liujuntuan xizhengde zhanlüe mudi" [On the strategic aims behind the Central Committee's decision to send the Seventh Army Corps north and the Sixth Army Corps west]. *Junshi shilin* 1:33–36.

"Yongding laixin" [Letter from Yongding]. 1937. In Zhongguo gongchandang Minxi'nan weiyuanhui jiguan bao, *Hongqi* 19, August 5. Mimeo. 052.1 813 15526 N 19.

Young, Lung-chang. 1988. "Regional stereotypes in China." *Chinese Studies in History*, Summer, 32–57.

Yu Boliu. 1983. "Xinsijun zujian shilüe" [History of the New Fourth Army's reorganization]. *Zhongguo xiandai shi yuekan* 9:132–38.

————. 1985. "Zhongyang genjudi sannian youjizhanzheng shulüe" [The three-year guerrilla war in the central base]. *Zhongguo xiandai shi yuekan* 9:60–65.

Yu Ge. 1980. "Dabieshande chunlei: Jieshao yizu Shangcheng qiyi qianhoude geming wenwu jizhi" [Spring thunder in the Dabie Mountains: Introducing revolutionary relics and sites from before and after the Shangcheng Uprising]. *Henan wenbo tongxun* 2:5–8.

Yu Ji'nan. 1982. *Zhang Guotao he "Wode huiyi"* [Zhang Guotao and "My Memoirs"]. Chengdu: Sichuan renmin chubanshe.

Yu Longgui. 1979. "Tingjinshi sannian youjizhanzheng" [The Advance Division's three-year guerrilla war]. *Zhejiang wenshi ziliao xuanji* 14:30–51.

———. 1984. "Diqiang worou e zhan duo" [Fierce battles fought frequently from a position of inferiority]. In Zhejiang sheng junqu, 108–31.

Yu Maoji et al. 1985. *Xinsijun shihua* [Narrative history of the New Fourth Army]. Beijing: Jiefangjun chubanshe.

Yuan Chen Yi tongzhi chu bufen gongzuo renyuan. 1977. "Qing song ting qie zhi: Shenqie huainian Chen Yi tongzhi" [The green pine is straight and firm: Commemorating Comrade Chen Yi]. In Renmin tiyu chubanshe 1977b, 190–217.

Yuan Guang. 1982. *Fengyan gunde suiyue* [Years of billowing wind and smoke]. Beijing: Zhanshi chubanshe.

Yuan Xuezu. 1980. "Chechu zhongyang genjudi yihou" [After withdrawing from the central base]. *Xinghuo liaoyuan congkan* 1:35–43.

Yue Qian. 1972. "You Chen Yi zhi si shuodao sanshinian qian 'Xinsijun shijian' " [Looking back thirty years to the "New Fourth Army Incident" on the occasion of Chen Yi's death]. *Zhanggu yuekan.* 4 parts. February 10, 12–14; March 10, 51–54; May 10, 54–57; June 10, 67–71.

Yue Shaohua. 1983. "Hongjun kangRi xianqiandui beishang jingguode baogao" [Report on the Red Army's anti-Japanese Northern Expedition]. In Fang Zhimin et al. 1983, 262–77.

Yue Xia. 1980. "Balujun zhu Jin banshichude shimo" [The whole story of the Eighth Route Army office in Shanxi]. *Geming huiyilu* 1:190–202.

Zai Tian. 1936. "Zai yingjie xinde xingshizhong wei shixian dangde jueyi meiyitiao wen er douzheng" [Fighting to realize the Party resolution in the new situation]. In Zhongguo gongchandang Minxi'nan weiyuanhui jiguan bao, *Hongqi* 10. Mimeo. 052.1 813 15523 N 9–11.

Zeng Jingbing. 1983a. "Yi Minbeide geming douzheng" [Recalling Minbei's revolutionary struggle]. In Fang Zhimin et al. 1983, 428–38.

———. 1983b. "Minbei dang tong Mindong dangde huihe wenti" [On the question of the meeting of the Minbei Party and the Mindong Party]. In Fang Zhimin et al. 1983, 515–16.

———. 1984 [1958]. "Dui Minbei geming douzhengde huiyi" [Recalling Minbei's revolutionary struggle]. *Fujian dangshi ziliao* 3:245–59.

Zeng Meisheng. 1985. "Dui Chang Jiang ju lingdao shiqi Fujian dang gongzuode jiben kanfa" [Basic views of Party work in Fujian during the period of leadership of the Chang Jiang Bureau]. *Fujian dangshi tongxun* 11:53–58.

Zeng Shan. 1980. "Huiyi Ganxi'nan suweiai shiqi" [Recalling Ganxi'nan's soviet period]. *Jiangxi wenshi ziliao xuanji* 1:1–13.

———. 1982. "Dao Deng Zhenxun tongzhi" [In mourning for Comrade Deng Zhenxun]. In Zhenjiang diqu, 247–49.

Zeng Sheng et al., eds. 1983. *Dong Jiang xinghuo* [Dong Jiang sparks]. Guangdong renmin chubanshe.

Zeng Shiwen. 1983. "Zai Gu Dacun tongzhi shenbian gongzuo" [Working by the side of Comrade Gu Dacun]. *Geming huiyilu* 9:72–79.

Zeng Zhi. 1982. "Tan Gantang baodong yu Mindong tudi geming" [On the Gantang uprising and the Mindong land revolution]. *Dangshi yanjiu cankao ziliao* (Fujian) 2:1–5.

Zeng Zhi, ed. 1986. *Changzheng nüzhanshi* [Women warriors on the Long March]. Vol. 1. Changchun: Beifang funü ertong chubanshe.

"Zenyang zuzhi fenliang douzheng" [How to organize the struggle to divide grain]. 1936. In Zhongguo gongchandang Minxi'nan weiyuanhui jiguan bao, *Hongqi* 1, May 30. Mimeo. 052.1 813 15523 N 9–11.

Zhai Zuojun. 1985. "Yi Mao zhuxi zai Yan'an jiejian Wei Lihuang" [Recalling Chairman Mao's meeting with Wei Lihuang in Yan'an]. *Dangshi ziliao zhengji tongxun* 6:32–34.

Zhan Huayu. 1984. "San cuo duwulü, zhijian biedongdui" [The thrice-defeated Independent Fifth Brigade destroys the secret agent squad by strategy]. In Wanxi geming, 95–105.

Zhang Dingcheng. 1936. "Guanyu Yongding gongzuode jiancha" [On work investigation in Yongding]. December 11. In Zhonggu gongchandang Minxi'nan weiyuanhui jiguan bao, *Hongqi* 10. Mimeo. 052.1 813 15523 N 9–11.

———. 1940. "Xinsijun ernianlaide zhengzhi gongzuo" [Two years of New Fourth Army political work]. *Balujun junzheng zazhi* 2 (2): 51–63.

———. 1982. *Zhongguo gongchandang chuangjian Minxi geming genjudi* [The Chinese Communist Party's creation of the Minxi revolutionary base]. Fuzhou: Fujian renmin chubanshe.

———. 1982 [1940]. "Xinsijun ernianlaide zhengzhi gongzuo—wei xinsijun chengli liangzhounian jinian er zuo" [Two years of New Fourth Army political work: On the occasion of the second anniversary of the establishment of the New Fourth Army]. In Zhenjiang diqu, 116–31.

———. 1984. "Xinsijun zai kangzhan fenghuozhong chengzhangzhe" [The New Fourth Army growing in the beacon fire of the Resistance War]. In Ma Hongwu et al., eds., *Xinsijun he Huazhong kangRi genjudi shiliaoxuan*. Shanghai: Renmin chubanshe. Vol. 2, 176–85.

Zhang Dingcheng and Tan Zhenlin. 1981. "Hongqi yueguo Ting Jiang" [The Red Army leaps across the Ting Jiang]. In Zhang Dingcheng et al., *Hongqi yueguo Ting Jiang*. Fuzhou: Fujian renmin chubanshe.

Zhang Dicheng et al. 1937? *Zhongyao tongxun* [Important bulletin]. N.p. 255.35 804 12266.

———. 1961. "Minxi sannian youji zhanzheng" [The three-year guerrilla war in Minxi]. *Xinghuo liaoyuan* 4:194–233.

———. 1983 [1936]. "Zhonghua suweiai gongheguo Minxi'nan junzheng weiyuanhui gao Minxi'nan gongren shu" [Letter to the workers of Minxi'nan from the Minxi'nan Military and Administrative Committee of the Chinese Soviet Republic]. In *Fujian gongyun shiliao huibian*, ed. Fujian sheng gonghui gongyun shi yanjiushi, Fujian sheng dang'anguan. N.p.

———. 1984. "Minxi sannian youjizhanzheng" [The three-year guerrilla war in Minxi]. *Fujian dangshi ziliao* 3:45–84.

———. 1985 [1937]. "Wei tingzhi neizhan yizhi kangRi gao Minxi'nan gejie renshi shu" [Letter to all circles calling for a cease-fire in the civil war and a united resistance to Japan]. In Zhonggong Fujian shengwei, 1–5.

Zhang Guangxin and Yang Shuzhen, eds. 1985. *Zhonggong dangshi shijian mingci renwu jianshi* [Introduction to events, terms, and people in Chinese Communist Party history]. Xi'an: Shaanxi renmin chubanshe.

Zhang Guotao. 1966–71. "Wode huiyi" [My memoirs]. *Mingbao yuekan* nos. 3–62.

Zhang Hai. 1986. "Jianku zhuojuede nanfang sannian youjizhanzheng" [The arduous and unsurpassed three-year guerrilla war in the south]. *Junshi shilin* 5:20–22.

Zhang Kai. 1980. "Qingsong tingli gandan zhaoren" [Straight as a pine, his daring lights up humanity]. In Renmin chubanshe, 113–24.

Zhang Lin. 1982. *Xu Haidong jiangjun zhuan* [Biography of General Xu Haidong]. Beijing: Jiefangjun wenyi chubanshe.

Zhang Liren and Ye Jianzhong. 1983. "Minbei suqu sufan guangdahuade yixie qingkuang" [Some facts about the broadening of the campaign to suppress counterrevolutionaries in the Mindong Soviet]. *Dangshi ziliao yu yanjiu* (Fujian) 4:40–44.

Zhang Qi. 1981. "Liangshi yiyou" [A good teacher and a helpful friend]. In Zhonggong Huanggang xianwei hui, 115–17.

Zhang Renyuan. 1958. "Zai Maoyangshanshang" [In the Maoyang Mountains]. *Hongse fengbao* 2:195–201.

Zhang Riqing. 1982. *Jiannande licheng* [Arduous course]. Beijing: Zhanshi chubanshe.

Zhang Tianrong. 1986. "Hongjun changzheng zhunbei wenti yanjiu pingshu" [Review of research on the preparations for the Red Army's Long March]. In *Changzheng xintan*, ed. Guofang daxue dangshi zhenggong jiaoyanshi. Beijing: Jiefangjun chubanshe, 1–35.

Zhang Wenbi. 1981. "Qian shan wan he xing" [The trials of a long and arduous journey]. In Tao Yong et al. 1–24.

Zhang Wentian. 1934. "Yiqie weile baowei suweiai" [Everything for the defense of the soviet]. *Hongse Zhonghua*. September 29.

Zhang Xiangbing. 1981. "Eyuwan suqu lishi yanjiuzhongde butong guandian" [Different views in historical research on the Eyuwan Soviet]. *Zhongguo xiandai shi* 6:38.

Zhang Xueliang. 1989 [1968]. "Penitent Confession on the Xi'an Incident." *Chinese Studies in History,* Spring, 64–76.

Zhang Yangui and Yuan Wei. 1987. *Zhongguo gongnong hongjun shilüe* [Brief history of the Chinese Red Army]. Beijing: Zhonggong dangshi ziliao chubanshe.

Zhang Yingpo and Wang Zhongyuan. 1986. *Chen Yide qingshaonian shidai* [Chen Yi's childhood and youth]. Henan renmin chubanshe.

Zhang Yunlong. 1984. "Xinsijun chengli chuqide jianku suiyue" [The New Fourth Army's hardships in the early period after its formation]. *Geming huiyilu* 11:48–65.

Zhang Zaoxun. 1982. "Youguan He Mingde yixie qingkuang" [Some facts relating to He Ming]. *Dangshi ziliao yu yanjiu* (Fujian) 11:45–47.

———. 1985. "He Ming wenti shi renmin neibu maodun" [The He Ming question is a contradiction among the people]. *Minnan geming shi yanjiu* 2: 19–23.

Zhang Zhaodi. 1983. "Yehuo shaobujin, chunfeng chui you sheng" [Not even a prairie fire can destroy the grass, it will grow again with the spring wind]. *Fengzhan hongqi* 3:55–66.

Zhang Zhixiu. 1980. "Yi Chen Yi tongzhide ersan shi" [Remembering two or three things about Comrade Chen Yi]. *Jindai shi yanjiu* 4:84–91.

———. 1983. "Yi Chen Yi tongzhi crsan shi" [Some facts about Comrade Chen Yi]. *Zhongguo xiandai shi* 10:209–13.

Zhao Rongsheng. 1985. *Huiyi Wei Lihuang* [Recalling Wei Lihuang]. Beijing: Wenshi ziliao chubanshe.

Zhao Zengyan. 1986. "Yuegan bianqu he Minxi'nan youjiqude nongmin tudi douzheng" [The peasants' land struggle in Yuegan and the Minxi'nan guerrilla area]. *Zhongguo xiandai shi yuekan* 6:79–83.

Zhejiang sheng junqu, eds. 1984. *Zhe'nan sannian* [Three years in Zhe'nan]. Hangzhou: Zhejiang renmin chubanshe.

Zhejiang sheng junqu dangshi ziliao zhengji bangongshi. 1987. "Hongjun tingjinshi zai Zhejiang" [The Red Army Advance Division in Zhejiang]. In Zhonggong zhongyang dangshi zhengji weiyuanhui, 229–53.

Zhejiang sheng junqu dangshi ziliao zhengji lingdao xiaozu. 1984. "Qianyan" [Preface]. In Zhejiang sheng junqu, i–vi.

Zhejiang sheng zhengxie wenshi ziliao yanjiu weiyuanhui, eds. 1987. *Dierci guogong hezuo zai Zhejiang* [The second Nationalist-Communist cooperation in Zhejiang]. Zhejiang renmin chubanshe.

Zheng Chuyun. 1984. "Mindong zaoqide geming huodong" [Early revolutionary activities in Mindong]. *Fengzhan hongqi* 4:97–101.

Zheng Danpu. 1983. "Huiyi Minzhe bian genjudide douzheng" [Recalling the struggle in the Minzhe base]. *Fujian wenshi ziliao* 7:60–77.

Zheng Fulong. 1983. "Guanyu Min'gan shengwei chenglide yixie shishide kaozheng" [Historical research on the establishment of the Min'gan Provincial Committee]. *Dangshi ziliao yu yanjiu* (Fujian) 6:47–49.

Zheng Guangjin and Fang Shike. 1987. *Zhongguo hongjun changzheng ji* [Record of the Chinese Red Army's Long March]. Henan renmin chubanshe.

Zheng Guiqing. 1984. "Zai mimide conglinli" [In the secret forest]. *Minxi dangshi ziliao tongxun* 3:8–20.

Zheng Jinhua. 1985. "Fujian dang zuzhi juti yunyong kangRi minzu tongyi zhanxiande jige wenti" [Some questions concerning the Fujian Party's concrete application of the anti-Japanese united front]. *Fujian dangshi tongxun* 12:41–48.

Zheng Tianbao. 1983. "Dong Jiang renmin yijiuerqinian qianhoude geming douzheng" [The revolutionary struggle around 1927 by the Dong Jiang people]. *Geming huiyilu* 9:41–55.

Zheng Weisan. 1982 [1941]. "KangRi zhanzheng yu nongmin yundong" [The Resistance War and the peasant movement]. In Fawubu diaochaju, eds., *Zhonggong "nongmin yundong"*, 125–50.

Zheng Xueqiu. 1982. "Longyan bao tian douzhengde chengguo" [The results of the struggle to keep the land in Longyan]. *Longyan wenshi ziliao* 5:46–47.

———. 1986. "Lun changzheng tuzhong zhongyang zhishidiande chuanda dui Minxi youjizhanzhengde zhidao zuoyong" [On the role of central directives radioed from the Long March in Minxi's guerrilla war]. Unpublished manuscript.

Zheng Zhong. 1987. *Tiantaishan bianyidui* [Plainclothes squad in the Tiantai Mountains]. Beijing: Jiefangjun chubanshe.

Zhenjiang diqu Maoshan geming lishi jinian'guan choubei xiaozu bangongshi, eds. 1982. *Xinsijun zai Maoshan: KangRi douzheng shiliaoxuan* [The New Fourth Army at Maoshan: A selection of historical materials]. Jiangsu renmin chubanshe.

Zhexuexi "Ye Ting zhuanlüe" bianxiezu, eds. 1977 and 1978. "Ye Ting zhuan-lüe" [Ye Ting: A biographical sketch]. 3 parts. *Zhongshan daxue xuebao (zhexue shehui kexue ban)* 1977(6): 49–66; 1978(1): 30–39; and 1978(2): 51–65.

Zhong Chenkun. 1982. "Gemingde Shecun, Tianfengting" [Tianfengting, a revolutionary She village]. *Ningde wenshi ziliao* 1:86–89.

Zhong Guang. 1981. "Maikai changzheng diyibu" [First step toward the Long March]. In Chen Yi et al. 1981, 530–31.

Zhong Liangpei. 1981. "Ruixi xiande jianli" [The establishment of Ruixi county]. In Chen Yi et al. 1981, 536–37.

Zhong Qiguang. 1987. "Zhandou zai Xiang'egan bianqu" [Fighting in Xiang'-egan]. In Wu Zaowen, 408–13.

Zhong ge junwei. 1986 [1934]. "Guanyu chengli zhongyang junqu fadong qun-zhong kaizhan youji huodongde zhishi (jielu)" [Direction on setting up the Central Military Region and mobilizing the masses for guerrilla activity (excerpt)]. In Junbo, 45.

Zhonggong Anfu xianwei dangshi bangongshi. 1987. "Xianggan bianqu sannian youjizhanzheng" [The three-year guerrilla war in Xianggan]. In Zhonggong zhongyang dangshi ziliao zhengji weiyuanhui, 254–69.

Zhonggong Anhui sheng dangshi gongzuo weiyuanhui. 1987. "Dierci guonei geming zhanzheng shiqide Anhui nongmin baodong" [Anhui peasant risings during the second revolutionary civil war]. In Zhonggong zhongyang dang-shi ziliao zhengji weiyuanhui, 142–53.

Zhonggong Anxi xianwei dangshi ziliao zhengji xiaozu. 1982. "Annanyong hongse quyu geming douzheng licheng" [The revolutionary struggle in An-nanyong's Red region]. *Dangshi yanjiu cankao ziliao* (Fujian) 5:26–37.

Zhonggong Chenzhou dangshi ziliao zhengji bangongshi, eds. 1986. *Xiangnan qiyi shigao* [Draft history of the Xiangnan Uprising]. Changsha: Hunan ren-min chubanshe.

Zhonggong Eyu bianqu tewei. 1938. *Wei baowei Henan baowei jiaxiang xuanyan* [Manifesto in defense of Henan and our native districts]. February 15. Mimeo. 224.1 812 13119.

Zhonggong Fujian sheng Longxi diwei dangshi bangongshi, Zhonggong Guang-dong sheng Shantou shiwei dangshi bangongshi, eds. 1985. *Minyue bianqu sannian youjizhanzheng shiliao huibian* [A collection of historical materials on the three-year guerrilla war in Minyue]. 2 vols. Hua'an: N.p.

Zhonggong Fujian shengwei dangshi ziliao zhengji bianxie weiyuanhui yanjiu-shi, eds. 1985. *Cong hetan dao beishang kangRi* [From peace talks to going north to resist Japan]. Fuzhou: Fujian renmin chubanshe.

Zhonggong Fujian shengwei dangshi ziliao zhengji weiyuanhui erzhanban. 1986. "Dierci guonei geming zhanzheng shiqi Minxi suqu 'suqing shehui min-zhudang' shijian qingkuang jianshu" [Introduction to the "purge of Social

Democrats" in the Minxi Soviet during the second revolutionary war]. *Dangshi tongxun* 5:2–4.

Zhonggong Fujian shengwei "Fujian geming shi huaji" weiyuanhui, eds. 1982. *Fujian geming shi huaji* [A pictorial history of the revolution in Fujian]. Fuzhou: Fujian renmin chubanshe.

Zhonggong Guangdong shengwei dangshi yanjiu weiyuanhui bangongshi et al., eds. 1986. *Nanyue yinglie zhuan* [Guangdong martyrs]. No. 2. Guangdong renmin chubanshe.

Zhonggong Huanggang xianwei hui, eds. 1981. *Huiyi Chen Tanqiu* [Remembering Chen Tanqiu]. Wuhan: Hubei renmin chubanshe.

Zhonggong Hunan shengwei. 1938. *Wei baowei Hunan xuanyan* [Manifesto in defense of Hunan]. August 13. 224.1 812 13120.

Zhonggong Hunan shengwei dangshi ziliao zhengji yanjiu weiyuanhui, eds. 1986. *Hunan dangshi dashi nianbiao (xin minzhuzhuyi geming shiqi)* [Chronicle of Party history in Hunan (new democratic revolution period)]. Changsha: Hunan renmin chubanshe.

Zhonggong Jianyang diwei dangshi bangongshi. 1985. "Minbei geming genjudide jianli ji qi douzheng qingkuang" [The establishment of the Minbei revolutionary base and its struggle]. *Fujian dangshi tongxun* 11:59–69.

Zhonggong Jinzhai xianwei xuanchuanbu, eds. 1980. *Lixiajie fenghuo* [Start-of-summer beacons]. Hefei: Anhui renmin chubanshe.

Zhonggong Lianjiang xianwei dangshiban. 1986. "Mindong hongjun haishang youjidui" [The Mindong Red Army's seaborne guerrillas]. *Mindong dangshi* 2:60–75.

Zhonggong Longyan diwei dangshi ziliao zhengji yanjiu weiyuanhui. 1987. *Minxi geming genjudi shi* [History of the Minxi revolutionary base]. Beijing: Huaxia chubanshe.

Zhonggong Lu'an diwei dangshi gongzuo weiyuanhui, eds. 1987. *Wanxi geming shi* [History of the revolution in Wanxi]. Anhui: Renmin chubanshe.

Zhonggong Minyue bianqu. 1937. *Guanyu xianwei shuji lianxi huiyi hou gongzuode jueding* [Resolution on work after the joint conference of county secretaries]. November. Mimeo.

Zhonggong Minyue bianqu tewei. 1937a. *Gao quan Minnan gejie tongbao shu* [Letter to all circles of Minnan compatriots]. November 29. 255.35 813 12787.

———. 1937b. *Wei kaizhan heping yundong gei geji dangbu ji hongjun yiyongjun yifeng zhishi xin* [A directive to Party branches and Red Army volunteers on developing the peace movement]. September 26. Mimeo. 244.2 813 2943.

Zhonggong Minzhegan bianqu wei. 1937. *Minzhegan bianqude xingshi yu dangde renwu jueyi* [Resolution on the situation and the Party's tasks in the Minzhegan border area]. December 27. Mimeo. 255.31 814 2509.

Zhonggong nanfang gongzuo weiyuanhui. 1985 [1937]. "Gei Minyue bianqu teweide zhishi" [Directive to the Minyue Special Committee]. In Zhonggong Fujian sheng Longxi, vol. 1, 198–204.

Zhonggong nanfangju. 1941? 1942? *Jinji tonggao* [Urgent communication]. Handwritten. 592–97 807 10369.

Zhonggong Ningde diwei dangshi zhengbianwei. 1986. "Zhongguo gongnong hongjun beishang kangRi xianqiandui tujing Mindong" [The Chinese Red Army's anti-Japanese Northern Expedition crosses Mindong]. *Mindong dangshi* 2:37–59.

Zhonggong Ningde diwei dangshi ziliao zhengweihui. 1986. "Mindong geming genjudide jianli ji qi douzheng qingkuang" [The establishment of the Mindong revolutionary base and its struggle]. *Fujian dangshi tongxun* 2:53–60.

Zhonggong Pingjiang xianwei dangshi ziliao zhengji bangongshi, eds. 1985. *Pingjiang can'an shiliao huibian* [Historical materials on the Pingjiang massacre]. Beijing: Zhongguo renmin jiefangjun zhengzhi xueyuan chubanshe.

Zhonggong Shangcheng xianweihui, eds. 1981. *Dabieshan fenghuo* [War flames in the Dabie Mountains]. N.p.: Henan renmin chubanshe.

Zhonggong Xianggan sheng weiyuanhui Xianggan bianqu junzheng weiyuanhui. 1937. *Lianhe xuanyan* [Joint declaration]. November. Mimeo. 224.1 812 12769.

"Zhonggong yanjiu" zazhishe bianjibu, eds. 1973. *Zhonggong wenhua da geming zhongyao wenjian huibian* [Important documents of the Chinese Communists' Cultural Revolution]. Taibei: "Zhonggong yanjiu" zazhishe.

Zhonggong zhongyang. 1986 [1935]. "Zhi zhongyang junqu dian" [Radio message to the Central Military District]. February 5. In Junbo, 45–46.

Zhonggong zhongyang dangshi ziliao zhengji weiyuanhui zhengji yanjiushi, eds. 1987. *Zhonggong dangshi ziliao zhuanti yanjiuji, dierci guonei geming zhanzheng shiqi* [Research materials on Chinese Communist history in the period of the second revolutionary civil war]. Beijing: Zhonggong dangshi ziliao chubanshe.

Zhonggong zhongyang dangshi ziliao zhengji weiyuanhui, zhongyang dang'anguan, eds. 1985. *Zunyi huiyi wenxian* [Documents of the Zunyi Conference]. Beijing: Renmin chubanshe.

Zhonggong zhongyang dangxiao chubanshe, eds. 1982. *Wannan shibian* [The Wannan Incident]. Zhonggong zhongyang dangxiao chubanshe.

Zhongguo dier lishi dang'anguan, eds. 1987. *Guomindang jun zhuidu hongjun changzheng dang'an shiliao xuanbian* [Selected historical archive materials relating to the chasing and blocking of the Red Army's Long March by Guomindang armed forces]. 2 vols. Beijing: Dang'anguan chubanshe.

Zhongguo geming bowuguan dangshi chenlie yanjiubu, eds. 1982. *Zhonggong dangshi zhuyao shijian jianjie (1919–1949)* [Brief introduction to important events in the history of the Chinese Communist Party (1919–1949)]. Chengdu: Sichuan renmin chubanshe.

Zhongguo gongchandang Ganyue bian weiyuanhui. 1937. *Wei kangzhan gao minzhong shu* [Letter to the masses about the Resistance War]. August 25. Mimeo. 255.35 824.

Zhongguo gongchandang Minxi'nan weiyuanhui. 1936. "Jiguan bao" [Administrative report]. *Hongqi* no. 8. November 7.

Zhongguo gongchandang Minyuegan bian sheng weiyuanhui. 1937. *Wei dui Ri kangzhan baowei Zhang Xia xuanyan* [Manifesto in favor of resisting Japan and defending Zhangzhou and Xiamen]. October 18. 224.1 813 4183.

Zhongguo gongchandang Minyuegan sheng weiyuanhui. 1937. *Wei dui Ri kangzhan baowei Zhang Xia xuanyan* [Manifesto in favor of resisting Japan and defending Zhangzhou and Xiamen]. October 28. 224.1 813 13141.

Zhongguo gongchandang Xiang'egan sheng weiyuanhui, Zhonghua suweiai gongheguo Xiang'egan sheng suweiai zhengfu. 1985 [1937]. "Wei heping hezuo lianhe xuanyan" [Manifesto for peaceful cooperation and alliance]. August 20. In Zhonggong Pingjiang xianwei, 45–47.

Zhongguo gongchandang Zhangzhou zhongxin xian weiyuanhui. 1940a. *Minnan gedi dangzheng dangju shu* [Letter to political and administrative authorities throughout Minnan]. August 12. Mimeo. 255, 35 814 13603.

———. 1940b. *Gao Minnan gejie minzhong shu* [Letter to all circles in Minnan]. June 16. Mimeo. 255.35 814 13603.

———. 1940c. *Wei A Yan tongzhi yuhai zhi gejie fulaoxiongdi shu* [Letter to all circles concerning the murder of Comrade A Yan]. September 30. Mimeo. 255.35 814 13603.

Zhongguo qingnian chubanshe, eds. 1954. *Daochu shi hongqi* [The Red Flag is everywhere]. Beijing: Zhongguo qingnian chubanshe.

Zhongguo renmin geming junshi bowuguan, eds. 1982. *Zhongguo renmin geming zhanzheng dituxuan* [Maps of the Chinese People's Revolutionary War]. Beijing: Ditu chubanshe.

———. 1986. *Chen Yi yuanshuai fengbei yongcun* [Marshal Chen Yi's monuments are immortal]. Shanghai: Renmin chubanshe.

"Zhongguo shaoshu minzu shehui lishi diaocha ziliao congkan" Fujian sheng bianjizu, eds. 1986. *Shezu shehui lishi diaocha* [Investigation into She social history]. Fuzhou: Fujian renmin chubanshe.

Zhonghua junwei Xiang'egan junqu renmin kangRi junshi weiyuanhui. 1985 [1937]. "Kuaiyou daidian" [Express telegram]. May 14. In Zhonggong Pingjiang xianwei, 43–44.

Zhonghua junwei Xiang'egan renmin kangRi hongjun. 1985 [1937]. "Junshi weiyuanhui bugao" [Proclamation of the military affairs commission]. August 20. In Zhonggong Pingjiang xianwei, 47–49.

Zhonghua renmin kangRi jiuguo yiyongjun daqi lujun diyi zhihuibu, eds. N.d. *Gao Minzhong minjun shu* [Letter to the people and the army in Minzhong]. Mimeo leaflet. 255.35 734 14118.

Zhonghua renmin suweiai gonghehuo Minxi'nan junzheng weiyuanhui. 1937a. *Gei Yu zongsiling Hanmou dengde yifeng xin* [Letter to General Commander Yu Hanmou and others]. Signed by Zhang Dingcheng, Deng Zihui, and Tan Zhenlin. May 15. 255.35 813.

———. 1937b. *Minxi'nan renmin kangRi jiuguo gangling* [Program for the Minxi'nan people's anti-Japanese resistance]. May 15. Mimeo. 255.35 813 15081 c.1.

———. 1937c. *Wei baohu chungeng zhunbei kangRi liangshi gao minzhong shu* [Letter to the people concerning the protection of spring plowing and the preparation of anti-Japanese grain]. March 1. Mimeo. 255 35 804 12266.

———. 1937d. *Wei tingzhi neizhan yizhi dui Ri san zhi Yuejun gonghan* [Three open letters to the Guangdong army calling for an end to civil war and everything for the resistance to Japan]. May 15. Mimeo. 255.35 813 15083.

———. 1937e. *Minxi'nan renmin kangRi jiuguo gangling* [Program for the Minxi'nan people's anti-Japanese resistance]. May 15. Mimeo. 575.2907, 813 14791 c.2.

————. 1937f. *Wei tingzhi neizhan yizhi kangRi zhi Minxi'nan gejie renshi shu* [Letter to all circles in Minxi'nan calling for an end to civil war and everything for the anti-Japanese resistance]. May 15. Mimeo. 255.35 813 15081 c.1.

Zhonghua renmin suweiai gongheguo Yonghejing junzheng weiyuanhui. 1937. *Gao Jinghe bian minzhong shu* [Letter to the people on the Jinghe border]. March 16. Mimeo. 255.35 804 12266.

Zhonghua suweiai gongheguo Minxi'nan junzheng weiyuanhui. 1936a. *Gao Yuejun guanbing shu* [Letter to officers and men of the Guangdong army]. Signed by Zhang Dingcheng, Deng Zihui, and Tan Zhenlin. October 25. Mimeo. 255.35 813 11789.

————. 1936b. *Wei kangRi jiuguo yundong zhi gejie gongkaide xin* [Open letters to all circles calling for a movement to resist Japan and save the country]. Signed by Zhang Dingcheng, Deng Zihui, and Tan Zhenlin. December 3. 255.35 813 11789.

Zhonghua suweiai gongheguo Minxi'nan junzheng weiyuanhui. 1979 [1936]. "Bugao. Dierhao. Xuanbu Minxi'nan renmin kang Ri tao Jiang gangling" [Second proclamation of the program for the Minxi'nan people's resistance to Japan and their punitive expedition against Chiang]. In *Zhonggong dangshi cankao ziliao* 3:183–88.

Zhongshan daxue "Ye Ting" bianxiezu. 1979. *Ye Ting*. Guangdong renmin chubanshe.

Zhongyang. 1982 [1937]. "Guanyu nanfang ge youji quyu gongzuode zhishi" [Directive on work in the guerrilla areas in the south]. In Shanghai renmin chubanshe, 14–17.

Zhongyang diaocha tongjiju. 1939a. *Diwu zhanqu xinsijun huodong gaikuang* [New Fourth Army activities in the Fifth War Zone]. December. Handwritten. 590.8026 815 17872.

————. 1939b. *Tezhong qingbao* [Special intelligence]. December 9. Mimeo. 270 10491.

————. 1939c. *Xinsijun gaikuang zhaiyao* [Digest of the situation in the New Fourth Army]. Mimeo. 590.8 815 4746.

————. 1940. *Xinsijun diaocha zhuanbao* [Special investigative report on the New Fourth Army]. Mimeo. 590.8026 815 475901.

Zhongyang junqu Xiang Ying. 1986 [1935]. "Guanyu dangqian gongzuo qingkuang zonghe baogao" [Summary report on the present work situation]. February 21. In Junbo, 46.

Zhongyang minzu xueyuan yanjiushi, eds. 1974. *Zhongguo shaoshu minzu jiankuang: Lizu, Shezu, Gaoshanzu, Jingzu* [Brief introduction to China's national minorities: Li, She, Gaoshan, Jing]. N.p.

Zhongyang shujichu. 1985 [1937]. "Zhongyang guanyu nanfang ge youjiqu gongzuo fangzhende zhishi" [Central Committee directive on the direction of work in the various guerrilla areas in the south]. October 1. In Zhonggong Fujian sheng Longxi, vol. 1, 263–64.

Zhongyang zhengzhiju. 1986 [1937]. "Duiyu nanfang youjiqu gongzuode jueyi" [Resolution on work in the southern guerrilla areas]. December 13. In Junbo, 14 and 46.

Zhongyang zuzhibu, eds. 1936. *Zhongguo gongchandangde huodong ji qi tezheng* [Chinese Communist Party activity and its special features]. N.p. Handwritten. 575.29 577 7263.

*Zhongyao tongxun* [Urgent communication]. 1937? N.p. 255.35 804 12266.

Zhou Aimin. 1981a. "Xingguo mofan xian" [Xingguo model county]. In Chen Yi et al. 1981, 439–45.

———. 1981b. "Zhuli hongjun changzhenghoude Jiangxi shengwei" [The Jiangxi Provincial Committee after the Red Army main force had gone on the Long March]. In Chen Yi et al. 1981, 534–37.

Zhou Junming. 1983. "Zhang Xingjiang yu Eyu bianqu hongjun youjidui" [Zhang Xingjiang and the Eyu Red Army guerrillas]. In Henan sheng minzhengting, vol. 4, 25–34.

Zhou Lan. 1981. "Chen Yi tongzhi sannian youjizhan suoji" [Fragmentary reminiscences of Comrade Chen Yi during the three-year guerrilla war]. In Chen Yi et al. 1981, 597–603.

Zhou Luo. 1977. " 'Xinsijun'de chengli ji qi neibu fenqi" [The founding of the "New Fourth Army" and its internal splits]. *Gongdang wenti yanjiu* 3 (12): 44–50.

Zhou Ti, ed. 1980. *Chen Yi zai Ganyue bian* [Chen Yi on the Ganyue border]. Beijing: Renmin meishu chubanshe.

Zhou Weisong, ed. 1985. *Zhongyuan fenghuo* [Beacon fires on the central plains]. He'nan renmin chubanshe.

Zhou Xiaojun. 1982. "Mindong guogong liangdang Ningde hetan jingguo jianshu" [The peace talks in Mindong's Ningde between Nationalists and Communists]. *Ningde wenshi ziliao* 1:48–52.

Zhou Yijin. 1986. "Hongjun tingjinshi zai Lishuide huodong" [The activities of the Red Army's Advance Division in Lishui]. *Lishui wenshi ziliao* 3:1–5.

Zhu Dongsheng. 1983. *Zhu De, Peng Dehuai, He Long, Chen Yi, Luo Ronghuan junshi huodong dashiji* [A chronicle of the military activities of Zhu De, Peng Dehuai, He Long, Chen Yi, and Luo Ronghuan]. Beijing: Zhanshi chubanshe.

Zhu Guodong. 1984. "Zhonggong Wanxi teweide douzheng shimo" [The whole story of the struggle of the Chinese Communists' Wanxi Special Committee]. In Wanxi geming, 143–49.

Zhu Yujin. 1982. "Huiyi Wannan shibianhou Zhou Enlai tongzhi zai nanfangjude jici jianghua" [Recalling some speeches by Comrade Zhou Enlai in the Southern Bureau after the Wannan Incident]. *Geming huiyilu* 4:139–44.

Zhu Yunqian. 1987. "Zai 'nanfang sannian youjizhanzheng' shiliao congshu huigao huishangde jianghua" [Speech at the meeting to collect manuscripts for the historical documentary series "The three-year guerrilla war in the south"]. *Junshi shilin* 4:58–59.

Zhu Zhongli. 1985. *Cancan hongye* [Magnificent red leaves]. Changsha: Hunan renmin chubanshe.

Zhuo Hongpo et al. 1986. "Shilun Mindong dang zai kangRi zhanzhengzhongde lishi zuoyong" [On the Mindong Party's historical role in the anti-Japanese war]. *Fujian dangshi tongxun* 2:39–48.

Zi Qin. 1938. *Chudongzhongde xinsijun* [The New Fourth Army sets off]. Hankou: Qunli shudian. 590.8 937 3945.

Zong Zhidi. 1980 [1952]. "Nanwangde sannian" [Three memorable years]. *Geming huiyilu* 1:137–71.

Zou Zhicheng. 1983. "Yi Wan'gan bianqu Fu, Ru, Qi diqude geming douzheng" [Recalling the revolutionary struggle in the Fu-Ru-Qi area of Wan'gan]. In Fang Zhimin et al. 1983, 527–29.

# INDEX

Compositor: Bookmasters
Text: 10/12 Baskerville
Display: Baskerville
Printer: Braun-Brumfield, Inc.
Binder: Braun-Brumfield, Inc.